£3.00

EVANGELISM
THROUGH
THE
LOCAL CHURCH

Reviewed: CA, 6/91.

EVANGELISM THROUGH THE LOCAL CHURCH

Michael Green

Hodder & Stoughton
LONDON SYDNEY AUCKLAND TORONTO

Bible quotations are generally taken from the RSV, unless otherwise indicated in the text.

British Library Cataloguing in Publication Data

Green Michael, *1930–*
   Evangelism through the local church.
   1. Christian church. Evangelism
   I. Title
   269.2

   ISBN 0-340-53667-5 hb
        0-340-52916-4 pb

Published by Hodder and Stoughton,
a division of Hodder and Stoughton Ltd,
Mill Road, Dunton Green, Sevenoaks, Kent TN13 2YA
Editorial Office: 47 Bedford Square, London WC1B 3DP

Photoset by Rowland Phototypesetting Ltd
Bury St Edmunds, Suffolk

Printed in Great Britain by Clays Ltd, St Ives plc

For Rosemary –
dear wife and true yokefellow,
a counsellor
who also does the work of an evangelist

Contents

Preface

Just as the Bible is the world's best seller, but often lies unread in the front room, so evangelism is essential to the nature of Christianity, and yet it is honoured more in the breach than the observance. At the intellectual level, evangelism has largely given way to dialogue. At the popular level, the majority of church members seem either to have little use for it, or alternatively have a bad conscience because they do not in fact do it. The same seems to be the case with the majority of clergy and ministers.

If evangelism happens at all in our Western society, it is likely to be in one of two main forms of presentation: the large crusade or the personal conversation. Some attempts are, of course, made by the churches to reach out to their locality with the Christian gospel, but all too often such attempts are fitful, short-lived, and ineffectual. On the other hand, the more aggressive evangelism of some of the para-church movements tends to be rather strong on heat and weak on light.

But whenever Christianity has been at its most healthy, evangelism has stemmed from the local church, and has had a noticeable impact on the surrounding area. I do not believe that the re-Christianisation of the West can take place without the renewal of local churches in this whole area of evangelism. We need a thoughtful, sustained, relevant presentation of the Christian faith, in word and in action, embodied in a warm, prayerful, lively local church which has a real concern for its community at all levels. This book has been written in the conviction that such evangelism in and from the local church is not only much needed but eminently possible. I believe it to be the most natural, long-lasting and effective evangelism that is open to us. If local churches were engaging in loving, outgoing evangelism within their neighbourhoods, many of our evangelistic campaigns, missions and crusades would be rendered much less necessary.

Evangelism has been part of my life ever since my twenties. It is so still. For decades now two callings have been struggling within me: that of the theological teacher, and that of the evangelist. But perhaps that tension is not altogether a bad thing, unusual though it may be. For most theologians do little evangelism, and many evangelists have little use for theology – to the impoverishment of both. If this book has any merit, it may well derive from a combination of theory and practice, of studying the Christian faith in some depth, and of sharing it with some consideration.

Some years ago I wrote a book, *Evangelism in the Early Church*. It sought to provide an accurate insight into the gospel the earliest Christians proclaimed and the ways in which they did it. This present book emerges out of many years of attempting to follow where those first evangelists blazed the trail. Through preaching, through personal conversation, through church work, through theological teaching, through writing, and through leading missions in churches, universities and towns, I have tried to *do* evangelism, not merely study it. As a result there is an unashamedly practical aspect to this book, which I hope may be acceptable. My deepest desire is not that the reader may agree with me, but that he or she may be stimulated to do evangelism in whatever way seems to be most appropriate in and from the family of the local church. *Extra ecclesiam nulla salus!* (outside the church there is no salvation). The church, the local church, is the womb from which healthy evangelism is born.

Jane Holloway has shared in the preparation of this book with me. She has read and made many helpful comments which have improved the main text of the book, and she has been responsible for much detailed work on the Appendices. She is currently the Field Work and Outreach Co-ordinator at Regent College, Vancouver. In this twin capacity she has masterminded and done a lot of the training for no less than five major missions in the past two years alone, along with numerous shorter ventures. Prior to her present appointment she worked with me as Rector's Secretary and Personal Assistant at St Aldate's Church, Oxford, where she played a large part in training teams of students who went out each year on a Pastorate Mission to some town or city where we were invited. These missions were large-scale and interdenominational. She also organised the training and co-ordination of those who led 'Discovery Groups' for the nurture of new Christians. She is therefore exceptionally well equipped to co-operate in the production of this book.

I owe so many debts of gratitude as I reflect on what lies behind a book like this. Gratitude to loving parents and a home dominated by Christian values. Gratitude to Richard Gorrie, who led me to a personal faith in Christ. Gratitude to the 'Iwerne Minister' house-parties where that faith was nourished in the early days; to Oxford and Cambridge which stretched me; to Professor Charlie Moule and Professor Sir Henry Chadwick who taught me theology. I am profoundly grateful for the privilege of having been able both to study and to spread the good news of Christ in many lands.

I am particularly conscious of the debt I owe to friends like Dr Os Guinness and Dr Graeme MacLean, Christian thinkers from whom I have learnt so much, as chapters 5–8 will make evident to those accustomed to reading between the lines. Graeme did me the great kindness of reading carefully through those chapters and making extensive suggestions, without which I would have made many more errors than I undoubtedly have. I am grateful, too, to the Revd Dr John Goldingay, Principal of St John's College, Nottingham, to the Rt Revd Peter Ball, Bishop of Lewes, and to the Revd David Winter, lately Head of Religious Broadcasting at the BBC and now Oxford Diocesan Missioner. They have all read parts of the manuscript and made helpful suggestions, as have my own colleagues at Regent, Dr Jim Houston and Dr Loren Wilkinson. I am deeply grateful to friends who have helped with the Appendices. The constant support and encouragement of David Wavre at Hodder & Stoughton means more than I can say. I am also very grateful to the many agnostics and atheists who have challenged me and made me rethink, in the course of finding their way painstakingly to Christ.

A big thank you, too, to Martha Jean Brodhead, who so kindly typed this book, and to my colleagues at St Aldate's Oxford (notably the Revd Bruce Gillingham and Paul Herrington, Director of Music) and more recently Regent College, Vancouver, from whom I have learnt much, and in whose company it has been a delight to celebrate our common Master Jesus Christ on many an enterprise. Most of all, I want to thank God for drawing me to himself and giving me the ministry of evangelism.

Part One of this book endeavours to examine the present situation, to clarify some of the issues, to examine the propriety of evangelism in our pluralist society, and to look at the quality of life which our churches need to exhibit if evangelism is to be credible.

Part Two concentrates on the intellectual challenges which face

Christians who seek to evangelise in the context of modern Western culture. But it ends with the reminder that it is useless to
answer the questions of the mind if we neglect the questions of the
heart.

Part Three is the practical section, dealing with evangelistic
preaching, personal evangelism, the nurture of new Christians, the
variety of methods open to us, and the possibilities of joint
co-operation between churches in reaching whole towns and cities
for Christ. It ends with the reminder that evangelism is not a matter
of human effort: it is God's work in which we are privileged to
share. And evangelism, to be real, must be local. The book
concludes with a number of appendices on specific practical issues.

I have tried to adopt non-sexist language; but reared as I am in
an educational milieu where 'man' is a matter of genus not gender,
I know I have failed. I crave the pardon of any reader for whom this
is a sensitive matter. I have not deliberately sought to offend.

The book could easily have been considerably extended: I am
well aware of its omissions. But it is long enough as it is. And it is
offered to the local churches of the West in the hope that it may be
of some service in stimulating evangelism, not least in a decade
which some of the largest denominations in the world have
challenged Christians to make a decade of evangelism.

Michael Green
Vancouver, 1990

EVANGELISM
THROUGH
THE
LOCAL CHURCH

PART ONE

ISSUES FOR THE CHURCH

1
Evangelism

Evangelism does not enjoy a good press. It literally means the sharing of good news, but for most people there is little good news about it. It conjures up images of strident, perspiring preachers, of smooth-talking televangelists, or of strange characters at street corners urging the passers-by to repent and meet their God.

In a word, evangelism seems something no self-respecting person would want to be involved in. It has overtones of manipulation. In a permissive age it smacks of wanting to change the way another person is. And that is an insult. It is unacceptable.

It is hardly surprising, therefore, that in many mainline churches evangelism is in eclipse. It belongs to the *demi-monde*. It is what unbalanced enthusiasts, with no theology about them, get up to. It is emphatically not respectable. A balanced, thoughtful church should have nothing to do with it. And yet, those same churches have second thoughts when they see bare pews where once there were people in their services. Sometimes they wonder afresh about evangelism when they reflect on the godlessness, materialism and selfishness which are becoming more and more rampant throughout society. And if their vision stretches to the fast-growing churches of, for example, East Africa, they may say, as David Jenkins, the Bishop of Durham, said to David Gitari, the Bishop of Mount Kenya East, after the 1988 Lambeth Conference, 'I need to learn from you.'

I find it very significant that no church has taken evangelism more seriously in the last decade than the Roman Catholic Church, that most institutional and respectable of all denominations! Perhaps the rest of us ought to take a leaf from their book.

What springs to mind, I wonder, when the word 'evangelism' is used? Do you think of a preacher, a Billy Graham, coming to take your town by storm? Do you think of a programme, carefully designed to reach all parts of your local community? Or do you think, perhaps, of two people (both looking a shade uncomfortable) locked in earnest conversation over open Bibles? And how do you feel when major world churches, including the Roman Catholic and the Anglican, designate the last ten years of this century as a decade of evangelism?

Maybe it would be a help, initially, if we were to clear our minds of some of the misconceptions which commonly cloud them when the subject of evangelism is under consideration. Let us at least recognise what evangelism is not.

WHAT EVANGELISM IS NOT

Evangelism is not the same as filling pews. Among pastors who are normally suspicious of this kind of thing, it springs to short-lived popularity only when the numbers and the finances of their church sink low. But the motivation of such 'evangelism' is suspect, and the results are not likely to be lasting.

Evangelism is not what is euphemistically called in Canada 'sheep-shuffling'. A great deal that passes for evangelism in fast-growing churches is nothing more than transfer growth from some other section of the fractured church of God. And that serves nothing but the self-esteem of the minister of the new church.

Evangelism is not an occasional raid by a visiting celebrity. If that happens, many of the congregation will vote against it with their feet, will keep their heads down while it happens, and will emerge at the end when the coast is clear. Such an invasion is more likely to polarise the church membership than to unite it in mission. Visitors can, of course, do much to mobilise and encourage evangelism, but not if they are regarded as the experts who have all the answers and are going to 'do evangelism' for the local church.

Evangelism is not a matter of impassioned and repeated calls for decision. If such challenges are repetitive they become powerless. If they do not rest on clear teaching they are shallow. I recall seeing a poster on a wall, 'Jesus is the answer', to which someone had not unreasonably appended a graffito, 'But what is the question?' The simplistic repetition of clichés or the issuing of biblical challenges unsupported by biblical teaching and unrelated to contemporary needs is not evangelism, however orthodox it may sound.

Evangelism is not a system. Too often it is presented as a package, involving three clear points, four spiritual laws or five things God wants you to know. I have no quarrel with such aids to the memory of those who are communicating the good news. The danger arises when the gospel is shrunk to the dimensions of such limiting and selective formulae. In the name of simplicity the door is opened to misconception, shallowness and even heresy.

Evangelism is not an activity proper to ministers alone, nor is it only a matter of preaching. But we often think it is. If evangelism is to happen at all, it should, we feel, happen in the church building on Sunday, and it should be done by the minister. It is healthy to recall that in the days of the greatest advance of the church they had no special building and no clearly defined ministers. It was seen to be the calling of all Christians, and it was realised that the good news could be communicated in a variety of ways – and not necessarily, or even primarily, in church.

Evangelism is not proclamation alone or presence alone. During the twentieth century, both in Europe and the USA, a disastrous chasm has widened between those who think of evangelism in terms of proclamation and those who, tired of the hypocrisy and exaggeration encountered in a good deal of such preaching, maintain that it is our presence as Christians in the midst of a hurting world that counts, not our words. A very similar dichotomy separates those who think in terms of a spiritual gospel or a social gospel. In each case, the distinction is either illusory or mischievous. To separate word from action is to put aside two things which God has joined together. To separate the spiritual from the social is to be blind to the fact that they are the outside and the inside of the same thing. As ever for Christians, Jesus is the supreme example. His social concern and his spiritual concern went hand in hand. His presence embodying the Kingdom of God was matched by his words explaining the Kingdom. The two are not opposed to one another; they are complementary. It is encouraging that 'liberal' and 'conservative' Christians are now realising as much, and are beginning to act in concert on this matter.

Evangelism is not individualistic. In the fragmentation of Western culture it often comes over that way. But so often in the history of Christian expansion evangelism has been a societal thing; whole villages, towns, communities of various sorts have, to a greater or lesser extent, been brought over into the faith together. This is in the past how whole countries have been won: currently, how whole tribes are being brought into the faith, be it the Aucas in Latin America or the Sawi in Indonesia. If secularised Europeans, strong in the brotherly solidarities of their trade unions, are to be brought to Christianity, it will be necessary for the church to engage with this corporate aspect of evangelism. For evangelism cannot and must not merely be 'plucking brands from the burning', but changing the direction of society towards the living God instead of away from him.

Evangelism is not an optional extra for those who like that sort of thing. It is a major part of the obedience of the whole church to the command of its Lord. He told us to go into all the world and make disciples. It is hard to see how we can realistically acknowledge him as Lord if we take no notice of what he tells us to do. The church, Peter reminds us, exists not least to 'declare the wonderful deeds of him who called you out of darkness into his marvellous light. Once you were no people but now you are God's people; once you had not received mercy but now you have received mercy' (1 Pet. 2:9–10). Such good news is for sharing, and any church worthy of the name must ensure that it happens.

It is sad but true that so much that passes for evangelism is nothing of the sort.

Evangelism is often too institutionalised, and can be seen, not inaccurately, as the church out to gain new recruits.

Evangelism is often too atomised, with the spiritual side cut off from the rest of life. Emphasis on the response of the spirit to Christ is not matched by care for the physical and moral well-being of the whole person.

Evangelism is often too fossilised: the package in which the good news is wrapped becomes mistakenly identified with the good news itself, and the result is culture-bound Christianity. This has happened all too obviously in the export of European trappings and denominations, along with the good news itself, to Africa and Asia.

Evangelism is, moreover, far too clericalised. *Evangelism* is generally seen as the preserve of the clergy. If a person is contemplating ordination, folk say: 'Oh, so you are going into the church, are you?' This virtual identification in many minds of the church with its ministers is one of the most serious distortions of Christianity hampering the spread of the gospel in our generation.

In some circles evangelism has become too secularised. As a reaction against simplistic, pietistic calls to repentance, many of the more radical Christians of our day have identified evangelism with taking the part of the poor and oppressed. That identification is utterly right and praiseworthy. But when it extends to supplying them with arms and embracing terrorist liberation movements, the case is much less clear. And when such action is described as evangelism, we have moved a long way from the Jesus who refused to take the sword and yet was crucified upon a freedom-fighter's gibbet.

At the other extreme, and more commonly, it is easy to see a Christianity which is 'pasteurised'. Like milk, it is treated and bottled before being served out. You get an 'evangelism' which is not definite, annoys nobody, challenges nobody, transforms nobody. An evangelism which is not about radical change, but a gradual osmosis into the ecclesiastical system. That is a very far cry from Jesus, the most extreme radical the world has ever seen, who was always challenging men and women to leave the cherished areas of their selfish lives and come, follow him. The church has often domesticated Jesus and emasculated the good news.

These are all expressions of impoverished evangelism. We need to get back to the breadth of the good news as Jesus himself proclaimed it to an astonished home synagogue in Nazareth: 'The Spirit of the Lord is upon me, because he has anointed me to preach good news to the poor. He has sent me to proclaim release to the captives and recovering of sight to the blind, to set at liberty those who are oppressed, to proclaim the acceptable year of the Lord' (Luke 4:18). Jesus shut the scroll of Isaiah 61 from which he had been reading this passage, and amazed his hearers by informing them, 'Today this scripture has been fulfilled in your hearing' (Luke 4:21). This was no ordinary good news, and no ordinary messenger. It was nothing less than God's long-awaited salvation, proclaimed by the Messiah himself. God had indeed come to the rescue of a world in need. No wonder, then, that it became known in short as *to euangelion*, *the* good news.

The passage in Isaiah was highly significant. It relates to the period after the Babylonian Exile; and the messenger, anointed with God's own Spirit, announces God's signal victory, his kingly rule. It betokens nothing less than the dawn of a new age, and one from which the heathen are not excluded. The days of salvation have arrived. The people of God are ready and waiting for him like a bride for her husband, their unworthiness covered by a robe of righteousness, their relationship with their God established by an everlasting covenant. They are days of liberation, days of healing, days of great good news which is meant to spread like wildfire. God is reaching out from a rebuilt Jerusalem to make his ways known to the Gentiles. All that, and more, is contained in the chapter of Isaiah from which Jesus read this manifesto at the inauguration of his good news for the world. Evangelism is a many-splendoured thing.

WHAT IS EVANGELISM?

There are three definitions of evangelism which I have found helpful.

The first is one word: 'overflow'. It gives the right nuance, of someone who is so full of joy about Jesus Christ that it overflows as surely as a bath that is filled to overflowing with water. It is a natural thing. It is a very obvious thing. Accordingly, it has that quality which so much evangelism lacks, spontaneity. Incidentally, 'overflow' is a very passable translation of a Greek word which occurs a good deal in the New Testament to describe the liberated confidence of the Christian, *plērophoria*. Paul reminds the Thessalonians that 'our gospel came to you not only in word, but also in power and in the Holy Spirit and in much *plērophoria*', much confident overflow (1 Thess. 1:5).

The second definition is a phrase attributed to C. H. Spurgeon, the famous nineteenth-century British preacher and evangelist. Evangelism, he maintained, 'is one beggar telling another beggar where to get bread'. I like that definition. It draws attention both to the needs of the recipient and to the generosity of the giver: God will not give us a stone when we ask him for bread. I like the equality it underscores. There is no way that an evangelist is any better or on any higher ground than the person to whom he is talking. The ground is level round the cross of Christ. The only difference between the two hungry beggars is that one has been fed and knows where food is always available. There is no great mystique about it. Evangelism is simply telling a fellow searcher where he can get bread. But there is another touch which is important in this definition. It reminds us that we cannot bring this good news to others unless we personally have come to 'taste and see that the Lord is good' (Ps. 34:8).

But perhaps the most all-embracing definition of evangelism, and one which has won the most wide-reaching acceptance, belongs to the English Archbishop William Temple. It comes at the outset of the report entitled *Towards the Conversion of England*, and it runs as follows: 'To evangelise is so to present Jesus Christ in the power of the Holy Spirit, that men shall come to put their trust in God through him, to accept him as their Saviour, and serve him as their King in the fellowship of his church.' If we accept that definition, it says some very important things about evangelism.

First, evangelism is not the same as mission. Mission is one half of the reason for the church's existence; worship is the other. In these two ways we are called to display what it means to be 'a colony of heaven'. But the mission of the church is, of course, much broader than evangelism. It embodies the total impact of the church on the world: its influence; its involvement with the social, political and moral life of the community and nation where it is placed; its succour of bleeding humanity in every way possible. This mission includes evangelism. The greatest thing we can do for anyone is to bring them face to face with the Christ who died for them. But it is clear that evangelism is one aspect, and one only, of the total mission of the church.

Second, evangelism is good news about Jesus. It is not advancing the claims of a church, a nation, an ideology, but of Jesus himself. As Pope Paul VI put it, 'there is no true evangelisation if the name, the teaching, the promises, the life, the death, the resurrection, the kingdom, and the mystery of Jesus Christ the Son of God are not proclaimed'. At the time of the 1960 Olympics a magazine carried an amusing cartoon showing the celebrated runner from Marathon arriving in Athens and falling exhausted on the ground while he mumbles, with a blank look on his face, 'I have forgotten the message.' Alas, that often seems to be the case with the contemporary church. Unless Jesus himself, who *became* the gospel through his death and resurrection, is the essence of our message, whatever we are doing is not evangelism.

Third, evangelism is centred in God the Father. Jesus Christ shares both God's nature and ours. He is a reliable indicator of what God is like. But he does not exhaust the Godhead. He said, 'the Father is greater than I' (John 14:28). Accordingly, any evangelism which is so Jesus-oriented that it leaves us with a forgotten Father is less than fully Christian. The Jesus Movement of the 1960s, for all its strengths, had a notable weakness in this area. It was a Jesus religion. But the religion of the New Testament is firmly trinitarian. It brings us to the source of the Godhead, the Father himself, through the agency of the Son, and at the instigation of the Holy Spirit.

And that is the fourth characteristic of evangelism, as defined by William Temple. It is something which depends entirely for its effectiveness on the work of the Holy Spirit. We human beings are quite unable to draw others to Christ. It is the prerogative of the Holy Spirit to convict people of their need of Christ, to make him real to them, to bring them to confess that he is Lord, to baptise them into Christ's body, the church, and to assure them that they belong. All this is the Spirit's work, not ours. That must never be forgotten. We can speak and challenge, urge and encourage as we will, but we are totally unable to bring anyone 'from darkness to light and from the power of Satan to God' (Acts 26:18). That is God's sovereign work alone.

Fifth, evangelism means incorporation into the church, the body of Christ. And here we encounter one of the very worrying features of so much televangelism. Viewers are invited to put their hands on the TV set, to open their lives to Christ, and so forth; but only a tiny fraction of those who make some profession of faith in this setting ever come into the family of the church. Yet evangelism in the New Testament is shamelessly corporate. You may come to Christ on your own, but as soon as you do, you find yourself among a whole family of brothers and sisters. It has been well said that a Christianity which does not begin with the individual does not begin: but a Christianity which ends with the individual, ends. This is something that Protestant Christians have to learn from their Catholic brethren. As Pope Paul VI expressed it:

> Evangelisation is for no one an individual and isolated act. It is one that is deeply ecclesial. When the most obscure preacher in the most distant land preaches the gospel, gathers his little community together or administers a sacrament, even alone, he is carrying out an ecclesial act, and his action is certainly attached to the evangelising activity of the whole church.

Sixth, our definition makes it very clear that evangelism challenges decision. It is not enough for people to hear the preaching of the gospel, and to be moved by the quality of Christian lives among them. They have to decide whether or not to bow the knee to Jesus as their King. The decision may be slow or sudden: that is not the point. It may be implicit if the person has grown up and been nourished from early years in a believing home and community: or it may be very explicit. In either case it has to be made. It does not matter whether or not I can recall the day of my surrender. What matters is whether or not I am in that relationship of commitment and obedience to him *now*. The teaching of Jesus and of the apostles, the evangelistic preaching of Christians down the centuries, has always had this element of challenge. There are two ways a man may travel. There are two foundations that a life may rest on. There are two states, darkness and light, that we may inhabit. Two, and not more. There is a choice which we cannot evade. Not to decide is in fact to decide. And that decision carries immensely important and far-reaching implications. Shall we or shall we not 'come to put our trust in God through him'? Shall we or shall we not 'accept him as our Saviour'? We must choose.

Finally, the definition which Temple adopted makes the important point that true evangelism issues in discipleship. It is not simply a matter of proclaiming good news, or of eliciting decisions for Christ, getting hands raised, or a cry of commitment made. The goal in evangelism is nothing less than fulfilling the Great Commission, and making disciples of Jesus Christ. A disciple is a learner. And evangelism which is truly evangelism issues in a life that is changed from going my way to going Christ's way. There will be many a fall, of course, but the direction is what matters. And the direction of the Christian is to be headed Christ's way and to seek to serve him as our King in the fellowship of brother and sister Christians in the church. The evangelist has no business to be looking simply for decisions, important though the element of decision undoubtably is. He is out for disciples – and not for himself, his church or organisation: disciples of Jesus Christ.

Such – and nothing less – is evangelism. And the earliest Christians were always at it: in the wine shops and the streets, in the laundries and on the sea-shore. In many parts of the world, especially Africa, Asia and Latin America, they still are. But in much of Europe and North America we hang back from forthright, warm, enthusiastic evangelism. Why is that?

WHY DO WE NOT DO IT?

Perhaps the biggest reason why church people are reluctant to evangelise is because they do not think it is their business to do so. The myth has emerged in the church of the West that religion is a very private business and we must not talk about it. If anyone is to break the sound barrier, it must be the clergyman, in a highly structured situation, clothed in his robes in the midst of a church service where he is permitted to preach for up to twenty minutes without interruption. In the growing churches of the developing world it is not so. Christians recognise that every believer is called to bear witness to his or her Lord. It will take place in a variety of ways. But it will take place. The church in the West will continue to diminish and may perhaps die unless it returns to the New Testament imperative to go and be witnesses to Jesus Christ. All are not called to preach. All are not called to evangelise: that is a gift for some Christians. But all are called to give testimony to the Lord they love and serve. All have their personal story to tell, and it carries a lot of impact. This is how growing churches like the Pentecostals are spreading so fast in many countries of the world. They may not have outstanding preachers. They certainly do not have outstanding education. But they do have a clear recognition that you cannot be a Christian without being a witness to Jesus Christ. And that is the biggest lesson which traditional Western Christians need to learn.

2.   A second reason why church people are reluctant to share their faith is that many of them may not have a first-hand faith at all. They may have been church members for many years. They may have no problems with the articles of the creed. They may be delightful, kind, good people. But they may still be strangers to Jesus Christ. I know that is more than possible. I was like that myself. The letter to Laodicea (Rev. 3:14–22) has more than a first-century relevance. It was written to a church which reckoned it was rich, prosperous and lacked nothing. But the Lord, with his searing gaze, knew it to be wretched, miserable, poor, blind and naked. The ascended Christ encouraged them to change all that, in a very simple way. The Christ they knew about, the Christ they believed in, but had no personal contact with, stood outside the door of the members of that church and knocked. The response could not be corporate. Each individual had to decide whether or not he wanted Christ to come and share life with him. The same is true today. 'Repent!' says Jesus, and then makes this marvellous offer. 'Behold, I stand at the door and knock; if any one hears my voice and opens the door, I will come in to him and eat with him, and he with me' (Rev. 3:20). That verse has been the means of many thousands of people coming from nominal church attachment into personal living relationship with Jesus Christ. It was for

me. But the verse is only one of the many ways in which the New Testament writers stress the importance of a vital relationship with Jesus Christ, so that we do not merely know about him: we know him. Like St Paul, we are privileged to say, 'I know whom I have believed . . .' (2 Tim. 1:12). We may be unclear on many of the things we have believed. We may be wrong about many of them. But on one thing we are clear and confident. We *know* him. To be sure, we need to know him better. But a personal bond unites us. We can introduce others to him because we know him for ourselves.

A third reason for the silence of many Christian people about the Jesus they believe in is that they are not sure where they stand. Ask them if they are Christians, and the answer is likely to be, 'Well, I hope so. I try my best. I go to church.' It is sad that many members of the Lord's family are uncertain about their parentage. Of course that does not stop them from being children in his family, but it does rob them of confidence in that relationship. Some people regard it as arrogant to have any confidence that you are a Christian. But they suffer under a misconception, it seems to me. If membership of God's family were something we earned or had to be good enough to inherit, which of us could possibly say that we belonged? But the whole New Testament unites to assure us that such a relationship is a free gift. We do not *deserve* it one little bit, but the heavenly Father is so full of love that he delights to *give* it to us, and for us to know that we have it. Would it not be ludicrous for my father to give me a car and yet mean me not to know that I had it? It is the same with membership of God's family. He has given us his word on the matter: 'God gave us eternal life, and this life is in his Son. He who has the Son has life; he who has not the Son of God has not life' (1 John 5:12). Indeed, John follows up this very explicit statement with a powerful confirmation. 'I write this to you who believe in the name of the Son of God that you may know that you have eternal life' (John 5:13). Not think, or hope, or try: *know*! Until you know, you can no more spread the good news of God's free grace than you can build a satisfactory house on uncertain foundations. Once you are sure that you belong, unworthy though you are, then you have something to shout about!

I guess that for many of us there is a further reason why we tend to keep quiet about our Lord. For much of the time we are not living very close to him. We feel too empty for the 'overflow' which constitutes true evangelism. Sometimes we are deliberately disobedient, and are full of other concerns and priorities. But at other times we are simply low and unenthusiastic. So, like tourists going through Customs, we have nothing to declare. I recall sitting in an aeroplane once, at the end of missions in Australia which had been exhausting. I certainly did not want to talk to anyone on that flight. But a still, small voice prompted me to talk to the lady on my right, an Indian woman. I resisted: 'Lord, I'm too empty. I need a rest . . .' Well, at length I gave in, and soon discovered why that still, small voice of the Holy Spirit had been prompting me. She was on the way to the funeral of her son, and was very open to the good news of the Jesus who had conquered death. She did not become a Christian, but she was very interested. I wonder what might have ensued had I been full of the Lord and his love, and had been obedient to this prompting as soon as I was aware of it.

A fifth reason is closely allied to the one we have just been looking at. We keep quiet because to do anything else would be too costly. It is too demanding, on our time, on consistency in our lifestyle. Alternatively, it would mark us out too distinctively. Frankly, it would be too embarrassing. So although we get many an opportunity to put in a word for Christ in the office, at sport, in the home, we don't do it. It is too much hassle. It was, of course, no less costly for the early Christians. I find it significant that in the period between the ascension and Pentecost, as recorded in Acts 1, the disciples were engaged in three costly prerequisites to evangelism. First, they were really united, not only within their very diverse group, but with Mary and the brothers of Jesus who had not been part of their number during the days of Jesus' life. I imagine that reconciliation was not easy. Then we are told they gave themselves to prayer, and that is always costly. And finally they obeyed Jesus implicitly. He told them to go and await the coming of the Spirit. They did precisely that. Take the opposite of those three qualities – prayerlessness, disobedience and disunity. They represent three very good reasons why many contemporary Christians are so reluctant to bear witness to Jesus Christ.

A sixth dissuasive is our fear. We are terrified of invading someone else's privacy, or of mentioning the name of Jesus – 'It will put them off.' We are afraid of standing up and being counted: that's the real trouble. And there is no need to be, because many people are all too ready to hear about Jesus, even if the church is unattractive to them. What is more, there is no need for us to be terrified. God has offered to give us his Holy Spirit so that fear may be banished: 'You shall receive power when the Holy Spirit has come upon you; and you shall be my witnesses . . .' (Acts 1:8).

That same Spirit brings not only power into our lives, but love: and 'There is no fear in love, but perfect love casts out fear' (1 John 4:18). We need to bring God our fear, and ask for his love to fill us and his powerful Holy Spirit to empower us. Then we shall be willing to witness. I write this just after a town mission when a totally untried team had come with me. On the first day one of the young nurses on the team said, 'I'm terrified.' You should have seen her five days later, standing up and saying to that same team what a joy and privilege it had been to help two other people come to Christ during the mission. There was no trace of fear: only a joy and a confidence bred in her by the Holy Spirit himself.

A seventh reason for our reticence is our ignorance. We fear being beaten in an argument. We would not know what to say: we would mess it all up. Such fears are groundless. We could not know less than the blind man whom Jesus healed at the Pool of Bethesda. He knew no theology, yet he was not afraid to engage in discussion with the professional theologians as represented by the Pharisees. Jesus, they said, must have been a sinner because he did the reputed cure on the sabbath. God does not hear sinners, therefore the cure could not have happened. To which the man who had been blind replied in those memorable words, 'Whether he is a sinner, I do not know; one thing I know, that though I was blind, now I see' (John 9:25). Could we not all give some such simple word of commendation to Jesus Christ? If that were a commonplace among Christians in the West, as it is in the growing churches of the Third World, the gospel would spread a lot faster. We are not in business to win arguments. Our doctrinal ignorance does not greatly matter, because people are rarely, if ever, argued into the Kingdom. What *is* eloquent is the personal testimony of someone whose life has been transformed by Christ. That is what excites the imagination and interest: the doctrinal part can come later, and if necessary from someone well qualified. Ignorance is no excuse for remaining silent. We each have our own story to tell.

An eighth reason which keeps us from evangelism is the cultural isolation in which many Christians exist. It is not, of course, that they do not have contacts at work, for instance, who are not yet Christians. It is simply that they do not have any close friends that are not Christians. They live in a Christian ghetto. And the church is often to blame for this state of affairs. Pastors ask lay people to go to far too many church midweek meetings, and the result is that they do not have the time to pursue friendships outside church circles. There is a dangerous tendency, in a church which in the

West is generally declining, to seek friendships, relationships and relaxation primarily, if not exclusively, within Christian circles. I recall how, in Bombay, I was once shocked to see a notice for a 'Christian Swimming Club'. But although we may not advertise it like that in the West, much the same attitude prevails. It is so much easier to spend our time and make our friends among those who share our Christian faith. But that is not the Jesus way. We are called to come out of the ghetto. The lamp has to get onto the lampstand: the salt has to get out as a preservative into the meat. The ghetto mentality, lauded as a virtue in some Christian circles, needs to be replaced by Jesus' own (difficult) prescription for his followers: they are to be 'in the world, but not of the world'. A lovely story is told of St Vincent, who wanted to reach the slaves in the Roman galleys with the gospel. He was notably unsuccessful – until he himself became a galley slave and was able to proclaim the good news when he was one of them, sharing their situation and conditions. You can, as one wise man put it – almost truly – only evangelise friends.

9. There is a final reason which succeeds in gagging most of us. We simply do not see the need of evangelising our friends. We live in an age of the global village. All faiths, and none, jostle one another in our streets. There is an exclusiveness about Christianity, claiming that God has come for us and died for us and calls us to allegiance to himself, which is very shocking. What about all the other religions? Are they not also ways to God? And does it matter, anyhow, what we believe so long as we are sincere? Sincerity has become one of the few values to survive in an age of disenchantment. Tolerance is one of the few qualities universally applauded in an age of unparalleled diversity. What, then, are we doing if we push our beliefs down the throats of others, who may perfectly well be quite happy as they are? Why should we bother with evangelism?

WHY BOTHER WITH EVANGELISM?

We need good reasons if we are to combat the forces of inertia, fear, embarrassment and distraction which keep us from evangelism. Well, there are many good reasons why we should bother: here are some of them.

The love of God

We Christians should bother because of God the Father's love. Evangelism follows from the nature of the God we worship. Did he keep himself in icy isolation from our predicament? Did he say, 'They are probably all right as they are'? Far from it. 'God so loved the world that he gave his only Son, that whoever believes in him should not perish but have eternal life' (John 3:16). The God we worship is the supreme lover.

All lovers will give anything, endure anything, do anything for the beloved. That is what our God is like. And if we are children of such a God, it stands to reason that we should mirror in our own attitudes that love of his for people who do not deserve it at all. Did God *like* the world as he saw it? Of course not. It consisted of human beings and whole societies marred and spoiled by sin. He did not – could not – like the world. But he could – and did – love it. The *agapē* love of God is not determined by the supposed worthiness of the object, as all other forms of love are, but by the nature of the lover. God is love, and he pours that love out indiscriminately on his creatures. His followers need to be infected by that quality of supernatural love for needy and often unpleasant people. It is one of the most notable indications of our parentage. 'Love your enemies', said Jesus, and in this way you will show yourselves to be the 'sons of your Father who is in heaven; for he makes his sun rise on the evil and on the good, and sends his rain on the just and on the unjust' (Matt. 5:44–5). That is the supreme reason for engaging in evangelism. We worship a God who had only one Son: and he gave himself to be a missionary. Such love becomes infectious.

The command of Jesus

A second reason why we should bother springs from the direct command of God the Son. Jesus told his disciples very clearly to 'Go . . . and make disciples of all nations, baptizing them in the name of the Father and of the Son and of the Holy Spirit' (Matt. 28:19). That was in fact his last injunction to them before he left this earth. Now the last words of a dear friend are very special. We pay a lot of attention to them. And these last words of Jesus rang very true to his whole character. He had been pouring himself out for others throughout his ministry. He intended his followers to do the same. I remember when my mother died. She had had a massive heart attack, but had managed to scrawl down on an old envelope some messages to me in case I did not reach her before she died. You can imagine how seriously I took those last wishes of hers. They were a sacred trust. That is how Christians are expected to treat the last command of Jesus, the Great Commission as it is often called. If Jesus made evangelism the subject of his last command to his disciples on earth, then it must be important. If we love him and seek to obey him, then we must carry it out.

The gift of the Spirit

A third motivation for evangelism is the gift of the Holy Spirit. The Spirit is intimately connected with mission. Jesus said, 'When the Counsellor comes, whom I shall send to you from the Father, . . . he will bear witness to me; and you also are witnesses, because you have been with me from the beginning' (John 15:26–7). And, 'As the Father has sent me, even so I send you . . . Receive the Holy Spirit' (John 20:21–2). Unquestionably there is a vital link between receiving the Holy Spirit and bearing witness to Jesus. This is not surprising. It is the work of the Spirit to glorify Jesus, and he builds that longing into our very being. Actually, this is a solemn barometer of our openness to the Holy Spirit. If we are full of the Spirit we will be full of the desire to share Jesus with other people. If we have no desire to share Christ with those who do not know him, there is every reason to doubt whether the Spirit is present in our lives at all, let alone filling us. For the whole purpose of the gift of the Spirit is to make us like Christ, and witnesses to Christ. He is given for mission. Without him the disciples would not have dared to venture out into evangelism. With him they could not hold back.

Those are three powerful reasons, three highly theological reasons, why we should bother about evangelism. They are rooted in the very nature of the Godhead. Father, Son and Holy Spirit are profoundly concerned for evangelism. The God we worship is a missionary God. And so we too should be committed to mission.

The climax of history

There is another profoundly theological consideration which thrills the Christian once it is understood. As I look back, I can see that it has been determinative in my own love for evangelism. The New Testament makes it clear that evangelism is in some way connected with the final return of Christ at the consummation of all history. It prepares the way for his return. He told his disciples as much in the apocalyptic discourse in Mark 13. Before the final coming of the Son of Man, 'the gospel must first be preached to all nations' (v.10). Such proclamation need not be by formal discourse. The context in Mark contemplates Christians being dragged before the authorities and having to give an account of their faith. Jesus promises that when they do, it will not merely be them speaking, but the Holy Spirit speaking through them (v.11). And that of course has happened throughout history. One thinks of the Russian hero Georgi Vins taking the opportunity of his trial to bear fearless witness to Jesus in the heart of the Stalinist repression of Christians – and being given a massive gaol sentence as a result.

Significantly, in the farewell discourse in John 14–16 the coming of the Paraclete, the mission of the church and the ultimate return of Christ are inextricably woven together. And when in Acts 1 the puzzled disciples are speculating about the end of history, Jesus strongly discourages them, tells them to wait in Jerusalem until they have received the power of his Holy Spirit, and then, armed with that Spirit, to go and be his witnesses in Jerusalem, Judaea, Samaria and to the ends of the earth. No less a commission must be undertaken before Jesus returns to wind up all history at his parousia. We can therefore in evangelism actually 'hasten' the day of the Lord, in the sense that we can fulfil his purposes in spreading the gospel and so facilitating his return. How human ministry of this nature can be reconciled with the sovereignty of God which controls the timings and destiny of history we may never know. But we are clearly given the assurance that the mission of the church in the power of the Spirit is a significant factor in when the final end of history will be. And that is a noble vision and a powerful stimulus.

Those reasons should be enough, and more than enough, to motivate our sluggish hearts and reluctant lips. But if not, there are other strong considerations.

The responsibility of the church

We should bother because of our responsibility. The only people who can make Christ known are those who already know him. He relies on us. 'We are ambassadors for Christ,' wrote Paul, 'God making his appeal through us. We beseech you on behalf of Christ, be reconciled to God' (2 Cor. 5:20). A country's policies are communicated abroad through its embassy, and 'we are an embassy from heaven' (Phil. 3:20). It is through his people that God means to communicate with those he longs to reach. The reality of what he offers is best seen in the lives of those who have begun to be changed by it. Conviction is best communicated by those who have themselves been convinced by Christ. Time after time in the New Testament the same theme is repeated. 'We are God's fellow workers' (1 Cor. 3:9). He relies on us. 'Therefore, having this ministry by the mercy of God, we do not lose heart' (2 Cor. 4:1). And the ministry he speaks of is the ministry of evangelism. We have a responsibility for it. If our close friends perish for lack of this life-saving good news, the responsibility will lie at our door. Paul was very clear about that. In Romans 1:14–15 he roundly declared, 'I am under obligation both to Greeks and to barbarians, both to the wise and to the foolish: so I am eager to preach the gospel . . .' And in Miletus he reminded his friends in the leadership of the church at Ephesus that he was innocent of the blood of them all, for he had not shrunk back from declaring to them the full counsel of God (Acts 20:26). Could we say the same?

The privilege of Christians

We should bother on account of the privilege that is ours. For we have, as Paul mused in 2 Corinthians 4:1, received mercy from God. Not only mercy, but we have received this ministry. What a privilege! Not only to be forgiven and reinstated in God's family, but also to be given employment in what we might reverently call 'the family business'. God does not appear to use angels for this task. He does not use men and women of great ability and power who have not bowed in surrender to him. No, he restricts himself for the most part to working through those who were rebels but have surrendered their arms and enlisted in his service. It is only pardoned sinners who can invite others to the cross of Christ. It is an amazing privilege to be given such a sacred trust. And Paul, for one, never forgot it. In 1 Corinthians 15:9 he is brought low by the memory that he had persecuted the church of God. Incredible that he should be taken on in the Master's service. Why, he was not worthy to be called an apostle!

But by the time he wrote Ephesians, a few years later, that sense of unworthiness had deepened. He speaks joyfully of the grace which has allowed him and empowered him to be a minister of the gospel. But he goes on to confess that he is less than the very least of all the Christians. His awareness of the privilege of the task was outweighed by his awareness of his own unworthiness (Eph. 3:7ff.).

By the time he wrote 1 Timothy, towards the end of his life, he had sunk still lower in his self-esteem. Once again he revels in the privilege of preaching 'the glorious gospel of the blessed God with which I have been entrusted' (1 Tim. 1:11). But once again he is desperately ashamed of the pride and rebellion which blinded him for so long to that same gospel. 'I formerly blasphemed and persecuted and insulted [Christ Jesus]; but I received mercy because I had acted ignorantly . . . The saying is sure and worthy of full acceptance, that Christ Jesus came into the world to save sinners. And I am the foremost of sinners' (1 Tim. 1:13–15). Do you see what has happened? As he has grown older in the faith, so he has grown correspondingly smaller in his own esteem. First, he was not worthy of the name of apostle; then, less than the very least of all Christians; last, the chief of sinners! There is a man who was well aware of the privilege of being God's messenger to a careless world.

The need of mankind

There is another reason which should motivate us powerfully in the direction of evangelism. It is the need of people without Jesus Christ. The New Testament is most unfashionable and most unflinching on this issue. It maintains that without Christ men and women are dead (Eph. 2:1) – spiritually defunct, although physically, mentally and socially alive. They are lost, like travellers in a fog (Luke 19:10). They are 'wretched, pitiable, poor, blind, and naked', though they think themselves 'rich, prosperous and in need of nothing' (Rev. 3:14–21). They are 'alienated from the life of God because of the ignorance that is in them, due to their hardness of heart' (Eph. 4:18). They are 'separated from Christ . . . having no hope and without God in the world' (Eph. 2:12).

Nowhere is the human predicament more clearly displayed than in a closely argued passage of Paul to the Corinthians where he says, 'if our gospel is veiled, it is veiled only to those who are

perishing. In their case the god of this world has blinded the minds
of the unbelievers, to keep them from seeing the light of the gospel
of the glory of Christ, who is the likeness of God' (2 Cor. 4:3–4).
Notice what he is saying. First, that those who do not know Christ
are perishing. They have not perished yet, but they are on the way
to perishing, like shipwrecked mariners adrift in the midst of the
ocean. Second, there is an unseen enemy whom Paul calls, like his
Master before him, 'the god of this world'. It is none other than
Satan, who has displaced God in so many peoples' hearts and
enthroned himself there instead. So people are not only on the
path to ruin but in bondage to a pseudo-god who in effect controls
the issues of their lives. But how could sensible people put up with
such a thing? Because their minds are blinded by enemy propaganda. Satan does not care how civilised they are, how kind,
how intelligent, how moral: if only he can keep them from 'seeing
the light of the good news of Christ' he is more than satisfied. Then
they will remain in his domain, and not 'convert' or cross over into
Christ's territory. Such is the Enemy's aim. The propaganda he
uses to keep men duped is manifold – 'Christianity will kill your
freedom', 'The Bible is a load of old wives' tales', 'You can't
believe in God these days', and so forth. And the result? Men are
perishing, captive, and blind both to their predicament and to the
glory of the good news Christ wants them to share.

It is hard, very hard, to believe this. We feel, 'It can't be as bad as
that.' But the New Testament assures us that it is indeed as bad as
that. It maintains that the comfortable middle ground on which we
would all like to live simply does not exist. There are two realms,
darkness and light. There are two rulers, Satan and God. There are
two ways, the broad and the narrow. There are two destinations,
life and destruction. There are two choices, for him or against him.
There are two groups, described variously as wheat and tares, wise
and foolish virgins, inside or outside of the feast, or the city, or
Christ. There are two foundations for life: either you build on
Christ, which is the only solid rock in the whole world. Or you build
on anything else whatever, and you will find that, in the last
analysis, it is nothing more than shifting sand. I wish it were not so.
I wish there were lots of broad middle ground. But the New
Testament in general, and Jesus in particular, warns us that such is
not the case. We have a fatal disease, called sin. There is one place,
and only one, where an antitoxin is distilled for that fatal disease.
And that is the cross of Jesus Christ. Without it we shall perish.
That is the unvarnished message of the New Testament, and

nobody who has taken the trouble to examine the documents can deny it.

Do you see that? Do you believe it? If you do, it will drive you out into loving, determined evangelism, day in day out. That is what motivated Paul to carry on, when he could so easily have rested on his laurels after his prodigious evangelistic labours. But no. 'We do not lose heart', he claims (2 Cor. 4:1). We do not draw back. He repeats the claim (2 Cor. 4:16). It is no less than the truth, and it is very near the heart of his unparalleled missionary dynamism. He is gripped by the sheer need of those who were strangers to his Lord Jesus. William Booth, the founder of the Salvation Army, was stung into wholehearted Christian service by a sceptic who said, 'If I believed what you Christians believe, I would not rest day or night from telling people about it.'

I recall reading a letter written by communists in Latin America. It displays some of the passionate commitment which should characterise Christians:

> We communists have a high casualty rate. We are the ones who get shot and hung and lynched and jailed, slandered and ridiculed and fired from our jobs, and in every other way made as uncomfortable as possible. A certain percentage of us get killed or imprisoned. We live in virtual poverty . . . We have been described as fanatics. We are fanatics. Our lives are dominated by one great overshadowing factor – the struggle for world communism.
>
> We communists have a philosophy of life which no amount of money could buy. We have a cause to fight for, a definite purpose in life. We subordinate our petty personal selves into a great movement of humanity, and if our personal lives seem hard, we are adequately compensated by the thought that each of us, in his small way, is contributing to something new and true and better for mankind.
>
> There is one thing in which I am in dead earnest, and that is the communist cause. It is my life, my business, my religion, my hobby, my wife, my mistress, my bread and meat. I work at it in the daytime, and dream of it by night. Its hold on me grows, not lessens, as time goes by. Therefore I cannot carry on a friendship, a love affair, or even a conversation without relating it to this force which both drives me and guides my life . . . I've been to jail because of my ideas, and if necessary I'm ready to go before a firing squad.

If communists will do that for their cause, what a challenge this poses to the Christian who sees not just the socio-economic but the eternal need and privation of his 'uninitiated' friends.

The joy of mission

I have found that there is a further incitement to mission. There is, frankly, no joy like it. That note of joy runs through the encounters with Jesus in the New Testament. Think of the joy of Andrew finding who Jesus is, and dragging his brother Peter along to meet him. Think of the joy of Zacchaeus, liberated from bondage to money and set free to be the friend of Jesus. Think of that same strain running through the parables: the joy of the pearl-fancier discovering the pearl of great price; the joy of the farmer striking a box of hidden treasure in what must have seemed a very dull field; the joy of the bridesmaids going in to the wedding feast, and so forth.

One of the most widely credited and wildly inaccurate myths is that Christianity is dull. It is nothing of the kind. Formal religion is as dull as ditchwater. But the friendship of Jesus, which lies at the heart of true Christianity, is the most exhilarating thing in the world. 'In thy presence there is fullness of joy, in thy right hand are pleasures for evermore' sang the psalmist (Ps. 16:11). And it is true. True when you find Christ for yourself. True when you are given the inestimable privilege of helping someone else to find him. It is certainly difficult at times. It can be very demanding. But there is no joy on earth to compare with that of leading a friend to Christ. If only church-people who are so timid and cautious about it could be persuaded of that, nothing could keep them silent. God's gagged people would become his confident people. But some of them have become discouraged, and many of them have never tried to help another person to faith. They are missing the greatest joy this world affords.

FURTHER READING

In considering the content of this chapter, you might find the following books useful:

Michael Green, *Evangelism Now and Then* (Inter-Varsity Press)
H. T. Hoekstra, *Evangelism in Eclipse* (Paternoster Press)
Lumen Gentium, in A. Flannery (ed.), *Vatican Council II* (Fowler Wright Books)
Towards the Conversion of England (Church Assembly)
David Watson, *I Believe in Evangelism* (Hodder & Stoughton)

2

Clearing the Ground

Before we go much further, we must clear a way through the theological and linguistic jungle. If we are going to talk about evangelism, a little clarification will be useful. We have seen in the previous chapter what evangelism is. But there are some related issues which will concern us a good deal in this book, and a chapter defining what we mean will save confusion later. There are four questions in particular which call for an answer: What is man? What is salvation? What is conversion? What is baptism?

WHAT IS MAN?

There is no question that will dominate the rest of the twentieth century more than this: What is man?

There are many who take an optimistic view of man. A few years ago, in the Reith Lectures in Britain, Dr Edmund Leach, Provost of King's College, Cambridge, maintained that men are now gods, and had better start behaving that way. Shakespeare put it rather more modestly, but with great flair, in *Hamlet*: 'What a piece of work is a man, how noble in reason, how infinite in faculties, in form and moving how express and admirable, in action how like an angel, in apprehension how like a god: the beauty of the world, the paragon of animals!'

This view of man is still somewhat evident among the scientific community. There has been such a remarkable development of human potential in the past century that some people feel 'the sky is the limit'. Man is glorious. Man is in charge of his destiny.

This assessment of man sprang from an evolutionary optimism, common at the beginning of the century, but increasingly threadbare as the century proceeded. H. G. Wells is a typical example. In 1937 he wrote, 'Can we doubt that presently our race will more than realise our boldest imaginations, that it will achieve unity and peace? What man has done, the little triumphs of his present state, form but the prelude to the things that man has yet to do.' By 1945, after the Second World War, things looked worse. In *The Fate of Homo Sapiens* Wells wrote:

> I see man being carried less and less intelligently and more and more rapidly along the stream of fate to degradation, suffering and death. The wanton destruction of homes, the ruthless herding of decent folk into exile, the bombing of open cities, the coldblooded massacre and mutilation of children and defenceless folk, the rapes and filthy humiliations, and above all the return of deliberate and cold-blooded torture has come near to breaking my spirit altogether.

A few years later, in his last book, *Mind at the End of Its Tether*, his conclusion was more sombre still: 'There is no way out, or round, or through.'

All of which leads us to the more common estimate of man as we approach the end of the century. A widespread pessimism is abroad, a profound fear about where the world is heading. Two world wars have convulsed the globe. Germany, one of the most civilised nations in the world, perpetrated the Holocaust on the Jews. We are ruining our environment with the poisoning of the seas, the destruction of the rain forests, the erosion of the ozone layer of our atmosphere. For the first time in history man has the capacity to destroy the planet many times over with nuclear missiles, and there is no reason to suppose he might not do it. Remember Hiroshima and Nagasaki . . . Optimistic humanists are therefore a much rarer species than they were half a century ago. The ugly facts of our world belie the hypothesis that we are all good folks at heart and are getting better all the time. Superman may be an entertaining figure in science fiction films, but mankind is manifestly not developing in that direction. The breakdown of marriage and family, the worldwide increase of torture and wanton killing, the mindless hedonism and greed and the emptiness of belief and purpose which characterise so much of the Western world do little to support an optimistic view of human nature.

The overwhelming difference between mankind today and a few centuries ago is the collapse of a sense of purpose. Of course there is purpose on a restricted scale: for today's programme, for our children's education, and so forth. But when one poses the question 'What is life for?' or 'Why does the world exist?' not many answers are forthcoming, in this age which is to all intents and purposes godless. Nobody has expressed this phenomenon and its consequences more clearly than Jean-Paul Sartre and Albert Camus.

They have looked into the abyss of atheism and have had the courage to draw the logical but chilling conclusion. If God is dead, as Nietzsche had maintained, then so is man. We come from nowhere and are going nowhere. Any pretence to the contrary is hypocrisy. And so you find in these very courageous thinkers who have honestly faced the implications of atheism a desperately low estimate of man. 'Every existent being is born without reason, prolongs itself out of weakness, and dies by chance,' wrote Sartre in *Nausea*. 'The essential thing is contingency. Contingency is not an illusion, an appearance which can be dissipated. It is absolute, and consequently, absolute futility. When you realise that, it turns your stomach over, and everything starts floating about.' Elsewhere in *Nausea* Sartre confesses:

> The world is not the product of intelligence. It meets our gaze as would a dirty, crumpled piece of paper, soaked in rain. It is absurd, nauseating . . . Man, too, has no divinely prepared nature to be fulfilled by action. What is he but a little puddle of water, whose freedom is death?

And Camus takes up the theme in *Caligula*: 'This world has no importance. Once a man realises that, he wins freedom.' But does he? Camus continues: 'What is intolerable is to see life drained of meaning, to be told there is no reason for existence. A man cannot live without some reason for living.' But alas, Camus could see no reason for living. Man is basically junk. He comes from plankton and is bound for extinction. That is all. Therefore his only hope is to make meaning where there is none, and to live it up – *vivre le plus possible*.

And this is the outlook of a great many modern people. Unconsciously they have adopted the views of Sartre and Camus. Though they could not express it like this, they think with Francis Bacon, the famous modern painter, that

> Man now realises he is an accident. He is a completely futile being. He has to play out the game without reason. Earlier artists were still conditioned by certain types of religious possibilities, which man now, you could say, has had cancelled out for him. Man can now only hope

to beguile himself for a time by prolonging his life, by buying a kind of immortality through the doctors.

The Nobel Prizewinner Jacques Monod strikes precisely the same note in *Chance and Necessity*: 'The universe was not pregnant with life, nor the biosphere with man. Our number came up in the Monte Carlo game.' So,

> man must at last awake out of his millennial dreams. And in so doing, wake to his total solitude, his fundamental isolation. Like a gypsy he lives on the boundary of an alien world, a world that is deaf to his music, and as indifferent to his hopes, as it is to his suffering or his crimes.

To believe this is a logical consequence of atheism. But the trouble is that we cannot entirely suppress the instinctive belief that such a view is false. In his very influential book *The Selfish Gene*, Richard Dawkins has argued for a thoroughly materialist explanation of even the generous, altruistic side of mankind. Human life is entirely governed by our genes, those 'unconscious, blind replicators'. But at the end of his book he expresses the hope that mankind may after all have the capacity for 'a genuine, disinterested, true altruism' – but declines to argue the case either way. He ends the book on this note. 'We, alone on earth, can rebel against the tyranny of the selfish replicators.' The high moral tone of hope and freedom in the last sentence is totally at odds with the whole of his previous argument that we are biologically determined. He is not convinced by his own pessimistic thesis. He cannot live with it.

And that is the trouble with atheistic humanism, optimistic or pessimistic. It is threadbare. It has no firm base for its noble precepts or brave hopes about the value of mankind. Keith Ward says it well in *The Battle for the Soul*:

> It tells us to respect humanity, in ourselves and others; to preserve the dignity of man. And yet, in a low but audible whisper, it tells us that it really knows, as we all do, that man has no dignity, in the perspective of eternity. There is nothing special about humanity: it will not survive. It is the chance product of random mutation. Our fondness for it is little more than a sort of magnified partiality, beyond rational justification.

The Christian faith is profoundly dissatisfied with both the pessimists and the optimists in the humanist camp. It refuses to see man as a god, knowing all too well our sin, failure and selfishness, and our propensity to foul even our own nest. The optimistic humanists have not paid sufficient attention to the dark side of human nature. On the other hand, Christianity can never agree with Sartre that 'man is an empty bubble on the sea of nothingness'. That takes away the glory of man – and there *is* glory in every person, however debased. 'I am fearfully and wonderfully made' sang the psalmist (Ps. 139:14, NIV). I believe that only the Judaeo-Christian revelation gives a credible account of man. It tells us that we are indeed created as a noble temple, fit for the Lord to inhabit. But we have become derelict: the marks of nobility are there still, but in terrible disarray. We are like a beautifully laid out garden that has run wild.

It is very important that we understand man in this way. For, as Elton Trueblood put it, 'Unless it is true that each person, regardless of race or sex, is one who is made in the image of God, much of the impetus for social justice is removed.' Only such a view of man gives us that respect for human life which alone can save our world from the madness of destruction. 'It is a serious thing', said C. S. Lewis, 'to live in a society of potential gods and goddesses. It is immortals who we joke with, work with, marry, snub and exploit – immortal horrors or everlasting splendours.' And that humanity, for all its ambiguities and pains, has been ennobled beyond belief by the incarnation. 'For whatever reason,' Lewis continued, 'God chose to make man as he is – limited and suffering and subject to sorrows and death. He had the honesty and courage to take his own medicine.' And because he did, we have a standard, an ideal by which to judge human nature. It is in the light of this that we see how substandard we all are, and how desperately in need of refashioning by the man of Nazareth. There is a superb assessment of the human condition in William Temple's book, *Citizen and Churchman*:

Man is both animal and spiritual. On one side he is the most fully developed of the animals; but if that were all, he would present, and know, no problems. Upon him is stamped the Image of God; he is capable of that communion with God which is eternal life. But here again we find two-sidedness; for the Image of God in man is blurred and distorted. How or why this should be so is a question too large for discussion here. The fact is certain. Man, capable by his nature as God made it, of communion with God as the author, centre, and goal of his being, does always in greater or lesser degree conduct himself as though he were himself his own beginning and end, the centre of his own universe. His 'sin' is not a mere survival or disproportionate development of animal tendencies, or an inadequate development of

rational control. It is a perversion of reason itself. His capacity for
divine communion is become a usurpation of divine authority. The
worst, the most typical sin, from which all other sin flows, is not
sensuality but pride.

Man is the vicegerent of God's world. He is also the rebel in
God's world, and the object of God's love. The image of God is
there, albeit so marred. The wonder of it all is that this image can
be restored in Christ. And that is a powerful motive to evangelism.

WHAT IS SALVATION?

This is a vast, broad topic, some of whose aspects I have tried to
address in *The Meaning of Salvation*. The word is commonly
applied to political and social movements, and to individual and
religious claims. How are we to conceive of salvation in the context
of evangelism? What aspect of salvation is the evangelist seeking to
realise?

In the Old Testament the theme of God as Saviour of his people
is central. And salvation wears many faces: rescue from narrow
and confining conditions, from distress, enemies, defeat, and occasionally sin. There is a future aspect to salvation, and it is progressively understood as the history of Israel unfolds. At no point
is salvation seen as coming to mankind through human effort or
religious cultus: it is always seen as the work of God himself, either
independently or through using some human agent.

In the New Testament the theme continues, only now salvation
is vested in the person of Jesus. His name means 'God to the
rescue' or 'Yahweh saves'. And the understanding of that salvation
is developed as the New Testament progresses. Its centre point was
the cross and resurrection of Jesus, but it stretches back to his
birth, and on into heaven. Indeed, it would not be inaccurate to
regard the famous story about Bishop Westcott and the Salvation
Army girl as a clear summary of what the Bible teaches about
salvation.

There was a day, so the story goes, when Bishop Westcott was
seated in a train, wearing his frock coat, gaiters and all. In got a girl
from the Salvation Army, and seeing that her travelling companion
was a bishop, she very much doubted if he were saved. So she
decided to pluck up courage and ask him. 'Bishop,' she said, 'are

you saved?' '*Sōtheis, sōzomenos ē sōthēsomenos?*' murmured the
Bishop, who was reading the Greek New Testament. He wondered
whether she meant, 'Have I been saved? Am I being saved? or
Shall I be saved?' The answer to all those three questions is not
necessarily the same!

There is, in fact, no New Testament warrant for someone
claiming to be saved in the final and absolute sense. It is perfectly
right to claim that because Christ died for me on the cross I have
been saved from the spiritual death which my self-centredness
richly merited. I have, if you like, been saved from the penalty of
my sins, though 'penalty' is an image much more common in
modern preaching than in the teaching and language of the New
Testament. I can be sure that 'my sins and iniquities he will
remember no more' and my accusing past will not rise to haunt me.
He has himself taken care of that. The word 'saved' is used in that
past tense, but only two or three times in the whole New Testament, and then with some such significant addition as 'in hope'.

But it is a good deal more frequent in the present tense, meaning
both protection in Christ and power through the Spirit. Salvation is
very much a continuing experience of relationship with the Saviour
God. I either am or am not, at any one time, drawing on his
resources and so being protected from the sin and selfishness which
constantly assail me. There is nothing predetermined or cut-and-
dried about it. Some of the time I am enjoying that divine aid; some
of the time I go my own way and decline it.

There is a third aspect to salvation, and it lies in the future. And
it is here, curiously enough, that the majority of New Testament
usage concentrates. Salvation is an eschatological concept, like
justification. But in the goodness of God I am enabled, if I trust
him, to anticipate here and now the ultimate verdict, and to enjoy
here and now something of the power of that salvation, however
imperfectly. But the day will come when we shall enjoy it together
in all its fullness in the Father's house. Salvation is a word which
points to heaven, and in that sense, of course, none of us can claim
it, for none of us on this earth has got there yet.

The Bishop was right. There are indeed three tenses of salvation, past, present and future. It is hardly surprising that the Bible
does not encourage us to say 'I am saved', and leave it at that. But,
it does allow us to say:

> I *have been* saved from the *penalty* of sin, by Christ's death and
> resurrection.

I *am* (sometimes) being saved from the *power* of sin, by the indwelling Spirit.

I *shall* one day be saved from the very *presence* of sin, when I go to be with God.

It is important for evangelists to understand this triple usage of the word 'salvation' in Scripture, and to proclaim it appropriately. It will save them from bad theology in evangelism, which is, alas, all too common.

If freezing salvation into a past experience is one danger to which evangelists are prone, another is to regard it as something very personal and individual. It is a curious fact that the man in the street so often shares with the evangelist at the street corner the conviction that religion is a very personal and private affair. For the man in the street it is so private that he feels it inappropriate even to discuss it. For the evangelist it is so personal and individual that one would never guess that salvation in the Bible is constantly seen as a corporate affair. The Old Testament's hope of the redeemed community is one where God's *shalom* reigns. The element of personal forgiveness is there, but so is the mutual belonging, the restoration of relationships, the social transformation, the victory over forces of decay and destruction, and God's healing touch. In the New Testament the societal aspect of salvation is strongly stressed, as is its link with healing. To be sure, community and healing will never be complete in this life, any more than salvation will. Their climax lies beyond the grave. But any evangelism which does not make clear God's will to rescue and transform the whole of life, physical and spiritual, and which does not make clear the mutual interdependence of those who are experiencing salvation, is deficient. Salvation is a mighty concept. It is God's sovereign act of rescue. It is tasted here and now, but only fully enjoyed in the life to come. It touches the whole of life: the notion of merely 'saving souls' is profoundly unbiblical. And it embraces individuals, in their lostness and fragmentation, and puts them into the family of God the Saviour which, in turn, is intended to exert a profound effect upon society at large.

WHAT IS CONVERSION?

Conversion as such is very rarely spoken of in Scripture. Perhaps as a result, it is understood in a very wide variety of ways. Is it a matter of Christian proclamation – or Christian presence? Is it a crisis – or a process? Is it a doctrine – or an experience? Is it initiatory – or continuous?

All these questions, and more, gather round the little word 'conversion'. How are Christian evangelists to use the word?

On the whole I try not to use it, because of the web of confusion over its meaning that befuddles many minds. It may make some sense to speak of a Hindu being converted to Christianity, but the word has very different undertones when it is used of someone who has moved in Christian circles and given assent to Christian teaching for many years. It conjures up the unhelpful image of itinerant tent based missions, or of a massive emotional high. If we are to use it at all, it is something far more profound than this. It is that encounter with the living Christ which can appropriately be described as a new birth, a radical restructuring of our lives by God himself. 'It cannot be a process only of enlightenment,' wrote William Temple. 'Nothing can suffice but a redemptive act. Something impinging on the self from without must deliver it from the freedom which is perfect bondage to the bondage which is its only perfect freedom.' 'I felt', wrote Monica Furlong, 'that I had been born for this moment, and that I had marked time till it occurred.' 'There may have been a neurotic element in the make-up of Saul of Tarsus, John Bunyan, and George Fox,' wrote H. G. Wood, 'and this may account for some of the features in the story of the conversion of each. But in all three examples, the man is re-made psychologically, morally and intellectually.'

Let us take the most famous of all such examples, Saul of Tarsus. His conversion gives us some important insights into both the meaning of the word and the experience.

In a letter to Timothy, Paul in later years looked back on his conversion and saw it not as the most bizarre exception to every known rule of religious experience, but as 'an example to those who were to believe in [Christ] for eternal life' (1 Tim. 1:16). Of course the specifics were not repeated, and should certainly not be looked for: the blindness, the falling to the ground, the voice from heaven and so forth – though some of them do occur in some conversions. No, Paul is claiming that certain *principles* which were active in his conversion are always active in every conversion. And it is not too difficult to see what they were. There are four factors which combined to bring about the conversion of Saul the persecutor into Paul the apostle and martyr.

First, God touched his conscience. He who had held the clothes for the men who stoned Stephen, the first Christian martyr, and had expressed solidarity with them, must often have looked back on that day with shame and guilt. On the Damascus Road, if not beforehand, he became aware that in persecuting Stephen he was really persecuting the one who stood behind Stephen, Jesus Christ himself. 'Saul, Saul, why do you persecute *me*?' (Acts 9:4). There were other things, too, weighing on his mind. He implies in Romans 7:7–11 and Philippians 3:6 that in his pursuit of excellence he could face all the first nine of God's commandments with equanimity; but the tenth slew him. He could see that he was riddled with covetous desires. He could see that he would never be good enough to stand before God. Awareness of need (not always of guilt – that may come later) is a precondition of coming to God to have that need met. Paul's conscience was touched.

Second, God illuminated his mind. He had long known, from Deuteronomy 21:23, that anyone exposed in death upon a wooden stake was perceived to rest under the curse of God. Very well, Jesus must have been accursed, for that is where he ended up. How could he be the Messiah? It was a blasphemous claim. And that is why Saul of Tarsus set himself to stamp out this earliest Christian movement.

But on the Damascus Road all that changed. He came to see that his premise was right, but his conclusion was wrong. Jesus was indeed accursed, but the curse he bore was *our* curse. (Paul developed this theme in Galatians 3:10, 13, and 2 Corinthians 5:21.)

Saul also came to see, on that Damascus Road, that the resurrection was no myth or deceit: it was God's great act of vindicating his crucified Messiah. 'Who are you, Lord?' he asked in awe. 'I am Jesus, whom you are persecuting' was the reply (Acts 9:5). That was the revelation which bowled him over on the Damascus Road. Jesus had borne his curse, his guilt, his sins. And Jesus was alive, addressing him personally. I doubt if he understood much more at that time. Later, of course, he became one of the greatest Christian thinkers ever. But it is comforting to reflect on how little he must have known when he was converted. He had some idea of the significance of the death and resurrection of Jesus. No more. It will be so with many whom the evangelist leads to faith. And that is totally proper. The growth in understanding can come later. You don't have to know how electricity works in order to turn on the light!

Third, God touched his will. Paul realised that a challenge like this, a sacrifice like this, a reality like this, could not be shrugged off. He had to decide. Was he going to continue to slaughter the Christians, or was he going to join them? It was a matter of his will. Which way would he go? He did in fact allow himself to be led, a willing captive, into Damascus. From now on it would be Christ's way, not his own. He had no idea of what the future held. He simply knew who held the future, and he put his life in Christ's hands. The element of will, of decision, is an ineluctable strand in Christian conversion. It may only be implicit, but it has to be there. When absolute Love addresses me, I have to reply. It is interesting that the phrase describing Saul as 'trembling and astonished' is present in some manuscripts but not the best ones. Emotion is not the thing that an evangelist should aim at. It may be there, or it may not. If it is not, he must not seek to work it up. If it is there, he should seek to get through the emotion to the citadel of the will. That is what needs to be stormed, not the emotions. An emotional response (alone) is the very opposite of authentic conversion. Conversion aims for a turn around in the will: any emotional stirrings are strictly optional and not necessarily even desirable.

Fourth, God transformed the whole of the rest of his life. First, his Christian initiation was completed through his baptism in water and the Spirit through the agency of Ananias. Immediately he sought Christian fellowship. He allowed himself to be helped by those whom, a day or two earlier, he would have despised. He wanted to tell others about Jesus. He was willing to face opposition for the cause. He found prayer a quite new and exhilarating reality. He grew in strength and understanding. He was willing to embrace a career of privation and suffering. All this we learn from Acts 9, which records his conversion. It was a total turn-round, which affected the whole of the rest of his life. Leo Tolstoy experienced something just as radical:

> Five years ago I came to believe in Christ's teaching, and my life suddenly changed. I ceased to desire what I had previously desired, and began to desire what I formerly did not want. What had previously seemed to me good seemed evil, and what had seemed evil seemed good. It happened to me as it happens to a man who goes out on some business, and on the way decides that the business is unnecessary and

returns home. All that was on his right is now on his left, and all that was on his left is now on his right.

That, no less, is Christian conversion. It is the human side of regeneration. God 'regenerates' me, or gives me his new life, when I 'convert', or turn to him in order gratefully to receive the gift. It is all part of the grace-faith reciprocal. It is man's response to God's initiative.

We are now much better placed to answer the confusions and questions about conversion with which we started. Conversion does not spring from Christian proclamation alone, or Christian presence alone. It springs from the two together. The presence needs to be explained in the proclamation. The proclamation needs to be sustained by the presence. Otherwise the presence is incomprehensible and the proclamation is incredible.

Conversion may be a crisis: it may be a process. Even crises like birth are really processes. An entirely 'sudden' conversion is so rare that I am tempted to hazard the guess that it never happens. Always there is some history behind the act of commitment. A grandmother's prayers, a teacher's example, a priest's kindness . . . But in any case, suddenness is not the heart of the matter. It would be stupid to argue whether birth or growth is the more important element in our experience. We are born to grow. And so it is in the Christian life. Some can remember the date of their conversion. Others cannot. What does it matter? Some people know their birthdays. Others do not. And none of us would know if our mother had not told us! The important thing is not the date of birth, known or unknown, but whether or not we are alive.

It is equally stupid to debate whether conversion is a doctrinal or an experiential matter. These are not authentic alternatives. There needs to be some doctrinal content, but it may be very small. There needs to be a genuine commitment, but it may be covert to begin with, and very tenuous. A finger-hold on Christ is enough to bring me into an initial relationship with him. But it would not suffice for a deep, satisfying, ongoing relationship. That develops over the years.

The debate about whether conversion is a once-for-all initiatory affair, or a matter of ongoing and lifelong re-turning to Christ, has a little more substance to it; but on inspection, not much. For the substance is merely verbal. We are all agreed that there needs to be both a beginning and a continuing, an initial turning and a constant turning back: that, after all, is what the two sacraments indicate.

Baptism speaks of the once-for-all incorporation into Christ, the unrepeatable beginning. And the eucharist speaks of the ongoing, constantly repeated turning back to Christ in order to be fed and nourished. Both are necessary. But I think it unhelpful to use the language of 'conversion' for the growing Christlikeness, the continued turning back to him that is an ongoing part of our Christian calling. To use language in such a way creates confusion. At all events, when used in this book – and, I would hope, when used by evangelists in general – the word 'conversion' will be used to mean the human side of regeneration, the initial turning to God in repentance and faith which launches us into Christian belonging.

Christian conversion has three faces, and they are not necessarily all shown at once.

First (logically, if not in temporal sequence), we experience *a conversion to God*. We turn back to the one from whom we have been estranged. We come humbly in repentance, adoringly in faith, and grasp the hand that is so unconditionally held out to us in love. (1)

Second, we find ourselves in a family of those who have taken that same step. There is, therefore, *a conversion to the church*. We may have been formal members of it already. We may not. But in either case, 'We know that we have passed from death to life, because we love our brothers [i.e. fellow Christians]' (1 John 3:14). And Christians who do not get converted to the church do not, normally, grow. Their faith stagnates, or shrivels away. In the Christian life, we are not intended to be islands, but part of the mainland of God's church. (2)

Third, we need *a conversion to the world* for which Christ died, to a society that remains out of touch with him. Far too many church people find life comfortable in the Christian ghetto, and simply do not move out in love and service to a needy world. But if we are converted to the likeness of our Master, we will steadfastly resist that 'stay in the womb' mentality. There is a threefold orientation to any conversion that is truly Christian. (3)

Not only has Christian conversion three faces, but it has three phases. If you ask me, 'When were you converted?', there are three answers I can give. All are correct. All are complementary.

I was converted, in the purposes of God the Father, when I was 'predestined in love', 'chosen in [Christ] before the foundation of the world' (Eph. 1:4, 5). Christian conversion is rooted in the elective love of God, the God who knows the end from the beginning, and whose initiative always antedates our response.

Alternatively, I could say that I was converted when Christ died upon the cross. That was the archetypal turning of mankind back to God, as the barrier of sin was broken down (Eph. 2:13–16). The cross of Christ is the efficient cause, as the philosophers would put it, which enables any of us to respond.

But equally I could answer the question by saying that I was converted when the Holy Spirit made these things real to me, and I responded. I turned to Christ, and 'was sealed with the promised Holy Spirit' (Eph. 1:13).

These are not three answers, but three aspects of one answer. They tell me that conversion is a big thing, like the gospel itself. They tell me that the whole Trinity was concerned not only in providing eternal salvation for sinners like me, but in enabling me to grasp it and be sure of it.

(1) We ought therefore to be circumspect in the way we use this language of conversion. We should beware of saying things like, 'Sixteen people were converted last night.' How do we know? Only God knows, along with the people concerned. All we can do is to note what people claim; and that claim may not represent the real state of affairs, for all sorts of reasons. It is much wiser, and more biblical, to say, 'Sixteen people made a profession of faith last night.' Time will tell the reality of that profession.

(2) Second, we ought to beware of leaving people satisfied with a mere profession. That is just the time that they need the most careful after-care and loving encouragement. The practice of calling for decisions, rejoicing to count them, and then going away and leaving them untended is one of the most scandalous aspects of modern evangelism. There is a great impropriety in evangelism without after-care.

(3) Third, we ought to beware of urging the necessity of here-and-now and once-for-all commitment. Conversion may come like a tornado striking down walls and ripping off roofs in its path. It may also come like a gentle spring dawn. Some will be aware of its onset. Others only aware that things are very different from what they were a year ago. It simply does not matter. What matters is that I should be walking in the light – not that I should be able accurately to record when the sun rose.

WHAT IS BAPTISM?

Many of the people who are keen to talk about baptism are very reluctant to speak much about conversion. Many of those who are at home in the conversion terminology are reluctant to give much place to baptism. Frankly, it embarrasses them. And yet, beyond doubt, baptism is *the* sacrament of Christian initiation. Paul makes it plain in Romans 6:1ff. that it is the sacrament of justification by grace through faith – a subject which has so engrossed him in the five previous chapters. Baptism is not the foe of repentance and faith or conversion: it is the bedfellow.

Baptism in the New Testament, like circumcision in the Old, is the covenant sign between God's grace and man's response. It is the sign and seal of both God's gracious initiative and man's glad acceptance. It is, moreover, the pledge of the Spirit coming to the heart. And yet there is only one baptism, and must not be more than one baptism (Eph. 4:5). It seals to us the three potentially different times of God's initiative, our repentance and faith, and the coming of the Spirit.

In divided Christendom there are three broad positions on this matter. There are the paedo-baptists, who stress the critical importance of God's initiative, long before we had any thought of responding: accordingly, they tie baptism firmly to God's side of the covenant, and baptise children of believers. Such children are born to those who are already in a covenant relationship with God. Therefore they have the right to the mark of the covenant. They will in due course, it is hoped, grow into appropriate response to the divine gift.

The Baptists see it differently. They point to the vast numbers of baptised children who show no signs whatever of the new life in Christ, and appear to have no more than a nominal Christian attachment – if that. They see baptism as being tied primarily to the human end of the covenant, when we respond in wholehearted commitment to the God who calls and the Christ who died. If the paedo-baptist stressed the divine 'justification', the Baptists stress the very real need for human 'faith', if justification by faith is to become real.

The trouble is that public profession in adult baptism does not necessarily bring about the new birth, any more than paedo-baptism did, though the correlation is a lot nearer. Accordingly, the Pentecostals, who have become a major force in world

Christianity since their emergence at the beginning of this century, emphasise that the really important thing is the gift of the Spirit of God. Without that, baptism is an empty shell. And to be real, it should have visible marks: the initial mark, so many (but not all) Pentecostals maintain, is the gift of tongues.

Now all three strands are saying something important. As a matter of fact, in the Acts of the Apostles, Christians are defined in each of these three ways. Luke could talk of them as the baptised, or as believers, or as those who have received the Spirit. And there was no embarrassment about it. He was clearly talking about three aspects of the same thing. Subsequent ages of the church have not been good at keeping the three constituents of Christian initiation together; but we must seek to remedy that today, and not to further the divisions by the way we preach the gospel. A Christian is a baptised believer whose life is indwelt by the Holy Spirit. All three aspects of that initiation are needed for Christian initiation to be complete. They need not all come at the same time, nor in the same order. But they are all needed. Repentance and faith (or conversion) is the *human side* in Christian initiation: we turn to Christ. Baptism is the *churchly side*: the candidate is received into the outward and visible community of the Christian church. And the gift of the Holy Spirit in our lives is the *divine side* of Christian initiation: it is what God does in regenerating us, in making us his sons and daughters. He sends the Spirit of his Son into our hearts to enable us to cry 'Abba, Father' (Gal. 4:6).

Evangelists are well aware that baptism in water without any real repentance and faith is sub-Christian. They are right. But they are in danger of making a number of serious mistakes in this delicate area of baptism. I have tried to write more fully about it in my book *Baptism*, and do not propose to repeat myself here. But I have heard a number of very inadequate presentations which are actually dangerously misleading.

I have heard evangelists suggest that the real mark of commitment is to come and receive a booklet, or to raise the hand, stand up, or give some other overt sign. The New Testament knows nothing of this. The New Testament has one badge of Christian belonging, and one only: Christian baptism. I am not saying that it is harmful to give a booklet or take a name. But let us not invest it with an importance that is not warranted.

I have heard evangelists suggest that the 'one baptism' received in infancy was not a baptism at all, but rather a 'christening' and not at all the real thing. There is of course no difference whatever between a baptism and a christening. And evangelists should be very careful before they denigrate a sacrament which Christ has instituted. There is one baptism, whenever it is administered. We may regret that it was not administered to the category of people we think most appropriate. If our convictions are Baptist, but the new believer was baptised in infancy, the proper thing, surely, is to establish fellowship on the basis of the one baptism, but to stress that there needs to be both an opening of the life to the Holy Spirit and the making of a public stand for Christ in repentance and faith before that baptism received in infancy has its full validity.

I know that there will be some who conscientiously will not be able to restrain themselves from rebaptising those already baptised, but it is very sad. You cannot repeat the sacrament of initiation. It is like being *re*justified or *re*adopted. If people want the psychological enrichment of going down into the water, could they be immersed 'in memory of their baptism', or whatever form of words seems to meet the need, rather than undergoing a repetition of that sacrament? In this way evangelists will be contributing to wholeness, not further division, within the body of Christ, and will be building up a deeper appreciation for the sacrament Christ himself left us. At the same time, they will be rightly stressing the response and opening up to the Spirit which are an essential part of the evangelistic task.

And finally, I have heard evangelists calling on people who are already baptised believers to be baptised with the Holy Spirit. This too is something we should avoid if we want to allow Scripture to be our guide. For there are seven references, and seven only, to 'baptism in the Holy Spirit', and they are all, without exception, describing becoming a Christian. John baptises with water to bring people to repentance: but Jesus will baptise with his Holy Spirit. That is what he did at Pentecost, and has been doing ever since, when men, women and children open up and ask the heavenly Father for the precious gift of his Spirit. Nowhere in the New Testament is the phrase 'baptism in or with the Spirit' used to describe an equipping of those who are *already Christians* with special power. Never is it used of an advanced or high-octane type of Christian living. It is always used as one of the word pictures (and more than a word picture!) of becoming a Christian at all. Look them up if you are in any doubt. The references are these: Mark 1:8, and its parallels in Luke 3:16, Matthew 3:11, John 1:33. Then there is Acts 1:5, where Jesus picks up the contrast between John's pre-Christian baptism and his own baptism in the Spirit and promises a speedy fulfilment – which came at Pentecost. Acts 11:16 refers back to this, and is again explicitly initiatory. And 1 Corinthians 12:13 makes it no less clear that it is the Spirit who baptises someone into Christ in the first place. Of course, what Pentecostal and neo-Pentecostal evangelists are getting at is entirely proper. They are insisting that nobody is a Christian in the full sense of the word until his body has become a temple for the Holy Spirit. I agree. But let us not muddy the water by calling it baptism. The New Testament writers do not. We should follow their example.

To be a Christian I need to be a believer, I need to be baptised, and I need to have made room in my heart for the life-giving Spirit of God. I am not a Christian in the sense of full Christian initiation until all three things are true of me. And the evangelist's job is to help people see that, and to put in place whichever of these three strands in Christian initiation is not there already. That is an enormous privilege and a wonderful calling. We must be very careful not to abuse it. We need to clear the theological and linguistic jungle for ourselves first, and then for those we seek to help.

FURTHER READING

For further reading on the issues considered in this chapter, you might care to consult:

George Carey, *I Believe in Man* (Hodder & Stoughton)
Michael Green, *Baptism* (Hodder & Stoughton)
Michael Green, *The Meaning of Salvation* (Hodder & Stoughton)
David Pawson, *The Normal Christian Birth* (Hodder & Stoughton)
Peter Toon, *About Turn: The Decisive Event of Conversion* (Hodder & Stoughton)
Jim Wallis, *The Call to Conversion* (Harper & Row)
Keith Ward, *The Battle for the Soul* (Hodder & Stoughton)
Ronald A. Ward, *The Pattern of our Salvation* (Word)

3

Evangelism in a Multi-Faith Society?

We live in an age of pluralism at every level, not least at the religious level. We are surrounded by a supermarket of faiths, and it is apparently up to us to choose what we think most appropriate for ourselves. Religion, along with values, has in most cultures been relegated to the private area of life. And in the private area, we can make our own choices and nobody bothers us unless what we do is a nuisance to others. Society in almost any Western country these days is extremely diverse – ethnically, and in terms of ideas, values and beliefs. In some countries, such as France, religion has comparatively little effect on daily life. In others, such as Iran, its impact is enormous.

In recent years a number of factors have brought pluralism into high relief. One is the fact that the world has become a global village. Buddhists and Sikhs, Mormons and followers of Hari Krishna are active everywhere. The sheer diversity of faiths, displayed before us in the persons of their representatives living down our street, makes pluralism a live issue whereas before it had remained largely theoretical. Another reason is the decline of convinced Christian belief in many parts of the Western world. Less grasp on Christianity carries with it less grasp on what makes Christianity special, and facilitates the assumption: 'We are all going in the same direction. One faith is as good as another – or indeed, as none.' There is also a new awareness of the need for world citizenship, of the search for what unites us rather than divides. Religion is undeniably one of the things that divides. Accordingly, dialogue (rather than evangelism) is seen as the only appropriate response to other faiths. Somehow we must draw together the various aspirations and beliefs of mankind if we are not going to damage our world irreparably. And in any case, how could it be credible that one faith is the right way and all others are wrong? What arrogance! The question which the pagan philosopher Symmachus asked St Ambrose in AD 384 has taken on added urgency sixteen hundred years later: 'If the Christian God is indeed a God of love who desires all to be saved, why did he wait so long to send the Saviour? Why have human beings been allowed to seek God along so many different paths for such a long time?'

HOW DO CHRISTIANS LOOK ON OTHER FAITHS?

The question of religious pluralism is extremely difficult for Christians. It seems almost ill-mannered to make exclusive claims for Jesus and his achievement, but do Christians have any alternative? And if he is the way to God, where does that leave other religious systems? There have been a number of attempts to resolve this question.

From evangelism to pluralism

The traditional answer, of course, has been evangelism. Those who belong to other faiths need the gospel: it is incumbent on Christians to tell them. There may well be much truth in their ancestral faith, but they will know nothing, in any faith they may belong to, of a God who cares enough about their estrangement and sin to come to this world and seek them. Nowhere else will they hear of a God whose love extends to burdening himself with their guilt. Nowhere will they hear of the possibility of such intimacy with that infinite, personal God that his Spirit can be welcomed into their hearts.

That great evangelistic vision of reaching the whole world with the gospel of Christ erupted in the Edinburgh Conference of 1910. Seventy-three years later the World Council of Churches met in Vancouver, under the slogan 'Jesus Christ, the Hope of the World'. It looked very much the same: but in fact it was utterly different. World Council officials uttered stern warnings against evangelism, because it imposed an obstacle to dialogue with other religions.

The study group of that World Council meeting revealed the

change in outlook on other faiths which had transpired since
Edinburgh:

> In the end, the great communities of faith will not have disappeared.
> None will have 'won' over the others. Jews will still be Jews; Muslims
> still Muslims; and those of the great Eastern faiths still Buddhists or
> Hindus or Taoists. Africa will still witness to its traditional life view;
> China to its inheritance. People will still come from the East and the
> West, the North and the South and sit down in the kingdom of God
> without having first become 'Christians' like us.

So Jesus Christ is *not* the hope of the world: he is an optional extra.
The phenomenon of conversion is both unnecessary and
distasteful.

The philosophical underpinning for this massive volte-face
about other faiths has been variously debated. Some think, with
Ernst Troeltsch, that all religions are relative. Truth has many
forms, and people should be left with the religious truth in which
they have been raised. Why should they be disturbed? It is 'true of
them'.

There are all sorts of difficulties in such a view. Maybe God has
given some revelation of himself to all cultures, through creation,
morals and reason. But if you are a Christian, are you not going to
maintain that at one specific point in space and time God gave a
definitive disclosure of himself in the historical form of Jesus of
Nazareth? Are you not going to maintain that on the cross he did
for mankind what no other has done or could do? And in any case,
from what standpoint can anyone confidently affirm all religions to
be relative? Where is that absolute base from which we could make
such a pronouncement? And when you say that all must be well if
something is 'true for me', are you not surrendering the very idea of
truth? When we say something is true, we do not mean, 'I like it. It
is fine for me.' We are making some claim for universal validity.

If all religions are not essentially relative, perhaps they are in the
last analysis all the same? They share a common essence. This is
the view of Arnold Toynbee, and has attracted a good deal of
support in some quarters. Let at any rate the five higher religions of
Islam, Buddhism, Hinduism, Judaism and Christianity drop their
particularities and join hands to save the world from destruction.
We ought, he argues, to purge our Christianity of the traditional
Western belief that Christianity is unique.

But this approach is no more promising than the last. Is there
really something common to all religions when some (like

Buddhism) are atheistic, and others (like Islam) are passionately monotheistic? And can we distinguish the essence which is supposed to underlie all faiths from the non-essentials which their worshippers cling to? How are we to do that? On what principle? Surely, on the ground that some elements in the faith are better than others. But from what vantage-point shall we decide which is better? And does not the whole question of truth get by-passed, and indeed swept beneath the carpet, by this throwing of them all into a saucepan, boiling them up, and straining off the essence? What if one religion actually does offer a fuller expression of that essence than another? How would that leave the common stockpot? And what about the astounding claims made by Jesus of Nazareth? What if the Absolute really *has* come into our midst? If that were the case, what should we make of the many examples of the relative? Jürgen Moltmann made an interesting point when he was lecturing in Vancouver in 1989. Challenged on the exclusive claims he was making for Jesus Christ, he replied that true dialogue emerges best from examining the uniqueness of one's position as a Christian, rather than what is held in common. He recalled a dialogue with East European Marxists in which they were prepared to defend the socio-economic aspects of the gospel. But what they really wanted to know was 'Why do Christians pray?' It was the uniqueness of the Christian claim which made for the most fruitful points of dialogue.

Another approach is adopted by Karl Rahner and Bishop John Robinson. They argue that all human beings are in fact implicit believers, though they do not know it and might not be flattered to be told it. All are embraced by Christ's work on the cross. All have been saved by him. The task of the church is not to enable people to respond to the gospel, but to inform them that they have already been rescued in Christ. And in Bishop Robinson's view the church should carry on its work as a co-operative effort with atheists and agnostics and members of all other faiths who are Christians in spite of themselves.

The strength of such a view is the centrality it places on the person and work of Jesus Christ. But its weaknesses are very apparent. It makes no room for the human response in faith to that justification which Christ crucified offers to all men. It insults members of other faiths, and none, by telling them that really they are Christians after all. As such it evacuates the term Christian of solid meaning.

All these views are inadequate. If you cast even a cursory glance over the religions of the world, the idea that they are all essentially the same, or veiled examples of Christianity, is seen to be ludicrous. To be sure, many world religions (though not all) have certain basic moral values in common. C. S. Lewis, in the Appendix to his book *The Abolition of Man*, shows that there is a considerable moral consensus underlying major religious systems. None, for example, advocate adultery, theft or murder. That broad ethical agreement is what you might expect if there really is a living, personal God who cares about the morals of his creatures and has put some understanding of his laws within their hearts. Even so, that basic moral consensus is a very blunt instrument. It masks a world of disagreement and contradiction between the religions over specifics. And none of it compares with the sublime ethical teaching of Jesus, with his 'Love your enemies,' 'Judge not, that you be not judged,' 'Forgive one another as I have forgiven you,' and 'It is more blessed to give than receive.'

Intimacy with God

However, contrary to the opinion of many, Christianity is not primarily about morals. It is about restoring the broken lines of communication between God and man. The Christian message of intimacy with God is strikingly different from the central affirmation of all other faiths. Whatever they are about, they are not about this. At the risk of dangerous generalisation, it might be useful to glance at the religions of the world and ask: Do they purport to offer that intimate, filial relationship with God which is at the heart of Christianity?

First, there are *occult religions*, such as animism, Tibetan Buddhism, witchcraft and so forth. These are concerned with spirits, usually evil spirits, which need to placated or manipulated. They may dwell in trees, sacred sites, or people. These spirits are as varied as the African witchdoctor, the Mongolian shaman, and the local sorcerer who seek to manipulate them. Occult religions are about spirits, not about God, let alone intimacy with him.

Second, there are what you might call *imperial religions*. They are not about God either. They are about the highest political authority which claims ultimate power and deference: from the 'divine kings' of Egypt and Mesopotamia, through the Caesars of ancient Rome and the Shinto emperors of imperial Japan, down to Hitler, Stalin and Mao in our own century. It is interesting to recall the numinous notes which both Hitler and Stalin struck. Stalin used to have giant photographs of himself projected on to low-lying clouds above mass rallies, and Hitler predicted a millennial Reich.

Third, there are *ascetic religions*, such as Jainism, Hinduism, Buddhism, and all the 'do-it-yourself' versions of Christianity from Pelagius to secular activism. They are not about God either, but about self-renunciation. The self is renounced and mortified in order to rid the person, and progressively the world, of evil and suffering. Sometimes that self-renunciation is so extreme that in, for example, the Buddhist *nirvana*, it implies the final elimination of man as a sentient, purposeful being. He is absorbed into the impersonal One, or Monad. It certainly has nothing to do with intimacy with God. For in most branches of these ascetic religions there is no personal God to be intimate with. That is certainly true of Buddhism and most forms of Hinduism.

Fourth, there are what one can only call *genital religions*. They worship sex. It is very old, this religion, and very modern. It ranges from the fertility cults of the Canaanite neighbours of Israel, through the lascivious statues in many Hindu temples, down to D. H. Lawrence and the porn merchants of Copenhagen, Soho and Los Angeles' Sunset Strip. They too have nothing in common with Christianity and the intimacy with God it offers.

Fifth, there are what we might call *bourgeois religions*, which satisfy the religious proclivities of the leisured classes and cost their adherents nothing apart from an expensive admission fee. They are bodies like Christian Science, Anthroposophy, Theosophy and many of the self-improvement cults. They are primarily about man, not God.

A sixth group is *prophetic religions*, which arise from the dynamic leadership and moral challenge of a great leader, and which tend to sweep across much of the world within a century or so of their origin. Islam is an excellent example, which made such enormous inroads into the Middle East and North Africa within a century of the death of Muhammad. Marxism is another. It profoundly influenced a third of the world's population within half a century of Russia first taking it on board. Although it is militantly atheistic, it inculcates a passionately held creed, high ideals, self-sacrifice, and a clear eschatology, in common with many religions. For communism, as for religions, its adherents will gladly die. Prophetic religions tend to be imperious, whether theocratic or totalitarian. Marxism is of course not about God at all. And even Islam – contrary to popular opinion – does not offer communion with God himself. 'God does not reveal himself. He does not reveal himself to anyone in any way. God reveals only his will.' So said Professor al-Farugi, a leading American Islamicist. Or, as Fathi-Osman, editor of *Arabia Magazine*, trenchantly put it, 'Allah reveals his message. He never reveals himself.' A relationship of love and intimacy with him is out of the question. It is blasphemy.

Finally, there are the *revelatory religions*. There have been only two religions in the history of the world which teach that God can be intimately and personally known, known through his own initiative. Only Judaism and its 'child' Christianity maintain that God has given a reliable and personal disclosure of himself to mankind. Judaism shows how God revealed himself through theophanies (e.g. to Abraham, Moses, and the prophets), through temporary charismatic endowment of particular individuals (e.g. Samson, Saul, David), and through self-disclosure to the prophets (e.g. Isaiah, Daniel, Amos). God's only permanent residence on earth was understood as being in the tiny space between the overarching wings of the cherubim above the 'mercy seat' on the ark; this was located first of all in the moveable tabernacle, and subsequently in the temple at Jerusalem. Of course Judaism is very differently placed today. There is no ark, no tabernacle, no temple. Modern Judaism is rooted in religious law, morality, and synagogue worship.

The other faith which developed this strand of revelation, so strong in Judaism, is Christianity – or rather Jesus Christ. He claimed to be the fulfilment of God's self-disclosure to mankind. He was Emmanuel, 'God with us'. 'In him', claims Paul, 'the whole fullness of deity dwells bodily' (Col. 2:9). In other words, if you want to see God, look at Jesus. In a derived sense, the Holy Spirit complements that quality of 'God with us' which Jesus embodied. For he is 'God in us', and brings about in the community of believers the power and love and healing of God almighty. He makes God real to believers and enables them to know him as Father and to cry 'Abba' as adopted children in his own family. Christianity alone among world religions, and Old Testament Judaism from which it sprang, is concerned with the intimate communion which can exist between God and man. It is the Spirit (i.e. God himself) that gives life: the flesh (i.e. humanity and human religious systems) has nothing to offer (John 6:63).

Even so cursory an overview as this makes it very plain that any attempt to syncretise all faiths cannot be made remotely plausible without a very great deal of special pleading. They are not all the same, and they do not profess to be.

Islam

But we have travelled too fast. Is not Islam supremely a religion of revelation? Does it not have as noble a view of God as you will find anywhere in the world? Does it not enjoy the highest ethical standards? And is it not one of the major religious forces in the modern world?

All that is true. Both Islam and Christianity believe in one God. Both believe Jesus was sent by God, and born of the Virgin Mary. Both believe in high morals. Both hope to gain God's forgiveness, and to go to paradise after death. With so much in common, cannot Christians and Muslims sink their differences?

This is a question which needs to be faced with great humility by Christians. When Muhammad was born in Mecca about the year AD 570, there was indeed a Christian presence in the Arabian peninsula; but this Nestorian church lacked the love, the purity of life and the spiritual effectiveness to make much impact among the Arab tribes, or to attract a man of the burning spirituality of Muhammad. As a result, Islam emerged from a background of unChristlike Christianity. Christians, when talking to their Muslim friends, should never forget that. Neither should they forget the Crusades, when Western nations, professing to follow the Jesus who never took up arms, heaped all manner of hatred, contumely, and physical assault on the followers of the Prophet. And long after the Crusades had built an all but impenetrable barrier between the two religions, ridicule and loathing for Islam pervaded European literature. It is only now beginning to recede. Is it any wonder that Muslims are sensitive to any slight on the Prophet from Westerners? I can only wonder at their forbearance over many centuries, and at their insistence that Jesus was a true prophet, come from God, who taught the same *islam*, or submission to God, as did Muhammad.

Nevertheless, it is neither true nor helpful to imagine that Islam and Christianity are saying much the same thing. Try persuading the Arab states or Nigeria or Pakistan of that proposition. Any trace of syncretism would be repudiated far more passionately by the followers of Muhammad than by most zealous and informed Christians. For the differences between the two cannot be bridged, or even glossed over. Christians have tried hard to enter into dialogue with Islam during recent years. Men like Kenneth Cragg have made this a fundamental purpose of their lives. But there has hitherto been little if any reciprocal study of Christianity by serious and sensitive Islamic scholars. It is hard for them not to despise a religion, albeit a 'religion of the book' (on which originally they looked more favourably), which appears to them to countenance three Gods; which blasphemously attributes deity to the prophet Jesus; which venerates a holy book written by men not by God himself; and which portrays God Almighty deserting his prophet Jesus and allowing him to die in shame on a cross. Moreover, Christianity seems to make few life-changing claims on its adherents. Christians are not noted for their prayer. Alcoholism and immorality abound in Christian lands. And there is a massive separation between religion and the rest of life. Such a religion is almost unworthy of the name. Consequently Muslims, far from being willing partners in dialogue, are often some of the most entrenched opponents of Christianity to be found anywhere in the world. Their own faith is submission to the will of Allah. It is a simple, uncomplicated religion, abounding in prohibitions, strong on reward and punishment, insistent on the unity of God, on prayer five times a day, on fasting (especially in the holy month of Ramadan), on ethical behaviour, on pilgrimage, and on the holy war against infidels, such as we have recently seen in Afghanistan. It is not given to a great deal of theologising: it is given to action. It is a militant, sturdy faith which has become a remarkable success story. Christianity, by way of contrast, begins from the failure of its leader and his disgraceful death on a gibbet, and continues as a somewhat feeble force in society.

Within a century of the death of the Prophet, Islam had captured Persia, Mesopotamia, Syria, Egypt, North Africa and Spain. It continued to advance for a thousand years, reaching Greece and Turkey, Africa and much of Asia, including China and India, Pakistan and Afghanistan. Today it is sending missionaries and making inroads into many traditionally Christian countries. There are more Muslims in Britain, for example, than Methodists and Baptists combined. They have great missionary zeal. They find apostasy intolerable. A Muslim who becomes a Christian runs the risk of being poisoned, and is almost sure to be banished from his home and his country. What lies behind this intransigence and passion? The question is all the more pressing when Muslims can affirm a good deal of the Christian creed.

A. Guillaume has shown in his book *Islam* how Muslims can accept the Apostles' Creed apart from the words in italics:

> I believe in God *the Father* Almighty,
> Maker of heaven and earth:
> And in Jesus Christ *his only Son our Lord*,
> Who was conceived by the Holy Ghost,
> Born of the Virgin Mary, *Suffered under Pontius Pilate, Was crucified*, dead, *and buried, He descended into hell; The third day he rose again from the dead*, He ascended into heaven, *And sitteth on the right hand of God the Father Almighty*; From thence he shall come *to judge the quick and the dead*.
>
> I believe in the Holy Ghost; *The holy Catholick Church; The Communion of Saints*; The Forgiveness of sins; The Resurrection of the body, and the life everlasting.

With a good deal in common between these two great monotheistic faiths, why are bridges so hard to build?

Islam has a very different understanding of God. To the Christian, God's will is the expression of his person. His gracious acts to human beings are the outcome of his character. Thus he may to some extent be known personally. To the Muslim, this is unthinkable. God does not reveal himself to anyone in any way. He reveals only his will. God is utterly transcendent, and to talk of self-revelation implies that he might also be immanent – and at once the 'otherness' of God is compromised. So there is in Islam no idea of a personal relationship with God.

Islam has also a different understanding of human nature and human sin. Sin is not a concept that Islam is much at home with. There are sins, to be sure, and they will receive punishment from God. But man is not essentially a sinner. He can turn back, and give in to God in *islam*, if he so chooses. To talk of human sinfulness looks to the Muslim like evasion of responsibility. Man should gird up his loins and obey God. Muslims have little conception of the destructive effect of sin on human relations with God. For Christians, sin is a power which grips one's life and alienates us from our source in God. It is not merely a list of misdoings. The difference is enormous.

Islam has a very different understanding of Jesus. To the Muslim, he is one of the prophets, and as such greatly revered (at least in theory), while of course being less than Muhammad. He was not the Son of God – the very idea, taken with crude literalness, they see to be blasphemous. He did not die on the cross – God would not abandon one of his prophets to such a fate. And he emphatically did not bear away the sins of the world. Every man will have to bear his own sins and face his own judgement. Accordingly, virtually everyone will have to spend some time, maybe the whole of eternity, in hell. The will of Allah (if he so chooses, and there is no reason why he should), the prayers of Muhammad and saintly Muslims, and the good deeds of the deceased person are the only hopes for escaping from hell to paradise, where the faithful may drink wine handed them by *huris*, or maidens of paradise, of whom each man may marry as many as he pleases.

Islam and Christianity have very different conceptions of the holy book. For Muslims, the Quran was written in heaven by God and revealed to Muhammad in the sacred language, Arabic, in which alone worship should be offered. It embraces the whole of life, for individual and society alike. It is infallible, penned by God, without textual variants, and without human intermediaries. The fact that it was revealed to Muhammad, himself illiterate, stresses the fact that man had no part in its composition. For Christians, the Bible was written by men of varied backgrounds and cultures, over a period of about fifteen hundred years. They were men in touch with God, but they were not mere channels of revelation: their own personality shines through their pages. This seems highly unsatisfactory to the Muslim. He sees the Christians' Scriptures as corrupt and unreliable. They must have been tampered with during their history. Anything that differs from the Quran must, *ipso facto*, be wrong.

Islam has a very different understanding of religious assurance. The Muslim can never know he is forgiven. Allah is utterly unconstrained, indeed arbitrary, in his display of mercy. So there is always fear in the Muslim heart, especially as he draws near to death. Always there is uncertainty. It is not surprising that this hunger for assurance in a somewhat cold and legalistic religious environment has driven many Muslims into non-Quranic devotions, the virtual worship of Muhammad and many of the *pirs* (holy men), the cult of the saints, and something very like charismatic worship.

There is in Islam no parallel to the Christian doctrine of the Holy Spirit indwelling the believer. The 'Paraclete' sayings in John's Gospel are thought to be indications of the coming of Muhammad. No, God is too great and too 'other' to indwell such a poor hovel as the human heart. Yet the presence of the Spirit in our hearts is what turns Christianity from law into good news, from duty into joy, from bondage into liberty.

Enough has been said to show that, for all their similarities, Christianity and Islam are fundamentally and irreconcilably different. Islam is in no doubt about the propriety of its missionary work in a multi-faith society. Nor should Christians be. For Christianity embraces the unity of God, the ethical code, the emphasis on prayer, the notion of accountability and judgement, and the social cohesion of Islam at its best. In addition, it offers to mankind a vision of a God who made atonement for our sins and is not ashamed to share our very lives. A God who blends love with law, treats men and women alike, and invites them into his family. A God who assures them that they belong, and that he has himself handled the problem raised by their inherent self-centredness. This is our God, and we need not be in the least embarrassed about making the good news of who he is and what he has done for mankind known to adherents of Islam as well as to everyone else. In Indonesia and Nigeria many thousands of Muslims are finding the fulfilment of their *islam* in loving submission to the great God who submitted to the cross for them. In many other parts of the Muslim world they have not so much rejected Jesus of Nazareth: they have never seen him.

The New Age movement

Nothing has been said thus far about the New Age movement, the most modern and the most comprehensive, joyous and eclectic of all attempts at syncretism. Surely here we have a faith that eclipses Christianity and makes it otiose, because many Christian tenets are taken up into the New Age?

New Age thinking is the fastest growing, most subtle and most influential new ideology to emerge for a long time. It is spreading like wildfire in the USA and Canada, and is beginning to make an impact on Europe. It is a loosely knit and constantly evolving world-view which is not easy to pinpoint precisely. Some of its leading proponents have virtually unlimited access to the media, such as the actress and author Shirley MacLaine, and Steven Spielberg with the *Star Wars* series. The main tenets of the New Age are as follows.

First, it is essentially monistic, like Hinduism and Buddhism. It believes that reality is a seamless garment, and that all differentia partake of *maya*, illusion. All is one. The problem of unity and diversity is solved by subordinating all diversity to a supposed underlying unity in the universe.

Second, the divine is not personal. God is not a 'He' but an 'It'. What is variously known as force, energy, essence, consciousness, the spirit, being, is totally impersonal. This is, of course, in total disagreement with the Bible, which sees God as the infinite who is also personal.

Third, everything is God. The all-pervading impersonal force which is God embraces everything in the universe. The traditional name for this belief, which has a very long history in human thought, is pantheism. In Scripture, of course, the personal infinite God is eternally transcendent. He is other than creation, though he is everywhere present in it (Acts 17:28). He is, in classical terminology, both transcendent and immanent. It makes a lot of difference! Under pantheism, when I see a lovely tree, I identify it with the divine. Under Christianity, I say, 'My heavenly Father is responsible for that. Glory to his name!'

Fourth, human beings are God. 'Kneel to your own self,' says the New Age guru Swami Muktananda: 'Honour and worship your own being. God dwells in you and as you.' 'Everyone is God,' writes Shirley MacLaine, 'everyone. To love self is to love God.' Those who come from the Islamic or Judaeo-Christian background are constantly amazed at the 'blasphemy' of such a claim. But it is consistent with the premises of monism. If all reality is one, so must God and man be one. All of us have a spark of the divine in our heart. Humanity is good, for it is a part of the divine. But so is evil, which is seen as an illusion, or negative vibrations or energy. There are no moral absolutes. And an enlightened person transcends moral distinctions. You can see why it is so popular!

Fifth, our resources are within us. It is up to us to tap the energies that lie there. Salvation is not by rescue from without, but by a realisation of what lies within human nature. It is in this respect that the New Agers join hands with the humanists and rationalists. Both see our destinies as shaped entirely by ourselves.

Sixth, the principle of *karma* holds good. This is derived from both Hinduism and Buddhism, and maintains that suffering is simply the inexorable effect of wrongdoing, which needs to be worked off in the next life. There is therefore a whole nest of implications which go with this implacable process of *karma*. It involves a cyclical view of history, whereas Scripture sees a clear beginning, a critical midpoint with Jesus, and an unambiguous end. It involves a belief in reincarnation, which not only has immense built-in philosophical difficulties, but is also in plain contradiction to the Bible's doctrine that this life is the time of decision and that 'it is appointed for men to die once, and after that comes the judgment' (Heb. 9:27). Logically, this doctrine of reincarnation makes good works the way of rescue, in total contrast to the whole biblical insistence that our rescue is the result of God's free grace and generosity to sinners who deserve nothing from his hand. What is more, it is bound to maintain, and it does maintain, that forgiveness is an illusion. Nothing can break the power of *karma*. And therefore Christ did not bear the world's sins upon the cross. Moral evil is not ultimately real, and therefore it does not need any forgiveness. The human problem is not sin but *maya*, the veil of ignorance. We need not salvation but illumination.

Seventh, the New Age movement lays stress on paranormal potential. We can experience ESP, telepathy, spirit-contact, healing and so forth, and there are gifted channellers to promote these phenomena. Spirit-guides manifest themselves by taking over the channeller. This is nothing different from the old-fashioned medium, outlawed by God so clearly in the Old Testament in passages like Deuteronomy 18:10–12, 'There shall not be found among you . . . anyone who practises divination, a soothsayer, or an augur, or a sorcerer, or a charmer, or a medium, or a wizard, or a necromancer. For whoever does these things is an abomination to the Lord.'

Eighth, religious syncretism is the order of the day. All religions are basically one (and maintain the tenets of the New Age!). Jesus was just one of the many mystical masters – though New Agers find it diplomatic to use a lot of Christian language like 'Christ-consciousness'. The uniqueness of Jesus is of course denied, thus dispensing with his incarnation as well as his atonement. The whole emphasis is not on God at all, and in this sense the New Age movement is 'a religion without being a religion' as R. J. L. Burrows put it. It is all about self-realisation, enlightenment, 'fusion with the One' and transcendence of normal human nature to self-divinity.

Ninth, the New Age movement is committed to belief in cosmic evolution. The human race is progressing towards the New Age of Aquarius, the age of planetary unity, peace and prosperity. And what are the hindrances? Not sin, but the lack of cosmic awareness, the cult of separateness, the illusory bonds of self, family, nation and matter. Reason and dogma in particular constitute barriers to the true perception of the One. They fragment reality, and must be swept away. And the means of progress towards the goal of universal brotherhood? Knowledge, *gnosis*, enlightenment: knowledge of the self by the self. But that will not suffice either: the self must become lost in the One as rivers are lost in the sea. So, in a way, enlightenment repeals the curse of life by embracing the curse of death. It undoes the structure of 'selfhood' by ending the separate existence of the person and freeing it to join the undifferentiated One.

Such are some of the outline assumptions in the New Age movement. But it is constantly changing in its presentation and details, and will, I believe, develop further.

It will be apparent to any who have studied the emergence of the early church that New Age spirituality offers startling parallels with the Gnosticism which nearly eclipsed Christianity in the second century AD and was already evoking strong warnings from the New Testament writers at the end of the apostolic age: the Johannine letters, in particular, are deliberately and decisively anti-Gnostic. There was no more subtle and dangerous foe which Christianity had to face than this. It was the main preoccupation of the second century church to do battle with this false teaching. And yet here it is again, dressed up in Christian-sounding terms as it was then, but embodying a series of teachings which are utterly opposed to every major tenet of the Christian faith. And so attenuated has our grasp on the faith become, that many people do not even see it as a danger. Thus five hundred of North America's largest corporations apparently meet regularly to discuss how metaphysics, Hindu mysticism and the occult can help their employees to success in the marketplace. Many large firms run motivation seminars, or send employees to the World Spirit University, which is entirely New Age in its orientation. Schools in North America which forbid Christian prayer nevertheless not only allow but actively promote yoga, Eastern meditation and visualisation techniques, which are nothing but Hindu forms of prayer, enthusiastically endorsed by the New Age movement.

Why is it so popular? For a number of reasons. It speaks to the hunger of mankind for unity in a desperately dangerous world. It speaks to the heart which has been reared on the values of materialism and realises that they are totally inadequate to live by. It speaks to important modern issues which Christians have been slow to address: the environment, various kinds of oppression, and

ᵈ) the sterility of the 'technological society'. It offers a spiritual dimension to life that is free from dogma, diverse in manifestation, full of celebration and 'fun' things, undemanding in lifestyle and emancipated from the claims of morality. That is a very powerful mix. It offers hope in a time of hopelessness, countering prophets of doom with the message of human potential and social trans-
ₑ) formation. And the biggest and reddest cherry on the top of the cake is this: self-deification. The primal sin has become the ultimate truth. I am divine. I can do what I like. As *Time* magazine (7 December 1987) observed:

> You can see the rise of the New Age [movement] as a barometer of the disintegration of American culture. Dostoevsky said anything is permissible if there is no God. But anything is also permissible if everything is God. There is no way of making any distinction between good and evil . . . Once you have deified yourself, which is what the New Age [movement] is all about, there is no higher moral absolute. It is a recipe for ethical anarchy, and it is a counterfeit religious claim.

ASSESSMENTS OF RELIGIOUS PLURALISM

Enough has been said to show that attempts either to relativise all religions or to reduce them to one are quite unconvincing in themselves and totally at odds with what Christianity teaches. Very well then, how does Christianity view other faiths? Christians have held a number of differing views.

· Before we look at them, however, it is important to remind ourselves of the heart of the Christian position. It is that God Almighty so cared for mankind in our alienation and lostness that he once and for all disclosed himself without distortion in human flesh, in the life of Jesus of Nazareth; that on the cross this same Jesus took responsibility for all the evil in the world, so that it could be affirmed with confidence that 'in Christ God was reconciling the world to himself' (2 Cor. 5:19); that he is alive today, ruling unseen in this world as Lord and Saviour; and that our human destiny is to know him and enjoy him for ever. That claim, as Stephen Neill observed in his *Christian Faith and Other Faiths*,

> is naturally offensive to the adherents of every other religious system. It is almost as offensive to modern man, brought up in the atmosphere of relativism, in which tolerance is regarded as almost the highest of the

virtues. But we must not suppose that this claim to universal validity is something which can be quietly removed from the gospel without changing it into something entirely different from what it is.

And he draws attention to Jesus' own assurance 'that he was in fact the final and decisive word of God to men . . . For the human sickness there is one specific remedy, and this is it. There is no other.'

Against this backcloth, let us examine some of the answers Christians have tried to give to religious pluralism and the status of other faiths.

Is there no other name?

Paul Knitter has produced a massive survey of the whole subject in his *No Other Name?* Throughout that book he wrestles with the normative and exclusive claims made for Christ both by himself and by his followers. Knitter's conclusion is disappointingly evasive and unsatisfactory. He maintains that it is all a lot easier if you move to a theocentric model, and relativise Jesus. The claims made about Jesus as Saviour are not *ontological* but *confessional*. That is to say, Jesus is not really Lord and God, but that is how I look at him. The language of uniqueness was coined by the early church because they were encapsulated in a classical culture and felt that if their claims about the overwhelming significance of Jesus were to be heard, they must either conquer or absorb all others. However, in the light of our 'new experience of pluralism', it is possible to affirm Jesus and his message without insisting that it is the final truth. What is more, Christians were in a minority in the ancient world, and so their exclusive claims for Jesus were an example of 'survival language'. They had to pitch it high if anyone was going to listen!

To achieve the desired result, Knitter has to abandon the once-for-allness of the incarnation, and quotes with approval Norman Pittenger's dictum: 'God is ever incarnating himself in his creation . . . It is all incarnation.' He also has to abandon the resurrection. He is reluctant to do so, but he calls it 'richly mythic'. The resurrection stories 'should not be taken literally'. They were 'symbolic attempts to express, to "picture" what had happened' (and he is extremely vague about what, if anything, did happen). Moreover, the resurrection 'does not necessarily imply "one and only"'. The Buddhists claim to sense the spirit of the Buddha, his real presence in their midst, even though their conceptual framework does not allow for an actual resurrection. And so a bright new era of missionary activity can evolve – 'not the "salvation business" (making people Christians so that they can be saved) but the task of serving and promoting the kingdom of justice and love by being sign and servant', along with people from other faiths. Great, and partly true, but a very earthbound conception of what Christianity and indeed every major world religion is about! It is not necessary, he claims, for Christians 'in their own faith and in their conversation with other believers to claim the "finality" or "normativity" of Jesus'. But he adds the tentative postscript that 'although such a claim need not and cannot be made, it may still be true. Perhaps something has happened in the historical event of Jesus Christ that surprisingly surpasses all other events.'

It is very difficult to imagine that such an assessment would have been regarded as a Christian option at all by the apostles, the early church, the leaders of the Reformation, or by the millions of people from all religious backgrounds who are currently coming to confess Jesus Christ as Lord and Saviour. For all its learning, Knitter's book does not present us with an authentically Christian way of looking at other faiths.

Praeparatio evangelica?

What unquestionably is a Christian attitude towards other faiths has recently been put forward in most moving terms by David Edwards in his book *Essentials*, an extended 'conversation' with John Stott. He stresses the humility Christians need to show before other faiths and other cultures. He does not in the least abandon the exclusive claims made for Jesus in Christianity, but he has a broad, loving and humble attitude towards truth wherever he can find it, and it is emphatically not confined to the Bible:

> I have argued in *The Futures of Christianity* (1987) that the glad acceptance of Christ as Saviour and Lord, as the One who can bring us to the Father as no other teacher can, is entirely compatible with a willingness to learn from other teachers. In the past Christians gladly learned from Greek philosophers and Roman poets. In our time Christians can be taught about community life under God by Jews, about devotion to God by Muslims or Hindus, about detachment from the passions by Buddhists, about the sacredness of nature by animists, and about goodness by atheists. Having learned these and many other

truths from traditions outside the church, we find that they are already taught in the Bible.

David Edwards is one of those who is impressed by the amount of truth that can be found in other faiths. He is perfectly right. No faith would enjoy wide currency if it did not contain much that was true. Other faiths therefore constitute a preparation for the gospel, and Christ comes not so much to destroy as to fulfil. The convert will not feel that he has lost his background, but that he has discovered that to which, at its best, it pointed. That is certainly the attitude I have found among friends converted to Christ from Hinduism, Islam and Buddhism. They are profoundly grateful for what they learned in those cultures, but are thrilled beyond words to have discovered a God who has stooped to their condition in coming as the man of Nazareth, and who has rescued them from guilt and alienation by his cross and resurrection.

This view has been widely held by Christians throughout the centuries. The apologists in the second century AD followed Paul and John in identifying Jesus with pre-existent Wisdom and the eternal Logos. This was language which had wide currency and enabled them to make Christian claims in non-Christian dress. Armed with these convictions, the early Christian intellectuals from John and Paul to Clement and Origen glow with the confidence of having found the key to understanding the universe: everything that was good and true in pagan writings they claimed for Jesus, the Light of the World. As E. L. Allen summarises it:

> Christ was present in every age and every race, but he was not known as such. Heathenism is related to Christianity as law to gospel, reason to faith, nature to grace. The heathen is like a blind man, feeling the sun's warmth but not seeing the sun itself. Christ was within heathenism as a natural potency but not yet as a personal principle.

And the one whose form and teaching was latent in the best of heathenism the Christians proclaimed openly and personally; he was Jesus, the fulfiller of the aspirations of mankind, and the Saviour of the world. The sun had risen on a dark world lit by many candles and lights. Their luminance was taken up and concentrated in the Light of the World.

There is something very liberating in this view of other faiths. It enables you to give a positive evaluation of all that is good or true or lovely within the tenets and practices of those other faiths, but at the same time to maintain the New Testament emphasis that the full light has dawned in Christ alone, and that salvation is in Christ alone. It is he whose death avails both for those 'who were far off' and for those 'who were near' – for those of other faiths and none, and also for the Jews. But if you believe this, as I do, then you cannot sit back and say 'They have good candles already. They are doing fine.' If you have any compassion, and love of Christ and of people in your heart, you will want to point them to 'the Light who enlightens every man'. You will want to evangelise.

Satanic influence?

A very different evaluation of other faiths is given within another strand of Christian teaching. If the emphasis of the *praeparatio evangelica* view which we have just looked at has been on the good in other religions, this view concentrates on the opposite. Such religions explicitly or implicitly deny the salvation that Jesus Christ offers. They espouse or allow moral practices some of which are revolting. They are open to infection from spiritual forces which do not come from God. Their truths are shrouded in much darkness. Indeed, some regard every non-Christian religion as a satanic product which keeps people from the true God. If this attitude seems extreme (and it is, though it was held by a good many of the nineteenth-century missionaries), then let Lesslie Newbigin, that experienced and highly intelligent missionary bishop who probably knows as much at first hand about other faiths as any man living, make two shrewd observations about the truth in this view, alongside the manifest exaggeration. They are to be found in his book *The Finality of Christ*. First, he sees that the demonic most shows itself precisely in the area of religion, and he remarks on the care with which converts distance themselves from their inherited practices for this very reason. And second:

> it is precisely at points of highest ethical and spiritual achievement that the religions find themselves threatened by and therefore ranged against the gospel. It was the guardians of God's revelation who crucified the Son of God. It is the noblest among the Hindus who most emphatically reject the gospel. It is those who say 'We see' who seek to blot out the light.

Human aspirations?

A third Christian view of other faiths is to see them not so much as preparations for the gospel or emanations from the demonic, but as aspirations of the human spirit. Buddhism, for instance, is an aspiration of the human spirit to counteract suffering in the world, animism to counter the dread forces of evil spirits. There is obviously truth in this view, and in some ways it brings out the differentia to which Christianity lays claim: the Christian gospel is not a religion in the sense of the human spirit reaching out to God. It is, rather, a revelation and a rescue by God himself. It does not begin at man's end and terminate on God, but the reverse.

However, on any showing, the view of other faiths as aspirations of the human spirit after God is inadequate. It does not make room for the element of natural revelation in other faiths. God does indeed, as Paul put it to the Athenians (Acts 17:27–8), intend that people should seek after him and find him. But equally he is not far from any one of us, for 'In him we live and move and have our being.' And Paul quotes with approval the pagan poet Aratus, 'For we are indeed his offspring.' And this God, who is not far from any of his creatures, has not left himself without witness (Acts 14:17). The heavens declare the Creator's glory, and the firmament shows his handiwork (Ps. 19:1). Moreover, human conscience and morality are part of God's general self-disclosure, for

> When the Gentiles who have not the law do by nature what the law requires, they are a law to themselves, even though they do not have the [Jewish] law. They show that what the law requires is written on their hearts, while their conscience also bears witness and their conflicting thoughts accuse or perhaps excuse them on that day when, according to my gospel, God judges the secrets of men by Christ Jesus. (Rom. 2:14–16)

So it would be misleading on Christian grounds to regard other faiths as simply the record of human striving after God. That would be unfair to other faiths, and it would not fit too readily with human nature as the Bible discloses it. We tend blandly to assume all people are eager seekers after God. It sounds good, and the judgement is charitable. But we know that we personally are not like that, and Scripture maintains that nobody else is either, for 'None is righteous, no, not one; no one understands, no one seeks for God' (Rom. 3:10). To be sure, the apostle is making his point very starkly. Of course people *sometimes* seek for God, especially in times of crisis. But very few set out *seriously* to find God and live their lives in conformity with his will.

The doubly astonishing thing that the Bible reveals to us is that we are not honest seekers after God at all. Very often we hold

down the truth in unrighteous living and do not see fit to acknowledge God even when we know perfectly well he is there (Rom.
1:18–20, 28). Light comes into the world, but we love darkness
rather than light because our deeds are evil (John 3:19). And that
holds good, in some measure, for all people. We embody a strange
mixture of longing for God and wanting to keep out of his way. No,
we are not single-minded seekers after God at all. That is one
embarrassing surprise. The other is absolutely astounding: God is
the single-minded seeker after us. He came to find us, lost as we
were.

Summary

I believe Sir Norman Anderson's judgement is wise when in his
book *Christianity and World Religions* he rejects any of these views
of other religions as sufficient in itself, but maintains that there is
truth in each:

> The non-Christian religions seem to me to resemble a patchwork quilt,
> with brighter and darker components in different proportions. There
> are elements of truth which must come from God himself, whether
> through the memory of an original revelation, through some process of
> cross-fertilisation which, I cannot doubt, God still vouchsafes to those
> who truly seek him. But there are also elements which are definitely
> false, and which I for one believe come from the 'father of lies' – whose
> primary purpose is not to entice men into sensual sin as to keep them
> back, by any means in his power, from the only Saviour. Yet again,
> there is much that could best be described as human aspirations after
> truth, rather than either divine revelation or Satanic deception.

WHAT IS SO SPECIAL ABOUT JESUS?

We can look at this briefly here, because we have already had
occasion to give it cursory attention, and will return to it in chapter
6. But what is so special about Jesus? Why are Christians so
unwilling to put him on a level with other great leaders in the
religions of the world? The answer is simple and straightforward.
The difference lies in who Jesus is, what he has achieved, and what
he offers.

Who is Jesus?

Jesus is not just a great teacher, or just a hero or martyr; nor is he just a prophet or a holy man authorised and sent by God. But in Jesus Christ we see no less than God made manifest in human flesh. All of the divine that could be concentrated in human form was embodied in that carpenter of Nazareth at the outset of our era. I shall not argue that now. I will do so in a later chapter. But it lies at the heart of the Christian claim both about Jesus and about other faiths. Jesus is in a totally different league from Buddha, Confucius and other great leaders. He is the man who was God, and in that lies a paradox. Yet it is this paradox which lies at the heart of Christianity. The Christian faith is the only one which rests entirely on the person of its founder: and he is no mythical figure, but a well-documented historical personage whose life, death and resurrection fully endorse the majestic claims he made about himself and others made about him. That is what makes Jesus so special.

What did Jesus achieve?

Boldly stated, he rescued the world. What does that mean? Simply that the world has from earliest days been operating under a dangerous bias: man has turned repeatedly, habitually, constantly to his own way. He has turned his back on God and on conscience times without number. This results in a parlous situation if God is, as Scripture and careful reflection would maintain, the supreme source of all that is good and upright and holy and just. This holy God cannot simply pretend that human wickedness and evil (as prevalent in our own generation as ever before in the history of mankind) do not matter. Of course they matter. And they will inevitably alienate us not only from each other, but from him who is utter perfection. There can be only one verdict for the whole human race: guilty. That applies to men and women of all religions and of none. 'All the world is guilty before God' (Rom. 3:19). That unholiness in us both evoked God's righteous judgement and called forth his mercy. It resulted in his own coming to this earth, not only to show us within the confines of a perfect human life what he is like, but supremely to fashion a way back to him for human rebels. What he did was to go to the place of degradation and shame, of the most terrible anguish and suffering; the place where innocent suffering would be experienced at its most acute; the place associated throughout Israel's history with God's repudiation and indeed his curse (Deut. 21:22–3). He went to the cross, that accursed instrument of torture. And he shouldered the curse – the curse, as Paul says, which should have been ours. For it was the curse of God's judgement upon those who had broken his laws; his personal, though not at all vindictive, verdict against human wickedness (Gal. 3:10, 13). And the whole New Testament exults in wonder at the generosity of a God who could stoop so low to conquer the hearts of his enemies, and could sacrifice himself so that we could go free. For by taking our place in the dock, he exhibited not only his grace but his justice: his grace welcomed us back, and his justice was fully met in all its claims against us – he had dealt with them on our behalf and in our place, at the cost of surrendering his own life.

No other leader in any of the world's religions ever did anything remotely similar. Nowhere else do you find the notion of a God who loves at such a cost that he has sacrificed himself for us. Nowhere else do you find the notion of rebels coming back free into the Father's house which they have deserted. Nowhere else do you hear even a whisper that there is nothing we can do to make ourselves acceptable. Our sin is too deep-dyed for that. But, praise be, God has done all that is necessary to bring us back and to enable us to stand unashamed in his holy presence, clothed in the goodness of Christ himself, as if it were our own.

Nor was that all. The perfect life of Jesus did not remain under the lock and key of death, as all other lives, maimed by sin, have done. Death could not keep him prisoner. And so you find, grounded in strong and consistent testimony from a horde of contemporaries, the astounding news that 'this Jesus God has raised up: and of that we are all witnesses' (Acts 2:32). So the resurrection shows he is the Son of God. The resurrection shows he overcame the sin barrier. The resurrection shows him as the conqueror of death. It makes him unrestrictedly available, and it points to the destiny God has for individuals and for the human race. That is what makes Jesus so special. What he has done in taking responsibility for the sins of the world could only be done by one who was in solidarity both with God and with man. What he achieved depends fairly and squarely on who he was. And such was his achievement that death itself was not strong enough to hold the crucified one. This is no mythology, but sober history. It is what started Christianity off and gave it its character. That is what makes the achievement of Jesus so special.

What can Jesus offer?

Jesus can offer forgiveness of sins, because he himself paid the price; he drank the draught of human wickedness to the dregs, and in return he can offer us the goblet of salvation's pure water.

Nowhere else in all the religions of the world will you find that. If you look to Hinduism or Buddhism, you will find that the principle of *karma* is inviolable. There is no forgiveness. You must pay your debts. If you look to Islam, you will find that 'God loves those who make themselves pure' – and what hope does that offer us? Moreover, God is utterly inscrutable. You cannot know how he will act. 'He punishes whom he pleases and grants mercy to whom he pleases.' Chill comfort there. It is only in Christ that there is an unrestricted, sure and just offer of forgiveness. But of course that is not all. By his resurrection he offers firm assurance as to who he really is (Rom. 1:3–4). He offers membership of a new community. That is not unique: most religions have some such community, though there are usually racial, class or financial restrictions. But that resurrection also offers the prospect of life after death with him and with fellow believers, a person-to-person relationship in which our lives will be taken up and transformed, just as his resurrection body was. Most of all, his resurrection paves the way for his Spirit to come and indwell our lives. That is utterly unique. Many other faiths rejoice in great teachers. But none offers unending friendship with that teacher irrespective of time and place, age and occupation. Yet that is just what the Spirit of Jesus can and does do to millions of people. He comes and indwells their lives, making Christ a constant companion and friend.

That is what is so special about Jesus. Who he is, what he has done and what he offers are all unique. Inevitably, therefore, Christians want to make him known.

WHAT BECOMES OF THOSE WHO HAVE NEVER HEARD THE GOSPEL?

There are three answers to this question which seem to me positively unChristian, though you will find Christians who hold each of them.

Are all inevitably 'saved'?

The first answer I have in mind is the view that people who have never heard the gospel (who must, of course, be carefully distinguished from those who have heard and have rejected it) will undoubtedly all be saved. This is called universalism. It is based on the conviction that the love of God will in due course break down all human resistance to him. All will be saved, because God in his love would never allow anyone to be lost.

Of course, we would all love it to be true. But universalism has never been part of mainline Christian belief, because the teaching of Jesus is so unambiguously opposed to it. He is constantly speaking of the two ways, the two destinations, the two futures awaiting the sheep and the goats, the wheat and the tares, those within the wedding feast and outside. Never in the teaching of Jesus or the apostles can you find any suggestion that all will inevitably be saved. What is more, it is very strange to argue this position of universalism from the teaching that God is love. How do we know that God is love? Basically because Jesus taught us so, and embodied that love in his own person and mission. And he is the one who taught most about the possibility and awesomeness of missing eternal life and making final shipwreck. There is something very odd, too, about the notion that in the end the God whose love did not preclude him from giving human beings free will is going to take that free will away, and dragoon us into his kingdom. To be sure, on the hypothesis of the universalist, it will eventually be a willing dragooning, as far as we are concerned. His love will have got through to us all in the end. But will it? How does he know? And how can he dogmatise in his assumption that nobody will use his God-given free will to resist God to the end? It is, I think, the overweening confidence and almost patronising attitude of the universalist that I find least like Jesus' own. In one place in his book *On Being a Christian*, Hans Küng scorns the agnosticism which many thoughtful Protestant theologians express on this subject 'with a supercilious "we do not know" as if it were no concern of theirs'. But surely it is the only attitude the creature can express before the Creator, when God has not given any direct light on the subject. I agree with Lesslie Newbigin's response to Küng in his *The Open Secret*:

> I find it astonishing that a theologian should think he has the authority to inform us in advance who is going to be saved on the last day. It is not

accidental that these ecclesiastical announcements are always moralis-
tic in tone: it is 'men of good will', the 'sincere' followers of other
religions, the 'observers of the law' who are informed in advance that
their seats in heaven are securely booked. This is the exact opposite of
the teaching of the New Testament. Here the emphasis is always on
surprise. It is the sinners who will be welcomed and those who were
confident that their place was secure who will find themselves outside.
God will shock the righteous by his limitless generosity and his
tremendous severity . . . There will be astonishment both among the
saved and among the lost (Matt. 25:31–46). And so we are warned to
judge nothing before the time (1 Cor. 4:1–5). To refuse to answer the
question which our Lord himself refused to answer (Luke 13:23–30) is
not 'supercilious'; it is simply honest.

Are all inevitably 'lost'?

If universalism will not qualify as an authentic Christian option,
what about its opposite, the conscious unending torment of all who
have never heard the gospel of Jesus Christ? There is no doubt that
many earnest Christians hold this view, but all the same I doubt
very much if it is a genuinely *Christian* option. What sort of God
would he be who could rejoice eternally in heaven with the saved,
while downstairs the cries of the lost make an agonising
cacophony? Such a God is not the person revealed in Scripture as
utterly just and utterly loving. To be sure, the New Testament is
emphatic about the possibility of eternal ruin. To be sure, it speaks
about hell in a direct manner. But it does not teach the conscious
unending torment of those who are eternally separated from God.
The language of 'destruction' is the most common description of
final loss in the Bible (Matt. 7:13; 10:28; 1 Thess. 5:3; 2 Thess. 1:9,
etc.). The most natural meaning spiritually is precisely parallel to
the literal meaning, i.e. to take away life, to liquidate. Immortality
is not, as Socrates thought, a quality which all people have naturally; it is, according to Jesus, the gift of God to those who trust him
for it. So there is no need to think of eternal ongoing enjoyment of
God being necessarily matched by eternal ongoing torment away
from God. It may well be – and the main thrust of Scripture
suggests that it is – final destruction. *Aiōnios*, the Greek adjective
for 'eternal life', is also applied to 'eternal destruction' in the
Bible. This does not primarily indicate unending quantity of life
or death, but ultimate quality. It means the life of the age to come,
or ruin for the age to come.

But does not the language about the lake of fire, and hell as a place 'where their worm does not die, and the fire is not quenched' (Mark 9:48), indicate constant unending torment? Not so. It is an allusion to the city rubbish dump called Gehenna, outside Jerusalem, where the maggots were always active and the fire always smouldering. It says nothing at all about constant unending torment; rubbish does not last long in a fire. The imagery indicates total ruin. But what about the lake of fire in the book of Revelation (Rev. 20:10)? That single reference in a highly pictorial book is not enough to hang a doctrine of such savagery on, particularly when you remember that it is said to be for the devil, the beast and the false prophet, who are not individuals at all, but principles of evil, which will be totally annihilated. Christians, therefore, should reject the doctrine of conscious unending torment for those who have never heard the gospel just as firmly as they reject universalism.

Will the heathen be judged by their deeds?

A third view found in Christian circles is that those who are not Christians will be accepted by God according to their works. They will be acquitted (or 'justified', as the New Testament would put it) by virtue of their proper adherence to their own religion and by their good deeds. Karl Rahner, an avant-garde Roman Catholic theologian, dubs them 'anonymous Christians' – a title which they would enthusiastically repudiate! Rahner was influential in the study which the Second Vatican Council gave to this matter, and concluded:

> Those also can attain to everlasting salvation who through no fault of their own do not know the gospel of Christ or his church, yet sincerely seek God, and, moved by his grace, strive by their deeds to do his will as it is known to them through the dictates of conscience. Nor does divine Providence deny the help necessary for salvation to those who, without blame on their part, have not yet arrived at an explicit knowledge of God, but who strive to live a good life thanks to his grace. Whatever goodness or truth is found among them is looked upon by the Church as a preparation for the gospel. She regards such qualities as given by him who enlightens all men so that they may finally have life. (*Lumen Gentium*, 2:16)

This is a very mixed statement. On the one hand it insists that other faiths are only a preparation for the gospel, and so maintains the supremacy of Christ. Three times it insists that a good life can only be lived by the grace of God. It also emphasises that people's ignorance of the gospel and failure to respond to it must be by no fault of their own. And it makes the customary (and often correct) Catholic distinction between implicit faith such as a baby may have in its mother, and explicit faith such as that baby could express in eloquent words twenty years later. But this Vatican statement gets very close to maintaining that a good life is all you need. It seems to promise salvation to those who 'seek God' (but how hard?) and who strive to do his will and live a good life. But who lives a good life? The Bible is very clear that nobody does. That is why a Saviour is needed. 'No human being will be justified in [God's] sight by works of the law, since through the law comes knowledge of sin' (Rom. 3:20). If leading 'a good life' and seeking the unknown God were enough, why should God have needed to stoop to the terrible depths of the incarnation and the cross for his fallen creatures? No. As Paul goes on to assert in Romans 3, God's own way of righting evil has been manifested in Christ. It is nothing to do with law-keeping and the religion of the prophets, though both the law and the prophets point forward to it. It is God's own righteousness. It is embodied in Jesus Christ. And it is intended for all who come in faith to claim it. Nobody deserves it, for the simple reason that there is no distinction: one and all have sinned and come short of the glory of God. But they can be justified, or acquitted, by his grace as a gift, through the redemption that is in Christ Jesus, whom God put forward as an expiation for sin through his death on the cross (Rom. 3:21–5).

Salvation is not achieved by works, and it is not rammed down everyone's throat whether they want it or not. But it is offered by a wholly just God, the Judge of all the earth, who always does right (Gen. 18:25). Therefore we may be confident that men and women will not be damned inexorably if they have had no chance to respond to the gospel.

Is there a door of hope?

How, then, can we make room both for the universal teaching of the Bible that nobody can merit God's heaven, and for the teaching that Christ died for the whole world and wants all to be saved (1 Tim. 2:4)?

The answer is, I think, hinted at in that extended passage of

Romans which I referred to above. Paul goes on, in Romans 3:25, to explain that Christ's work of sin-bearing on the cross demonstrated that God really had been just in times past when he had seemed to overlook sin. The cross showed that he had not overlooked it at all, but was waiting for the right moment to deal with it. In that act of rescue on the cross God demonstrated two things. One, that he was utterly just: so just, that he could not bear to pretend that sin does not matter. But he was also the justifier of the person who trusts in Jesus: so generous, that any who ask can share in that acquittal. And Paul goes on in the next few verses to make it plain that the great men of the Old Testament, like Abraham and David, were 'justified' in this way. They had nothing to boast of in their obedience, their law-keeping or their cultic religion. They were accepted because they put their whole trust in the Lord. They were 'justified by faith', is Paul's way of putting it.

> 'Abraham believed God, and it was reckoned to him as righteousness.' Now to one who works, his wages are not reckoned as a gift but as his due. And to one who does not work but trusts him who justifies the ungodly, his faith is reckoned as righteousness.

That is what Paul says in Romans 4:3–5, and he goes on to apply the same reasoning to David. These Old Testament men of God were not put right with God because of anything they did. Rather, they trusted that somehow God would find a way to accept them even though they knew they did not deserve it.

And now the eyes of Paul have had the cataract removed, so to speak. He sees how it is possible. David and Abraham, and millions like them in the Old Testament days, were saved because they trusted the living God whom they perceived with varying degrees of unclarity. How could God accept them? Because of what Christ *was going to do* on the cross. And how could he accept you and me? Because of what Christ *has done* for us on the cross. That mighty cross and resurrection are situated at the mid-point of history. Their shadow is cast both forward and back. They are both retrospective and prospective. That is how we may believe God can with perfect justice and in perfect love welcome all, from every religion or philosophy, who genuinely want to find him. If they do not rely on their own fancied goodness, but cast themselves on his mercy, they may well be among those who are surprised on the day of judgement to find themselves sheep rather than goats. For Christ died not for our sins only, but for the sins of the whole world (1 John 2:2). We are saved not by our knowledge of how God was able to manage it (Abraham and David had no inkling of such a thing), but by trusting our case wholly to him – that is to say, by faith. And that is not to make faith the supreme 'work' to compensate for the failure in all our other works. No, faith is the hand that gratefully receives the gift proffered us by this amazing God who shows his love for us in that while we were still sinners Christ died for us (Rom. 5:8).

There is a great deal of merit in this understanding of how God deals with those who have never heard. I have believed it for many years, and am glad to find support for it expressed in Sir Norman Anderson's book *Christianity and World Religions*. Such a view shows that God is consistent in how he treats mankind over the ages. It shows the seriousness of sin. It shows that we cannot save ourselves, but are perishing without a Saviour. It shows that Jesus is the one and only Saviour we sinners need, whatever our race and religion. It shows that God is scrupulously fair, and that he has made such abundant provision for mankind's salvation that nobody who casts himself on his mercy need miss it, however limited his knowledge. In a word, it validates the justice and mercy of God the Father, the universal need of mankind, the unique efficacy of Jesus' sacrifice and his being the only source of eternal salvation for all who reach the Father's house, whether they have heard of him or not. At the same time, it does not make the false assumption that people in other faiths are all right as they are, that they do not need the gospel, or that they will be saved by the profession of their own religion. Nor does it maintain that dialogue, valuable as it is, has replaced evangelism. If such good news awaits a needy world, how can we bear to keep silent? And that is the subject we must turn to as this chapter draws to an end.

Is the missionary nerve cut if some who have never heard the gospel may be saved?

The answer is an emphatic 'No'. There are some hints in Scripture, as we have seen, which suggest that the scope of salvation may well be a lot larger than the church, utterly dependent though that salvation is on Jesus Christ. The New Testament looks to the day when Christ crucified will draw all men to himself (John 12:32), when God the Father will unite all things under Christ's suzerainty (Eph. 1:10), when every knee will bow to him and every tongue confess that he is Lord (Phil. 2:10–11), when 'all Israel', will be saved (Rom. 11:26) and God will be everything to everyone (1 Cor. 15:28).

That teaching is there as a strand in the New Testament hope, and we must neither omit it nor exaggerate it. But what is certain is that the New Testament writers who used those words were assuredly not inhibited in their preaching of the good news. The fact that they believed that God desires all men to be saved and to come to the knowledge of truth (1 Tim. 2:4) did not for one moment mean that they got slack about preaching the gospel. The fact that they believed that Christ died not for our sins only, but for the sins of the whole world (1 John 2:2), did not imply that they sat back and waited for God to do his own work in his own time without any co-operation from themselves. Nothing could be further from the truth. These men and women of the first Christian centuries poured themselves out in preaching and teaching, in dialoguing and in persuading. Their zeal is one of the most wonderful things the world has witnessed. And they did not do it, in the main, because they were obsessed with the conviction that everyone would go to hell if they had not consciously responded to the gospel. They had other motivations, and so should we.

We will glance at those other motives in a moment, but first it is worth reflecting on Romans 10:12–18, a most instructive passage in this regard. It is part of Paul's passionate three chapters about the condition of Israel, his beloved nation. In Romans 10:13 he quotes Joel 2:32 to the effect that 'every one who calls upon the name of the Lord will be saved'. That 'every one' includes Jews who know about the true God, and Gentiles who do not. But there is no distinction between Jew and Greek. The same Lord is Lord of all, and bestows his riches upon all who call upon him. There is nothing narrow about Paul. He has a tremendously broad conception of God's mercy. But does that mean he is slack about evangelism? The verses that follow go on to maintain that just because God *does* want all to be saved, just because he *is* longing to bestow his riches on those who do not know him, it is incumbent on those who are Christians to be messengers of the gospel. 'How beautiful are the feet of those who preach good news!' (Rom. 10:15). In the very passage where he is daring to hope that one day – he knows not how – 'all Israel' (however that 'all' be construed) will be saved, and that whoever among the heathen calls on the name of the Lord shall be saved, he rises to a purple passage of challenge to go and tell this good news of salvation. No missionary nerve is cut for him by the possibility that God may save some of the heathen who call upon the name of the Lord as best they can, but do not know the name of Jesus – through whom, nevertheless, they are reached by God's salvation.

Just as the evangelists were not made idle by the expressed desire of their God that all men may be saved, equally they were not induced to sit back by the pluralism which was even more prevalent then than now. It amazes me to read theologians like John Hick suggesting that we must reinterpret the gospel in the light of modern pluralism because our situation is so different from what it was in the world upon which Christianity first dawned. What utter nonsense! The pluralism of the first and second centuries AD was the greatest in extent and intensity that the world has ever seen. The Jews refused to bow to it, and they were tolerated in the Roman Empire because Julius Caesar had conferred on them special privileges, which successive emperors respected. So the Jews were allowed to pray to their God for the health of Rome and the emperor, but were not expected to offer sacrifices to the pagan gods, which was required of everyone else. When the expanding Roman Empire met peoples with gods of which they knew nothing, their procedure was very simple. They either added the local gods to their already extensive pantheon, or else they identified them with deities already within the pantheon. But they found they could not do that with Christians, who refused to say both 'Jesus is Lord' and 'Caesar is Lord'. Such refusal cost thousands of them their liberty and their lives. They were imprisoned, tortured, thrown to the lions, crucified – but it made no difference. It was no good telling them that Jesus was just another charismatic prophet like Honi the Circle-drawer, or miracle-worker like Apollonius of Tyana. They steadfastly refused all efforts to make them compromise either in ethics or dogma. Jesus Christ was Lord. He was Son of God and Saviour. And few though they were initially, they claimed the whole of public life for him. They would not go to educational establishments that taught polytheism. They would not attend bloodthirsty gladiatorial shows. They would not worship the imperial statue. This made them very suspect, but they persevered, and in the end they won, and won most handsomely. Not by compromise, not by syncretism; but by enthusiastically persuading their hearers that Jesus is Lord and that he transforms the lives of those who trust him.

That is precisely what is happening all over Asia, Africa and Latin America these days. Millions of people are coming to Christ in these continents. Try telling the local evangelists there that they do not really need to preach the gospel, because all other faiths are as good, or that Christ must be relativised, or that the pagans are perfectly all right as they are – and see what an answer you receive! Christianity in much of the West is sick. It has lost its drive. It no longer really believes in the Saviour passionately enough to proclaim him with vigour. It no longer believes that men and women need this Saviour desperately. And so this dynamic gospel is shrunk into a suburban captivity of the churches and a virtual surrender by the church intelligentsia of the uniqueness of Christ and the importance of proclaiming his gospel. Alas, many of them may never have been responsible for leading anyone to Christ, and seeing the transformation which ensues. If they had, they would not so speedily give up their birthright. Last night I had the joy of doing just that – and to see the liberation in the person's face when she entrusted her shattered life to Christ, and to hear her start praying aloud with joy and confidence to God for her friends who are not yet Christians, was wonderful. This is what lit up the early Christians. They left to God the issue of who would or would not ultimately be saved. They recalled that Jesus had refused to answer the question whether the number would be large or small, but had bidden them enter in themselves (Luke 13:23–30). They did just that, and they turned the world upside down encouraging others to follow them. Why did they burn themselves out as they did?

Four powerful motives

First, they had a clear command from Jesus their master. They were told to go into all the world and make disciples, baptising them into the name of the Father and of the Son and of the Holy Spirit (Matt. 28:18–20). It was to this enterprise that Jesus lent his authority. It was to these missionaries that he promised his constant presence. It was no good calling Jesus Lord if you did not do what he told you. But they did what he told them: they went in the power of the Spirit and proclaimed the good news as Jesus commanded them.

Second, there was another good reason which must have motivated them. For every Cornelius who was just longing to trust Christ the moment he heard of him, there were hundreds who did not want to know. And so the apostles laboured among them assiduously. It is really not much comfort to know that God will save those who trust him, however little they know, because it is abundantly obvious that many people are determined to remain in rebellion against God. And the early evangelists went out to reach them. It was an uphill struggle. They did not find themselves surrounded by noble pagans seeking the truth. All too often their hearers were 'filled with all manner of wickedness, evil, covetousness, malice'. They were 'full of envy, murder, strife, deceit, malignity'. They were 'gossips, slanderers, haters of God, insolent, haughty, boastful, inventors of evil, disobedient to parents, foolish, faithless, heartless, ruthless'. Though they knew full well 'God's decree that those who do such things deserve to die', they not only did them but they approved those who practised them (Rom. 1:29–32). That was the sort of society which the apostles turned round by means of this dynamic gospel.

Third, there was in fact a profound sense of indebtedness which led the early Christians out in evangelism. 'I am under obligation both to Greeks and to barbarians, both to the wise and to the foolish: so I am eager to preach the gospel . . .' (Rom. 1:14–15). They were ambassadors for Christ, as though God were beseeching people through them to get reconciled with him (2 Cor. 5:20). They did not say, 'Well, pluralism is a problem, and no doubt God will save all these people in the end. Meanwhile, let them continue in the worship of Apollo.' They left no stone unturned in passion, in argument, in proclamation, in pleading, to win people to the Saviour. Whatever might or might not be their status hereafter was not too clearly revealed to those disciples – or to us. It lay in the hands of God alone. But in the meantime their contemporaries had no hope and were 'without God in the world' (Eph. 2:12). They were in the kingdom of darkness (Col. 1:13) and they needed to be transferred to the kingdom of God's beloved Son. What a change that would bring! In the old heathen days they lived in anger, wrath, malice, slander, foul talk, impurity, fornication 'and covetousness, which is idolatry'. And these are the things which evoke the righteous wrath of God (Col. 3:5–8). So Paul and his colleagues were very keen to see these lives transformed. He wanted them to come to Christ and 'Put on . . . as God's chosen ones . . . compassion, kindness, lowliness, meekness, and patience, forbearing one another and . . . forgiving each other . . . Above all these things put on love . . .' (Col. 3:12–14).

Finally, we come to the supreme reason why the early Christians did not allow the current pluralism and syncretism to impair their preaching of the gospel: the love of God spurred them on. They had known that love warm their own hearts like sunshine on a summer morning. They could not simply bask in it selfishly. They were impelled to call people out of the chill cellars of darkness into that glorious sunlight. 'We love, because he first loved us' could almost be the theme song of the entire New Testament. It certainly explains the missionary passion of the early church. They had been dragged from the highways and hedges into the Great Supper. They had experienced the generosity of the host and the joy of the meal, and they simply had to go out and tell others who were blind to it what they were missing. Gratitude and love mingled in the hearts of these evangelists of early days. And so they do today in parts of the world where the gospel is spreading like wildfire.

Believers do not evangelise because they have carefully calculated the probabilities of universalism, annihilation or unending torment, or because they have weighed Christianity in the balances with Buddhism or Islam. They go because they have fallen in love with the great Lover. They go because they have been set free by the great Liberator. They love him, and they want that love to reach others. It is far too good to keep to themselves. Evangelism in a pluralistic world? But of course! Far from closing our options, pluralism allows us to proclaim an undiluted gospel in the public square and in the supermarket of faiths, allowing others the same right. Let the truth prevail: but let craven silence be banished. If we have discovered Jesus for ourselves, there can be no alternative but to offer him to others. Freely you have received: freely give!

FURTHER READING

J. N. D. Anderson, *Christianity and World Religions* (Inter-Varsity Press)

David Edwards, with John Stott, *Essentials* (Hodder & Stoughton)

William Hocking, *Rethinking Missions* (Harper & Row)

Paul Knitter, *No Other Name?* (Orbis Books)

Hans Küng, *Christianity and World Religions* (Collins)

Christopher Lamb, *Belief in a Mixed Society* (Lion Books)

Stephen Neill, *Christian Faith and Other Faiths* (Oxford University Press)

Lesslie Newbigin, *The Finality of Christ* (SCM Press)

Lesslie Newbigin, *The Gospel in a Pluralist Society* (SPCK)

Lesslie Newbigin, *The Open Secret* (Eerdmans)

Karl Rahner, 'Christianity and the Non-Christian Religions', *Theological Investigations*, vol. 5 (Seabury Press)

A. H. Strong, *Systematic Theology* (Fleming Revell)

Arnold Toynbee, *Christianity Among the Religions of the World* (Scribner)

4

The Church God Uses in Evangelism

THE CHURCH GOD CANNOT USE

Mahatma Gandhi once said to some missionaries in India, 'You work so hard at it. Just remember that the rose never invites anyone to smell it. If it is fragrant, people will walk across the garden and endure the thorns to smell it.'

Now that is not the whole story about evangelism. But it is an important part of it. Nobody is going to want the Saviour we proclaim if they cannot see that he makes a difference to our lives, and that our churches are really attractive.

A few years ago Dr Billy Graham visited England, and part of the year of preparation was a study entitled 'Is your church worth joining?' A tough question, but a very proper one. For many churches, frankly, are not worth joining. And lots of people must share that view. The shrinking figures for church attendance in much of Western Europe bear testimony to the fact.

Alas, many churches seem to be rather like the stringy and parched pot plants that are all I manage to raise in my house! It is obvious enough what they are meant to be, but it is equally obvious that they are very unwell.

Here are some of the characteristics that are all too commonly found in churches, characteristics that are hardly calculated to draw new members in and make them feel at home.

You could go to many churches for weeks on end, experiencing nothing more than a verbal welcome. Nobody is interested in you. Nobody asks you out to lunch. Nobody visits you. It does not seem to matter very much whether you are there or not.

The service is likely to be highly predictable in pattern, hardly changing from week to week. Moreover, it is run from the front, rather like a performance – but a performance in which very few people take any spoken parts.

You may well sense some malaise in the air. Some of the people seem tense and unfulfilled. There may well be tension between the minister and elders or lay leaders. There is quite likely to be tension between the minister and the organist. And that is symptomatic of a lack of real love, a lack of personal warmth, in the place.

If you examine the leadership structure in many of our churches, you are likely to find one of two extremes. Either it is a one-man band, where nothing can be decided, perhaps even where services cannot be taken, without the vicar or minister in charge. He may well be very gracious, but he is firmly in control of everything that happens – or doesn't happen. Alternatively, in reaction against that sort of leadership, you may find that the church has taken refuge in the anonymity of committee structures. Nothing can be decided without the appropriate committee. A marvellous expedient. It means that nobody has to carry the can for decisions, and nobody can be seen to be the leader.

Little attempt seems to be made to reach those who do not darken the doors of the church, but who live nearby and daily pass its walls. The church itself may well be open only on Sundays for a couple of hours in the morning and evening. Or, if it is open during the week, the church members have no use for it, and so it is hired out to worthy organisations like Alcoholics Anonymous or Day Care.

Such churches will often be found to have little praise of God, little joy about them. It is all rather solemn, a Sunday ritual that has to be conducted, but nobody could say that the proceedings are dominated by any great sense of discovery or tinge of excitement.

The church is clearly concerned with the Bible and with prayer. These are well-known traditional Christian activities. So they happen. But the Bible does not leap to life. It is read, often in the beautiful but mildly incomprehensible Authorised King James Version, by someone who does not put much life or expression into the reading, and it does not have any noticeable effect on the hearers. It is not made much of in the preaching. It seems to come from another world. Prayer, likewise, lacks vitality. Someone is sure to pray for the peace of the world, for the sick (but without expecting anything to happen), and for the church. But it is not likely to be characterised by expectancy, variety, specificity or confidence.

It gradually becomes apparent that the Sunday worship has little relevance to the concerns of the ordinary people during the rest of the week – family, job, teenagers, and so forth. It does not seem to affect the lifestyle of the church members. There is nothing noteworthy about them during the week to signify that the Sunday church service has made any real change. Holiness of life is neither likely to figure in the preaching schedule of the church nor to characterise the lives of members. Indeed, most of them would give you a very odd look if you raised it.

The members of the church would be likely to be drawn from one social stratum, probably the middle class, and you would soon see that a small proportion of them carry almost all the responsibility for the life of the church and do nearly all the work. Moreover, this faithful central core is likely to be composed very largely of women. The men seem to have a distinct scarcity value, and so do the teenagers and young marrieds.

Last, but not least, you would be likely to assess the prevailing mood of the church as one of cautious conservatism. When wondering what a course of action should be, they would be more than likely to ask, 'What did we do last year?' The Holy Spirit, so prominent in the early days of the church as recorded in Acts and the epistles, would be unlikely to gain frequent mention, and if anyone claiming his inspiration were actually to say something during a church service, stunned amazement would result, speedily followed by strong disapproval.

That may be a bit of a caricature: but it is all too readily recognisable in many a congregation. Imagine drawing new believers into such a church. They would not stay for long. Therefore it is imperative to try to find some of the marks of a church that God will be able to entrust new believers to. There is an old saying that you don't put live chicks under dead hens. Maybe God doesn't, either!

Recently one major denomination put out a study course entitled 'Rafts and Trawlers'. It was asking the shrewd if painful question, 'Is your church a raft or a trawler?' Many people with Christian convictions look to the church to provide stability in a period of rapid social change. It is a raft to cling to in the waves of a stormy sea. That is why change is resisted so strenuously. It is not so much that any particular example of change is especially irritating: the whole principle of change is the really threatening thing. The trouble is that people do not have their faith in the right place. To be sure, we need something that is stable in a fast-moving world. But that 'something' is not the ancient version of the Scriptures or a liturgy hallowed by centuries of use. It is Jesus Christ, the same, yesterday, today and for ever (Heb. 13:8). He, and he alone, is the proper Christian anchor. No, this is not the sort of church that God can afford to use. He looks for something very different.

THE CHURCH GOD CAN USE

We are fortunate to live in an age where massive Christian shrinkage in some parts of the world is matched by massive Christian growth in others. A great deal of study has been devoted to this in recent decades. Notable among the researchers in this area are the Church Growth leaders Donald McGavran and Win Arm, followed by Peter Wagner and Eddie Gibbs at Fuller. Dr Glenn Smith has also put out a collection of some of the most exciting growth stories, mainly in the Roman Catholic Church. His three volumes, *Evangelising Adults*, *Evangelising Youth*, and *Evangelising Blacks* (published jointly by the Paulist Press and Tyndale Press), give an amazing insight into what is going on – often in unexpected places. In Britain the writing of David Watson has been outstanding, particularly his two books published by Hodder & Stoughton, *I Believe in the Church* and *I Believe in Evangelism*. If ever a Christian leader in our generation knew about these two areas, David did. And now, internationally, MARC Europe has put out a remarkable series of stories of growing churches: *Ten Growing Churches*, *Ten Worshipping Churches*, *Ten Growing Soviet Churches*, *Ten Sending Churches*. They make fascinating reading. A recent Anglican book published by Hodder & Stoughton, *By My Spirit*, consisting of contributions from across the world and edited by the previous Archbishop of Cape Town, Bill Burnett, makes much the same point. There is a remarkable unity in the picture we are getting of those churches which God allows to grow not only in numbers but in depth, vitality and mission. I believe that almost all the points which modern Christians are recovering are foreshadowed in the New Testament church at Antioch.

We read the story in Acts 11:19–30 and 13:1–3. It repays careful study, for it encapsulates many of the principles, found throughout the New Testament, of the type of church that God can use.

Antioch was a great city. It was the capital of Syria, Queen of the East, and was situated as a most important sea port at the mouth of the river Orontes. There were only two cities larger than Antioch in all the ancient world, Rome and Alexandria. The city has been well excavated, and we know a lot about it and its attitudes. It was a military stronghold. It housed an extraordinary number of Jews, who had full citizen rights alongside the Gentile Antiochenes. It was devoted to business and commerce. It was dedicated to sex. It was swathed in superstition. All in all, it was a very modern city. And this is the place that became the springboard for Christian evangelism in Asia, Europe, and eventually worldwide. Had it not been for Antioch, Christianity might have shrivelled to become only a small sect in Judaism. It was in Antioch that Christianity, the world faith, was born (Acts 11:26). It was from here that missionary journeys went out in ever-widening arcs.

What can we learn from the planting of the faith in Antioch? How was it won for Christ? One might imagine that it was the target of careful planning, of a major crusade or a five-year plan. No. Or was it converted through the brilliance and self-sacrifice of the leading apostles? No. It was won through a handful of wandering Christians moving up the coast from Jerusalem. They had no money, no plans. They simply loved Jesus very much and wanted to share him with others. So they did. It was all very spontaneous. Antioch became a most exciting church. If we want to learn about the sort of church God can use, we could profitably study what went on in this most open congregation.

It was open to change

We must begin at the beginning, with the people who came to evangelise the city. They were Hellenists, friends of the first martyr, Stephen. They were men who had been raised as Greeks, and were imbued with Greek culture and language. They thought big. They thought fresh. Stephen had taught them to do this. The gravamen of the charge which cost Stephen his life was this: he had advocated change! That change has been sufficient to unseat many in the church since Stephen's day. He dared to maintain that God was not confined to a building, nor to a book, nor to the customs of the worshipping community. He was perceived to speak 'against this holy place' (i.e. the Jerusalem temple), 'against the law' (i.e. the Torah), and he had the effrontery to suggest that Jesus would

'change the customs which Moses delivered to us' (Acts 6:13, 14).
It would be hard to find three more volcanic targets than those!

Most churchmen would want to stand foursquare against change
in one or more of those three areas. Some largely identify Christianity with a building. 'Where is St John's Church?' we ask. 'Down
the street; that building there,' they reply. But of course that is not
St John's Church. It is simply the meeting-place of St John's
Church, and if the church building were knocked down, the
congregation would continue elsewhere.

Others would see Christianity very much as the religion of the
book. It might be the Bible. It might be the 1662 Prayer Book, or
the Roman Missal. But it is Islam, not Christianity, which is the
religion of a book. Christianity is the religion of a Person.

As for changing the customs we have inherited – how painful
that is for all of us. But especially if we have placed our confidence
and sought our security in those same customs, any change is very
bad news indeed. And so it seemed to the conservatives at
Jerusalem, the Twelve and their colleagues. But not to Stephen.
That is why Stephen was killed, while the apostles did not even get
kicked out of Jerusalem. A traditional sort of faith is acceptable in
a tolerant, unbelieving world. But a radically different faith, and
consequently a different lifestyle, is such a threat that it courts
opposition. So it was here. The apostles were free to stay. The
followers of Stephen got hounded from the capital . . . and went
everywhere chattering the message (Acts 8:1, 4).

Against all appearances, it was these Hellenists who would win.
The future lay with them, not with the conservatives who were
impervious to change. They believed in a God who is always on the
move – not housed in a building. They believed in a Jesus who is
the Son of Man, Lord over the whole of mankind, not simply the
Jewish Messiah. They believed in the God who makes all things
new, and does not tie us to the customs of the past. They believed
in a faith which was as good for Gentiles as it was for Jews, not
restricted to those who were already 'insiders'. Their message and
their way of life was striking and indeed radical. But it turned the
world upside down. They were very manifestly open to change.

For any congregation that is at all settled, change is one of the
hardest things to face. And yet it is a prime necessity. Had not
those Hellenists been open to change there would have been little
or no missionary activity. We owe them an enormous debt. They
have blazed for us a trail we may be unwilling to follow, but follow
we must. Unless there is openness to change in the modern

Western church we will get nowhere. The message is plain. People have voted with their feet. They do not want to be where most of us currently are. I do not blame them. What excitement is there in a normal traditional church service? Are there not alternatives on a Sunday morning? Our attitudes must change. Maybe our music must change. Our robes may well need to be discarded. Our building-based mentality may need to change. Our ministerial pattern of 'six days invisible, one day incomprehensible' needs to change. Our idea of one-person ministry needs to change. The only thing that does not change is a cemetery. Every living thing changes, and so will a living church. It is a very exciting thing to be part of. But it must be open to change wherever the Lord indicates.

Such change may be very radical, and it may be very costly. I think of a church in the USA situated in 'yuppy' country, and keen to grow. They asked themselves, 'When would people in this area come to church, if they ever thought of coming?' They concluded *?(see are/)* that the answer was Sunday morning. They then asked themselves, 'Why do so many of these people, who have a residual faith in God, not come to church?' The answers they came up with were that such people did not want to be noticed; they did not want to sing anything; and they did not want to pay anything. On this basis they set about constructing an entirely new worship service. It lasted for just an hour. Nobody was singled out. There were no collections. No congregational singing was expected. The aim was excellence. The preaching was very carefully crafted, and precisely gauged to the needs of those whom they hoped would come. And come they did! When I last heard, they were getting some six thousand people on a Sunday morning, mainly from this young, upwardly mobile group that they had set out to reach. The remarkable thing was that the people who would not have called themselves Christians at all were thrilled with this, and told their friends, 'We have found the sort of church we've always been looking for. You must come along.' They themselves proved to be the evangelists! And the minister never made a challenge to commitment. He would have agreed with René Padilla's remarks at the Lausanne Congress in 1974:

> The task of the evangelist in communicating the gospel is not to make it easier, so that people will respond positively, but to make it clear. Neither Jesus nor his apostles ever reduced the demands of the gospel in order to make converts. No cheap grace, but God's kindness which is meant to lead to repentance, provides the only solid basis for discipleship. He who accommodates the gospel to the mood of the day,

does so because he has forgotten the nature of Christian salvation – it is not man's work, but God's.

No cheap grace was offered at this church. The challenge of Christ was faithfully transmitted. And after six months or so, one of these young business people would take a friend out to lunch after the service, and ask, 'Isn't it about time you committed yourself?' That is how the outreach of the church grows. But the change for the regular congregation has been massive. It has meant moving their main service of worship to a weeknight evening. But they were even prepared for that in the cause of the gospel. They were open to change.

It was open to lay initiatives

I find it amusing, indeed almost ironic, that the Western church, with its hierarchies, its pomp and circumstance, was brought into being by a bunch of nobodies who were all lay people. Of course, the distinction between laity and clergy, which has so distorted Christianity, was quite unknown in those far off New Testament days. Christianity was entirely a lay movement. The Antioch church not only gave vast scope to laymen: it was founded by laymen. The nearest thing to clergy were the apostles: and not one of them was to be seen at Antioch. They were all keeping their heads down in Jerusalem. But the wandering refugees who had 'hazarded their lives for the Lord Jesus' brought this exciting church into being. Surely there is something for us to learn here? Most churches give only the most limited scope and responsibility to lay members: the key tasks are carefully reserved for the clergy. This is disastrous. It not only creates a two-class society, but it gives the impression that the clergyman or minister knows it all, and the layman is an amateur. Nothing could be further from the truth. In many ways the laity know far more about life, about celebration and friendship, about natural contacts with their friends than the clergy do. They have between them many skills that the clergy lack. It is sheer folly to endure the cork-in-the-bottle situation which bedevils so many churches – where the minister is the cork! He *is* valuable, just as valuable and no more valuable than any of the rest of the congregation. But he must not be permitted to quench lay initiatives, or the church will regress. The laity will say, 'Very well, if he wants to play it that way, the best of luck to him.' That may be comfortable for his self-esteem, but I can assure you

of one thing. That will not be a growing church. Effective evangelism takes place in churches which know full well that every
member is a minister, that everyone is a limb in the body of Christ,
and every limb has a job to do, different from and complementary
to that of other limbs in the body.

I went to a Canadian church recently where there was the
unusual phenomenon of about eight hundred people gathered for
an evening service. It was then followed by a gathering of about a
hundred and fifty young people – even more amazing! I wanted to
know the secret of this, so I asked the minister late that night while
I sat at his table. The answer lay in the laity. He told me that of the
six hundred or so members of his church, all but about twenty had a
clearly defined ministry for Christ either inside the church or
branching out from it. Churches like that not only grow: they
deserve to grow!

It was open to faith

Those Christians who evangelised Antioch really knew what it
meant to trust the living God. They simply laughed at problems.
How could they found a church? Yet they did. They were so few, so
poor, so ill-educated, so powerless. Yet they founded the church at
Antioch. The problems they faced were so daunting: problems of
race, class, decadence, politics. Yet they founded the church at
Antioch. Their message seemed so ludicrous: of a crucified peasant
who, they asserted, was alive and was God come in the flesh for the
rescue of men. Crazy it might be, but it was the founding charter of
the church of Antioch. They must have been men of enormous
faith, these Hellenists who endured, as seeing the invisible. They,
like the heroes recorded in Hebrews 11, sought a city which had
foundations, whose builder and maker is God . . . and in so doing
they founded a church in the city of Antioch. They laughed at
difficulties. They shrugged off the impossible. They had learned to
trust the Lord, to obey him, and to put their lives on the line. God
honours faith like that.

That is how the faith is growing today in Zambia, in Colombia, in
Korea. It is growing apace, because men and women are on fire for
Jesus Christ and are fearlessly trusting him to give the increase.
Some of us here in Western Canada are church-planting; we are
seeing churches begin where there were none before, seeing
churches start with no members but the founding couple. And

these are among the most dynamic churches around. They are the churches which draw people. They are the churches which send missionaries out. The Korean Church, which is such a model in the Christian world today, was founded through an intrepid Welshman who went out there armed with tracts written in the Korean language, of which he knew not a word! He was promptly martyred, but not before he had scattered his tracts at the feet of his executioners. One of them picked some of the tracts up, and used them as decoration in his house. The inevitable happened! Those tracts brought first one and then another to Christ, and so the Korean church was born. Great faith, crazy faith if you like, faith that was prepared to pay the supreme price, had once again triumphed, as it has throughout the centuries of the church's history. For God loves to respond to the loving faith of his people, faith that is spelt 'R-I-S-K'.

It was open to speak about Jesus

'Jesus' is almost an unmentionable word in some churches. They feel that it is an embarrassment. It will put people off. It is indelicate. Such direct talk must at all costs not take place. But this is a great mistake, a mistake which those early evangelists of Antioch did not make. You see, they were shameless enthusiasts for Jesus. They had been speaking of him as they wandered up the coast from Jerusalem to the north; but they had confined their conversations to Jews, telling them the amazing news that their long-awaited Messiah had come, and that he was Jesus. But when they got to Antioch, where Jews and Greeks were so much on a par, they could hold themselves back no longer. They preached the Lord Jesus 'to the Greeks also' (Acts 11:20). It was very fruitful. 'The hand of the Lord was with them, and a great number that believed turned to the Lord' (Acts 11:21). This personal chatting about the subject of their greatest joy, Jesus, led many to believe in him. It still does. It is the best way of evangelism, when one person is talking about Jesus to one person who is interested in listening. A few nights ago I led an interested person to the Lord Jesus – and that person is busy telling all her friends what they are missing. It is causing a lot of interest. People are beginning to want to find him for themselves. That is what happened in Antioch. One of the greatest tragedies in the ossifying Western church is that people do not, by and large, talk about Jesus. That is extremely foolish. Jesus is the supremely attractive one. If we exclude from our conversation the only real winning card that we have, we are of all people the most to be pitied. If a church seriously wants to evangelise, my advice would not be to hire a famous preacher or invite the Archbishop: it would be to open the mouths of the people in the pews. Everyone has a story to tell, the story of God's dealing with their own soul. Everyone can invite a friend to a meeting. Everyone can say what a difference this Jesus has made to them. It is not difficult. It springs naturally to many who have recently discovered the beauty of Jesus for themselves – until they discover that 'mature Christians' no longer do such bizarre things!

I think of friends of mine in Tanzania, where the gospel is spreading so fast through lay witness to Jesus that the Anglicans alone are opening a church a week. I think of another friend in Sri Lanka who leads to Christ some hundreds of Buddhists a year through personal testimony, his own and that of members of his church, often at street corners. I think of the Pentecostals in Australia, out on the streets among the passers-by and confidently bearing testimony to Jesus – and not a minister among them! I think of students at Oxford, a city where I used to work, often bringing friends to Christ by their own conversations in the middle of the night, the time when students are at their best! I think of those same students on a two-week mission, enthusiastically preaching Jesus in the streets, in home meetings, in bingo halls – just like the founders of the church at Antioch. And I thank God that he has not left this task to the highly skilled and profoundly educated (though these too have a most important place in the church), but to ordinary men and women who love him, trust him, and are prepared to open their mouths about the 'Jesus' who must be 'Lord'. When a church becomes open to speak about Jesus, then things happen. In the early days of my evangelistic preaching at Oxford I used to rely on inviting people to come and meet me afterwards. Later on, I was more than happy to ask people to turn to their neighbours in the pew and discuss the claims of Christ at the end of a sermon, knowing full well that so many lay people in the congregation were perfectly capable of leading an enquirer to the Saviour. As a result we saw a large number of new conversions every year. It was the fruit that resulted from people willing to talk about Jesus.

It was open to training

News of the substantial turning to Christ of Gentiles as well as Jews in Antioch reached the Jerusalem authorities. They sent Barnabas to see what was going on, and he was thrilled with what he saw. But he realised that the new believers needed training, so he collected Saul from Tarsus and 'For a whole year they met with the church, and taught a large company of people' (Acts 11:22–6). They realised the need of training the congregation if they were to be at all effective for God.

Many modern congregations and their leaders do not realise that. The level of training in many of the older mainline churches is very weak. The standard of preaching is low and uninspiring. Little effort is made to equip the congregation in different areas of Christian service. Apologetics is unknown. How to handle the cults from the perspective of biblical Christianity is an ever-increasing need, but one which does not get addressed. In a word, we are very weak on training.

Training needs to happen in three distinct ways. First, there needs to be training in the Bible. It is the foundation document of Christianity and one of the main nutrients of the Christian life. Believers need to develop a regular personal time of daily Bible study. There are plenty of notes to help with this: from Scripture Union notes, the Bible Reading Fellowship's notes, the Soldier's Armoury, and the like. The Roman Catholic Church has moved light years ahead in this respect recently, with the publication of *Share the Word* (both Bible reading notes and audio cassettes). This understanding of Scripture can also come through courses of sermons, and home Bible study groups. Many churches seem not to have considered planning courses of sermons. They stick to the lectionary if they are liturgical churches, or allow individual choice to preachers if they are not: they might, perhaps, elect to teach their way through a book of the New Testament. But a well-planned, well-publicised series of addresses based on Scripture and designed to meet the felt needs of the congregation could be a valuable teaching method, could attract passers-by into the church, and could be a stimulus to regular Bible study among the congregation.

We shall be examining the place of home-based Bible study groups later. But they are a valuable way of promoting fellowship and understanding in a church. The home group will have about a dozen members, so it is small enough to facilitate close relationships. And the study itself has guidelines, but enables and indeed necessitates full participation by members. Such Bible study outlines are available from the Scripture Union and from Inter-Varsity Press in England, and from Harold Shaw Publishers in the USA. All three publishing houses specialise in providing this material. Unless the congregation are getting rooted in Scripture, they will not have the remotest hope of influencing others to Christ, and may well fall prey to one of the many attractive-looking imitations of real Christianity which are on the market, awaiting gullible buyers.

All-age Sunday schools are one of the most helpful features in American Christianity. The concept is very simple, and potentially very effective. Members of the congregation offer two or two and a half hours to the church on a Sunday morning. One hour is spent in worship, with a shortish sermon. A coffee break follows. The second hour is spent in a Sunday-school class. Several options may be on offer at any one time, and they can be directed to whatever the needs in the congregation may be – ethical, doctrinal, educational or apologetic. This greatly sharpens the understanding of the members. It gives choice to the customers, and it makes good use of the teaching gifts of lay members of the church. Why should Sunday school stop in the early teens? This is a training method that deserves to be used widely throughout the Christian church. And if there are two morning services, you simply have the coffee break between them, continue with the all-age Sunday school, and members take in a worship service of their choice before or after the class.

The second main way of training is by having evening courses on specific matters, geared to target groups. A short course for new believers; one for leaders of home groups; one for Sunday school teachers, or youth workers; one in personal evangelism; some on moral dilemmas, and some on the cults. Spread through the year, these can be an enormous help to the spiritual diet of members of the congregation. Short courses of not more than two months are often best, so that there is no danger of burn-out. Some of the courses will be practical, some apologetic, and some designed to further congregational or individual growth in Christ.

The third main way of training is to take younger people with you on some specific item of Christian ministry and train them on the job. This was the apostolic method, and it is still the most effective. They learn from the strengths (and the weaknesses) of the senior partner, and discover the joys and the challenges of encounter with real situations. The Antioch church was clear about that. They sent out Saul and Barnabas, with John Mark to help and learn the trade. And that pattern continued throughout the New Testament period. It is a very good one.

Staid Englishman that I am, I continue to be amazed by the amount of church-planting that goes on in Western Canada. Some of it is based on personality splits, which is regrettable. Some of it is sheep-stealing, which is no less regrettable. But much of it is primary evangelism in a post-Christian situation. I suspect that these conditions are likely to increase in Western Europe. We might all need to learn from these Antioch pioneers, and sooner than we imagine. I think of friends in Canada and the USA who have formed churches simply by starting with two couples. Sometimes they have advertised in the press, or visited, or used the telephone to ring round some thousands of people in the area (local phone calls in Canada being free!) to invite them to check out their new church if they currently belong to no other. One of my friends who is experienced in this area of church-planting is George Mallone. He is clear that the learning climate needs to be 'hot'. That is to say, it is best to learn on the job with a more experienced colleague, rather than from the 'cool' medium of books. He and others like him have hammered out five principles which they believe to be vital elements in this 'hands-on' training. First, do the ministry yourself, learning as you go, and reflecting on how others can be involved. Second, draw others into doing the ministry with you. Third, let them do the ministry, as you stay alongside, supervise and encourage. Then comes the transfer of the responsibility for the ministry to them: they report back to you on how they got on. And finally, the responsibility for training others is passed on to them. Does that leave you wondering what sort of people you can invite to help you in the first place? John McClure, one of the Vineyard Fellowship leaders, has a simple and helpful acrostic, FATSOS. You are looking for FATSOS, people who are

Faithful to God, to his Word and to the leadership.
Available to God in the use of their time and opportunities.
Teachable by the leaders, circumstances and the Spirit.
Sound in New Testament Christianity, both orthodoxy and
   orthopraxy.
Outgoing in social skills, so as to maximise their impact.
Spirit-led in the development of character and obedience to Jesus.

I fancy that is a passable description of the layfolk who went out and planted the church at Antioch!

It was open to love

Love is the most attractive quality in the world. And it lies at the heart of Christianity. It is the most notable trade-mark of the great Lover. Without it a church is nothing at all. And clearly love flourished at Antioch. Love drove those early missionaries to come and chat the good tidings. Love drove Saul and Barnabas to drop everything and teach them. Love knit Jewish and Gentile Christians together in a table-fellowship which was something entirely new in the ancient world. Love drove them to support the poor in Jerusalem and to equip and support their friends going out on the first missionary journey. The fellowship between the Christians at Antioch was something very special and very attractive.

But it is not always thus. Many churches have a very low level of love flowing through them. There is politeness, yes. But deep caring, no. People meet for an hour or two on Sundays, but feel no need to get together in the week. There is not a lot of laughter together, prayer for each other, eating in each other's homes, and so on. But there could be. And where there is, where love reigns, then churches grow.

Love is the climate which allows gifts to bloom and people to feel loved for themselves. But how is it to be achieved?

To some extent it comes with a warm welcome at the door as you go in. To some extent it comes from invitations to lunch after the service. To some extent it comes from coffee at the back of the church, joint occasional picnics and pot-luck suppers. To a large extent it comes from the leadership: if it is apparent that the leaders really love one another, then that is going to catch on in the congregation at large. But essentially love grows in the small group where everyone can be known, welcomed and recognised for what they are. In any congregation of more than fifty you can't hope to get to know everyone in depth. So it is wise for the congregation to be broken up into small groups meeting weekly in homes for fellowship in Christ.

These home groups will comprise several elements. There will be some worship, some food, and time to share personal news. There will be some Bible study and perhaps a house communion. Members may come up with some service they can render to one of their number, like painting a room; or they may agree to try to meet some need in their immediate locality. There will be 'fun' things, which will include the children. There will be care for one another in loneliness and illness. Above all there will be the chance for members to share aspects of their lives with one another. They will gradually allow trusted friends within the group to see deep into the places in their hearts where hurts persist, and they will experience the healing this mutual sharing, praying and loving can bring.

Such loving fellowship is very therapeutic. We need it. And it is very hard to find outside the small group. You can't love everybody without devaluing the meaning of the word 'love'. But you can love a dozen people.

The home group has proved to be the key to love in many churches, and a major factor in the growth of the church world-wide. In the great churches in Korea, which number many thousands of members, the congregations are broken down into multiples of twelve. Thus everyone matters, everyone is cared for. The small home group is the primary agent of pastoral care as well as the essential sphere of Christian fellowship. David Prior has written a most stimulating book, *The Church in the Home*, which is required reading for any who want to get such groups going in their own churches; and I have tried to write about the setting up of such groups, the training of their leaders, and the maintenance of their life within the overall programme of the church, in *Freed to Serve*.

There are, of course, tasks which these home groups can undertake within the local church: sometimes they can corporately lead a service, decorate the church for a festival, host a banquet. Sometimes there will be occasions when two or three such groups get together for an evening, so as to broaden the circle of friendship, and to provide an opportunity for the gifts of group members to be exercised.

If all this seems far away from where the country pastor finds himself, it really is not so. He can get a group of believers in his church to meet on a regular basis in the homes of one of the members. He can lead it to begin with, gradually turning over the task to others within the group as their confidence increases and their gifts emerge. Prayers will be answered, fellowship will increase, brainstorming on advances in parish life will take place; and before long that group will spawn another, even within a small congregation.

It is exciting to see how one minister in the heart of the Suffolk countryside in England is making use of additional home-based meetings in the three small rural parishes of which he has charge: the scope is endless. There are already house fellowship groups, which study the Bible and worship and pray. But he has devised a wider net, called *The Way In*. It is a four-week discussion programme for church members and those on the fringe of the church to discuss four central themes in any church's life: worship of God, witness to Christ, service of others, and use of resources. The aim is of course to inculcate these basic themes into the minds of the villagers, and to work out clear goals for the village churches as a result. People are invited to come to a nearby home, share their views, and listen to one another: and they are responding in a big way.

Of course there will need to be careful teaching and 'apprentic-ing' of leaders for these groups in any church, small or large. Close liaison between the home group leaders and the pastor needs to be maintained by regular meetings for teaching and encouragement. Otherwise they could spin off into orbit, and disunity could replace love. It is this fear that stops many pastors from allowing such groups in their church. But they are shortsighted. Given the right safeguards, I know of no means of growing love in a church like the way of small groups. Significantly, whether you look at church growth in Europe, in Latin America or in Asia, the small group is the basic element in Christian structures of love. The good that has been done by agencies like the Cursillo Movement or Marriage Encounter, to mention but two ways of drawing Christians together for lively and loving interchange, is incalculable. And these home groups, like the church itself, should be made up of 'unlikes' as well as of 'likes'. It is easy to love those who are like us: not so easy when they are not. But we are not called in the Christian church to have fellowship only with those who are like us. Antioch did not. The Jews and Gentiles who ate together were not like each other. The smooth Antiochenes were not like the wild prophet Agabus who descended unawares upon them. Saul was not like Barnabas. There was no 'homogeneous unit principle' at work in the growth of this church. Love is colour-blind. Love is a family affair, God's family: in a family you do not choose your brothers and sisters! And the home groups that have learned most of love have trodden this at first sight unattractive path. They have embraced the unlikable and the unattractive, and in so doing have become agents for their transformation. For when we are loved unconditionally, that is when we begin to grow. When we know we are accepted just as we are, then we have confidence to face change.

It was open to need

One of the saddest accusations which can be laid against Christians is that of hypocrisy. They say we are hypocrites. It is often unfair, often unthought out. But if it were verbalised, I think the charge would lie in two main areas. Our behaviour is a long way from our belief. And we tend to carry on with our hymns and our services without doing much to alleviate the need around us in the hurting world out there. Many churches are wonderful in this respect, but many others are not. The fact is that the unbelievers pay us a great compliment. They really expect Christians to be concerned about the needs of people they do not even know. They really expect us to lead attractive lives that are somehow different.

At Antioch nobody could have called the believers hypocrites. As we shall see, they called them 'Christians' instead, impressed as they were by the Christlikeness of their lives. And this showed up nowhere more than in their generous response to need. No sooner did they hear of the need that would soon hit Jerusalem through the famine which a visitor named Agabus predicted, than they amassed a substantial offering and sent it to Jerusalem through a couple of their members, Barnabas and Saul (Acts 11:27–30). This is very remarkable. The Jerusalem Christians were probably suffering as a result of financial mismanagement – they had, after all, shared out their capital in a splendid gesture . . . and in due course it ran out. So these Antiochene Christians, many of them Gentiles, many of them, no doubt, businessmen, might have decided that the Jerusalem church had made a mess of things and might best be helped by being left to sort the mess out and learn from it. They might equally have been suspicious of a need whose only evidence was a remarkable visiting prophet! But no. They gave, and they gave at once, most generously, to meet an impending social need. It was just the same when Saul and Barnabas went out on that first missionary journey. I do not suppose the Christians at Antioch wanted to lose two of their best leaders. But they agreed at once, and they raised finance and collected supplies for them and sent them off. I love these two glimpses that we are given of their generosity, their willingness to meet unexpected need.

Churches which put themselves out to meet social needs grow.

Churches which live for themselves die by themselves. The amount of the giving may be small because the congregation is tiny: that does not matter. It is the attitude that counts with the Lord who sees a widow's mite as more value than a rich man's big gift. If our evangelism is to be effective, the church must be concerned to meet the surrounding need. This may consist of lonely shut-in people. It may require the provision of nursery space. It may be educating immigrants in literacy. It may be providing somewhere for street people to go. It may be offering adopting agencies for unwanted pregnancies. The local need should be discerned, and the church should show that it cares and that it is trying, however inadequately, to meet that need. Then it will be seen to be relevant. Then people will want to hear its message: not before then. The introversion of the churches is one of the main reasons for their ineffectiveness in our generation. It was not so in previous chapters of the church's life. It is not so in many parts of the world today. But in Western Europe it is often, alas, like that. The church seems to meet on Sundays but to take no notice of the signs of need all round it. It simply is not in touch. No wonder it cannot evangelise. But once a church's members begin to get released from the bonds of materialism, once they learn to tithe their income and sense the joy of giving to the Lord's work, then the whole spirit of a church changes. It becomes open to need. It begins to see with the eyes of Christ, to care, and to do something about it. God can use a church like that. And he does. (See the Appendix on Evangelism and Social Justice.)

It was open to shared leadership

As we have seen, leadership in Christian churches often presents one of two extremes. It is either dominated by the minister, or it is lost in a committee. The pattern of leadership in the church at Antioch is very instructive. It was shared, not individual. That is a very important matter. One-man leadership is bad for the man and for the church. The man tends to imagine he has gifts that God has not given him, and that he is nearly indispensable. The congregation see that he thinks that way and find it convenient to go along with it. It means less work for them. So everyone loses in a one-man leadership. Even if everything seems to be highly successful while he is in charge, it folds once he is gone.

Shared though it was, however, the leadership in Antioch was not faceless. Decisions were not hidden in the bowels of an anonymous committee – which always makes people angry! There were five high-profile leaders at Antioch (Acts 13:1) but they worked as a team.

They came from several different countries, if you can believe it. What a way to start the leadership of a new church! Barnabas came from Cyprus, Manaean from government circles in Jerusalem, Saul from Tarsus, Lucius (probably of Arab stock) from Cyrene in North Africa, and Simeon the Swarthy was a black man, doubtless a Nilotic from East Africa. Such was the leadership. Varied indeed, but united in ministry. They embodied the quality of togetherness that they were seeking to inculcate in the congregation at large. It is incumbent on the leadership of every church to be like that. Avoiding the dominance of the one man and the facelessness of the committee, Christian leadership should be both varied and united. It should model a plurality of leadership striving to outdo one another in love and service. Nobody in that leadership ministers without being ministered to.

Before we leave these Antiochenes, note two things more. The diversity is greater than we might ever have imagined. For one thing, that leadership was international and cross-cultural. For another, it seems to have had somewhat different theological emphases. We are told that 'prophets and teachers' led the church at Antioch. Now these are very uncomfortable bedfellows. Prophets are unpredictable. Teachers are not. Prophets want freedom in worship. Teachers usually want stability. Prophets think teachers are dull and uninspired. Teachers think prophets are a little wild, a little unrooted in Scripture, and they never prepare anything! All the possibilities for discord were there. But apparently it did not happen. They worked together wonderfully well. And their variety enriched their leadership.

Having worked for the past twenty years in two teams which comprised both men and women, ordained and lay, British and other, charismatic and non-charismatic, and having enjoyed the unity (sometimes strained almost to breaking point) and the mutual encouragement and correction of such groups, I would never want to go back to one-man leadership. Shared leadership, for all its difficulties, is the way ahead. And the mutual stimulus within that leadership facilitates evangelism. I think they realised this at Antioch.

But many ministers either do not realise it, or are not prepared for what it takes. If you are the pastor of a small country church, for example, and you have to do everything yourself, from arranging the heating to typing the bulletin – all this talk of shared leadership may seem like cloud-cuckooland. But it need not be so. What is to prevent you from inviting two of the senior Christians in the congregation to have breakfast and prayer with you, say, on a Saturday morning each week? You could talk over problems, share some responsibilities, and come up with suggestions for the decision-making body of the church on possible ways ahead in the life of the parish. If there is a will to share leadership, there is always a way.

It was open to dynamic worship

The description of the Antiochene church at worship is instructive, though it is brief. From Acts 11:27–8 and 13:2–3 seven things are apparent about the worship.

First, it was ordered. The Greek word used here for 'worship' is *leitourgein*, from which our word 'liturgy' is derived. This did not of course indicate in the earliest period of the church an agreed form of words; rather, a recognisable pattern of events. There was both a dignity and an order about their worship.

Second, it was serious. They did not just worship: they worshipped 'to the Lord'. He was the centre of their vision. Their minds and hearts were fixed on him. And this of course drew the congregation together. The seriousness of their purpose is shown by their fasting. It was a regular part of their Christian lives. We find it here in the account of their worship, and subsequently, before they sent Paul and Barnabas off on their mission.

Third, it was prayerful. It was in prayer that the vision for the mission emerged; it was on prayer that they concentrated before that mission began. It was clearly a matter of top priority in their lives.

Fourth, it was expectant. They must have been on tiptoe to see what God would reveal to them during their time of worship. They expected to meet him, to hear from him. And it was into this expectancy, this waiting on God, doubtless in silence, that his Spirit was able to communicate what God wanted from them – the first missionary journey.

Fifth, it was open to intervention. It was not all tied down and buttoned up to the precise minute before the service began. I don't suppose any of them knew – or cared overmuch – when it would end. They were just losing themselves in wonder, love and praise. And God made his message plain to them. How that intervention came, we do not know. It may have been by everyone getting a similar conviction; much more likely it was through a prophecy which was uttered by one of the congregation and which commended itself as right to everyone else. What we do know is that here was a church that expected God to show them things, and that welcomed his intervention.

6. charismatic

Sixth, it was charismatic. It was open to spiritual gifts like visions or prophecy or whatever sparked the missionary journey. It was open to prophetic characters like Agabus arising and making predictions in their midst. Not that we should think of the Antiochenes as crazy charismatics swinging from the chandeliers. There was, as we have seen, a very ordered and solemn side to their worship. But they welcomed the Holy Spirit's presence and gifts. They wanted him, not themselves, to be in charge.

7. Obedient

Seventh, they were obedient to what God had shown. That is, alas, an unusual streak in a church. We hear some teaching and promptly forget it, or do nothing about it. They heard, were convinced, and immediately set about facilitating the journey that had been laid upon them. They fasted again, prayed again, laid hands on their two dear fellow leaders, and sent them on their way.

I believe we need to take on board those seven factors from the Antiochene church. Our worship really is the shop window, indeed the barometer, of our spirituality.

Most modern churches, apart from those on the more charismatic fringe, don't need to be told that worship is ordered. They know it very well. It is often tight shut, so tight that nobody could take part in it if it had not been prearranged, let alone the Holy Spirit. But our churches are on the whole very weak in the area of prayer and fasting. Yet it is here that spiritual battles are won. I know of no church that is growing deep which does not have a deep prayer life. Are there prayer meetings in your church? Do you have prayer breakfasts, silent retreats, half nights of prayer? Do you expect answers to prayer? Do you sometimes allow the congregation to split into groups during the prayer time just to pray to God? Do you welcome people standing up to pray in their own words? Is prayer a way of life? If it is, it will not be long before God's blessing begins to show. Last night I found myself at a two-hour time of prayer and praise in a very new congregation, only a few months old. We have a very long way to go, but already we are seeing answers to prayer, already people are coming to faith, already we are being knit together in love and partnership. I find prayer hard work. To my shame, I would rather do than pray. But I know that without the praying the doing is of no avail. I do not believe that any church can be effective in evangelism until and unless it gives itself to prayer.

True prayer has two faces. One is expectancy. We need to be a congregation of people who expect God to act. It is this faith that he delights to answer. The other is resolution. That is where fasting comes in. Isaiah 58 is perhaps the most marvellous passage in Scripture about fasting: it will repay study. Maybe they studied it at Antioch. Anyhow, they knew it was an important part of the spiritual armoury.

The charismatic dimension is important, too. It is sad that the charismatic movement has led to some division, as well as to much blessing. It is true to affirm, with the Bishop of Pontefract, that 'all Christians are meant to be charismatic; however, not all Christians are meant to be part of the charismatic movement'. But to live in the expectancy that God may reveal himself in some unexpected way during the worship, to welcome genuine manifestations of spiritual gifts, and to be prepared for mistakes to be made and picked up in love – all this is important. It shows the openness of the congregation. It exhibits a flexibility that will make it very attractive to those who come in. Such a church may well have a singing group as well as a formal choir – or instead of it. It may have neither, and rely on congregational worship entirely. It may use an orchestra instead of a piano or organ – or it may use unaccompanied singing all the time. It may from time to time use drama or sacred dance in the worship. It may have congregational meetings where people are invited to discuss how the church is doing in one area of its life or another. The actual contents are not so important. What is important is the flexibility under God which makes it possible for him to show himself and to mould the worship as only he can.

It was open to outreach

There are three particular aspects of outreach which meet us in the short record we have of the church in Antioch. No doubt there were many more. But here are the three.

First, the church was founded by conversational evangelism.

Visitors chatted about the Lord Jesus, and gradually people began to find him for themselves.

(2)

Second, the church was strongly associated with overseas missionary work. Indeed, it was born there. Antioch became the centre for outreach with the gospel, a centre where Christians criss-crossed from all parts of the Empire.

(3)

Third, little teams went away from Antioch for a short or a longer time with the gospel.

Each of these methods will be looked at more fully in subsequent chapters. But here let me simply say that almost any church can get involved in all three ways if only the will is there. Person-to-person evangelism is not beyond any of us. I know of a conversion through the witness of a handicapped teenager who could only speak ten words a minute! There must be almost no church that cannot encourage and give some help in personal evangelism like this. It is just the same with missionary involvement. It is not possible for every church to have a member away overseas. But it is possible for every church to have a living link with such a person: a number of churches can combine to support one missionary in prayer and giving. Many societies have 'mission links' to facilitate just this.

It is no less possible for even very small churches to take little teams away on some enterprise for God. Suppose the minister is asked to preach somewhere. Why should he not take three people with him from his congregation, pray and plan with them beforehand, and give them a share in the speaking or leading? They will return with joy, having learned a lot, and with a deep enthusiasm to do more. The report-back to the church next weekend will bring others forward, asking why they were not invited! They can come another time. Meanwhile the idea of a shared ministry grows in the hearts of the congregation. And when evangelism takes place locally, it fits in naturally with this atmosphere which has been created.

It was centred on Jesus

The disciples, we read, were called 'Christians' for the first time in Antioch (Acts 11:26). It was a nickname. They got it because they clearly loved Jesus. They talked about Jesus. They reminded people of Jesus. They became progressively more like Jesus. There was a genuine transformation going on inside them. And it showed.

If we are to be a church which, like the rose with which this chapter began, has a fragrance that draws people in, then the link between Jesus and all the members of the congregation needs to be constantly deepening. Those in leadership have a particular responsibility here. They must teach that nothing less than Christlikeness will satisfy the God and Father of our Lord Jesus Christ. They must model Christlikeness, showing in their own lives something of what it might look like. That will mean passing their habits and attitudes under the spotlight of his scrutiny.

They must encourage this Christlikeness in the congregation, with quiet but steady insistence on prayer and Bible study, fellowship and communion. Ignorance of Jesus and disobedience to Jesus are two of the great enemies of Christlikeness.

Finally, leaders must exhibit Christlikeness in their decision-making. The Lordship of Jesus needs to extend to every aspect of church life. He is well able to guide a committee to a unanimous decision if all the members are really looking to him for guidance. I know that from many years of personal experience. That is why lots of growing churches make it a rule not to take any new step in the church's life unless and until they get unanimity among the decision-makers. It is a very practical way of keeping open to Jesus.

Of course the Antioch situation need not necessarily be normative. But it is full of instructive insight for us twentieth-century Christians. The gospel has been around a long time. We have got very set in our ways – and they are not always God's ways. But if a church is to move out in evangelism, it really has to flow with love. It has to have worship that is flexible and warm, nourishing and varied. There must be an expectancy that people will meet the living God, and appropriate structures will need to be created for that to happen, including a proper emphasis on Scripture, silence, praise and openness to ministry being offered by others than those at the front. Prayer needs to become a way of life in the church. And Jesus needs to be kept at No. 1. If these conditions are more or less in place (and they never will be perfectly realised), then that is a church which can expect God to add to its numbers regularly. It is a church God can use.

FURTHER READING

On Church Renewal

Robert Banks, *Paul's Idea of Community* (Paternoster Press)
Peter Cotterell, *Church Alive!* (Inter-Varsity Press)
Michael Green, *Evangelism Now and Then* (Inter-Varsity Press)
Michael Green, *Freed to Serve* (Hodder & Stoughton)
Graham Kendrick, *Worship* (Marshalls)
Donald B. Kraybill, *The Upside Down Kingdom* (Marshalls)
Pat Lynch, *Awakening the Giant – Evangelism and the Catholic Church*
    (Darton, Longman & Todd)
Michael Marshall, *Renewal in Worship* (Marshall, Morgan & Scott)
James Nikkel, *Antioch Blueprints* (Mennonite Brethren Press)
Howard Snyder, *Liberating the Church* (Marshalls)
Andrew Walker, *Restoring the Kingdom* (Hodder & Stoughton)

On Lay Leadership

Philip King, *Leadership Explosion* (Hodder & Stoughton)
Howard Snyder, *Liberating the Church* (Marshall, Morgan & Scott)
Paul Stevens, *Liberating the Laity* (Inter-Varsity Press)
Frank Tillapaugh, *Unleashing the Church* (Regal Books)

On Openness to the Holy Spirit

Bill Burnett (ed.), *By My Spirit* (Hodder & Stoughton)
Michael Green, *I Believe in the Holy Spirit* (Hodder & Stoughton)
Richard Lovelace, *Dynamics of the Spiritual Life* (Paternoster Press)
John Marshall, *So Send I You* (MARC Europe)
J. I. Packer, *Keep in Step With the Spirit* (Inter-Varsity Press)
David Pytches, *Come, Holy Spirit* (Hodder & Stoughton)

On Drama

Patricia Beall, *The Folk Arts in God's Family* (Hodder & Stoughton)
Paul Burbridge and Murray Watts, *Lightning Sketches* (Hodder &
    Stoughton)
Paul Burbridge and Murray Watts, *Red Letter Days* (Hodder &
    Stoughton)

Paul Burbridge and Murray Watts, *Time to Act* (Hodder & Stoughton)
The Lamb's Players, *Developing a Drama Group* (World Wide Publications)
The Lamb's Players, *15 Surefire Scripts* (World Wide Publications)
J. Gattis Smith, *Drama Through the Church Year* (Meriwether)
Steve and Jane Stickley, *Footnotes* (Hodder & Stoughton)
Steve and Jane Stickley and Jim Belben, *Using the Bible in Drama* (Bible Society)

On Movement

Madeleine Berry, *Know How to Use Dance in Worship* (Scripture Union)
Gordon and Ronni Lamont, *Move Yourselves* (Bible Society)
R. Gagne, T. Kane, R. VerEecke, *Introducing Dance in Christian Worship* (Pastoral Press)
Geoffrey and Judith Stevenson, *Steps of Faith* (Kingsway)

On Home Groups

E. Griffin, *Getting Together* (Inter-Varsity Press)
C. K. Hadaway, S. A. Wright and F. M. DuBose, *Home Cell Groups and House Churches* (Broadmore)
David Prior, *Bedrock* (Hodder & Stoughton)
David Prior, *The Church in the Home* (Marshalls)

On Music

G. Kendrick, *Worship* (Kingsway Publications)
A. Maries, *One Heart, One Voice* (Hodder & Stoughton)
R. Sheldon (ed.), *In Spirit and in Truth* (Hodder & Stoughton)
J. Stein, *Singing a New Song* (Handsel Press)

Good music books include:
Church Family Worship (Hodder & Stoughton)
Hymns for Today's Church (Hodder & Stoughton)
Let's Praise (Marshall Pickering)
Mission Praise 1 and 2 (Marshall Pickering)
Songs and Hymns of Fellowship (Kingsway Publications)

PART TWO

THE SECULAR CHALLENGE

5

Getting to Grips with the Secular Mind

It is one thing to have a church where love flows, where all members are expected to engage in some sort of ministry, and where people are anxious to share the good news of Jesus Christ with their friends. It is quite another to get inside the minds of these same friends, and to move them in the direction of Christian commitment. The Christian gospel seems, at least at first sight, to be very alien to the way most Western people think these days, and you will need to win your way not only into their hearts but into their minds. This is partly achieved by persistent prayer, partly by friendship, partly by allowing the sheer joy of Christian living to be seen in you. But sooner or later you will need to get to grips with the secular mindsets all around you, and to face up hard-headedly to some of the major stumbling-blocks to faith which many of our contemporaries have.

So I shall devote the next four chapters to this matter. We will only be touching on some of the most common problems which people have before becoming Christians, and will be suggesting ways in which the thoughtful evangelist may approach them. The number of issues handled could have been greatly increased: I have chosen four which I find most commonly raised. They are the existence of God, the person and uniqueness of Jesus, the incredibility of miracle, and the problem of suffering. But before trying to tackle them, in chapters 6 and 7, I offer this chapter as a direction-finder for those who seriously want to help intelligent non-Christians.

If we do not have any great confidence in defending our convictions, and if we are unable to give convincing reasons for holding them, we shall never be able effectively to challenge others with the central question which Christianity poses, 'What shall I do with Jesus?' We are going to need some understanding of Christian apologetics. The intellectual assault on the unbelieving mind is an important element in the evangelistic assault on the unsurrendered will. We cannot hope to reach thoughtful people who are not Christians unless we cultivate some skills in Christian apologetics.

There is nothing 'apologetic' or defensive about Christian apologetics. The word derives from the Greek word *apologoumai*, which means to give a reasoned account of your beliefs. It is the sort of thing you find Stephen doing in Jerusalem (Acts 7), Paul doing in Athens (Acts 17), and Peter advocating in his first letter (1 Pet. 3:15). There he calls on his readers to reverence Christ as Lord in their hearts, and always to be ready to give an answer to anyone who asks them the reason for the hope that they cherish – but to do so not in an argumentative spirit, but modestly and gently. Throughout, they must keep their conscience clear, so that even when abuse is hurled at them for their views, their adversaries may be astonished at the quality of their Christian lives. Such is the attitude in which Christian apologetics should be conducted.

There are, however, a number of questions which arise as soon as the subject is raised in Christian circles.

THE PROPRIETY OF CHRISTIAN APOLOGETICS

Is apologetics a proper Christian pursuit?

The hesitation about the propriety of apologetics arises from two dogmatic convictions. The first is that the human mind is irreparably fallen, and the second is that preaching is the uniquely appointed means of reaching people with the gospel. Let us look at these in turn.

It is perfectly true that the mind is fallen, and that 'the unspiritual man does not receive the gifts of the Spirit of God, for they are folly to him . . . because they are spiritually discerned' (1 Cor. 2:14). The human mind shares in all the consequences of the fall. It is very far gone from its pristine state. There are traces of corruption throughout every aspect of our mental process, just as there are in every side of our character. In that sense it is true to say that we are totally corrupt. There is no part of us that is free from the entail and the taint of sin.

But it is not true to say that every part of us is as corrupt as it could possibly be. That goes well beyond the teaching of the Bible. If that were the case we would not be able to judge between true and false, right and wrong. The mind has fallen, but we must not forget that it is also God-given and very necessary. People will not accept something which their mind tells them is rubbish, nor should they. The proper function of the mind, as far as God is concerned, is to come to grips with his revelation and then in faith to respond affirmatively to it. Our mind matters. It is one of God's highest gifts to mankind, and any attempt to devalue it into a position of no importance is both insulting to the God who gave it, and ultimately also self-defeating. For if the mind is unimportant, truth cannot matter much.

It is equally true that preaching is a God-given means of bringing people to faith. That is why Jesus engaged in it so assiduously. That is why the apostles valued it so much. 'Since, in the wisdom of God, the world did not know God through wisdom,' wrote Paul, 'it pleased God through the folly of what we preach to save those who believe' (1 Cor. 1:21). And it stands to reason: if God offers us salvation as a free gift, then we need to hear about that wonderful offer. Proclamation is obviously essential. If we were able to earn that recognition from God, preaching would be correspondingly less significant. But since we cannot, the good news of what God in his generosity offers to do for us must be passed on. So preaching is important.

When Paul calls the gospel 'folly', he is not claiming that it lacks intellectual content or rigor: merely that it seems foolish at first sight to Jew and Gentile alike. Preaching in New Testament times had a strong intellectual content. You only have to look at the words used in Acts to describe this activity to realise as much. One word means 'proclaim good news', another 'argue strenuously', another 'ransack the Old Testament for texts'. Obviously, the apostles took pains to get inside the mental attitudes of those they spoke to, so that there would be no unnecessary stumbling-blocks to the message. They adapted themselves to the philosophical, social and historical background of those to whom they spoke, and this required great apologetic skill if they were to remain faithful to the gospel message, and yet convey it in terms that made sense to their hearers.

I have tried to give some examples of this kind of presentation of the gospel in chapters 3–5 of my *Evangelism in the Early Church*. It engaged the best minds of the day. And if we, in our day and generation, are to reach through the mists of scepticism and confusion, misunderstanding and prejudice which keep people blind to the gospel, we too shall need to examine as carefully as we can where people stand, to show them the inadequacy of the position they espouse without Christ, and to demonstrate not that the gospel can be deduced by reason alone (how could such unmerited grace be postulated by reason?), but that it does not run counter to reason, and that there are no intellectual barriers which are sufficiently serious to stop us from responding to it. That is the task of Christian apologetics.

Is apologetics biblical?

Did not Jesus simply proclaim the Kingdom, rather than seek to argue for its truth? Does Scripture not assume God's existence rather than tease it out in argument? If we get too far into argument, shall we not distance ourselves both from faith and from the New Testament?

Of course, there is a danger of that. But frankly, not much. I do not sense that today's church suffers from an overdose of competent apologetics. We have a long way to go before our arguments for the faith become so all-absorbing that faith itself is squeezed out! The reverse is much nearer the truth. But as a matter of fact we do find apologetics being used in Scripture. We find it in the stringent assaults on idolatry presented by Isaiah and Jeremiah. We find it in the controversies between Jesus and the Jews in the middle chapters of John's Gospel, particularly chapters 7–9. John Stott has shown this clearly, both in *Your Mind Matters* and in *Christ the Controversialist*. We find it in Paul's approach to the Athenians in Acts 17 and to the Romans in Romans 1–3. An equally potent apologetic confronts us in Ephesians 1–3 and parts of the Corinthian epistles. This is no 'simple gospel' stuff. It is passionately, brilliantly argued, with a sharp understanding of where the other people are coming from, and a determination both to destroy what is false in their position and to build up all that is good. All reputable apologetics has both a destructive and a constructive role.

In some Christian circles today people follow Karl Barth in a deep suspicion of and antipathy to natural theology. Barth was a giant, and at the most profound level he met theological liberalism with Scripture, and reliance on works with utter dependence on the sheer grace of God. (The emphases on grace and on Scripture were an important part of the Lutheran and Calvinist strands in his spiritual inheritance.) But Barth's rejection of natural theology was disastrous. You cannot get to God by nature alone, yet nature bears constant testimony to its Creator. That is the thrust of Romans 1:20, 'Ever since the creation of the world [God's] invisible nature, namely, his eternal power and deity, has been clearly perceived in the things that have been made.' And nowhere is the book of God's revelation in nature and the book of his revelation in Scripture brought more emphatically together than in Psalm 19. The first half of the psalm speaks of the created order, with its mute testimony to its Creator. The second half goes on to speak of the 'law' of the Lord, his 'precepts', his 'testimony' his 'ordinances' – which bring joy to the heart and illumination to the eyes, for they reveal the living God to mortal men and women. The God of nature is the God of grace. Hold the two together, and you make sense both of this world and of redemption. Split them, and you are in big intellectual trouble.

That trouble is constantly apparent in Christian circles. You hear people talking about saving souls (never a biblical concept) instead of spreading the Kingdom. You find people regarding spiritual work as more important than secular employment: 'vocation' is generally applied primarily to missionary work or the ministry, rather than to any and every job where the Christian can serve his Lord. And this dangerous split between the secular and the sacred, between creation and redemption, allows you to argue about the niceties of the millennium instead of getting involved in housing refugees, feeding the starving, or creating hostels for AIDS patients. You will tell me that these latter things are not part of the gospel? They most certainly are. We find Jesus both healing and caring for the needy, and at the same time preaching the Kingdom. His acts and his words went hand in hand. Of course, when Christ returns the care of lepers will become irrelevant. But until then it is not irrelevant at all. It is what Jesus would be doing if he were here today. For he refused to separate the spiritual into a special small compartment that is isolated from the rest of life.

And in a profound way, the truth of the incarnation is the supreme answer to those who tell you that apologetics is not biblical. For the incarnation shows that God has climbed into our world, into our shoes, into our thought forms, in order to win us to himself. And if we profess to be his disciples, we must do the same for those who do not know him.

Is apologetics important?

Apologetics is very important, and for this reason. The Christian faith claims to be true, true for all men everywhere, true irrespective of age or outlook. And yet, for a variety of reasons, it has become very implausible to Western man. Apologetics represents an attempt to come to grips with that sense of implausibility and to turn it round. The gospel and its values used to dominate the legal system, business practice, legislative presuppositions, employer-employee relationships and, to a degree, international relations. Now all that has gone. Christianity is hardly discernible in public life. There are, to be sure, some traces of it in some Western countries: Britain, for example, retains the Queen as the titular head of the Church of England; prayers are said in Parliament, and the church retains some influence in establishment circles in the country. But the gospel and the values of Jesus Christ are not applied to economic policies, the framing of legislation, international relations or any of the affairs of state. For all practical purposes your values and your religious beliefs are part of a private world that must not impinge on public life but which you are welcome to cultivate as you wish in your spare time. Religion has become a private interest for a minority, like gardening. Values have followed, and the ethical scandals in so many Western countries in recent years, involving insider trading, nepotism, lies, bribery and breach of promise, have been enormously on the increase.

Lesslie Newbigin has given a careful and very important analysis of this process of privatisation in his book *Foolishness to the Greeks*. There is a disastrous separation between facts and values in our culture. Facts are deemed objective, values subjective. Facts belong to the public arena of life, values to the private. 'There are no "right" or "wrong" styles of life. Perhaps the only thing that is really wrong is condemning as wrong the lifestyle of another. In the field of personal values, pluralism reigns.' Such is Newbigin's sharp analysis of current attitudes. They have been moving in this direction ever since the Enlightenment. His book makes a powerful case for reinstating values in the 'public' arena of life: there *is* an objective difference between right and wrong. God is either Lord of the whole of life or he is not Lord at all. We must not settle for a peaceful life in a corner, maintaining a 'spiritual gospel' which does not touch real life. We must make strong claims for Christ in the public ground: and that will require the most cogent apologetics of which we are capable. Newbigin has a great passage in which he makes this point, in the course of an attack on the privatisation of values:

> That the development of the individual person is governed by the program encoded in the DNA molecule is a fact every educated person is expected to know and accept. It will be part of the curriculum in the public school system. That every human being is made to glorify God and enjoy him for ever is an opinion held by some people but not part of public truth. Yet if it is true, it is at least as important as anything else in the preparation for their journey through life.

Apologetics is indeed important. It is a powerful tool, and if properly used it can show sceptics that their way of looking at life, God and the world is wrong and potentially disastrous. We believers certainly cannot afford to be marginalised into those who 'like that sort of thing because they were brought up to be religious'. The crown rights of the Redeemer extend to every aspect of life, and apologetics is one of the means of driving that home.

Is apologetics neglected?

Apologetics is in such low esteem that in many leading universities and seminaries nobody of any stature can be found to teach it. Lord Russell, the philosopher, observed: 'Today, there are only a few old-fashioned Catholics and a few fundamentalists left arguing with reason for faith. Most Christians blunt the force of logic and appeal to the heart, not the head.' This is a strange decline, for apologetics has had a long and honoured place in our history. Many of the great theologians have been stalwart apologists. Not so today. There is a virtual abandonment of Christian apologetics, in the face of a conservative tendency to proclamation rather than persuasion, and a liberal tendency to dialogue rather than defence. Neither position has any time for apologetics.

The conservative tendency is to be found in evangelical, char-ismatic, neo-orthodox and some Catholic circles. As the sceptical philosopher Antony Flew said of Barth's writings, 'In Barth, belief cannot argue with unbelief: it can only preach at it.' And that, of course, carries an inborn tendency to devalue apologetics. There is no point in trying to persuade: our task is to proclaim the truth!

In liberal circles the same conclusion follows from very different premises. There has been a determined movement away from apologetics. Liberals no longer pursue a *rational* sense of certainty: the traditional proofs for the existence of God are not deemed to be watertight. They abandon a *historical* search for certainty: scepticism reigns over the New Testament record in general and the person of Jesus in particular. And they have moved away from any *cultural* sense of certainty: colonialism in mission has been given a rough ride, and a new tolerant attitude towards other faiths, as equally valid approaches to God, has come in.

It is manifest, therefore, that in such a climate there is no use for apologetics. Dialogue, not defence of the faith, is the order of the day. And let us be clear what is meant by dialogue. It does not embody any attempt to change the other person's view (or to be changed yourself) at the end of the discussion: it is, rather, a sort of radical openness, and a search for clearer mutual understanding.

Neither the conservative nor the liberal versions of Christianity have any use for apologetics these days.

And maybe that is why the name of C. S. Lewis stands out so clearly in this regard. Quite apart from the fact that he was the most brilliant, silver-tongued (albeit non-professional) theologian and apologist, there simply is not anyone else in the English-speaking world of this century who begins to aspire to similar stature. Apologists are indeed an endangered species.

And such apologetics as is practised has a strictly limited appeal. It is directed to the open and the interested, and has little persuasive power for those who are neither open nor interested. It is directed to those in need, and plays upon that need. Interestingly enough, such apologetic material as was available met a remarkable need in the 1960s, because that decade of exciting experimentation ended in despair, and our apologetic literature spoke to that despair. But the succeeding decades have been marked not so much by existential despair as by sheer apathy or selfishness; and our apologetics has been notably less successful in cracking apathy and selfishness. It is not that people have powerful arguments against the truth of Christianity these days. They simply do not want to know.

Moreover, our apologetic strategies and techniques, such as they are, are not merely directed to the open and the interested, do not merely touch those who have a sense of need, but they speak only to those who share our world-view. There is no point in laboriously arguing the truth of the resurrection to an existentialist. He will simply say 'Fine. You may well be right. But so what?'

There is no point in trying to induce a sense of sin in an atheist. He may well be aware of things he would prefer to have done otherwise, but the whole concept of guilt is bound up with that of a living, holy, personal God who will one day call us to account. With the decline of belief in God it is not at all surprising that the sense of guilt should have become one of the less common expressions of human need.

Indeed, if we were being strictly self-critical about the efficacy of our apologetic literature, we would have to admit that it suffers from two failings. Most of our apologetics is directed to those who are literate, middle-class, rational thinkers. But the majority of our countrymen do not read books at all; they are not middle-class; and they are not used to abstract thinking. They are immediate, visual people, non-sequential thinkers. They do not lack intelligence. They are often very shrewd. But the way in which we Christians argue our case leaves them cold. The Christian presses pour out more and more books for a reading public that is, if anything, shrinking: such books have very little impact on our society in a television age which relies less and less on the written word.

And so to the last, rather sombre, point. Most of our apologetic material is directed towards the Christian public. It may well be intended for those who are not yet Christians – but it never reaches them. It is published by Christian presses for sale in Christian bookshops or in university and college Christian Unions which are often not at all good at moving out of the Christian ghetto into the rough and tumble of secular university life – let alone taking Christian literature to them.

Yes, in the light of all these considerations, it is hard to deny that apologetics is in low water in Western Christianity, just as the church itself is.

Why this decline?

The reasons for this decline in apologetics are not hard to identify.

First, we have uncritically accepted the assumptions of the Enlightenment. For two hundred years and more an erroneous metaphysic, claiming support from Newtonian physics, has beguiled us into giving all our explanations in terms of cause and effect, while neglecting the concept of purpose. 'Reality' is restricted to the natural world which we can see and measure: and the scientist is the priest who can unlock its secrets. Science, and the technology which springs from it, has been so successful, particularly in this century, that we have tended to buy into the myth that it is the only way of looking at the world, and that anything which does not get caught in its net does not exist. A moment's reflection will show how foolish that is: romance, reliability, friendship, honour, beauty – those personal qualities which make life worth living – are quite incapable of being dredged up in a scientist's net. Scientific knowledge is not the only form of knowledge, and we should never have allowed ourselves to be forced into assuming that it is.

Second, we have demonstrated our inability to come to terms with pluralism. We live in a world where there is a multiplicity of cultural 'languages'. And like the monoglot English or American, when people do not understand, we speak slower and shout louder. We don't manage to get inside their frame of reference. And in this respect, as in so many others, we show how far short we fall of the versatility and imagination of the early church. They were more like the Swiss than the English, getting inside the language and thought forms of those they sought to bring to faith. They became 'all things to all men, so that [they] might by all means save some' (1 Cor. 9:22). A marvellous description, that. It shows the immense flexibility of those early missionaries on the one hand; and it shows their single-minded aim on the other, to win men and women to Christ. But we lack their flexibility, and our 'monoglot' approach so often fails, for obvious reasons. And then we give up. Failure undermines confidence.

Third, we have abandoned our biblical moorings. No longer is the Bible seen in many Christian circles to derive in some way from God and to bring his absolutes into our world of the relative; supremely to tell us of his invasion of our rebel globe with rescue for the lost. No, it is just one more great religious book: it gives some people's views about God! Yet having abandoned the Bible, we have no place to stand.

Apologetics is not always seen as a reasoned commendation of biblical faith. But that is what it is. It would be a great mistake to see it as abstract intellectual argumentation – a different world from biblical proclamation. No! As we have seen, apologetics is rooted in both Old and New Testaments. The proclamation of the gospel can never happen in a vacuum. It must occur in the midst of some cultural milieu. Very well, what happens when that proclamation is rejected? In the New Testament they argued, they persuaded. And that is where apologetics comes in. It is at its most

potent when the gospel is controverted. It is a ministry of clearing
the ground, so as to remove barriers to understanding and response. Apologetics seeks to open up the door for faith. It is
directed towards not only the head but the heart of unbelief. For
unbelief is what blinds people from seeing who God really is. And
apologetics seeks, if not to remove that blindness (only God can do
that), at least to render it inexcusable and untenable.

Apologetics is the intellectual, moral and spiritual prosecution
of unbelief. It seeks to break down road-blocks on the way to faith.
And that is necessary. You need, all too often, a negative, destructive job to be done on unbelief first, making the person profoundly
dissatisfied with its consequences, before you can lay the positive
foundation of the good news. Only when your friend sees he is
naked will he want to be clothed in Christ. Apologetics at its best
lovingly but firmly strips him naked, and shows that the clothes in
which he once boasted are nothing but insubstantial rags.

AN APPROACH TO CHRISTIAN APOLOGETICS

If we are even to begin to make any headway, we must know where
people are living (intellectually speaking) in this modern world.
We must then adopt a rather different approach from that which
has been practised in recent history. I want therefore to take five
typical faces of modern secular man, and follow that overview with
five faces of Christian apologetics, concluding the chapter with five
suggestions which may be of help.

Five faces of secular man

Monism
Many people will never have heard of monism, though it is
everywhere about them. It is the philosophical position underlying
both Hinduism and Buddhism. It is sweeping many parts of
America and Canada in the shape of the New Age movement. It is
exciting and liberating for many people. It is part of the reaction
against materialism.

We are manifestly not just collections of chemicals, and materialism is neither intellectually convincing nor personally satisfying.

It is greatly to the credit of the New Age movement, with its celebrated devotees like Shirley MacLaine, that they have led an emphatic rejection of materialist philosophy and brought celebration, personhood and spirituality back into the centre of the stage. Many people are puzzled by the illogicality of the New Age movement, embracing as it does so many contradictions. But that simply shows its heritage. It is part of Eastern monism, the view that everything in the world is basically a unity: good and bad, the divine and the human, truth and falsehood. There is something very attractive about this longing for unity in the universal One, in this world of ours which is so fractured and divided. There is something very appealing in the idea that there is a truth which transcends logic and nullifies the law of non-contradiction. There is something very unitive in the idea that we are all going the same way, and all belong together no matter what we do or what we believe. To have a spirituality without corresponding ethical claims has a charm all its own. And these are some of the reasons for the amazing growth of this movement which derives from the East, and which ultimately denies the reality of the personality. The destiny of the human race is not to have an I-Thou relation with a personal God, but to be sucked back into the impersonal One which embraces everything. My personality will eventually be wiped out. I shall be united with the undifferentiated sea of being.

How are we to approach a world-view like that? First, we should rejoice in its recognition of spiritual values after decades of barren materialism. Second, we should make friends with members of the New Age movement, go to their bookshops and foodshops, and get to know them. This is not difficult. They are essentially open people. One of my friends goes to such meetings regularly, and has been asked to read pieces from the Bible each week on the topic chosen for the evening. These readings make a lot of impact. There is an openness, and we need to take advantage of it. But basically it seems to me that a movement like the New Age movement is a judgement on the Western church for its rationalism and deadness. We are so weak on the transcendent: they are not. We are so feeble and dull in worship: they are not. I believe we will get nowhere with such people by argument. They are devotees of experience. And we have to show that in Christianity there is an experience just as dynamic but far more credible and reasonable.

So I would want to take such a person with me regularly to really deep, exciting Christian worship, preferably with a strong charismatic dimension, so that my friend could sense and feel as well as understand and listen to the reality of the living God. And then I would want to spend time with such a person, talking about the infinite personal God who does not want to obliterate his ego but to redeem it, cleanse and transform it, and draw him into an eternal I-Thou relationship with himself. I would hope to be able to show him that he is right in postulating a God that is infinite. But he is wrong in supposing that the infinite cannot be personal. The fact that we are persons suggests that the source of our being is no less than personal, however much that source may transcend personhood. Part of the marvel of the good news is that this personal, infinite God longs to have us in lasting relationship with him and with all others who know and love him. That makes wonderful sense of our hunger for immortality, our sense of personhood and our longing for unity, fulfilment and celebration. We will not find these things intelligibly combined in the New Age movement. We will find them in the living God who speaks, who saves and who sends.

Humanism

Humanism is almost a religion in many parts of the Western world. It is, to all intents and purposes, the worship of mankind by man. A humanist does not believe in God, heaven or hell. This life is all there is. All mankind's problems were caused by man and can be solved by man. It is a world-view that belongs to the able, the liberated, the sophisticated, the wealthy. It has never made great progress among the mass of mankind. It has never been noted for missionary zeal in promoting faith in mankind in the dark places of the world. Though many individual humanists are extremely generous, ethical and kind, I have not found many of their number staffing hospitals in remote areas of Africa and Latin America. It is a faith that belongs more to the senior common rooms of universities than to the *haciendas* of Guatemala.

Nevertheless, it is a viewpoint that many in the West will meet. It is well presented, attractively argued, and often supported by blameless lives. How are we to approach such people?

First, by the recognition that there is a basic split among humanists. Some are very optimistic: often they will turn out to be scientists. And why not? Science has produced the most amazing results for human advancement in this century. Is it not reasonable to suppose that it might solve *all* our problems? 'No!' say the pessimistic humanists, many of them belonging to the artistic community. It is, after all, the most technologically and scientifically advanced nations which have, in our own lifetime, perpetrated the greatest and most horrific wars in all history; and these same advanced scientific people have resorted to torture and genocide in a way unparalleled during the entire history of the world. How can we believe that the world is getting better? It lives on the edge of total destruction – ecologically, through population explosion and through the wanton waste of non-renewable resources, if not by nuclear war. Two world wars, and the atrocities of death-camps like Auschwitz (committed by one of the most intelligent and sensitive nations in Europe), have for many people knocked the bottom out of optimistic humanism.

But can we not present the gospel as the true humanism? It was proclaimed as such in the late Middle Ages by men like Colet, More, and Erasmus. Christianity has every claim to the noble name of humanism. For in the last analysis you can only give honour to man if you believe him to be inherently valuable. And atheistic humanism cannot do that. On that view, man is simply an aggregate of chemicals held in suspension for a few short years. He came from plankton and is headed for extinction. There is nothing inherently valuable about him. Why then treat him with exaggerated respect? There is, and there can be, no reason. Some, holding those atheistic presuppositions, will liquidate their fellow men if it is convenient, and if it does not bring down excessive judgement on their heads. Other humanists will show their fellow men tremendous kindness and care. You can take your choice. But if men and women are in fact made in the image of God, then you *cannot* take your choice. You value them as beings of infinite personal value. There is a sense, therefore, in which Christianity is the true humanism. It has a genuine reason for respecting human beings: they are God's creatures. Christians rightly claim to be neither optimistic nor pessimistic humanists. They are the realists. They know there is much evil in mankind, and their gospel takes care of that. They also know that there is much good in man – after all, God made him. So they are never surprised by evil, even in highly educated fellow humans; nor are they prone to dismiss or devalue the genuine goodness to which optimistic humanists rightly draw attention.

And from that perspective the Christian apologist can proclaim the good news in a way which makes a lot of sense to thoughtful humanists. We can concur with their high ideals about mankind, but show why those ideals hold water. We can explain both the nobility and the sinfulness of man, taking account of the full story of Genesis 1–3. We can draw attention to the contingency of this world in which that incredibly valuable object, humanity, resides. Creation came from God's free choice, and shows how important choice is in a world which is not, whatever some scientists say, exhaustively defined in terms of cause and effect. Choice is a Godlike faculty for which we are going to be held responsible by the giver. We could point to the complementarity of man and woman in the divine plan: God's image is represented in neither of them on their own, but in their interdependence (Gen. 1:27). Men and women were made for fellowship with each other and with God – hence the loneliness on our own, and the sense of alienation deep within us, if we do not get reconciled with God. Humanists greatly value love, and we can trace that love back to its source in God. His love is of the highest order and continues despite human disobedience. Above all, we need to present the humanist with the person of Jesus Christ as he is brought before us in the Gospels. He is the proper man. He is man as he should be. There has never been a man like him, nor ever will be. What was there in his genes, or in his environment, that produced such a life? How are we to explain it? Is not the most reasonable explanation the one which the New Testament writers give us? That there is a God who made and cares passionately for this world. That he came to seek us personally in and through Jesus of Nazareth. That the life and teaching of Jesus bring before us all of God that we are capable of taking in. That he is not merely the ideal man, but the best insight we could possibly have into the nature of the God we cannot see.

'To look only at God breeds pride,' said Pascal. 'To look only at ourselves breeds despair. But when we find Jesus Christ, we find our true equilibrium, for there we find not only God but ourselves as well.'

Narcissism

Narcissism is the preoccupation with self. It is a pervasive characteristic of Western culture. It lies at the heart of the 'Me' generation. The ancient myth of Narcissus is instructive. Ovid has a sensitive version of it in Book Three of the *Metamorphoses*. He was a handsome youth, in love with the nymph Echo. He was promised a long life so long as he never gazed at an image of himself. One day he passed a pool, looked at his image reflected in it, and fell in love with himself. He was infatuated with himself, and could no longer respond to Echo. He tried to embrace his reflection, fell into the water, and died. Ate, the Greek goddess of retribution, slew him. And he was condemned to eternally frustrating infatuation with his own image in the river of the underworld, the Styx.

It is not difficult to see much modern society reflected in that ancient myth, particularly in North America. The narcissistic temperament is often blind to the needs of others, always seeking an audience to impress, manipulative in relationships, and utterly self-absorbed. There is an underlying insecurity in such people which drives them towards those who radiate charisma. A brilliant book on this subject has been written by Christopher Lasch, and it was a nationwide bestseller in the United States. It is called *The Culture of Narcissism*, and subtitled 'American life in an age of diminishing expectations'. Have we, asks the blurb, fallen in love with ourselves? Have we bargained away our future for self-gratification now? Have we lost intimacy, joy, insight and shared loved in a frantic search for ourselves? The answer to all three questions can only be Yes. That is an embarrassingly accurate analysis of a major strand in contemporary culture. And it is very ugly, and in the long run very dangerous. For we are not just individuals, islands among a sea of people. We belong to one another. We are part of the mainland. Without strong relationships we head for destruction. And the narcissist is not only selfish to a degree; he is hostile to authority, and fearful of dependence. He is preoccupied with his private world of self-reliance, self-love, self-fulfilment. Narcissism is profoundly unrealistic, too, because it affects to turn a blind eye to the failures in its character: for these it blames other people. Anna Russell's doggerel captures the attitude well:

> At three I had a feeling of ambivalence towards my brothers,
> And so it follows naturally I poisoned all my lovers.
> But now I'm happy. I have learned the lesson this has taught:
> That everything I do that's wrong is someone else's fault.

In Christian circles, narcissism is widespread. You see it in the insecure people gravitating towards those with charisma. You see it in the hostility towards the leadership that is commonly displayed. You see it in the manipulation and the self-centredness of many in our churches. You see it in the poverty of relationships in church. You see it above all in the religious hedonism which says, 'Well, I like going to church on Sunday mornings. It makes me feel good.' Narcissism exists for the promotion of the self. It hates authentic Christianity, which calls for the renunciation of the self.

Of course, the irony of it all is that narcissism starts with optimism and ends in loneliness, emptiness and despair. Christianity, on the other hand, begins with self-abandonment and ends in joy.

If we are to get through to such people, our message must major on the cross. There we see that 'I' crossed out. We see the principle of dying-to-live, or new birth coming through life sacrificially laid down. It is at the cross that we are initiated into the profound paradox that you only find your life when you are prepared to lose it. You can only take it up when you have laid it down. That is the challenge of the cross to the narcissist.

But he needs to hear the comfort of the cross before he can bear to respond to its challenge. And the comfort is very wonderful. For it tells this poor man or woman (so weak in relationships, so starved of love that self-love is the only recourse) that they really matter. God loves them, unconditionally. They are beautiful in his eyes, the most important eyes in the world. Hostile they may have been to him, the source of all authority. But that has not alienated him. God commends his love towards them in that while they were still rebels Christ died for them. They need no longer hang on to loving themselves because of the deep-seated fear that nobody else will. God loves them so much that he went to the cross for them. It is at the cross that I see I really am somebody, independent of whatever I may or may not subsequently achieve. It is at the cross that I recognise how extravagantly God loves me. And it is at the cross that I find a company of rebels such as I, captivated by the same generosity, ennobled by the same divine self-giving. And so I can begin to escape from the bondage of my autonomy into the fellowship of a group of mutually dependent people for the first time in my life.

Agnosticism
It is difficult to know how prevalent agnosticism really is. It is constantly professed: how deep-seated it is, is another matter. Many young people throw out the idea of God by their teens. The utilitarianism of Mill, the romanticism of Rousseau, the dialectical materialism of Marx, the evolutionary hypotheses of Darwin and the psychological studies of Freud and Jung all combine to make agnosticism a very attractive position. It is intellectually respectable. It is highly liberating (no God, no after-life, no moral absolutes, no conscience). And it is very fashionable.

The word 'agnostic' seems to have been coined by the scientist Thomas Huxley in the nineteenth century. It is fascinating that the world should have managed to do without it until then! Huxley meant by it not simply that he did not know about the existence of God, but that it was impossible to know. There is insufficient evidence. The traditional proofs for God's existence had been regarded as less than watertight since the work of Immanuel Kant. And agnosticism seemed to be rendered impregnable by the recognition that man in his insignificance and limitations could never reach a position where he pontificated with assurance about the source of the whole universe – in which he is so insignificant a speck. As Herbert Spencer, another of the early agnostics, was fond of maintaining, 'The Infinite cannot be known by the finite.' So agnosticism is secure.

But is it? What Huxley and Spencer failed to recognise is that their position overlooks a possibility of staggering significance. It is true that man cannot hope to take in the divine. The creature cannot begin fully to understand the Creator – if there is one. The Old Testament prophets were clear on that! But there is no reason why God, if he exists, should not condescend to show himself to his creatures. Agnosticism is not logically secure at all. What if God has shown his hand? Surely the Christian thinker and preacher can make a very good case for God having done just that. He has shown his hand in fashioning the world, in the emergence of mankind, in values, in conscience, in the religious instinct, and in history. But supremely he has shown his hand in the coming, the character, the dying and the rising again of Jesus of Nazareth. That is God's conclusive word to man, spoken in his clearest tones. 'No one has ever seen God': that is the agnostic's very proper complaint. But 'the only Son . . . has made him known' (John 1:18): that other half of the verse is the proper Christian response.

The way in which we can help an agnostic is not by extended arguments at a philosophical level. These may be necessary, but they will not be conclusive. He can only be convinced by personally facing up to the one place in the history of the world where the claim is responsibly made that the Beyond has come into our midst, and that agnosticism is, therefore, not an option we can allow ourselves. We cannot plead ignorance of the ideal if the ideal has come. And come he did. We date our era by him.

I have found that time and again the genuine agnostic is brought to faith by exposure to the person of Jesus as recorded in the Gospels. The sheer power and beauty of that figure shine out of the page and have their own appeal. The patent honesty of the record in the Gospels breaks through prejudice. And the evidence for the resurrection underlines and validates the claim made for the ultimacy of Jesus Christ. The person and the resurrection of Jesus Christ is the way in to the agnostic . . . if he is really genuine about his agnosticism.

But many agnostics are not genuine. It is a convenient cloak for their personal selfishness. It is not that they can't believe in God. They don't dare to, because it would make too much of a challenge to the way they live.

I shall never forget these words from another of the celebrated Huxley family. It was Aldous, in his book *Ends and Means*, where he writes:

> I had motives for not wanting the world to have a meaning; conse-quently assumed that it had none, and was able without any difficulty to find satisfying reasons for this assumption. The philosopher who finds no meaning in the world is not concerned exclusively with a problem in pure metaphysics. He is also concerned to prove that there is no valid reason why he personally should not do as he wants to do, or why his friends should not seize political power and govern in the way they find most advantageous to themselves . . . For myself, the philosophy of meaninglessness was essentially an instrument of liberation, sexual and political.

It is not often that you find an agnostic writing as honestly as that about the dishonest reasons for his agnosticism. However, there are many who do not have Huxley's courage, but who share Huxley's dissimulation about the real cause of their agnosticism. And such dishonest agnosticism needs to be challenged, not only at an intellectual level but at a moral one. Something of the holiness of God needs to come into the conversation, and a warning that he is not to be trifled with. The counterpart of freedom is accountabil-ity, and we shall all be accountable – the agnostic included – to the one who gave us freedom. I have found numbers of agnostics who have come to faith in Christ when the root of their unwillingness to face God was exposed and dealt with. Once that unwillingness is removed, the living God will not neglect the honest cry of the agnostic heart, 'Is anyone there?' He will make himself known. I have myself met dozens of people who, out of the darkness of agnosticism, have prayed like that, and are joyful confident Christ-ians today. The God who invented communication has spoken to their hearts.

Pragmatism
This is a deeply rooted attitude in both British and North American

hearts. They are not so much interested in theory. They are very interested in practice. Their question is not so much 'Is it true?' but 'Does it work?' Now no Christian will be satisfied with that attitude, but it is an indicator of where to start. We need to scratch people where they itch. If their question is 'How can I cope with my loneliness?' or 'Where can I get the strength to handle this over-whelming temptation?', it is no good giving them ten reasons why they should believe in Jesus Christ. We should begin where they are, and in due course help them to see that the Christian faith only 'works' because it is true. Truth has priority over relevance. But in today's climate relevance shouts louder than truth. We need to heed the cry, and take the person through the perceived need to the living God who is truth.

This is essentially the age of the pragmatist. Our society abounds in self-help schemes, self-fulfilment programmes, positivism. And many who have dismissed truth as relative are all too willing to ask of any new idea (yes, especially a new idea), 'Is it any good? Does it work?'

Judged by this standard, how does Christianity fare? There is no doubt how the churches at large fare. People who used to attend have voted in massive numbers with their feet. They have not been persuaded that church-going makes any difference. For them it has not 'worked'. That is why they are so quick to call church-goers 'hypocrites'. There is a deep suspicion that these same church-goers are acting a part that is not real. It does not change anything in the ordinary life of work and home. There may be God on Sunday, but not God on Monday.

The only way of meeting this very proper challenge is by the Holy Spirit. We must explain to our friend that if the Christian story is true, God's Holy Spirit is alive and available to enter and transform the lives of those who open up to him. To be sure, not all church-goers have done that: and therein lies some of the dis-crepancy of which the sceptical pragmatist is all too well aware, and which leads him to call churchmen hypocrites. But we cannot get off the hook that lightly. We need to explain that in those who genuinely have opened up to the Spirit of God there is still a fatal flaw in their character and life. God is at work on it. He has not finished with us yet. But in all of us there is a gap (diminishing all the time, hopefully) between what we profess and what we do. We have not yet attained the purpose for which Christ laid hold of us: we are, however, on the way.

Having said that, we need to be able to point to the difference that

Christ makes, in the most practical of terms. This is where our personal testimony to his life-transforming power comes in. There is something very attractive and powerful about testimony, if it is not overdone. For it takes things out of the realm of theory and earths them in personal experience. That really helps the open-minded seeker. The thought that this gospel might actually change the way people live is very arresting. I remember once leading someone to Christ in my house through introducing him to a couple who were in the adjoining room. The husband had just come out of prison for a horrible offence, and the wife, who had believed in him all through those difficult years of imprisonment, even though she was all too well aware of his guilt, was thrilled to have him back. Prison had brought them both to Christ. She came through the ministry of the church. He came to the Lord in his own cell. And to see them together again after his sentence had been served was something very special. It simply amazed the enquirer I had with me when I took him next door and introduced him to the couple. He could see the difference that Christ had made to this ex-offender. It shone out through his face. And that same joy and radiance was there in the wife too. It is not surprising that the enquirer came to Christ himself that very afternoon. He was a pragmatist. He saw that Christianity made a real difference. It was not just talk. It worked. And in committing himself to the Jesus of whom he knew all too little, he began the adventure of finding that transforming power at work in his own life.

Any Christian looking back can think of some such occasions. The amazement in hospital when somebody had been healed through prayer and the laying on of hands. The astonishment in the face of a social worker on seeing a person set free from demonic powers in front of their very eyes. And of course the most obvious things, like the impact of Mother Teresa on the poor and needy in Calcutta (and indeed through her sisters in the wider world nowadays), are eloquent. It is changed lives, radiant with the power of the Holy Spirit, that validate the gospel for the pragmatist. We should be glad that it is so. If there is no cash value in our supposed good news, then it is not much good. I, for one, am happy to accept the testing question, 'What difference does it make?'

In our evangelistic apologetic with the pragmatist, then, we need to draw his attention to marked examples in our own experience and that of others, preferably those he knows personally or has heard of, where the Spirit of God has made a noticeable difference. And then we need to urge him gently but firmly to 'taste and see that the Lord is good'. He can never know until he trusts. It is like walking on to a frozen lake: will it bear my weight? You can never know for sure until you entrust yourself. The knowing springs from the trusting. And the shrewd pragmatist will see the point of that. I have often known such a person pray a prayer of commitment something like this: 'Lord, I'm not sure that you are there, or that you can do anything about this situation. But if you are, and if you can, please do. I'm open for anything you have to show me.' Very tentative. Very pragmatic. But it is the way that many have trod into the Kingdom of God.

Those are five faces of modern unbelief. They are very common. In each case I have given some slight indication of how I think it might be appropriate to try to help such a person. They all demand different treatment. There are of course many other common mindsets we shall find. There will be the Muslims. There will be the communists or fellow-travellers. There will be the relativists, who are convinced (until they have to face up to Jesus Christ) that there are no norms in truth or character. There are the materialists (though genuinely consistent materialists are hard to find). There are the atheists. And above all there are the sheer hedonists, out for pleasure, but not at all sure what happiness consists in. I could have given some suggestions for coping with each of these stances, but I have given a sample, and it will suffice to make the point that we are in a very diverse world and we need to be very flexible in the way we approach people. Examine the flexibility of Jesus' personal dealings with the very wide variety of people who came his way. He never seems to have adopted the same approach twice. Maybe we need to emulate him in this respect as in all others, and not to box people into ideological pigeon-holes.

Five faces of the Christian apologist

Identification
Of course we can never fully identify with any other person or their experience. But we can get very close to them and empathise with them. The trouble with so much apologetics is that, like politics, it is adversarial. Two embattled positions are facing one another. And victory becomes more important (for self-esteem) than truth. That is a disastrous state of affairs. We need to maximise the common ground we have with the person we are talking to. We need to read the sort of material they read, be aware of the

television programmes they watch, experience some of the pressures to which they are subject. Jesus Christ did not shout advice or commands at us from far away in the glory. He did not send a newscast on television which, arguably, would have been a very efficient way of reaching a lot of people simultaneously with an important announcement. No, he came as one of us. He lived our life, ate our food, shared our limitations and died our death. That gave him every right to be heard. He knew our condition from the inside.

But Christians are often unlike their Master in this respect. We are very bad at identifying. We feel out of place in the working-men's club or the pub. We do not fit. So we retire into a ghetto. And the Christian world in the West is very like a ghetto, self-sustaining, self-related, and well able to use up the energy of its members. We must renounce the mentality of the ghetto. We must be able to mix easily, naturally and knowledgeably with those we hope to help to the faith. It is very hard for a white missionary to do that in, say, Angola. His best contribution will probably be made by pouring himself into the Angolan church leadership, who in turn will be much better than he could ever be at reaching their compatriots with the good news in a way that will minimise its 'strangeness'. It is very hard for the clergyman living in a large rectory in a city centre to identify with the working people all round him who are crowded into small and unattractive homes. To point out that he has very little money and that the house hangs round his neck like an albatross makes no difference whatsoever. He is perceived to be different: 'not one of us'. And it makes it very difficult for the working man to identify with the church when its leadership is so obviously very different from him.

I recall hearing a Christian man from a rough working-class situation explain how, before he could get round to coming to church (even when he wanted to), he had to have a number of stiff drinks to nerve him for the venture! On the first Sunday he only got as far as the nearest pub. The next Sunday he stopped off at another pub, a bit nearer the church. But by the third Sunday he had worked up sufficient courage to enter the building and tentatively feel out what these church people were all about. We must do all in our power to minimise these stumbling-blocks. We need to accommodate ourselves to where the other person is, not expect him to fit into our system. And that is something the churches are notably bad at doing.

Investigation

We must find out where the person we are trying to help lives. It may be no bad thing to find out where he lives geographically: that is the first step on the way to getting to know him. But it is much more vital to get to know where he lives emotionally and philosophically. What makes him tick? What are his attitudes about life? How far are they conditioned by his experience?

It is unfortunately the case that many of us are far more prone to talk than to listen. If we have any zest at all to share the gospel with others, then we tend towards getting on with it enthusiastically. A moment's thought shows how short-sighted that is. We have two ears and only one mouth, and we should bear that proportion in mind as we come to Christian apologetics. It is only the very inept doctor who prescribes before he has diagnosed. That happened to me once, and it was very damaging. I collapsed after preaching in Durban one night, and two doctors came to my aid. The one filled me up with antibiotics. The other asked if he could come and see me the next day. It was the latter whose careful investigation showed that I had got meningitis, and the overzealous action of the first doctor queered the pitch badly. It was impossible to tell for several days whether I had contracted the viral or the bacterial type of the disease. I guess we are often guilty of similar ineptitude in spiritual doctoring, because we rush in with our prescription before fully assessing where the patient is and what he is suffering from.

Provocation

Asking provocative insightful questions is today a lost art in many Christian circles. But it is a very necessary one. For sheer self-protection in a world that is often hostile and always fast-moving, we very quickly develop some armour, a world-view which we assume is correct so long as it is serviceable. When some of our assumptions are questioned, and above all when they are shown to be misplaced, then we are made to think hard. We are vulnerable at that point. And this is what the apologist needs to bear in mind. He should constantly be seeking to make his agnostic friend ask himself, 'I wonder if I am right about that?' Or, 'Has Bill got a point here that I need to consider?' We are trying to plant doubts in the unbeliever's mind. Doubts about whether his world-view is sound. To do this we certainly have to identify with him, or we shall only succeed in alienating him. And we certainly have to investigate where he lives, so to speak, or we shall not know the way in. But having got in, we want to arouse these existential questions in his mind, and show him through his own painful realisation that the house he has built for himself as a shelter from the approach of God is leaky and uninhabitable: he had better evacuate!

One of the most skilful people at doing this whom I have ever met was Dr Francis Schaeffer. He was one of the most accomplished apologists of the middle of the twentieth century, and he asked far more questions than he gave answers. He was always trying to discover what the basic presuppositions were of the person he was talking to; and he would then drive that person relentlessly towards the logical conclusions of his presuppositions. In this way he showed the person how wrong those assumptions were; and then, and not until then, the man was willing to sit down and examine an alternative, the alternative of the gospel of Christ. One day Schaeffer was arguing with a young man who protested the relativity of morals and the virtues of free sex. Schaeffer's immediate riposte was to ask for the name and telephone number of his live-in girlfriend. The young man was furious, until he realised that he was hoist with his own petard, and that the virtues of free sex paled somewhat when they were turned against himself and someone he loved.

On another occasion Schaeffer was arguing with a dedicated anarchist who advocated violence, if appropriate. So Schaeffer and friends held him down, and Schaeffer produced a cudgel and asked him why, on the anarchist's presuppositions, he should not beat his brains to pulp. Of course, the man had no answer. He abandoned his anarchism because he had felt in his own person its utter inadequacy. He was more human than his theory, and accordingly he left his theory and was drawn to that most human of saviours, Jesus Christ. But Schaeffer would never have got through to him had he not taken pains to find out where the man lived, intellectually, and then to provoke that most agonising of questions in his mind: 'Am I wrong, utterly wrong, after all this time? Have I totally missed the way?' Schaeffer was always very careful to do this work of provoking devastating questions very gently. It was, he reminded his hearers, the modern way of preaching hell. For it showed the person in question that he was lost. He was living in a condemned house, and it would not keep out the hail. Apologetics, Schaeffer used to say, was like taking off the roof of such a house and letting the hail of truth in. And it ought always to be done with tears of compassion. He did it that way, and his influence survives him.

Translation

We must never forget that, owing to the decline of Christian influence in state, churches, homes and schools, a great many people are reared without having any understanding of a Christian world-view. We literally live in different worlds. And therefore it is important that we become adept at translation. Translating our language, for one thing. People do not have the vaguest idea of what we mean by so fundamental a thing as 'the cross'. 'The resurrection' means little to them. 'Jesus' is simply a swear-word, or at best denotes a great teacher of long ago. Words like 'redeemed' and 'saved' are total gibberish in a society many of whose members do not know what happened on the first Christmas day or Easter day. Such is the captivity of the churches that they do not realise that other people simply have no idea of the message that they count dear. It is hard to overestimate the ignorance of the gospel in modern Western society. And it is getting worse. Soon that understanding will vanish almost entirely, and then we shall be better off. We will, in a sense, be able to start again, and the gospel may regain that freshness which broke like a thunder clap upon first-century society.

But in the meantime we must be careful to demythologise our language. We need to go for two-syllable words rather than three-syllable, unless we are speaking to a person who knows a lot about the faith. We need to make sure that the words we use are readily understood. The early Christians were superb at this, giving synonyms for difficult concepts like 'the Kingdom of God', a very Jewish idea not readily assimilated by their Greek hearers. So they translated it into 'eternal life', which was something the ancient pagan world was deeply hankering for. The translation was accurate and brilliant. It touched men of a different culture, and they were hungry to take it in.

It is not only the words we use. It is the ideas we employ. Those too need radical overhaul. Most people today have no use for the abstract nouns that Christians love to use, 'salvation', 'justification', and the like. It means little or nothing to them. They go for verbs and concrete nouns; and so must we. They think pictorially; and so must we. We need to be constantly illustrating what we have to say by concepts within their mental furniture. If you are talking to a carpenter, major on the fact that Jesus was a carpenter, and tell him the good news in language that a carpenter can take in. If you are dealing with an existentialist, then you need to take over and use his categories of encounter, relationship, ultimate experience and so forth, filling them with Christian meaning. You find St Paul doing this time and again in his epistles, taking over the language of his opponents or of secular people round about, and filling it with Christian meaning. We simply have to be translators if we are to gain a hearing these days. And that means we have to be thoroughly modern men and women. Our play-reading, our current affairs, our political and social awareness, our appreciation of the world about us – all this will be invaluable in our task of sharing the gospel with those who do not know it. In a word, we need to dress *our* message in *their* clothes.

Relation

We must relate the many-splendoured Christ to the felt need of the person we are working with. That is sure not to be his only need, maybe not his most important need. But it is the need he is aware of at present. Often these days it is meaninglessness and emptiness. Often it is a lack of purpose in life. Often it is the sense of not being loved and valued for himself, only for what he can do or produce. Fear is far more common than we imagine.

What we have to do is to seek to apply that aspect of our Lord Jesus Christ which is the most immediately relevant to the person we are talking to. It will often be helpful to ask ourselves if there is a New Testament situation which is similar to that which we have discerned our friend to be in. If so, the Scripture will speak to him with a powerful immediacy. But in any case we need to look to that quality of Christ which particularly fits his need, and then go with that. Thus a humanist may not be impressed by arguments for the existence of God. However, he may well be impressed and brought to faith by exposure to Christians in dynamic worship, and by exposure to a modern translation of one of the Gospels, given him for thoughtful, unhurried reading. A scientist will be much more likely to be persuaded by the evidence for the resurrection, and by taking a Gospel and reading it to see if it persuades him that Jesus was more than a man. The lonely person is likely to be struck by the friendship of Jesus for someone who was lonely, like Nicodemus, Zacchaeus, or the woman of Samaria. A person gripped with demonic forces will be profoundly moved by the story of the Gadarene demoniac, and I have known that passage lead such persons to Christ.

In short, we come back to flexibility. We must be flexible. Evangelism and apologetics are not a matter of intellectual fire-power and technique. They owe a lot more to friendly relationships and laughter, honesty and directness. It is a mistake to imagine that people are hardened against the gospel. They are simply bored by the way it is so often presented – too rigid, too rationalistic, too uncomprehending of other world-views, too small-minded. Let us make sure that no such accusation can be levelled at us. It is imperative that we do not forget either the rational or the non-rational factors in this whole area of evangelism and apologetics. Most people are not moved by reason alone, perhaps not even by reason primarily. There are powerful non-theological factors which we ignore at our peril. The gospel of Christ is more often caught than taught, and this is especially the case in our own day, when non-linear thinking has robbed logic of a lot of its effectiveness. People are more touched by atmosphere, love, welcome, surprise – rather than argument. That does not mean we should neglect intellectual argument. It does mean that we should not rely on it alone. We shall often have to travel through the intellect in order to discover the reasons of the heart, and it is by these that the person is usually dominated. There are many who do not want the gospel to be true, and who rationalise their rejection accordingly.

As I was typing this chapter, a doctor rang up. With a child's innocence and fearless directness, her seven year old son had been telling the good news of Jesus to his atheist grandmother. There then followed a long and difficult conversation between the Christian mother and the grandmother! But what fascinated me was the fact that this senior woman, who was a charming, well-educated humanist teaching biology at doctoral level in a university, came out with the most arrant nonsense about Christianity. 'The gospels were all written hundreds of years after the event'; 'We can't possibly know if there is a God or not'; 'All religions are the same', and so forth. Those were the rationalisations of the head. The reasons of the heart also began to emerge, and they were the real things. There had been desperate hurt in childhood: her mother had died of cancer, untreated, because she was a Christian Scientist and was taught to believe that pain was unreal. That left great bitterness, and Christianity was branded with the stigma of Christian Science. If we neglect the reasons of the heart, we shall never help people into the Kingdom of God. We shall certainly never succeed in introducing them to the Kingdom by argument alone.

Five suggestions for Christian apologists

I would like to conclude this chapter with five suggestions which I offer only because I have found them helpful in my own ministry.

Begin where the person you are talking to is
We should have the flexibility to use any road as a path to Christ. It does not matter where we start from. If we are thought to be producing some carefully prepared sermonette, it will be disastrous. Evangelism is all about personal relationships, personal sharing in an honest and real way. We must learn to begin where the person we are talking to wants us to begin – where the conversation springs up from. We must also learn to take our opportunities when they occur. If we defer them to a more convenient time, that time will not happen! And let the other person make the running. We do not have to lead the conversation. He is seeking direction for his life. Let him take the lead. Follow him sensitively and helpfully, as occasion offers. And do not mind in the least if the conversation wanders off spiritual things. It may well wander on again, later in the evening. Or maybe it can be picked up another time. What will prove injurious for the relationship is pressure by you if the other person does not want it. But if you find it possible to be as natural when talking about God as when talking about cricket or baseball you will find that your friend will be only too willing to return to a question which is, after all, one of the most fundamental in the world.

Do not be embarrassed to open your Bible
'Oh no!', I hear you say, 'That will put them off for ever.' No it won't. It all depends on how you do it. If you speak from authority, the authority of the Bible, then you can expect a strong reaction in this very anti-authoritarian age. But if you use it in a non-authoritarian manner (although believing passionately in its authority yourself), you are likely to be well received. 'Well now, that's a very interesting question you asked. Let's look at what Jesus had to say about that, and see if it helps at all.' Or maybe your friend has been making some astonishing assertions about what he or she thinks Christianity is about, and you can say, 'Well, it's fascinating to swap ideas about this, but why don't we get back to the original source-book, the New Testament?' And invariably the person will agree. It is the academically respectable thing to do in all such endeavour: get back to the original source. That is all you

purport to be doing. But actually you are doing something more. You know, though your friend does not, that the Word of God is sharp and powerful. You know that its words can get through to places your words can never reach. So you want your friend to be exposed to the laser beams of Scripture. It will have its effect.

This open-ended and non-dogmatic approach is very necessary. You are showing that the Scriptures are perfectly intelligible if you come to them with an open mind, assuming only that the witnesses who wrote them were honest men. You are showing that Christians do not make up their faith as they go along, but that they go back to the original teaching of Jesus. And you open their eyes to what that teaching, that life, death and resurrection mean. What is more, you begin to give your friend the suspicion that there is something unusual about this book, something that has a ring of truth about it. He feels, 'Here is a book which understands me, which speaks to my condition.' When he recognises that, he is well on the way to conversion.

Major on Jesus and the resurrection

That is what Paul did with the Athenians – so much so that the untutored among them thought that he was wanting to add two new deities to their pantheon, Jesus and Anastasis (Acts 17:18). I doubt whether anyone could misunderstand the contemporary apologist so! But I have found that these are indeed the two cardinal issues to concentrate on. The person of Jesus is the most attractive in the world. And the evidence for his being more than just a man is overwhelming. I love to face enquirers with that. And then I encourage them to go away and read the five accounts of the resurrection, to see how it reverberates from practically every page in Acts, and then to attempt to argue against it. It is a formidable case to dismantle, and they do not succeed. God has not given us the answer to all manner of questions we would love to have unravelled. But he has seen fit to provide very strong supporting evidence for the divinity of Jesus Christ and the fact of his resurrection from the dead. And those two points are almost enough. I well remember a young postgraduate medic in one of the Agnostics Anonymous classes I used to run at Oxford University. He had come to the group in order to examine ethical issues with which he knew he would inevitably be caught up in his profession. He had gone away the week before to study the evidence for the resurrection. And as he came into the room the following week he said to his friends: 'Well, I'm not a Christian yet, but I am persuaded that Jesus Christ rose from the dead.' Before he left that evening, he asked me when the next 'Discovery Group' (for new Christians) started. 'I think I can't hold out any longer,' he said. 'I'm committed.' He is an active Christian doctor today.

Distinguish between smokescreens and real problems
We shall have more to say about this in a subsequent chapter, but the distinction is crucial, though not always easy to make. If a person has a real problem, and you solve that problem to his satisfaction, he should have no further reason for holding out against the truth of Christ. But if what purports to be a real reason for hesitation is in fact a smokescreen behind which your friend is wanting to hide, then a very different situation emerges. Solve that problem, and he will assuredly produce another. Solve that, and another will grow. It will become apparent that his heart is unwilling to move, and so his head is devising rationalisations in support.

The difficulty is that sometimes what is a real problem for one person can be a smokescreen for another.

Take the problem of pain and suffering, for instance. That is the classic thing that Christians cannot fully answer: it is therefore an excellent stick to hit the Christians with. So your friend comes up with the question 'Why is there so much evil as suffering in the world?', and sits back to watch you squirm and you attempt a lengthy answer. For him it is probably only a smokescreen. And if you answer it he will move on to 'What happens to those who have never heard the gospel?' or 'What if there is life on Mars?' But another person might produce precisely the same issue, the problem of suffering; and for him it is not an academic problem to keep you at arm's length. It is a desperately painful hurt – because only last year his mother died in great pain of cancer. If you treat an excuse as if it were a real reason, you will find that another one grows in its place and at the end of the day nothing is accomplished. You need to puncture an excuse, not feed it. But on the other hand, if you treat as an excuse what really is a genuine problem, and seek to puncture it, you will hurt the questioner very deeply. Remember too that some people have a whole constellation of genuine problems, and to regard their second, third or fourth problem as mere evasion would be quite disastrous. All of which goes to show how sensitive we must be in dealing with questions which are raised. If possible, we need to see what lies behind the question and why they ask it. Only so can we answer it in a way that will really help that particular person. But the distinction between genuine difficulties and mere excuses is vital to grasp if we are to engage at all effectively in apologetics. We must understand the distinction, and act accordingly.

Be direct
Here again I can hear someone saying, 'But that will put people off.' That is what I was told by some Christians when I came to Canada. 'Be very oblique and laid-back, Michael. Canadians will not take directness.' I believe I have evidence sufficient to show that this advice, though well meant, was quite wrong. Canadians are very polite, but they appreciate directness just like anyone else. The religious scene is bedevilled by endless talk. It is like a breath of fresh air when someone comes and speaks about Jesus, his cross, his living presence and his claims on our lives – and then asks us what we are going to do about it. Of course we need to use tact. Of course we need to be sensitive to the wind of the Spirit, and only follow where we sense he is leading. But directness does not alienate if it is allied to love. Love someone, really love them, and you can afford to make endless mistakes, to drop barrow-loads of bricks, and you can still get away with it. The point is that you love them, and they know it. You want the best for them, and they know it. And so they do not take umbrage, as they certainly would if that vital ingredient of love were missing. The gospel of Christ concerns matters of the utmost importance, matters of life and death. We dare not beat about the bush and hedge every statement with a thousand qualifications. We need humbly but clearly to tell it like it is. In the last analysis it comes down to the question Pilate had to face: 'What shall I do with Jesus who is called the Messiah?' That is the question we must help our friends to face, with love and with directness, once we have penetrated their mindset, which may well be very different from our own.

FURTHER READING

You may find the following books a useful introduction to getting to grips with the secular mind. They are only a sample of the vast array on offer.

At a popular level

H. Blamires, *The Christian Mind* (SPCK)
D. G. Bloesch, *Faith and Its Counterfeits* (Inter-Varsity Press)
Colin Chapman, *The Case for Christianity* (Lion)
R. Gange, *Origins and Destiny* (Word)
M. Green, *World on the Run* (Inter-Varsity Press)
M. Green, *You Must Be Joking* (Hodder & Stoughton)
C. S. Lewis, *Mere Christianity* (Collins Fount)
C. S. Lewis, *The Pilgrim's Regress* (Collins Fount)
Stephen Neill, *Christian Faith Today* (Penguin Books)
F. Schaeffer, *Escape from Reason* (Inter-Varsity Press)
F. Schaeffer, *The God Who Is There* (Hodder & Stoughton)
John Stott, *Christ the Controversialist* (Inter-Varsity Press)
John Stott, *Your Mind Matters* (Inter-Varsity Press)

At a more advanced level

Peter Berger, *A Rumour of Angels* (Penguin Books)
Langmead Casserley, *Graceful Reason: The Contribution of Reason to Theology* (University Press of America)
Charles Colson, *Against the Night* (Hodder & Stoughton)
Charles Colson, *Kingdoms in Conflict* (Hodder & Stoughton)
William Dyrness, *Christian Apologetics in a World Community* (Inter-Varsity Press)
Os Guinness, *The Dust of Death* (Inter-Varsity Press)
Os Guinness, *The Gravedigger File* (Hodder & Stoughton)
Lesslie Newbigin, *Foolishness to the Greeks* (SPCK)
Lesslie Newbigin, *The Gospel in a Pluralist Society* (SPCK)
Clark H. Pinnock, *Reason Enough* (Inter-Varsity Press)
Alan Richardson, *Christian Apologetics* (SCM Press)
James Sire, *The Universe Next Door* (Inter-Varsity Press)

6
Handling Agnosticism About God and Jesus

In the previous chapter we looked at the more common secular world-views we are likely to encounter, and at possible ways of approaching them. I want now to examine some of the major intellectual problems that are most frequently put forward by thoughtful people when you seek to bring the good news of Christ to them. There are five which I constantly meet.

First, there is the ultimate question: Does God exist? If you get past that one, the person of Jesus is sure to need scrutiny. Who is this Jesus? Why do Christians regard him so highly? Third, there is the question of miracle, and supremely the miraculous resurrection of Jesus Christ from the grave on the first Easter day. That lies at the very heart of the Christian claim, and for many modern people it is frankly incredible. Fourth, there is the problem of suffering and evil in this world that purports to derive from a good and loving God. And finally there is the question of other faiths. We live in a highly pluralistic world. How can we – how dare we – make claims of ultimacy for Jesus Christ?

The question of pluralism has already been considered quite extensively in chapter 3. I propose in this chapter and the next to offer some suggestions about how we might approach the other four questions, as and when people raise them. I do so, not because I have any special competence, nor because any of the questions is susceptible of direct knock-down proof, but because there is a weight of evidence in favour of the Christian explanation which renders it highly probable, and which means that people can commit themselves to it without any surrender of intellectual integrity.

THE EXISTENCE OF GOD

We need to have a good deal of sympathy with modern people who say they cannot believe in God. God seems a very implausible hypothesis in today's society in the Western world, though we need to retain some sense of proportion when we make this observation. Not only are atheism and agnosticism statistically negligible worldwide, usually to be found in sophisticated and comfortable urban centres, but neither has ever been able to characterise any known culture throughout history. The theists therefore have no need to be on the defensive.

But they are on the defensive. The intellectual calibre of atheists like Bertrand Russell, Jean-Paul Sartre and Simone de Beauvoir combines with the psychological dismissal of God by men like Freud and Jung, and Darwin's replacement of a purposive Creator by blind evolution, to produce an atmosphere where belief in God is not easy to justify and atheism can be both intellectually and personally convenient. I combine the personal and intellectual dimensions because it is worth recalling the psalmist's comment that 'The fool says in his heart, "There is no God"' (Ps. 14:1). Generally that is not merely an intellectual conviction but a rebellious attitude which does not want God to exist. Atheists hate being told this, but it is frequently the case, just as among some theists belief in God may grow from wishful thinking.

There are other reasons which encourage atheism. High among them is the problem of so much pain and cruelty in a world which, through intercontinental travel and television, has shrunk to a global village, so that we know, as never before, the anguish of mankind. The plurality of religions has, equally, been brought forcibly before us through the same two factors of travel and TV. Where there is such diversity, perhaps all are wrong?

But maybe C. S. Lewis identified the greatest reason for the practical atheism which characterises so many moderns. It is the sheer material comfort and the lack of any compelling need (except in times of crisis) to consider the great questions of life and death, of origin and purpose for ourselves and the world. We are so caught up in the urgent and the trivial that we do not give time to the ultimate.

In the first of *The Screwtape Letters*, Screwtape reminds Wormwood, his junior associate devil, that he need not make his candidate on earth think 'that materialism is *true*. Make him think it is strong, or stark, or courageous – that it is the philosophy of the future. That's the sort of thing he cares about.' Screwtape goes on to tell of an atheist he nearly lost to 'the Enemy' when this man was working one day in the British Museum and was being dangerously carried towards God by a certain course of thought. So instead of arguing, Screwtape made the man remember he was hungry, and that anyhow this was far too important a matter to deal with at the end of the morning. So out he went into the 'real' world of the road, the midday paper and a No. 73 bus; and before long he was convinced 'that all "that sort of thing"' which he had been thinking about in the Museum could not possibly be true. Screwtape concludes: 'He knew he'd had a narrow escape and in the later years was fond of talking about "that inarticulate sense for actuality which is our ultimate safeguard against the aberrations of mere logic". He is now safe in Our Father's house.'

For these and other reasons atheism is probably on the increase. How are we to meet it as thoughtful Christians? Here are some suggestions.

Discover the reason

Why is this person an atheist? I think of one of the atheists I met who became one overnight through the death of the father whom he idolised. No amount of intellectual argument would avail. He had to be helped to allow Christ's love, mediated in this case through me, to get through to him in his hidden pain and anger.

I think of another celebrated atheist with whom I was due to debate. During the dinner beforehand, it became evident that the cause of her atheism was a series of terrible experiences in a Catholic school as a youngster.

Another was a survivor of Auschwitz. Another was brought up in a strongly anti-religious home and had imbibed his parents' attitudes uncritically. Others have been deeply influenced by Nietzsche, Feuerbach or Sartre. Others have been philosophers, impressed by what they take to be Immanuel Kant's destruction of the traditional 'proofs' for God's existence, though it is noteworthy that other philosophers of religion are far from convinced that Kant damaged the traditional proofs in any substantial way. We must be people-centred in our approach, and discover, if possible, what lies behind the atheist front. It may of course be sheer reasoning, but I have found that rarely to be the case. Whatever the cause, we need to find it out before we can hope to deal with the person appropriately.

Examine the logic

Whatever the reason for the person's atheism, he will be convinced that he has rational grounds for it. And the loving but firm application of some rigorous logic can have a very salutary effect.

Very likely your friend will say, 'You can't prove God's existence.' You need to show him gently but inexorably that there are very few things he can prove. To prove something you have to show that it is so certain that it could not be otherwise. 'Proof' is a very final form of certainty. You cannot prove that the sun will rise tomorrow. You cannot prove that your wife loves you. You cannot prove that there is a necessary link between cause and effect. You cannot prove that you are alive, still less that you are the same person you were ten years ago. The philosopher David Hume attempted to prove the link between cause and effect, and that he was the same man he had been ten years earlier; and he had to confess to failure. The fact of the matter is that firm proof is only to be found in rather rarefied areas of mathematics and philosophy where the conclusion is concealed within the premises of the argument. It follows with certainty only because it is actually entailed already.

Your friend may complain, 'Nonsense. Scientific method proves things.' Oh no, it does not. Scientific method is inductive: it begins with observed uniformities and seeks to establish the general 'law' which accounts for them. You can certainly demonstrate a very high degree of probability through the inductive procedure, but not certainty. The fact that repeated experiments lead to the same conclusion does not allow for the one contrary instance which may throw a wrench in the whole proceedings, and show that your supposed 'general law' needs to be reworked. The coelacanth was, by all empirical investigation, shown to have been extinct for millennia – until one was caught deep in the seas off Madagascar in the middle of this century. This one instance sufficed to show that the scientific conclusion 'The coelacanth is extinct, and has been for thousands of years' was wrong.

To put it in more technical terms, no inductive procedure can lead to absolute proof. That is to say, no procedure which begins with observed uniformities and works back to the supposed general law which is held to explain them, is certain. As in the case of the coelacanth, a single contrary instance can upset the whole string of observed uniformities. No, the only certain proof is deductive. That is to say, you have to show that your conclusion follows logically from some anterior truth which *is* certain. In the end that brings you back to axioms, things you cannot prove but cannot doubt without obvious absurdity. Now it may be that God's existence is axiomatic, and that is what some of the traditional 'proofs' for his existence sought to demontrate. But irrespective of their success, of which I am doubtful, it is obvious that you cannot *prove* God in the sense of showing him to be logically entailed by something more certain. For, by definition, God is the ultimate in the universe. There is manifestly nothing greater or more certain from which his existence could with certainty be deduced.

But our inability to attain absolute certainty does not reduce us to a morass of scepticism. We are in no doubt that we exist, that the sun will rise tomorrow, or that cause and effect prevail in our world. None of these things can strictly be proved, but there is excellent reason to believe in them, just as there is to believe in God. Not conclusive proof, but very good reason all the same.

Indeed, if you want to tease your friend a little, you could take him a lot deeper into this inability of ours to prove any of the more interesting things in life. In a brilliant series of lectures at Regent College, Vancouver, Dr Graeme MacLean encouraged us to take our agnostic to four different types of things that he thinks he knows, and show him that he cannot demonstrate his knowledge in a single case!

How does he know when William the Conqueror won the Battle of Hastings? He thinks he knows it because of unbroken testimony going back to 1066. But there are all sorts of alternative explanations which show that that conclusion, while highly probable, is not proven. There might have been a mistake over the dates; there might have been a conspiracy to deceive. The evidence might be faulty. And so forth. To credit the date of the Battle of Hastings we are driven to assume the reliability of testimony. But we cannot actually prove it.

How does he know what will happen when a match lights a piece of paper? He knows what happened when he lit paper in the past. But he cannot be certain that it will happen in the future without counting on another axiom, another assumption which he cannot prove – the uniformity of nature.

How does he know where he was at midday today? He is

confident about that matter: he remembers it. But memory often plays tricks with us. Such supposed knowledge is far from proven. It relies on the presupposition of the reliability of memory, which may well generally be the case but is not always so. And proof cannot depend on a 'perhaps'.

How does he know that there are other people in the room? Again, the answer looks obvious, and he is sure of it. But he cannot prove it. He is forced to rely on two assumptions which he can never demonstrate – the existence of other persons, and the reliability of sense data. Hume, for example, found he could not give any firm proof of his conviction that the materials suggested by his senses were real. And he found that he could not prove the existence of other people. Indeed, he found himself drawn towards a philosophical position which it is impossible to disprove but equally impossible to credit. It is called 'solipsism', and it maintains that the only things you can actually know are the goings on of your own mind. They may or may not be connected to the external world, if there is one: you have no way of making sure!

We make all these assumptions, but in the last analysis we cannot justify them. They form a sort of network which underlies our whole system of belief. These axiomatic assumptions, which we take for granted and which we cannot prove, are perfectly natural and are almost unavoidable. Indeed, we regard anyone who does not share them as deranged. But they are themselves ungrounded in any knock-down certainty. You have to take them on faith. As one wise man put it, 'The unjust as well as the just shall live by faith.'

You could go on and suggest to your friend that the only sufficient reason for relying on these basic presuppositions is if they spring from a reliable, personal God who is the source both of the physical universe and of our own complicated selves. Challenge him to come up with another satisfactory explanation. He won't be able to!

Another common atheistic charge is crudely expressed in the question you are sure to have met, 'Then who made God?' Put in a more sophisticated way, it maintains that believers in God are involved either in a contradiction or in an infinite regress. If we argue that every event must have a sufficient cause, and seek to derive God's existence from that, then either God must be the exception to the rule of cause and effect, being the Uncaused Cause, or else the question 'Who made God?' must drive you back for ever and ever.

But the Christian refuses to be impaled on the horns of that dilemma. We are not saying that all things must have a cause, but that all *finite* things must have a cause. That does not lead us into either contradiction or an infinite regress. It is an eminently reasonable position.

'Well,' he may say, 'all the undeserved suffering in the world proves there is no God.' It sounds powerful, but on inspection it will not hold water, and you need to show him that it will not. After all, it is theoretically possible that all suffering is deserved and that it is only through God's mercy that there is not more suffering in the world. What is more, it could be the case that suffering is our battle school before attaining the best of all possible worlds, in heaven. If that were the case, suffering would not in the least eliminate the concept of a good God. Nor is this special pleading. It is often our experience in ordinary life that the most worthwhile things only come to us through pain and hardship. Why should that not be true of life as a whole? But you could go further. If your atheist friend presses the claim that suffering and evil are *ultimately* unjustifiable (which is what he must do if he is to eliminate the existence of God by means of the existence of evil), then he is in big trouble. For if some pain or evil in this world is ultimately unjust, there must be some *ultimate* standard of justice by which to judge it. And does that not bring you right back to God?

These are just some examples of what I mean by 'examine the logic'. You cannot demonstrate God's existence by logic. Neither can you demonstrate his non-existence. But so many of the arguments turn out, when examined, to be illogical and self-defeating. I have given an example of three such arguments. The Christian apologist needs to unpack the atheistic argument with which he is faced, and to use logic not as a shoe-horn into the Kingdom of God (it won't work as that), but as a small charge of dynamite that knocks over an unsafe and dangerous building. You are out to show your friend that the sooner he evacuates such a building the better.

Outline the consequences

It is very liberating to throw out the idea of God. It leaves you free to please yourself. No threat of heaven or hell hangs over you. There is no God, like a policeman, looking over your shoulder, taking note of your actions. You are free!

But such a view certainly lands a person in deep problems. And it is the part of the Christian evangelist's task to show them to his friend. He may think that he is going to have a trouble-free existence, but such is not the case. Here are a number of problems that he will have to live with.

1. The problem of the world he lives in. If there was no Creator, how did it originate? From the Big Bang? But then where did the Big Bang (which looks dangerously compatible with purposive creation!) spring from? What lies behind that? Press him hard in this area. He will wriggle, and probably tell you that evolution supplies the answer. That is very unconvincing, not primarily because it is a theory that is unproven, full of missing links, and by no means universally accepted in the scientific community; but because you have to have a starting-point for the evolutionary process. Darwin himself at the outset of *The Origin of Species* acknowledged God as the source of the evolutionary process.

If he takes refuge in DNA or the atom, you press him as to why DNA should possess the remarkable properties it has, and why there should be any atoms rather than none. Philosophically speaking, this argument says that all contingent facts must, in the final analysis, be based on a necessary cause.

Every finite thing is caused. Behind all those contingent things, like the rain, and beings like you and me (who could so easily have been otherwise), there must be a ground of all being from which everything derives. The philosopher Nelson Pike put it baldly: 'If there is no necessary being, nothing exists.' He is saying that there cannot be a causal sequence with an infinite number of members. It has got to start somewhere. To admit that you and I are contingent beings (i.e. we might not have existed had our parents never met, or we might have been very different had our circumstances changed) drives us logically to admit that a necessary being exists, and we call him God the Creator. The philosopher Goetz put it very clearly:

> As a contingent being, I have what appears to be a conclusive reason for acknowledging the existence of a necessary and personal being. As a person God will have to be immaterial. And he will necessarily be omnipotent, for what more powerful being could there be than one who can create something out of a state of affairs where nothing exists but himself?

In a word, if there was no Creator, how can your friend give a rational explanation of the world he lives in? Having got rid of a

Creator, he must do without one. So the world must have arisen by chance. Even more amazing is the emergence of sentient, intelligent life, apparently on this planet alone. That must be due to chance as well – if there was no Creator. Impersonal matter, that is to say, given aeons of time and unlimited chance, produced personal life, did it? The world is a fluke, and the greatest of all flukes upon it is man?

He will not like that alternative. It does not seem very reasonable. It does not give a good account of the reasoning mind with which he puts the argument forward. And it does not begin to answer the question of why, in a random universe, the very opposite principle of cause and effect is everywhere apparent.

2. Your friend faces another and closely allied problem. He lives in a world which seems to be designed for mankind to inhabit. There is nowhere else in the universe like it, so far as we know. This world is remarkably fashioned to support life, and human life in particular. Modern science is recognising this as the *anthropic principle*. It means that had the circumstances of our physical world been one tiny fraction different, it would have been impossible for life to exist on this planet. John Polkinghorne is a distinguished scientist who has done a lot of work in this area. A few years ago he left the Chair of Mathematical Physics at Cambridge University to become ordained, and has since returned to teach at that university. He is an outstanding example of the compatibility of Christian faith and scientific eminence. He wrote, 'There is a very tight knit series of constraints . . . on the way our world must be in order that we are here to observe it.' (Why not read his book *The Way the World Is*?) Wherever you look in the world you see evidence of design: in the laws of physics, in the development of an embryo, in the delicate balance of an ear, in the radar of a bat, in the uniqueness of each snowflake. You have to be very hard boiled and very determined in your rejection of God to argue that all this evidence of design in the world is illusory or simply exhibits adaptation in the unsupervised evolutionary march. If you see design in a watch, in a car, in a camera, how much more in the world, in a human being, in an eye? Your agnostic friend has a problem on his hands.

3. The problem of personality. Mankind is an impressive, if marred, pointer to the God who made us in his own image. That is an intelligible and forceful argument. But if the atheist is right, and there is no God, what is man? Just a higher form of anthropoid

ape? Reducible in the last analysis to a small amount of chemicals, with no remainder?

One of our basic convictions is that there is a distinction between mind and body. I am an immaterial substance who possesses a body. That distinction between mind and body is one of our few basic intuitions, and all attempts to reduce the body to the mind (idealism) or the mind to the body (materialism) are unconvincing. The other basic distinctions we are intuitively confident of are those between finite and infinite, necessary and contingent, human and divine, particular and universal. Nothing can cross those divides. Very well then, what are we to make of human personality? All attempts to derive our intelligence, reason, joys, and loves from mere matter are totally unconvincing. Are we just a collocation of atoms? Just a bunch of grown-up genes? To say so is not only flying in the face of all the evidence; it constitutes the ultimate trashing of human dignity.

It is not without significance that Nietzsche's claim at the end of the last century that God is dead was followed with impeccable logic and great courage by Sartre, Kafka and the existentialists in general, when, during the first half of this century, they drew the painful conclusion that in that case man, too, is dead. Man is an entirely futile being, devoid of personal origin, value or destiny. When you recognise that, the only logical conclusion, if there is no God, is that it hurts . . .

4. The problem of values. We all have certain values: many of them are not just personal to us but universally prized – qualities like truth, goodness, beauty, creativity, love, communication. The obvious explanation is that they are placed in our world and in our personalities by God the Creator, and that each of them sheds light on some aspect of his nature. But once dispense with God, and how are you to explain them? It is very hard to see virtues as somehow inhering in and springing from atoms! For on the atheist view, life itself sprang from chance and matter, and has no inherent value. Creativity is inexplicable, since there is no Creator. Human beings have speech, but there is no ultimate communication in which they share: speech sprang out of a silent planet. Truth has no real meaning. Beauty is simply one manifestation of primal chaos. Goodness apparently emerged from plankton. Love must be attributed to nothing more than chemical attraction. Personality, too, sprang from impersonal matter. Challenge your friend. He can believe this if he likes, but let him not pretend that it is the most likely or rational explanation of the origin of our values. For the

very mind which enables him to make that judgement has no
independent validity. It, too, is nothing more than matter, a mass
of neurological pulp composed of infinite complexity but without a
Designer. How much more probable it is that our values spring
from a personal Creator.

5. The problem of religion. No race in history has ever existed
without belief in God. It is often, as in Islam today, the most potent
force in a society. What can account for this universal phenomenon
if not God? Religion is one of our deepest instincts. All our other
instincts have realities to which they refer: hunger, sex, and so
forth all have that which satisfies them. Is religion the only one of
all our human instincts which has nothing to which it relates? I
suppose it could be so, but that would fly in the face of all the
parallels. It would make it very hard to understand how the
religious sense survives slavery, persecution, torture and every
attempt that is made to crush it: witness the vitality of faith in
totalitarian states today like Russia and China, where the most
strenuous persecution has been carried on for decades. In a novel
called *The Sleeping Partner*, Winston Graham, the novelist,
observed:

> Science, I suppose you would say, begins with observed facts, system-
> atically classified. Right? Well, there is one fact about man that has
> distinguished him from his first appearance on earth. That is, he is a
> worshipping animal. Wherever he has existed there are the remains, in
> some form, of his worship. That is not a pious conclusion: it is an
> observed fact.

Let your friend attempt an explanation!

6. The problem of conscience. Agnostics have a real problem
with conscience. Don't we all? But believers at least know whence
it derives. It seems to them to be a powerful pointer to a holy God
who is concerned with ethical behaviour and has placed in every
human being that moral direction-finder of conscience. But what is
the agnostic to make of conscience?

Is it a subjective statement about how we feel, like: 'I have a
stomach ache'? No, that is very different from saying: 'Torturing
children for fun is wrong.' You can argue about the propriety of
torturing children. You cannot argue with me whether or not I
have a stomach ache.

If morals cannot be grounded in subjective feeling, how about
community regulations? Will that explain conscience? Manifestly
not, or we would never be able to compare one moral system with

others. It would be impossible to ask if what the community does is right – if 'right' means what the community does.

Can we ground morality, then, in sheer self-interest? That would not account for the noble acts of self-sacrifice which are done for conscience sake, like Captain Oates walking out into the snow to die. Then is conscience an instinct, perhaps? That will not do either. Often, for conscience sake, we will go against our instinctive love of security, pleasure, or even life itself.

Is it perhaps just some evolutionary development which enhances the survival of our species? But it does not necessarily do anything of the kind: think of self-sacrifice to the point of ostracism or even death. What evolutionary instinct could lead Wilberforce to labour most of his working life for the liberation of slaves? It was against his financial interests and those of his peers. It had not been done before. And it cost him dear. Yet he did it, for conscience sake. And this is the way in which all moral advance has taken place. There is an imperative in conscience with which the best moral philosophers, including atheists, agree. But they are hard put to find a ground for conscience, having done away with God. And so will your agnostic friend be.

7. The problem of mankind. What is man? Christians believe that human beings are made in the image of the Creator, and their inherent value lies in just this fact. They are marred, but not totally destroyed, by the evil in the world. They remain the objects of God's love, and he plans to spend eternity with them.

But remove God, and what you have left looks very different. Man springs from no loving personal source. As the Nobel Prizewinner Jacques Monod put it, 'Man must wake up to his total solitude, his fundamental isolation. Like a gypsy he lives on the boundary of an alien world, a world that is deaf to his music, and is as indifferent to his hopes and fears as to his sufferings and his crimes.'

Moreover, man has no inherent value. From matter he comes, and to matter he returns. 'Man has no divinely prepared nature to be fulfilled by action. What is he but a little puddle of water whose freedom is death?' So wrote Sartre, with rigorous frankness. 'Life', wrote Hemingway, 'is just a dirty trick, from nothingness to nothingness.'

And that, of course, is where it all ends. 'On humanist assumptions life leads nowhere, and every pretence that it does is a deceit.' So wrote that very honest humanist H. J. Blackman. There is no purpose for the world in general or for us in particular.

Modern man 'believes in nothing, enjoys nothing, finds purpose in nothing, and remains alive because there is nothing for which he will die'. Dorothy Sayers, who said that, never spoke a truer word.

And while he lives, modern atheist man perceives all round him, and in his own heart, an increasing collapse in ethics. 'I have done no wrong,' claimed Klaus Barbie, the 'Butcher of Lyons'. 'Is there no God?' asked Dostoevsky. 'Then everything is permitted.'

In May 1987 a whole issue of *Time* magazine was devoted to the question, 'Whatever happened to ethics?' It examined the astonishing prevalence of massive corruption in high places in government within the USA. The answer to the question is simple. Ethical collapse is a natural and frequent result of decline in faith. If you do not believe in a personal, holy source of the world and all that is in it, then nobody should be surprised if the contents of ethical behaviour disappear. They did in Nazi Germany, in Stalinist Russia, and in Maoist China. You see, the motivation for ethics has evaporated: why should I bother to seek the good if the bad pays me better? To be sure, there will always remain many noble, kind, moral atheists whose very lives are a refutation of their assumptions. But on their assumptions there is no *reason* why they should behave that way. It is up to them. If mankind has no divine Creator or eternal home, but is a totally expendable biological accident, then in the long run it does not matter how you treat him. Love him or liquidate him, as you choose. He has no inherent value.

Some atheists would contest this. They would claim that they do have a reason for ethical behaviour: the self-evidently binding character of moral obligation. But that will not do. The claims of morality are by no means self-evident. Whole countries see nothing wrong in liquidating thousands of people if they are inconvenient. As I write, the Chinese Government has just gunned down thousands of its own unarmed citizens in Beijing, in the interests of an atheistic political theory. No sense of moral obligation there! In 1989 France extravagantly celebrated the bicentenary of the Revolution where liberty, equality and fraternity, the supposed humanist qualities of a people liberated at last from God, led to the Reign of Terror in which hundreds and thousands of innocent people were slaughtered for the sadistic gratification of the mob. Danton and Robespierre, nourished on Rousseau's 'rights of man', cheerfully guillotined any who got in their way. When the supernatural ground for ethics is removed, 'social contract' theories and 'self-evident moral obligations' prove to be a very poor alternative. What happens is that ethics becomes more and more a matter of what most people want, or what I want. It is a tendency that is becoming increasingly evident in the socio-political legislation and the personal lifestyle of Western nations. Ethical behaviour has never survived the demise of belief in God by more than a generation or so. You can live on acquired moral capital for a while. And then it runs out.

It is hardly surprising that consideration of these implications of rejecting God often leads thoughtful people to despair. 'Only on the foundation of unyielding despair can the soul's habitation safely by built,' claimed Bertrand Russell, that massively erudite thinker. It may have been a particularly purple patch of prose, but he was being utterly logical. As B. F. Skinner realised, if there is no God, 'to man, as man, we can readily say "Good riddance"' – and he proceeded to develop a behaviourist philosophy which embodied that conviction.

These are some of the uncomfortable facts that the atheist needs to face up to. He has no convincing explanation for the world he lives in, for human nature, for values or for conscience. You could extend the list. For on his assumptions he has no adequate explanation, either, for Jesus Christ, for the phenomenon of conversion, or for the subsequent fruits of the Spirit.

But it might be interesting to face your friend with the writings of Peter Berger, a very open-minded and perceptive sociologist.

In his book *A Rumour of Angels*, he drew attention to a number of 'signals of transcendence' which we all acknowledge, but which it is very hard to explain if there is no God.

One is order. All societies dislike chaos. We have a natural human instinct for order, and we postulate it in the world we see around us. 'Human order in some way corresponds to an order that transcends it . . . an order man can trust himself and his destiny to,' writes Berger. 'Thus man's ordering propensity implies a transcendent order, and each ordering gesture is a signal of this transcendence.'

Another is play. It suspends, for a moment, our serious 'living towards death' as we experience again the 'deathlessness' of childhood. Play, he suggests, is a very odd thing to find in a world which has no Creator and no goal.

Hope is a third signal of transcendence. It is a universal part of human experience. It continues to the bitter end of our lives. It is like a silver thread, interwoven with our experience at every point, but coming from outside us.

A fourth strand of the transcendent in our experience is what Berger calls the argument from damnation. He thinks of situations where our humanity is so outraged by actions like the Holocaust that we think no punishment is enough. That is a very interesting phenomenon, if death is the ultimate sanction.

> There are deeds which demand not only condemnation but *damnation* in the full religious sense of the word – that is, the doer not only puts himself outside the community of men; he also separates himself in a final way from a moral order that transcends the human community, and thus invokes a retribution which is more than human.

Fifth, humour. What an astonishing thing to find in a world that had no personal Creator! Humour recognises the imprisonment of the human spirit in the world, and also, for a moment, liberates it. It gives a sense of proportion which makes our predicament bearable.

What we have considered so far are some of the approaches which may lead an atheist friend to see the consequences of his position. They may force him afresh to question whether or not his atheism makes sense of the totality of his existence. Used sensitively, this drawing out of the consequences of atheism is a powerful apologetic tool. It may well be necessary before your friend is able to listen with an open mind to an alternative interpretation of the evidence, against which his mind may long have been closed.

Suggest an alternative

When I reach this point I sometimes outline a number of facts which point strongly towards the existence of a living personal God such as the Bible reveals. The fact of the world, of design, of values, of conscience, of religion, of humanity, and so forth. It is a powerful way of deploying evidence which he may not have looked at carefully before. There is force in each consideration, and their cumulative impact is very great indeed.

But often it is better to come at it in a more allusive way. Seek to get him on your side. Say to him, 'Just suppose for a moment that the vast majority of mankind across the world and down the ages is right, and that there is a God, a supreme source from whom all else flows. Go further and imagine yourself as that God. What would you do if you wanted to reach out to the human beings you had made in your own image, but who did not want to know you? How would you try to get through to them?

'First, you might create a marvellous world, a world full of beautiful things, a world that shouted out loud the love, the wisdom, the skill and the power of the Creator. God has done that.

'Second, you might create people who are able to respond to love. People with the dangerous gift of free will, with the ability to decide for you and to love you. But of course that implies the opposite possibility: they might decide against you and rebel. They would have that almost divine faculty of self-determination and free choice. Well, God took that risk. He has done just that.

'Third, you might instil into their hearts values which spoke of God. Values like beauty, goodness, harmony, creativity, speech, truth, love. They all point the recipient to the Giver: the Person who is unutterable beauty, supreme goodness, total harmony, unceasing creativity. The God who is truth and life and love and who speaks. Well, God has done that.

'Fourth, you might well build in a conscience that would alert your creatures to right and wrong. A conscience that would approve when they went the right way, and would prod them and warn them when they went astray from your will which was their highest good. A conscience which would persevere however much they tried to dull its force and refuse its directions. God has done that.

'Fifth, you might instil a God-shaped blank in their hearts, a space that nothing can fill apart from the living God himself. A space that cries out for satisfaction and fulfilment, however much rubbish they crowd into it. A space that would elicit from them the cry that came to Augustine's lips, "O God, you have made us for yourself, and our hearts are restless until they find their rest in you." God has done that, too.

'Sixth, you might show your hand in the course of history. You might ensure that arrogance in a civilisation led inevitably to decline and fall. You might perhaps concentrate on one man, one family, one tribe, one nation that would trust you and obey you, and which in time you could train to receive and perhaps even obey your message. They might have to go through flood and captivity as they learned those lessons, but the stakes being high, you would persevere with them, and take pains over them. So much would depend on their understanding and their lifestyle if you were going to be able to reach out to a world that had gone astray. God did that.

'And finally, just conceivably, you might come in person to their world. You would have to come as one of them, for if you disclosed yourself in your unutterable beauty they would be blinded by the sight. You would need to come in disguise. You would need to learn their language so perfectly, without the trace of a foreign accent, that you could be mistaken for a native. It would be very costly. You would have to love them an awful lot if you were going to shrink yourself down to their level. It would be like one of us becoming a rat or a slug in order really to communicate with such lowly creatures. It would be an almost unthinkable sacrifice. But God did that too.

'Listen to one of the oldest bits in the New Testament, Philippians 2:6–11 (NIV). It tells us about the fantastic stoop we are contemplating:

> Jesus Christ, being in very nature of God, did not consider equality with God something to be grasped, but made himself nothing, taking the very nature of a servant, being made in human likeness. And being found in appearance as a man, he humbled himself and became obedient to death – even death on a cross. Therefore God exalted him to the highest place and gave him the name that is above every name, that at the name of Jesus every knee should bow, in heaven and on earth and under the earth, and every tongue confess that Jesus Christ is Lord, to the glory of God the Father.'

Such an approach often draws the enquirer along with you, and enables you to see his sticking points as you work through those seven steps. Best of all, they culminate in Jesus. And that is very important. For vital as the sensitive use of apologetics is, it can leave the mind convinced but the heart untouched; and exposure to the person of Jesus Christ does touch the heart and challenge the will. An intelligent Creator, personal, moral, the source of values, concerned for our morals, our worship and our companionship, nevertheless remains the unknown God unless he chooses to disclose himself.

And this he has done in the person of Jesus Christ:

> No one has ever seen God; the only Son, who is in the bosom of the Father, he has made him known. (John 1:18)
>
> In him the whole fullness of deity dwells bodily. (Col. 2:9)
>
> In many and various ways God spoke of old to our fathers by the prophets; but in these last days he has spoken to us by a Son, whom he appointed the heir of all things, through whom also he created the world. He reflects the glory of God and bears the very stamp of his nature, upholding the universe by his word of power. (Heb. 1:1–3)

That is the last and greatest fact which points with irresistible force to God's reality and care for us: Jesus Christ. It is noteworthy that the Bible never tries to prove God. But it does constantly point us towards the one place where we can meet God, in the person of Jesus his Son. And to that we turn next.

THE PERSON OF JESUS

There is a perennial fascination about Jesus of Nazareth. Currently Hinduism is making room for him. Judaism is producing a wealth of books about him. The New Age movement cannot evade his spell.

> Every letter you write, you date from Jesus. Commerce is intricate and keen, yet commerce ceases the day when Jesus rose. On every hospital Christ is written large. On every orphanage his name is graven. Through every provision for the friendless and fallen the pity of his heart is shining still. Think what you will of Christ, there is the fact that history has been powerless to hide him. You cannot avoid him. He confronts you everywhere. He is magnificently and universally conspicuous. And yet this Christ was meek and lowly and shrank from popularity and clamour. (G. H. Morison, *The Return of Angels*)

What are we to make of Jesus? His existence cannot be doubted by any informed and rational person. It is attested by Roman, Jewish and archaeological as well as Christian sources. 'The historicity of Christ', wrote Professor F. F. Bruce, one of the most outstanding biblical scholars of the twentieth century, 'is as axiomatic for the unbiased historian as the historicity of Julius Caesar. It is not historians who propagate "Christ myth" theories.' And Otto Betz, another very distinguished Continental New Testament scholar, put the matter tartly when he said, 'No serious scholar has ventured to postulate the non-historicity of Jesus.' Pliny, Tacitus, Suetonius, Bar-Serapion, Thallus, Lucian, Josephus, and the Talmud all combine to attest his historicity and many of the things we read of in the Gospels. But it is only in those same Gospels that we get a contemporary and thorough account of his life. What do they reveal?

They reveal a very human Jesus. He was born, and he worked as a carpenter. He was tired and slept from exhaustion in the back of a boat. He had family ties like anyone else. He loved, and he wept.

He suffered and he died. He was very human. He was one of us, our brother. But is that all? Many people today want to leave it there. Jesus was a great guru. Jesus was a witty rabbi. Jesus was the man for others. Jesus was a fabulous teacher. But no more. Well, his contemporaries could not leave it there. They realised that the human category was not sufficient to embrace him. That is why he was killed. And that is why his disciples were willing to go through fire and blood to follow him as their Lord and their God. The original disciples could not rest content with the assumption that Jesus was just a man like us. That would not explain the phenomena they had personally witnessed.

All the New Testament writers were convinced that Jesus was more than man. Listen to Paul:

> He is the visible representation of the God we cannot see. He holds the primacy over all created things. By him everything in heaven and earth was brought into being. The whole universe was made by him and for him. He exists before all things, and the whole universe has its principle of coherence in him. (Col. 1:15–17)

Listen to John: 'In the beginning was the Word, and the Word was with God, and the Word was God . . . And the Word became flesh and dwelt among us . . . [and] we have beheld his glory, glory as of the only Son from the Father' (John 1:1, 14). Listen to Jude (who seems to have been the brother of Jesus) at the end of his short letter:

> Now to him who is able to keep you from falling and to present you without blemish before the presence of his glory with rejoicing, to the only God, our Saviour through Jesus Christ our Lord, be glory, majesty, dominion, and authority, before all time and now and for ever. (Jude 24–5)

That is how the disciples thought of Jesus. And this is totally amazing. For one thing, they had lived alongside him, and the thought that he might be more than man must have been shattering beyond words. But more important, as Jews they were conditioned to reject as impious the very suggestion that he might be more than man. God was so great that you did not mention the divine name if you were a Jew. So great that no image adorned his holy of holies in the temple. So holy that the scribes in the Dead Sea community at Qumran washed their hands every time they wrote the name of God in their manuscripts. The Jews were passionate monotheists. They were the hardest people in the whole wide world to convince that Jesus was more than man. Yet they became convinced. What did it? There were, I think, seven considerations which combined to move them inexorably to this conclusion, and they have the same force today.

Jesus' influence

He has been the dominant person in the world from that day to this, dominant over all types and nationalities. He has been universally recognised as the ideal for human life. Of no one else could that to be said. To be sure, Muhammad has had profound influence, and so has Socrates. But nothing like Jesus. Jesus has captured the heart and allegiance of peasant and king, of intellectual and illiterate the world over, all down the centuries. It makes no difference whether you go to the Naga tribesmen of the hills of India, the warrior Masai in Kenya, black and white in South Africa and the USA, the Maoris in New Zealand or the Eskimo in the Arctic. It makes no difference whether you travel to Sebastopol or Singapore, to Fiji or to Finland. Everywhere there are Christians, captivated by the man of Nazareth.

You could say much the same of Lenin or Mao. They have a tremendous following in certain parts of the world. But their appeal has been to one class of persons only. Mao offered hope to the workers, yet nothing but doom for the bourgeois. Jesus too offered justice, love and hope to the poor; but he also reached out to the rich and disillusioned. He challenged and in due course changed them. But he did not threaten them or require of them the rejection of their class. Moreover, the philosophy behind a Lenin or a Mao has a lot of envy and hate about it, a lot of ruthlessness, and a terrifying indifference to the truth.

Where do you find in the whole history of mankind a character that approaches that of Jesus of Nazareth? His life and influence are utterly without parallel.

Do you know that anonymous piece called *One Solitary Life*? Here it is:

He was born in an obscure village, the child of a peasant woman.
He grew up in still another village, where he worked in a carpenter's shop until he was thirty. Then for three years he was a wandering preacher.
He never wrote a book. He never held an office. He never had a family or owned a house. He did not go to college. He never visited a big city.

He never travelled two hundred miles from the place where he was born. He did none of the things one usually associates with greatness. He had no credentials but himself.

He was only thirty-three when the tide of public opinion turned against him. His friends ran away. He was turned over to his enemies, and went through the mockery of a trial. He was nailed to a cross between two thieves. While he was dying his executioners gambled for his clothing, the only property he had on earth. When he was dead he was laid in a borrowed grave through the pity of a friend.

Nineteen centuries have come and gone. Today he remains the central figure of the human race, and the leader of mankind's progress. All the armies that ever marched, all the navies that ever sailed, all the parliaments that ever sat, all the kings that ever reigned, put together, have not affected the life of man on this planet so much as that *one solitary life*!

Can you deny it?

Jesus' teaching

It was memorable. Nobody had ever taught like this before, nor have they since. It was so vivid and memorable. It was so power-fully authoritative – 'Truly, truly I tell you . . .' Who was this 'I'? He taught them, says Mark, as one who had authority, and not as the scribes (the clergy of the day). The content of his teaching was no less staggering. He taught that the long-awaited Kingdom of God had actually arrived with himself! He invited those who were weary and heavy laden to come to himself. He said that he would satisfy those with deep inner thirst. He told them that there was nothing they could do to make themselves acceptable to God. On the contrary, God had done all that was necessary. He was like a king who forgave his debtor an incalculable debt simply out of the kindness of his heart. He was like a nobleman who threw a great wedding party for his son, to which he invited not only friends and relations but the scum off the city streets. God is like that. And, said Jesus, he is not merely that generous, but he is sensitive to how people feel when confronted with great generosity. So he provides not only the wedding reception free, gratis and for nothing; but also the clothes for people coming in to wear, so that all are the same and none need be embarrassed at his rags, and none can be proud of his finery.

'No man ever spoke like this man!' said the soldiers who had been sent to arrest him, when they returned without having accomplished their task (John 7:46). And they were right. There has been no parallel in the history of the world to the quality, the power and the authority of the teaching of Jesus. Nobody has been able to show any evil contained within it. Nobody has been able to show any good that is not contained, explicitly or implicitly, within it. Nobody has been able to surpass it. People were amazed at it. 'How does this man know so much, never having been to university?' they asked. Jesus' answer was simple and devastating: 'My teaching is not mine but his that sent me. If any man is willing to do his will, he will have no doubts about where the teaching comes from – whether I speak from God or whether I speak from myself' (cf. John 7:15–17). If you are still in doubt, take a slow read through the Sermon on the Mount in Matthew 5–7. And spend time reflecting on the closing verses and their implications.

Jesus' conduct

Jesus' teaching, the highest ever given, was backed up by a flawless character. So flawless that when at his trial they put up false witnesses to arraign him they could not agree in their testimony. So flawless that Pilate three times declared him not guilty, and Pilate's wife had nightmares about the judicial murder of this innocent person. So flawless that the centurion at the cross, hardened as he was to bloodshed, declared: 'This man was innocent'. So flawless that his friends – his friends, mark you – maintained that he was completely without sin. Indeed, tough fisherman though he was, Simon Peter once fell at his feet and begged him to depart from a soiled person like himself. So flawless that when faced by an angry crowd out for his blood, Jesus could calmly ask them: 'which of you can point to anything wrong that I have done?' – and get no reply. So flawless was his character that unlike the great saints of any religion, who are always the first to recognise their own shortcomings, Jesus could say, 'I always do what is pleasing to [my heavenly Father]' (John 8:29). Such was the man. Such was his conduct. There was no shadow of wickedness or failure in it. No other great teacher had ever managed to practise fully what he preached. Moses, Confucius, Plato – and in our own century Martin Luther King, Pope John Paul, and Billy Graham – have all taught wonderful things, and men have hung on their words. But none of them have managed to carry out what they taught. In all of them there has been some consciousness of failure and falling short of their own high ideals, let alone God's. But Jesus was different. He taught the highest standards that any teacher has ever formulated, and he kept them through and through. He utterly practised what he preached. His life was a moral miracle, and it has never been matched. Perhaps that is why when he quietly claimed to be the supreme self-disclosure of God to men, and the only way to enable men to know God as their Father, they believed him. He told them not to believe him if his 'works' did not match his 'words'. They did. He not only taught people to love their enemies: he did it. He not only claimed that the highest thing a man could do for his friends was to lay down his life: he did it. He not only taught that it was more blessed to give than to receive: he lived that way. It makes him the most remarkable of all teachers. Here was one who taught the most exacting standards and embodied them completely. He claimed to bring God into our midst; and his life lent credibility to his claim.

Jesus' miracles

You cannot disentangle Jesus from miracle. In the last century people tried hard to so pare away at the gospel records that they left us with a non-supernatural Jesus, meek and mild, and never doing anything out of the ordinary. Schweitzer and Barth, however, at the beginning of this century, showed that it cannot be done. At every point in the story of Jesus, and in every strand of the gospel record, you stub your foot against miracles. The miracles began at his conception and birth: he was God's Son, according to Mark; God's Word and agent in creation according to John; the full repository of the Godhead according to Paul (while none the less being 'born of a woman'); the one who came into the world without the agency of a human father, according to Matthew and Luke. The miracles continue in his ministry: miracles of knowledge, miracles of healing, miracles of exorcism, miracles over nature, and even some miraculous cases of raising people from the dead. Artlessly and naturally they are interwoven with the whole account. So much were they part of Jesus' self-disclosure that John chose seven of them, called them 'signs' (i.e. pointers to who Jesus really is) and built his Gospel around them. By giving an account of each of them, together with an explanatory discourse, he shows us what Jesus' real significance is, and what he can do for men. The one who fed the five thousand can certainly feed the hungry soul.

The one who opened blind eyes can do as much for men and women blinded by pride and prejudice. The one who raised the dead can bring new life to someone who is spiritually dead. The miracles were never done for selfish purposes. They were never to show off. They were evoked by Jesus' compassion for human need and they were intended to show that the long-awaited Messiah had indeed arrived, and also that Jesus was the liberator who could unlock the various shackles of mankind.

The miracles were so well attested that we find the opponents of Jesus unable to deny them, and forced to assign them to an evil power. 'Through the ruler of the demons he casts out the demons,' said the Pharisees. 'But how can the devil cast out the devil?' asked Jesus. 'In that case his control would collapse in ruins' – which is manifestly not the case. The interesting thing to note is that his opponents did not and could not deny the efficacy of Jesus' cures and exorcisms. In later years they said that he had learned magic in Egypt, and that he was crucified on the eve of Passover for having practised sorcery in Egypt. That was the official party line in the Jewish Mishnah. But so clear was the power of his miracles that we find Jewish people trying to make use of that power without yielding their lives to Jesus. In the Acts of the Apostles we find some of these people attempting exorcism 'by the Jesus whom Paul proclaims' (Acts 19:13–16). We read, with a touch of amusement, that the man with the evil spirit flew at them shouting, 'Jesus I know, and Paul I know; but who are you?', overpowered them, and handled them so roughly that they ran out of the house stripped and battered! There are several prohibitions in later Jewish literature against healing in the name of Jesus: 'A man shall have no dealing with the heretics [i.e. Christians] nor be cured by them even for the sake of an hour of life.'

The miracles of Jesus are hard to deny. Of course they are all secondary to the great miracles of the incarnation and the resurrection, but they stand as mute though powerful indicators of who Jesus is. When they saw the miracle at Cana his disciples, we read, believed on Jesus (John 2:11). The raising of Lazarus to life had the same effect: 'Many of the Jews who had come to visit Mary, and had seen what Jesus did, put their faith in him' (John 11:45, NIV). And on another occasion, when he was besieged by an angry crowd, furious because of his claim to be God's Son, he said, 'My deeds done in my Father's name are my credentials . . . I and the Father are one . . . If I am not acting as my Father would, do not believe me. But if I am, accept the evidence of my deeds, even if you do not believe me' (John 10:25, 30, 37–8). The miracles of Jesus bore powerful testimony to his person as Son of God. They still do.

Jesus' fulfilment of prophecy

Jesus' fulfilment of prophecy was something which hit the first disciples between the eyes. So much so that they found themselves writing like this: 'This was done in order to fulfil the words of the prophet Isaiah . . .', and so on. It is a recurring theme in the New Testament. Jesus is the fulfiller of the ancient scriptures. Now this is a very remarkable claim. It is impossible to exaggerate the respect which the Jews had for the Old Testament. These were the very oracles of God. Yet they were manifestly incomplete. Those scriptures spoke of a day when God would judge the earth. They spoke of a king of David's stock whose dominion would be without end. They spoke of all the families of man being blessed in Abraham, the man of faith from whom the Jewish nation had sprung. They spoke of one like a Son of Man coming to the Ancient of Days, and receiving a kingdom that would never be destroyed, together with power and glory and judgement. They spoke of a prophet like Moses arising among the people, whose teaching would be beyond compare. They spoke of a Servant of the Lord whose suffering would be intense and whose death would carry away the sins of the people. They spoke of a Son of God whose character would measure up to that of his Father. This coming one would fulfil the role of prophet, priest and king for ever. He would be born of David's lineage, but of a humble family. His birthplace would be Bethlehem. He would both restore the fallen in Israel and be a light to the Gentiles. He would be despised and rejected by the very people he came to rescue from their self-centredness. He would die among malefactors, and his tomb would be supplied by a rich man. But that would not be the end of him. He would live again, and the Lord's programme would prosper under his hand. When he saw all that would be accomplished by the anguish of his soul he would be satisfied, for he would have forged a new agreement between God and man by his death; indeed, his death would open up the possibility of ordinary men and women having the Spirit of God come and take up residence in their lives.

All of this came true with Jesus. Not some of it: all of it. There is no example in the history of the world's literature where the

prophecies made centuries beforehand in a holy book were fulfilled by a single historical person in this way. It amazed his
followers, but it convinced them. They came to see in him, the
humble carpenter of Nazareth, the fulfilment of all those ancient
predictions. He was born in Bethlehem of David's stock. His
teaching showed him to be the prophet like Moses. He was the
Suffering Servant of the Lord whose anguish on the cross brought
pardon for all who would believe, as Abraham had believed. He
was the one who would restore the fortunes of Israel and open up
the way of faith for the Gentiles. He had established this new
covenant between God and man, sealing it with his blood. His
death had made the ultimate sacrifice, and no priesthood was ever
to be needed again – for he had once and for all reconciled men to
God by his own self-offering. His kingly rule would last for ever:
veiled now, but apparent when he comes to judge. His Spirit was
already at work transforming the lives of his followers.

In the centuries which followed, the argument from prophecy
had an enormous impact, and so it should. Many distinguished
pagans were won to faith in Jesus as the Son of God by the way he
fulfilled prophecies made in these writings of an Old Testament
which seemed so much older and more noble than their own
writings of Homer and Plato. As Professor C. F. D. Moule, one of
the leading New Testament scholars in the world today, put it in his
book *The Phenomenon of the New Testament*:

> The notion of the 'fulfilment' of Scripture in a single individual, a figure
> of recent history, and he a condemned and disgraced criminal, who
> claimed to be the coping stone of the whole structure and the goal of
> God's whole design, was new.
>
> And it was the Christian community which first related together,
> round a single focus, the scattered and largely disconnected images of
> Israel's hope. It was utterly new for images like 'Messiah', 'Christ',
> 'Son of God', 'Son of Man', 'Suffering Servant' and 'Lord' to be seen as
> interchangeable terms all relating to one figure.

The fulfilment theme goes a lot deeper. It stretches to the names
and titles given to God Almighty in the Old Testament. For
instance, in Isaiah God calls himself 'the First and the Last' (Isa.
41:4; 44:6; 48:12), but in the New Testament this title is applied to
Jesus (Rev. 1:17; 2:8; 22:13). 'I am' is the special name of God in
the Old Testament (Exod. 3:14), and it was too sacred to be
pronounced, so that the Jews used the word 'Adonai' (Lord) as a
substitute. But we find Jesus again and again claiming to be the 'I

am', notably in the fantastic statement of John 8:58, 'Before Abraham was, I am.' So much so that when at a crucial stage in his trial he was asked whether he was the Messiah, he replied: 'I am. And you will see the Son of Man sitting at the right hand of the Mighty One and coming on the clouds of heaven' (Mark 14:62, NIV). This produced an understandably extreme reaction in the high priest and his colleagues, because it was seen to be a claim to personal deity on the part of Jesus.

Again, who is it in the Old Testament who is the Shepherd of his people? God, of course. 'The Lord is my Shepherd' is how the famous Psalm 23 begins. But Jesus calmly uses the title himself. 'I am the good shepherd' (John 10:14). And other New Testament writers such as Peter and the author of Hebrews speak of him as 'the chief shepherd' and 'the great shepherd'. They had got the message.

Perhaps the most remarkable function of God in the Old Testament was to create the world. 'In the beginning God created the heavens and the earth' is, after all, the opening sentence of the whole Bible. But listen to Paul: 'By [Christ] all things were created: things in heaven and on earth . . . all things were created by him and for him' (Col. 1:16, NIV). Listen to John: 'He was in the beginning with God; all things were made through him, and without him was not anything made that was made' (John 1:2–3). Listen to Hebrews: 'In these last days [God] has spoken to us by a Son, whom he appointed the heir of all things, through whom also he created the world' (Heb. 1:2).

Yes, Jesus fulfilled the scriptures written centuries before. Nothing like this has ever happened before or since. There must be something very special about this person who is the centrepiece of all history.

Jesus' claims

Jesus is unique among the teachers of the world, in that he has so much to say about himself. He did not conform to the usual pattern of religious teachers who had some new things to say about God (though he did that too). But the remarkable thing was the place he gave himself in the whole picture of mankind's relationship with God. He dared to assert, 'No one knows the Son except the Father, and no one knows the Father except the Son and any one to whom the Son chooses to reveal him' (Matt. 11:27). What an astounding claim! It is very similar to one in John's Gospel: 'In truth I tell you, in very truth, the man who does not enter the sheepfold by the door, but climbs in some other way, is nothing but a thief and a robber . . . I am the door; anyone who comes into the fold through me shall be safe' (John 10:1, 9).

More, he claimed to have a relationship with God that nobody else could lay claim to. We find it in his use of the word *Abba*. Nobody had addressed God in this way throughout the many centuries of Israel's history. Why? Because it was too intimate. To be sure, Jews were accustomed to praying to God as Father of Israel. But the word they used was *Abhinu*, a form of address which was reverent and essentially an appeal to God for mercy and forgiveness. But there is no trace of that in Jesus' term *Abba*. It is the familiar term of closest intimacy. It means 'Dear Daddy'. And Jesus differentiated between his own relationship with God as father and that of anyone else. He never said, 'Our Father', aligning himself with his disciples, but rather referred to 'My God and your God, my Father and your Father'. He was the Son of God in a quite different way from other men who were merely God's creation. This word *Abba* takes us to the heart of the good news Jesus had come to bring. It meant that he had a unique filial relationship with God and was prepared to share it with the utterly unworthy if only they committed themselves to him.

The passage of time from the first century to this has dulled the sense of shock that such claims must have made on Jesus' contemporaries. Here was a peasant teacher saying in sober, earnest tones, 'I give [people] eternal life, and they shall never perish, and no one shall snatch them out of my hand. My Father, who has given them to me, is greater than all, and no one is able to snatch them out of the Father's hand. I and the Father are one' (John 10:28–30). Such was the breathtaking claim of this unique man. But there was more to come.

He claimed to be able to forgive sins in the absolute sense, and of course this was the prerogative of God alone. That is why the Jews were so furious when Jesus looked with love at a man whose friends had let him down on a stretcher through the roof into the house where he was teaching, and Jesus said, 'Your sins are forgiven you.' Here was someone who was either guilty of blasphemy or actually was authorised to proclaim on earth what God Almighty was affirming in heaven. And that is precisely what Jesus went on to claim. 'But that you may know that the Son of man has authority on earth to forgive sins' – he said to the paralysed man – 'I say to you, rise, take up your pallet and go home' (Mark 2:10–11). The astonishing healing validated the astonishing claim. Here was one who did the unthinkable. He forgave sins. We find just the same thing happening with the woman taken in adultery, whose story is recounted in John 8. When the males who had so enthusiastically accused her all began to slip away because of their own guilty consciences, Jesus asked her, 'Woman, where are they? Has no one condemned you?' She said, 'No one, Lord.' And Jesus said, 'Neither do I condemn you; go, and do not sin again.'

More, Jesus took it for granted that he is entitled to divine worship. When Peter falls at his feet in adoration after a fishing expedition and says, 'Depart from me, for I am a sinful man, O Lord' (Luke 5:8), Jesus does nothing to stop him. When Thomas falls at his feet after the resurrection and exclaims, 'My Lord and my God!' (John 20:28), Jesus does not rebuke him – except for needing the evidence of his eyes to come to that conclusion. No good man would do that. Indeed, we have examples in the New Testament of two good men, Peter and Paul, both of whom found themselves being worshipped by ignorant pagans, and they reacted violently against it, telling them to worship God alone. But Jesus seems to have taken such worship as his due.

Even more staggering, he sometimes made it clear that the final destiny of his hearers depended upon their relation with himself. One of the most famous of such cases is the parable of the sheep and the goats, which begins with Jesus as Son of Man, coming in glory to judge mankind (Matt. 25:31–46). Another is at the end of the Sermon on the Mount, where Jesus declares that on the day of judgement men will apply to him for entry into the Kingdom of heaven, saying 'Lord, Lord' – and if they do not know him, they will not find access (Matt. 7:21–3).

C. S. Lewis put the force of those claims very powerfully:

The things he says are very different from what any other teacher has said. Others say, 'This is the truth about the universe. This is the way you ought to go.' But he says 'I am the Truth and the Way and the Life.' He says 'No man can reach absolute reality, except through me. Try to retain your own life and you will inevitably be ruined. Give yourself away and you will be saved.' He says 'If you are ashamed of me, if, when you hear my call you turn the other way, I will look the other way when I come again as God without disguise. If anything whatever is keeping you from God and from me, whatever it is, throw it away. If it is your eye, pull it out. If it is your hand, cut it off. If you put yourself first you will be last. Come to me, everyone who is carrying a heavy load, and I will set that right. Your sins, all of them are wiped out. I can do that. I am Re-birth. I am Life. Eat me, drink me. I am your food. And finally, do not be afraid. I have overcome the whole universe.' That is the issue.

That is indeed the issue: what are you to make of those claims of Jesus? That is the key issue with which to face an enquirer. Many accept Jesus as a fine man and a great teacher, but those claims of his rule such an interpretation out of court. To quote Lewis again:

> I am trying to prevent anyone saying the really foolish thing that people often say about him. 'I'm ready to accept Jesus as a great moral teacher but I don't accept his claim to be God.' That is the one thing we must not say. A man who was merely a man and said the sort of things Jesus said would not be a great moral teacher. He would either be a lunatic – on a level with the man who says he is a poached egg – or he would be the devil of hell. You must make your choice. Either this man was and is the Son of God; or else a madman or something worse.

Jesus' death

Jesus had predicted that if he was lifted up from the earth, he would draw all kinds of people to himself, and this has proved abundantly true. Until the cross of Jesus, the faith of his disciples was weak and vacillating. The cross, which might well have dashed to the ground such fragile faith as they had, in fact lit it into an inextinguishable blaze. Now that is a very remarkable thing. Remarkable to start believing in your leader once he is dead and gone. Remarkable to start believing that he is God's anointed rescuer once he has so signally failed to produce the goods and has ended in disgrace on a gibbet. Most remarkable of all when you remember that in the Old Testament it says that anyone exposed on a gibbet rests under the curse of God (Deut. 21:22–3). Remarkable, but true. The Christian movement only took root once Jesus was crucified. The cross became the symbol of the new movement. The symbol of death and shame turned into the most glorious badge of discipleship. How did that happen?

It was as they saw him die that understanding began to dawn. The sheer self-sacrifice of it; the gentleness, the horror, the love, the pardon, the victory intertwined with that cross quickened their insight. Listen to Peter, who was there. He is writing years later to scattered Christians throughout Turkey and Southern Russia. 'He himself bore our sins in his body on the tree,' he exclaims. And a little later: 'Christ has once and for all suffered for sins, the just for the unjust, that he might bring us to God' (1 Pet. 3:18; cf. 2:24). Peter had come to see that Jesus did indeed die in the place of cursing, that awesome gibbet: but that the curse was ours and not his own. He did indeed bear sins: but they were our sins, not his own, for he had none.

It is astonishing that through this squalid murder on Calvary the followers of Jesus should have received such lasting assurance about who he was. But such is the case. Mark tells us of the death of Jesus and then immediately goes on, 'And the curtain of the temple was torn in two, from top to bottom' (Mark 15:38). That curtain was there to keep people out from the presence of God, manifested in the holy of holies. When the curtain was split wide open, at the death of Jesus, it was a symbolic gesture to show that the way into God's presence had been opened for all. And immediately we find a Gentile soldier, who had personally killed this same Jesus, going, so to speak, through that split curtain into God's presence with the awed confession on his lips: 'Truly this man was the Son of God' (Mark 15:39). The author of Hebrews cannot affirm the full deity of Jesus (which he does very powerfully in Heb. 1:1–3) without continuing, 'When he had made purification for sins, he sat down at the right hand of the Majesty on high.' And Paul was no less clear that in the cross he saw God Almighty dealing with the basic human problem, sin. 'In Christ God was reconciling the world to himself, not counting their trespasses against them' (2 Cor. 5:19). That is precisely what Jesus himself had said he would do. Three times in Mark's Gospel he predicted his passion, and then capped it with the explanation: 'The Son of man . . . came . . . to give his life as a ransom for many' (Mark 10:45). It was in that supreme act of self-sacrifice and sin-bearing that the disciples saw straight through to the heart of God. God had come to them in Christ, and God had saved them through his cross.

Those seven things about Jesus, his influence, his teaching, his conduct, his miracles, his fulfilment of prophecy, his claims, and his death all mount up to a formidable case that he is indeed the Christ, the Son of the living God. There was one further crowning demonstration, his resurrection, and that will be considered in our next chapter.

FURTHER READING

At a popular level

F. F. Bruce, *The New Testament Documents: Are They Reliable?* (Inter-Varsity Press)
C. H. Dodd, *The Founder of Christianity* (Collins)
Michael Green, *World on the Run* (Inter-Varsity Press)
Michael Green, *You Must be Joking* (Hodder & Stoughton)
Rosalind Murray, *The Good Pagan's Failure* (Collins)
Lesslie Newbigin, *Honest Religion for Secular Man* (SCM Press)
Lesslie Newbigin, *Foolishness to the Greeks* (SPCK)
John Polkinghorne, *The Way the World Is* (SPCK)
A. E. Taylor, *Does God Exist?* (Collins)
David Watson, *Is Anyone There?* (Falcon)

At a more advanced level

J. N. D. Anderson, *The Mystery of the Incarnation* (Hodder & Stoughton)
D. M. Baillie, *God Was in Christ* (Faber & Faber)
J. A. Baker, *The Foolishness of God* (Darton, Longman & Todd)
Paul Barnett, *Is the New Testament History?* (Hodder & Stoughton)
Peter Berger, *A Rumour of Angels* (Penguin Books)
F. F. Bruce, *Jesus and Christian Origins Outside the New Testament* (Hodder & Stoughton)
George Carey, *The Great God Robbery* (Collins)
James Dunn, *The Evidence for Jesus* (SCM Press)
R. T. France, *The Evidence for Jesus* (Hodder & Stoughton)
Michael Green (ed.), *The Truth of God Incarnate* (Hodder & Stoughton)
Anthony Hanson (ed.), *Vindications* (SCM Press)
John Polkinghorne, *One World: The Interaction of Science and Theology* (SPCK)
Keith Ward, *Holding Fast to God* (SPCK)

7

Facing the Problems of Miracle and Suffering

In the previous chapter we have looked at two of the most common stumbling-blocks which the Christian evangelist will have to encounter, and which drive him into a study of apologetics. This chapter is an attempt to sketch how we might face two other such objections which are very commonly made. They are the question of miracle and the problem of evil and suffering. Both issues are deep and complex. Both land us in general philosophical problems at the same time as being critically important for Christian belief. We all have our own preferred way of handling them. What follows is but the merest sketch in an area in which I claim no expertise.

THE QUESTION OF MIRACLE

Definition

How shall we define 'miracle'? The word is very loosely used in common parlance. Literally it means a marvel, an object of wonder. But why so? Because it is a break with the normal pattern of events. It defies natural explanation. It supersedes, or at all events suspends, what we call the 'laws of nature'. If an event is susceptible of a natural explanation, it is not, we feel, a miracle.

But that will not do. A miracle is not the same as an anomaly, which also appears to go against the laws of nature and has no known explanation. An anomaly does not embody any truth claims, which a miracle does. Moreover, miracle has nothing to do with magic, which is basically human manipulation of super-human forces, and brings glory to the practitioner, not to God. What is more, miracles are different from satanic signs and wonders (where these are authentic), for we use the word 'miracle' to denote a good result, and one that springs from divine intervention.

A miracle, therefore, is an event which is an exception to the normal pattern of events, but not necessarily a contradiction of it. It makes some truth claim for God. It is intended for a good end. And it brings glory to God by manifesting some aspect of his character.

It goes without saying that it is often hard to identify a miracle. Things may fall outside our contemporary understanding of nature's laws and yet be perfectly explicable later on when our knowledge is more comprehensive. Think how miraculous space travel or penicillin would have seemed to our grandparents. Space travel is rather a good example, because it involves weightlessness. We all know that gravity draws all unsupported bodies to the ground: yet in space, unsupported bodies float around. Is this defiance of the laws of nature? By no means. It is precisely what a sound understanding of gravity would lead us to expect . . . but nobody could have guessed it a century ago.

Does this mean that there must be an explanation for every-thing, even if we never discover what it is? Not necessarily. Why should we submit to the assumption that there must be a rational explanation for everything? What if some things – what if one Reality – just happens to be? If there is a self-subsistent, transcen-dent reality which we call God, then there is no reason whatever why there should not be miracles in the world he has created. If there is God, there may well be miracle.

Possibility

But the very possibility of miracle is vehemently denied in many quarters today, and has been since David Hume's famous essay on miracles in his *Enquiry Concerning Human Understanding*. Hume's basic objection to miracles is that if they occurred they would be violations of the laws of nature. And the laws of nature are built on the highest degree of probability. Indeed, they are built on 'the firm and unalterable' experience of mankind. There is, therefore, the lowest degree of probability for miracle.

'Uniform experience' militates against it: otherwise, says Hume, it would not be classed a miracle. A miracle is so improbable as to be negligible. It is far more likely that the witnesses were lying or mistaken than that a miracle occurred.

This looks like an impressive argument, but it is a lot less impressive than it seems. First, it assumes that a 'law of nature' is *prescriptive*, determining an immutable way in which things *must* happen. Instead, of course, it is *descriptive*, explaining how through constant observation we discern that a thing *does* happen. The former excludes the very possibility of miracle. The latter allows it. Second, why should Hume assume that the prudent man should always base his conclusion upon what has happened in the past, rather on the evidence of the present which may be before his eyes? But underlying both these objections is the fact that Hume is assuming what he wants to prove. If there is 'uniform experience' against miracles, there is nothing more to be said. But we can only be assured of this 'uniform experience' against the miraculous if we happen to know that all reports of miracles are false. And of course we could only know this to be the case if we knew that miracles have never occurred and never do. And that, of course, is to argue in a circle!

Hume's whole treatment of probability is vitiated by the assumption of what he seeks to prove. He assumes the uniformity of nature, and from that basis argues the extreme improbability of miracle. It is no good saying that because our experience tends to confirm our belief in uniformity we may reasonably expect that it will always be confirmed. Why should it – unless there is indeed that uniformity in nature which we are seeking to establish? The fact that things have happened in a certain way many times in the past says nothing whatever about future probabilities unless we can assume the uniformity of nature. If nature is not uniform, nothing is either probable or improbable. C. S. Lewis' argument is very forceful when he considers this point in Hume's position:

> If we stick to Hume's method, far from getting what he had hoped (namely the conclusion that all miracles are infinitely improbable) we get a complete deadlock. The only kind of probability he allows holds exclusively within the frame of uniformity. When uniformity is itself in question (and it is in question the moment we ask whether miracles occur) this kind of probability is suspended. And Hume knows no other. By his method, therefore, we cannot say that miracles are either probable or improbable. We have impounded *both* uniformity *and* miracles in a sort of limbo where probability and improbability can

never come. This result is equally disastrous for the scientist and the theologian; but along Hume's lines there is nothing whatever to be done about it.

That same fallacy bedevils all subsequent attacks on miracles. Antony Flew, a modern rationalist philosopher, has tried to update Hume's argument. He maintains that miracles are by definition particular and unrepeatable events; that scientific laws of nature are constant and repeatable; that evidence for the latter is always greater than for the former; and that therefore we should never believe in miracles. Once again this conceals a circular argument. What Flew is saying is, in effect, that everything that happens in the natural world is caused by the natural world. But this begs the question. The whole point about a miracle is that it happens in the natural world (otherwise we would not be able to perceive it) but that it comes from divine intervention from beyond the natural world. Flew has given us a classic example of an unfalsifiable position. No amount of evidence would convince him that a miracle has happened: such a thing would assail his naturalistic unbelief!

But if we admit God, must we admit miracle? That is the question which comes to mind at this juncture, and it is one which C. S. Lewis ably answers in *Miracles*.

But if we admit God, must we admit Miracles? Indeed, indeed, you have no security against it. That is the bargain. Theology says to you, in effect, 'Admit God and with him the risk of a few miracles, and I in return will ratify your faith in uniformity as regards the overwhelming majority of events.' The philosophy which forbids you to make uniformity absolute is also the philosophy which offers you solid grounds for believing it to be general, to be *almost* absolute. The Being who threatens Nature's claim to omnipotence confirms her in her lawful occasions. Give us this ha'porth of tar and we will save the ship. The alternative is really much worse. Try to make Nature absolute and you find that her uniformity is not even probable. By claiming too much you get nothing. You get the deadlock, as in Hume. Theology offers you a working arrangement, which leaves the scientist free to continue his experiments and the Christian free to continue his prayers.

Richard Purtill in his book *C. S. Lewis's Case for the Christian Faith* has some interesting commentary and a brilliant illustration to illuminate this passage in Lewis. First, he reminds us how Lewis objected to defining miracles (as Hume had done) as violations of natural law. He thought of them as interventions by the God who set natural laws in motion.

Second, he underlines the importance of the observed uniformities which go to make up natural law. In an unordered, chaotic universe the word 'miracle' could have no meaning. It needs the regularity of nature's laws. Exceptions to rules positively require the existence of rules for them to be exceptions! Science shows how ordered this world is, and that in itself, as we saw in the last chapter, constitutes a powerful evidence for God. But if the natural world and its laws are the result of God's action, why should he not, if there is sufficiently good reason, occasionally intervene in the world and the order of general uniformities which he himself has created? We allow the particularly gifted child to skip grades – that is an exception to the normal rule. President Ford granted a presidential pardon to Nixon, but that does not invalidate the normal legal procedure, nor is it rendered impossible by that system.

And this is an analogy which Purtill pursues effectively. The scientist, *qua* scientist, must ignore the possibility of miracle, just as the lawyer, *qua* lawyer, must ignore the possibility of a presidential pardon for his client, since there is nothing he can do as a lawyer which could ensure such a pardon. A pardon is a free action by the President which cannot be guaranteed by any legal procedure, but equally cannot be ruled out of court as impossible. The same is true of miracle. A presidential pardon does not violate any laws, nor does it suspend the laws. It simply makes an individual exception. So it is with miracle. Again, a presidential pardon cannot be compelled; it can only be asked for. It cannot be predicted, and gives no ground for future assumptions. So it is with miracle. And finally, we could not settle whether presidential pardons are possible by looking at the day-to-day business of the courts. No, we must ask what kind of legal system we live under. It is like that with miracles. We cannot settle whether they occur by looking at the ordinary course of nature; we must ask what kind of universe we live in. And one relevant consideration in resolving that question is this. A universe made by God leaves room for human reason, whereas a universe derived from natural necessity is hard put to do so. If we decide that it is reasonable to believe in God, then miracles are obviously possible. The issue then will be one of evidence, not of possibility. Indeed, if God wants to emphasise some particularly important message he has for us, there would seem to be no better way than through miracles. A God who could never intervene would be worthy neither of our worship nor of our prayers. But the living God whom the Bible describes – why should he not underline his message with miracles? Why should word and deed not get together? The question is not, therefore, 'Is it possible?' but 'Did it happen?'

Evidence

The Bible is quite unembarrassed about miracles. It records them frequently as elements of God's self-disclosure. He is the God who acts, and his actions are sometimes highly unusual. Nowhere in the history of salvation would we expect those miracles to concentrate more than in the supreme intervention of our interventionist God, in the coming, the living, the dying and the rising of Jesus of Nazareth. And that is precisely what we find.

This is not the place to discuss the general reliability of the evidence about Jesus' miracles of knowing, of healing, of delivering from demonic forces, his abilities over nature and ultimately over death. We have glanced already in the previous chapter at the miracles of Jesus, and seen that they were not just 'acts of power', as the synoptic gospels describe them, but also 'signs', as John puts it, of who Jesus is and what he can do for mankind. There is a particularly helpful piece in one of the sermons of C. S. Lewis which may help us to understand the status of these miracles. He quotes Athanasius:

> Our Lord took a body like ours and lived as a man in order that those who had refused to recognise him in his superintendence and captaincy of the whole universe might come to recognise from the works he did here below in the body, that what dwelt in this body was the Word of God.

In other words, the miracles of Jesus, far from opposing the workings of nature, concentrate into a single instant what normally happens over a long time, in order to draw attention to the God who is behind both, and who calls for their allegiance.

Lewis takes the example of the vine. God makes it absorb water through its roots, and its ensuing fruit, ripened by the sun, turns eventually into wine. But men fail to see it. Either, like ancient pagans, they refer the process to some finite spirit, such as Bacchus; or else, like modern pagans, 'they attribute real and ultimate causality to the chemical and other material phenomena which are all that our senses can discover in it. But when Christ at Cana makes water into wine, the mask is off!'

It is the same with corn. Every year God makes a little corn into much corn. The ancient pagans honour the Corn God, and the modern pagans the laws of nature. But 'the close-up, the translation of this annual wonder, is the feeding of the five thousand'.

It is the same with miracles of healing. Contrary to much of our mythology, the doctor does not heal. All he does is to facilitate the natural healing processes of the body, implanted by God: 'All who are cured are cured by Him, the healer within. But once he did it visibly, a Man meeting a man.

You could say the same about the miracles like the stilling of the storm. The Old Testament God is seen as the stiller of the storm. But men take no notice. They regard it as a natural happening when the storm has blown itself out. So Jesus concentrates in a single, sudden, dynamic act that stilling of the storm which God has been engaged in from time immemorial within the wonderful world he has made.

That insight of Lewis has helped me to understand something more about the miracles of Jesus. I am not affronted by them, and never have been. If he really is God incarnate, it is not surprising that there should have been some rather remarkable events attending his coming among us. They point to who he is and what he can do for us. But Lewis has helped me to see the essential continuity of Jesus' miracles with God's ordered world in which they took place. They are the exceptions which draw attention not merely to the rule but to the One who set the rules and whom we manage so effectively to leave out of account.

But all other reputed miracles of Jesus fade into insignificance before the two greatest miracles of all, the incarnation and the resurrection.

THE INCARNATION

The account given us in the Gospels, of God breaking into our world in the person of Jesus who was born to the Virgin Mary, is so staggering as to be almost incredible. Can we credit a miracle of that magnitude? Told of anyone else, it would be utterly incredible. But if God really exists, and cares for us so much that he came to make himself known to us in the human terms we could understand, and to rescue us from the results of our foolish

rebellion, then, yes, it is just credible. The question is, is the evidence good enough? It cannot be a matter to be settled *a priori*. It cannot rest on what we think would have been appropriate. Bishop David Jenkins of Durham once said on TV: 'I very much doubt if God would arrange a virgin birth.' That is totally to miss the point. Christianity is not concerned with our guess-work: it is concerned with what actually happened. We are not at liberty to rewrite history to fit our presuppositions.

'We believe God was born of a virgin,' wrote Jerome, 'because we read it.' Where so?

We read it in the two quite independent accounts which we have in the Gospels of Matthew and Luke. Both draw on material current well before AD 70. It circulated, therefore, well within the lifetime of contemporaries and colleagues of Jesus, and was subject to their corroboration – or otherwise. The two independent accounts differ in many respects, but are agreed on three major particulars. First, the birthplace is Bethlehem; the later home Nazareth. Second, the mother is Mary, a virgin; the 'foster father' is Joseph. Third, the child Jesus was conceived by the Holy Spirit of God.

This core of material must therefore antedate the divergent accounts of Matthew and Luke, which it underlies. It seems probable that Luke tells Mary's story (concentrating on the angel's annunciation to her, her perplexity and obedience) while Matthew gives us Joseph's (concentrating on the angel's annunciation to him, his perplexity and obedience). We therefore have in Matthew and Luke two early, separate accounts of the virginal conception of Jesus, independent and complementary, the one going back to Mary and the other to Joseph.

'Ah,' your friend may say (if he knows enough!), 'but the rest of the New Testament knows nothing of the virgin birth.' There is some truth in that. The virgin birth does not seem to have been part of the *kerygma*, the evangelistic preaching of the early church, if we are to credit the sermons in Acts. The Christians concentrated on the fact of the incarnation, not on its mode. It may well have been not very widely known. But there are indications in other parts of the New Testament. Mark 6:3 speaks of Jesus the carpenter, 'the son of Mary'. In Judaism, to call someone the son of his mother was normally a massive insult. Interestingly enough, both Matthew and Luke change the phrase, out of reverence. But 'son of Mary' is precisely what Jesus was. Again, in Galatians 4:4 Paul makes great play of Jesus having been 'born of a woman' – a

very odd phrase if he was not alluding to the virgin birth. And Revelation 12 sees 'the woman' bring forth 'the man child' who is caught up to God and his throne. Hints, nothing more. But maybe significant hints. The apostolic church was well aware of the virgin birth of Jesus.

When we turn from the New Testament to the Apostolic Fathers who followed, then there is a great deal of emphasis on the virgin birth. The origins of the Apostles' Creed go back to before AD 150, and so 'Born of the Virgin Mary' would have been part of the baptismal confession of every believer. Irenaeus and Tertullian, Justin and Aristides, are strong on the virgin birth, and Ignatius is almost obsessed by it: 'For our God, Jesus the Christ, was conceived in the womb by Mary, of the seed of David but also of the Holy Spirit.' He sees the virginity of Mary, the child-bearing by Mary of the Saviour, and the death of the Lord as three mysteries that were wrought in the silence of God but which need to be cried aloud. By AD 110 the virgin birth was clearly a very important element of Christian belief. Significantly enough, the non-Christians recognised that Jesus was not born in the normal way to Joseph and Mary. The second-century Jewish leader Trypho and the pagan philosopher Celsus both put his birth down to marital infidelity by Mary; and in Jewish literature before AD 70, preserved in the Talmud, Jesus is called 'the bastard of a married woman'. That is good historical evidence that there was something very unusual about his birth.

But are there not plenty of parallels to the virgin birth story? No, there are not. Great play was made of this in the last century, but on inspection the case cannot be maintained. J. Gresham Machen's *The Virgin Birth* makes mincemeat of it. To Jews the idea of a divine incarnation was utterly foreign, and by means of a virginal conception it would have been utterly revolting. There are no parallels at all in Judaism. The divine does not have intercourse with a woman. And even in the famous passage in Isaiah 7:14, *almah* seems to mean 'young woman' rather than 'virgin'. There is no pre-Christian interpretation of that verse which sees it as a reference to a virgin conceiving and bearing a son. That was a Christian reading of Isaiah's prophecy in the light of how Jesus actually was born . . . and *almah* was perfectly patient of the meaning 'virgin'.

But what about the Greeks? Did they not have vivid myths about Zeus and his amours with mortal women? Did they not have endless 'divine men' or 'sons of God' wandering around the place?

But the pagan myths were highly sexual. They majored on the union of the god, usually in some sort of disguise, with the woman. But of this there is no hint in the Gospels. The whole account is modest and restrained. It is the creative word of God, as in Genesis 1, which brings life to Mary's womb. The whole way the story is recounted is profoundly Jewish, even though the idea of an incarnation is so very unJewish. We are not dealing with any pagan myth, but with something which emerged in the heart of Judaism. As for the 'divine men' with which the ancient world was populated, according to the overheated imagination of Wetter and Bielter, they are not to be found. Every instance that can be pointed to in the second century (and there are none in first-century sources) is influenced by Christianity. The account of the virgin birth is utterly unique and has no parallel anywhere in the world. It was an eminently fitting way for God to have entered his world. Fitting, but not necessary. It is possible to believe in the real incarnation of God without believing in the virginal conception (the New Testament nowhere suggests that there was anything particularly unusual about the actual birth). Lots of people do. It was not necessary for God to have come to our world in that way. But it was entirely congruous, as Justin put it in the second century, 'that the Firstborn of all things should, by incarnation in a virgin's womb, truly become a child'.

That propriety is picked up by C. S. Lewis in a continuation of that sermon of his quoted above. In the normal act of generation a tiny sperm from the father impregnates the woman's ovum. Within that microscopic organism of the sperm lie coded 'the colour of his hair and his great grandfather's hanging lip . . . Behind every spermatozoon lies the whole history of the universe: locked within it is no small part of the world's future.' That is God's normal way of making a man. It takes centuries. Indeed it goes back to the beginning of time and the creation of matter. And now, in the incarnation, God achieves this process not over millennia, but in an instant. Not through a genetic chain, but without a single spermatozoon. The long process of generation had produced a mankind deeply tainted. Now God intervenes to give humanity a new start. 'This time he was creating not simply a man, but the man who was to be Himself: the only true Man.'

Is that beyond belief? I do not see why it should be. It is the concentrating in a single person and a single moment of the essence of what God had been doing down the centuries at a much slower pace. It is another example of the divine intervention which brought mankind into being at the first. It is congruous both with the love and the humility of God that he should come into our world in the ovum of an unmarried girl, the object of ridicule by those he came to save. You cannot prove the virginal conception of Jesus Christ. All you can say is that it is exceedingly well attested very early, and that it is exceedingly fitting that the Christ should so clearly share God's nature (no sperm) and ours (Mary's ovum). Christ, the bridge over troubled water, can only be a reliable bridge, open for traffic each way, if he is firmly rooted both in God's reality and nature, and in our own. The virginal conception asserts that he is.

THE RESURRECTION

The supreme miracle of Christianity is the resurrection. Unlike the virginal conception of Jesus which (though important) is rarely mentioned in the New Testament, assurance of the resurrection shines out from every page. It is the crux of Christianity, the heart of the matter. If it is true, then there is a God; the claims of Jesus are vindicated; he has saved us; there is a future for mankind; and death and suffering have to be viewed in a totally new light. If it is not true, Christianity collapses into mythology. In that case we are, as Saul of Tarsus conceded, of all men most to be pitied.

Once again we must refuse to be guided by what we judge to be probability. There is nothing merely 'probable' about the resurrection of Jesus. It is true or false: no nonsense. And in assessing the claims made by the Christian church for the resurrection of Jesus, we need to reject both theological prejudice and scientific prejudice.

Scientific prejudice is very hard to escape from as we consider the resurrection of Jesus. For we know that dead men don't rise. Science is sceptical about miracle. However, science concerns itself with evidence. No top-class scientist would say 'The resurrection can't be true' without examining the evidence. Such blind dogmatism would be the very antithesis of scientific enquiry. And that is all the Christian is asking for: open-minded examination of the evidence for this astounding claim that in one man, Jesus of Nazareth, the power of death was rolled back and he rose to a new dimension of life from the chill of the tomb.

That brings us to the second and most important point. Christians do not make this claim for anyone else. They are well aware that dead men don't rise. They are claiming that in this one person, a very special person who was more than man, the forces of death met their match. We have seen that there are good reasons to suppose that Jesus Christ shared God's nature as well as ours. Very well, in that case how could we possibly be so sure that he could not rise from the grave? We have seen that he alone among mankind lived a perfect, unsullied life. How can we be so sure that a life like that, a life which gave no foothold to sin, could not master death? There are no other such lives to compare it with. Jesus made his whole credibility depend upon that resurrection which would follow death. Just as Jonah came back from his three-day 'death' inside the great fish, so Jesus himself would come back from the jaws of death (Matt. 12:39–41). So for the true scientist the question is 'Did it happen?' And that is a matter of evidence.

But there is another type of prejudice: theological prejudice. Many theologians come to their task with sceptical presuppositions, for a variety of reasons which are not important at the moment. It is commonly held in such circles that Jesus could not have risen from the dead, but that in some sense his cause lived on or his spirit continued to influence his followers: the 'resurrection' was so spiritual that it was compatible with Jesus' body remaining rotting in the tomb. We can get back by historical means to the first outbreak of Easter faith, we are told, but not to any Easter event which may underlie it. We should not be interested in the empty tomb, but in the living Lord who meets us in the preaching of the gospel. Christianity must not be brought into an area where it stands or falls by historical or scientific explanation.

I find all this most unconvincing. If we are to grant the importance of the Easter faith, how can it be thought inappropriate or irrelevant to enquire into what gave rise to that Easter faith, if not the Easter event?

If Jesus did not rise from the tomb and reverse the grip of death, what sort of sense does it make to encourage people to meet him in the preaching of the gospel?

And if history and science disprove Christianity, the sooner we admit it, and abandon a faith which has been discredited, the better.

No, we should abjure prejudice from whatever quarter, and examine the evidence. And the evidence is very powerful. Indeed, it is so powerful that although attempts have been made to crack it ever since the first century, no single alternative explanation has ever survived for long. The alternatives simply do not bear the weight of critical investigation. But there are many useful accounts of the resurrection faith and its rationale on the market today. If the person you are seeking to bring to faith is of a legal turn of mind, then take him to Professor Sir Norman Anderson's *The Evidence for the Resurrection* or *A Lawyer among the Theologians*, or the solicitor Val Grieve's *Your Verdict*. If he is a churchman, show him Archbishop A. M. Ramsey's *The Resurrection of Christ*. If he likes detective stories, John Wenham's *Easter Enigma* is a fascinating reconstruction which makes sense of all the different resurrection accounts to be found in the New Testament. If he is a journalist, Frank Morison's *Who Moved the Stone?* is the book for him, written as it is by one who once did not believe the resurrection at all. Many substantial theological books come regularly from the presses on this the central tenet of Christianity, and I have added to them myself in *The Empty Cross of Jesus* and a more popular treatment, *The Day Death Died*. There is obviously a vast amount that could be said on the matter, but the heart of it can be expressed fairly simply and succinctly.

The evidence of the cross

For there to be any possibility of a resurrection there must first have been a death. And there are those throughout history who have suggested that Jesus did not really die. He recovered from his swoon in the cool of the tomb, left it, and allowed his followers to imagine that he had risen from the grave. The most celebrated modern exponent of this position was H. J. Schonfield, whose book *The Passover Plot* was a best-seller. But it is as old as Celsus in the second century AD, who explained the resurrection by supposing that a not-quite-dead Jesus was nursed back to health again by Mary Magdalene; forty days later his wounds got the better of him, and he died and was buried secretly, but not before he had assembled his friends, and walked off into a cloud on a mountain top! Such explanations are of course psychologically incredible, imaginative without a shred of evidence, and neglect completely the finality of the brutal Roman method of execution on a cross.

Jesus was executed in full view of a large crowd by four soldiers who had had a lot of experience at this grisly task during the

Roman occupation of Judaea. Crucified men did not escape death. There is, in fact, only one occasion in ancient literature where a crucified man was rescued from death. Josephus (*Vita*, 75) tells us of a time when he saw a number of captives being crucified; and noticing three of his friends among them, he asked the Roman commander, Titus, for a reprieve. This was granted, and the men were immediately taken down. It seems that they had only just been crucified, but despite being given every care by the most expert physicians available two of them died. It is incredible that Jesus – who had not eaten or slept before his execution, who was weakened by loss of blood and the savagery of the most brutal scourging, who was pierced through his hands and feet by a six-inch nail (one has recently been unearthed, still impaling the ankle of a crucified man) – could have survived unaided, had he been alive when he was taken down from the cross after at least six hours of exposure in the scorching sun. It is even more incredible that he should have been able to emerge from a guarded tomb and persuade his followers that he was conqueror of death. There can be no doubt that Jesus was dead.

As a matter of fact there are indications in the Gospel accounts which demonstrate it conclusively. In the case of Jesus the execution squad saw he was dead already and so did not break his legs. That was a barbaric way of ensuring that crucified wretches did not continue to raise themselves on their crosses (by pressing on their feet) and gulp in breath. Instead, and just to make sure, they pierced his side with a spear, and out came 'blood and water' as an eyewitness expressed it (John 19:34–5). It is clear that the eyewitness attached great importance to what he saw: it is no less clear that he did not understand it. Hardly surprising. Nobody did until the rise of modern medicine. But any doctor will now tell you that the separation of the blood into clot and serum is one of the strongest indications of death. Had Jesus been alive, strong spurts of bright arterial blood would have emerged after the spear wound. The 'blood and water' is proof positive that Jesus was dead. If we wanted more, we could have it. Not only did the centurion report to the governor that the job was done (and he knew a dead man when he saw one: if he made a mistake, he could be on a capital charge himself), but Pilate allowed Joseph of Arimathea to take the body away and bury it (John 19:38). This would have been inconceivable had there been any doubt over the death of so notable a prisoner who had predicted his own resurrection! Significantly, the word here used for the 'body' of Jesus is *ptōma*, a word in Greek reserved for a corpse. Yes, the evidence of the cross makes it certain that Jesus was dead.

The evidence of the church

In his book *The Phenomenon of the New Testament*, Professor C. F. D. Moule points out a fascinating thing about early Christianity. It had nothing whatsoever to add to the Judaism from which it sprang, apart from the conviction that the Messiah Jesus had risen from the dead! All the earliest Christians were Jews, of course, Jews from every country under the sun (Acts 2:5–12), including large numbers of the official priesthood (Acts 6:7). They all went to the synagogue and to the temple. Their ethics were Jewish ethics. Only one thing caused this new religion (as it became) to erupt. It was the conviction that Jesus must be the long-awaited Deliverer of the nation, foretold in the Old Testament scriptures. He was the Messiah, the Son of Man, the Son of God, the Prophet like Moses, the King of Israel. He was 'the coming one'. His resurrection from the dead proved it (Rom. 1:4). Nobody else had done anything remotely comparable. He was declared by that resurrection to be 'Son of God'. He had a right to the name 'Lord', normally applied to God Almighty in the Old Testament.

That church, armed with such an improbable claim, and beginning from a handful of uneducated fishermen and tax-gatherers, swept across the whole known world in the next three hundred years. It is a perfectly amazing story of peaceful revolution that has no parallel in the history of the world. It came about because Christians were able to say to enquirers: 'Jesus did not only die for you. He is alive! You can meet him and discover for yourself the reality we are talking about!' They did, and joined the church. And the church, born from that Easter grave, spread everywhere.

The church had three characteristics. They had a special day, Sunday. They had a special rite, baptism. They had a special meal, the Communion. And each of those three special differentia is rooted in the resurrection. Sunday, called 'the Lord's Day' in Revelation 1:10, was so named because it was the first day in the week, the day on which the Lord had risen from the tomb. Jews from time immemorial had kept Saturday special, to celebrate the completion of God's work of creation. Indeed, its observance was laid down in the ten commandments, and remains one of the distinguishing features of the Jewish people. Yet these Jews who knew that Jesus was risen reckoned, reasonably enough, that God's new creation in the resurrection of Jesus was even more memorable and significant than his act of creating the world in the first place. It is quite something to change the day of rest after thousands of years. It needed nothing less than the resurrection to trigger it off.

Then there was Christian baptism. What did it mean, as you went into the river confessing your sins and professing your faith in Jesus? What did it mean as you emerged from the waters? Simply this. That you, as a disciple, were indissolubly linked with the Lord who went down into the river of death and came up again. It was an initiation ceremony which would have been impossible without the resurrection.

It was just the same with the Holy Communion, or Lord's Supper, which they regularly celebrated. This was no memorial feast in honour of a dead hero. The bread was broken and the wine poured out to recall the cross of Jesus. But it would have been unbearable had they not been convinced that the Risen One was in their midst. That is why they broke bread with *agalliasis* (Acts 2:46), with 'exultant joy'. Death was conquered and the Conqueror himself, albeit unseen, was feasting with them at his table.

Sunday, baptism, communion: all point to the resurrection of Jesus from the grave which acted as a launch pad – the only launch pad – for the whole Christian rocket which soared into orbit about the year AD 30.

The evidence of the tomb

Everyone is agreed that the tomb of Jesus was empty on the first Easter day. Had this not been the case, the Jews or Romans could very easily have silenced the infant church as it began to preach the resurrection of Jesus. They would have disproved the claim by producing the body, and that would most conveniently have nipped the new movement in the bud. But they were not able to do this. Incidentally, the fact that they could not produce the body shows that the Jews had not moved it. Not that they would have wanted to: they were only too pleased to have got Jesus dead and buried at last. Equally the Romans did not move the body of Jesus. They, too, wanted a quiet life and were far too sensible to do anything so stupid. If by any chance they had, they would have been able to point to the correct tomb with its decomposing occupant when the disciples began, six weeks later, to disturb the peace with large open-air preaching meetings which soon led to major riots.

This really only leaves open the possibility that the disciples rifled the grave and removed the body of their Master. But is this credible? Could they have got through the guard which Matthew says was posted on the tomb to prevent precisely just such an eventuality (Matt. 27:65; 28:11–15)? And even if they could have done it, is it credible that they would? These men who were so craven that they had all deserted Jesus in his hour of need and run away: can you imagine them doing such a thing? And why should they? Their hopes were dashed by the death of their leader, and there was no expectation in Judaism that any prophet might come back from the grave – until the expected great and general resurrection at 'the last day'.

Although he had predicted it, Jesus' disciples were not expecting the resurrection. That is certain. And if they had been trying to give the impression that he had come to life again, how are we to explain the fact that none of them cracked in the face of whipping and torture and death? They were radiantly confident. They were fearless. They were willing to be imprisoned for this faith, torn limb from limb, thrown to the lions, or turned into human torches in the Emperor Nero's gardens for this conviction that Jesus was alive. Would they have endured all that for a claim they knew was fraudulent? How are we to account for the note of discovery and unselfconscious joy which pervades the pages of the New Testament, and particularly the account of the growth and spread of the church in Acts, if the whole thing is based on a fraud? No. That will not do. I am not aware of any unprejudiced person who has gone into the evidence carefully and emerged with the belief that this explanation will hold water.

Very well then, if the body of Jesus was not removed by his disciples, or his enemies, that leaves only one possibility. It is the one to which all the Gospels bear testimony. The grave of Jesus was visited early on Easter day and it was found to be empty.

Actually, not quite empty. There were the grave clothes lying there, and John in his account is clearly highly impressed by them. He and Peter had run to the tomb after Mary's message that Jesus was alive. They 'saw the linen cloths lying, and the napkin, which had been [around] his head, not lying with the linen cloths but rolled up in a place by itself' (John 20:6–8). That is what so impressed them and brought them to faith. Why? Because the wrapping seemed to them like a chrysalis case when the butterfly has emerged. The grave clothes had encircled Jesus and were interlaced with a great load of embalming spices. The head covering was a little way away, retaining its original shape surrounding the head of Jesus. But the body was gone! No wonder they were convinced and awed. No grave-robber would have been able to enact so remarkable a thing. It would never have entered his head. He would have made off with the body, complete with its clothes and valuable spices. Had Jesus merely been resuscitated, he would presumably have used the clothes, or conceivably he might have laid them aside. But as it was, all the signs pointed to Jesus having risen to a new order of life, a new sphere of existence. He left the grave clothes behind as the butterfly, emerging to a new dimension of life, leaves the cocoon behind it. That sight in the tomb on the first Easter day utterly convinced Peter and John, as well it might.

The evidence of the appearances

Not only was the tomb empty, but Jesus appeared unmistakably to a great many people after his resurrection. Paul gives a list of them in 1 Corinthians 15, a letter he wrote about twenty years after the event, when plenty of eyewitnesses were still alive. What is more, he reminds the Corinthians that there is nothing new about what he is telling them. He brought them just the same message a few years earlier, when he evangelised them (1 Cor. 15:1–8). And there was nothing new about that either. He had received it as a firm tradition when he was himself converted in the mid 30s. We have struck here some exceedingly valuable and early evidence. What does it say?

'I delivered to you as of first importance what I also received, that Christ died for our sins in accordance with the scriptures, that he was buried, that he was raised on the third day in accordance with the scriptures, and that he appeared . . .' To whom?

First in the list he mentions Peter, referring to him by his ancient Aramaic name 'Cephas'. Jesus appeared to the Peter who had denied him. Then to 'the twelve', presumably a group description omitting Judas (dead) and Thomas (absent). Then he appeared to more than five hundred 'brethren' at one time, probably in Galilee, where most of his followers lived. Most of them are still alive, Paul assured the Corinthians – as if to say, 'Go and check them out for accuracy, if you like.' Jesus then appeared to James, his brother.

He appeared to 'all the apostles', presumably including Thomas this time. He appeared also to Paul, his sworn opponent. The Gospels record additional appearances, to women in a garden, to walkers on a road, to his fishermen disciples on a lake, to a gathering in an upper room, and finally in an early morning farewell on a hilltop. Examine the diversity of those appearances, and then see if you can brand them all as sheer imagination, or hallucination maybe. Hallucinations tend to happen to individuals: here was a large group. Hallucinations tend to be found in particular types of people: here was massive emotional and psychological diversity. Hallucinations tend to be allied to wish-fulfilment: that was notable by its absence in this case. Hallucinations tend to recur: these appearances ended after forty days. Hallucinations belong to the sick world: there was nothing sick about these early preachers of good news, maintaining with conviction the 'salvation', or full health, that their risen Messiah had brought to them. There has never been a parallel to the resurrection appearances of Jesus Christ. They point as clearly to the empty tomb as the butterfly does to the chrysalis case. Nowhere else in all the religious literature of the world will you find anybody, let alone so great a diversity of people, claiming to have had intimate personal contact (even to go as far as eating fish and honeycomb) with a friend recently killed. And it will not do to suppose that these were mere subjective visions. At least one of the apostles, Paul, was used to having visions, and was very proud of them. And he was very sure that this appearance of the Risen One was no vision (1 Cor. 9:1; 2 Cor. 12:1–4). It was generically different. It was for real.

The evidence of transformation

This has always been one of the strongest demonstrations of the truth of Christ's resurrection. Those who claim to have met with him have had their lives transformed. Not completely. It is never complete in this life. But there is evidence of substantial change in every true Christian. Jesus validates his claim to resurrection power by changing people. Paul writes to the Ephesians recalling 'the immeasurable greatness of his power in us who believe', nothing less than 'the working of his great might which he accomplished in Christ when he raised him from the dead' (Eph. 1:19). And Paul ought to know. His life had been turned upside down by

Jesus of Nazareth. From being a dyed-in-the-wool opponent, he had become the most passionate advocate of the crucified Jesus – all because that same Jesus showed himself to Paul in all his risen glory on the Damascus road. Peter was changed from a coward to a man of rock, and became the centrepiece of the apostolic church. The twelve were transformed from a rabble into one of the most effective missionary organisations the world has ever seen. All the apostles, including Thomas, came from unbelief to ardent faith. This was particularly notable in the case of James and Jude: both were brothers of Jesus and were not among his disciples, but distinctly distanced from them, in the days when Jesus walked the streets of Palestine. However, after his crucifixion, we find them at the heart of the Christian community. They were convinced – because of the resurrection. In the list of witnesses of the resurrection recorded in 1 Corinthians 15, Paul in verse 7 laconically observes: 'Then he appeared to James . . .' That was what made all the difference. James became leader of the church in Jerusalem, the church which worshipped his brother as Lord and Saviour.

It might be possible to dismiss such testimony of transformation if it were confined to an era long removed. But it is not. All down history the risen Christ has been transforming the lives of those who trust him. Of course there are many hypocrites in the church: men and women who profess to know Christ but clearly do not. That is scandalous and off-putting, but it cannot invalidate the change in those who really have met him. Forgeries do not banish genuine banknotes. Of course Christians are not yet what they should be. But equally they are not what they were before they met Christ. I should be surprised if any enquirer about the faith with whom we might discuss these things cannot name several men and women of his acquaintance whose lives he knows to be changed, different from what they were – and it is all to do with Jesus. He may not be very articulate about it, but the transformed life has been a silent and powerful pointer to the resurrection of Jesus Christ. It happens all the time.

The evidence of massive testimony

It would be remarkable if one person, or even one hundred people, claimed to have encountered Jesus of Nazareth after his death in a way which drove them to the conclusion that he was still alive. It would be most arresting if one generation of mankind, or one type of person, or one nationality, made such a claim. But of course the combined testimony to the risen Christ runs into billions. They consist of every race and tribe and tongue and nationality in the world. They are not confined to any particular personality type. They stretch from the third decade of the first century to our own day at the edge of the third millennium. And despite the variety of their formulations of faith, despite their disagreement on a vast array of issues, despite their various intellectual and social backgrounds, they unite in the conviction that Jesus Christ is alive. That is the central affirmation of the Christian church throughout the world. Jesus Christ is Saviour and Lord. Saviour because of what he did upon the cross. Lord, the title associated with God the Father, because of his resurrection from the tomb to a life that will never end. That is what Christians believe, and there are some 1500 million of them on earth today, about a third of the population of the globe.

The more you think about it, the more remarkable it is. If Jesus were physically present on earth, and had had extensive media exposure, it would be no foregone conclusion that so many people would acknowledge his reality. But we are talking about a Jesus whom nobody has ever seen and yet whose invisible power has made such an impact on them that people have been constrained to conclude that he is alive. It is an impressive point to put to an enquirer. What alternative explanation would he care to offer for this remarkable phenomenon?

Indeed, one can press this point even more sharply. With any normal historical event, the testimony of witnesses tends to pale as the years go by. In subsequent generations the memory of it grows dim and nobody is going to be willing to go to the stake for its veracity. But how different with Jesus Christ. As the years and centuries have rolled by, the number of witnesses to Jesus and his resurrection, far from diminishing, has grown. That remains the case worldwide today, despite the decline in Western Europe. In many parts of the African and Asian continents the gospel is spreading faster than the birthrate. And not only is the conviction of his resurrection spreading in terms of numbers, but also, it would seem, in terms of intensity. It would be very difficult to find one person in the world today who would stake his life on the historicity of Julius Caesar. But this generation has seen more men, women and children martyred for their unshakeable faith in the risen Jesus than all the previous Christian centuries put together. There is indeed overwhelmingly massive evidence available in ordinary people the world over that Jesus Christ is alive.

The evidence of encounter

There is one way above all others that will convince me you exist: if I meet you. That is the crowning argument for the resurrection, and one towards which the Christian apologist is always seeking to lead his friends. 'He appeared also to me,' claimed Paul in 1 Corinthians 15:8. Every Christian is able to corroborate that claim. And every Christian is able to say, as Paul did later on, 'I know whom I have believed' (2 Tim. 1:12). I may not be able precisely to articulate what I have believed. I may not be sure how I am sure. But I know whom I have believed. I not only know about him. I know him. That is very different, and a whole lot more satisfying and convincing. All down the ages, from the first century until now, people have been encountering Jesus for themselves. It has made an enormous difference to their joy, their moral power, their family and work life, their hopes and fears. It still happens. It has happened to me.

It is difficult to explain the difference between a dry, intellectual faith in the resurrection, and the awesome joy of knowing the risen Lord. For it is as different as day from night. That is the cause of the joy which marks believers in Albanian prisons or on Korean prayer mountains. And the enquirer will never turn from a 'seeker' to a 'finder' until this encounter takes place. It is not difficult. He is not far from us. He is as near as a prayer; the prayer of the penitent sinner, the prayer of the humbled intellectual – 'Lord, I believe. Help my unbelief. And if you really are alive, come, make yourself known to me.' He will. He has been doing it in response to prayers like that throughout the centuries. That, no less, is the way to become sure of the resurrection of Jesus Christ. The evangelist will use some or all of those first six arguments as he talks with the enquirer (the evidence of the cross, of the church, of the tomb, of the post-resurrection appearances, of personal transformation, of massive widespread testimony). But it is when the seventh step (of personal encounter) is taken that the light begins to dawn. It is what Kierkegaard called 'the autopsy of faith'. You see for yourself. When in trust you welcome the one you have long and earnestly desired to shun, you discover to your amazement that he is indeed alive. But not till then.

THE PROBLEM OF EVIL AND SUFFERING

Why does God allow evil and suffering?

We shall often meet people who think that evil, with the suffering it brings, is an insuperable barrier to belief in a good and sovereign God. The problem can be put like this:

A God who is good and loving would not want to allow evil and suffering in his world.
A God who is all-powerful could remove evil and suffering from this world.
Therefore, if God is both good and powerful, there would be no suffering or evil in the world. But there is.
Therefore a good and powerful God does not exist.

This argument is superficially impressive. But it has one fatal flaw. The third point does not follow from the first two. There could be all sorts of reasons why God might *for a time* allow both evil and suffering in his world (especially if, as Scripture teaches, man has free will). All that we could really deduce from the first and second premises of this argument is that evil and suffering would not exist for ever if there is a good and powerful God. God would at some time deal with it and remove it from his creation.

Suppose for a moment that God were immediately to wipe out all evil. Where would we stand? Would not humanity be destroyed? For which of us is free from evil? Far from remaining an abstract intellectual problem, evil is a very pressing moral problem within each of us. *We ourselves are the problem of evil!* And if simple eradication were the answer, we would have no hope.

Or just suppose for a moment that the problem of evil and suffering in the world drives our enquirer to reject the existence of a loving God, and to imagine that some heartless monster rules our destinies, or that the stars are in charge of our fortunes, how does that help? He may have got rid of one set of problems (evil and pain) – though he still has to live with them; but he has replaced them with a much bigger one. How is he to explain the kindness, goodness, love and humanity, unselfishness and gentleness in a world that is governed by a horrible monster or by unfeeling stars?

On any showing, evil and pain constitute a massive problem for any world-view. None has an exhaustive answer. But Christianity offers a greater insight into the problem of pain and suffering than can be found anywhere else. For the Bible maintains that God our Creator is no stranger to the pain his creatures suffer.

Christianity apart, however, Buddhism comes nearest to giving a profoundly thoughtful account of the problem of evil and pain. For the whole faith of Buddhism is an attempt to answer the problem of suffering from which the young Guatama had been so carefully protected, but which hit him so profoundly when he came across it. He saw that suffering was writ large on every page of life. And when he received his enlightenment he came up with the following answer. There are four noble truths: first, all life is suffering; second, the reason for suffering is desire; third, the way to end suffering is to end desire – in Nirvana, or personal extinction; fourth, the way to mortify desire is the eightfold path of self-reduction.

I do not believe the Buddhist answer. Nirvana removes suffering but it removes the sentient self as well. The cure is worse than the disease. But I profoundly admire the way Buddhism grapples so courageously with this critical problem of suffering in the world.

Very well, how does the Christian faith attempt to make sense out of suffering? It believes that God is good, utterly good. For man at his best can be good, and God cannot be less good than his creatures. Jesus Christ is in any case the best evidence we have that God is good.

What is more, Christianity dares to maintain that God is omnipotent. He is the God of creation, the God of the atom, the maker of life. But let us not mistake the nature of omnipotence. It is not the ability to do everything (however contradictory): it is the ability to achieve purpose.

Imagine a nursery with several children playing together with bricks. One builds a tower. One knocks it down. A quarrel ensues: then a fight, resulting in a nasty accident. What is the father to do as he comes into the room and surveys the shambles? Is he to kick them out and build the brick tower himself? Is he to intervene and forcibly prevent them quarrelling ever again? Is he to beat up the ringleaders? Or is he willing to take the long haul, and see it built slowly, and with many a disaster; wrecked time and again by pride and bad blood, impatience and jealousy? And all the while he patiently teaches them to build again, showing them how to do it and how to relate co-operatively with one another. Would that not be the way of 'omnipotence'? And why might it not be so with God? Could it be that he weaves our sufferings and failings into his great purpose so that there will be no regrets when the finished article is revealed? The omnipotent one is not he who waves the magic wand to do any bizarre thing; rather, he is the one who can bring his good purposes to fruition whatever the hindrances on the way.

So let us enquire whether perhaps the love and goodness of God can be united in a theodicy which takes full account of the suffering in the world. We need to come humbly when we cry out against God. For we know so little of his working, and we are so limited in our understanding. It is as if I should walk out of a play after ten minutes and then fancy I had the right to quarrel with the whole plot. In many mystery stories we are having to grapple with real or apparent contradictions until the *dénouement* in the very last chapter. Why should it be any different with the mystery of suffering? The Bible warns us sharply against making premature judgements, and against the clay pot blaming the potter. It hints that the world is not as God made it, nor as it shall be one day, in the fullness of his purpose. It is in the process of being transformed in such a way that none of us need be ultimately dissatisfied, and none will be able to claim that God is unfair. And then God's purposes will ultimately prevail over suffering, evil and death. He has not finished his work of creating the universe yet; and pain is part of his incognito as he does so.

There are a number of considerations that may help an enquirer as he wrestles with the problem of a good God and the prevalence of pain and evil. The Bible makes it very clear that God wants the utmost good for his creatures. Suffering and pain are never the direct will of God for us. He may permit them, but he does not send them. 'He does not willingly afflict or grieve the sons of men' (Lam. 3:33). There are, however, four limitations on God's designs for our good.

The nature of our world
It is consistent. It works to regular laws, and we should be thankful that it does, or life would become impossible. But that means that if a knife will cut bread it will also cut a finger. If a shotgun kills a rabbit for our food it will also kill a man. The useful force of gravity which keeps me on this earth is not suspended for my benefit when I fall out of the window. So at least the possibility of pain is built into the very structure of the world we live in, where cause and effect prevail. This is inevitable. It is also invaluable. Pain can so often be nature's warning light. Were it not for the pain in your inflamed appendix it might well burst inside you and you could die.

The existence of Satan

You cannot make any sense of evil and suffering in the world on Christian presuppositions if you neglect the existence of this great anti-God force which the Bible calls Satan, the devil, Beelzebub and the prince of this world. The Bible is emphatic on this point, and I would have thought that there is enough evidence in our world to support that claim to the hilt. I have attempted to show good reasons which lead us to recognise the existence of Satan in my book *I Believe in Satan's Downfall*.

Not much is told us of Satan's origin. He appears to be one of God's angelic spirits which rebelled and brought other spirits with him into the opposition camp against God. He is manifestly still very much in business behind disease, hatred, war, oppression, and all the evil in the world. This is not to throw responsibility for all our failures on some supernatural force of evil. It is simply to affirm that when you have made full allowance for the evil in our own hearts and for the pressures of society around about us, you are still driven towards postulating an organising force of evil, the devil. The church has always seen that our battle is with an anti-trinity, the world, the flesh and the devil. But the Bible which asserts the reality and power of Satan is no less clear that the devil is not an equal and opposite figure to God. There is no dualism here. The devil remains 'God's devil' as Luther called him. He is on a chain, albeit a long one. His eventual destiny is destruction, but in the meantime he is out to spoil God's world in every way possible. He spoils personal life by sin, family life by discord, social life by greed and jealousy, national life by war, physical life by disease, and could ruin cosmic life by nuclear destruction. Although Jesus made it clear that individual illness is not necessarily the result of individual sin, he left us in no doubt that suffering as a whole is largely due to sin as a whole. Moreover, the devil can have a hand in disease. When Jesus healed one woman on the sabbath day, he referred to the bondage in which Satan had held her for eighteen years (Luke 13:16). And in Acts we read of the way in which Jesus 'went around doing good and healing all who were under the power of the devil' (Acts 10:38, NIV). So this is one aspect of suffering we cannot avoid taking note of. There is a devil. He is out to spoil and mar God's world in every way he can.

The fact of free will

That, too, has to be taken into account when we are wrestling with suffering and evil. For free will is a major cause of pain and evil in the world. God was constrained by his own loving nature to give us free will. You cannot love a tailor's dummy: it can't reciprocate. And God who is love cannot possibly be satisfied with creating human beings who could never respond freely to his love because they were programmed. There could be no love, no goodness, if humans ran inevitably along moral railway lines with no possibility of independence. But once grant that independence, and you have a situation where man can rebel against God just as easily as respond to his love. So human free will, necessary if we are to be human at all, allows for the possibility of human error and evil. And by far the preponderance of evil and suffering in the world is due to man's misuse of human free will. Why does God allow wars? Because men determine to fight each other. Why does he allow thalidomide babies? Because man uses his free will to market products (in pursuit of gain) before they have been fully tested. God cannot suddenly intervene to veto man's free will when man misuses it. Otherwise it would reduce us to robots, and Love cannot be satisfied with robots. The man who blames God for the mess in the world is generally pointing to things that cannot be laid at God's door at all, but are the plain result of mankind's misuse of freedom. But that does not cover all suffering. It does not explain natural evils such as hurricanes and earthquakes, for example, and there is therefore a fourth factor which we must take into account.

The interdependence of a fallen world
The world is not as God made it. It is not as he meant it to be. The Architect's plans have been scrapped by man in revolt. The story is told as early as Genesis 3, but it is always contemporary. Adam, meaning 'man', is not just a figure of long ago, the progenitor of the race; Adam is me. I, too, have chosen to rebel. And chaos results from our rebellion. This chaos affects every aspect of our rebel world. In the picturesque story of Genesis, man's disobedience results not only in his shame, his alienation from God and his fellows, and in his banishment from the goal of his ambition; but also in the disruption of nature. Man and his environment belong together, as ecology is belatedly discovering. Human evil, human rebellion, human self-centredness have affected our habitat. We are not just individuals. We are part of a common humanity, and it is a tainted stock. That is one important reason for the prevalence of evil and suffering in the world. It is not an exhaustive explan-ation, but it is illuminating. Discord, disease, rape, war, and hatred affect other people, innocent people. We are all suffering from a

disease, the 'human disease' of self-centredness, and its results are devastating.

If you care to think of it this way, the poisonous virus of wilful independence from God has invaded the bloodstream of humanity, like smallpox in the body. Once the body has contracted the disease, the actual spots will emerge at random. There is no sense in enquiring, 'Why should this spot be on my toe and not my ear?', just as there is no sense in asking, when illness or disaster strike, 'Why should this happen to me?' There is no rhyme or reason to the actual occurrence of the spots, or to the disasters in life. In both instances you have to go to the root of the disease. Suffering as a whole is linked with sin as a whole. They constitute a massive problem not merely for the intellect, but for action. What is to be done about them?

What has God done about evil and suffering?

The cross of Jesus Christ is the profound and mysterious, but wonderful, answer to this question. No other faith suggests anything remotely comparable. And from the cross four beams of light shine out into the darkness of the problem of evil and pain.

The cross shows that God is no stranger to pain and evil

God does not allow us to go through what he himself avoids. He came face to face with concentrated evil in this world when he came among us in the person of Jesus. He is the suffering God, the one whose royalty is supremely displayed in suffering and in dying. 'In all their affliction he was afflicted' (Isa. 63:9), just as a father agonises over a sick child or a teenager's wild oats. But in a much deeper way Jesus shared our agony when he came to this world and suffered and died on that terrible cross. The cross shows that he knows all about suffering. The cross shows that he has been through the worst suffering that human beings can take, and was crushed by the greatest evil that anyone has ever had to bear. And he still suffers in all the suffering of humanity. Ever since the incarnation he has remained one of us. Isn't that just like God? He did not give us an exhaustive answer to the problem of suffering: he shared it. He did not explain it: he accepted his full part in it.

The cross shows that God loves on through pain and suffering
Often people feel that the fact of their suffering is some punishment from a vengeful God who is determined to exact his pound of
flesh. The pain indicates to them that God has turned against them.
That is entirely understandable, but quite wrong. Jesus died in the
utmost agony on the cross, and yet the heavenly Father never loved
him more. It was into his Father's hand that Jesus commended his
spirit. And Peter encourages Christians to do the same (1 Pet.
4:19), for God does not leave his people unloved and desolate in
their sufferings. We may not understand the experience we are
having to endure, but the cross of Christ assures us of the undying
love of the heavenly Father.

The cross shows how God uses pain and transforms evil
Nothing was more evil than the combination of people, events and
attitudes which took Jesus Christ to the cross. He faced
monumental evil on that Good Friday, and by accepting it he
transformed it. The New Testament seems to suggest that the evil
forces which combined to bring him to that cross would not have
laughed so loud if they had known how fruitless their efforts would
prove: 'None of the rulers of this age understood this; for if they
had, they would not have crucified the Lord of glory' (1 Cor. 2:8).

Evil though suffering is, God makes good come out of it in a
number of ways. He does it in nature: think of the way the oyster
uses the irritation of grit within the shell to turn it into a pearl. He
does it in human character: think of the qualities like courage,
self-sacrifice, and endurance that would have been impossible
without it. These qualities spring only from the soil of suffering.

And God does it in the spiritual life too. Sometimes he uses pain
to *reach* us. I have met people who would never have paused to
listen to God, and would never have come to know Christ, were it
not for some tragedy that stopped them in their tracks and made
them reflect.

Sometimes God uses pain to *teach* us. 'Let God train you, for he
is doing what any loving father does for his children. Who ever
heard of a son who was never corrected? If God doesn't punish you
when you need it, as other fathers punish their sons, then it means
that you aren't really [his children] at all – that you don't really
belong in his family' (Heb. 12:7–8, Living Bible). Many of us could
affirm that. Most of the really important lessons in our lives we
have learned through the discipline of suffering.

Sometimes God uses pain to *equip* us. Paul came to realise that a terrible experience he had been through was intended by God to equip him to comfort others with the comfort by which God had comforted him (2 Cor. 1:4). The experience of suffering, of facing and dealing with evil, can equip us to help others in this world where we are all interdependent. Supremely that happened on the cross. But it happens still, and it is one of the significant ways in which God uses the pain which he permits but does not will.

Sometimes God uses pain to *draw us closer* to himself. Peter tells his readers not to be surprised at the fiery ordeal which is clearly about to come their way (perhaps literally: Christians were burned alive during the fire of Rome by an emperor seeking a scapegoat). They must not think that something strange is happening to them. After all, their Master suffered. They must suffer too. 'But rejoice in so far as you share Christ's sufferings' (1 Pet. 4:13). And Paul writes, 'Now I rejoice in my sufferings for your sake, and in my flesh I complete what is lacking in Christ's [sufferings] for the sake of his body, that is, the church' (Col. 1:24). Mysterious words, but at least they mean that suffering, willingly accepted, plunges him deeper into the suffering Christ. It is not an unmitigated disaster. It unites him more intimately with the Suffering Servant who is, of course, the supreme exemplar in all history of innocent suffering at its most unjust.

The cross shows how God triumphs over pain and evil

The cross can never be separated from the resurrection. It points steadily, at the mid-point of time, to that ultimate victory over pain at the end of all time. Because of the cross and the resurrection we can be sure that God will not ultimately be defeated by evil and suffering, and neither will his followers be. We have seen that suffering as a whole is primarily due to evil as a whole. On the cross Jesus dealt with sin and suffering at its root. He shared the suffering of his people to the full: he drained the cup of suffering to the dregs, and it failed to poison him or make him distrust his heavenly Father.

But not only did he share the suffering *with* man; he took responsibility for the evil in the world *for* man. He fought Satan and won. He bore the sin and drew the Dragon's teeth, presaging his ultimate victory at the end of time. Good Friday was followed by Easter day. Suffering and evil, if this world were all there is, would be inexplicable and unjustifiable. But this world is not all there is. It is the ante-room of heaven, 'the vale of soul-making', as Keats once called it. The evil we face and the pain we suffer can be turned into the gold of character if we take them right. What is sown in tears will be reaped in joy. It was so for Jesus. It will be so for his beleaguered and suffering followers. If we suffer with him, we shall also reign with him, Paul assures us (2 Tim. 2:12). No tears fall unnoticed on the ground of Calvary.

That is what enables Paul, who certainly had more than his fair share of suffering, to exult so joyously in Romans 8. With, so to speak, his feet in the stocks and his head in heaven, he writes this personal confession about the problem of pain, or, as he would have put it, the privilege of suffering:

> Since we are his children, we will share his treasures – for all God gives to his Son Jesus is now ours too. But if we are to share his glory, we must also share his suffering. Yet what we suffer now is nothing compared to the glory he will give us later. For all creation is waiting patiently and hopefully for that future day when God will resurrect his children. For on that day thorns and thistles, sin, death and decay – the things that overcame the world against its will at God's command – will all disappear, and the world around us will share in the glorious freedom from sin which God's children enjoy.
>
> For we know that even the things of nature, like animals and plants, suffer in sickness and death . . . as they await this great event. And even we Christians, although we have the Holy Spirit within us as a foretaste of future glory, also groan to be released from pain and suffering. We, too, wait anxiously for that day when God will give us our full rights as his children, including the new bodies he has promised us – bodies that will never be sick and will never die. (Rom. 8:17–23, Living Bible)

Exaggeration? Pie in the sky? Not so. Paul looks steadily at the cross and resurrection of Jesus, and in them he sees the certain ground of hope for the future and final answer to the problem of pain and suffering.

We moderns do not see that answer nearly so clearly as Paul did. We have lost faith in ultimate meaning. We have, as we have had occasion to observe several times in this book, ceased to think teleologically: we have given up thinking that the world as such has any meaning. And therefore we do not see suffering as a means of purification but as the ultimate obscenity which refuses to fit into our analytical explanations.

We have also been beguiled by a false view of the supreme good. Almost all the ages of mankind have seen this as virtue, being good. But we see it as happiness, or feeling good. On the former view suffering was a necessary part of being good, and therefore it was tolerable. But on the modern view, suffering has no place in feeling good: so we excoriate it.

We moderns have forgotten human solidarity, especially in the West. We glory in our individualism and autonomy. And suffering comes to remind us sharply that there are no exemptions from the school of pain. It comes to all of us alike in our common humanity. And it tells us in no uncertain terms that we are frail human beings and not autonomous at all.

We have trivialised sin in this twentieth century. We have explained it away in terms of heredity, environment, mental imbalance, psychological disorder, and the like. We have chosen to reject the link which all previous generations have seen more clearly than ourselves – the link between justice and penalty, between sin and suffering. And this is one reason why we find it such an offence to our hedonistic lifestyles.

And we are earthbound. If the Victorians made too much of heaven and hell, we make far too little. We live as if this earth is all there is. What if we are wrong? Having ceased to believe in life after death, we are not making a very impressive showing at living life before death. We have no long-term perspective on this problem of suffering. We fail to see it in the light of eternity. And so we cannot hope to understand it.

Most of all, we are blind to the cross and resurrection of Jesus, the God-man. It is there we see the heart of the suffering God. It is there we see the hope of suffering mankind. Nowhere else will the enquirer find so profound an insight into the twin mysteries of suffering and evil. Nowhere else will he find a key which opens their doors: but only at the cross of Christ. The cross is the key.

FURTHER READING

You may find the following books useful as a starting-point for further reading.

At a popular level

Michael Green, *The Day Death Died* (Inter-Varsity Press)
Val Grieve, *Your Verdict* (Inter-Varsity Press)

C. S. Lewis, *Miracles* (Collins Fount)
C. S. Lewis, *The Problem of Pain* (Collins Fount)
C. S. Lewis, *A Grief Observed* (Collins Fount)
C. S. Lewis, *God in the Dock: Essays on Theology and Ethics* (Eerdmans)
Frank Morison, *Who Moved the Stone?* (Faber & Faber)
Sheldon Vanauken, *A Severe Mercy* (Hodder & Stoughton)

At a more advanced level

J. N. D. Anderson, *A Lawyer Among the Theologians* (Hodder & Stoughton)
David Cook, *Thinking About Faith* (Inter-Varsity Press)
C. Stephen Evans, *The Quest for Faith* (Inter-Varsity Press)
Antony Flew, *Hume's Philosophy of Belief* (Routledge)
Michael Green, *The Empty Cross of Jesus* (Hodder & Stoughton)
Peter Kreeft, *Making Sense Out of Suffering* (Hodder & Stoughton)
H. D. Lewis, *Philosophy of Religion* (Hodder & Stoughton)
Jürgen Moltmann, *Theology of Hope* (SCM Press)
Jürgen Moltmann, *The Crucified God* (SCM Press)
C. F. D. Moule (ed.), *The Significance of the Message of the Resurrection for Faith in Jesus Christ* (SCM Press)
A. Plantinga and N. Wolterstorff (eds), *Faith and Rationality* (Notre Dame)
I. T. Ramsey, *Miracles* (Oxford University Press)
Alan Richardson, *Christian Apologetics* (SCM Press)
Andrew Walker (ed.), *Different Gospels* (Hodder & Stoughton)
John Wenham, *Easter Enigma* (Paternoster Press)

8

Reaching the Reasons of the Heart

'The heart has its reasons,' said Pascal. They are very powerful, the more so when they remain unacknowledged. It is important to consider them, albeit briefly, before we leave this area of the intellectual climate of our day. For they often underlie an enormous amount of the resistance to the gospel of Jesus Christ that we encounter.

THE IMPACT OF THE ENLIGHTENMENT

We drew attention in chapter 5 to Lesslie Newbigin's shrewd book *Foolishness to the Greeks*. His is just one of the many modern studies which draw attention to the massive shifts taking place in what is being called 'postmodern society'. The process has been perceptively examined by men like Peter Berger, David Lyon, Bryan Wilson and Os Guinness.

The present era is a fascinating and yet confusing time in the history of the world. The consensus which held sway among most thinking people until the Enlightenment has dissolved into a myriad strands. Now 'pluralisation' holds the floor. For the past two centuries the gospel has been growing increasingly alien to Western man. It all began when human self-sufficiency removed God from the centre of the universe, a process which can be traced back to the Enlightenment, and indeed to the Renaissance. 'Glory to God in the highest' gave way to 'Glory to man in the highest.' No longer must we think of our destiny as to know God and enjoy him for ever. This world is all there is; this life is all we have. No longer should explanations be given in terms of purpose, as if this world had a grand Designer. They should be in terms of causation and origin. No longer are there objective standards of right and wrong, no longer any true religion. Pluralism in religion and in ethics has become the order of the day. Choice has been multiplied in a society which has outgrown its rural and feudal roots and become increasingly urbanised and industrialised. Liberated now from divine supervision, we are autonomous: we are men come of age. It is up to us to decide whom we will talk to, where we will live, what we will do or think, value or believe.

Nevertheless, this freedom to choose which marks the pluralism of the modern world has strict limits. It exists only in the private domain, not in the market-place. A sharp dichotomy has developed between the public world of scientifically verifiable facts which are value-free, and the private world of home and family, relaxation and interests, where values are all-important. The latter are considered to be a matter of preference. Anything goes, so long as it does not interfere with other people. In a word, pluralism reigns in the area of personal values.

In the public arena, however, it is a very different story. This is the world of hard facts, of commerce and bureaucracy, a world which has been enormously advanced through science and technology. Now science is inductive in its method of enquiry. It depends on three factors: accurate observation, the uniformity of nature, and the link between cause and effect. Science sees no need for God in this procedure. It has abandoned teleology, the exploration of purpose in the world. It is concerned, rather, with what a thing is composed of or how it originated. To modern secular man, natural law has replaced divine purpose. Purpose is strictly irrelevant to scientific enquiry. And since science has made the modern world what it is, and has no need of recourse to purpose, most people have ceased to ask ultimate questions about the purpose of life or the destiny of man. These, along with any talk of God, are thought to be an intrusion in the market-place. They are matters of opinion, and belong, if at all, to the private domain, the value-laden sphere of life.

The virtual banishing of values from the public sector has had serious consequences for our society. It means that scientists can pursue 'pure research' without feeling any responsibility for how the results of that research may be used. The creation of a nuclear bomb can be justified as a triumph in physics without any consideration of its power to destroy the very world we live in. Our worship of the GNP can be pursued in the name of progress without considering what it will do to the Two-Thirds World, or to our rivers, our forests and our atmosphere.

It is imperative to bring values back into the public domain. They are an essential complement to scientific advance and technological development. But what values? There is no agreement. Who, for example, has the rights to Canadian land? The whites who have taken and developed it, or the dispossessed Indians who have been marginalised and are now waking up to the full extent of their loss? We shall not long survive if we do not address ourselves to the purpose for which the world and human life exist. It is rather ironic that many scientists who unashamedly pursue their research projects with dedicated purpose should deny that the purpose of life itself is a proper subject for enquiry! Instead, modern Westerners have ceased to ask ultimate questions and have been turning increasingly towards the religions of the East. These appear congenial, for they too are not oriented towards purpose, and do not believe that the world is going anywhere.

Science has brought us immeasurable benefits. But it has had negative results as well. It has been largely responsible for the growth of a generation which is very suspicious of the reality of anything that cannot be measured or touched. Enriched as we are by comforts which our forefathers could not have dreamed of, we have succumbed to the delusion that material well-being is all that matters. The results have been catastrophic. They are apparent in the destruction of our environment, the collapse of the family, the trivialising of sexual relations, and the emptiness of belief and purpose which mark our society.

Moreover, modern secularism has replaced the notion of God's sovereignty with that of 'the rights of man'. When people still recognised that God was on his throne, and was the source of the world and all the people that were in it, human beings naturally enjoyed a place of high dignity. They were the crown of God's creation. They were the regents in his universe, who owed him the obedience of responsible stewards. But when God was dethroned – what then? It was then that we began to hear strident claims being made for 'the rights of man'. Since the eighteenth century they have become more and more prominent, numerous and difficult to weigh. Indeed, if there is no God, and man is simply a material phenomenon upon the face of the globe, it is hard to see on what grounds one could maintain that he has any inalienable rights at all. However, an increasing galaxy of natural rights are being claimed these days: the right to life, the right to abort unwanted foetuses, the rights of surrogate parents, of sexual preference and the like. No longer do we think in terms of the mutual relationships of giving and receiving in the human family of which God is the head. Now it is everyone for himself, pursuing his private goals in a world that is basically purposeless. And let the devil take the hindmost.

A SCHIZOID SOCIETY

The effect of the Enlightenment is hard to exaggerate. It has permeated every level of society. It is part of the air we breathe. And it produces very schizoid people.

We are all caught up in the sharp divide between the public world of 'facts' and the private world of 'values'. We are convinced that God is an implausible hypothesis, and yet we have a God-shaped void in our hearts. We are clear that there is no ultimate purpose to life or to the universe, and yet we act as if there was. We are persuaded that all values are relative, and yet we passionately believe in our own: we cannot bring ourselves to believe that they are valid only for ourselves. The notion of absoluteness which we deny with our minds nevertheless refuses to be banished from our subconscious. Never has the world so needed its citizens to pull together, and yet individualism is not only endemic to us all: it is on the increase.

In the light of these tensions so characteristic of the modern world, is it surprising that the heart has its reasons? People are torn. They have been injured by their experiences of life. Often as infants and children they have been abused by others who have been pursuing their own selfish aims. They are lonely and confused. They are able to manage their public performance, but are sadly adrift in their personal lives. They publicly acknowledge one level of acceptable morality for society at large, but in fact practise a very different one. They talk about freedom, but are trapped in bondage to habits they cannot break. They subordinate everything to making money, to enjoying sexual licence, or to achieving power. But there is ultimately no point to any of it, and they know it. Death will take us all, sooner or later. We come from nothing, and we go out like a light. What is it all in aid of?

To suppose, therefore, that the difficulties people have with the Christian faith are primarily intellectual is very naive. That would be to surrender to the very rationalism which has been wreaking increasing havoc in society. Reason is absolutely necessary, but absolutely inadequate. We do not live by reason alone. Our emotions and our will are every bit as significant as our mind. One of the main reasons for the decline of optimistic humanism lies in the discoveries of Jung and Freud that we are profoundly influenced by emotional and volitional factors of which we have no rational knowledge but which nevertheless govern our actions.

It would, therefore, be the height of folly to attempt the task of evangelism without paying careful attention to these non-rational elements in the great divorce between God and modern man. It is sad that evangelists in general, particularly the more thoughtful of them, have tended to be weak in diagnosis at this point. Evangelical Christians often argue the existence of God, the deity and humanity of Jesus, and the truth of the resurrection as if these were premises from which one could logically and inexorably proceed to a conclusion. Jesus rose from the dead: *ergo*, commit your life to him! I recall being asked to help in the case of an undergraduate whom some Christians had been seeking with great enthusiasm and reasoning to bring to Christ. They had given a strong defence of the resurrection. And their friend, influenced as he was by existentialism, had replied to this effect: 'Right, I am convinced. Jesus Christ did rise from the dead. But so what?' Evangelical rationalism had rebounded on those who had relied on it. As a matter of fact that young man did come to Christ, but only when the clamant reasons of his heart had been addressed.

We are, in general, very cautious about getting involved in the emotional life of somebody else, especially in evangelism. Let us stick to the intellect. It is straightforward. Emotions are complex, we feel, and usually messy. They will demand of us time and a level of commitment we shrink from offering. And so we steer clear. As a result modern men and women can be forgiven for thinking that Christianity is more an intellectual stance than a love relationship with the Jesus who touches our hearts and lives, not merely our minds. I received a letter this week which expresses that very contemporary longing for the feelings to be met, for the emotions to be touched, for the life to be changed:

> I must ask you this. Is your relationship with Jesus one of belief alone, or do you experience the bliss of union with God? The old saints talked of raptures, ecstasies, flights of the spirit – experiences which I also claim. Direct communion and union makes a mystic what he is – the Son of God!

Do you share this ecstasy, or is yours an intellectual conviction? To me it makes no sense to be intellectually convinced, without experience. My whole pathway involves more and more openness with God, experienced as bliss and effortless love flowing. I met with so many who do not have this connection and yet they can quote scriptures and fulfil church expectations. This is really the big issue in a person's life – is it real or is it pretend? Is your God-hunger satisfied?

That seems to me to be a marvellously honest cry from a very modern heart, a person who has drunk the waters of the New Age movement, has looked East, and has had a mystical experience. It saddens me greatly that Christians can ever give the impression that their faith is merely a matter of church-going, correct belief, or intellectual conviction. How tragic, and how empty! It is very significant that in the eighteenth century, when scepticism was as rife as it is now, it was not the painstaking orthodoxy of Bishop Butler's refutation of deism, but the passionate, heart-directed evangelism of Wesley and Whitefield that changed the face of England within one generation. But that passion has cooled. It has been codified. We have almost made an object of the gospel and thrown it at the people. Nobody has been more guilty of this than those of us who are evangelicals. We are the modern scribes and Pharisees. We have boxed the living Jesus in with intellectualism and legalism. We have objectified the gospel and made it into a series of steps to be taken, a number of things to be believed, rather than the liberating, joyful, life-transforming friendship with the radical Jesus. And one of the ways we have done it is by succumbing to this rationalism which has neglected the deeper reasons of the heart and has concentrated on trying to argue about the faith. To our shame, it is the evangelicals, who rightly protest at the ravages of the Enlightenment, who are among the most obvious children of the Enlightenment.

A MAN FOR ALL SEASONS

When we stop to think of Jesus, the Jesus we profess to love and follow, the differences between the modern evangelist and the Master are so great as to make us wonder if we are on the same team. It is hardly an exaggeration to say that our understanding of truth has been propositional. But his understanding was personal.

This emphasis on personal integrity and character is one of the great marks of truth as seen in the Old Testament, where truth, *emeth*, is already preparing us for the declaration, 'I am the Truth.' But we are bound into the classical mindset so clearly displayed by Pontius Pilate in his question, '*What* is truth?' The truth stood in front of him, and he could not see it. He was simply incapable of taking in the fact that final truth is not a matter of propositions but a quality of life. And it is here that we are so unlike Jesus. Our mindset has been that of Pilate. We have assumed that truth consists in doctrinal statements which can be packaged and need to be disseminated. Not so Jesus.

Jesus revelled in creation, the good creation of his heavenly Father. We Christians have not been notable for our care about the environment. The Green movement has not been led by Christians. We have so concentrated on redemption that we have failed to understand or revel in creation. The results are catastrophic: a false other-worldliness, a suspicion of the arts, a dichotomy between 'ordinary jobs' and 'full-time service', and acquiescence through a conspiracy of silence in the rape of the earth. We are only now beginning to repent of this attitude. But our repentance may yet prove to have begun too late. If any people ever had the chance to understand the interdependence of man and nature, the balance between mankind's headship over creation and his servanthood and stewardship to God, then it was those who professed the Christian faith and lived by the Christian Bible. But we have failed.

Jesus was such a happy man. True, he was at times 'a man of sorrows and acquainted with grief', especially as the cross drew near. But the prevailing impact he makes in the Gospels is one of life and love and joy. That is what drew people so irresistibly to him. Joy is infectious. It has been well said that Christianity is more often caught than taught. But by our rationalism and formalism, by the absence of radiant and carefree celebration in our ranks, we have not had that magnetic impact which Jesus undoubtedly possessed. We have hidden him in doctrine and in churchianity. If people saw deep, unselfish joy in us Christians, they would be predisposed to listen when we explained where that joy comes from.

Jesus had profound empathy with people in their feelings. He wept at the tomb of Lazarus. We read that he was filled with compassion (literally 'he was moved in his guts') at the sight of helpless, purposeless people, lost and unaware of where they were heading. He felt so much for the lepers that he did the unthinkable, and touched them. He felt for that rich young ruler who loved his money more than Jesus. He really loved him. Jesus did not keep his feelings under lock and key. His empathy drew people to him. They felt that here was someone who cared, someone who understood. But, alas, that is not the universal impression of the Christian church or the Christian evangelist. The church is too formal, too busy with its programmes, to bother about the feelings and heart-cries of ordinary people. The evangelist is too preoccupied with his message, his delivery, his impact, to bother too much about the individual. If he does, in a 'time of ministry' after he has issued his challenge, that time will probably be short and perfunctory. We have ceased to feel the heartbeat of hurting people. We have ceased to care. At least, that is the impression we have managed to give. No wonder evangelism does not seem to be the sharing of good news, but the quest for new members.

Jesus was a secular person. He did not keep himself in splendid separation from the defilements of secular society. He knew where the prostitutes and the soldiers, the tax-gatherers and the poorest of the poor were to be found. And he got among them. He completely fulfilled the ideal he taught of being 'in the world, yet not of the world'. People did not feel that he was talking down to them or manifesting superiority. They were drawn by his naturalness, his integrity, his unshockability, his friendliness, his holiness. For true holiness is the greatest magnet of all. And we? We tend to keep our evangelism for church, if we do it at all. We talk of God in church, but rarely outside. We move in church circles, and simply do not know where or how to get among the vast numbers of utterly unchurched people around us. Our churches have many programmes for members, but little that the man in the street can identify with. An invisible wall separates the church from society. We are not, in the best sense of the word, secular people. Yet if the incarnation means anything to us, it should have spelled the collapse of any dividing wall between the secular and the sacred.

Jesus was a caring person. It was not all talk and no action. Preaching and acts of compassion and power went hand in hand in his ministry. He healed broken people. He liberated demonised people. He met lonely people. On occasion, he raised dead people back to life again. Practical caring is not always associated with Christian evangelism. We are perceived to be people who have something to say, maybe, but who do not do anything. There is a marvellous article in V. Samuel and A. Hauser (eds), *Proclaiming Christ in Christ's Way* by the professor of evangelism at Fuller

Seminary, Bill Pannell, in which he stresses the need not only for a Billy Graham but for a Martin Luther King in evangelism. The latter would not see the garbage heaps in Manila as merely a pressing incentive to preach the gospel:

> He could tell us about garbage and garbage workers. He could make the connection between the dump and politics. He could show us the connections between poverty in Manila and racism in Washington D.C. He could remind us that there is a difference between righteousness and relief, between preaching and martyrdom. He could demonstrate that you can see the promised land from a garbage heap much better than from a cathedral, or a well furnished hotel down-town. Christians who act in solidarity with the denizens of garbage dumps get themselves shot. Hardly anyone shoots evangelists any more, as long as they stick to the simple gospel, anyway.

Jesus was a community person. The community of the three close followers, the community of the twelve, of the seventy . . . You find him in homes as diverse as those of Lazarus, Martha and Mary on the one hand, and Jairus on the other – with Zacchaeus and Simon the Pharisee thrown in for good measure. You find him with the crowds. You find him founding a new community, bound together by a new covenant. He was the very antithesis of individualism. And yet, supreme irony, his Western followers are shameless individualists. So individualist that many of us treat church as an optional extra. So individualist that meeting in a home for Christian fellowship of an informal nature, or even greeting one another with a handshake or embrace in church, are seen as a threat. So individualist that we sit as far apart from one another as we can when we gather for worship. And on top of it all, we are split up into endless – and proliferating – denominations. And yet we are the people whom God has chosen to show to the world a foretaste of heaven, a pattern of his new society! Is not this almost total lack of Christian solidarity why trade unions have largely separated themselves from their Christian roots? Is this not why Marxism is more appealing to the poor of the world than Christianity? Is this solidarity not what binds Muslims together into such a formidable force while Christians have so little to show in terms of fellowship and unity? Evangelism will not be effective unless it springs from community, and draws people into community: a community which is warm, accepting, unjudging and supportive. That will touch people at a level reason alone cannot reach.

And finally, Jesus was a passionately committed person. He

came proclaiming and embodying the Kingdom of God. All he did, all he said, was directed towards extending its boundaries. There was nothing impatient about his manner, nothing brash about his insistence, nothing insensitive about his relationships. But it was impossible to mistake the purpose of his life, and the joy and conviction he had in sharing it. That is not the impression which generally emerges from contemporary Christian circles. But when it is present, it speaks. It is so real, so authentic, that it cuts through arguments and excuses. It is very attractive. In a grey world, people long for sunshine; and when they see it shining brightly and unashamedly in another person's life, they are drawn to enquire about it. Evangelism then becomes easy.

A CURE FOR ALL HURTS

In the light of the attractiveness of Jesus, it is hardly surprising that men and women flocked to him. Jesus was surrounded by crowds, presumably because they felt that in some way he held the key to community: he was a wonderful person to be with. Jesus met and transformed the loneliness of Zacchaeus, a man whose relationships had become frozen because of his pursuit of money and his ruthlessness in dealing with people. Jesus met and transformed the woman taken in adultery: unlike the religious leaders, he neither sought her out in her sin nor condemned her when she was brought before him. He understood her. He cared about her. He knew the hurt she had suffered and the guilt she felt. It was not condemnation she needed, but acquittal. He offered her just that, together with the pointer towards a better life, and the power to achieve it. Jesus met and transformed the impetuous Peter, making this mercurial man, dominated by his emotions, into a stable leader of Christ's new community, a rock on which he could build. Jesus met and transformed John the dreamer, making him a mystic and a visionary who became the apostle of love. Jesus met and transformed the household of Jairus in its disappointment, its grief and bereavement. He met and transformed beggars like Bartimaeus, prostitutes like Mary Magdalene, crooked businessmen like Matthew. In every case his approach was tailored to the individual. In every case he entered into the need and the hurt which had marred that person's life, and spoke his word of healing and renewal.

And that is the heart of effective evangelism. Not many people are brought to Christ via the route of the intellect, though some are. Vital though the intellect is, most people are won when they sense Christ coming to touch broken places and torn feelings in their lives. This may be at a point of perceived, long-standing need. Or it may be that only when some aspect of Jesus is seen does the person recognise how empty or needy he has been all along.

A great many people today have never experienced love without strings attached. They have been appreciated when they have performed in a certain way, or made certain achievements. But they have known nothing of being loved for themselves, warts and all, alike in success and in failure. The unconditional love of Jesus for all and sundry can surge like a flood into a heart like that.

A great many people have a tremendously low self-image. It has been inculcated in them by parents who have dominated them and have failed to praise and love them: instead, a critical attitude has surrounded their childhood and youth. They have been made to feel no good. And this happens to people who are great achievers just as much as it does to poor achievers. External accomplishments tell us nothing about the inner feelings of the person concerned. It is when people who feel so inadequate and unimportant see that Jesus rates them very differently that the skies begin to clear. If he valued them so highly that he came for them and died for them – why, they must be something very special after all! And that realisation brings new life to many who are dogged by this spectre of a low self-image.

A great many people have been abused in their childhood. It is becoming increasingly plain in our supposedly civilised culture that enormous numbers of youngsters are abused verbally, physically and sexually by the very people who should be their most ardent protectors, their parents. Is it any wonder that we are witnessing such a rise of counselling services in our society? It is to respond to the crying need from so many broken people, broken when they were too young to understand what was happening, but not too young to be scarred and crippled by it. Logic and argument will not help such a person towards Christ. But once they sense that Jesus not only cares but can take the pus out of those wounds, through what he did on Calvary and the power of his indwelling Spirit, then something very profound happens: there is a new creation.

A great many people are lonely. It matters not one whit whether they have many friends or few, whether they are the fortunate in society or at the bottom of the pile. 'Why am I so lonely when there are so many people here?', a plea scratched on a school desk, is the agonising question of many hearts. The answer, of course, lies in the friend who sticks closer than a brother, the one who will never leave us nor forsake us once he is welcomed into our life. That companionship of Jesus, risen from the dead, alive for evermore, is the ultimate answer to loneliness. Millions the world over have proved its staying-power: be they politicians at the centre of the action, invalids on their beds, or believers incarcerated in solitary confinement. It will be the image of Jesus the friend which attracts such people. They do not need to know the evidence for the resurrection. They need to see in other lives, and wonderingly to accept for themselves, the possibility that this living Jesus would be willing to accompany them personally.

A great many people feel despised. Maybe they sense they are despised by others (for their looks, their achievements, their station in life). Maybe they despise and even hate themselves. When they come to see the Jesus who loves the unlovely, who despises nobody, who was himself despised and rejected and understands their situation from the inside, then gradually their defences go down and they dare to believe the almost incredible, that he accepts them though they feel themselves to be totally unacceptable. And what is that but the New Testament doctrine of justification? But the truth of doctrine needs to be mediated through the reality of feelings. Only when they feel it, perhaps through the loving service of a friend, can they come to believe it and experience it for themselves.

A great many people feel defeated. Defeated by habits too strong to break, defeated by the past catching up with them, defeated by inherited defects in character. They had imagined that Christianity was for good people, who dressed nicely and went to church on Sundays, not for the likes of them. God forgive us that such an impression could ever have got abroad, but it has. They need to see that Jesus takes failures and makes them saints. They may see it in the reclaimed lives of some of their friends and acquaintances. They may become assured of it in the loving perseverance of the person who is trying to bring the good news to them – often in the face of their own opposition and acrimony. But it is when they feel within themselves that Jesus is willing to take failures like themselves on board that new hope is born, and new life begun.

I hope enough has been said to show that what really matters is that the healing hand of the great physician should be brought gently into touch with the emotions as well as with the mind of the person concerned. A great deal of our evangelism is a total failure because it does not touch the heart and show where the Saviour can reach the hidden fears and hurts which plague us human beings – all of us.

How, then, is the heart reached, and its deep reasons addressed? There is of course no single answer to that question.

REACHING THE HEART

Often people are touched by the testimony of a friend. They expect ministers to talk about God, but they do not expect their friends to do so. And they certainly do not expect to hear a close friend claim a living and personal relationship with the God who to them seems so very distant. You can argue against an intellectual position. You cannot argue against testimony. If someone assures you from their own experience of the difference Christ makes, you can only believe them or disbelieve them. Testimony produces an existential challenge which argument cannot, and which often helps a friend to commitment.

Sometimes it is worship that achieves the breakthrough. When someone who has successfully barricaded his life against God's advances is brought into contact with a church where people are genuinely lost in wonder, love and praise of the living God, it can have the most dynamic impact. Equally, it can happen when such a person ventures into a monastery or abbey and is touched by the worship, holiness and lifestyle of the monks or nuns. The same thing can happen when a rebellious teenager breaks into his parents' room only to find them on their knees in prayer. These things are eloquent. Sometimes it is just going into a building where prayer has been made for generations that does it. But worship is the highest activity of which human beings are capable, and often it draws the observer in the same direction, however hard he or she strives to evade the magnetism.

Sometimes it is through friendship that the love of Christ breaks through. The experience of a friendship which accepts you in all circumstances is very wonderful if you have been let down often in the past, or injured because people valued you simply for what they could get from you. Real friendship touches the areas of loneliness and self-distrust which plague so many people beneath their surface poise.

Sometimes it is the way a Christian believer handles fear or the approach of death which touches the observer. He wonders, 'How would I handle this situation if I were in his shoes?' It was the peace and poise of the Moravian missionaries sailing with John Wesley to evangelise America that so struck him and made him realise how little he knew of that peace in his own heart, and how intellectual was his perception of the gospel which to them was a medicine for the heart as well as for the mind. And many have been brought to faith by watching a loved one die, full of joy and faith in God. On the whole, the claim is justified: 'Our people die well.'

Sometimes it is the fact of reconciliation which strikes deep into the heart of other people. When you see a murderer and the wife of his victim journeying to another country to spread the gospel (as happened with Elizabeth Elliot and the Auca tribesman who speared her missionary husband to death), you sit up and take notice. When children see their parents, whose marriage had been torn apart by bitterness and hatred, reconciled through their surrender to Christ and recommitment to each other, they cannot but be impressed. These things happen. They draw people to Christ. But they do not travel by the route of the intellect. They address the reasons of the heart.

Perhaps the bottom line is to return to the Renaissance. It was there that God was dethroned and man was deified. It was there that individualism was born. When God is dethroned, and individualism becomes supreme, purpose dissipates and values become relative. An individual's purpose and values become a matter of private choice, and have nothing to do with the public world of facts; hence that disastrous dualism which we are witnessing today. If modern unbelieving man, the child of the Renaissance and of the Enlightenment, is to be attracted back to the gospel which is his despised heritage, it must surely be through God being brought right into the centre of the picture by those who claim to follow him. It is only as God is made central in the lives of the church at large, and individual Christians in particular, that members of a cynical, materialistic and disenchanted culture will be challenged to reconsider the gospel they have jettisoned. This may seem simplistic, but I believe it to be fundamental. Only a church, only individual Christians who genuinely put God in the centre of the whole of life, will be able to have a lasting impact for him. People are sceptical about words and propaganda. They have not been treated to a great deal of holiness in the Western church in recent years. When they see God-centred lives, reaching out to them in love, they will feel the reasons of their hearts being addressed. It will no longer be a matter of talk, but of relationship.

CONCLUSION

That last point is an important one to remember as we move on to look at various ways in which modern men and women in a predominantly post-Christian culture can be brought face to face once again with Jesus Christ. We must be clear what we mean by evangelism (as we saw in Part One), be clear about its propriety, and be part of a church which embodies what it proclaims. We must also, as we have seen in Part Two, seek to wrestle with the genuine and massive intellectual problems which modern people find in the Christian claim. We can never argue anyone into the Kingdom of God: but we are called to give as good a reason as we can for the faith which is within us. However, we must never forget that the heart, as well as the mind, has its reasons. Rejection of the Christian faith may not be due primarily to intellectual stumbling-blocks, even when these are presented as the cause of unbelief. It may be due to very different reasons, often heavily concealed. We must never forget that the heart is a rebel: that although men know perfectly well that God exists they do not thank him or glorify him or want to know him. As a result, hearts become dark, and reasonings futile. It is natural for mankind to erect all manner of idols in the place which God has the right to occupy. It is natural for mankind to be sceptical about God, and to prefer any and every alternative. Three times in the terrible passage in which Paul reflects on these things in Romans 1:18–32 he says, 'Therefore God gave them up' (vv.24, 26, 28), gave them up to every kind of wickedness, evil, greed and depravity. Mankind gets what it chooses. And the evil and wickedness we cherish hurts us. Human beings are both prone to do evil and are crippled by the hurt which results from evil done to them. Therefore, if we wish to reach them with the good news of a comprehensive Saviour, we must remember that there are three sides to the transformation which Christ longs to bring us in our brokenness. They concern the intellectual, the emotional and the conative aspects of our personality. The gospel has to satisfy the enquiries of the intellect, to be sure: God is beyond reason, but he does not ask us to accept the unreasonable. But the gospel must go deeper than the reason. It must address the hurts and needs of our injured personalities: it must touch us where we have been wounded, and bring Christ's unique healing with the touch. And we must never forget, either, that we possess the priceless gift of freedom. We are able to make choices. We will be held accountable for them. Choosing is one of the most God-like aspects of humanity. Evangelism, accordingly, addresses not only the mind and the emotions, but the will.

FURTHER READING

Peter Berger, *The Heretical Imperative* (Doubleday Anchor)
Peter Berger, *The Sacred Canopy* (Doubleday Anchor)
Anthony Campolo, *A Reasonable Faith: Responding to Secularism* (Word)
Jacques Ellul, *The New Demons* (Seabury Press)
Os Guinness, *The Gravedigger File* (Hodder & Stoughton)
David Lyon, *The Steeple's Shadow* (SPCK)
Lesslie Newbigin, *Foolishness to the Greeks* (SPCK)
Bryan Wilson, *Religion in Secular Society* (Oxford University Press)

PART THREE

CHURCH-BASED EVANGELISM

9

Preaching for a Verdict

I have devoted the last four chapters to apologetics because it is both important and neglected. The Christian faith rests on solid foundations, and we really need to know and be able to show others the strength of those foundations before we have the right to invite them to build the house of their lives on Christ. But apologetics alone will never win anyone to Christ. It will clear away all manner of rubbish which is in his way, keeping him immobilised in unbelief. But it will not by itself get him moving towards Christ. That requires evangelism. And in the latter part of this book we shall examine some of the ways in which a local church can engage in evangelism. By far the most widespread and commonly used form of evangelism in a local church is, and is likely to remain, the evangelistic sermon on the special occasion.

There is good sense in this. The early Christians made their greatest impact around the fringe of the synagogue. And all our churches have a fringe. The people who come three times a year on cultic or civic occasions. The spouses of members of the church who have no faith themselves. There is great hope that these people can be reached. They already have some link with the church. It is not entirely unfamiliar territory. It is not a major obstacle for them to enter the building – as increasingly it is for many others. These fringe people are the folk most likely to be helped by a straightforward evangelistic address in church. Of course, plenty of people will not be seen dead near the church, and so we shall have to devise other ways of reaching them (see chapter 12). But right now we are considering how to preach for a decision in church. Let us ask, and try to answer, a number of questions on this vexed matter of evangelistic preaching.

IS PREACHING IMPORTANT?

That is a fair question in a television age where word and picture always go together. And on television you will rarely find one person speaking uninterrupted for half an hour. Should we even contemplate doing such a thing in church? And in any case, the very assumption behind preaching is authoritarian. Should we not have discussions instead? One person's view about the subject of God is obviously as good as another's. Preaching is an archaic survival from a previous age.

You will have heard all those objections and others like them. Yet preaching *is* important, for at least three reasons. For one thing, God is the supreme communicator. Indeed, he is communication. That is part of what the doctrine of the Trinity means. But quite apart from his internal relations within the Godhead, he communicates with mankind. The heavens are not unfeeling and brazen. The universe is not silent. God has spoken. And down the ages he has used men and women to be his messengers. He did it through the prophets of Israel. He did it through the apostles. He has done it through preachers ever since. As the apostle Paul expressed it with humility and wonder, 'We are Christ's ambassadors, as though God were making his appeal through us' (2 Cor. 5:20, NIV). What an incredible privilege preaching must be, if it is to be God's messenger.

Not only is God the supreme communicator, which is one good reason for preaching; but Christ has explicitly commanded us to do just this. He gave us an example. He sent out the twelve and the seventy to preach. And his last command enjoined that very calling on his apostles (Matt. 28:19–20). The promise of his power, the promise of his presence, is for those who will go into all the world and make disciples of the people who are strangers to his love.

As if that were not enough, the Holy Spirit, who inspired Scripture, clearly works through those who make it known. That is obvious as we turn the pages of the Acts. It is implicit in 2 Corinthians 4:4–5 – only the Spirit can open the eyes of those blinded by 'the god of this world'. Colossians 1:28 shows the Spirit using preaching to build mature people up in Christ.

Yes, there is a trinitarian basis for preaching. It has great authority, the authority of God himself. And it has great power. The Christian gospel concerns things God has actually done for sinful humankind. And someone needs to go and tell them. That, at its most basic, is what preaching is all about.

CAN PREACHING BE EFFECTIVE?

Just think of Jesus for a moment. It was the powerful preaching of Jesus that drew such crowds. Here was this man, so sure of his God, dynamic in his teaching; clear and relevant, profound and yet simple. People had never heard anything like it. 'He taught as one with authority, and not like the scribes' (i.e. the clergy!). Cast your mind back to the Sermon on the Mount, the parables, the controversies, the synagogue preaching of Jesus. Jesus came telling the good news of the Kingdom, and the common people heard him gladly.

It was much the same with the earliest church. It was born in preaching, open-air preaching at that. It was confident stuff, with an assurance derived from a relationship with Jesus (Acts 4:13). It did not lull people to sleep. It stirred them to decision. Sometimes they decided to imprison the preachers, or kill them. Sometimes they decided to believe them, and join them. But there was nothing insipid about it. It was powerful, often confrontational, rooted in the teaching of Jesus and of the Old Testament, and bathed in prayer and awareness of the Holy Spirit. It had a clear aim: to bring men and women to Christ, or to build them up in him. And the preachers did it in many different places. They could do it in the streets at Pentecost. They could, like Stephen, do it before an execution. They did it in law-courts, like Paul. They did it in the temple after a healing, or in the lecture hall of Tyrannus when it was vacant. But most of all they did it in the synagogues, and sometimes they got invited back next week (Acts 13:42).

No wonder the apostles avoided getting too caught up in administration, but gave themselves to prayer and study and proclamation of the word. More than thirty times in Acts we read that the word grew, the word flourished, the word prevailed. Luke means by this, of course, the proclamation of the gospel. This is how the faith spread. Paul saw preaching as the way in which people came most frequently from darkness to light (compare 2 Cor. 4:4, 6 and then reflect on verse 5; see also Acts 26:16–18). And so Mark's longer ending puts it, 'They went out and preached everywhere' (Mark 16:20, NIV). Our last glimpse of Paul is in prison in Rome. But the word of God is not bound. This intrepid preacher evangelised his gaolers and his visitors. He was in prison, that is true. But he was 'preaching the kingdom of God and teaching about the Lord Jesus Christ quite openly and unhindered' (Acts 28:31).

Nor did this cease at the end of the apostolic age. In his book *I Believe in Preaching*, John Stott gives a short sketch of the way in which the glory of preaching continued to shine out through the centuries: Chrysostom, Wycliffe, Luther, the friars, Wesley and Whitefield, Jonathan Edwards and the like. He gives two lovely quotes which have stuck in my mind. Francis of Assisi said to his preaching friars, 'Unless you preach everywhere you go, there is no use in going anywhere to preach.' That man and his friends certainly had an abiding fruitfulness through preaching. The same is true of Martin Luther, who remarked somewhat contentiously, 'I simply taught, preached and wrote God's word. Otherwise I did nothing. While I slept, or drank beer with my friends, the word so greatly weakened the papacy that never a prince or emperor inflicted such damage upon it. I did nothing. The word did it all.'

In our own day Billy Graham and Pope John Paul II are by far the most famous preachers. Both of them influence the hearts of men more than any politician on the globe. 'Preaching the good news of Jesus Christ', wrote Will Sangster, author of *The Craft of the Sermon*, 'is the highest, holiest task to which a man can give himself. It is a task for which the archangels might forsake the courts of heaven.'

HAVE WE THE RIGHT TO PREACH?

Where is the authority for preaching? The answer lies in that little phrase 'the word' which has popped up time and time again in this chapter. A preacher worth his salt does not give his bright ideas about God. He is a man under authority, the very authority of God's revealed truth in Scripture. By definition we, his very finite creatures, can know no more about God than he has chosen to reveal to us. We need to drink deep at the well of that revelation if we are to have anything solid and thirst-quenching to offer to others. The presupposition of the evangelistic preacher is that

Scripture contains God's self-disclosure. It tells us not all about God that we would like to know, but all we need to know. It is a revelation, and it concerns a rescue.

Almost all Christian denominations affirm in theory that Scripture embodies God's self-disclosure and is normative. In practice it is a very different matter, and biblical preaching is in low water. But the declared position of the churches recognising the authority and inspiration of Scripture, coming as it does from the God who speaks, springs unequivocally from the attitude of Jesus. He studied it. He framed his life by it. He regarded it as inspired by God. He treated it as authoritative and utterly reliable. This is not the place to argue those claims. I have done so elsewhere, in *The Authority of Scripture*, and so have others, far more adequately, such as Sir Norman Anderson (*God's Word for God's World*), John Wenham (*Our Lord's View of the Old Testament*) and R. T. France (*Jesus and the Old Testament*). I do not believe that a fair examination of the evidence can come up with any other conclusion. Jesus' respect for the authority and inspiration of the Scriptures was total. It can only be evaded by making use of either the accommodation or the kenosis theories, which assume respectively that he accommodate himself to the ignorance of his contemporaries about the real unreliability of the Scriptures, or that the conditions of his incarnation blinded him. Neither seem to me to be tolerable *Christian* explanations. They savour more of desperate attempts to escape from the overwhelming evidence (contained in all strands of the gospel material) for Jesus' reverence of the Old Testament. It was normative even for him who came to bring it to fulfilment.

That is one reason why Christians give such weight to Scripture. Jesus, our Lord, did. The other reason is pragmatic: it works. This book, the Bible, has a power and trenchancy which my words do not have. And that is the assumption behind biblical preaching. This book contains the truth of God. We are there to make its message heard. The evangelist is not, essentially, the originator of new ideas. He is not a guru, nor is he a prophet. He does not get his message from his own mind, or from gathering other people's ideas, but from the Bible. He sows the word. He teaches the word. He is a steward of the word. He is a herald of the word. He cuts a straight furrow through the word. These are some of the images which Scripture itself gives of the preacher. There is a *givenness* about his material.

WHY IS PREACHING IN SUCH LOW WATER?

There are a number of reasons. Here are five.

First, there is, in Western Christendom, a collapse in belief. Many clergy seem hardly to believe in God, let alone the articles of the creed or the Christian Scriptures. They are hollow men, and inevitably their message sounds hollow.

Second, there is a revolution in communication on our hands. The instant visual communication of the television age makes the preacher look old-fashioned and dull. How can he compete? Knowledge on a wide variety of topics is instantly available on television from experts: how can the preacher's education keep up?

Third, ours is an age which rejects authority. How dare a man or woman get up and harangue their hearers uninterrupted for twenty minutes? Why not have a discussion group instead?

Fourth, the growth of relativism and pluralism is a massive disincentive to preaching. What is the point of proclaiming One Way if there are many ways, and if none of them is more than relative anyhow?

Fifth, there is a very obvious change of priorities among churches and ministers these days. Churches place much more emphasis on worship, on clubs, on social functions and social action. Ministers major more on further degrees, on non-directional counselling, on amateur political, social or psychological activity, and above all they give themselves to administration and committee meetings – not to preaching. As a result modern preaching tends to be dull and defective. Dull, because it is so tentative, so undistinguished. Formal clothes, formal language, formal manner and subject-matter – yawn. But get a Billy Graham, get Archbishop Bloom, or the Pope, and people flock to hear. There is a hunger in the human heart which most of us preachers do not manage to touch. And our preaching is not only dull, it is highly defective. It does not bridge gaps. It does not affect real life. It is part of the 'show' for church-goers, but does not seem to be vital for the life and growth of the church. It is, on the whole, irrelevant for Monday to Saturday life. This is tragic when, as we have seen above, preaching can be such a mighty instrument in God's hands.

WHAT ARE THE PATHWAYS TO EFFECTIVE PREACHING?

First, I must believe in preaching. I must see it as a God-given weapon in the spiritual warfare in which we are engaged. I must see that it is God's chosen way of bringing people to repentance and faith. I must believe in the power of this strange activity. I must expect God to act through it.

Second, I must trust the Scriptures. All great preaching down the centuries has been biblical preaching. I must believe that the Bible contains the words of eternal life. If not, I should abandon preaching altogether. We are not in the pulpit to show off our learning, or to entertain people for a while, or to enjoin good moral behaviour. We are there in Christ's stead to say to people: 'Be reconciled with God.' 'If anyone speaks,' said Peter wisely, 'he should do it as one speaking the very words of God' (1 Pet. 4:11, NIV).

Third, I must keep Jesus in the centre of my sights. He is the supremely attractive one. I must speak often of him, and make clear who he is and what he has done. I must show what are the costs and the joys of following him, and I must show people with utmost clarity how they can find him for themselves.

Fourth, I must build bridges. Bridges between what I see so clearly and what my hearers see so dimly. Bridges between world-views and cultural divides. Bridges between the New Testament and the current world. Bridges between the agenda God has and the very different matters that are at the top of the human agenda. Bridge-building is our calling, with one end of the bridge firmly anchored to God's revelation in Christ, and the other end planted equally firmly in the condition and concerns of our hearers.

Fifth, I must be definite, vulnerable and bold. Definite in content, in aim, in thought, in language. Definite in prayer and expectancy. I must expect that sermon to do something.

But equally I must be vulnerable. I must speak as a poor weak sinner to poor weak sinners. I must not conceal my own fears and doubts and weaknesses. When preachers are definite they are often hard. There must be no trace of that in me.

But I must be bold, too. Bold in preaching for a verdict. Bold in appealing to the wills of the people. Bold in making use of the unexpected. Bold in debate. Bold in open-air work. Bold in applying the message directly to the hearts of the hearers.

Bold in being willing if necessary to go out on a limb while expecting the Holy Spirit to act. Preaching is no task for cowards.

WHAT ATTRACTS PEOPLE TO JESUS CHRIST?

There are many factors. I have noticed a number of them artlessly displayed in John's Gospel.

There is the sense of discovery. You see it in Andrew (John 1:41). It immediately made an impact on his brother Peter and brought him to Jesus. When people have made a life-changing discovery in this rather jaded world, it is news. It attracts attention. Others want to know. That is why new believers are among the best evangelists. They have so many friends who are not Christians, and the difference in their own lives and priorities is eloquent and invites curiosity.

There is the sense of wonder. That is what struck the disciples when Jesus turned water into wine (John 2:11). Any situation which brings the transcendent into focus can achieve that. Worship is an obvious example. When people are caught up in wonder and love and adoration of their God, when it shows in their body language and their faces, this has an enormous power to attract people to Jesus. When the water of a very ordinary life is changed into the wine of a transformed character by the power of the Spirit, this too is an obvious and great attraction to Jesus.

There is the sense of love. That attracts to Jesus like nothing on earth. John 3:16 is archetypal. If people can see themselves as the recipients of a love that sought them and sacrificed for them when they were in total rebellion, that has its own marvellous way of breaking down opposition and melting hearts. When Christian individuals and churches know that quality of love, people get attracted (see 1 John 3:16).

There is the sense of power. Think of the paralysed man in John 5, or the blind man in John 9. The sheer power of Jesus to deal with bodily complaints, his miraculous power, in short, was what drew them, and many like them, to Christ. That is one of the important lessons which so-called Power Evangelism has to teach us in this generation. God's power is still released from time to time to set people free from physical, emotional and psychological bondage.

And when that happens it is a powerful magnet towards Christ the healer.

There is the sense of need. That comes through strongly in the story of Nicodemus in John 3, or the woman at the well in John 4. That need may be for forgiveness and acceptance; it was with the woman taken in adultery (John 8:1–11). But it may be the need for acceptance, for power over habits too strong for us, for meaning in a world that seems not to have any. There are many shapes of human need, and some people are drawn to Christ by seeing the way in which he is the answer to the need which is so clamant in their hearts.

These are some of the ways in which people recognise the 'pearl of great price'. We would be wise to make full allowance for their variety if we want to be effective in evangelism.

WHAT IS THE HEART OF THE GOOD NEWS?

I suppose you could sum up the essence of the gospel in four propositions.

First, we believe in a God who speaks. He has revealed himself in many ways: in nature, in human personality, in the history of Israel, and above all in Jesus. The Bible is all about the God who refuses to hide himself. It is about revelation. And on the basis of that revelation, we have something to say.

Second, we believe in a God who rescues. Scripture and experience join in convincing us that all is not well with *homo sapiens*. Our words, deeds, thoughts, inclinations, attitudes and our character are all infected by the 'human disease' of self-centredness and sin. It is very dangerous. In fact it is lethal. And there is nothing we can do to rescue ourselves from its clutches. As with AIDS, there is no cure. Religious questing and moral behaviour are both admirable but inadequate. They cannot get us to God. They cannot make us fit to be seen in his presence. And they cannot deal with the virus of sin in our lives. But the amazing testimony of the Bible is that God has stepped in, in the person of Jesus, to do for us what we could never do for ourselves. If we look hard enough we will see that God was in Christ reconciling the world to himself. And the cross was where it happened. On that cross God took full responsibility for our failures and sins. He burdened himself with them.

They crushed him. But that was not the end of the story. He rose from the grave, offering forgiveness and the power of his Holy Spirit to those who will turn to him and ask for them. This again is one of the central themes of the whole Bible. The God who reveals himself is the same God who rescues mankind. He is the God who acquits the ungodly, and he can do so with perfect propriety because he has himself shouldered our debts and drunk the poison of our sins to the very last dregs.

Third, we believe in a God who gives life. He puts his Spirit within us, and that makes a real difference. It is marked in the Hebrew, where *nephesh* is the word which is used for our human spirit, while *ruach* is used for God's Spirit which he offers to instil. Things are not the same as they were before. When the Spirit comes, there is a new understanding, a new liberty in prayer, a new sense of belonging, a new power over evil habits, a new desire to tell others, a new love for Christian fellowship, a new humility, boldness and desire to learn. That is the result, variously and gradually evidenced, of the new birth which God brings about in those who 'convert' or turn to him in repentance and faith.

Fourth, we believe in a God who sends. All through Scripture, and all through history, people who have found – or rather been found by – this living, triune, redemptive God have had something to declare. They cannot keep quiet. They do it because they must. They have found treasure: they want others to know. The Lord loved them and gave himself for them. The least they can do is to seek with all their power to introduce others to him. And that is what lies at the heart of evangelism: the God who says, 'Whom shall I send, and who will go for us?' The evangelist replies, humbly, but with love and wholeheartedness, 'Lord, here am I, send me.'

The good news of the gospel contains a lot more than that. But I submit to you that those four propositions lie very near its centre.

HOW CAN WE PREPARE
FOR AN EVANGELISTIC SERMON?

The preparation is at least threefold.

First, as we have seen, there is the vital need to prepare the congregation. If that is neglected, nothing will be achieved. We have thought in chapter 4 of the love that needs to characterise us. Without that, nobody will want to get very close, and any attempt at evangelism will look hard and maybe resemble a modern form of head-hunting. Love must flow, and be seen to flow. Warm welcomers will be needed for the doors, refreshments available afterwards; everything must be designed to make those who do not normally come to church feel as much at home as possible. Prayer must accompany love. It would be good to mobilise a system of prayer triplets, where three people get together on several occasions to pray for three friends each, whom they hope to invite. There could be a night or half-night of prayer beforehand, too. The congregation needs to be full of the Lord, so much so that they are willing to go and open their mouths for him, to invite others, and to say something of what Christ has done for them if opportunity offers. There needs to be an expectancy that God will work, a happy confidence in the Holy Spirit who loves to glorify Christ. I believe that before God is likely to bring large numbers of converts into a congregation the church needs to demonstrate that their fellowship is deep and real, and that they are able to welcome and assimilate the new life. That is where the 'Fellowship Groups' come in – groups of a dozen or so people who meet regularly within homes for fellowship, learning, prayer, encouragement and service. But even where this structure is in place in a church, one thing more is needed. We need people to lead Discovery Groups, that is to say, small groups of those who have just committed their lives to Christ and need to be built up. We shall devote a half chapter to the setting up and running of those groups, but in the meantime it is worth noting that part of the preparation for an evangelistic sermon is the preparing of people to lead these groups – who at the moment have no members in them! That in itself is a declaration of faith in the living God. When I worked at a church set in the midst of Oxford University, we always used to prepare for one or two such groups to emerge immediately after an evangelistic address: sometimes as many as eight groups, when our faith was strong! And we trained leaders in the confidence that God would answer prayer and provide their group with members.

Second, preparation of the congregation needs to be matched by the preparation of the occasion. You need to choose it with care, going for a time when it is likely that unbelievers may be around in large numbers and could, if they were so disposed, come to church. Such occasions need to be carefully planned in the calendar of the year's activities – maybe three or four a year. And the publicity needs to be good. There is the publicity within the church, and the publicity to those you want to invite. Of these the former is the more important. If you can fire up the members of the congregation to invite people, with enthusiasm, love and persistence, and to bring them with them, then you have solved your publicity problem. But, in addition, you will want to have some attractively produced material which you can hand to prospective visitors, and distribute round homes if you have a visiting team who would like to do that; and above all you will need a large and attractive notice outside the church with a bold, provocative title on it. On the whole, people will not be interested that the sermon will be preached by the Reverend Bill Jones, BD, which is the sort of thing you often find outside a church as the only notice that is evident. Frankly, who knows or cares about the Reverend Bill Jones, BD? But if there is a notice featuring the question 'Is there hope in a world that is falling apart?' or something that touches people at the point of felt need, interest or weakness, then people will be attracted. On the whole, publicity does not bring a lot of people in: personal invitations do that. But unless the publicity is good, expectancy will be low, nobody will know about it, and it will be an inconspicuous and probably ineffective event.

The third area of necessary preparation is the service itself. It needs to be very carefully prepared, and everything needs to be subordinated to helping those who are visitors and making them able to participate without feeling that they are being gunned at on the one hand, or mystified by the in-house language and liturgy of the church on the other. A delicate balance should be our aim. The service will need to be different from normal, but not so different that if and when they come next week to a 'normal' service it will be a totally different world! If liturgy is used, the page numbers of the books where it is found must always be announced. Remember that if you want people to use a Bible it is likely to be quite unfamiliar to them. The very furniture of a church is odd to many these days. Choir and clergy robes are usually a turn-off. The same is true of old-fashioned language and 'the language of Zion'. As for the clerical voice – it must be avoided at all costs. Organs are not the only effective ways of accompanying singing, unless you are in a large church or a cathedral. The use of a piano or a guitar or a small orchestra is often a more attractive alternative. It is no good singing psalms at an evangelistic service. That will be a different world from the one inhabited by those visitors you are trying to accommodate. Equally, the endless repetition of choruses may not edify them either! And powerful though the Holy Communion is to nourish believers, it is not the thing to have when you are directing your whole service towards guests. Canticles are out, and so are long classical choir anthems. This does not help Mr and Mrs Average these days. So a great deal of thinking needs to go into the service. We have forgotten how out of touch with ordinary people all our church services have become.

Some of the things I have found helpful to do in such an evangelistic service are as follows. Dispense with service books: people only get lost in them. Instead, if the architecture allows, use the overhead projector for songs, hymns, and any parts of the service where the people participate together. Alternatively, print the corporate parts of the service in the bulletin. Have a singing group praising God for a quarter of an hour or more before the service starts. Cut notices to the minimum, or remove them altogether by putting them in a bulletin which is placed in the hands of everyone as they come in. And that same bulletin should have details in it of anything else you want to let your visitors know – especially the leaders' names, the locations and the starting times of the Discovery Groups that you hope to start in the coming week. Ensure that someone with real sensitivity in worship and warmth of manner leads the service. It may be good to make use of a couple of testimonies, with stories from people of contrasting sex and age, because testimony to the power of God by lay people is a very attractive thing. If there is a solo or choir-music item, it should be short and very up-beat. The accompaniment of the hymns, or, better, the modern scripture choruses which are springing up all over the world church, needs to be strong. It does not matter if people do not know all the songs (and you don't want too many). They can be taught them very easily, for most of these songs have very simple and catching melodies. Remember that some of the great old hymns have a power which most modern choruses cannot equal. The Scripture reading is very important and should be read by someone who can read well. The sermon is your responsibility: we will come to that in a minute. But the final hymn should be optional. You may want to cancel it in the light of how the sermon closes.

People need to be available after the service to counsel any who wish it, and they need to have received some training beforehand. You will naturally want to meet with such folk and all leading participants three quarters of an hour before the service begins, so as to finalise all details, make sure nothing has been forgotten

('Who was going to bring those evangelistic booklets? . . . You mean, they aren't here?' is the sort of thing that can easily happen), and have time to commit the whole venture to God in prayer, along with the musicians, and those who are leading, reading, praying, and giving testimony. When we have been immersed in worship for half an hour, it shows on our faces as we go in to lead the congregation. When we have not, that shows too!

HOW SHALL WE PREPARE THE ADDRESS?

Preaching is truth mediated through personality, so different people will approach it in different ways. But some general things stand out. All great preaching has been biblical preaching: not that it is Bible-thumping, but that it enshrines the message of the Bible in the course of the address. All great preaching has been in demonstration of the power of the Spirit. So prayer and utter dependence on God is vital. So is the prayerful support of the congregation as you prepare and as you preach. Often in Oxford, when doing an evangelistic address to a large number of people, we would have a prayer service going on across the road in the Rectory for those who felt the call to prayer, or had not managed to bring any visitors with them. That prayer time was an immense support to the preacher. Once or twice in the course of the service a member of the congregation would go across and tell them what was happening, as fuel for prayer! All good evangelistic preaching really engages and interests the hearers, and it ends by challenging them to encounter the living Christ.

A good evangelistic talk is crisp: it wastes no words. It is interesting: it grabs attention from the opening sentence and maintains it throughout. It is biblical: Scripture has a power our words do not. It is relevant to the needs of the hearers, and it is immediately perceived to be so. And it challenges people to decision.

Here are some things I try to bear in mind as I prepare. I often think of a single individual whom I would dearly love to lead to Christ and who I know will be in the congregation, and have him or her in the forefront of my mind as I prepare.

1. *First, start where they are.* It is important that the content of what we preach is biblical, but it is a great mistake to start with a

text of Scripture. You need to get the taste buds working first! Start where they are. That is good educational method. You then have some hope of taking them where you want them to go. I wrote a book some years ago which embodied this inductive approach. It was called *You Must Be Joking!*, and the chapter titles were all things I had heard people say, things which admirably lent themselves to an evangelistic talk, things like: 'You can't believe in God these days,' 'Jesus was just a good man,' 'All religions lead to God,' 'Nothing can alter the past,' 'When you're dead, you're dead,' and so forth. Those titles and that book have had a continuing interest and appeal because they are addressed to questions people really are asking. There are many ways in which you can capture interest with your title.

Take an assumption and destroy it. A good example would be: 'It doesn't matter what you believe, so long as you are sincere.'

Take an interest and develop it. I think of a Valentine's party where I spoke evangelistically on love, or a Christmas party when I tried: 'Yes to the manger, no to the occupant.'

Take a modern concern. For example, 'Can there be peace in our world?', or 'How to be married and stay that way.'

Key into some of the questing songs of the day. With apologies to Bruce Cockburn, I am about to preach an evangelistic address on 'Rumours of Glory'.

Take a perennial fascination and give it a new twist. 'Is life worth more than the funeral expenses?', or 'Is there life before death?'

Tailor your title to your audience. I have spoken to businessmen more than once on titles like 'Nobody's fool', expounding the story of the rich fool. All businessmen like to think they are nobody's fool!

It is good to fit in with a feeling that is prevalent in society. I shall never forget the power I unwittingly released when I stumbled upon the subject of 'Jesus spells freedom' in Africa in the 1960s. It was beginning to be *the* subject of the continent. The same decade saw the counter-culture in full swing, and subjects like 'Jesus the Radical' or 'The Revolutionary Jesus' were very big draws. I think of a sermon for new students at Oxford which drew enormous numbers. It was 'Confirmed too young – agnostic too long'. It just keyed in with where many people were at. But it is important not to be dominated by needs. And it is important not to cheat with them. If you are going to take a subject like 'Jesus the Radical', you really have to do it full justice, or people will rightly feel cheated.

One final word about maintaining and retaining interest. I find it very helpful to use testimony in my addresses, and also to use dramatic sketches. These can be used at an earlier part of the proceedings, and have great value there. But I have found that to interview someone on a key point in the middle of the sermon can be a great attention-grabber, and the use of a short dramatic sketch, appropriately introduced and picked up, makes a point sharply, often humorously, and not only saves you time but gives that change of voice and medium which is so valuable.

2. *Second, shape your material.* Once you have found your title, see what there is in Scripture that speaks to it. Last autumn I spoke to university students on a title that I was given, 'Money, Sex and Power – what more does a body need?', and as I reflected on it, I saw that it was precisely addressed by the letter of Christ to the church at Laodicea in Revelation 3:14–21. So that became the biblical thrust of my sermon. But I did not begin with Laodicea!

When shaping your material in an evangelistic address there are a number of things to keep in mind.

First, your aim. You should have a clear, single aim, and that should govern everything you say. If you do not have a crystal-clear aim, you will be surprised how good people are at missing it. And of course, if you aim at nothing, you are sure to hit it!

Second, your plan. Break the material up to make sure that people can easily latch on to what you are saying. Make it palatable. And be sure that every point subserves the aim of the whole address. Failure to do this results in a disorganised and confusing message. A clear plan is absolutely vital.

Third, your structure. This, too, must be clear. Not so clear that people can follow it, but so clear that nobody can fail to follow it. You need to advertise your points with great freeway signs, not inconspicuous little sign-posts. And if you can work it so that each one of your points leads naturally and apparently inevitably into the next one, you are likely to make a great preacher. The well-constructed address hammers home the main point relentlessly, and its subheadings seem utterly right and obvious – once you have heard them. Structure is an important part of preaching. Time spent on it is not wasted.

Fourth, your illustrations. These are very important – and easy to mess up! Never illustrate the obvious. Always illustrate the unknown by the known. Never use illustrations which sound incredible – even if they aren't. Never use illustrations which glorify yourself. Never use illustrations that are too involved; and shun exaggeration like the plague. If you follow Jesus' example, you will draw a lot of your illustrations from the natural world and the ordinary commerce of mankind. The book of nature and the book of Scripture do, after all, have the same author. It is not surprising that they illuminate one another. The local paper, current affairs, plays, films, TV and songs all furnish good material for illustrations. Books of illustrations usually disappoint and do not sound real. But it is a good idea to note down outstanding illustrations which you hear, and use them appropriately later on yourself. None of them are copyright!

Fifth, your start and your conclusion are both critical. The start has to be really arresting – a situation, a humorous anecdote, a problem. It should be brief, arresting, and intriguing in itself. It is your hook into some fish which may be very wary. Give good thought to it. It may be wise to try it out on a friend before you preach it. As for the conclusion, never moralise. Do not go on too long. Take note of Jesus' parables, which never drew the moral, but forced the hearers to think furiously. Sometimes a verse of Scripture can be used at the end. Sometimes even an illustration. But the conclusion should never try to add new material. It should encapsulate and drive home the theme of the whole sermon. It should provide the final hammer blow to the nail which is your aim and which has been going steadily in since you began. I believe this applies to almost all types of preaching. But the evangelistic sermon has some peculiarities of its own, and we shall turn to them in a moment.

Sixth, your language. Words matter to the Holy Spirit (1 Cor. 2:13), and they should matter to us. I find it helpful to word-prepare my major sermons, but never to read them. Detailed verbal preparation helps me confidently to negotiate the difficult places in the address when I get to them. I have faced them head on and in detail during my preparation, and so I am the more likely, when I preach, to carry people with me over the difficulty. Our words in preaching should not be starchy or churchy. They should be in the sort of language that local people speak. A sermon should not be an artistic creation: it should be an impassioned procla-mation. It is not something to admire, but something to act on. So the language should be gripping, vivid, simple. Go for familiar words, evocative words that can bring home a familiar truth in a fresh way. Determine that there shall be no possibility of your being misunderstood.

Seventh, your manner. The New Testament images of a

preacher are very varied and very illuminating. He is an ambassador (2 Cor. 5:20), a herald (1 Tim. 2:7), a father (1 Cor. 4:14), a
steward (1 Cor. 4:1–5), a servant (1 Cor. 3:5), a witness (Acts
2:32). Different styles are appropriate to different ones of those
images. You must select the right mood for your subject-matter,
and blend your manner with it. Ask yourself how Jesus would
speak if he were in your shoes. Let there be warmth, and utter
sincerity. Let there be a profound sense of earnestness, but never
of dullness. You will need courage (to say 'you' when you mean
'you') and humility and compassion. Get friends to check you for
irritating mannerisms, and iron them out so that you do not distract
the hearers: the stakes are too high to have stupid little mannerisms
putting people off.

3. *Third, be Christ-centred.* Speak much of him. He is the
supremely attractive one. He promised that if he were lifted up
from the earth he would draw all sorts of people to himself. And he
does. So we need to take care to make much of who he is, and of
what he has done, and to make it very clear that he is alive and
willing to come to us personally if we will allow him. The early
Christians had an outline in those sermons recorded in Acts which
they used a good deal. It is a wise one. They spoke to a need once
they discerned it; they told of a person, Jesus Christ, no less; they
proffered the twin gifts of forgiveness and the Holy Spirit; and they
looked for a response, a visible response of repentance, faith,
and baptism into the Christian community. We could profitably
emulate them.

4. *Fourth, watch the balance of your evangelistic preaching.* The
gospel of Christ is both big and broad. It is easy to miss great areas
of it because we are comfortable with particular aspects of it. It is
wise from time to time to check out whether we have not only a
biblical message but a biblical balance in our message. Here again
discerning friends can be a help to us. Evangelism without much
doctrine, with no mention of the cost of discipleship, with no
depth, no warmth, no social content and no sensitivity is a travesty
of the real thing, and we must do our best to avoid aberrations by
coming constantly back to the balance and overview of Scripture,
with the help of friends who know the truth in depth.

5. *Finally, leave time to conclude.* It is all too easy to miss this
vital ingredient out, and to come to the end of your talk, when you
need time, and find that it has flown.

Preparation that is as careful as this will give you a lot of
confidence as you go into the pulpit. There are other little things

that can help. Preach into a mirror occasionally, and watch your expression and manner. You may get a shock! Allow a group from the congregation to criticise one of your sermons in detail with you, checking your aim, content, use of Scripture, structure, manner, application and illustration. That is tremendously helpful – and humbling. Time yourself as you preach through the completed sermon to yourself – and remember that it always takes longer on the day that it does in preparation.

But the most important essential in preparation is prayer. Get church leaders to pray for you daily in the week when you are preparing a major address. Ask the congregation to remember you in prayer. Make it a topic for prayer at the prayer meeting. Prayer burns the message into you. Prayer will burn it into the souls of some who hear you. The Holy Spirit can work powerfully when much prayer is being offered. He inspired the very Scripture you are going to preach. He moved you as you worked on it in preparation. It is his task to commend it to the hearts and wills of men and women when you preach it. Prayer enables him to do just that. And I, for one, go with much greater confidence into the pulpit when two or three of my colleagues gather round me in prayer just before I stand up to preach. It is not only an encouragement to me: it is a demonstration to one and all that we depend utterly on what God does, not on our own efforts.

I love the words of an old Methodist local preacher on the subject of sermon preparation: 'First I reads meself full; then I thinks meself clear; then I prays meself hot; then I lets go!'

HOW CAN WE HANDLE THE CONCLUSION OF AN EVANGELISTIC SERMON?

This is an important and delicate matter. It is vital to draw the address to a challenging conclusion. But we are not salesmen: we are dealing with the living God and his claim on people's lives. Here are some of the lessons I try to bear in mind – and often have to relearn.

I only offer a challenge to commitment when there has been a clear and reasonably rounded presentation of the gospel. Human need, the cross, the cost, and the availability of the Spirit need at least to have been touched on.

I try to leave myself plenty of time at the end of the sermon. If I am going to call for an explicit response, I explain what I am about to do before I do it, so that it does not come as a shock to people, and so that they are mentally more prepared to respond.

I try to be open to the possibility of pleading with people to return to Christ. There is a lot of that loving, pleading compassion in the Old and New Testaments, but I find that it is little used today. Many preachers just tell you how it is, and then stop. It hardly seems to matter to them whether you respond or not. That is very different from Jesus: 'O Jerusalem, Jerusalem . . . how often would I have gathered your children together as a hen gathers her brood . . . and you would not!' (Matt. 23:37). It is impossible to miss the note of pleading there. We need to allow the warmth of Jesus, the seriousness of the issues, and the awesome alternative to coming to Christ to be reflected in what we say at this juncture. Kindle their imagination so that you can reach their will. That is your goal.

Watch people's faces, and try to read their minds. It is not as difficult as it might seem. Learn to answer questions which you think may be in their minds. 'Are you wondering what it will cost to follow Christ? Good. Let me try to answer that question . . .'; '"But, Mr Green," you may say, "I'm a churchman!" True, but so were the Pharisees to whom Jesus spoke. Even better churchmen than you!' This divining of what is going on in minds and speaking to it is very effective. It can, I believe, be a spiritual gift from God to the preacher. We should ask for it. It is particularly valuable in dispelling objections against a positive response to Christ, and the place for it is as the sermon comes to an end.

Your attitude should be a mixture. On the one hand you need to be fearless and bold. On the other hand you need to be warm and sensitive. Pray for that balance.

Trust the Word of God. It is very powerful. Placard the promises of God and the cross of Christ before the eyes of your hearers. Faith is, after all, trusting the promises of God. And these promises are very new to them. They need time, and they need you to be extremely clear, if they are to take it in.

Use appropriate illustrations at this delicate time. The best ones are personal illustrations, those which depict meeting and encounter. The marriage analogy between the Lord and the believer is very clear and readily comprehensible. The image of opening the door of heart and life to Christ is one which has helped millions to commitment. The 'in Christ' imagery is helpful too, though a bit more difficult to take in. But it makes very clear both the unity with him and the need of a leap of faith if you are going to move from being 'without Christ' to being 'in Christ'. Another biblical image which is helpful to many is the idea of the sperm and the egg, or the seed and the soil. It is from the marriage of these two that the new life is born. But never get boxed into a corner by using just one image. It may help some but leave others cold. So vary it. 'Give and take' is a simple commitment image we can use. You give yourself to him and you gratefully take his pardon and his Spirit in return.

Be broad in your appeal at the end of the sermon. There will be a great variety of people in the church, and you want to be of maximum help to them all. You could call on people to entrust their lives to Christ for the first time, and then add: 'There may well be others of you who did that long ago, but somehow you have drifted away. Come back to him now. Ask his pardon. Put yourself without reserve in his hands, and you will know again the joy of the Father's house which you may have walked out of.' It is sometimes helpful, with people who genuinely are not sure whether they have committed their lives to Christ or not, to suggest that whatever pencilled commitment there may have been in the past, now is the time to ink it in and get clear about it. So make a broad and a challenging appeal. But do not press. It is the job of the Holy Spirit, not of the preacher, to do that. Human pressure can do great damage.

Usually at the end of a talk I suggest a time of silence as folk kneel or sit. Silence is not only golden. It is powerful. It gives the Spirit of God a chance to speak to individuals. I may well repeat the verse of Scripture that has been foremost in the sermon and then give one or two minutes of complete silence, inviting people to face up to the challenge, and those who are already committed Christians to pray silently for those who are not. I eschew emotionalism, especially at this critical time. I try to make it seem the most natural thing in the world to accept Christ into one's life, or to pray for others to do so. If I am matter of fact about it, the congregation will not feel that any emotional pressure is being exerted, and the Holy Spirit will be free to act. Often in the silence people will break into quiet sobbing. But that is fine. The Spirit is at work on their spirit, and almost invariably it leads to real repentance and new life.

After a time of silence I may well suggest a prayer of commitment for those who want to use it, *and only for them*. I say: 'If you feel you don't know how to put it, why not use something very simple like this? You could say it after me under your breath if you like. "Lord, please forgive me and come and take up residence in my life. Amen."' I then thank God that he keeps his promises, and that if any have taken him at his word he will never leave them or forsake them; and then I draw the service to an end, with or without the optional final hymn. It is not always needed at such a juncture, and it may detract from – or enhance – the impact. After the blessing I normally say, 'One thing more, as you go. If you have taken that step of opening up to Christ, and if you have prayed that prayer with me just now, I would love to meet you briefly. I want to invite you into what we call a Discovery Group. It is an eight-week course on Christian foundations, and we have one or more groups starting this coming week. I think you will find it a great help to join a group like this where there is plenty of chance for questions and discussion, but where we take a major theme of the Christian life and study it each week. If you intend to be serious with Christ, come and join one of these groups. You need it, and you will benefit from it a great deal. I have the details here at the front (or the back, or wherever you think fit). Come and sign up, and I'll see you have the details about which group you are in by tomorrow.'

This 'gathering of the fruit' is absolutely vital. You don't so much want people to make a hasty decision on the spot about Christ. But you do want them to sign up for a group, because there they can have a chance to receive warm care by fairly experienced folk over a period of two months. Experience shows that if they join a group, however uncertain they may be at the beginning, they tend to come to Christ in the course of it, and then they grow. Accordingly, I do my best to draw them into a Discovery Group; for it is especially designed for new believers. I shall have more to say about these groups in chapter 10. For the moment, suffice it to say that those who are going to lead the Discovery Group would be ideal people to have alongside you after the service. This means that the people who chat to those who come forward are therefore the same people who will lead the Discovery Groups, and that begins to form the basis of a relationship which can be built on later.

If there are enough people for one Discovery Group only, do your best to ensure that the group is scheduled to start at a time when your leaders and all the prospective members can come. If the numbers warrant several groups, it is wise to get first and second preferences for the starting time. It may not be possible logistically to give all of them their first preference, so you need to know two times they could manage. It is probably a help to have duplicated beforehand a simple form explaining what a Discovery Group is all about, and the subjects that will be covered during the course. That part of the form they hold on to. There needs also to be a detachable portion which you get them to fill in then and there, and collect it from them before they leave. It will have room for their name, address, phone number and their first and second choice of a time for the group (unless you have already determined that beforehand).

Sometimes there may be a large response to such a challenge. In that case the sorting out of names afterwards is a skilled job. Attention needs to be paid to the balance of the group by sex, age and perhaps locality and background, within the limits of the times they can manage. It would be good if they could be contacted later that very day and told which group they are in (if there is more than one). That will give them a sense of confidence at a time in their lives when they are probably feeling unsure of themselves. It will also show your care and efficiency. It is important, too, because the Enemy of souls is sure to be busy that day. Why give him an advantage?

As you invite people to the front, avoid any sense of pressure. Be laid-back about it. But train your congregation to ask their visitors at this juncture, at the end of the service, 'Would you like to join a Discovery Group? They are a real help. I'll come with you up to the front if you would like company.' I sometimes go up to a visitor who I can see has been touched by the Holy Spirit and personally invite him or her to join a group. And I like to have experienced colleagues standing at the door to say farewell to people as they leave. Often a person who has not plucked up the courage to sign up for a Discovery Group may have been deeply moved, and it shows on their face. Then a tactful word and a chat can greatly help, and can result in that person joining a group.

With all this activity going on at the end of the service, it makes it very easy for those who want to pray or reflect to stay in their seats without embarrassment. And it makes it easy for those standing with you to chat to the individuals who come forward, not only about the Discovery Group, but about what particularly helped them in the service. Often immediate ministry like this after an evangelistic challenge is invaluable, and information gained through such a conversation, however brief, can be an important initial help to those who are going to lead the groups.

I have not mentioned, hitherto, the use of evangelistic materials such as tracts or booklets at the end of an evangelistic address. I very often offer something appropriate, and indeed I have written a little booklet, *Come, Follow Me*, for precisely such occasions. John Stott's *Becoming a Christian* has had wide circulation all over the world in this connection. Billy Graham's *Steps to Peace With God* is simple and attractively produced. You may have others, perhaps, which you prefer. It does not greatly matter. But to put something of this sort in the hand of a person who has been touched by the evangelistic address is very useful. If at the end of your talk you mention that you have such material, it gives them something to come and ask for, and therefore minimises the embarrassment of going to talk to a minister about God at the end of a service! What is more, material such as this takes the person in a coherent manner through the steps to a living faith, and therefore enables him to revise the elements he understands and have a cool look at the parts which were obscure or only partially understood in the sermon. The thing to avoid, I think, is making the taking of a booklet the mark of having put faith in Christ. At this stage people may well be staggered by the immensity of what Christ is offering them, and frankly they are often not in the position to know if they have 'accepted Christ' or not. It is all spinning round in their head. There will be, and there must be, a proper occasion for confessing Christ publicly later on, but now is not the right moment. You want to make it as easy as you can for them to get the help which a clearly written booklet affords, and to make that initial contact which will, one hopes, result in their being drawn into a Discovery Group, where these things can be sorted out in a far more careful and leisurely way over the next couple of months.

I have spoken throughout this chapter as if the minister of the church is giving the evangelistic sermon. This will often be the case, but is by no means necessarily so. It may be a visiting speaker, in which case it is very important to see that he is fully conversant with your local ground rules as to what he should do at the end of his address. He may prefer to hand it over to you at that point, and you then invite people to come and meet you so as to get signed up for a Discovery Group. It is easy to make such an announcement pleasantly low key. 'I'd like to give you something, and take something from you in return! I'd like to give you this little book, which goes through the steps to a living faith and is something you may find helpful. And I'd like to take your name and address, so that I can give you an invitation to the Discovery Group we have been talking about.'

It may well be, however, that the preacher on any given occasion is neither yourself, as minister of the church, nor a visiting preacher, but some other member of your own congregation who perhaps has gifts in evangelism which you may lack. It is not a question of position, but of gifts. I know some ministers who have no evangelistic gifts themselves, but they use other members of their congregations to preach on such occasions, and see a steady crop of new believers coming to join the church. These wise pastors allow those whom God has gifted in evangelism to use that gift for the good of the church, and without any twinge of pride or jealousy.

There are, of course, other ways of ending an evangelistic meeting. Some favour getting people to raise their hands or to stand up, but this seems to me to be calling for a public confession of commitment before that commitment may have been understood or taken. I much prefer, therefore, a Discovery Group to which new believers, those not yet quite sure, and those who want to rededicate their lives can all be invited. It makes it much less threatening, and it immediately places them into a context where they can be built up. Evangelists need to remember that the Lord is not interested in decisions. He is seeking disciples. And all our evangelism must lead in that direction.

I am reluctant to leave this chapter without one final word. It will be stressed strongly in chapter 14, but it needs saying now as well. A chapter like this on preaching for decision can leave the impression of a very man-centred, almost a contrived approach to evangelism. This is one of the great dangers facing anyone who seeks to engage in evangelism. We can by ourselves achieve nothing. It is only God who begets new life. And he loves to do it through his Word. Peter knew that. 'You have been born anew,' he writes, 'not of perishable seed but of imperishable, through the living and abiding word of God . . . That word is the good news which was preached to you' (1 Pet. 1:23–4). The proclamation of God's good news, whether in a specific evangelistic service or not, has enormous power. And the wise pastor will give himself to expository preaching, that is to say, allowing the Word of God to be so clearly placed before his hearers that it does its own inscrutable work. Given that, he will find that people come to Christ at all sorts of times after being exposed to the Word of God. It will assuredly not be restricted to evangelistic services. The divine Word has a power to which our words can never attain. Our supreme privilege and calling as ministers of the gospel is to allow it to speak. Much preaching is a very far cry from that. We are called to be 'servants of the Word'. And when that happens, God has a way of drawing people to himself.

FURTHER READING

Among books on evangelistic preaching that have helped me are:
Martyn Lloyd Jones, *Preachers and Preaching* (Hodder & Stoughton)
W. E. Sangster, *The Craft of the Sermon* (Epworth)
James Stewart, *A Faith to Proclaim* (Hodder & Stoughton)
James Stewart, *Heralds of God* (Hodder & Stoughton)
John Stott, *I Believe in Preaching* (Hodder & Stoughton)
Alan Walker, *Evangelistic Preaching* (Zondervan)
   There is also much value to be gained from occasionally reading the sermons of great preachers from the past, such as C. H. Spurgeon. Also recommended is Spurgeon's *Lectures to My Students* (Zondervan), which is extremely shrewd, and very amusing.

10

Person to Person

If evangelistic preaching is perhaps the most usual way of spreading the faith to those who do not share it, personal evangelism is the most effective. The reason is simple: it is *personal* evangelism, the sharing of good news between two friends. That is the most natural thing in the world. It is also one of the most joyous.

The New Testament is insistent that every Christian is a witness. Not every Christian is a preacher: maybe that is something to be thankful for. But we are all called to bear witness to the Lord who is in charge of our lives. Good news, as Leighton Ford puts it in the title of his book, is for sharing.

A WORLD WITHOUT GOD

It is important not to blind ourselves to the fact that a great number of people these days live to all intents and purposes in a world without God. They have, as the astronomer Laplace said to Napoleon, no need of that hypothesis. Their needs are catered for by the comforts of modern urban society. They may not be atheists: not everyone thinks things out as clearly as that. They may be agnostic or vaguely believe that 'there must be something out there' but never bother to pursue the matter. That tendency has grown apace in the past century under the influence of Darwin, Nietzsche, Freud, and Sartre, and it has been accelerated by two world wars and the Holocaust. The absence of God is now taken for granted in both thoughtful and popular circles.

That makes a great deal of difference, when you come to think of it. If you believe in a living, personal God, the Creator and

Sustainer, the Origin and Goal of all there is, it makes a lot of sense of the things and the people in this world. Both spring from this unified source, God. You have a frame of reference which is big enough to embrace atoms and personalities, crystals and values, rocks and religion. But once you throw God out you have a problem, indeed a nest of problems. You are torn apart. Your view of the world has to assume that the personal sprang from the impersonal, that what you can touch and measure is real, and what you feel and value is not. You are torn between the personal aspects of life, which must be treated as secondary or even illusory (remember, we have got rid of a personal Creator), and the 'real' world of the test tube, the world of big business and technology. And it is not easy. Try relating to your wife in the evening as you have related to your boss or your subordinates in the day, and it won't make for a happy marriage. Try evaluating your marriage relationship in scientific terms of measurement, analysis and experiment, and you are heading for a divorce. Divorces have become nearly as common as marriages these days, because people are so torn. They live in a dichotomy, a world which essentially has no inherent value, no personal creativity, no morals, no destiny – and yet nobody can live that way. If they try, it ends in despair. For so many sensitive and perceptive modern painters and poets and musicians and playwrights it has been the path to suicide.

I suggest that you think through the shape of the world, the world without God, which most people inhabit. It has profound implications for our lives. I could illustrate each point profusely from modern plays, films, literature. But those illustrations would be out of date in a year or two. Others would have walked upon the stage to play out the same tragic part. If you listen to pop music, read modern poetry, go to modern plays, you will find the following seven implications of the modern Godless world-view cropping up time and again. They are built into the logical structure of a mindset that leaves out of consideration a living, personal, Creator God.

A world without love

Of course they fall in love; they enjoy friendships, they care for children and parents, to some extent at least. But if they are being consistent, the love they feel is just part of the structure of an unfeeling universe. Love is, in this world-view, no more than chemical attraction; and this is coming through more and more strongly in modern music and song. And yet you can't live that way without anguish. Anguish there is in so many modern lives, so much modern writing. It comes over powerfully in this short poem by Steve Turner:

> My love
>> she said
>> that when all's considered
>> we're only machines.
> I chained
>> her to my bedroom wall
>> for future use
>> and she cried.

A world without values

Once again, of course, they have values. But in the last analysis these are arbitrary and subjective. Nothing is absolute. All is relative. How can you get values out of the primal abyss from which we came? Remember we have removed the possibility of a Creator. Sartre saw the force of this clearly: 'If God does not exist, man is, in consequence, forlorn. For he cannot find anything to depend on either inside or outside himself . . . Morals are for us both unavoidable and impossible.' And Alvin Toffler, in *Future Shock*, confessed, 'On the edge of a new millennium, on the brink of a new stage in human development, we are racing blindly into the future. But where do we want to go? What would happen if we actually tried to answer this question?' Values have to be arbitrary in a world where, by definition, there is no Absolute. And that hurts people in their guts when they come to see it. For on this matter their guts refuse to listen to their heads. They cannot unwaveringly believe what they think they are driven to believe, that all values are, in the last analysis, baseless.

A world without meaning

It sprang from nothingness and will return to nothingness in due course. It emerged with a Big Bang which might easily not have happened. The existence of our planet is a random, uncaused event – from which, nevertheless, our causally chained world emerged. People feel the lack of meaning intensely. It is known to be a major cause of depression and suicide. 'Everything lacks meaning,' wrote Nietzsche (quite properly, if his atheistic hypothesis is right). 'The goal is lacking. The answer is lacking to our "why?"' The Theatre of the Absurd is the artistic expression of this 'death of man' which follows Nietzsche's 'death of God'. Ronald Conway, one of Australia's leading psychologists, put it in very down-to-earth terms:

> We have in parts of Melbourne the highest barbiturate dependence in the world, the highest suicide rate among young males between eighteen and thirty, the highest declared rate of rape in the world, and one in four women and one in ten men are suffering from depression. Australians have everything, and yet they have nothing to live for.

A world without freedom

Despite all the furore for social, political and personal freedom, people are vaguely (or sometimes acutely) aware of the bondages under which they live. In countries where there is severe sexual or racial discrimination, or where there is a strong curtailment of personal liberties, the absence of freedom is clear enough. But in the so-called free world political bondage, media bondage, role bondage, mind control are very much at work. And behind all that is the assumption that we are conditioned, perhaps totally conditioned, socially, economically or chemically. After all, if there is no God, then values like freedom have no real meaning. 'All in all,' as Pink Floyd sang, 'you're just another brick in the wall.' Or as Jacques Monod puts it in *Chance and Necessity*:

> Recognise the split in modern man: chance and values. No society before ours was ever torn apart by such a conflict. In both classical and primitive cultures people saw knowledge and values stemming from the same source. For the first time in history a civilisation is trying to shape itself by clinging desperately to the ancient tradition in its values, while at the same time abandoning it as the source of knowledge, of truth.

A world without fulfilment

People are hungry for something, they know not what, even when they appear to have everything. Advertisers promote gifts 'for the man/woman who has everything'. People put all they have into climbing to the top of their particular tree. If they do not make it, they develop a chip on the shoulder. If they do, they are still empty inside. Sophia Loren spoke for more than the Hollywood community when she said, 'My life is what I have dreamed of. Films, marriage to Carlo, bearing his children. Marvellous. I only lack one thing – I do not know how to describe it. But in my life there is a void, *impossible a combler*.' Despite having all they wanted, people are, as John Lennon put it in his memorable song, crippled inside. If you were to contrast the faces on the London Underground with those in rural Tanzania, you would notice a tremendous difference in the apparent, and I believe real, sense of fulfilment. We in the West have everything, and yet we have nothing. We can survive in our professional life, but not in our personal life.

A world without truth

Objective truth, which people used to believe in and search for with all their hearts, has been dissolved into relativism – 'Well, it's true for me; it may not be true for you.' It has faded into the new mysticism, which offers some satisfaction but no rationale. It has been swallowed up into the new syncretism in which contradictory world-views are held in tension when they are totally incompatible. The law of non-contradiction is jettisoned. Truth has disappeared from the intellectual map. Many people take refuge in the trip within: hence the drug culture and the New Age movement and the thousand and one new cults which constantly emerge. And if 'truth' language is still used, it is used by connotation, not direct applicability. The coinage of truth is still in common use. But it is devalued. It is just paper money. There is no gold standard to which it corresponds.

A world of despair

They try to get away from it most of the time by keeping busy and not thinking about it. Like the Roman Empire on the eve of dissolution, there is a frenzied search for 'bread and circuses'. But deep down people have little hope for the future. The ecological threat; the nuclear threat; the increasing violence in cities; the awesome possibilities of human engineering; the spread of famine and the growth of population. At a more personal level, the six elements mentioned above (and there are others, including personal tragedy) lead many people to despair, self-hatred and a sense of futile helplessness or longing to end it all. And yet, man's spirit is so constituted that it cannot long allow the collapse of hope. But is there a hope that has promise for the individual, for society and the cosmos? Is there a solidly based and credible hope like that? You and I believe there is. That is why we are bound to share it with those who have no hope. And this is not normally best done within the walls of a church, which may bring to their minds all sorts of unhelpful memories or associations. It is best done where the two of you can talk comfortably, the two of you together. And that is personal evangelism at its most basic.

PREREQUISITES

That is the mental climate in which many people live. If we are going to be of service to them, there are some basic things to bear in mind.

We need to lead attractive Christian lives

This has, somewhat belatedly, become evident to those who are seeking to evangelise. The scandals that have disfigured the scene, particularly in the highly publicised televangelism industry, have drawn attention to what we must be if people are even to begin to listen to what we say. Holy living, warm, friendly living, joyful living, compassionate living, is essential if we are to commend the good news of Christ. This will take many forms, according to the situation of those we are trying to help, but it is indispensable. If our lives do not attract people, our message certainly won't. And a loveless, joyless, legalistic, narrow Christianity is going to do more harm than good to the cause of Jesus, that delightful and liberated friend of publicans and sinners.

So important is this that a whole new approach to evangelism is now being advocated: it is called 'lifestyle evangelism'. You will find it advocated in J. C. Aldrich's *Lifestyle Evangelism*, Don Posterski's *Friendship*, and notably in Becky Pippert's *Out of the Saltshaker*. This current emphasis is a reaction against the heavily structured 'programme evangelism' on the one hand, which seeks to give a tight, sometimes rather shallow, methodology for people to shoot at their friends (and foes) with; and, on the other, against the dull, legalistic, loveless, and unChristlike living which, alas, marks so many Christians and churches. As such it is an emphasis that is much needed. There is a lot of truth in the saying, 'You can only evangelise friends,' and the 'friendship evangelists' are saying just that. Lifestyle is an essential precondition of evangelism at any level. So this modern emphasis, welcome as it is, contains nothing new. It is simply getting back to an aspect of New Testament Christianity that had been lost through other emphases. Look at those early Christians. Their lifestyle was eloquent indeed. They showed tremendous practical love. They had a joy that overflowed. They cared for the poor and the needy. They were not in bondage to past custom. They knew Jesus personally, and it showed in changes in their personality and way of life. They were generous to a fault, and untouched by the materialism of the day. Their company was good to be in. They bothered about justice. And there was no sniff of the Christian ghetto about them: they kept looking outwards. Lifestyle evangelism, friendship evangelism? Yes indeed. It is vital. But one caveat is needed. By itself lifestyle will not do the trick. Plenty of people lead delightful and generous lives without any faith, and unless life and word go together we shall not see the changes in our friends that we hope for. We need to talk to them, once we have won their friendship. 'Lifestyle evangelism' tends to be strong on life, but weak on lip.

We need to ask sensitive, probing questions

If people are living in a basically Godless world, they are actually on the wrong path. They are stumbling along in the dark. And this sense of loneliness, frustration, alienation, lack of purpose, deprivation of love and so forth springs from a wrong attitude to God. But they do not see that, and they will not thank us at first for pointing it out. They have got to be brought to see it for themselves. So we need to show profound compassion and understanding of where they are, emotionally and spiritually. But we cannot, if we care about them, leave it there. We need to ask them probing questions, questions which begin to open up to them the possibility that they may be on the wrong track. We have looked into this a little in chapters 5 and 6. In my experience Dr Francis Schaeffer was the master of this Socratic method. By asking carefully directed questions, he had a remarkable gift of enabling people to realise they were basing their lives on a false set of presuppositions. We need to listen. We need to empathise. But we need, gently yet firmly, to point out where what is being said will not stand up. It can be very painful. Nobody likes to realise that they have been resting their life on foundations which cannot bear its weight. But until they do realise that, you and I will not get very far in evangelism. It is here that we find the proper place for the use of apologetics, frequently an indispensable prerequisite to direct evangelism.

We need to suggest an alternative

From our position alongside our friend we need to suggest that there could be an alternative way of looking at the world. What if there is a God who cares for men? What if he has actually got involved in our world, and through creation, conscience, values, personality and so forth is seeking to get through to us? What if he has actually come to find us? What if he has broken the wall of alienation that your friend may well be so conscious of? What if he is alive and able to be met? Do not dogmatise. That will get you nowhere. Suggest an alternative scenario. It is probably one that he has not seriously considered for years, if at all. And do not be embarrassed to open your Bible with him. I am amazed at how many Christians seem to be terrified of doing this. Whether they are terrified of exposing their own ignorance, or terrified of putting their friend off, I am not sure. Both fears I believe to be ground-less. You know some key verses or chapters in Scripture, do you not? And you know where to find them? Use what you have, and your repertoire will increase (especially with the help of an organ-isation like the Navigators who specialise in personal evangelism and the memorisation of appropriate and useful texts of Scripture). And as for putting others off, I have never found that to be the case. So long as I do not ram texts down their throat, but invite them to come alongside me and see what Christianity according to the earliest members of the Christian church, and of Jesus himself, looks like, I have always found people to be both interested and unembarrassed. You see, the Bible has its own power and im-mediacy. We do not need to engage in a defence of its reliability before we dare use it. We simply need to let it be known and read and understood. It will do its own work. For whether our friend knows it or not, *we know*: it is the Word of God and it will get through.

We need constant dependence on the Holy Spirit

No skill of ours is going to be able to lead an enquirer to Christ. That is the sovereign work of the Spirit himself. We never know whether our frail attempts to make the truth and challenge of the gospel plain to a friend will be crowned with success or not. The marvellous thing is that we do not have to concern ourselves too much about it. Our call is to be faithful stewards of the treasure of the gospel which has been given into our charge. The Spirit's task is to apply it. When we fail, we should indeed look and see if there was any obvious mistake or lack of love or directness on our part. There may well have been. On the other hand, it may simply be that the time was not yet ripe. The Spirit did not make the whole thing luminous to him. We can trust God's Spirit to do his own work in his own time. We are not called to go round, like Atlas, carrying the world on our shoulders. We are called to be happy, sensitive witnesses to Christ, and to leave the results to him.

We need constantly to be building bridges

It is one of the merits of Leighton Ford's book *Good News is for Sharing* that he makes much of this imperative. And in his own life he resolutely carries it out. He has a graciousness, a shrewdness, a charm, a sensitivity that does establish quick and easy relations with other people from a wide variety of backgrounds. This is a quality we should covet and cultivate. People need to see us not only as examples of what Christ can do, but as bridge-people to help them get there too. How often do I hear people say, 'Michael, I wish I had your faith.' I tell them that they do have precisely my faith: it is simply put in the wrong place! This often encourages them to examine how they can put it in the right place.

Leighton Ford makes some helpful points about this sort of bridge-building. God wants me to be his person: that is basic, or he could not use me. But equally he wants me to be myself, not to copy others or emulate their gifts. He is the God of infinite variety, and he can use every type of personality. It is important for us to accept ourselves if we are to help others to find God's free and liberating acceptance. He goes on to urge would-be bridge-builders to forsake the castle of the Christian ghetto and to reach out in authentic friendship to people who are not yet Christians. He has wise things to say if people ask you to events inconsistent with your standards. Instead of saying, 'I don't do that,' why not invite them to some alternative shared activity? He is certainly right in warning against the all-consuming nature of the activities of many churches, leaving little time to cultivate relationships with people who are not Christians. We need to love people, and love them in a practical way, if we are to be able to share Christ, the Christ who washed his disciples' sweaty feet, with them. And we have to show that we are people who are as happy to receive as we are to give. And never must we forget that bridges are meant for crossing: building them is not enough. But how are we to begin to do that?

A FLEXIBLE APPROACH

Years ago in World Council of Churches circles there was an adage: 'Let the world set the agenda.' Despite its inadequacies as a total Christian programme, it has real merit when applied to personal evangelism. It is simply disastrous if we move into conversation with someone armed with a packaged formula. We need to use every and any path as a path to Christ. There is enormous flexibility in the way the New Testament presents its message. There is no excuse for us to be wooden.

Casual contacts may well present themselves, and we need to snap up these fleeting opportunities, because they may not recur. Directness, humour, sensitivity and love are the main ingredients, together with a taste of that salt or a flash of that light which Jesus Christ has brought into our lives. I sometimes think it is like the craft of the fly fisherman. He casts a fly over a fish. If the fish is hungry, it will take. If not, the wise fisherman does not continue to flog the water. He moves on, knowing that one of these days that fish will rise. We are not called to storm the gates of unbelief. We are called to move humbly, sensitively and observantly behind the Holy Spirit, and to be ready to offer a word in season when he opens up the way. Chances to turn the conversation may well come our way after a TV programme or a film, or perhaps during a discussion about a moral issue like abortion or big-business profits. Wearing a discreet badge, or leaving a Christian magazine lying around the room, can open up a good discussion. There is a lot of power in a simple testimony to the reality of Jesus Christ in your own experience: 'I have found . . .' is something which cannot be gainsaid. It is, after all, your own experience which you are contributing to the conversation. He must make of it what he will.

Sometimes the person we are talking with will go quiet and not want to pursue the conversation. It is worth leaving the matter there, but just giving him something to reflect on. 'Right, let's leave it, but I wonder whether you are perhaps being a bit short-sighted?' Above all, be natural. Do what feels right for you.

Sometimes you will find that he is keen to open up and discuss things. He may have been secretly wanting to talk about Christian things for some time, but not found the opportunity hitherto. If so, give him space, be a good listener, and take it from there. Sometimes you will find one of the old chestnuts being brought up in response to your initiative. This is likely to be a tactic to keep you at arm's length. A touch of self-deprecating humour, a brief but shrewd response, will leave the way open for another occasion. Sometimes the smokescreen needs to be penetrated, and the poverty of the excuse revealed, but you would be wise not to do that in public. You never help people forward by humiliating them. Of course, the person may be ready for a thoughtful talk then and there. If so, try to drop any other priorities and move with the flow. Treat him as you would a friend.

And with friends, it is often a long haul to win them to Christ. We need to earn the right to speak by caring, by shared interests, by prayer and by the silent testimony of our lives. As time goes by, we shall discover how he ticks and where, spiritually and intellectually, he lives. As we saw in a previous chapter, it is good to try to discover the felt need in a person's life, and then relate Jesus Christ to that. Some people will maintain that they have no felt need. It is not wise to try to manufacture one! Go for the truth issue. Did Jesus Christ, or did he not, come from God? Did he or did he not rise from the dead? If these things are true, then it is not simply a matter of perceived need. If Jesus Christ is God and came to this world for the likes of us, then we were in need, in deep need, whether or not we realise it.

After discovering where our friend *is*, we need to seek to

stimulate his desire. Jesus is never dull; nor should our talk of him be. Fascinate your friend by showing him what he does not expect, that Jesus is alive and highly relevant to his everyday life. Tell him something of the difference he has made to you and to friends that you and he have in common. See if you can think of some biblical passage where Jesus approaches and captivates a person of his type. Note the flexibility of Jesus' own approach to different people. To Nicodemus, a bland theologian who knew it all, he spoke of the revolutionary concept of a new birth (John 3). To the Samaritan woman, disenchanted with men and the outcast situation in which Samaritans felt themselves, Jesus offered free acceptance: he drank from the same utensil as she, demonstrating his lack of any prejudice, and he spoke to her of the inner sparkling water of life that could transform her daily trudge to the well (John 4). To the thief, dying alongside him in terrible agony, and reaching out in faith that he was going to receive a kingdom after death, Jesus offered the man the relief and joy of being with him in paradise, God's garden, that very day (Luke 23). This was all the more welcome because crucified victims often lingered for days in their agony. Or think of Zacchaeus, so aware of hostility and alienation and trying to compensate for his loneliness by ill-gotten gains; Jesus offers to come and have a meal with him (Luke 19). I wonder how long it had been since anyone had done that? The paralysed man needed healing: but much more he needed forgiveness, and Jesus saw that, and touched him on this raw and unsuspected area of his life. The healing followed (Mark 2). The woman caught in the act of adultery did not need any reminder of her guilt (John 8). What took her breath away was the free word of forgiveness which Jesus gave her.

A totally different approach on each occasion, you see, but just right for the individual in question. We shall not get it right every time. Far from it. But it is a good goal to have. Jesus is the way to God. But there are many roads to Jesus. Fear, hope, trust, and love are four of the main motivating forces of mankind. They can very well provide a way in to the heart. Some people are very fearful: it could be right on occasion to move this to a different plane of fear. There is such a thing as proper fear of God (Luke 13:1–5). But if we are going to use that tack, we need to be intensely sensitive, and to remember that it is love which casts out fear (1 John 4:18). Many people are hopeful by temperament, but they have little grounds for their optimism. There is in Christ, who has entered heaven on our behalf, a hope which is the steadfast

anchor of the soul, and we need not be embarrassed to affirm it
(Heb. 6:19). Point trusting people, who are so often deceived
because of the trustful nature they possess, to the utterly trustworthy one who will have never let them down (Rom. 5:1; John
6:37). And the warm, loving people we meet – they will be most
helped and wooed by the love of Jesus which seeks them however
little they have hitherto responded to it (John 3:16; Gal. 2:20).
Seek the appropriate 'way in' to each individual.

It is most important to ensure that you are communicating.
Christians often think they are when they are not. So people hear
but do not understand (cf. Mark 4:12, NIV). We need to translate
both our language and our thought forms into what makes sense
for our friend. We need to illustrate copiously from the realm of his
experience. We need to have one foot in the New Testament and
one in his dramatic, musical, intellectual and social world. If we
care enough, we will ensure that we are understood, indeed that we
cannot be misunderstood.

And then we need to relate Jesus Christ to the person we have
been 'investigating'.

Is he a Jehovah's Witness? If so, he will know parts of the Bible
very well, but he will basically be very short on hope, and will be
relying on his own good works to get him right with God. Paul's
treatment of justification in Romans could be very helpful.

Is he a humanist? The optimistic variety reject authority, absolute values and of course the future life, and major on love and
kindness. Do not collide with him. Point him to the perfect human
being, and explore the teachings and the character and the standards of the Man of Nazareth with him. He may well soon find that
he cannot, if he is being honest, keep his own high standards, and
that he has no genuinely rational grounds (as an atheist) for his
belief in the supremacy of love. Well, you can show him some.

Is he an existentialist? Many of them are humanists of the
pessimistic variety. There is no need to talk to them about sin and
deadness, for they know all too well the darkness and despair of
modern man. A person like that will be looking for significance,
identity, relationship. Show him that they are to be found in Jesus.
He probably thinks Christianity is assent to somewhat improbable
propositions, and at best an attempt to live out those ideals. Show
him that it involves relationship, commitment and new life. These
are all concepts he is strong on and understands very well.

Is he a scientist? Show him the solid evidence underlying the
Christian claim. He has access to it in the Gospels. Let him conduct

an experiment. Jesus claimed that his teaching derived from God and that if anyone's will was open, he would know the truth (John 7:17). And the Gospel of John was written to provide that evidence, from an eyewitness source, to show why he had believed and to provide a point of departure for later generations to commit themselves (John 20:31). The scrutiny of the evidence, the self-commitment to the theory that it is reliable, and the subsequent verification is very much the scientific method. Do not imagine that hard-headed scientists are difficult to win to Christ. That is not the case, provided they are shown the evidence, are persuaded of its reliability, and commit themselves to it as they would to a possible scientific advance.

Is your friend apathetic? Show him the lack of integrity in such a position. The Christian claim is monumental in its implications. Just to shrug your shoulders and say 'maybe' is not a tolerable response for anyone who professes to value truth. Nor is it a grateful response from anyone who professes to value love.

Is he lonely, worried, schizoid, unhappy? Show him the difference, from the gospel stories, that Jesus can and has made to such situations. It is important not to exaggerate. Christ offers to share our situations in partnership with us. He does not always remove the difficulties, but he gives us the grace to handle them.

You have won your friend's confidence. You have discovered his basic position, stimulated his desire and related Jesus Christ to where he is situated. Now is the time to gently open his eyes to the basic cause of all his malaise. He is out of touch with God. The New Testament has different words for this human disease of sin in which we are all born, and to which we all give way. It speaks of *hamartia*, falling short of God's standards; *parabasis*, breaking God's rules; *akrasia*, lack of self-control; *anomia*, rebellion. With this disease in our lives, no wonder things go wrong. God seems unreal, or a threat. We need to get right with him. And with supreme generosity, God has made that possible.

LEARNING FROM JESUS . . . AND PHILIP

At this juncture it could be helpful to see Jesus himself engaging in this delicate task of drawing an individual to faith. Perhaps the most celebrated example in the Gospels is to be found in John 4, where Jesus is in discussion with a woman of Samaria. The passage is well known, and often preached about, but it certainly has some important lessons to teach us.

First, it is clear that Jesus had a fire burning within him. He had a passion to share the good news of the Kingdom, and he probably had a presentiment that it would be with someone from Samaria. 'He had to pass through Samaria,' we read (v.4) – well, he didn't actually *have* to. Through Samaria was the direct route, but so bad were the relations between Jews and Samaritans that orthodox Jews went to the trouble of making a large detour to avoid getting defiled by going into this country of mixed race and religion, Samaria. Not so Jesus. He had a passion to reach those in need.

Second, I see that he bothered about one single individual (v.7). He defied convention and spoke with a woman alone. He defied exhaustion too (v.6), and took the opportunity when he must least have felt like it.

Third, curious though it certainly seemed to her, Jesus asked the woman to do him a favour (v.7). This is often the way into somebody's confidence, and in due course into their heart.

Fourth, Jesus began where the woman's interest was – with water. She was not looking for a spiritual conversion. She had come to get water. And with consummate tact and shrewdness Jesus led her on from there. Natural avenues are the ones to travel down.

Fifth, he drew out the woman's curiosity, making her spiritually thirsty: 'If you knew . . . who it is that is saying to you, "Give me a drink" . . .', said Jesus (v.10). We need to look for ways of eliciting that initial curiosity that will get a person moving in the right direction. Worship is one such way, testimony another, and if there is a healing or a tongue and an interpretation, or a prophetic utterance, and there is in many Christian circles these days, then that too will often elicit the initial curiosity in people who appear utterly unconcerned on the surface.

Sixth, the next thing that is apparent here is the way in which Jesus began to thrill her with the possibilities of a real spiritual life: the 'spring of living water' in her own parched heart was an image that must have been well-nigh irresistible to this woman who was so tired of the drudgery of going to the well. This sense of excitement enabled her to be satisfied with a very brief answer to her question about the proper place of worship, which was mildly irrelevant to the issue in hand.

Seventh, I note that Jesus was not embarrassed to point to her sin. He did so graciously and obliquely (v.16), but firmly all the same. If people are to turn round and find Christ, there does need to be an act of repentance. We cannot eat at his table, so to speak, with unwashed hands.

Eighth, the woman had a difficulty which she raised at this point (v.19). No doubt it was a real problem to her, but raising it as she did at this juncture suggests it may have been something of a smokescreen as well. We may assume, I think, that she did not want to have Jesus continue the enquiry into her matrimonial affairs. Jesus dealt with her question, whether or not it was an evasion, with great succinctness and brought her back to the question of himself, the living water, and what she was going to do about it.

Ninth, we then see Jesus, with great simplicity and sureness of touch, leading her to faith. That faith was not very well formulated, nor very extensive. Its content was doubtless deficient, but it sufficed to enable her and the Saviour to begin contact. She had some idea who Jesus was (v.26), and she had some inkling of the transformation he could effect through that 'living water' (v.14). That was about all. Not extensive, but sufficient. You do not need to know your way through Calvin's *Institutes* or Aquinas' *Summa* before coming to Christian commitment. The content of belief may often be minimal. But the encounter is always crucial, just as it was for this woman.

Tenth, two lovely things bring this instructive story to a conclusion. First we find the woman giving a testimony to others of what she had begun to find, so thrilled was she with Jesus (v.29). That is very frequently the outcome of someone finding Christ. They can't keep it quiet, but want to pass it on. And then we find the men of Samaria responding to Jesus themselves (vv.39–42), partly as a result of what the woman had to say, and partly as a result of meeting him for themselves.

The whole story is a marvellous paradigm of personal evangelism, a lesson from the Master himself.

But if we feel we cannot begin to match the skills of Jesus, let us glance at Philip as he is brought before us in Acts 8. Luke evidently intends us to see him as a model of that personal outreach by the early Christians which had such a lot to do with the spread of the church.

First and foremost, here was a man in touch with God (vv.26, 29, 39). God could lead him because he was abiding in Christ, and sensitive to his voice.

Second, that sensitivity led to obedience (vv.26–7). He went where he was told, and he responded to the gentle nudge of the Holy Spirit to leave Samaria and move far to the south. It would have been very easy for him to find good reasons not to do what God was telling him.

Third, he was obviously a humble man. One of the seven 'deacons' of Acts 6, he had clearly found that his greatest gifts lay not in administration but in preaching, and the early part of Acts 8 is full of his exploits in Samaria where something like a revival seems to have taken place. Maybe he was reaping what Jesus had sown there. At all events, he was prepared to leave all this behind, to abandon the limelight, and to journey seventy miles into the desert with no prospect of an audience, because one person there needed him – and he did not even know it. He was prepared to be the servant of an Ethiopian eunuch for Christ's sake. There was certainly nothing stuffy or prickly about Philip.

Fourth, he was enthusiastic (v.30). You have to be enthusiastic to run in that desert, where the temperature can rise to as much as 140°F in the shade. His zeal must have sprung, at bottom, from realising the need of that man, without Christ and without hope, as he read aloud in his chariot while it moved along. Something of Christ's own compassion gripped Philip and spurred him into action.

Fifth, he was tactful, a virtue that does not always go with enthusiasm. He did not rush in, but listened, asked a lot of questions, and offered his services (vv.30–5). Then he began precisely where the man was. Tact like that springs from love, from really caring.

Sixth, he was well-informed. He knew his Bible well enough to recognise the passage which was so surprisingly being read aloud in the desert air. It was from Isaiah 53, and he was well able to preach 'Jesus' from that launch-pad. There is no short cut to learning at least a few passages of Scripture by heart in order to be able to use them to help others. Of course, not every casual contact will be reading Isaiah 53! But the point stands. We need to be prepared for whatever approach is suggested by the presenting situation of those we seek to serve.

Finally, he was very direct (v.35). He gave this needy but seeking man not ideas or religion, but Jesus, the living, loving person of Jesus. Directness seems to have been a characteristic of Philip (vv.5, 12). It is still effective if we do it in love. Certainly Jesus himself must be the burden of what we have to communicate to people. He, and he alone, can transform their lives.

THE ROLE OF THE MIDWIFE

It is to be hoped that the time will come in our conversation with a friend when we can actually help him or her over the border into faith in Christ. We have the immense privilege, sometimes, of being midwives at a birth. Every birth is special. Each one is a thing of surpassing wonder. And when you put it like that, it is easy to see two contrasting errors to which you could possibly fall prey. One would be to treat all births alike, with professional competence, but miss the individual needs and be blinded to the glory of it all. That way is sad, and potentially disastrous, especially if there are any complications in the birth; and spiritually there usually are! The other mistake would be to be called upon to act the midwife and yet not have the slightest clue what to do! Some ministers are like that with spiritual births. It is not an enviable position to be in. Somehow, therefore, we need to have the flexibility of Jesus or Philip on the one hand, and also to have some idea in our minds of how to bring a person from unbelief to faith. We must not offer people a hard-line, tightly-packaged, programme: but we must not be like the fisherman who was asked by his wife on his return home, 'How many did you catch?' and had to reply, 'None actually. But I influenced a good many.'

What follows must therefore not be taken for a technique. We are not manipulators but introducers. We have reached the point in conversation when our friend genuinely wants to start a relationship with Christ. How can we help him to begin?

I generally have the first four letters of the alphabet at the back of my mind at this point. However flexibly I approach it, however often I am diverted by his questions or concerns, there are four things that seem essential if he is to come to know Christ. There is something to *admit*: his falling short, and its consequences. There is something to *believe*: that God in Christ has done everything for his restoration. There is something to *consider*: what it will all cost to be a disciple. And there is something to *do*: reach out in faith and personally appropriate the proffered gift.

There is something to admit

Our friend needs to be brought to appreciate that he has the 'human disease' of sin. It consists in breaking God's law, coming short of his standards, and rejecting his love and authority over us (1 John 3:4; Jas. 4:17; John 3:18). The results of this disease are very serious. We are estranged from God (Isa. 59:1–2, Eph. 2:1), and we are enslaved to self-centredness (John 8:34; Tit. 3:3). The disease is fatal, if it is not dealt with (Rom. 6:23). In order to begin a living relationship with Christ, our friend needs to admit the truth of this biblical diagnosis of the basic problem in his life. He needs to recognise that he is in the wrong with God, and to be willing for changes to be made. Nothing he can do will be able to remedy this bad situation. Even if he could live a perfect life from today onwards, that would still leave unrelieved the guilt of the past. As the epistle to the Romans laconically observes, 'None is righteous, no, not one' (Rom. 3:10). And a God who is holy and just cannot overlook such a thing. He cannot have defilement in his holy presence. It stands to reason.

There is something to believe

As we saw in the interview between Jesus and the woman of Samaria, the contents of belief are not necessarily large, though they are demanding. It is not possible to be a Christian, surely, unless you recognise who 'Christ' is. He is no less than God come to our rescue. The earliest baptismal confession was 'Jesus is Lord'. That says it all, really. It is proclaiming that Jesus (and the word *means* 'God to the rescue') is exalted as Lord over all. The one who became incarnate for us, died on the cross for us, is alive for ever through the resurrection, and calls for our allegiance. We need to take time to show our friend that Jesus came to deal with the fact of human sin. He died on the cross to atone for the guilt of human sin. And he rose from the dead in order to be able to break the power of sin. You will need to spend time explaining the cross. Few people understand the heart of it. Not surprising, for it is the ultimate mystery! But it is certainly not just an example of how much God loves us. It is certainly not a good man coming to a sticky end. It is certainly not a martyr stoically enduring his fate. It is God himself dealing with our sins by taking the weight of them on his own shoulders. Verses from the Bible like Romans 5:8; 2 Corinthians 5:18, 21; Galatians 3:10, 13; Mark 10:45 all help to show some sides of the mystery. I find it almost incredible that God should love people like us enough to come among us and stoop to the most horrible death that could ever be designed by the brutality of man.

More, that he should allow the world's evil to be poured out in vile concentration on his sinless head. But he did. And that is why it is Good Friday for us, terrible though it was for him. That is why we can cry with confident exultation, 'There is therefore now no condemnation for those who are in Christ Jesus' (Rom. 8:1). But one of the verses I find most helpful in taking people to the heart of what Christ did for them on the cross is 1 Peter 3:18: 'Christ has once suffered for sins, the just for the unjust, to bring us to God.' Immensely simple, and extremely clear. The sufferer on that cross was none other than the Christ for whom the world had been waiting since the Garden of Eden. It was the supreme rescuer who ended up in naked agony on that terrible tree. Why was he there? 'For sins.' He, the just one, took the place which should rightly have fallen to us, the unjust, if we really got our deserts from a holy God. And why was it needed? 'To bring us to God.' Had there been any lesser way, we can be sure he would have taken it. But there was no lesser way. There on the cross, he did all that was necessary to bring us back to the one we so earnestly desire to keep away from. And it happened 'once'. The Greek word does not mean 'once upon a time', but 'once and for all'. The job has been done. The rescue is complete. Christ's death can clean up the sheet of our past, guilty life. Christ's resurrection can release in our lives the power to effect radical change. The risen one offers to come and take up residence in our lives, so as to release in us the power of his resurrection (Rom. 5:10; 1 Pet. 1:5; Phil. 4:13). He will progressively break down that bondage to self-will which spoils us, and set us free to be sons and daughters in his family (John 8:36). That is what we are asked to believe. Not many things, but things of vast significance!

There is something to consider

That is, the cost of discipleship. The entrance to the Christian life is free, but the annual subscription is everything we possess. Jesus is not merely Saviour, he is Lord. And we shall save ourselves and our friend a lot of trouble later on if we make very plain at the outset that it will be a costly thing to follow Christ. Jesus laid it on the line very clearly in Luke 14:25–35, immediately after emphasising in the parable of the great supper that the Kingdom is gloriously free for all comers. He asked the crowds to consider whether they were prepared to face obedience to himself, even before family and self. Were they ready for a lifetime of commitment? Were they willing to be opposed, and to cope with being a minority movement? Dare they be salt in society? Such were some of the elements in the cost of discipleship which Jesus stressed.

Of course, all this lies in the future. Your friend cannot at the moment of commitment have any realistic idea of what it will cost him, any more than the bridal couple have any idea of what it will cost them to be pledged to one another for better for worse, for richer for poorer. But there needs to be that willingness in principle to put the other first, come wind, come weather. And it is like that with Christian commitment. Jesus himself put it very sharply in Matthew 6:24: 'You cannot serve God and mammon' (the Carthaginian god of wealth). It is costly to be a Christian. We must not disguise the fact. But it is also costly to reject him, very costly indeed. It is interesting that despite the cost of mutual commitment for life, most married couples do not regard it as prohibitive! I often summarise it in three questions: Are you willing to let Christ clean up the wrong things in your life? Are you willing to put him in the No. 1 slot? And are you willing to be known as a Christian and join the Christian community? That is about as far ahead as he will be able to see, for the present.

There is something to do

Your friend needs to receive the gift which is Jesus Christ. All God's other gifts are wrapped up in him (Eph. 1:3). There are many metaphors in the New Testament for the way in which we in our weakness and Christ in his love and power get together. We 'believe in Christ' (John 3:16), enter 'into Christ' (Eph. 2:12–13), accept the juridical verdict of 'acquitted' (Rom. 8:1), receive 'adoption' (Gal. 4:5), 'find access' (Eph. 2:18), 'come to Christ' (John 6:37). I often find it a help at this stage of the discussion to begin with John 3:16; stressing as it does God's great love, man's real need, and the importance of a step of belief. It has the advantage of being probably the best-known verse in the Bible. My friend may well think he does 'believe', so I take him back a page to John 1:12, to show what 'believing' in biblical terminology means. It is tantamount to 'receiving'. He may believe about Jesus in his head, but never have received him into his life. His faith in Jesus is intellectual but not volitional. He has assent but not affiance. It is worth making this very plain to him. Hold out a banknote to him and say, 'Do you believe this is for you?' He will smile, and say 'Yes' – without making any move. You reply, 'Then you don't believe at all!' – and withdraw the note! In a short time he will see the point: real believing means receiving. It is when he reaches out and takes the note that it really becomes his. And that is what he needs to do about God's divine gift, the Spirit of Jesus Christ. And before I move on, I use verse 13 of John 1 to show how you do *not* get into the family and become a child of God. It is 'not of blood' that you are born into this family – it never comes automatically with parentage or nationality. It is 'not of the will of the flesh' – no amount of effort, hair shirts, trying hard, and religious observances can make you a child of God. It is 'not of the will of man' either. Nobody else can do it for you – no parent, no priest. It is 'of God'. He alone adopts us into his family alongside his one and only Son Jesus Christ. And he does it for those who 'receive' Jesus. But how can that be done?

Revelation 3:20 is a verse that has led millions to faith. The imagery is so basic and so clear. It forms part of a communication from the risen Christ through his servant John to the church at Laodicea. That church is very formal. The members congratulate themselves, 'I am rich, I have prospered, and I need nothing'. But they do not realise that they are 'wretched, pitiable, poor, blind, and naked'. Christ offers to meet them in their need, with 'gold . . . that you may be rich, and white garments to clothe you and to keep the shame of your nakedness from being seen, and salve to anoint your eyes, that you may see'. But as things stand, Christ is the excluded party. They represent that paradox – a church which has everything except Christ. He tells them that they need to make haste and repent, and then to receive him into their lives as they would receive a visitor into their city or their home. 'Behold, I stand at the door and knock; if anyone hears my voice and opens the door, I will come in to him and eat with him, and he with me' (Rev. 3:20). Jesus is the one who can give life and reality to this churchly but spiritually dead community. And he stands outside, knocking. His hand is scarred. He died for them. He lives to make a difference to them, if only they will let him in. It is up to them.

The imagery is superb and wonderfully clear. Your friend will get the point at once. He will see that he too has left Christ out of his life. He may well know about him, believe about him, but he has never 'received' him. He has never let him come in. And the marvel of this illustration is that it is more than an illustration. For when a person opens up to Christ, then his unseen but real Spirit *does* come in. The image is not only pictorial but ontological. Something happens. The person is not the same as before. The Spirit of Christ has come in.

Some people object to the use of this verse because it is written to a church and therefore cannot illuminate initial commitment. I beg to differ. The whole point about this church is that it was a Christless church. The Saviour was excluded by their insane self-satisfaction. They were very much in the place of the non-committed, although they went to church. The religious and the pagan are precisely on the same level if they have not 'received' or 'believed in' Jesus. In a word, if they have not asked him into their lives.

So it is not difficult to point out to your friend that he can think of the house, in the imagery of Revelation 3:20, as his life. The Lord who made the house, the Lord who bought it back when it had been wrenched wilfully from his ownership, stands knocking for admission. He is willing to enter and cleanse the house. He wants his light to shine out from its window. But he will not act without the agreement of the tenant. The promise is unconditional, 'I will come in.' The offer is universal, 'If anyone opens the door.' Christ will not force himself upon us. He will not enter by his Spirit until and unless he is invited. When he is, that brings a person into the family of God (John 1:12). He must decide what to do with the Saviour who stands at the door and knocks. Shall he ask him in? Or not? To respond to him is urgent (Heb. 3:7–8). It is indispensable (1 John 5:12; Acts 4:12). It is unrepeatable (Heb. 10:14). 'Receiving Christ' or 'commitment to Christ' is, like marriage, instantaneous, though there is much that lies behind and precedes it, and a lifelong adjustment that follows. Your friend needs to see that clearly.

COMMITMENT ANXIETIES AND PROBLEMS

When lovingly confronted with the powerful challenge of the gospel, your friend is likely to make one of three responses.

He may say 'Yes', and if so it will be your privilege to help him into the new life with Christ, beginning then and there. We will look at that at the end of this chapter.

But he may very well say 'No' or 'Not yet'. If so, he is likely to need help on one of three 'Rs'.

He may be implying a 'No' to *repentance*. Maybe he thinks he is all right as he is. I have found that to go through the ten commandments or the standards of the Sermon on the Mount with a person in that situation is very valuable. Both are powerful at humbling the proud. Other verses of Scripture that you might like to work through with him may include Jeremiah 17:9; Luke 13:3; Matthew 7:21–3; Romans 3:10–20. It is very important to remember that commitment without repentance soon melts away. Remember too that you are not seeking to arouse guilt over petty sins: you are wanting to encourage 'repentance to God' as Paul puts it (Acts 20:21). Our whole life has been centred on self, and God is calling us to centre it on him. That is what is called for in repentance.

He may, of course, evidence no *realisation*. He may never have understood what Christ did for him on the cross. How could that death so long ago affect him personally? Show him that the offering of the infinite Christ more than covers all the finite number of sinners that the world could ever hold (Heb. 10:11–14; 1 John 2:2). Maybe he still thinks he can earn salvation by church-going or a good life (but see Eph. 2:8–9). So long as we are proud of ourselves and our achievements, we cannot give glory to God: but that is what the redeemed delight to do for all eternity (Rev. 4:9–10; 5:12–14). It is the same old problem of the primal sin, the number one thing that God hates, pride. That is his problem, and 'God opposes the proud, but gives grace to the humble' (1 Pet. 5:5). Maybe he has never realised that the full power of Christ's resurrection is available in his own life? In that case, you could well use personal testimony, the resurrection material in the Gospels and the epistles, and verses such as Revelation 1:17–18 and 2 Timothy 1:12.

But perhaps his 'No' is to *receiving*. He is not yet ready to receive Christ. Maybe he confuses it with intellectual agreement (but see Jas. 2:19), emotional experience (but see Luke 11:13), sacramental initiation (see Rom. 2:28; Acts 8:15–16; 1 Cor. 10:1–5), or suddenness (see Rom. 8:1 – what matters is not the date of his birth but whether or not he is alive).

I have often found that the person who is not yet ready to respond to Christ may be helped in one of the following ways. You could say, 'Fine. You don't feel ready yet. I fully respect that. What do you think is standing in your way? If we can sort that out to your satisfaction, would you then be ready to open your life to

Christ?' Another person might respond better to something like this. 'Right, you feel you need more time? Great, if you want to give the matter more reflection. But not so good if you want to postpone doing anything about it! Isaiah 55:6–7 has something important to say about that. Why not continue to think it over, and then let's meet for a meal in a couple of days to take it from there?' This respects the person's request for more time, but does not allow him to slip gently back off the hook!

If you sense that the 'Not yet' response is really ducking out of surrendering to Christ, but not exactly liking to admit it, a rather tougher approach might be warranted. 'You want to put it off? What would you say if someone for whom you had risked your life simply did not want to meet you? Would you not think it desperately ungrateful? I wonder how Christ feels? He did not risk his life for you. He gave it. In any case, it is foolish to keep him at arm's length. He wants to enrich our life, not to rob you.' I have, on occasion, used each of those responses effectively with people, but it is crucial to be very sensitive to the unspoken things that are going on under the surface and to pray constantly for the wisdom of Solomon as you handle someone at a very critical juncture in their spiritual life.

Of course, your friend may be different, and fall under none of those categories. He may, for instance, come from a Catholic background. It is best not to get involved in discussing doctrinal niceties at this point; rather to stress the areas that may have been obscured by his background. His faith may be more in the Virgin than in the Saviour. He may be weak on grace, and under the impression that if he goes to Mass all will necessarily be well. He may be weak, as many Catholics are, on God's assurance of our salvation – in which case take him to the promises of God, Romans 5:1, 8 and 8:1 being no bad place to start.

He may actually be a Christian, but very unsure of it. If so, go for the promises, like John 6:37, Revelation 3:20 and Ephesians 2:8. Point to the cross (Heb. 10:10–14): bills do not require to be paid twice. And look with him for the signs of the new life. He is meant to know where he stands (1 John 5:13) and not to wallow in uncertainty throughout his life. Actually, the marks of new life as outlined in John's first letter are well worth going through. There will gradually emerge in the child of God a new sense of pardon, a new desire to please God, a new attitude to other people, a new love for other Christians, a new power over evil, a new joy and confidence, and a new experience of answered prayer (1 John

2:1–2; 2:4, 6; 3:10; 3:14, 16; 4:4; 1:3–4; 4:16–19; 5:14–15). He is meant not just to feel, or hope, but to *know* he belongs.

He may have been 'hit' by the Spirit of God. It is fascinating to meet people who have had a major spiritual experience totally independent of any human agency. Acts 10:44 is a classic New Testament example. The Spirit does not need our co-operation, though he often graciously uses it. He is well able to do his own work in his own way (1 John 2:27). We need to help someone in a position like this to see that any spiritual gift given him at a time like this is intended to be used for the common good, humbly and in love. The emotional 'high' will pass: the Spirit will remain. He needs to grasp that important distinction. If the person has been involved in the occult, he may well need a ministry of deliverance, and we shall consider that in another chapter.

Of course, your friend may bring forward one or more of the classic difficulties or excuses. There is a fundamental difference between the two, though the presenting 'symptoms' may be identical. Thus, as we saw in chapter 3, for one person the problem of pain may be an excuse to avoid facing up to Christ; whereas for another precisely the same problem may be an agonising reason for legitimate doubt – perhaps he saw his brother slowly die of a painful cancer. The difference between the two is this. If you dispose of a real difficulty, then the person will quite easily come to Christ: the barrier has been removed. But if you knock down an excuse, he will produce another excuse, and hope thereby to keep you at arm's length! So the genuine difficulty needs to be handled with sensitivity and care. It needs a lot of empathy, the loan of suitable literature, maybe the sharing of personal experience of your own. The excuse, on the other hand, needs to be shown up for the paltry thing it is.

Pray that you do not make a mistake in diagnosis here. If you treat a real difficulty as if it were an excuse, you will cause hurt; if you spend too much energy in answering a problem which is really only a smokescreen, you will only get more smoke puffed into your face. It is well worth spending time studying some of the more common difficulties and excuses. They do not vary a great deal. You will see some attempts to give answers to them in the following books: Cliffe Knechtle, *Give me an Answer*; R. C. Sproul, *Objections Answered*; Michael Green, *You Must Be Joking!*; C. S. Lewis, *Mere Christianity*; Josh McDowell, *Evidence That Demands a Verdict*; F. F. Bruce, *The Real Jesus*, and *New Testament Documents*; and James Dunn, *The Evidence for Jesus*.

Excuses

Common excuses include the following. 'I haven't time to take Christianity seriously.' The answer is, 'Yes you have. In this respect all men are equal: we all have the same amount of time, and we make time for what we really prize' (Isa. 55:6; Gal. 6:7). Or he may come up with, 'There are too many hypocrites in church.' Swallowing down the temptation to say, 'Come along, and make one more,' I often prick that bubble by asking which hypocrites he knows in the congregation, and how does he know they are hypocrites? Romans 14:12 is a valuable corrective here.

Another excuse is, 'I can be a Christian without going to church.' To this the answer is short: Jesus couldn't (Luke 4:16). But the whole attitude of minimalising (how much can I get away *without* doing?) is the very antithesis of someone who has been touched by the grace of God. Christianity is corporate.

Again, when you get to the point of challenging your friend to make a commitment, you may well find him saying, to your astonishment, 'Well, I've always been a Christian.' When you investigate a little, you may find that he is identifying being a Christian with going to church (but see John 1:13; 2 Tim. 3:5), having been baptised (but see Rom. 2:28; Acts 8:13, 21), or doing his best (but see Jas. 2:10; Matt. 22:37–9; Gal. 3:10). All these variations of 'I'm already a Christian' are normally excuses to hide the real reason for rebellion against God. That is what you will seek patiently and lovingly to unearth. Romans 1:18–32 is, of course, a devastating indictment of man in revolt.

Excuses such as these, and there are plenty more, generally spring from a mixture of pride and prejudice. They are helped by fashion, laziness, ignorance, fear and materialism. These factors help to confirm man in his rebellion. The amazing thing is that God should continue to offer pardon freely to those who are so un-willing to receive it (Rom. 5:6–10).

Difficulties

Of course, some of the problems you will meet which inhibit commitment are not excuses at all. They are real difficulties. Here are a small selection.

Often a person will say, 'I really am trying hard to be a Chris-tian.' This is an offshoot of the Pelagianism which lies so deep within us. We always want to do, rather than to allow anything to be done for us. And the gospel is good news of what God has done for us. It is not 'try' but 'trust' which is at the heart of Christian living; not performance but relationship. A lot of the New Testament is devoted to making that plain. Verses such as Romans 4:3–5, Acts 16:31 and Isaiah 12:2 point it up.

'But I don't understand it all,' some people say at this juncture. Of course they don't! How could mortal man take in what Almighty God has done to make him acceptable? ' "What no eye has seen, nor ear heard, nor the heart of man conceived, what God has prepared for those who love him," God has revealed to us through the Spirit' (1 Cor. 2:9). I do not need to understand electricity before availing myself of it!

'I've tried it before and it is no good,' is something that may come up. It needs a sensitive and loving touch. What is the 'it' which he has tried? Is he confusing a deep turning to God with something less? Maybe he 'went forward' during a Crusade, but it never made any lasting difference? That could have been because his emotions were stirred but his will was untouched. Or it could be because there was no subsequent nurture. Maybe he really did entrust himself to Christ, but never grew, and so has gradually become indistinguishable from those who never began. Maybe he has never got involved in the Christian community, and has shrivelled as a result. Maybe he has never understood the power of the Spirit in one's life to break the grip of sinful habits. Maybe the chill winds of personal doubt and the scepticism of others have withered the tiny shoot of faith. You will need to exercise great care with such a person. Show that 'If we are faithless, [God] remains faithful – for he cannot deny himself' (2 Tim. 2:13). Show him that his state does not depend on his feelings, but on the dependability of God, who has given us his word that 'He who has the Son has life; he who has not the Son of God has not life' (1 John 5:12). Has he or has he not welcomed the Son of God into the partnership of his life? If he has, however long ago and however feebly done, Christ *has* come in; and he can know that because of the Lord's promises. Feed him on the promises of God. Let him learn some of them with you. They will prove invaluable in the early days of definite discipleship. If, as he looks at his life, he concludes that he has never really begun the life of repentance and faith in earnest, then lead him to it, as you would anyone else.

'I could never keep it up,' your friend may say. That is a noble sentiment. It shows he wants to keep it up, but is doubtful about his

ability. He needs to be shown that Christ will keep *him* up (1 Pet.
1:5; John 10:28–9; Jude 24). Once again he needs to learn the
unfamiliar but utterly necessary path of faith. It is Christ's job to
keep me. It is my job to trust him to do so.

Often you will get down to the bottom line, and he will admit to
you that he is scared. That is a difficulty nearly everybody faces.
Scared that nothing might happen? In that case, take him again to
the Saviour's promise, 'I *will* come in!' He will not, he cannot break
his word. Scared that he will be letting himself in for a miserable,
narrow time? Far from it. In his presence 'there is fullness of joy'
and at his right hand 'are pleasures for evermore' (Ps. 16:11).
Scared of being in a minority? Sure, but one plus Christ is always a
majority. And since when has the majority always been right?
Scared of what his friends will say? That is usually the problem.
And it is very real. Show him that any friends who are worth their
salt will not desert him. Show him that he is not called to drop
anyone – simply to be among them as before, but with Jesus just
beneath the surface of his life. Show him that perfect love casts out
fear (1 John 4:18) and that he is about to welcome perfect love into
his life.

Commitment

The time has come when things seem pretty clear, and the flow of
questions and anxieties has dried up a bit. Ask him gently, 'Do you
think you are ready to say "yes" to the Lord now?', or 'Is there
anything that is still keeping you back from him?' If he can't think
of anything, say, 'Right, then let's kneel down right away and ask
him to come into your life' (or whatever analogy you are using).
Alternatively, you can ask him if he would prefer to make that
solemn act of commitment on his own, maybe by his bedside, and
tell you when he has done so; or whether he would like your help
and presence at this important time. Mostly he will opt for your
help (though respect his wishes if he prefers to go the other route).
If so, sit or kneel together. Pray for him that he may be truly
brought into the family of God. Then encourage him to pray for
himself, admitting his sins and asking Christ's Spirit to come into
his life. I have already suggested that you use some promise such as
John 1:12, 3:16, or Revelation 3:20, and get him to claim it. It is no
better if he prays out loud rather than silently, of course, but many
Christians do, and he might as well start as he means to go on. I

have found that people who make their initial commitment to Christ out loud never have any problems in the future about joining in extempore verbal prayer. In any case, to pray out loud will help him in precision; it will break the sound barrier, and it will show him that he is well able to pray to God in his own words without necessarily depending on some book of prayers. It will also help you to be aware of what is going on in his heart.If he says, 'I can't pray aloud,' I sometimes say, 'Then pray silently, and give me a prod when you have taken the step of opening up to Christ.' Soon, a hand prods me! Alternatively, I may say, if I sense that it will really help him to pray aloud but that some blockage is in the way, 'May I pray that God will open your lips? Why not join me?' Then I pray for him, and almost always he will burst into verbal prayer, released by God's gracious Spirit from whatever was holding him back. It is a great privilege to be alongside as these broken, sometimes sobbing words of commitment come flooding out. I often find myself weeping in empathy, and it does not one whit of harm! Then I pray for my friend, that the Holy Spirit will baptise him deeply into Christ, fill him with spiritual gifts and never leave him.

It is a very moving time. There are often tears and laughter. It is important that in the sheer joy of the moment we do not omit vital things which require to be attended to. I turn to him and ask, 'Has he come in?' Mostly they know the answer without a shadow of doubt. But not always. In that case I take them back again to the promise of Christ. 'It says, "If anyone opens the door I will come in." Did you open the door?' 'Well, yes, as best I know how.' 'Then what has he done?' 'Oh, I see, he *has* come in, even though I don't feel very different.' 'Exactly,' I say. 'And be thankful for this first of many lessons that you will get in your Christian life, that you live and grow by trusting the promises and faithfulness of the Lord, and not your own volatile feelings.' I then do with him what I do with the person who is already happily sure. I get him to thank the Lord for coming in. 'Dear Lord, thank you for coming into my life. Thank you for your promise never to leave me. Help me to be true to you all my days.' A prayer like that, trusting Christ's promise, standing upon it and thanking him for it, is a valuable lesson of trust at the very outset of his Christian walk, and it teaches him to look to the Lord in gratitude and praise, and not only to come to him with requests.

After that, I normally give him a tract or booklet like *Come, Follow Me*, summarising the step he has taken, along with one verse of Scripture to take away with him. It might be John 6:37, Matthew 28:20 or 1 John 5:12. The last one is so clear and such a prophylactic against doubt: 'He who has the Son has life; he who has not the Son of God has not life.' Beautiful simplicity and clarity, is it not? Just the initial uncomplicated assurance that the new believer needs. He is sure to be attacked by doubt, the Tempter's first and very powerful weapon. At his first appearance in Genesis 3 we find him at it: 'Did God say . . . ?' And the sooner the new believer learns, like his Master, to counter doubt with the promises of God (cf. Matt. 4:4, 7, 10), the sooner he is likely to find his feet as a Christian and to grow.

Two final things as you bid him farewell. He has had enough for one session! But he will need tender loving care very soon (and we shall consider the nurture of the new Christian in the next chapter). Therefore, arrange to meet him tomorrow. But as he leaves, encourage him to tell someone else what has happened. It will help to confirm him in his assurance, and will fulfil the injunction of Romans 10:9–10. It would be best in the first instance to tell someone who is friendly and understanding, and who will rejoice with him and encourage him. Probably he knows some such person, who has very likely been praying for him. I am constantly amazed at the number of new believers who know very well of certain people who have been doing just that. So let him select one and tell them the good news that he has begun the most exciting of all relationships, with Jesus Christ as his Saviour and Lord.

FURTHER READING

While talking about the faith with individuals is essentially a personal matter, where any whiff of a prepared package is highly unproductive, some of the following books may be of help simply as direction-finders.

John Bright, *Revolution Now* (Campus Crusade)
John Bright, *Witnessing Without Fear* (Campus Crusade)
John Chapman, *Know and Tell the Gospel* (Navpress)
Robert Coleman, *The Master Plan of Evangelism* (Revell)
T. N. Eisenmann, *Everyday Evangelism* (Inter-Varsity Press)
Leighton Ford, *Good News is For Sharing* (Cook)
Michael Green, *Come, Follow Me* (Inter-Varsity Press)
James Kennedy, *Evangelism Explosion* (Tyndale Press)
Paul Little, *How To Give Away Your Faith* (Inter-Varsity Press)

H. C. Pawson, *Personal Evangelism* (Epworth Press)

Jim Petersen, *Evangelism for our Generation* (Navpress)

Rebecca Manley Pippert, *Out of the Saltshaker* (Inter-Varsity Press)

Don Posterski, *Friendship* (Project Teen Canada)

Don Posterski, *Reinventing Evangelism* (Inter-Varsity Press)

Don Posterski, *Why Am I Afraid to Tell You I'm a Christian?* (Inter-Varsity Press)

John Stott, *Becoming a Christian* (Inter-Varsity Press)

R. A. Torrey, *How to Work for Christ* (Revell). This is old and very uncompromising, but highly suggestive

C. G. Turnbull, *Taking Men Alive* (RTS). An old book, but full of wisdom.

There is also an enormous amount to be learned from the two major composite productions emanating from the congresses led by Billy Graham: see J. D. Douglas (ed.), *Let the Earth Hear His Voice* (World Wide Publications), and J. D. Douglas (ed.), *The Work of an Evangelist* (World Wide Publications).

11

Christian Nurture

There are few areas in the Christian church where we fail more catastrophically than in the care we give to new believers. Perhaps it is that we are so rarely in the position of having new believers to care for. At all events, we do not do it well. They are, on the whole, expected to sink or swim. When asked to lead missions in different parts of England, the USA or Canada, I always ask what regular plans they have for the nurture of new Christians. And they look at me with stares of blank astonishment. The idea never seems to have crossed their minds. Christian education, for all practical purposes, ends with the reception of adolescents into the full membership of the church – and the day of their commissioning is all too often seen as a passing-out parade. Yet it is an area to which the early church gave tremendous care. They had a full-blown catechesis for new members, even in the earliest period of the apostolic age. Traces of it remain in the New Testament letters. Today, however, it has become a very neglected area.

Yet it is a very critical area. The culture gap between the church and the rest of society is widening all the time in the Western world. New converts must not be expected to learn without any assistance a new culture, a new set of standards, a new language, a new use for their Sundays. They should not be expected simply to conform to what the church has become accustomed to doing and saying and assuming. Moreover, the church is a confusing place where little is explained and much is taken for granted. It is distressing to go into a liturgical church and find that, though books are provided, no indication even of page numbers is given to the worshippers. That speaks volumes. It shows that the church has ceased to think of itself as a school for sinners, but has become the closed society of the like-minded. It has lost its outward orientation, and with it, its vitality. Those who do find their way into the church, and manage to stick at it, are much to be admired, but even so they have got a very poor foundation. And without a strong foundation you are going to be in trouble when the storms of life arise. You are also not going to be much use in helping other people to enter the worshipping life of the church.

It is apparent, therefore, that this care of new believers is a very necessary area for any church to give attention to. People need a lot of help at this watershed of their lives, when they may have entrusted themselves to Christ, but are very confused about what they have done, and unclear about what it will involve to live as his disciples in a world which has little time for him. They need information. They need encouragement. They need to be drawn into the community of Christians. They need to get to know people in the church. They need help in developing a devotional life. They need to get into the habit of worshipping, and to know what they are doing. They need to learn the reason for the hope that is within them. They need to be nourished by the Word and the sacraments. They need someone to look after them and help them over the initial hurdles. They need examples of Christian living to emulate. They need, above all, to be loved. How can we best help them? I would like to suggest two approaches which I have found helpful in a wide variety of circumstances.

NEW TESTAMENT PRECEDENTS

The New Testament has a lot to teach us in this regard. From the day of Pentecost onwards we find the Christians giving great care to the nurture of new believers, and seven ways of doing it stand out.

Baptism

First, believers were baptised into the church. We read that on the birthday of the church 'those who received [Peter's] word were baptized, and there was added that day about three thousand souls' (Acts 2:41). Unless Luke is being very impressionistic, it is clear that someone actually counted these new Christians. Their faces were recognised, their names assimilated. Somebody took an interest in them, and they were baptised into the church. Repentance and faith was not enough. They needed to undergo the rite of initiation which Jesus himself had inaugurated. They were baptised. That is the badge of Christian belonging, and it should be conferred as soon as possible after the person is clearly committed to Christ. At least, that is what the early Christians believed. They baptised upon profession of faith. There was certainly careful catechesis, but it seems to have happened after baptism, not before. It might be argued that this is a risky procedure. It is. But they did it because the new Christian soldier had every right to his uniform. They did it because baptism was not the mark of mature Christian discipleship but of raw Christian beginning. They did it because they saw repentance, faith, the reception of the Holy Spirit and baptism as very much a unity, and the closer they could be kept together the better. So closely did Peter and Paul construe the link that they sometimes speak of baptism in instrumental language. It is the means whereby people become Christians. That is the plain meaning, for example, of 1 Peter 3:21, 'Baptism . . . now saves you', or of Galatians 3:27, 'as many of you as were baptized into Christ have put on Christ'. The apostles were not operating on an *ex opere operato* assumption, as if baptism was all that is necessary in becoming a Christian – an error into which some mainline churches have slipped. Nor did they imagine, as one small denomination stipulates, that no profession of conversion must be allowed until the candidate is actually in the baptismal water! But they did see baptism as the sign and seal of the new life in Christ, and the means whereby it became manifest to others and assured to the recipient.

New believers need to be baptised. If they have already been baptised, perhaps in infancy, most Christian churches are clear that they do not need to be baptised again. There is 'one baptism' (Eph. 4:5). But they do need the opportunity to confess Christ publicly. That is the confessional aspect of baptism which they have, by definition, been unable to take part in yet, for they had no living faith to confess! In the church where for many years I had the privilege of ministering in Oxford, we had a large number of young men and women, mostly Oxford undergraduates and graduates, coming to faith from a variety of backgrounds. It was our practice to baptise them shortly after profession of faith, while they were undergoing grounding in Christian basics. This was a marvellous witness to their friends, and a great encouragement to them. It gave them a chance publicly to nail their colours to the mast, and to give personal testimony during the ceremony to their discovery of

Christ. If they had already been baptised, we gave them the opportunity, shortly after commitment to Christ, to bear witness to that new-found faith in the context of the congregation at worship, and then to reaffirm their baptismal vows. We laid hands upon them, and prayed that the Holy Spirit would come and fill their lives. This proved an invaluable foundation for the ongoing nurture which took place in the Discovery Groups in which they were all incorporated, and which will concern us in the second part of this chapter.

Before we leave the controversial subject of baptism (on which I have tried to write more comprehensively in my book *Baptism*), it ought to be noted that baptism is never an isolated act separated from the life of the church of God. It is the doorway into that church, and this is very evident in a Jewish or Muslim community when someone is baptised. They can believe in Jesus until the cows come home, and nobody gets upset. It is when they cross the Rubicon of baptism that the insults begin to fly, and usually the candidates are thrown out of house and home, disinherited, and a funeral is held for them. Baptism is inescapably corporate. It brings you into the Christ in whom others are engrafted. So it should not be administered without the intention of incorporation into the church of God. That is what happened at Pentecost. Those who responded to Peter's sermon were baptised and added to the church.

Teaching

The first converts, we are told, continued in the apostles' teaching (Acts 2:42). What was it, we may wonder?

First and foremost, it must have been teaching about Jesus. The sort of material which has been recorded for us in the Gospels. Who was this Jesus whom they had come to trust? What did he teach? Why did he die? How sure could they be about his resurrection? Where was he now? Where lay the future? Those were obvious questions which would have sprung to the minds of new believers. They still do.

Second, it seems to have been teaching about fulfilment. That is where Peter's Pentecost address began: 'This is what was spoken by the prophet Joel . . .' (Acts 2:16). By 'this' he meant the fulfilment of Old Testament prophecy embodied in the gift of tongues, the radiant joy and praise on the streets, the evident sense of newness and discovery. Healing and prophetic gifts were to follow, along with fearless and unquenchable evangelism. This all sprang from the sense of fulfilment which marked the infant church. All the strands of truth in Judaism and in pagan philosophy had reached their culmination in the Man of Nazareth whom God had made both Lord and Messiah (Acts 2:22, 36). In that confidence of fulfilment the early Christians could confront the Jews and Gentiles alike with deep composure, sure of where they stood. They did not need to surrender to the pluralism and syncretism all around them. They had been discovered and set free by nothing less than the Truth incarnate. They found their sense of that fulfilment in a combination of the Old Testament scriptures and the Holy Spirit's illumination. That is very evident from Peter's sermon, where he cites passage after passage from the Old Testament with a brand new confidence. It is not just words in a scroll now: it is truth which he *knows* from its fulfilment in Jesus, and from the witness that the Spirit gives to that. This sense of fulfilment in Christ is a very important element in the spiritual growth of new Christians. It forms a basis from which they can face with assurance the many '-isms' by which they are confronted daily.

Third, the teaching given by the earliest Christians concerned the new life in Christ and the ethical imperatives it involved. In Colossians there is the sequence: 'Put off the old nature' (Col. 3:9), 'Put on the new nature' (Col. 3:10), 'Submit' (Col. 3:18), 'Watch and Pray' (Col. 4:2), and 'Stand' (Col. 4:12). This may look like an arbitrary selection, until you notice a similar pattern elsewhere. Ephesians has much the same: 'Put off' (Eph. 4:22) 'Put on' (Eph. 4:24), 'Submit' (Eph. 5:22), 'Stand' (Eph. 6:11) 'Watch and pray' (Eph. 6:18). 1 Peter begins with a strong emphasis on the new birth (1 Pet. 1:23), and follows it with 'Put off'' (1 Pet. 2:1), 'Worship' (1 Pet. 2:4–9), 'Submit' (1 Pet. 2:13 – and he spells it out until 5:9 as it applies to husbands, wives, citizens and leaders), 'Watch and pray' (1 Pet. 4:7), 'Resist' (1 Pet. 5:8–9). James also starts with the new birth (Jas. 1:18), and follows it with 'Put off' (Jas. 1:21), 'Be subject' (Jas. 4:7), 'Resist the devil' (Jas. 4:7) and 'Pray' (Jas. 5:16). All these passages have strong reference to love for the brethren, and this is spelled out in detail in Ephesians, Colossians and James. While we cannot be too sure about the details of this 'catechism', it is certainly significant that broadly the same pattern recurs in three such different writers as Paul, Peter and James. What a marvellous teaching course this material could make.

First, a session on the new birth, and the radical transformation it will bring with it. The convert needs to be sure about this, otherwise he will build on a shaky foundation.

Second, an examination of some of the things from the old life that need to be laid aside as inconsistent with the new allegiance to Jesus.

Third, a lesson on the image of God in which man was made; lost through our disobedience, restored in the person of Jesus, and gradually imparted to the believer by the Spirit as he transforms us into likeness to Christ. This new life needs to be put on deliberately, daily, like a suit of new clothes.

Fourth, Christians are not called to boss others around, but to live in submission to their Lord and to one another. The husband must as much submit to his wife in loving care and protection as she must to him as leader in the family. And the same applies in our relationships with the state and with one another. Jesus lived the life of the Servant, and the disciple is called to tread the same path.

Fifth, the new believer needs to be taught to 'stand' or 'withstand' the evil one. The devil is a reality and needs to be resisted in the new-found power of Christ. Discipleship is not disclosed in sudden enthusiasm, but in long-term standing up for Christ.

Sixth, the new Christian needs to watch and pray. It is interesting that the two should come together. But unless he watches he will not pray: the prayer time will get squeezed out. And unless he watches in another sense, he will not go on praying. For he will not notice the answer to his prayers, and will become discouraged.

Finally, the Word of God and love for one another were two main subjects covered by the basic teaching of the early Christians. What a magnificent study course for new Christians that would make.

Fellowship

The earliest believers continued in the apostles' fellowship, we are told (Acts 2:42). That fellowship was very warm. They shared possessions, they sold property to care for one another's needs, and their love and unity were something of which the ancient world had not seen the like. That fellowship took three forms, and all three of them are important today.

First, there was the personal attention that all of us need, but more especially when we move into a new situation. And the new believer has moved into an entirely fresh world, and very much needs a lot of personal care at that stage in his or her development. I recall regular meetings, one-on-one, with the person who helped me to Christ, and I could gain encouragement and advice from him at the same time as raising my doubts and difficulties. I owe him more than he will ever know. In the earliest days it was the same. Where would Timothy and Silas have been without Paul? Where would Paul himself have been without Ananias or Barnabas? We need that personal care, and all too often the new Christian does not get it. If each new believer had a time with a friend who was a more experienced Christian once a week for two or three months, a time where a bit of the Bible could be read, prayer could be made, and problems discussed, their growth would be solid and remarkable. That is not theory. It is experience.

Along with the personal attention, there needs to be the fellowship of the small, caring, relaxed group of fellow Christians. The earliest believers met for fellowship in homes, and that has a tremendous amount to commend it. The informal atmosphere, the naturalness of meeting, the food, the conversation, the friendships, the joint activities all make it easy to move on and off spiritual topics, and help the new Christian to adjust to the new society of which he has become a member. It is a notable fact throughout the world that the churches which are growing fastest are those where there are natural meeting-places for small sections of the congregations – normally meeting in homes. It is in this way that relationships can be forged, problems talked over, personal and maybe financial needs addressed, and individuals can feel that they matter and are loved.

A third area of fellowship, and the one that most naturally springs to mind, is the fellowship of the church congregation. New believers need to be introduced gradually to the congregation, and in a way that does not embarrass them. 'I want you to meet Bill. He's our newest convert,' is the surest way to frighten anyone off. But gradually to draw them into the life of the congregation at large in a way that enables them to find their own feet and in due course to display their own gifts and talents for the common good, that is just what is required. It sometimes helps to have a Welcome Desk at the back of the church, manned after services, especially in a large congregation where it is easy for people to remain unwelcomed. This Desk will have details of what is going on in the church, fellowship groups, nursery arrangements, sectional interests and forthcoming congregational special events. When we

started one in Oxford, we kicked ourselves for not having thought
of it earlier. It was in constant use, and funnelled people into a
weekly Welcome Meeting where they were able to get to know one
another and get known by the team who ran it. At this there would
be the sharing of personal information, material about the church
and its life, and usually a simple inductive Bible study and prayer
time. This enabled the team to recommend where the newcomers
should be placed in the system of home fellowship groups which
was a major feature of church life. At all events, it was a concrete
attempt to integrate new people into the ongoing life of a large
congregation without their being swamped or feeling lost. And
people need that. Love is the most crucial of all Christian qualities,
and it is likely to flow most copiously in the congregation at large if
it is already experienced in the small group.

Worship

The earliest Christians took part in what Luke calls 'the breaking of
bread', doubtless the Holy Communion, Eucharist, or Lord's
Supper, as it is variously known today. That was what Jesus had
commanded. And that is the activity by which Christian worship
came most specifically to be recognised. New converts need to be
brought speedily into the eucharistic fellowship of the church.
They are physical beings, and much about the Christian faith is
'spiritual' and hard to get a grip on. But eating is the most basic
human activity. We may be sure that that is one of the reasons why
Jesus chose it for us to remember him by, and to meet him in. It is a
meal of the utmost profundity: we shall never plumb all its mystery. But the new believer can begin right away. He can readily
understand how that broken bread indicates the body of Jesus
broken for him on the cross, and the poured-out wine his spilled
blood. And his heart will be warmed in gratitude. He can readily
understand that as bread and wine feed his body, so Jesus, the
bread and wine of life, is the nourishment for his soul. Just as he
takes the bread and wine into himself and makes it part of him, so
he needs to feed on Christ, take him deep within his being, and
make him part of his own person. Again, it is not too difficult for
him to understand that this meal is a foretaste of the final banquet
in heaven, presided over by the Father, with all his family present.
Each Communion brings us a little nearer that day. And if he
understands that much, he is not doing too badly for the early days.

There is, of course, much more to come in this inexhaustible sacrament. But that much is a reasonable start.

Most churches hedge their tables. They have special rules governing who may and who may not take part. The minister is the person to approach about this, and it will be a good opportunity to get your friend acquainted with his spiritual leader and ready to learn from him.

Christian worship does not consist in the Holy Communion, though there are some Christian denominations which seem to have almost no other services. But just as in Judaism, where the synagogue service of the Word balanced the sacramental worship in the temple feasts, so it should be in the church. There should be non-sacramental services for the new believer to attend where praise and teaching, Scripture and prayer can mingle with other elements, and worship can begin to become a reality and a joy to him.

The older I get, the less important it is to me what type of worship I engage in. It is all provisional this side of heaven. But it does matter more and more to me that I engage in it. Worship is half of the purpose of the church: the other half is mission, in its broadest sense. Worship of God and ministry to mankind are the two supreme callings of the Christian body, and our friend needs to be introduced to the joys and disciplines of regular worship immediately after coming to faith. Many, of course, will already be used to church worship. Indeed, it may have been one of the major factors in drawing them to Christ.

Prayer

Prayer is rather foreign to most people. They may pray in a crisis. They may pray more than they would ever let on. But it is not as natural to them as breathing. It isn't a way of life. And one of the first marvellous changes that comes with the new relationship to Christ is that prayer does become these things. The one mark given to Ananias to assure him that there had been a substantive change in Saul of Tarsus was this: 'He is praying' (Acts 9:11). The Spirit within the new Christian teaches him to address the Father with the intimacy proper to members of the family – 'Abba, dear Father' (Rom. 8:16). So the propensity will be there in every new Christian, but it will need a lot of coaxing along and instructing. They are sure to have lots of problems with prayer. Does it do any good?

Would God not act in the same way whether they prayed or not? Where does confession come in, and what on earth is adoration? What about when prayer does not get answered? And does sin affect all this?

These and other such questions are going to need a lot of patient answering. But above all, new Christians need to be immersed in an atmosphere where they do pray and find others praying naturally, confidently, and in faith. The most natural way of understanding Acts 2:42 is that they continued in 'the prayer times'. There were set times for prayer in the temple at Jerusalem, as in Islam today, and there is evidence that the Christians made use of them. They gathered for prayer, sometimes in the temple and sometimes in a private home, or even on the sea shore or at a river bank. Prayer was not only individual but corporate, and they soon learned that there is a special power to be released, and a special presence of Christ to be claimed, where two or three are gathered together in his name to make their requests to the Father. Prayer needs to be taught, and books such as those by E. M. Bounds, Metropolitan Anthony and Sister Margaret Magdalen are wonderfully helpful in understanding it and in motivating it. But prayer also needs to be caught. And involvement in a small prayer group, a prayer breakfast or prayer chain, or a half night of prayer, will make an enormous difference to the prayer life of the new Christian.

Witness

One of the most striking differences between the early church and the modern church lies in the attitude to witness for Christ. Today it is seen as rather over the top: something for the real enthusiasts who are rather short on tact, and who will, in due course no doubt, grow out of their intemperate zeal. Then it was seen as the mark of all Christians. On the day of Pentecost, Peter was doing the preaching, but he maintained roundly that 'we all are witnesses' of the risen Christ (Acts 2:32). There was nothing sickly or egotistical about such witness. It did not mean to imply that 'Once I was very bad and now I am very good,' or anything of that sort. It was witness to Jesus and the fact that he was alive. And that is something that every Christian needs to be able to do. In Third World countries, particularly Latin America and Africa, this is indeed the norm. There is a massive lay witness to Christ. In the

West we are crippled with embarrassment even to mention the name of Jesus. Until we get over that, the church will not grow. And new believers are extraordinarily good at witnessing, if they are given a modicum of encouragement. After all, they have the enthusiasm of new discovery. They have not yet discovered that Christians are fashionably inhibited about their Lord, and the change in their own style of life inevitably calls for some sort of explanation. They should be encouraged to give that explanation in their own way, as naturally and as warmly as they can. They will not lose many friends that way. They are likely, instead, to bring a number of friends over into their newly found faith. It is my experience that the best evangelists are normally those who are new believers themselves and have never been spoiled by going to courses on evangelism!

Oversight

The seventh feature which seems to have been constant in the pattern of nurture to be found in the New Testament is pastoral oversight. The new Christian had someone to look after him in those vital early days. A Mark had his Peter, a Silvanus his Paul. We are suspicious of oversight in this egalitarian age. But we need not be. It is one of the gifts which God gives to his body, the church (Eph. 4:11). Leaders are offered to us not to inhibit our initiative or to squeeze us into a pattern, but to 'equip the saints for the work of ministry' (Eph. 4:12). In the New Testament we find them setting an example, exercising discipline, taking young Christians on missionary journeys, encouraging them, and writing letters. All of this needs to be borne in mind by those who have the privilege of helping to lead new Christians into mature discipleship. We have the tremendous privilege of helping to mould disciples.

A moment's thought will show how much help a new believer needs. First and foremost, he needs immediate help over doubt. And doubt attends every profession of commitment to Christ. Who has not asked himself, in the aftermath of that encounter, 'Was it real? Is Anyone there? Did Christ really accept me? Am I good enough? Can I be sure? What if I mess it all up?' Such questions must be all but universal. And they need prompt handling, or they will fester.

When that initial doubt has been dealt with, and Christian assurance seen to depend on the promise of God and the finished work of Christ, and the pledged coming of the Holy Spirit, there will be other urgent matters that require attention. The new believer will need to be introduced into Christian company, and that may need considerable finesse. He will certainly need to be helped towards developing a devotional life. He will need to learn to pray, and will want help in getting to grips with the Bible devotionally. It would be good to introduce him to Bible-reading notes such as those produced by the Scripture Union or the Bible Reading Fellowship which suggest a passage of manageable length for each day, and provide helpful notes on it designed to help the reader to gain spiritual nourishment (as opposed to intellectual problems) from it. Then there may well be ethical issues which need to be addressed sooner or later. As the 'lifestyle gap' between the church and society widens, it will be no surprise if the new Christian brings with him habits every bit as alien to the gospel as the Gentile vices of the first century. The weaning process will require lots of love and tact. And then there will be a host of problems – some intellectual, some ethical, some concerned with Christian life in society and especially in the home and at work, some sexual, some financial – all of which desperately need the help of some wise Christian friend who has been a disciple of Christ for some time. The most natural person for such a role is the one who has led the new believer into the faith. But this may not be possible, for a variety of reasons. At all events, some wise and loving person who is relaxed, non-threatening, and unshockable is needed to be a model, a leader for the new Christian. The need is urgent. Someone should spend time with the convert the very next day. The Enemy of souls will not be idle, even if we are. When, however, there are a number of new members of the Christian family it becomes increasingly difficult to find mature people who have the skills and the time to look after them one-on-one. And over the years I have come to the conviction that one of the most helpful things for the new believer is to join a group under competent leadership where all the members are also new Christians or on the edge of commitment. Such groups are growing in popularity, and are variously known as Beginners' Groups, Nurture Groups, Follow-up Groups or, best of all, Discovery Groups.

DISCOVERY GROUPS

The Discovery Group is very simple. It is nothing more than a number of new Christians meeting together for learning, study, prayer and encouragement under the leadership of some experienced Christians, preferably laypeople. Over the years at St Aldate's Church, Oxford, we developed these groups until they became the main way of helping new Christians to grow. They were valuable teaching tools, great fun, and built relationships which flowed over into dynamic life for the church.

The value of such groups is not hard to recognise. For one thing, the use of Discovery Groups ensures that competent people are helping the new Christians onwards, people who have a responsibility towards those in their group and also to the church which has entrusted them with that delicate and thrilling task. For another, it teaches the new Christians the importance and the joy of Christian fellowship almost before they have ever heard the word. Moreover, it incorporates the one-on-one care which we have examined above, but transposes it into a different key because of the group dimension. Each of the leaders makes himself personally responsible for discipling one or more of the group, and does this informally outside the group meeting-time. So the new believer gets his personal care, but he is greatly enriched also by the group. For it is here that he can share his fears and discoveries. It is here that he can grow and see others grow. He can hear of, and share, answers to prayer. He can raise problems, and listen to the answers as others voice matters he feels but has not articulated. Another great advantage in running such groups is that they lead naturally into the network of home fellowship groups which are such a healthy dimension in the life of most growing churches – but are not particularly suitable for slotting raw new disciples into, until they have found their sea legs, so to speak. And that is precisely what the Discovery Group enables them to do.

The aim of the group is clear. It is to 'present everyone mature in Christ' (Col. 1:28), in so far as that can begin to be realised within a period of two months, the optimum length for such a course. Mature enough, at least, to know he is a Christian disciple, and to begin to be able to give some account of why. Mature enough to have a regular devotional life, and to have had a shot at sharing his faith with someone. Mature enough to know what the church is about and to be able to take his place within its fellowship. Mature

enough to want to serve the Lord in some way or other. That is
what one may expect to come out of these Discovery Groups, and
it very often does. Our experience shows that only a very small
number of those who make a Christian profession fall away if they
attend one of these courses for new Christians. It seems to provide
a foundation for their Christian lives.

The numbers involved will be large enough to form a viable
group even if one or two are away through illness or some other
cause; but small enough to ensure that there are no passengers in
the group. Everyone has a part to play. The ratio of leaders to
members is very important. Because the leader's task is not simply
to lead the various activities of the group, but also to care pastorally for some of the members, it is important to see that no leader
has to look after more than, say, three people: otherwise it would
be too heavy a demand on his spare time. These leaders are lay folk
with regular jobs, in most instances, and therefore cannot effectively be responsible for more than two or three members. So you
need, in a large group, four leaders for ten to twelve members.
Two leaders could manage a group of six.

The members of the group will be varied in age, sex, background
and situation. This does not matter in the least. I have found that
groups that contain doctoral students and unemployed alcoholics
go well. The Christian family is very mixed: and we do not choose
our brothers and sisters! Variety is in fact an asset in the group.
And assuredly they will be at a variety of stages spiritually. Some
will be there for a refresher course in Christian basics. Some will be
there because they have just put their faith in Christ. Others will
have allowed themselves to sign up as no more than interested
enquirers. And particularly if the group emerges from an evangelistic address, there are sure to be some people who do not know
why they agreed to come. They were under some impulse of the
Spirit of God but they cannot explain it, and may well be embarrassed about it. The first meeting, if skilfully conducted, should
handle that!

The course material will be found in the Appendices at the back
of this book. It has no particular merits apart from having been
tried and used a great deal in many parts of the world. I include it
there because it may be a helpful starting-point for a church that is
wanting to begin Discovery Groups, but I should be surprised –
and disappointed – if you stayed with it for too long. It was devised
by one church for a particular constituency, and although it has
been used very widely, it is only an example of the sort of thing that

can be done. It is not copyright, and you are welcome to use it and adapt it as you see fit. And then write your own. This one lasts for eight weeks, and members should have it made plain on the joining form at the beginning that they are committing themselves to come weekly. Each week has a theme for the evening, and all constituent parts of the evening subserve that theme. There are notes for members of the group to take away with them afterwards. These serve as a concise reminder of what took place; they enable members to check out the scripture verses which bear on the theme; and by the end of the eight weeks they provide a sketchy but not inconsiderable series of flysheets on a number of basic doctrines. From time to time you will find that members of the group spontaneously start their own group among their friends and use the material that they have so recently grasped themselves!

Though a single theme is studied each night, there are several aspects to the evening. One of the leaders will give a short talk on the theme, using some of the verses from the New Testament which bear upon it, so as to get the essence of the teaching clearly into the minds of the group. (Suggested talk outlines are given in the notes.) This will be followed by questions, objections and difficulties.

A second element we have found it helpful to have is another form of learning about the same theme, through an inductive Bible study. This is again compered by one of the leaders, but his skill here lies in doing the minimum himself and maximising the opportunities for members of the group to discover for themselves what Scripture is saying, to wrestle with it personally, and find how it speaks to their situation. This is a very exciting part of the evening.

A third element which has been found very useful is the teaching of a verse of Scripture which encapsulates the theme of the evening. There is an incalculable value in hiding portions of Scripture away in the heart: it is done all too little these days. And if new Christians start it right away, they are going to learn a very good habit, and will rapidly be able to help other people.

A fourth element in the evening is the mention of suitable books which the leaders will have brought with them for loan or sale in the group. This is another means of growth: to get into the habit early on of assimilating a bit about the faith. It does not so much matter what the particular books are: the valuable thing is to get people reading and therefore thinking intelligently about their faith, and to feed people the books that are appropriate to their condition and the questions they are asking. If a small shoebox of books is brought each week from a local Christian bookstore on a sale or return basis, and if the books are well introduced by one of the leaders, there should be a steady sale each week, and growing interest.

A fifth part of the evening will be prayer, perhaps in silence, but more often extempore. It will help people in the group to begin to voice their prayers and praises, and they will be encouraged by finding that others are prepared to do it too. The prayer time emerges from the inductive Bible study, so people pray over the thoughts that have struck them from the pages of Scripture. This is of course all good modelling, unconsciously assimilated, for their own daily Bible reading and prayer.

The evening will end after prayer, but usually the coffee time comes into its own, and people are in no hurry to go. This is a valuable time for the leaders to chat informally with members over issues that may have been raised and shelved during the evening, or to arrange to meet for a meal or a chat during the week.

People join the course in several ways. They may be fed in from an evangelistic address in church, or from an outreach dinner. They may find their way there through personal evangelism. They may join because it has been announced in church, and joining forms (indicating the length, purpose and outline of the course) have been made available. They may join because of personal recommendation.

So much for the members. What of the leaders? How are they recruited? The best way is to look out for Christians who are fairly experienced but not necessarily particularly knowledgeable. Their friendliness, tact, sensitivity and unshockability is more important than their detailed knowledge. It is helpful to ensure that the leader of the team is a person who has done it several times before, and is well instructed, but I have found that assistant leaders may well be drawn from the ranks of those who not so long ago were themselves going through a Discovery Group. In a word, the middle ages had it right: apprenticeship is the best way to learn. If you are starting from scratch, and nobody has done it before, go for people who have had experience in a small group, and all its dynamics. I tend to make a point of choosing assistant leaders to work with me who are teachable rather than indoctrinated, and who are 'people's people' rather than intellectuals. Paul gives the right nuance when he speaks of those engaged in this sort of work as first nurses and then fathers (1 Thess. 2:7, 11). They must be able to relate with ease and sympathy to people emerging from secular culture – and many good church people cannot.

There are some 'Notes for Leaders' in Appendix B, but if I were asked what are the most important things for leaders to bear in mind in running these groups, I think I would want to suggest the following points.

Your relationship with the other leaders

Leaders need to know and trust each other and have an easy working relationship. So it is good to meet for a meal, and share your life situation and the story of your own spiritual pilgrimage with one another, as well as finding out each other's interests, strengths, likes and dislikes, and experience. Time invested this way will be amply repaid later on. The evening should end with prayer for one another, for the course, and for the people who will be joining it – by name, if they are known yet. This bonding of the leadership together will model something important for the group to assimilate.

Your relationship with the members

They signed up. They may well be regretting it. They need, first and foremost, to be phoned up and, if possible, visited before the first meeting of the group. This will allay their fears, and allow them to know at least one person in the group before they arrive. That first visit may well be the foundation for a friendship that will develop throughout the next two months: alternatively, you may feel that whoever takes pastoral care of that person, it should not be you! In either case, valuable information has been gained, and contact established.

That contact needs to be developed both in the first meeting and throughout the coming weeks. People will feel very shy when they first come, and need a tolerant, happy, non-threatening atmosphere in the meetings. They need the chance to talk, to express views, to be listened to. And you need to get inside them and find out what makes them tick. What's more, they need some 'fun' times – a boating party, maybe, or perhaps a dinner party where everyone shares in preparing the food.

Most important of all is your relationship with the members of the group for whom you are assigned personal responsibility. The leaders will decide which of them looks after whom, but of course the member will be quite unaware of this gentle 'shepherding', and so it is up to you to make the running. Book him or her up at the first meeting for a meal and a chat, and aim to have a second such talk before the two-month course comes to an end.

The first talk should enable you to see where the person stands spiritually. If they are not yet professing commitment to Christ, they need to be encouraged to feel that this is perfectly acceptable so long as they are moving in the right direction. You are available to help them over any hurdles that you can. It is often the case that however brilliant the public teaching may have been on the way to Christ, your friend simply may not have had the spiritual insight to take it in. And your personal ministrations, patiently taking him through some of the salient points, finding out where his difficulties lie, and exposing him to the power and comfort of key verses of Scripture, may well lead him to that understanding and step of faith which had seemed so elusive to him when the preacher tried to explain it.

It may well be that he is not yet ready to make any such commitment. In that case, encourage him to stay with the group for the eight weeks and see what emerges. It is highly probable that by the end of that time he will have come to a clear faith in Christ, especially as he sees others in the group grow. It may be a help to give him something appropriate to read, and fix a time in two or three weeks to discuss it.

If the person is clear on commitment to Christ, then that first session with him or her should go through again the grounds of assurance, for without that no confident Christian life can be built. And it is important to show them how to read the Bible devotionally, and how to pray. They may have particular problems that they want to talk over, and these should of course be addressed at once: most new Christians have a host of such things that they will bring out once they trust you. But your main aim in this first time together is to plant the beginnings of a regular devotional life in the heart and in the habits of someone who is quietly confident that he has begun to be an authentic disciple of Jesus Christ.

It may well be that all this takes more than one session. Fine. The important thing is to give the person what they need in terms of time and advice: not overwhelm them with it. But at all events you will need to have a final session with your friend near the end of the course. Problems may have arisen which it will be important to talk over: and you have by now earned the right to be their counsellor, so they are likely to take more from you on spiritual issues than from anyone else. They have, after all, seen you at close quarters for a couple of hours every week for two months. Whatever their own agenda may be, you too will have things you want to clear up. How is his or her devotional life progressing? Have they been reading any Christian literature? How are their non-Christian friends reacting to this new faith? What about his girlfriend or her boyfriend? Is there encouragement at home, or the reverse? And perhaps most important of all, is he or she thinking ahead to the end of the Discovery Group? Is there some home fellowship group in the church which they could join? If so, then it is your job to consult the appropriate authorities in charge of the groups and arrange the contact. They are going to need a personal and relaxed time of introduction to the leader of the home group. These times of transition from one group to another are perilous. They are the time when people are most likely to fall away. And they need a lot of tender loving care at that point. It might also be good to discuss whether he or she needs to be baptised, or whether they are permitted by the rules of the denomination to partake in the Holy Communion. It is very important to settle these matters as quickly as possible. And then there is the question of Christian service. They should be beginning to think ahead to some area of Christian ministry in society at large. At all events, it will be something which they would not be doing were it not for faith in Christ. And to have some such sphere of ministry is a major means of ensuring growth and stabilisation in the period after they are transplanted out of the Discovery Group, a time which many find traumatic. They have never found such close fellowship before, and they fear they never will again, so they are reluctant to contemplate its dissolution. But dissolve it must, and they need to be injected, like fresh arterial blood, into the mainstream of the church's life. Your caring relationship with those members for whom you have been given responsibility will be the best way to bring this about.

Your responsibility

Reliability is a vital quality in the leadership of these groups. It shows in the careful preparation of your particular part in each evening. It shows in seeing that the physical preparations for the evening happen: that the food and drinks are there, that the notes

and books and a few Bibles are available for loan. It shows in
keeping the ministers (or whoever set up the Discovery Group)
informed as to how it is progressing, and if any member who signed
up has failed to appear. When someone fails to show up, the best
way is for one of the leaders to visit him with the notes from the first
evening's meeting, saying how they had all missed him, and
offering to come and pick him up next week. In this way it is rare
that someone is not incorporated in the group. But it may well be
that they have unwittingly signed up for a time they find it
impossible to honour: in which case the person administering the
Discovery Groups needs to know speedily, so as to assign that
person to a different group. And that will not happen unless you, as
a leader, are reliable in passing on such information as this to the
right quarter very fast. Reliability shows too, of course, in the
pastoral care offered without stint to the individuals who are
assigned for you to look after. 'It is required of stewards that they
be found trustworthy,' writes Paul (1 Cor. 4:2), and a steward of
God is precisely what you are as a leader of one of these Discovery
Groups.

Your leadership

Leadership in these groups needs to be unostentatious, but it is
important. The members are looking for a lead, and will trust
someone they have confidence in. Your leadership will show in a
variety of ways.

The partnership between the leaders will be such an important
factor. If there is tension or jealousy, it will immediately be
apparent to the members of the group, and it will be disastrous.
Your love for one another, your modelling of what you teach, your
manner, your example, your handling of questions, your unshockability and unstuffiness will all have a silent eloquence.

The conduct of the first evening is very important, and the most
experienced leader should handle it. It is crucial to make people
feel at home. And they will be feeling anything but at home when
they arrive. They are not used to talking about God in a private
house before a bunch of strangers on a weekday evening! No
wonder they sit on the edge of their chairs and spill the coffee . . . It
is your job as leader to take the tension out of the situation. A good
way to do this on the first evening, after about ten minutes of
milling-around time, is to ask people to grab a chair (don't have

them put out in serried ranks beforehand: let people circulate), and have everyone gather round in a circle. Then say something like this: 'It would be fascinating if we could all say a bit about ourselves and what brings us here, as a bunch of complete strangers, tonight.' Then kick off yourself – 'Maybe I'd better begin . . .' Say a little about yourself and your situation, and succinctly explain how you came to faith in Christ. Then pass to another of your leaders, sitting next to you, who will tell a little of his story. The scene will be set for others to follow suit, and you will be intrigued to hear stories, some of them utterly amazing, of the work of God in bringing these people here. Some of them will have come clearly into Christian faith. Others will be there but do not realise it. Others will not be sure. Others will be on the brink of decision. Others will have some serious obstacle to faith. All need to be made to feel comfortable about what they have contributed. Some deft comments by you, as leader, can facilitate this, and occasionally somebody's story makes a valuable teaching point for you to underline. Make it plain that you will not be doing this sort of thing each week, lest they get the wrong idea about how these evenings will proceed. But you will have gained such a lot through this simple exercise. Everyone will have given some sort of spiritual testimony as to where they stand or do not stand with God. Everyone will have trusted others with that information. And as a result they will have broken the ice, and be willing and able to talk about the most intimate spiritual things with those who earlier in the evening were strangers to them.

Leadership is then required in the short talk on the subject for the evening. On the first night it is commitment and assurance, though you might care to alter the order given in the Appendix, and do a short opening study devised by yourself to fit the first evening: an outline of salvation, perhaps, in the most simple and gripping terms. It has to be intriguing. It must not sound like a sermon. It needs to be short and crystal clear. It needs to get Scripture in front of them, so that they see that this book packs power. Your biggest danger will be to go on too long, or to assume too much. Do not assume they will bring a Bible with them on the first night, even if they have been asked to on the joining form. They won't. So you need to have some Bibles ready to lend them (as well as some to sell them, on your little bookstall). And you would be wise to have them all the same version, or you will waste endless time responding to querulous and unprofitable complaints 'My Bible doesn't say that. It says . . .' All small points, no doubt, but for them all to flow so naturally that they are not even noticed requires leadership, and very careful preparation. And so great today is ignorance of the Bible that you will probably need to say, 'There are two parts to this book, the Old Testament and the New Testament. We'll find out more about it later on, but for now let's turn to page . . . of the New Testament.'

If you manage on that first evening to get across to the group the essence of what Christian commitment means, and how they can be sure about it, then you will have done well. There may well not be time to do an inductive Bible study on the first night, but it is good to do it if you can, depending on how long the introductions have taken. For it begins to cut their teeth on using the Bible for themselves and sensing its relevance, and it will be a good launch to their own devotional reading in the subsequent week.

The inductive Bible study can be tricky, and it calls for leadership of a relaxed yet vigilant kind. If you have a big group, it would be wise to split into two, with a couple of leaders in each. These Bible studies are not so much a teaching exercise as a learning one – on the theme of the evening. You are there to stimulate, to referee, and to encourage – not to dominate, and certainly not to preach. Lead from behind. Trust the Holy Spirit, and allow the members to make mistakes. Initially it does not matter much what they say, so long as they say something and get used to the sound of their own voice talking about God and the Bible!

So get the small group gathered round, with Bibles open at the right place. Offer a brief prayer for light and understanding. Get members to read the passage to themselves, or out loud, perhaps a verse each, going round the circle. Then say, 'We are going to have three minutes of quiet now, when we can read it through again, and see what most strikes us. Then we'll pool those thoughts and learn from one another.' Give them the time you indicated – though someone will be sure to say something before the three minutes are over, so unused is modern man to silence, even for so short a time. Don't let him get away with it. 'Hang on,' you say. 'Let's just give time for everyone to make their choice, and then you can begin when I give the word!'

Your heart may miss a beat or two, waiting for someone to start after that three minutes; but somebody will, and then you're away. It may well be hard to stop them by the end of the evening. It is good to get people to say what verse they are finding a help. This both concentrates their own ideas and enables others to concentrate on the same thing. The big things to avoid are red herrings and cross references to other parts of Scripture. If you go for a cross reference, you will lose them irretrievably, deep in Numbers or 2 Chronicles! If you allow 'red herring fishing', you might as well give up and go home. Everyone will air their own ideas on matters about which they know little. They will never learn that way how to feed on the Word of God and let it inform their attitudes. When you get some particularly irrelevant comment, enquire innocently, 'Yes, and which verse do you find that in, Bill?' You won't have to do that very often! But you will often find that people fail to apply to real life the thoughts that are coming to them from the Scriptures, and you need to say gently, 'Great. But what could that mean for us at work tomorrow, Jill?'

I find it good to encourage contributions in the first person singular: 'I like verse seven because it shows that . . .' It teaches people to allow the Word to address them personally. As their spiritual insight grows, it is often a good idea to push them a little further. 'Why do you like that verse, Bill? What difference might it make if we actually acted on it?'

The questions which are set out in the notes for these inductive Bible studies are merely a second line of defence. You may not need them at all: the whole thing may flow. But if it dries up, you may be glad to use one or more of these questions. They are calculated not to produce a yes or no answer, but to stimulate discussion. As such they can often be helpful in taking the study to a deeper level.

There are, of course, particular problems to be encountered in these inductive Bible studies, particularly when the whole idea is so fresh to them all. Some people will come up with problems all the time. It may be helpful, for the sake of teaching, to discuss one of these occasionally, but generally they prove a distraction from feeding on the Scriptures, which is your prime aim. It is best to say, 'Well, that's an interesting point, but I doubt if we can follow it through now. Let's get together to talk about it afterwards.' And mind you keep your word! Then there is the garrulous person whose plentiful contributions intimidate others. 'Great, John, but you've had a couple of opportunities to share already this evening. May we see if someone who has not spoken yet has something they would like to share with us?' And how are you to help the very shy person? They must not be pounced upon. Leave them quietly to absorb it all for the first week or so, and thereafter venture a question in their direction. It will be such a joy to see the whole group begin to get thrilled with the Scriptures, and unself-consciously discuss it and their attempts to live it out.

The prayer time which follows is very important, and is another test of your leadership. Badly introduced, it can silence one and all. But if it is done naturally, prayer will flow. I have found it natural to say something like this. 'Well, we must be drawing to a close soon. But wouldn't it be nice to talk directly to the Lord before we go? We have been talking about him for much of the evening. Why not just take the bit of this Scripture passage that you have found most helpful, read it out, and then say a simple prayer out loud, "Lord, please make this true in my life," or "Thank you, Lord, for this." Of course it doesn't reach God any more easily if we pray out loud: but it does enable the rest of us to enter in to what you are saying, and we'd like to say Amen to it.' Then say, 'James (your fellow leader) will kick off, and I'll close in a few minutes. But do use the time in between to pray yourself if you would like to.' And the amazing thing is that several of them will do just that. They may or may not offer the simple 'Please' or 'Thank you' prayers, as you have suggested. Indeed, they may launch out into a very heartfelt and moving address to God which almost has you in tears because it is all so fresh and so real. But a threshold will have been crossed that evening. Several of them will have crossed the Rubicon of praying in a group with others, and in the mercy of God they will often see answers to those prayers in the next few days, and will come back next week full of joy at answered prayer, an experience they had never dreamed was possible. As the group develops you can lengthen the time of prayer a little (but never let it drag) and can move on to praying for one another's needs. It is amazing how speedily new Christians get into this.

After the prayer time, the evening is over in one sense, and in another it is not. You will give them the notes for the evening, but you'll find that most of them are in no hurry to go. They browse around the bookstall which one of you introduced earlier in the evening. They ask your advice about acquiring a Bible, or joining the Scripture Union (which has a special series of undated notes designed for new Christians, called *Come Alive to God*). Or they may just be basking in the new experience and not in a hurry to leave. It has, after all, been an evening of many new experiences. Coming to a private house to talk about God. Listening to a talk on how you can get to know God and be sure of it. Sharing where you are personally in Christian things. Discovering something of Christian fellowship. Finding that the Bible speaks today. Learning a verse of Scripture by heart. Daring to pray, and really meaning it. Quite an evening! And few of them will need reminders to come back next week. They will be there.

As people drift away, you will want to arrange to meet those for whom you are going to be pastorally responsible, for a personal meal and a chat. And then when they have all gone, the leaders, exhausted and probably rejoicing, will get together to pray for the individuals committed to them, for the development of the group, for any who appeared ill at ease, for criticisms and suggestions about how the evening went, and to plan who does what next week. By the time next week comes, God will have been doing some significant things in the lives of a number of the group, and as you give them time and opportunity to tell the rest about the joys they have had or the problems they have encountered, the sense of group trust and cohesion will grow, and the questions will flow with increasing ease. It may be good to have a shared meal on the second or third week: this helps the group to 'gel'. It is also an attractive feature for the one or two people who intended to come, but for some reasons did not turn up on the first occasion. But it is unwise to have people join the group after the second week. They have missed too much in content and in experience, and their coming tends to spoil the group cohesion. Let them wait until the next Discovery Group begins.

I have gone into considerable detail about the conduct of Discovery Groups because I find that many churches are strangers to this concept which proves so very effective in the nurture of new believers. The group acts as a stimulus and as a cementing bond. The personal pastoral care is given full play. And as members see other people in the group growing in faith and experience, it encourages them even more than being under the solitary guidance of an experienced Christian.

I am conscious that after saying a lot on this subject I have only begun to scratch the surface. But it will suffice if this encourages others to start Discovery Groups, and find the joy and the fruitfulness that such an approach to initial Christian nurture can bring.

FURTHER READING

Not nearly enough has been written on the nurture of new Christians. We seem to assume that they will assimilate all they need as they progress: fortunately they often do, but that is no excuse for incompetent follow-up.

You will find material about the nurture of the Christians as practised in the early church in S. L. Greenslade, *Shepherding the Flock* (SCM Press), R. C. Worley, *Preaching and Teaching in the Earliest Church* (Westminster Press), and my *Evangelism in the Early Church* (Hodder & Stoughton). Recently a training course for nurture group leaders in Mission England was published jointly by Scripture Union and the Bible Society, entitled *Caring for New Christians*.

See also the appendix on Discovery Groups (pp. 429–58) and how to set them up and lead them.

Scripture Union also provide what are probably the best initial notes to help new Christians get into Bible reading. *Come Alive to God* is the most suitable, or *Newness of Life* for the slightly younger reader.

Inter-Varsity Press (USA) provide a series of simple Bible study booklets, *Lifeguide Bible Studies*, as well as their more advanced study course, *Search the Scriptures*.

The following books may well prove valuable for background information and attitudes:

J. C. Aldrich, *Lifestyle Evangelism* (Multnomah Press)
Dietrich Bonhoeffer, *Spiritual Care* (Fortress Press)
F. F. Bruce, *The New Testament Documents: Are They Reliable?* (Inter-Varsity Press)
F. F. Bruce, *The Real Jesus* (Hodder & Stoughton)
James Dunn, *The Evidence for Jesus* (SCM Press)
R. T. France, *The Evidence for Jesus* (Hodder & Stoughton)
Michael Green, *New Life, New Lifestyle* (Hodder & Stoughton)
Michael Green, *Was Jesus Who He Said He Was?* (Servant Books)
Michael Green, *You Must Be Joking* (Hodder & Stoughton)
Cliffe Knechtle, *Give Me an Answer* (Inter-Varsity Press)
C. S. Lewis, *Mere Christianity* (Collins Fount)
Josh McDowell, *Evidence That Demands a Verdict* (Campus Crusade)
Don Posterski, *Reinventing Evangelism* (Inter-Varsity Press)
F. Schaeffer, *The God Who is There* (Hodder & Stoughton)
R. C. Sproul, *Objections Answered* (Regal)

12

More Ways Than One

The speaker was an American. He was talking about methods of evangelism. Americans are usually very strong on methodologies of all kinds, so I was particularly intrigued by the different line this man took. 'Have you ever been out in a Kansas dust storm?' he asked. I had not. But in the next few minutes he made me acutely aware of what it must be like. When one of these palls of summer dust bears down upon you, there is nothing you can do to keep it out. You may be in the most up-to-date of cars, with the best fitting doors. You may hermetically seal the windows and tape over the entire grille. It makes no difference. That dust gets in: everywhere. There is no stopping it.

That is what it is like when the people of God have the wind of the Spirit behind them. Like a Kansas dust storm, they effect penetration. They do not need long courses of instruction on evangelism, any more than a messenger needs elaborate coaching in how to tell a piece of good news, or a lover needs a manual to equip him to tell his beloved that he wants to marry her. Where there's a will there's a way. And that is true of evangelism.

Many people think that we are in need of a new method these days. That could be true, but is profoundly unimportant. We need integrity of lifestyle. We need prayer. We need confidence in the gospel. We need every-member ministry. We need to work out from a centre that is already hot with Christ's life. Yes, we need those things. They are basic. We have looked at them in chapter 4. But having said that, our crying need is not for a new methodology. God forbid! I get distressed these days by the hyphenating of evangelism. We get project-evangelism, church-based evangelism, friendship-evangelism, crusade-evangelism, power-evangelism and the like. There is only one evangelism, the sharing of good news about a God who cared and came and died and rose and knocks. As David Wells put it so clearly in his book *God the Evangelist*, it is the Holy Spirit who initiates evangelism, motivates for it, and empowers it. The ways of carrying it out are legion. No, it is not methods we need, but a close walk with the Spirit of God, a willingness to launch out and if necessary fail, a passionate longing that others shall come to share what we enjoy in Christ. The crux of the matter lies in motivation, not methods. If an individual, if a congregation is motivated to evangelise, they will find ways of doing it. Those ways should never become boring. There is scope for infinite variety. In this chapter I offer some suggestions. They have proved effective in many places. But they may not suit your situation. If not, wait on God, and seek his face until he shows you what is right for you in your part of his harvest field. And then launch out, and do it.

EVANGELISM IN CHURCH

If your church is warm and welcoming; if there is an outward look to it, accompanied by prayer and expectancy on the part of the minister and congregation alike, then it should become a magnet in the locality. People will want to bring their friends along. It will grow in the normal course of events. It will not grow if there is little love, if there is a lot of 'insider' language and attitudes, and constant appeals for money.

We have already considered in previous chapters two of the most obvious ways of evangelism in church. One is church planting, which is happening increasingly in Britain now, as well as in North America; within the Anglican Church as well as outside it. Holy Trinity Church, Brompton, in the heart of London, has, for example, founded two new congregations by each time hiving off a sector of their own large congregation and transplanting it into a church destined for closure. And Roger Forster's new church, Ichthus, has spawned a number of vibrant new congregations in tough and very de-Christianised parts of London.

The other is evangelistic preaching. This has been considered extensively in chapter 9. Many churches will find it the easiest and most natural way to start an ongoing evangelistic ministry. But as we saw, so much depends on the quality of the worship, the love, the prayer, and the openness of the congregation to change, and to the Holy Spirit. If no headway is being made in these areas, despite loving persistence, then a case might be made for starting a new congregation in the same church building. In many parts of the world there are no evening services. The thing would be, in that case, to start one. I live in a city where there are few evening services. But there is a church which regularly draws more than 1,500 young people, complete with brass band, massed choir, the lot! So much depends on the neighbourhood and whom you are seeking to reach. The appropriate way in must be found. It is often found most easily by starting a new congregation within the same church, where you can make radically new structures and approaches without the fear that the traditionally minded will either be put off or will oppose the new initiatives. I have recently had experience of just such a situation. The church had about sixty people in it, none of them under the age of about sixty, and was deeply wedded to traditional Anglican worship. A number of attempts were made through some intensive visiting to draw others from the neighbourhood into this service. They were unsuccessful. People came once and did not return. It was too far removed from their own outlook and preferences. So, starting very small, we began a very informal family-based service at 9.00 a.m. with warm fellowship, a cross section of ages, clear teaching and a definite orientation to those outside the church. It is growing apace, and is now much larger than the other congregation which, however, has been able to continue its style of worship undisturbed.

There are many other ways of spreading the knowledge of Christ among the not inconsiderable number of people who from time to time find their way into a church without having any relationship with Jesus. One is to make good use of the 'rites of passage' which occur in every type of church. Baptisms, weddings, and funerals, in their different ways, all afford opportunities for the gospel not only to be proclaimed but to be seen to be relevant to people's lives.

Churches which baptise only believers need no encouragement to use this ordinance evangelistically. They already do so, and they take pains to baptise nobody unless they have come, so far as human eye can discern, to put their faith in Christ. It is much less common for the gospel message to make a significant impact in services of infant baptism, particularly in mainline churches where this has become something of a social and cultural tradition – complete with christening robe and Jordan water. Actually, of course, infant baptism gives a marvellous opportunity to explain the truth of the gospel. You can explain it to the parents beforehand in a baptism preparation class. You can make it plain to them how hypocritical it would be to make those promises for the little one without meaning them for themselves. You can show how empty it would be to come to the baptismal ceremony without any intention to continue in the worshipping life of the church to which baptism is the doorway. I find that people are often very open at this time in their lives, and have often discovered that these times of preparation for a child's baptism have led to the conversion of the parents. The instruction can be given either by the minister, or by lay leaders in the church – which is often better.

But it is not only the preparation class which can have evangelistic overtones. So can the service itself. Naturally, baptism will only take place in a main service of the church, when the vigour of the congregational life can be experienced not only by the parents (whom you have already been working on), but by the baptismal party, the friends and aunts and cousins, who tend to appear on such ritual occasions. A clear explanation of what baptism means, how it embodies God's initiative, how it calls for personal response in repentance and faith when the child is old enough, is clearly called for on such an occasion, and it is often fruitful in stirring consciences among those who rarely go to church, and occasionally in bringing them right through to faith.

I have found confirmation services can be just as fruitful. They can, of course, be the most dreary of rituals, but in the right hands they can be powerful agencies for the gospel. It is to be hoped that the candidates have already been brought to a living faith during the confirmation classes by those who prepare them. They need to be encouraged to bring not only their parents and family but also their friends to the confirmation service. The bishop or senior church official who admits the candidates into their full membership has a delicate task: he must be a man who knows how to speak to people who are not committed to Christ, as well as to the candidates. Given that combination, and a packed church with dynamic worship; given personal public confession of Christ by the candidates themselves, and you have a very effective agency for spreading the gospel.

I recall one such occasion in Oxford. It had been a mighty service. Some of the candidates had even begun to speak in tongues as the bishop's hands were laid upon them! And we held a reception on the lawn outside the church after the service. I walked up to the parents of one of the candidates, who had been converted during the previous few months, and asked the father if he shared the same living faith as his son. He was embarrassed, and confessed that he did not. 'Cheer up,' I said, 'there is no reason why things should stay like that.' So I went into the church and got him a book to read on the truth and the challenge of the Christian gospel. Within three days he had rung up to ask me more. A few days later he drove down to see me, and I had the privilege of seeing this big businessman come humbly to the Saviour who had made such a difference to his son, and ask for forgiveness and incorporation into his family. But each year, in this particular church, we used to find people coming to faith because of the impact of the confirmation service.

Marriage is another critical time. The alert pastor, or whoever is taking the wedding preparation, will have plenty of opportunity to spend time with the couple and explore with them the spiritual dimension of marriage as well as its other aspects. The couple may imagine that they are only coming to fix up a church wedding: they will discover that this involves them in a number of sessions with the minister, or other Christian leader, who will make it his prayer and his business to seek to lead them to Christ. I have known several couples where one or both of them have come to Christ through such wedding preparation.

As in baptism, the service lends itself to an evangelistic dimension. If marriage really is the counterpart to the relationship between Christ and the church, then the challenge of that relationship forms a very natural part of what the minister may properly preach about at a wedding. I make it a habit to leave material on becoming a Christian at the back of the church for people to take away on such occasions, and frequently people do. This is particularly effective when one or other of the couple has become a Christian in the previous year or so, and is keen for you to make this known at the wedding – to the surprise of their friends who knew them in the old days, and are intrigued to find out what has made the difference. I have often helped people to faith in the wake of a wedding like that. On one occasion I recall leading to Christ the chief bridesmaid, who worked in the Paris fashion industry, because she came back into the church (during the extensive photo session outside) to find out more about the living Christ she had heard about during the address! I think of another occasion when I was able to lead a trade unionist to Christ during the course of a wedding reception. He had already been profoundly influenced by the life of my son Tim, who worked in the same factory, and of his own son who had come to faith through a combination of Tim's friendship and his invitation to a Billy Graham rally.

Funerals, too, give opportunities for making known the good news of divine love and comfort. The message of the resurrection speaks, as nothing else can speak, to grieving relatives. It is my experience that they do not tend to ask questions about the fate of their departed relatives: they take it for granted (rightly or wrongly) that all is well with him or her. But they are often driven to reflect on the resurrection of Jesus Christ, and what that says about life and death. And they can often be led to Christ through the trauma of bereavement. Great sensitivity is needed. People must never be taken advantage of, least of all when they are as vulnerable as they usually are at funerals, but with love and care and clear teaching it is often possible through the service itself or through the visiting before and afterwards to help grieving survivors to find the risen Christ.

The Holy Communion service is another occasion when people come to an active faith. In one sense this is surprising, since of all Christian activities this is the one most designed for those who are already members of Christ's flock. But in another sense it is not so surprising. Cranmer saw the Communion as a 'converting ordinance'; and the 1662 Anglican Prayer Book, based on Cranmer's rite, makes it very clear that in the Communion Christ's sacrifice for the sins of the world is offered to us personally in his body and blood, and that this needs to be personally appropriated as we feed on him in our hearts by faith. At all events, there could be no more graphic embodiment of the gospel message than to have the elements of bread and wine, representing all that Christ is and has done for us, presented to us so that we may take them into our very being. Quite often, therefore, people will catch the divine spark at such a time, and the wise pastor will be on the lookout for it. I recall seeing a visitor to the church one day coming up to receive Communion. She was visibly disturbed. I asked one of the sidesmen to find a sensitive counsellor. He did, and the two of them sat side by side, talking and praying as the service progressed. She came to Christ that day, and has been a pillar of the church ever since. I do not suppose she could tell you just why she was in tears that day. But the Spirit of God was drawing her to himself, and fortunately there were people available who could help.

An incident like that underlines how important it is to have experienced members of the congregation available after services to pray with those who ask for it. When this is known to be a regular feature of a church's ministry, all sorts of things get handled in these after-church times, and a steady trickle of people come to the Christ they do not know but are groping towards. They can then get linked up with the next Discovery Group and incorporated into the life of the church.

One final word about evangelism in church. It is not uncommon to find people drawn into church by the warmth and vitality that exudes from it, and being so moved by the whole experience that they come to Christ. Where there is deep worship, heartfelt prayer, a sense of joy and love and freedom, people are very attracted, and they come to the source of these things without knowing quite what they have done. It is the task of the wise pastor to sense when this is taking place, and to see that this implicit faith becomes more explicit through the Discovery Group or some other medium of teaching. But there is no doubt that it happens. It takes place sometimes even in an empty church! On two occasions I knew of people coming into our church in Oxford, a place where prayer and worship had been going on for a thousand years and more, and being so moved by the Spirit of God and the atmosphere that they became Christians. Of course they needed a lot of help and instruction. But the turning-point for them had been coming into that church where a thousand years of prayer somehow exercised its own powerful grip on their imaginations and their wills. It led them to Christ.

EVANGELISM IN THE HOME

The home is probably the main place where friendships flower into the sharing of the good news, and where personal conversations about Christ are most likely to take place. We have already considered this a little in chapter 10. Personal conversation about life in general, and the most important issues in life in particular, is undoubtedly the best way to share the gospel, and the current move towards emphasising friendship as the bridgehead for evangelism is very healthy.

But 'events' as well as friendship can happen in the home. Here are some that I have found to be effective, but the home is such a flexible tool that all sorts of other ways of using it could readily be dreamed up.

The easiest thing is to have one or two people in for a meal, and look for a chance to share your faith. Another route is to throw a party. It might be a supper party. It could be for dessert. But it would be for friends and acquaintances. You might well choose to organise it in partnership with one or two other friends or couples, and this would widen the range of those invited. It is important to be very open about the purpose of such a party. Nobody must be there on false pretences. But if you have, for example, a judge to speak on the ultimate basis for law, or a Christian politician to speak on politics and the gospel of Christ, or a leading businessman on 'My God and my job', or an ex-convict on the difference Christ has made to him and his family – people will be interested. They will want to come, and you will get a high response rate to your invitation. The rest depends on prayer, a welcoming atmosphere, a clear address, and the opportunity for people who have been struck by the evening to take the matter further in personal conversation. Often a small bookstall is appreciated as well, with carefully chosen books designed to help people to faith.

Another way to use the home is to have an investigative Bible study there on a regular basis. Some of the para-church organis-ations like Inter Varisty and Navigators produce particularly good material for interesting friends and neighbours in this sort of thing. I know of a whole church in Canada which was founded through this method. A few Christian friends visited on a new estate, and said they were going to hold an investigation into the basis of Christianity. They invited their neighbours to come along and look into the Gospel of Mark with them, the first of the Gospels. The result astonished them. Many people wanted to come. The course was much enjoyed. The longer-term result was the founding of a church. And further still down the track it has now founded two other churches, one with several hundred members. Not bad for one home Bible study!

Another way to use the home is to mark some particular crisis or discovery. I think of a crisis where a man's only son had been killed in a farm accident just before he was due to go up to university. The parents – and the son, too, for that matter – were Christians. And the father decided to mark the tragic event by inviting all his dead son's friends (seventy of them!) to the house for a reception. He asked me to speak on this occasion, and he gave each person a copy of a little book I had written about the resurrection of Jesus and what it can mean for us. It was a very moving and very fruitful evening, and wonderful use of the home in a time of great adversity.

I think of another couple who threw open their home to celebrate. They wanted to express their joy at welcoming Christ into their lives. It had been a slow business, talking, arguing, reading the Bible for a number of weeks in their front room. But they reached the point of clarity about Christ and immediately wanted to share that joy with their friends, none of whom were Christians. So they invited a house-full, and in the context of the wonderful supper they produced, I spoke of Jesus' parable of the great supper and the many excuses offered for non-attendance (Luke 14:15–24).

Another way of using the home is to have an Enquirer's Group meeting there. It needs someone with a fairly good knowledge of the Christian faith, and of the reasons for believing in its truth, to lead it. It is best not to have more than one, or at the most two, Christians present, and to dare others to join this Agnostics Anonymous group for, say, six weeks. All sorts of people who have some links with the church, usually through a personal friend or relative, can be drawn into such a group. For one thing, they think they can shoot you out of the water. For another, they are emboldened by the company of other agnostics. The very name sounds good. Offer some food and a warm and friendly atmosphere, and then you can handle it in a variety of ways. I have made some suggestions in Appendix A. You could perhaps produce a series of crucial subjects, ranging from the existence of God through the meaning of the cross, suffering, other faiths, and the resurrection, to Christian commitment. You could study some key passages from a hard-hitting and controversial Gospel like John. You could make use of David Watson's short TV documentaries produced on videotape and entitled 'Jesus Then and Now', which are on Christian basics. There he gives some potent input on a number of crucial issues for about fifteen minutes; so you could show one, then switch the VCR off and allow the discussion to rage! Or you could ask them what they do not believe about the Christian faith, and work out your group agenda from there. This is a good idea, for you will find that they all tend to have different blockages, and their arguments will tend to cancel one another out! It is a short step, but a humbling one, to move from one of these Agnostics Groups to a Discovery Group. But many make the transition. It is a very effective use of the home for evangelism.

PERSONAL CONVERSATION

A good deal has already been said about personal conversation in a previous chapter. But we cannot afford to omit it when talking about methods of reaching people with the good news. For personal conversation is without question the most effective way of doing it. I remember taking a mission in Cape Town University once when the publicity was so good that at the climax of their preparations they even had helicopters coming and hurling bundles of flyers on to the campus. But even that did not bring in the people in large numbers. The great Jamieson Hall only gradually filled up over the week as Christian people came out of their holes in the woodwork and actually pestered their friends to come along. It is very hard to gainsay the enthusiastic invitation of someone who has clearly found something very worthwhile.

If that is so, we should be doing a lot more chatting naturally about Jesus Christ than we do. I find it a natural thing to do with petrol attendants, in planes or trains, with shop workers, bank clerks, or whenever the conversation gives an opening. I do not recommend making a big thing of it, or introducing a heavy note into the conversation. I mean just naturally making some comment about Jesus Christ and the joy of serving him and the difference he makes. If we Christians did more of this, a lot more people would be intrigued and want to know what we have found in a faith that they think is hopelessly *passé*.

We do not necessarily even need to say anything. A fellow professor friend of mine was visiting China, and went to see the pastor of one of the fast-growing Baptist Churches there. He asked him how he went about evangelism. The answer surprised him. The man said, 'I don't do much searching out of people. They come to me!' Why? The reason became plain as the conversation proceeded. During the Cultural Revolution this man had been conscripted to work in a soul-destroying factory making parts for radios. He was not allowed to speak about Christ at all. But he whistled as he worked. Nobody else in that factory could summon up the joy to whistle. So when the days of the Cultural Revolution were over, and the man returned to his work as a pastor, he found a steady trickle of people from the factory knocking at his office to find out what was the secret of his joy. If it could carry him serene through such unpleasant circumstances, it must be worth hearing about.

But China is a long way away, and your circumstances are doubtless very different. Are you saying to yourself, 'But I'm not an evangelist'? That is exactly what my wife Rosemary says, so I am asking her to take over at this point!

BUT I'M NOT AN EVANGELIST . . . !

There are clearly some to whom God gives the gift of evangelism. Michael is one of them. He combines an ease in opening up conversation about Jesus, and in leading right through to commitment to Christ, with the sensitivity to know the right moment to push for decision or to hold back.

I began to recognise this at the end of our first three years of ministry together in a parish. He had led scores of people to faith. As far as I was aware I had led only one (who has since become a missionary in Iran and in Afghanistan). At the time I felt a failure, but I have since seen that our gifts are different, and complementary. I curl up inside at the prospect of having to be part of the onlooking crowd during an open-air outreach, then approaching a total stranger with 'What did you think of that?' Others, however, would run a mile from some of the chronic depressives with whom I am willing to spend many hours. It is right that we seek to recognise, and use obediently, the gifts that God has given us.

Timothy appears to me to be a person whose gifting was primarily teaching and pastoral, and whose temperament was not naturally that of the forefront evangelist. But Paul encouraged him to 'do the work of an evangelist' (2 Tim. 4:5). And even those of us who are not gifted evangelists are called to be witnesses to our Master and to share our good news with those who 'have no hope and are without God in the world' (Eph. 2:12). After all, one of the primary functions of the Holy Spirit is to enable us to testify to Jesus (John 15:26–7). Some years ago, at the end of a training course on different aspects of practical Christian service, a group of us were praying together. One of the members had a picture of a field of ripe wheat. A combine harvester was covering a lot of ground, sweeping up everything in its path, not noticing individual stalks of grain, or stopping for the wildlife. Round the edge of the field were reapers, working carefully by hand. We knew that in the room there was one gifted evangelist; this picture encouraged the rest of us to work patiently with the ones and twos.

Behind the easy excuse 'That's not my gift' there is, for most of us, the inhibition of fear; fear of making fools of ourselves. I often think of Moses at the burning bush, in Exodus 3. He must have been thrilled when he heard God saying that he had heard the cry of the oppressed Israelites (v.9) – and then shocked when he was told that God was sending *him* to lead the people out of Egypt. One excuse after another tumbled out of him. 'I'm a nobody' (v.11); 'I shan't have the right answers' (v.13); 'What if they won't believe me?' (Exod. 4:1). To each one God patiently gave the promise of his presence and his power. Moses tried again. 'I'm no good at speaking' (Exod. 4:10). After all, he hadn't had much experience, after forty years as a shepherd in the desert. Back came God's reply, 'I gave you your mouth. I'll help you speak and teach you what to say' (Exod. 4:11–12). But Moses still argued. 'Please send someone else' (Exod. 4:13). And then God got angry. He allowed Aaron to become the spokesman – but as we think of the later incident of the golden calf, we can see that it might have been better for Moses if he had not had to rely so much on Aaron. We can label Moses as a coward – and then turn round, and make identical excuses for ourselves and our failures and fears. I am encouraged that so often in Scripture we find the Lord saying, 'Fear not.' That tells me that he recognises how prone we are to fear. But it also tells me that we do not need to continue to fear, as he says to us, 'Don't be afraid . . . I am with you . . . I have got things under control.' In my early days as a Christian I learned a good deal about personal evangelism, and was a zealous Christian student. In more recent years a renewed love for Jesus has enabled me to bubble over much more freely and naturally in conversation about him. We would be wise, too, to know the basic framework of the gospel, and to be able to explain it in everyday language, using Scripture but without being stuck with Christian jargon. It helps to try some role-playing with a friend. Let one of you pretend to be the enquirer, and the other see how good you are at showing the way to Jesus.

What are some of the situations in which I find myself speaking about the gospel? It may be in conversation with friends, when a Christian viewpoint can be slipped in when discussing a news item about abortion, AIDS, an earthquake, a train crash. It may be with a casual contact in a shop or on a plane. On one recent flight across Canada, Michael and I had (typically!) checked in fairly late, and were unable to sit together. Before we had even taken off, I heard him chatting with his next-door neighbour, who turned out to be a Christian with a fascinating story who recognised him from the TV! It did not take me much longer to get talking with one lady next to me. In showing interest in her life, and in exchanging the reasons for our journeys, there was the chance to speak a little about my faith and to ask about hers. Later in the flight, I was working with my New Testament out, and the Chinese lady on my other side asked if I was a Christian. That was not evangelism – she was already a believer! But the basic readiness to talk with a stranger was there. Another time, we were flying from England to Australia. I soon got chatting to the man next to me – the reason for the journey made an easy opening gambit. It turned out that he had been a Christian for about three years, but he said that his wife, who was travelling with him, was pretty antagonistic. I leaned across him, and talked with her about their children and their home – and about her phobia of flying. A twenty-four hour flight is a long way, and it seems longer if you have that sort of fear. During the second eight-hour hop, I was specifically praying for a chance to talk with her about Christ at the next airport stop, when the man turned to me and asked if I would be willing to talk with his wife if he moved to a different seat for a time. He didn't know what else he could say to help her. As I began to talk with her gently, about apparently irrational fears (from my counselling experience), and then a bit about God, I asked whether she would be willing for me to pray for her, then and there. She readily accepted, and at the next stop she told Michael what a help it had been.

You may well find a situation where someone who is not yet a Christian is nevertheless ready for you to pray, aloud, and on the spot, at a time of crisis. One evening a relative phoned to tell us that her husband was very seriously ill in hospital. Here was a person, brought up in a Christian home, whose current church-going was probably limited to Christmas and Easter (and her husband even less). Cautiously she asked whether we could 'spare a thought for him at bedtime'. So I plunged in. 'Of course we will pray together for you then – but would you like me to pray for you now, over the phone? Or would you think that too odd?' She readily agreed. I cannot remember in what terms I prayed, but I do know that next evening she phoned again. She had seen his temperature drop dramatically in the night; she recognised God's hand in this, and she asked me to pray and give thanks then and there on the phone. A few days later she called again – and this time, she was the one who prayed aloud. That couple are now regular at their local church – largely untaught, but I believe that that prayer was used to get her in touch with God.

A few days as an in-patient in the hospital also brings us into contact with strangers in immediate need. Two years ago, when I had to undergo an operation, I did not ask for prayer for miraculous healing, because I was sure that God had a purpose for my undergoing surgery, and I went into hospital with two evangelistic booklets in my bag. My faith was too small – I needed more! In the next-door bed was a single woman, aged about thirty-five, rather fed up with life. One day when she was in tears, I just went to give her a hug. Another time, there was prolonged crying coming from the next room, and she gave me a gift question. 'That gets me down. What makes you able to cope?' So very simply, I told her the outline of the gospel, offered her a booklet to read – and then switched to playing a game of cards that she taught me; before she went home we returned briefly to talk about Christ. The next occupant of the same bed was younger; a nominal Roman Catholic. She had a mother who had recently had a charismatic experience and was thrusting her faith and her religious activities down the throats of her family. So I had to be cautious! But her fear of surgery became the opportunity to pray with her about that. (To be honest, I missed that one – but Michael picked it up when he was visiting me!) On my final day, the cleaner, a lady of Polish origins, was expressing the hope that the weekend would be fine, for her eight year old's first Communion. Again, a chance to rejoice with her that Roman Catholic and Protestant share the same God, and to give her a booklet, which she took enthusiastically.

Other scenarios flash across my mind. A boss at work with a painful back was intrigued by a book on healing which a friend of mine was reading. A shop assistant, trying to wrap elusive Brussels sprouts in the small pages of a tabloid newspaper, complained, 'Not much good for wrapping sprouts.' I replied, 'And not much good for the sort of stories it carries, either.' That was a marvellous opening! A bank official, entertaining friends to dinner, left a Christian book on the coffee table. Most left at midnight, but one stayed on for the next three hours to discuss the faith which that book embodied. A young woman, rehearsing for amateur dramatics, discovered an enormous area of need in the life of another as they waited in the wings and talked: this led to an invitation to supper and conversation about how Jesus could meet her in her need.

Stories could be multiplied, but I want to finish with a poem, whose author I do not know:

> Not merely in the words expressed
> Not only in the deeds confessed
> But in the most unconscious way
>   Is Christ expressed.
>
> Is it a calm and peaceful smile?
> A holy light upon your brow?
> Oh no! I felt his presence
>   When you laughed just now.
>
> For me, 'twas not the truth you taught,
> To you so clear, to me so dim,
> But when you came to me you brought
>   A sense of Him.

THE MEDIA

Some people have access to the media, and these are a valuable, though by themselves inadequate, way of spreading the gospel. Valuable because they reach a very wide spectrum of people, getting into their hands if they are a book or a paper; getting into their living rooms or their cars if they are radio or TV. No Christian can afford to despise communicating the gospel through the media. Jesus or Paul would certainly have used them if they had been living in our day. And I have nothing but admiration for TV programmes like those of Billy Graham or Terry Winter and David Mainse in Canada where a clear presentation of the Christian faith is combined with sensitive handling of phone enquiries or written responses, and, of course, money is not solicited. It is hard to exaggerate the harm that has been done to the cause of the gospel by unscrupulous and worldly-minded televangelists in the United States during the 1980s. It has made things much harder for everyone else who is trying to use the media for Christ. And if Christians do not take such opportunities as they can garner, there are plenty of others who will, both among the sects and in the ranks of secular humanists, who often seek influence through the media.

Wherever you go, even in small villages, you see evidence of the proliferation of video cassettes and their recorders. These are immensely popular, and of course they communicate very clearly to those who cannot read – a section of society which is actually growing alarmingly, and one which Christians are very weak at reaching. There are now some very good Christian films on video, and some courses, such as David Watson's *Jesus Then and Now* (mentioned earlier), are specifically designed for outreach by use in homes. The number of such quality video cassettes is not high, but it is on the increase. They can make an interesting and arresting beginning to an evening's discussion about Jesus with a roomful of friends or neighbours.

Equally, books and newspapers are an invaluable way into people's minds, and sometimes into their hearts. The courage of Christians opposing a communist government in China, the generosity of Christian organisations like TEAR Fund or World Vision, the personal generosity and money-raising talents of well-known artists like Cliff Richard to people starving in the Third World – all these get occasional coverage in the press. More often, however, it is the bad news and the scandals that make the columns, and if there is a fair-minded story which is positive about the Christian faith, more often than not it is somewhat garbled. However, if it is possible to get a column once a week in the local paper, or, better still, in a national paper, that can have a steady and lasting influence. The same is true in the world of magazines. When a skilful and sensitive Christian journalist gets access to an 'agony column' on a regular basis, thousands of lives are touched.

But the value of specifically Christian literature, designed to reach those who are not yet Christians, is still one of the most effective ways of using the mass media. You never know into whose hands that piece of literature may fall. Many Christians have been brought to faith through a tract handed them on the street. Before throwing it away, they decided to read it – and it changed the whole course of their lives. Those who display Scripture texts on railway hoardings have similar stories of lives transformed by what to many seems a crude and ineffective instrument. And books and magazines written by Christians for the uncommitted have an astonishing effect at times. I can recall my own amazement when a couple of my books, written in a thoughtful but racy style, really took off, neared the half-million mark apiece, and were translated into many different languages. I was astonished. But I was also delighted that my feeble attempts to commend the Christian faith could travel to so many places where I would never be able to go. I still meet people who became Christians because of reading those books, and I never cease to be thankful. I know that literature, as well as the press, radio and TV, can be a means of passing on the good news.

Having said that, I must reiterate: the media are in themselves inadequate. The Christian faith is essentially communal. It is all about being incorporated in the family of God, the army of Christ, the vine, the flock, and all those corporate images which keep recurring in the pages of the New Testament. And all approaches through the media are essentially impersonal. They reach people in the isolation of their rooms, their cars, or wherever they do their listening, viewing and reading. They do not bring people into the community of God's family. That is why evangelism through television is very necessary, but by itself is very inadequate. Unless the written, seen, or spoken word through the media leads the recipient to join the church of God and become part of a visible, local community of Christians, it cannot be judged to be evangelism in the New Testament sense of the word. But needless to say, as an adjunct to other forms of evangelism, it is invaluable. Particularly good use is being made of the media in countries where Christianity is a tiny minority religion. I think of some of the aggressively Muslim states where open preaching is not allowed. But nobody can stop Christian teaching coming into the country by radio, and there are organisations such as FEBA which concentrate on such an approach. People are invited to write in and enquire about the faith. They are incorporated into a correspondence course. Many of them do in fact commit themselves to Christ, and are then asked if they would like to be put in touch with others who are coming out of Islam into Christian faith. Many thousands of people are reached in Muslim and Hindu lands each year through this combination of media contact and careful teaching through the correspondence course, culminating in commitment both to Christ and his community.

VISITING

Visiting has largely fallen into disuse in many a local church. The community is so fragmented. The rate of moving on is so great. Those with the heart for visiting are so few. Its results seem so meagre.

The disenchantment with visiting which marks so much modern Christianity is both understandable and misguided. It may not be true any longer that a visiting pastor produces a church-going people, but it is certainly true that a church which does not visit in its neighbourhood becomes more and more of a ghetto, and its members more like patrons of a club than soldiers of Jesus Christ.

Visiting pays in all sorts of ways, especially if it is shared between the staff of a church and its members. It shows people that the church cares. It reminds people of God in an age when it is all too possible to squeeze him out. It begins to build relationships in the locality between church-goers and those who do not go. It opens the eyes of the church people to the needs around them. It reveals some areas where help can be offered. And it draws some people into the church.

Young people have shown the way in visiting. Two of the most vigorous para-church organisations are Youth With A Mission and Operation Mobilisation. Both make great use of visiting and street work. They do it with young volunteers from the West moving into Europe, Asia or the Americas to work with local young people from indigenous churches. This brings a tremendous infusion of confidence to local Christians who might never have ventured on such a bold and direct approach. Often it is very simple: giving or selling Christian literature in the streets and shopping malls. On each of those pieces of literature is an address where the reader can learn more. And this apparently crude approach is proving one of the most effective ways of reaching into countries dominated by one of the other major world religions. And the enthusiasm rubs off on the local Christians. The leadership of OM in India, for example, is wholly in the hands of Indian Christians now.

In the USA, Evangelism Explosion is an evangelistic method based on visiting. It hinges on two basic questions, which receive slight modification from time to time. But the first is: 'Have you reached the point in your spiritual life where you would be sure of going to heaven if you died tonight?' And the second is: 'Why do you think God should allow you into heaven?' Those are brilliant diagnostic questions, for they enable the visitor to learn an awful lot about the assumptions and real faith – or lack of it – of those who are visited. It works well in a culture where there is still a residual belief in heaven and hell. In strongly post-Christian cultures such as Canada, and to a large extent Britain, it is a less effective tool. Nevertheless it has had very good effects even there. It has given a simple but shrewd method of approach to ordinary Christians, which they can introduce into conversation at an appropriate point and see it produce a reaction. It gets Christians out visiting – minister and people together. It produces results. And when it fails, it drives the visitors back into renewed prayer and research so as to be better at it next time.

A useful and less heavily structured approach has been devised in Britain by Michael Wooderson, Vicar of Chasetown. He discovered it by accident. It all began with a man at a funeral at which he was officiating saying, 'I would be interested in finding out more about the Christian faith.' That man was totally outside the ambit of the church, and his question got Michael thinking. How could such a man find out what he wanted to know? He was not the sort to read books. Church would be a totally alien world to him. How could he find out?

And then Michael Wooderson hit on an idea which he has developed ever since. It is highly successful, and he has written about it in *The Church Down Our Street* and *Good News Down Our Street*. He was influenced by some aspects of James Kennedy's *Evangelism Explosion*. For that was a method which mobilised the whole church for evangelism, was built on the concept of learning by doing, took the good news to people in their homes, and made evangelism a continuous activity and a normal part of church life. He was also influenced by the Jehovah's Witnesses, visiting on his estate. They embodied three important principles. One was systematic visiting, aimed at uncovering interest. A second was setting up study groups in the homes of interested people. And the third was immediately sending out new converts visiting, giving them no time to become lukewarm.

He developed these principles into a very simple method. Michael himself has a flair for making relationships, and discovers people in the area who would like to learn a little about the Christian faith in the course of a home visit, and would be willing to welcome a small team coming to their home. Michael trained the congregation in running a simple course for six visits in the homes of interested people, giving them enough information about Jesus to enable them to make a decision for or against him. It was all very informal. In home contexts, questions flow and misunderstandings are cleared up. People are surprised to see lay folk like themselves feeling so enthusiastic about the gospel that they are willing to take the time and make the effort to share it. They go in threes in order to train inexperienced people on the job, to incorporate new converts immediately, and to deepen fellowship among church

members. That is an evangelistic strategy that is making solid
headway in some of the most unchurched parts of England. How
effective this course has been can be seen from the following
figures. Of the first two hundred people visited (by eighty-nine
teams comprising 120 members of the congregation), five failed to
complete the six-week course, fifteen were already Christians, 136
made a commitment to Christ, four have made a commitment
subsequently and forty made no positive decision. They have now
reached the point where church members regard evangelism like
this as a normal part of their Christian life, and feel deprived if they
are not assigned to a visiting team fairly frequently. As Roy Pointer
of the Bible Society says in his Foreword to *The Church Down Our
Street*, 'This story reads like the Gospels and the Acts of the
Apostles all over again.' But there is nothing that any local church
could not emulate – if it had the will and the commitment.

COMMUNITY SERVICE

The good news of Jesus is communicated not only by word, but also
in action. It is when people see the difference Christ makes that
they begin to listen to what he has to say. It was when he saw water
gushing from the drill which TEAR Fund had brought into his
parched village in Sudan that the headman said, 'Now I believe the
gospel of Jesus.' It is not accidental that there are a great many
conversions in the refugee camps set up after disasters in Thailand
and the Sudan. Roman Catholic Christians have been far ahead of
their Protestant brethren in this matter, as a rule. I recall the
terrible shanty towns spreading all around Lima, Peru. A mass of
humanity flowed down from the Andes to seek illusory wealth in
the capital, and ended up on the streets with homes made of little
structures of sticks and corrugated iron. In the midst of all this
misery a genial Catholic friar made breakfast free for all comers
each day, and Catholic teachers started a school for the shoe-shine
boys, the poorest of the poor. That is very attractive. It is very like
Jesus.

And that is one of the best ways in which a local church can make
an impact on its area. It must discover what the real needs are, and
set out to meet some of them, however weak it may feel, and
however scant its resources. It may be to run a coffee house for

unemployed youngsters. It may be to visit in the local prison on a regular basis, and perhaps to inaugurate a half-way house for prisoners upon their release if they have nowhere else to go. I know of one prison chaplain, who is also a Baptist minister, who shares his chaplain's responsibility with a dozen and more members of his congregation. How he has got this past the prison authorities, I do not know, but I have seen both him and some of them at work in that prison, and it is highly impressive to witness the love of Christ being communicated so naturally and so relevantly in a very difficult situation like that. The very success of one ministry like this in England led to the creation of a half-way house, so that those who had come to faith had some initial nurture and continuing Christian teaching and fellowship in the early days after their release, and were not simply turned loose one morning on the street.

I once knew a group of doctors who wanted to make Christ known through meeting genuine need. They were unwilling on principle to take innocent life, by performing abortions on their patients. But they did not leave it at that. They set up an adoption agency for unwanted pregnancies.

I was with a friend the other day whose church wanted to do something about the unsavoury reputation that the local beach was getting. So they are proposing to run open-air services there all summer, and to provide food for penniless youngsters who haunt the beach, and accommodation for the old men who doss down there. A church like that has a right to be heard.

Many churches run youth clubs and gymnasia. But what about running your own restaurant? Churches like St Michael's Chester Square, London, and St Aldate's, Oxford, do just that. It is a lot of work, and continuous hassle! But it meets a local need and provides a warm, welcoming atmosphere in which friendly conversations of all kinds can go on. My predecessor sensed the need for overseas students to have some much-needed accommodation in the heart of Oxford, where the church was situated. And his initiative achieved housing for more than sixty such. There was a small but steady trickle of conversions within that housing complex, but that was a secondary aim. The primary aim was to relieve need, and when the church does that, the hearts of people are often open to what the church has to say . . . and they often are not!

Another aspect of community service which is appropriate in some areas is to hold community events like street parties, *fiestas*. These fun occasions catch the spirit of the community, and they show that the church has a heart which beats with the heart of the people all around. There may well be no immediate result in spiritual terms. But in due course it would be surprising if some people did not start moving into the life of the church, perhaps becoming part of it gradually, by osmosis. The same is true when the church initiates marches to protest against injustice, or inhuman conditions for the people. The prime moving of the Catholic Church in Poland in the rise and success of Solidarity, or in the Philippines through the bloodless expulsion of the notorious president Marcos, is not only a mark of moral leadership in the respective nations, but is a powerful spiritual attractor, as the passionate Christian commitment of the Poles and Filipinos amply demonstrates.

THE OPEN AIR

Jesus Christ was an open-air preacher. Most of his followers are not. The infant church was born in the streets on the day of Pentecost. Most church members these days would not be seen dead in the streets. We are very different from our founder and our forebears. And we are impoverished as a result. For churches like the Pentecostals, who do make a big thing out of getting out on the streets, win both respect and converts. I remember teaching on evangelism one Sunday afternoon in a large Australian city. The church had glass doors, so that it could look out on the busy world passing by. A good number gathered for this teaching session. I made it very short, and got them out on the street to join me in open-air witness to the crowds outside. We had song, some basic drama and dance, and preaching along with testimony, and they were thrilled to bits. This was a red-letter day. But later that afternoon my wife and I walked a little further along the street and found a Pentecostal open-air witness in progress. It was ragged, loud and theologically illiterate. But it was passionate. I enquired how long they had been Christians, and for most of them it was all very recent. I enquired how often they did this. The answer was every day. No wonder they grow. They deserve to.

But there are many ways of using the open air effectively. One is to have a Christian pop concert in a sunny climate on a Sunday afternoon when everyone is out enjoying themselves. Another is to have a walk of witness, say on a Good Friday or at Pentecost, preferably binding all the churches in a town together for this act of witness. If somebody is carrying a great cross, the point is made all the more sharply. There is power in the cross of Jesus. One of my erstwhile colleagues, Canon David Hawkins, actually held an open-air service in a shopping precinct one Good Friday when a member of the congregation was erected on a cross, with hands and feet bound to it. You can imagine the impact that made, and the way the preacher's words went home. In a lighter vein, he had been known to lead a procession down the street while dressed as a clown and playing his violin. On his front was 'A fool for Christ'. On his back 'Whose fool are you?' There are many ways of using the open air.

Another is a public eucharist in a large football arena, or a public baptism in the sea or river. Most baptisms used to be conducted in this way, and the habit of doing it within the four walls of the church is in some ways rather regrettable. It misses out on one of the most dramatic acts of witness that a Christian can ever give. We would sometimes conduct open-air baptisms in the river in Oxford. A procession would start from the church, growing in size as it moved down the towpath on a busy Sunday afternoon. When we reached the appointed place there was a large crowd in attendance, drawn by the spectacle and by the singing and joy of the participants. Each of the candidates would give a testimony to what Christ had come to mean to him or her, and then my colleague and I would immerse them in the river in the name of the Trinity, and there would be great praise and rejoicing as each emerged from the water. It was unusual if other conversions did not spring from those public baptisms.

There are many other ways in which the open air can be captured for the gospel. It may be a quiet giving out of leaflets advertising some event: that often leads to profitable conversations. It may be going on to the streets, two by two, with a simple questionnaire: see Appendix D for a sample. It may be going with love, literature and a guitar to work the bus queues in the centre of some town. That too has its own value. It may be a major procession, a Praise March, when hundreds or thousands of Christians combine to march through the city, as they did in London, England, in 1988, or in Cranbrook and Victoria, British Columbia, in 1989, singing the praises of God and flowing with his love to passers by. Such marches make a major impact both on the local population and on the television station sent to report them. These are all opportunities for evangelism which derive from an imaginative use of the open air.

But the sort of open-air work which I love most is the most basic of all. It consists of a group of Christians proclaiming the good news of Christ in a very earthy way in the shopping malls or market squares of a city. It can, of course, be disastrous, especially if you choose a place where people do not normally go. But if you go to a populous area and are loving, happy, relaxed, self-effacing and confident in the message you are charged with, many people will listen. It can be done in a wide variety of ways. Drama is perhaps the most important ingredient. It always draws a crowd, and if your group performs a sequence of short street playlets, each lasting a few minutes and making one clear, arresting point, it is only too easy for a compere to draw out the implications of what has been seen and apply them to the crowd which has gathered. Meanwhile members of your congregation are mingling with the crowd, chatting with onlookers. Singing can help, but curiously enough it often drives people away in the open air. A visual aid, progressively unmasked if possible, is a big attraction, and some people are brilliantly gifted at painting in the open air while they preach. Sometimes a juggler or karate expert can be invited to operate first of all, and that is guaranteed to draw a crowd. The secret is a fast-moving, attractive, relaxed presentation of the heart of the gospel in terms that people really understand. I often find myself preaching from the road signs or the names of shops: I seem to have the sort of mind that can take such things and turn them to advantage in what I want to say!

The main value of such open-air operations is to heighten the Christian presence in the community, to sharpen the courage and zeal of those who take part, and to broadcast the good news that was intended not for the churchman but for the man in the street. But often it goes further than that. I have seen many people quietly put their faith in Christ when hearing in the streets of his love and sacrifice and his claim on their lives. I have seen people kneel down on the pavement and ask the Lord to accept them. And I have seen many people drawn from such meetings to hear the gospel in another place which gave them more opportunity for a considered response. I think of May Morning in Oxford, when all the city is alive and on the streets by 6.00 a.m. So were we, complete with jugglers and singers, speakers and dramatists. It was such a joy to proclaim Christ in that historic main street of the ancient university city with hundreds of people clustered round. And it was a further

joy to invite them back to the church hall where we offered all and
sundry a free breakfast and a talk on Christian commitment. An
operation like that led people to the Lord year after year. And we
did not restrict it to May Morning. The gospel is good news. It is
too good to confine within the four walls of a church.

NEUTRAL GROUND

One of the important lessons the modern church needs to relearn
comes from the school of Tyrannus. We know nothing about this
Ephesian pedagogue except that the apostle Paul made daily use of
his school at a time when Tyrannus had no use for it. One ancient
manuscript tells us when he did it: 'from 11 a.m. to 4.00 p.m.'
When you consider that in Ephesus more people would be asleep
at 1.00 p.m., during the midday siesta, than at 1.00 a.m., that says a
great deal for the attractiveness of Paul's dialectic! But the most
noteworthy thing is Paul's use of secular ground. People would feel
quite comfortable in going to cross swords with this tentmaker-
teacher in the lecture hall of Tyrannus. That is the point. And we
need to take it very seriously. Many of our attempts at evangelism
are doomed before they start, because we insist on doing them on
our own property, where many unchurched people feel very ill at
ease. We Christians believe that Jesus Christ broke down all
barriers between the sacred and the secular by his own incarnation.
Right: we should therefore carry out that principle in our evangelism. We should reach out to where people are, not expect them to
come to where we are. In a word, much of the best evangelism will
not happen in church at all.

   There now follow some suggestions for evangelism on neutral
ground. They are not by any means exhaustive, but I hope they
may prove suggestive for your own creative thinking on the
subject.

   Debates are a marvellous way of stirring interest, which can
ripen into commitment. They are particularly valuable as a centrepiece in a mission or campaign. They are attractive because
Christians come out into the open and are not afraid of having their
position exposed and criticised. They are attractive because there
is opportunity for many believers to get up and say their piece from
the floor. They lend themselves to refreshments afterwards and the

chance to take things further at a more personal level. They are easy to publicise, and readily draw a crowd which would not normally attend a religious meeting. The more well known the person with whom you are debating, the better. I have found that when debating with politicians, celebrated atheists or well-known personalities all manner of people turn up for the fun, and stay out of interest. The danger in this sort of enterprise lies in the very nature of debate. It is eristic. It is designed for victory. And if you gain victory in argument about Christ but alienate or fail to show love to your opponent, you have lost everything. Consequently, great courtesy is called for, along with rigorous logic, and if it is possible for you and your opponent to have dinner together beforehand it is all to the good in building some relationship between you. Jesus engaged in a stringent debate, and on neutral ground at that. We are neglecting a wonderful opportunity if we fail to do likewise. And it is so profitable for the cause of the Kingdom of God. I think of one occasion in Australia where a friend and I took on all comers for several hours one night – and there were hundreds of them. The outcome? Much interest, the continuation of the genre, and six people signing up for a Discovery Group. Only the other day I debated with a remarkable New Age artist, a delightful character, and very well known locally. This packed the hall and provided an excellent opportunity for two very contrasting world-views to meet head on, with great grace and goodwill, but with considerable trenchancy. It was broadcast, all two and a half hours of it, the next night, and without doubt it stirred the interest of the city where it took place more than almost anything else we did all week.

If Christians often shy off debates, they are even more cautious about bars and pubs. Yet this is where so many normal citizens go for recreation without any thought of getting drunk. Should Christians not be among them? Conversations move very easily in such a setting: people are not wary and defensive, and it is not hard to move the discussion on to things that matter. Alternatively, by arrangement with the management, it is sometimes possible to bring in a singer who can communicate the gospel in folk music with occasional comments, and that tends to open things up for talking about Christ. If the local minister goes in, and becomes trusted, he will have endless pastoral opportunities opening up before him. On one occasion I sat myself down in a pub, was asked what my job was, and that developed into a marvellous conversation about Christ. Soon the whole bar was involved, either taking part in the discussion or watching. One man came to put his faith in Christ then and there, as he sat on a bar stool. I think of the sportsmen's club in Oxford, and of the many evenings I spent there with university athletes, speaking on some aspect of the Christian faith, and then repairing to the bar, where the whole conversation all round the room was about Christ, and where twice in succession somebody came to Christian commitment then and there in that bar. Sometimes some music, drama, or poetry helps. But bars can be places of great opportunity in the cause of the gospel, if we will have the courage and imagination to make use of them. You don't have to drink. You do have to be at ease – and then others will feel at ease with you.

Public lectures are another way of drawing a crowd to think about the claims of Christ. It helps if the lecturer is well known, if he is speaking on his subject, if the event is well advertised, and if Christians are primed to bring friends. It may be a Christian bishop or a Christian trade unionist, a Christian cabinet minister or a clean-up-TV activist. I have invited all four, and a good many more, to relate the Christian faith to some aspect of life in which they were expert. It has always drawn a crowd and proved a very valuable evangelistic or pre-evangelistic enterprise. I am sure a lot more could be done in that way.

Luncheons are very popular. Business people use them regularly in the course of their work, so for them it is a very natural form of meeting. A local church can host such luncheons for the leaders of management or labour in any local enterprise with which they have any links, or for the police or lawyers. It is simple enough for a few committed Christian lay people in business to get together across denominational boundaries and put on a monthly Christian Businessmen's Luncheon. I have known towns where this was so much the thing to belong to that there had to be a waiting list for people longing to join! If speakers are chosen with discretion, and the proceedings kept strictly within time, and if literature is made available, and the opportunity to talk things over is regularly offered, there can be a continual trickle of people coming to faith through such means. Recently in the USA I met a lady who had felt it right to start women's lunches across the country, and they are spreading like wildfire. But it does not even have to be an event. When you take a friend out to lunch, or entertain him or her in your home, it is an ideal opportunity to talk about Christ if the conversation moves that way. You can always stop if your friend does not want to pursue it. But all too often he will want to talk, and will be thankful that at last he has found someone willing to listen, and able to help him.

If lunches work well in the midst of a busy day, it stands to reason that dinner parties are even more fruitful, coming at the end of the day, when people are more relaxed. I have often found that professional people like to meet others in their own walk of life to hear a talk on the Christian faith: lawyers, doctors, and teachers especially come to mind, but I shall never forget a Town Hall reception full of builders who had come to hear Sir John Laing, the architect of the British motorway system, speaking simply and powerfully on building your life on the rock of Christ. Some years ago a dentist, a hotelier, a doctor and I planned a series of evenings during the course of a winter when we would welcome a hundred or so of our friends into a large private home for a dinner and then to listen to a Christian in some walk of life speak about how his faith interacted with his work. On another occasion my wife got called in to speak to a gathering of doctor's patients, young mothers who wanted to teach their children about God and prayer, but had no idea where to start. The evening gatherings begun there led several of them into Christian commitment. The point is clear. Evening events in private homes are very useful in evangelism today, just as they were in the first days of the church, when homes were all they had.

Music is such a powerful medium. There are all sorts of ways in which it can be deployed in the cause of the gospel. One way is to get a popular singer who writes his own songs, such as Glenn Allan Green in the USA, Garth Hewitt, Martyn Joseph or Cliff Richard in England, or Michael Hart in Canada, to come and sing and explain why he wrote the songs he did, and what is most important in life to him. People flock to carefully chosen events like these. They pay good money to come in, which looks after the finances of the enterprise and allows you to concentrate on making the most of the impact. Complimentary tickets need to be given to people who are thought to be not far from the Kingdom! If the artist has not himself got the gift of evangelism, an appropriate evangelist may be sought to draw things to a conclusion, though this is a particularly delicate task after such an evening, and if done badly it can easily backfire. If done well, it can be extremely productive. Carol singing is another very popular musical medium which many churches do not make enough of. Let it take place by candlelight. Let there be drama and dance as well as song. Let there be an address about the one who came at Christmas and still seeks access to the hearts of men. And it will remain as popular as ever: but it will be far more fruitful. The same applies to something like Haydn's *Creation* or Handel's *Messiah*, especially if sung by an all-Christian cast who really mean what they sing. The effect can be immense, and the drawing power is formidable. It is sometimes appropriate to weave a challenge into the ending of such an evening, especially if it is closely related to the Christian commitment of the composer. And with Handel that is not difficult.

Dancing is one of the most popular of all recreations. It can get out of hand: hence the common Christian distrust of dance. But it need not. And why, when people are rejoicing and celebrating together, should it be inappropriate for the world's greatest cause for joy and celebration to be mentioned? It takes a very charming and relaxed evangelist to draw people together in the middle of a dance and speak of the Lord of the Dance. But it can be done. It has been done. And it has led to firm conversions. I like it. It shows initiative and imagination, and they are often sorely lacking in evangelism.

If dancing is one of mankind's favourite recreations, sport is another. That area, too, needs to be permeated by the gospel. Top sportsmen are so wrapped up in their sport that they are very hard to reach except by those within it. In recent years this has been recognised on both sides of the Atlantic, as well as in Africa, and organisations like Christians in Sport and Athletes in Action have gone a long way towards spanning the yawning gap which normally exists between sports people and Christianity. In America now there are Christian 'chapters' in many of the top-line football, basketball and baseball clubs. At the international level, the Christians are getting together in the athletics, soccer, cricket, tennis and golf worlds, to name but five. Just before the 1980 Olympics, representatives from more than 120 nations met together in Seoul with the purpose of setting up sports ministries at school, club and national level throughout the world, and I believe that since then more than ninety nations have begun this type of outreach. It is something in which the local church can get fully involved. One of the early meetings of Christians in Sport for English professional soccer players took place in my Rectory, and Andrew Wingfield-Digby, its National Director, has kindly contributed Appendix G on how churches can get involved in this type of outreach if they feel called to it. Athletes and sports people are no more important in God's eyes than anybody else, but it is undeniable that they are high among the cult figures of modern society, and if Christian values and faith are represented widely in sport it is going to make a great difference to the views which the man in the street has about the faith.

Holidays are of great importance to us all, and yet we are sometimes at a loss to know what to do with them and whom to go with on holiday. This is where the parish holiday or youth camp comes into its own. There is a tremendous amount to be said for a parish organising its own holiday for all ages. This brings members of the congregation together in the most relaxed and natural of circumstances, and the fellowship of the church will benefit from it for a long time to come. But a holiday like that also gives every opportunity to invite people who are on the edge of the Christian community, or not part of it at all, to come and join in. It is a very attractive and effective way of making use of neutral ground.

These are only a few suggestions in an area which is limitless. We are called to use our imagination in the cause of Christ. One church I know did it by gaining possession of a shop in town, and making that a drop-in centre for coffee: it was thronged by youngsters. Further suggestions about a youth outreach are to be found in Appendix C. Another church had some gifted musicians and dramatists who found a regular welcome in the local schools, places that are so often devoid of any positive Christian teaching these days, but which often are not averse to a Christian message in a fresh medium. I think of another church that was always making new contacts for Christ through hiring a space in the local market and taking a barrow of Christian books down for sale there each Saturday. Others find that a simple creche and investigatory Bible study for hard-pressed mums (and exuberant toddlers) is not only a service to what can be a lonely sector of society: it is also a very natural way in for people who already have so much in common to find Christ as the one who binds all life together.

Perhaps the last word is this. We should cultivate godly opportunism. If we are people who are not dominated by church buildings and religious hours, but are free to talk about our Lord and seek to introduce others to him wherever we are, then the opportunities will come. Willingness is the key to usefulness. If we get into the habit of praying, 'Lord, use my life and lips as you want to today,' more often than not he will. And he may not wait until we are in the church on Sunday to provide the opportunity. For there are more ways than one to communicate the good news of Christ; and most of those ways occur on neutral ground.

FURTHER READING

Material on the Cursillo Movement, originally designed for Latin Christians, is now widely disseminated among the churches. A good centre to approach would be National Episcopal Cursillo, P. O. Box 213, Cedar Falls, Iowa, 50613, USA, who can provide you with the *Lay Talk Workbook* and the *Spiritual Advisor's Workbook*, along with descriptive material about the Movement.

For a preliminary investigation of some current Christian videos, Needoak Ltd, 61 High St, Alton, Hampshire, GU34 1 AF, England, has a lot on offer. The widely acclaimed *Person to Person* video on helping others to faith, along with much other material, can be had from P. O. Box 240, Swindon SN5 7HA, England.

On Praise Marches, their aim and conduct, see Graham Kendrick, *Make Way* (Marshalls). Kendrick is not only one of the most outstanding modern hymn-writers and musicians. He is one of the main architects of Praise Marches.

A selection of titles on imaginative aspects of renewal and outreach will be found on pp. 104–5 above.

The following books are a mine of information which will stimulate a wide variety of evangelistic approaches:

J. D. Douglas (ed.), *Let the Earth Hear His Voice* (World Wide Publications)

J. D. Douglas (ed.), *Proclaim Christ Until He Comes* (World Wide Publications)

J. D. Douglas (ed.), *The Work of an Evangelist* (World Wide Publications)

Glenn C. Smith (ed.), *Evangelising Adults* (Tyndale Press/Paulist Press)

Glenn C. Smith (ed.), *Evangelising Blacks* (Tyndale Press/Paulist Press)

Glenn C. Smith (ed.), *Evangelising Youth* (Tyndale Press/Paulist Press)

13
Missions

A church-based mission is what a lot of people think of when the subject of evangelism is raised: 'It is about time we had another mission in our parish.' They are not confident that it will do a lot of good, but it seems to be the thing to do if numbers are decreasing and if some new oxygen seems needed in the system. On the other hand, a number of churches have been burned off by missions, and are very doubtful indeed about allying themselves with a week or so of frenzied activity which can even be counter-productive to ongoing congregational life. So what part, if any, can we give to a mission in the life of a local church?

It may be apparent by now that I am using the word 'mission' ambiguously. It could refer to the church or team which is bringing the mission to some other place. It could equally apply to the receiving congregation. I would like to think that the two uses are not only compatible but complementary. It is when a church has been lit up by a mission which has taken place in its midst that it is best equipped to carry out a mission elsewhere. I think of an English village some years ago where a team which I was leading took a mission. It just so happened that the timing was right, in the providence of God, and the results were remarkable. The next thing we heard was that lay people began testifying in the ordinary services of the church to what God had done in their lives. And a little later we learned that their church was itself sending out teams with the good news into the surrounding countryside. Receivers become givers, in mission as in so much else.

TOWARDS A PHILOSOPHY OF 'MISSION'

First of all, what are we talking about? A mission is not an invasion from outer space by some supposed expert, but an overflow of Christian life, an extended attempt over a number of days, or even weeks, to make the Christian gospel the major issue in a given area. It is not propaganda, but celebration. It is not best conducted by one person, but by many. It could be based on one church, or on many churches working together. It need not take place only in the church building, but in all sorts of venues. It is not designed to fill pews but to open mouths and mobilise the people of God. It is not a duty but a joy. And therefore it will comprise central meetings and meetings in homes. It will get into the local schools and factories. It will reach business people and doctors, lawyers and teachers, young people and old, sports people and handicapped. It will make use of radio and TV if available, along with personal conversation, drama and dance. It is, ideally, the uninhibited and happy opening of flood gates by a church that is full of the Holy Spirit.

Missions like this have a real value. After all, God invented mission in its broadest sense, and this is one way in which the divine mission can be channelled. And, let us face it, in many places little evangelism happens, so it is no bad thing for a concentrated effort to call us back to what is part of the basic and continuing calling of the church. Such a mission draws the participants together in a fellowship that is rarely found outside shared evangelistic activity. It fosters love and interdependence among those who take part, be they the members of one local church or of the churches of a city. It brings people to faith. And it drives others out to enquire into whether or not there may be some truth in all this. It gives members of long standing an example of how to continue to share the good news with their friends and acquaintances. And it deepens their faith in the power of the gospel, and stimulates their courage to be bold in the cause of Christ.

Evangelism is best done by the local church. They know the people in the area and can build up relationships with them. Those relationships are ongoing, and should provide solid credibility for the message which the Christians want to share. Witness-bearing is God's call to all Christians: all are asked to manifest their faith in some way appropriate to them. And nobody should take that away from them, least of all the visitors who come to town for a mission.

Nevertheless, evangelism by a visiting team has a real value,

limited though it be. At its worst it can look like an air bombard-
ment, when wise people take cover and emerge after it is all over!
But at its best it can focus the attention of a church or a town on the
Christian gospel in a way that would not have been possible during
the normal run of events. I received a letter as I was writing this
chapter, telling me of the publicity for Billy Graham's June 1989
mission in London. My correspondent writes, 'The buzz in London
created by a very clever advertising campaign has been terrific:
there can be very few people who do not know what is going
on . . .'

Another advantage that can accrue, if the mission is trans-
denominational, is joint action among the churches. It is not that
previously they were apathetic to one another, or in competition;
but somehow they rarely did things together. However, when a
mission comes, it draws together the various groupings in a parish,
or the churches in a city. And out of joint mission comes deepened
fellowship. Several missions I have recently been engaged in have
left the churches in the city committed to ongoing partnership in
common enterprises.

Another advantage of a mission is that the incoming team can
often model a freshness, an imagination, a partnership and a
courage which rubs off on the town or parish where the mission
takes place. And finally, a mission can become a catalyst for
congregational participation and for heightened commitment to
every-member ministry in the future.

The alternatives to a mission

It is probably true to say that the main form of evangelism by which
it has been traditional in North America and on a smaller scale in
Britain to complement the work of local churches, has been the
'crusade', when a prominent speaker takes a church or an arena for
a number of nights and preaches the gospel in the context of music
and testimony. It is also probably true to say that these crusades are
likely to diminish in effectiveness. There is really only a tiny
handful of men in the world, of whom the most famous is Billy
Graham, who can pull in large crowds of non-Christians. For
others the attenders are for the most part Christians already –
which is not the aim! Many ordinary people are chary of these large
meetings. They do not have any relationship with the person who is
speaking. They suspect that it will be emotional. They fancy they

may well get urged to do something they do not want to do. They are simply not attracted by the thought of going to a large meeting where they will be talked at by one man without the right of reply, or even the chance to meet him.

If the large meeting or crusade is one type of evangelism, the other approach most commonly in use today is the precise opposite. It is low key, relational, relaxed. They call it 'friendship evangelism'. This is obviously a most important emphasis. But it easily degenerates into all friendship and no evangelism.

The advantages of a mission

In the light of these contrasting backgrounds, a mission has real merit, and the more so if it is conducted by a team, and not merely by an individual. For members of a team can manifest the reconciliation of which they speak. Their love can overflow and wing their words. And the variety of gifts on a team makes the impact far greater. Moreover, a team exhibits the 'body life' which it is part of the aim of the mission to promote.

If, then, the members of a mission team, perfectly ordinary Christians who love God and are prepared to make him known, give up, say, a week of their lives to go to a church or a city, a number of things tend to happen. It gets the church or churches loving, praying, and preparing opportunities into which this team can be poured. It liberates all sorts of unsuspected talents both in the home congregation and in the team. People come forward with amazing offers and suggestions at such a time as this. Moreover, most of the work is done by the home church people themselves. The mission is not done *for* them, but *with* them. They make the openings, and these will be dependent to a large extent on the relationships they have been cultivating over the previous months and years. When they have made the openings, members of the team get in there with them.

There are other significant advantages. A mission gives each congregation in a town, or each group within a local church, the freedom to build the programme its own way. The visitors do not come with a prepared package. They have a lot of ideas, and these are shared in depth with the organising committee. But the programme is made by the local Christians, using the visitors in the way that is most suitable in their situation. And every mission is different, very different, precisely for this reason.

Other advantages in a mission are not hard to perceive. It can, if properly promoted, capture the attention of a community. It facilitates fellowship both among the receiving churches and with the visiting team. It heightens faith and expectancy. It brings the lay people into their own. It does not depend on big names: it is a team event. And people latch on to the idea. It intrigues them that a large number of complete strangers should bother about them enough to come and give a week, free of charge, to talk with them about God!

A mission promotes imagination. People are stimulated to do some brainstorming about reaching their community for Christ. They are jolted into more radical thinking than they have done for a long time. They begin to think big, and bold. They learn to think in terms of a team, not an individual preacher (though one or two of those are an important part of the team). They wonder where they could find openings for the lay Christians on the team to gain a hearing. In a recent city-wide mission there were meetings for doctors and for doctor's wives, for hospital staff, for an MS support group, the mentally handicapped, cancer patients, youth, a fitness club, Rotary, dental workers, bankers, lawyers, the Chamber of Commerce, hunters, mountaineers, guides, beauty queens, and even *habitués* of the local hot tub! Shopping malls, foreign language classes, judo groups, bingo clubs are all fair game, and of course most of the meetings are in private homes among groups of friends who want to introduce to them a couple of members of the team for an evening's chat. And those who really have made good friendships in the locality are the ones who have wonderfully productive house meetings. The relationships are already in place; the trust is there. And the visitors simply act as a catalyst for profitable discussion.

A mission is costly. This must not be minimised when plans are being laid. Even if the team refuses any remuneration on principle, a mission will be costly in money, costly in commitment, costly in hospitality, in planning, in spiritual warfare, in boldness, in visiting and in follow-up. But the costliness of the enterprise is part of its power. So much of our Christianity in the West involves what Dietrich Bonhoeffer called cheap grace. It is the religious counterpart to the quest for happiness, ease and comfort which bedevils Europe and America. The sheer challenge of a mission is very bracing for a congregation, and draws forth unsuspected reserves of commitment, generosity and inventiveness.

A mission demands unity. That is both its glory and its cost.

Christ prayed for unity among his people. The early Christians went to great lengths to maintain it. They saw it as a gift from the Holy Spirit which they were not at liberty to break. But a very different attitude prevails today. Protestant Christianity has shattered to smithereens since the Reformation, though Roman Catholicism has done much better and has maintained the form of the church. Unity is the exception rather than the rule today, both within churches and among different churches. They pray for God to supply their need of ministers, money and buildings, and to bless their work. But why should he? There are plenty of ministers, money and buildings, if people will unite. And why should he bless disunity? It stands as the very antithesis of that reconciliation which Christ died to bring about. It is when churches and their ministers will get together in common work for the Kingdom that God may be expected to bless them. And he does. It is very good for a town to see that what unites Christians is so much greater than what divides them. That is why an *ecumenical* mission is so desirable whenever possible. And when churches unite round the unvarnished message of the New Testament, they are actually enabled to recapture much of the unity which denominational allegiances may have tended to erode.

A mission is pluriform and incarnational. It makes use of lots of approaches, and draws in lots of people. The ways into a community include drama, open-air work, debate, worship, preaching, lectures, discussions, dinners, youth gatherings, concerts and so on. The people involved incarnate the message. God seems to love and honour the incarnational method. After all, he so loved the world that he did not send a committee or a telecast: he sent his Son, and Jesus was the embodiment of his message. That is what happens, in a derived sense, when a mission team goes out. The members of the team *are* the gospel they proclaim. The only impression of the eternal gospel which many in the town will gain is the impression they personally make. And very ordinary people full of love and the Holy Spirit can carry a great deal of conviction.

Finally, evangelism, particularly in missions, is a partnership. It is a partnership between being, telling and doing. What we are counts most. By the end of a week or two, the sheer love and dedication of the team and the local Christians will have brought many cynics to their knees: it is not only in the ancient world that people marvelled and said, 'See how these Christians love one another.' But that being is accompanied by telling. The team members tell their story in home groups. They visit where they are asked to. They give testimony in the open air, the home, or even the factory. They preach in the churches. They challenge people in personal conversation. If the early Christians had laid all their emphasis on being rather than telling, they would not have got very far. But if their telling had not been backed up by their being, they would have got nowhere at all. Equally, theirs was not just pious talk, but caring action. They cared for the sick, the prisoners, the lonely, those in danger. And the same is required of Christians today. Christlike action needs to be part of the work of any mission: we must do the work of Christ and not just talk about it. That may include finding housing for the homeless, helping people off drugs, investing time and effort with the drunks. It is when the faith is seen to produce costly, unselfish action for others that people sit up and take notice.

But there is another sense in which evangelism in missions is a partnership. It is a partnership between intellect, heart and will. The intellectual understanding of an increasingly secular society needs to be redirected. The heart of an increasingly hedonistic society needs to be touched. And the wills of men and women, who for all their charm are rebels against their God, need to be challenged, so that they may turn 'from darkness to light and from the power of Satan to God' (Acts 26:18). Evangelism without any rigorous intellectual content, any personal warmth or any challenge to the will is sadly deficient.

At the most profound level of all there is another partnership at work. It is between the Holy Spirit and prayer. No human being can bring another to faith in Christ. It is supremely the work of the Holy Spirit himself. He is the evangelist. But it is in prayer that his power is released. The Western church is very slow to act on this truth, luminous though it is throughout the Bible. We rely on our wealth, our committees, our *savoir faire* to make things happen. Our church meetings are almost indistinguishable from secular meetings in the way they are conducted. And we wonder why we are so powerless! Growing Third World churches know full well that they do not have the power, the expertise, the financial resources to evangelise. So they choose the better part, to pray. And God honours it. People are added daily to the church.

Those are some of the requirements in a mission, and the benefits that spring from it. Of course, missions need careful preparation and follow-up, and we will consider these in the latter part of this chapter and in Appendices C–F. But one cannot simply mount a mission from cold. There are a good many intermediate steps between the place where many parish churches find themselves and the place where they can properly receive a mission, let alone take one elsewhere. To these we now turn.

TOWARDS THE POSSIBILITY OF A 'MISSION'

Many churches have found that the steps towards a full-blown mission follow some such pattern as this.

The dawning of vision

First comes the dawning of vision. We begin to ensure that our church's energies are directed into mission, not maintenance. Our eyes become opened to the fact that current church life is not proving very attractive to those who are not members. And that is often a painful realisation, because we all love patterns we have become accustomed to, and are reluctant to change.

There may well need to be changes of all kinds: in those who greet people coming in at the door, in the hospitality offered to newcomers, in the creation of a team to extend a welcome to visitors during the week following their first appearance. Change may well be called for in the type of service offered. The preaching may need to be radically changed in style and content, and perhaps illustrated with an overhead projector. The style of the music may need to change. A family service may need to be set up, or a new congregation started at another time of day. The dawning of vision may have all sorts of uncomfortable but profitable implications for the life of the local church. And this vision may be stimulated in a number of ways. If we have the humility, we may learn from adapting what other churches do when they grow. There may be one or more such growing churches in our neighbourhood, and if so then a lengthy lunch with the minister and one or two of the lay leaders could be very useful.

Alternatively, we could read about some examples of growing churches and learn from them. MARC Europe has done us a great service by putting out a whole series of books of this nature, such as *Ten Growing Churches, Ten Worshipping Churches, Ten Growing*

Soviet Churches, and so on. Many important principles can be gleaned and adapted from such books.

But perhaps the most helpful way of all to encourage the dawning of vision is to invite a team of people to come from a church you trust where renewal is already under way. I know from experience that a visit like that, if properly prepared for and if a large number of the receiving congregation turns out, can be a tremendous step forward. Careful liaison needs to take place beforehand. But an initial visit might usefully include the following elements.

A gifted teacher should be sought from the church to which you turn, along with one or more musicians, and possibly three or four people who are skilled in the Christian use of drama and dance. One or two others might be added to the team to meet your specific needs as a church, depending on what they are. The team would come for a weekend, arriving on the Friday afternoon and staying until late Sunday night or Monday morning. They would be accommodated in the homes of your congregation.

On the first night, the visiting team might be spread around, speaking at three or four evangelistic supper parties. Members of the congregation could invite a number of unchurched friends to come and have supper and meet a couple of the visitors who would be speaking on 'A faith for today', or some such subject. It is often wise to place the talk on such occasions between the first and second courses of the meal, which allows conversation to develop on the theme of the evening. The probable results will be that a few people actually come to the point of commitment, while others are fascinated and determine to come to hear more from these people on Sunday.

While all this is going on, the leader of the team and, if he is a clergyman, one of his lay leaders, spends the evening with the decision-making body of your church, opening their eyes to shared ministry, body life, the growth of love in a church, the need for and possibilities of training, pastoral care, and ways of reaching out into the community in obedience to Christ's commission. It is important that a 'three line whip' be issued to all members of the leadership, because until their eyes are opened and their hearts warmed to the possibilities of constructive change in the life of the church, they will oppose it, and instead of unity there will be disarray in the parish.

The next day, Saturday, could well be used as follows. It will consist of a parish conference, say from 9.00 a.m. to 4.00 p.m. It will begin with a plenary meeting for worship which is fresh, open and warm. This will be led by the visitors, and will include encouraging teaching on the need for all Christians to be involved in the life and ministry of the church, illustrated by recounting how this has come about (along with all the accompanying failures and hurts) in the church from which the visitors come.

The conference will then break up into a number of workshops for which people have signed up beforehand. The local minister will have planned these with the visitors well in advance, according to the perceived needs of the church. A workshop on prayer is fundamental; others might well be offered on lay witness, on leadership, on preaching and speaking, on drama, on youth work, on home fellowship groups, and on adult training in the church. One of the visiting team will be allocated to each of these groups and will lead it appropriately, paying much attention to where the members of the congregation are coming from, and to their hopes, fears and doubts. There will be the chance for a good time of prayer together. After lunch, either the seminars can continue with a further session, or people can join a second seminar, and so make the contribution of the visiting team broader in its impact.

The afternoon could fittingly end with an informal eucharist where personal ministry is offered to those who so desire, and opportunity given for members to bear testimony to what they have learned from the day. All this will have greatly kindled anticipation for the following day. The visiting team can have the evening off or, better, run something special for the youth of the neighbourhood at a barbecue or concert.

Sunday is an opportunity for the visitors to lead much of the services, both morning and evening. This gives a wonderful opportunity to experiment and show new things to the congregation, without their feeling that any innovations are set in concrete. But very simple things like extempore prayers by two or three of the team, a solo or duet sung to guitar and piano accompaniment, an address which includes short contributions from one or two others in the team, have a great impact and point the way to what could happen in the local congregation from time to time.

It may be appropriate to make that Sunday morning service a 'Guest Service' where members of the congregation really seek to draw their friends to church with them for the special occasion of the visiting team. If so, an evangelistic address could well be given, and this would perhaps draw to Christ some who had already been attracted through the Friday supper parties, as well as others who may have been in church frequently (or rarely) without having made any personal commitment to Christ. If this approach is taken, it would, of course, require the prior preparation of one or two tried leaders within the congregation who could run a Discovery Group for those who come to faith through the sermon (see chapter 11 above). The weekend comes to a fitting close with an evening service of high celebration and praise, led by the visiting team. It needs to give scope for testimony from those who have been blessed through the visit, and personal ministry should be available at the end of the service.

The way ahead

In the wake of such a visit, all sorts of possibilities open up. People will surface who have been thrilled by the weekend. If there is not already a prayer meeting in your church, one will be likely to emerge, and it is something to foster with great care. It is the place where you can gather the keenest members of the congregation, while being sure to announce it at each service so that nobody can accuse it of being a clique. People may now be open to the singing of some modern worship music alongside the traditional music in church. The people who have come to faith during that weekend will add new imagination and vitality to the church as they settle in. Occasionally it may well be possible to allow for testimonies from members of the congregation. Someone may have experienced a healing or want to share some verses of Scripture or some picture which they feel God has given them, for the benefit of the congregation. New ministries may spring up. Somebody may come and offer to start a youth group, or a mothers' and toddlers' club.

Be sensitive to what God is doing in your midst. Be much in prayer to see what his developing vision for the church may be. It could be useful, after a few months, to have a day of prayer and discussion about the life of the congregation. You could plan another evangelistic occasion and this time mount it from the local resources. And the planning of invitations, the subject-matter, the advertising, the music, the shape of the service, and above all the prayer, would do much to nourish the new life within the congregation and heighten the expectancy of faith. That is a crucial thing. God delights to answer the trusting dependence of his people. And we are not very good at trusting God. We are inclined to trust almost anything else: the service, the music, the minister, and so on. It is when the congregation gets to the point of expecting that God will do something through them and their worship that his hands seem to be freed to act and to draw people to himself.

The training of leaders

By now the vitality in the congregation should be on the increase. People will be wanting to serve the Lord, without knowing quite how. They will sense that every Christian has a ministry, but will not know how to exercise it, nor even, in most cases, what it is. Some general principles may well be learned through the weekly prayer meeting, where you will be taking the core of the congregation deeper by your teaching. But the time will come when the pastor will want to provide some specific training of lay members of the congregation for the various areas of leadership into which God is leading them. He will want to put on a training course.

It is probably wise to set your sights high and send personal invitations to the key people in the church, including the office bearers. Go for a whole evening each week, perhaps with dinner provided in the middle to break it up and to provide the opportunity for fellowship to grow. You could make it a three-month course, with twelve evenings, each divided into three parts.

The first part of the evening would be a time of informal worship, planned and led by three or four different people from the course each week. There should be time for vocal prayer, and a deep sense of worship in the singing and waiting on God. The second part of the evening should be a well-prepared address; for this, duplicated notes should be provided, or the main points written up on the overhead projector. Since such a course must inevitably be somewhat general, space needs to be found within it to service the head, the heart, the knees and the feet of the participants. The head needs to be taught; the heart needs to be warmed; the knees need to bend in prayer and worship; and the feet need to be equipped to step out.

Accordingly, subjects such as these might usefully be included. Every-member ministry; reasons for Christian belief; how to meet common objections to the faith; how to lead a home Bible study; how to help someone to Christ; how to prepare and give a talk; how to learn the art of listening; how to visit and help the bereaved, the abused and the depressed; how to lead an outreach meeting in the home; and one or two evenings on the body of Christ, first looking at the role of the family, the singles and the extended family, and then looking at how to enable a group to function well.

There are other subjects that need to be covered. It may be good to handle these after the meal and for this third part of the evening to split the course members up into small 'tutor groups' (i.e. about six members round a leader), in which they stay for the whole of the three months. These groups will tease out the practical implications of some of the talks. For instance, the group members will all have their own problems to air on reasons for belief, and common objections that they meet with. The devotional life of members will need strengthening, and so one or more evenings in the tutor group could be devoted to a communal time of Bible reading, prayer and sharing. On another night the group could do a role-play on faith-sharing with an interested enquirer. The care of the new believer would occupy another evening; a listening exercise another night, and so forth. One night would look at the practical outworking of every-member ministry; another might help each member to discover their own gifts through the perception of others in the group who have come to know and value them. And the course might end with a Communion service and a commissioning.

Two other features in such a course have proved valuable. First, you could build in a full day-conference on one Saturday during the course, when you can tackle, at a practical level, some of the major doctrines they need to know: the nature of man; the reason for the cross; the fact and implications of the resurrection; and the person, gifts and graces of the Holy Spirit.

Second, let each tutor plan a weekend away in another church where he can take his small team and minister in the way that seems appropriate. They could at least join in leading the Sunday services and Sunday schools. That sort of thing takes a fair amount of planning, but it is eminently worth the trouble. It takes the whole thing out of the realm of theory into the realm of practice. It scares the team members and teaches them to pray with passion and to trust God. It binds them close to each other. They give a real boost to the receiving church, and they return thrilled with what they have seen God do through themselves, when they scarcely imagined such a thing remotely possible.

A course like that will have immense repercussions among the congregation, and will certainly throw up leaders you had never anticipated, and gifts and ministries which had not crossed anyone's mind. It will all help in preparing the congregation for the next stage in what God plans to do with it.

Faith-sharing teams

The next step may be to gather some of those who have been through your training course, and have them as a pool from which you can draw colleagues when you are invited to speak elsewhere. This can, of course, be done without the backing of the minister at all, and in various parts of the world there are acknowledged teams of lay people who go to parishes on request to share what their faith means to them. But it is better if it is done with the full support and active encouragement of the minister, because then it can be co-ordinated into the ongoing and developing life of the church, and not be seen as simply a piece of private enterprise.

It is very simple to arrange. Suppose the minister is asked to speak at Thanksgiving, or at a Harvest Festival in a neighbouring town. He could well reply by agreeing, provided he is allowed to take a team with him. The other church may be puzzled, but is unlikely to refuse. So a group of you get together, and plan and pray how best you may be used on that visit. Try to maximise it. Ask if you can have someone sing, or lead prayers in the service, or maybe speak at a meeting of the young people. Will they allow participation in the Harvest Supper the night before? Offer, perhaps, to produce a dramatic sketch in the course of the service, or to have an after-church meeting at which some of your team could speak about the growing vitality that has been taking place in their own congregation.

In a word, you make what was a solo event into a team event. And everyone is delighted. The receiving congregation is pleased and surprised to see lay people like themselves coming to share in taking a service. They see a team in action. They notice the power of even halting lay testimony to Jesus. They are really helped if the team do well. If not, they may well be stimulated to react by saying, 'I think we could do as well as that.' Either way, your object has been achieved! And your team will return thrilled to their home church, and should be given a brief opportunity next Sunday to stand up and bear testimony to what God had done through them. The minister will then find that people besiege him, asking to be invited on the next team of this kind.

I can think of one dear doctor friend who was a very loosely attached church member when I first knew him. Gradually over the years, through increasing commitment, lay training courses, and going away on teams like this, he has not only become confident in evangelism but now leads such teams himself with a quiet poise and assurance. Multiply growth like that throughout a congregation, and the results are very significant. That church will be ready to go further with missions.

TOWARDS THE IMPLEMENTING OF A 'MISSION'

What I want to do now is to sketch possible ways of running a mission. The principles seem to me to hold good whether it is a mission to a university, a parish or a city. I hope that what follows will be of help both to organisations and churches which are looking for missions, and also to those who are being called to lead them.

During the past few years I have had the joy of taking part in nearly twenty such missions, and in most of them a good deal of the training, organisation and preparation has fallen on the able shoulders of my colleagues, the Rev. Bruce Gillingham, now Birmingham Diocesan Missioner, and Miss Jane Holloway, now Outreach Coordinator at Regent College, Vancouver. Jane has prepared some detailed Appendices on the subject, at the back of this book, which will repay careful study. My approach here will be more impressionistic.

A church-based mission

It is impossible to define how a mission in a single local church takes place, because all churches are different. The basic rule is that it should be in a manner that is appropriate for the church in question.

The Anglican Church's Board for Mission and Unity produced in 1987 a useful document, *The Measure of Mission*, with ten specific examples of how a mission might be carried out in different parts of the country and sectors of the community. And the Archbishop's Commission on Evangelism produced a classic on the subject as long ago as 1945, entitled *Towards the Conversion of*

England. It has never been seriously implemented, unfortunately, but it is full of wisdom. So are the writings of Roland Allen, that great missionary strategist who lived before his time, and whose books such as *Missionary Methods – St Paul's or Ours?*, have a lasting value in making plain the often uncomfortable principles of mission as found in the New Testament. The School of Church Growth at Fuller Seminary, California, has put us all in its debt through the writings of Drs McGavran, Arn, Gibbs and Wagner on the subject of how churches grow. Their experience world-wide is encyclopaedic. In England, Dr Roy Pointer has done sterling work in this area from his post in the Bible Society, and his book *How Do Churches Grow?* is particularly useful. In comparison with these men, the suggestions which follow will be amateur. All that can be said for them is that they come from a modicum of experience.

Initial preparations
There is basically little difference between a mission based on a single church, to which we shall now turn our attention, and one based on a town, which we will look at a little later. Both depend on the church members praying, and inviting friends to events. But the mission to a single denominational church does not have the same wide impact in the community as a venture embracing virtually all the churches. It still looks too much like a particular church searching for new recruits. It has a real value, but a limited one. That is why I have come to prefer a town mission, with all the churches involved. In this way every section of the community can be reached, every house visited, and people begin to sit up and take notice of what the churches, together, are mounting in their town.

Here, however, we are looking at the mission based on a single church. The first thing I do, when asked to lead such a mission, is to pray about it and then meet the leadership. I want to know if there is a steady trickle (however small) of people coming to faith within that congregation: you cannot mount a mission effectively if nothing much is happening in the church by the way of outreach already. Intermediate steps, such as I have outlined above, need to be taken first.

The same holds good with university missions. I recall being asked to take a university mission some years ago. When I went to talk it over with the people in charge, it became apparent that they had neither seen anyone come to faith in the past year, nor were they really expecting anyone to! So I said that I would not lead a mission, but that I would come and give some talks on helping others to faith. This took place, and within a few weeks they had three new believers, much to their joy. Imagine what this did to their faith and expectancy. They did have the mission a year or so later, though, because of other commitments, I did not take part in it. It was very fruitful. But they would not have been able to mount it were it not for that intermediate step.

If there are some signs of outreach from the church I would next want to know why they thought a mission was appropriate at that time. A mission will only have real value to a congregation which is already on the move and wanting to progress. The measure of that desire is not the enthusiasm of the minister, but the solid backing that he has in the first instance from his decision-making body, and then from the church at large. Visitors cannot effectively do a mission for a local church. They can only help the local Christians with their own evangelistic responsibility to their neighbourhood, and if the church is not ready and willing to undertake that, then a mission is sheer folly. I am unwilling to engage in such a mission unless the decision-making body of the church is virtually unanimous in requesting it.

Next, you must determine what time of year is possible and appropriate for the mission, and how long it should last. At least nine months need to be set aside for the preparation of such an event, and church activities need to be geared towards it with increasing publicity and intensity as time approaches.

The receiving church needs to have a number of points made abundantly plain to it early on in the negotiations.

First, that this is a labour of love, and that no monetary reward will be received by the visitors. They will give their time and effort free. But the receiving church will need to provide hospitality, and to finance the whole venture. This financing should be done by church budgeting, special offerings and personal gifts, and should be complete before the mission begins. It is most undesirable to hold collections at events where one is stressing the grace of God and his free offer of Christ! A mission will cost a good deal of money. The team will need to be put up in the homes of the congregation, and whereas that may well be at no charge to the church, their feeding will cost something, as will their travel costs, the necessary publicity and perhaps the hiring of premises or p.a. equipment. But in financial terms a parish mission is not an expensive thing if it is run along these lines. At least, not in terms of money. It will, however, be costly in other ways.

Second, they need to start praying regularly for the mission. And

I do not mean saying prayers in church on Sunday. I mean having special gatherings to pray for it. I mean having prayer breakfasts or a concert of prayer (music, singing, prayer, silence, on a variety of topics concerned with the mission). Prayer triplets have been found to be particularly valuable. This is a simple expedient whereby three Christian friends get together to pray for three friends each as the mission approaches. This targeting of those where there are already bonds of affection and friendship is very effective. It generally leads to the conversion of some of them before the mission even starts.

Third, a great deal of practical preparation is needed for an event of this sort. Appendix C shows how it can be approached, and in what order. But let there be no doubt about this: it means lots of work for everyone. For, contrary to many people's expectations, the job will not be done in the main by the visiting team. It will be done by members of the local church. It is they who should plan the programme, in consultation with the visitors. Naturally, for it is their locality, and the mission needs to build on their gifts, their friendships, their openings into the community. And the better and more thoroughly that work is done, the more fruitful the mission will be. For a missioner to take a house meeting where there is a real bond of friendship and carefully cultivated relationships between those present is sheer joy. It is easy to speak of spiritual things, because people like and trust one another. Indeed, the host himself may have such an ease of manner with his friends that he or she is able to get them to talk about their own religious situation in the most natural manner. In a recent mission one of us was in just such a home meeting, and for the first hour and more the visitors did not need to say anything! It all flowed from the leadership of the host and the ready participation of those present. Contrast that with the nervous and duty-ridden host or hostess who feels obliged to invite some neighbours in at the last moment so as to have a house meeting to notch up! A high proportion of them will not actually come, and those who do will be reluctant and nervous. That house meeting is unlikely to go well. The difference lies in the effort made to forge relationships during the previous months and even years. You reap what you sow. And if you are not prepared to work at it, then there is unlikely to be much of a harvest.

Fourth, a small committee needs to be set up to oversee all the preparation. Lay membership is generally more effective. But the pastor's backing and active promotion of the mission are very important indeed. The chairman has a key job. It is crucial to have someone who is deeply spiritual, who is widely respected, and who can work with the pastor. He would also be the major means of liaising with the visiting team.

Each member of the committee should have a particular responsibility: prayer, finance, publicity, training, youth work, accommodation, programme co-ordination and follow-up. It would be good to have a secretary who can really give himself or herself to detailed work. Early on in the proceedings this committee needs to produce a detailed profile of the church, so that the visiting team can have as accurate a picture as possible of the needs to be addressed.

Further preparations
It always takes the receiving parish some time to understand that this is not a one-man band by a famous preacher who will do it all in church services each evening. That old-fashioned way of conducting a mission still has value, especially in some places, but it is on the way out. People simply will not come to be harangued in church these days. But they will come to a home, a dinner, a sports club or their normal meeting ground, and will probably not object to meeting one of the visiting team and discussing Christian things in such a setting. The key to effective work in missions is diversification of the team. In so far as you penetrate different aspects of the life of the church and its surrounding area, you will have effective impact. And it needs to be done on the community's turf, not the church's.

There are some very specific preparations that need to take place at both ends as the mission draws closer. In the receiving parish there needs to be a growing commitment to prayer, increasingly specific publicity, the careful selection of accommodation for team members, and the planning of any main meetings and their titles. Members of the congregation need to offer to arrange a meeting with a few of their friends in a pub, a home, a club, perhaps over lunch or dinner. Training will need to be offered in how to help a friend to faith, and how to tell their personal 'faith story' appropriately. So much will depend on what follows the mission week, and therefore it is important to train two lots of the most sensitive and instructed Christians available. One group needs to be able to run Discovery Groups for new believers after the mission. A second group needs to know how to lead a group for enquirers (see chapter 11 above). A possible course for enquirers is included in Appendix A.

Equally, there needs to be a lot of preparation among the visitors. The missioner will need to surround himself with a team, probably drawn to a large extent from his own congregation. He will need to weld them into a loving, interdependent group. They do not all need to be very experienced or knowledgeable. They *do* need to have a personal faith in Christ, a willingness to make him known, and a commitment to give that week wholeheartedly to the mission.

The team will have regular sessions for training. Each session will aim to bind them together in worship, to give them a deep confidence in the Lord and trust in one another, to explore one another's gifts, and to get practical training for things that will be required of them in the mission. They will all need at some time or other to tell their spiritual story: so they need help in knowing how to present it. They will all give a talk: but they may not know how, until they have had both instruction and some opportunity to practice. They may all be called upon to help someone who wants to know the way to faith: so they must learn that way with simplicity and confidence. They will all have to contend for the faith among people who do not believe a word of it: so some exposure to basic Christian apologetics is required. They will all be thrown in at the deep end, far beyond their capabilities and experience: so they need to be made aware of the power and the gifts of the Holy Spirit. They will need to know about first steps in nurture: so they must be clear about the arrangements that have been made for local Discovery Groups after the mission.

In addition, there are all sorts of other practical things they need to know. How, for example, should they try to bring a meeting to a conclusion? What books will they find useful? I find it a real help on a mission to have everywhere available a small comment card (and I have given a suggested format in Appendix B). It is then easy to say something like this at the end of a meeting: 'You received when you came in (or 'You will now be handed by one of my colleagues') a simple card. We should very much like you to fill that in with your name, address and phone number, and tell us frankly what you made of this evening. How could we improve it? Where did we go wrong? In particular, if you are seriously considering Christian discipleship and will commit yourself to an eight-week course on getting started as a Christian, tick the box that says,

"Count me in". If you feel you are not there yet, but would like the chance to talk matters over with someone, then tick the little box that says "Tell me more", and we will contact you in the next couple of days.' That can all be done without the least embarrassment. Amazingly, people respond!

Some time before the mission, it is advisable for the missioner and a few of his team to come and lead a day-conference for the parish. There will be things that need talking over, and he, himself, needs to give some training to the key members of the host congregation, set minds at rest over problems, and motivate those who are not sure about the whole project. Time spent in the building of relationships and confidence in this way is not wasted. People in the congregation will be much more likely to risk inviting their friends to hear a visiting missioner if they have already gained some confidence in him.

I have not yet mentioned another vital part of the preparations of the visitors. They need to develop, if at all possible, the use of the arts in evangelism, in particular the three main areas of music, drama and dance.

Music is a very powerful agency, and a judicious use of instruments and songs and modes of music is required, a good deal of it 'up-beat' for a mission. It should embrace the best of traditional and modern material.

The use of drama in the presentation of the gospel is very old: witness the mystery plays in the middle ages. It is reviving strongly these days, and those who want to begin to get a drama group together for use in church and in the open air would be wise to avail themselves of the books of Paul Burbridge and Murray Watts, *Time to Act, Lightning Sketches* and *Red Letter Days*, or *Scene One* by Ashley Martin, Andy Kelso and others, together with *Using the Bible in Drama* by Steve and Jane Stickley and Jim Belben. As the group develops it will probably want to write its own material, but to begin with you could not do better than to get a performing licence for these brilliant short sketches which go to the heart of the matter amusingly and powerfully. They are a marvellous adjunct to preaching. I often use two such carefully selected sketches in the course of an evangelistic address.

Dance is a sensitive medium. It is a powerful communicator of feeling, and can be a great help in directing the hearts and emotions of the congregation towards God. There are occasions in a mission where its use can be breathtaking. A valuable book on this subject is *Know How to Use Dance in Worship*, by M. Berry. Many congregations are entirely unprepared for this medium, so if it is used it will need careful explanation beforehand.

But preparations in these three areas all take a lot of time, a lot of co-ordination, and close working with the main speaker. There is much to prepare at both ends before a mission takes place.

The mission itself

But what about when the mission comes? The week will have been carefully planned by the local committee, who will have agreed all the main matters with the visiting team. There is a lot to be said for having a central meeting on the first night, so as to motivate the church people afresh for their full involvement in the week. Experience tends to show that it is not best to have central meetings every night. They tend only to attract church members and a small 'fringe'. It is much more effective to go for small meetings, hosted by members of the church in their homes, workplace, clubs, and so forth. And the evangelists are the team! They go in pairs (if possible) to these events. They liaise carefully beforehand with the host, and learn as much as possible about who will be there. They arrive in good time, armed with appropriate literature for sale or giving away.

If the meeting is in a home, then after the refreshments one of the team will speak for a few minutes, while the other may well say a few personal words about the difference he or she has found Christ to be in daily life. The meeting could then be thrown open to questions, and usually it is hard to stop it at the predetermined time! All manner of objections and red herrings come up, and it is part of the skill of the team members to handle them as best they can. One of them should end with a brief summary of the evening, and a warm, natural explanation of the way to faith in Christ.

Comment cards could then be used, if appropriate. And it often is appropriate. I have become convinced of the value of them, although I used to be very wary. If introduced in a relaxed way, and if all are invited to fill them in, there is no embarrassment, and those who have been touched by the talk and want to take it further can tick their box 'Count me in' and thereby join up for a Discovery Group without attracting unwelcome attention. These cards become very valuable. They are the only tangible way of assessing response, and team members need to gather them up and hand them in daily at their team meeting.

Preferably, this daily meeting for the whole team takes place in the morning. If the team are going to be any use during the rest of the day in giving out to others, they need to be nourished by God and encouraged by each other earlier in the day. A good plan might be for the mission team leaders to meet with their host minister and his close colleagues each morning at 8.00 a.m. for news, a review of the way the mission is going, and to go over the plans for the day. This would be followed by a meeting of the whole team for worship, prayer, teaching, news, encouragement and forward planning. All administrative details can be handled then, before the team disperses to lunch meetings, afternoon visiting and so forth.

Other team members will be involved in the youth events that have been planned. I shall have more to say about that below, but it is crucial to remember the importance of young people. Statistics show that by far the highest proportion of conversions take place before the age of twenty-five. Evangelism that does not major on young people is courting failure in the long run.

The visiting missioner is likely to be the main speaker at the central meetings, assisted by the musicians and dramatists. The programme should be varied, and notably different from a normal church service. Use should be made of testimony, and it is often helpful if someone answers one of the common objections against Christianity. There should be a great time of celebration on the last night, which invariably draws a large crowd. In between the first and last night's central meetings, it may be sensible to include one other. But it may not. The missioner may be better employed in smaller, sectional gatherings which meet on neutral ground, like a restaurant or club. These could include business colleagues and friends of, say, a businessman or lawyer in the congregation. These people would be most unlikely ever to come to a central rally.

Maximum use needs to be made of the Sunday services. In a parish mission there is a lot to be said for a major evangelistic challenge on a Sunday morning, when many visitors can be expected, arising from the impact of the past few days. A challenge to commitment, followed up by an invitation to join Discovery Groups, is frequently very fruitful at such a juncture. On the last evening a Communion service may be appropriate, but one which includes unusual elements such as testimony, exultant praise, the opportunity for people to say what the week has meant to them, and prayer in small groups throughout the church rather than being led from the front, followed by personal ministry for those who so desire. The theme ought to be forward-looking, concentrating on going on with Christ, and reiterating the challenge to join Discovery Groups. If comment cards are plentifully scattered throughout the seats of the church, large numbers of them are likely to be filled in, and the church is going to be left with a major job in nurturing the new believers, and continuing, perhaps through Enquirers' Groups, the ministry to those who are 'almost persuaded'.

A mission such as this will do a great deal to stimulate the Christians. It will breathe fresh life into the structures of the parish. It will show what a team can do, as the body of Christ, as against one talented individual. It will draw many people to Christ. It will make a lot of others think. And it will heighten expectancy in the congregation that the God who acted so powerfully in the mission can be counted on to continue with them in the future under circumstances of less frenetic activity.

The next stage

After a parish mission, what next? Well, a parish mission involves only one church, representing only one denomination. It would obviously be ideal if the whole town or city could be reached with the gospel, instead of just one church. Is that feasible?

Yes it is. But not without much loving preparation. Most of the churches will belong to the local council of churches, and their ministers to a minister's fraternal or similar gathering of clergy, who congregate once a month to discuss matters of common interest. Sometimes there is a real depth of fellowship in these fraternals. Often there is not. Sometimes there is a real pulling together among most of the church in town. Often there is not. They do not know who each other's members are: so there could well be a considerable number of Christians who live in the same apartment block, or in the same street, without any of them being aware of it. Churches tend to mind their own business. The amount of ecumenical worship and ministry is usually small, and is generally confined to some moral welfare projects and the occasional shared service (which many members of the constituent churches do not attend if it does not happen to be in their own building). You cannot mount an effective town-wide mission on that basis.

If, then, anything really corporate is to be done in a town, there are several steps that should be taken. The first is to sense if there is any genuine longing in town for a joint presentation of New Testament Christianity free from denominational slant. Such a thing may be dearer to the hearts of the people than of the ministers. But unless that longing is there, a mission is not going to be effective.

Even if the longing is there, the churches are frequently too separate to trust one another and work together. So a good next move is to offer the same sort of leadership training course outlined above, not this time to a particular parish, but widely across the city, using as tutors leaders, ordained and lay, from different churches. This has a great bonding effect, in addition to its educational value. I know a church which began by running its own leadership training course, but before long was sharing in the promotion of such a course for churches right across the city and beyond.

In addition to the joint training courses, the next stepping-stone towards a town-wide mission is often a series of joint celebrations. A parade on Good Friday, with a combined procession through the town, is one possibility. Another is a joint open-air celebration at Pentecost, followed by a transdenominational service with an inspirational speaker in the largest church in town. The sheer planning of such a service, and the equipping of people to counsel those who come for prayer afterwards, is a marvellously unitive act. So is the growing fellowship among the fraternal, as together the clergy and ministers plan and pray for these joint ventures. Advent is another good time to have a joint celebration. It is, after all, the beginning of the church's year, and yet not a major festival in most denominations. To take the local cathedral or large cinema for an evening of 'Advent Praise' would be a concrete move towards a city-wide mission.

And such a mission is invaluable. It transcends sectional interests. It gets the Christians of different denominations to know and trust one another, and to work together. It shows the un-believers that the things which divide Christians are comparatively trivial compared with those that unite. It gives a far stronger handle for approaching the city authorities. It carries a lot more weight than any one church could muster. And by now such a project has become feasible, whereas before such joint action was undertaken it would not have got off the ground.

The town-wide mission

Importance
As I write, I look back on two town-wide missions conducted in the

past six months, and I thank God for them. We had a team of over a hundred in one, and fifty in the other smaller location. You should have seen the joy on their faces as they came back after these missions! They had seen God at work. You should have seen, too, the tears of local Christians as they bade us goodbye. After only a week we had become fast friends, with that depth of relationship that you find most profoundly among Christians engaged on their Master's business. These were most challenging and exciting times as we worked with churches right across the denominational spectrum, from Roman Catholic to Pentecostal. Ecumenism had come alive through mission.

As I write today, the *Update* of Africa Enterprise has come on to my desk. Africa Enterprise is a remarkable evangelistic organisation combining blacks and whites in South and East Africa, under the twin leadership of Bishop Chitemo of Tanzania and Michael Cassidy of South Africa. They are jointly leading a mission to the capital city of Zambia, under the title 'Lusaka Back to God'. There has been the most careful preparation for this venture. The first week concentrates on the leadership circles of the capital city, the second on all other sectors of the city. The President of Zambia, Dr Kenneth Kaunda, is behind the venture, and himself undertook to host a presidential prayer breakfast for the leaders of the city. The mission team itself comes from East Africa under a black bishop, and from South Africa under a white layman. What an embodiment of the gospel of Christ! What a living witness to his power to save and to unite!

Missions like that are taking place all over the world. I think of a Tanzanian bishop who spends his time training teams to go into the villages with the good news of Christ, and then visits those villages to encourage, lead and nurture those who come to faith. It is only in our own cynical, *déjà-vu* Western world that such missions are regarded with a jaundiced eye. But when they comprise virtually all the churches, and are town-wide, then they make a very considerable impact. The publicity makes an impact. The open-air witness makes an impact. The lay invitations to endless home and professional meetings make an impact. A march through the streets by Christians of all denominations, praising God with music and banners, astounds people who associate Christians with gloomy buildings, and have never seen them erupt with joy on to the streets. The use of local radio and TV stations ensures that everyone knows what is going on. They may like to come to a big debate, a large public rally, a concert, or a meeting in the home of a friend. There is plenty of variety. And there is all the authenticity of a united campaign, mounted jointly by all the churches.

Planning and preparation
The planning and preparation of such a mission is basically similar to that required for a parish mission. But it is more demanding. It requires much more time (at least eighteen months) to organise the detailed support from each participating church. Much persuasion is needed to get churches as different as, say, the Baptists and the Roman Catholics to work together. Moreover, Catholics and Anglicans are unlikely to give widespread backing unless their hierarchy supports it. So that needs to be worked on. Mutual tensions among the ministers need to be resolved. The whole habit of thinking town-wide and corporately instead of for one's own individual church needs to be developed, and it is a difficult lesson. Planning is that much harder when you are working with a whole variety of leadership styles and decision-making bodies. But it is worth all the hassle!

This is not the place to go into detail about the preparation of a town-wide mission: it is addressed in Appendix C. The principles are much the same as we have already seen. The first requirement is unity, trust and commitment among the participating churches. So the missioner is going to need to spend time with them and win their confidence. He is going to need to persuade them of the value of a team. And he will, if he is wise, not agree to come unless he has an almost total support from the churches of the town. Of course, that support will vary in enthusiasm, but unless something like a unanimous invitation is issued, the impact of a united approach for Christ to the town will be eroded. All of this will take time, love and prayer. It will also require, fairly early on, a definite commitment from the participating churches to join in the mission. The mission team needs to know whom they are dealing with. And, as in the case of parish missions, it is vital not to rely on the supportive voices of the ministers alone. They must be required to go back to their decision-making bodies and get substantial backing for the mission. Unless people and pastor are together in this it will not work. Conversely, however, those parishes that do put a lot into such a venture inevitably get a lot out of it. Those who invest little, gain little.

Each participating church not only needs to undertake to be part of the mission: they also all need to be ready to share in raising the requisite finance. This is needed for exactly the same things as in the parish mission: nothing for the team, but money is needed for travel, food, publicity, hire of halls and a good deal of incidental expense, such as substantial phone bills. The town churches must agree to raise this: it is, after all, their mission, with which the visitors help. And when they put money into it, they are more likely to own it.

Once the die is cast, a committee needs to be set up immediately, under a good chairman. People should be chosen to serve on it not because of their denomination, but because of their gifts for the task in hand. Each area of responsibility is headed up by one person on the committee, who co-opts others talented in that area. In this way the work can be parcelled out without anyone getting overloaded. The portfolio holder knows what is happening in his department and can represent it at committee meetings. More details on how to set up a town-wide mission of this sort are to be found in the Appendices, along with an outline of the sequence of events in planning. Training is essential, for visitors and hosts alike. It helps to have one day, six months before the mission, when the missioner comes to meet all the clergy of the supporting churches. That is followed by a training weekend for lay people from the supporting churches on the Friday evening and Saturday, culminating in a public rally on the Saturday night. This gives them a taste of what to expect when the mission comes.

As with the parish mission, the programme is a mixture of a few central rallies and a multitude of meetings in homes and hospitals, offices and sports clubs. But because each of the participating churches devises its own programme, and decides where the team members can best be employed, co-ordination is much more difficult than it was in a parish mission. One person needs to head this up, and to be in close and constant touch with the missioner (or whoever organises him!). It is up to the committee to decide how many central rallies there should be, and where the team and its main speaker(s) can most strategically be used in the course of the week. It is up to them to model the priority of prayer and see to it that prayer is given a very high priority in the preparations for the mission. A book like Frank Peretti's *This Present Darkness* would open many eyes to the reality of the spiritual conflict that a mission stirs up, and the vital importance of prayer if anything at all is to be achieved.

Of course, when you are operating at a city-wide level, certain things become a lot easier. It is much easier to organise events for sectors of the community who have a lot in common, such as the judges, the athletes, the doctors and the city leaders. It is much easier to get permission for the use of shopping malls, or for closing the streets for a praise march.

Youth work

Another thing that it is much easier to organise is effective ministry among young people. Many churches do not have flourishing youth groups; some have none at all. A mission provides an ideal opportunity to gather all the youth leaders in the town and get them to pull together. This they may never have done, and it may take both time and patience. Hopefully, however, in the run up to the mission, they will come to see the value of a co-ordinated and co-operative approach to the young people of the town.

They may decide to take over an old shop, make it a 'dive' for the young, and hold events there on a daily basis after school and in the evening. They may decide to get a top-rank Christian singer (and you can afford one if the project is town-wide). He or she can spend the week playing in the schools, running lunch-time concerts and youth evenings. Music is a superb vehicle for the gospel. So put a number of the team to work with such a person, because the impact among young people will be great. It may also be ephemeral, so particular care needs to be taken against false professions of commitment to Christ, based on personality cult.

A coffee house and drop-in centre may be developed. It needs to be based around a group of young people whose hearts have been set aflame by Christ and who are keen to share him with their friends. This does not happen overnight, and it cannot be manufactured. Ownership by the youth themselves is fundamental for this outreach. Let them decide possible spots to have the coffee house. Let them plan how it shall be organised, help to prepare the place, fix up lighting and so forth. The programme should be varied. Interview some of the Christian young people on a topic, and then mix it with a current song on the same subject. Music is vitally important. Videos have a place, as do panel discussions on issues like sex, parents and 'Who is Jesus?' Loving, imaginative, flexible work in such an environment can be profoundly useful in drawing the friends of Christian youngsters to Christ.

One recent mission in Western Canada hired a government ferry, and took eight hundred young people round the Gulf Islands at the beginning of the mission, thus laying a superb foundation for the further youth events scheduled later in the week.

It would be good if these shared events during the mission could lead to similar joint activity in the future. Young people are not denomination-bound. They care more about their friends than their ministers. It is so important that we do not allow denominational rivalries to stand in the way of effective youth work. In one Canadian town I was greeted by more than a hundred young people. I was surprised that any church should have so many. The answer was that no church did. But the Anglican, the Pentecostal and the Baptist youth leaders brought their youngsters together every Sunday night and met by rotation in each other's churches. Those young people will grow up as Christians first, and as Baptists, Anglicans or Pentecostals very much second.

Ministers
In a town-wide mission like this it is very important to show care for the clergy and ministers. They have done a great deal in preparing for this week, and they need encouragement. Some time during the week should be set aside for a special meeting with the ministers, learning from mistakes and successes, discussing problems and looking forward to what they plan to do after the mission.

Ministers' wives are often neglected because of church work, and resentment may well simmer beneath the surface. The pastors themselves may hover on the edge of burn-out. All of this may provide opportunities of personal counsel during the course of the mission. And whereas they might not want to open up to another minister in their own town, it is a different matter when a mission leader comes to their area: he may well be chosen as a confidant, and what is done in the privacy of some of those conversations may become very important in the ongoing life of whole churches in the town, through a new lease of life in the minister's home.

Another matter which needs to be gone through with the ministers, both in the initial stages of planning and again when the mission is in progress, is the handling of names. All names of those helped during the mission should be passed through shortly after the end of the mission to any minister with whom there are any links. It is then up to the minister to visit such people and strengthen church ties with them. But more sensitive is the question of Discovery Groups. Some ministers want to run their own groups for new believers and enquirers. While this is a possible option, it is far from ideal. For one thing, the new believer may not yet be linked up to any church. For another, the weak churches would scarcely be in the position to run effective groups: they need the help and expertise of leaders from the stronger churches.

Moreover, if the groups are run interdenominationally for those eight weeks, you are offering a second string to the local church in initial nurture. Any particular church may or may not be suitable for the new believer. But in any case, the Discovery Group is expressly designed for such a person, and should adequately meet his early needs and struggles. By the end of eight weeks he should be in an excellent position to get closely involved in the local church and make a real contribution. But this policy needs to be sensitively talked over with the ministers, and their minds set at rest.

Nurture
It is hard to over-emphasise the importance of follow-up in a mission like this. New believers are left in a very vulnerable position, and need immediate, appropriate and sensitive care. This is all the harder to ensure when they have been reached by a town-wide mission. It is all too easy for names to fall through the cracks which exist in even the best run organisation.

All team members, and any local Christians who offer counsel in homes or main meetings, must be made to realise how vital the comment or response cards are, if what has been begun in the person concerned is to be carried further. All cards should be handed in, when properly completed, to one central co-ordinator. This is a most responsible job, and needs to be in the hands of someone who has great spiritual sensitivity and cool organisational ability. For it is basically this central co-ordinator who sorts out names and puts them into the groups. By the end of the mission week it will be seen where the main concentrations of preferences for days and times to join Discovery Groups are coming, as well as the parts of town where response is heaviest. The groups can then be arranged accordingly. Those filling in response cards will have all been asked to offer a first and second choice of when they could be available for a group. It may simply not be possible to give everyone their first choice. It will depend on various considerations such as the mix of male and female, old and young in a given group, not to mention geographical factors and the suitability of the particular leaders for the members who are envisaged. But by the morning after the mission ends, it should be possible to see where everyone who has signed up can be placed, and the list of names phoned through to the leader of each Discovery Group. Until now, of course, they have all been on tenterhooks. They have been trained in the conduct of a group, but have had no members, and no assurance of any. It is only at the end of the mission that people can be assigned to them. Now, with the names and phone numbers, in their hands, the leadership team of each Discovery Group can visit all their members prior to the first meeting of the group, which will take place that very week.

I like to spend time with all the leaders of these Discovery Groups on the last afternoon of a mission, which is usually a Sunday. They are the 'under-shepherds' who are charged with looking after these new lambs in Christ's flock – along with some who are still struggling towards birth. They need all the help and encouragement they can get. In their hands much of the short-term fruit of the mission will lie. I try to impress on them the importance of immediately contacting those assigned to them, the need for personal interviews as well as group meetings, and the delicate time of hand-over at the end. They will be sure to find that some who have signed up for the day and time of their Discovery Group cannot make it after all. Such names will need to be passed on to the central co-ordinator at once, so that they can be reassigned to another group at a time they can manage, and not miss the vital first meeting.

The last night of such a mission is always an exhilarating time, and it tends to bring forward a lot of names for Discovery and Enquirers' Groups: people have been wavering, perhaps, for some days, but who on the last night decide to commit themselves. The building is usually packed, and combines a final challenge to commitment with help for going on in the Christian life. It allows room for those who have been blessed during the week to get up and say so. Praise is a notable feature of the evening, and so is the commissioning of all the local ministers for their future ministry together in the town. They will have been drawn closer together by this mission than ever before, and this is a great gain which must not be lost. Having tasted the fruit of unity in mission, they are not likely to want to return to any semblance of separatism. The bonds have grown too strong for that. But the new depth of togetherness needs to be carefully nurtured by joint action, joint prayer, and occasional joint celebrations. These will be among the long-term blessings of a town-wide mission.

FURTHER READING

Not enough has been written about the parish and town-wide missions described in this chapter, although much helpful information will be found in J. D. Douglas (ed.), *Let the Earth Hear His Voice* (World Wide Publications) and J. D. Douglas (ed.), *The Work of an Evangelist* (World Wide Publications), and in three books edited by Glenn C. Smith *Evangelising Adults* (Tyndale Press/Paulist Press), *Evangelising Blacks* (Tyndale Press/Paulist Press), *Evangelising Youth* (Tyndale Press/Paulist Press). These books bring together many evangelistic approaches in both the Roman Catholic and Protestant churches. There is much to be gleaned, too, from the series published by MARC Europe, with titles such as *Ten Worshipping Churches*, *Ten Growing Churches*, *Ten Sending Churches*. For books on drama and the arts, see pp. 104–5 above.

There are many different aspects of mission, to which the following may be an introduction:

Roland Allen, *Missionary Methods – St Paul's or Ours?* (Eerdmans)
R. S. Armstrong, *The Pastor as Evangelist* (Westminster Press)
R. S. Armstrong, *Service Evangelism* (Westminster Press)
Ray Bakke, *The Urban Christian* (Inter-Varsity Press)
Board for Mission and Unity, *The Measure of Mission* (Church House Publishing)
Robert Coleman, *The Master Plan of Evangelism* (Revell)
Harvie Conn, *A Clarified Vision for Urban Mission* (Zondervan)
Orlando Costas, *Liberating News* (Eerdmans)
John Dawson, *Taking Our Cities for God* (Creation House)
Eddie Gibbs, *I Believe in Church Growth* (Hodder & Stoughton)
Roger Greenway and Timothy Mousma, *Cities: God's New Frontier* (Baker Books)
E. M. Griffin, *The Mind Changers* (Tyndale Press)
Bob and Betty Jacks, *Your Home a Lighthouse* (Navpress)
J. E. Kyle (ed.), *Urban Mission* (Inter-Varsity Press)
Michael Marshall, *Renewal in Worship* (Anglican Book Centre)
Donald McGavran, *Effective Evangelism* (Presbyterian & Reformed)
Frank Peretti, *Piercing the Darkness* (Kingsway Publications)
Frank Peretti, *This Present Darkness* (Kingsway Publications)
Roy Pointer, *How Do Churches Grow?* (Marshalls)
John T. Seamands, *Harvest of Humanity* (Victory)
Patrick Sookhdeo, *New Frontiers in Mission* (Paternoster Press)
D. R. Veerman, *Youth Evangelism* (Victor Books)

14

God the Evangelist

Ours is a pragmatic age. We tend to think, not least if we live in North America, that whatever the problem, we can fix it. We will fix AIDS, we will fix the problems of the environment, just as we have overcome the problems of space travel. And we tend, almost subconsciously, to assume the same about evangelism. We have the message, the manpower, the methodology, the money: let's go.

But it is not like that. God will not give his glory to another. And the pragmatism of so much modern evangelism is an insult to the Almighty. He does not need our publicity drives, our booklets or our appeals. He may well make use of them, in his grace, from time to time. But it is God Almighty we are talking about! Evangelism is supremely his work. He so loved the world that he became the first evangelist. And there are three areas in particular where the mystery of his working, and his alone, are most evident: the sovereignty of his choice, the authority of his Scriptures, and the power of his Spirit.

THE SOVEREIGNTY OF GOD

When evangelism is being discussed, it is not uncommon to find one or other of these two attitudes, and they are as old as Arminius and Calvin. The first claims: 'We won seventeen people to Christ this afternoon.' The other is embodied in the famous response of a Baptist deacon to William Carey's concern for the evangelisation of the heathen: 'Young man, sit down. When God is pleased to convert the heathen, he will do it without your aid or mine.'

The Christian world is sadly divided on this matter. Calvinists stress the sovereignty of God in salvation, and tend to be quietist. Arminians stress the responsibility of man, and tend to be activist.

A candid look at the Bible shows that there is truth in both positions. Salvation flows from God alone. He devised it. He revealed it. He purchased it at immense cost on the cross. He applies it by his Spirit to the human heart. That is fundamental. On the other hand, God does not force his will upon his creatures. That is the surpassing glory of our humanity. We have the ability to choose. Throughout Scripture we see men and women exercising that right, sometimes for God and sometimes against him. We see the prophets pleading with a recalcitrant people in the name of the Lord who loves them. We see the challenge of Jesus to the wills of men. We note the insistent appeal to repentance and faith in Acts and, implicitly, in the epistles of the New Testament. To be sure, men and women cannot repent and believe unless it is given them by God: but then we cannot do anything without his enabling capacity and the life that he alone gives us. Nevertheless, we are called to make the response that he enables. There is a human strand as well as a divine strand in evangelism.

One particular saying of Jesus embodies this paradox very clearly. 'All that the Father gives me will come to me,' he says in John 6:37. You could not have divine election more clearly spelled out than that. But the verse continues, 'and him who comes to me I will not cast out'. That speaks very directly of the human choice we have, to come or not to come. I sometimes think of salvation as a walled garden. There is a little door into the garden, and emblazoned on the outside of that door it reads, 'Him who comes to me I will not cast out.' I enter. I marvel at the beauty and fruitfulness of this garden – so unsuspected by me hitherto, so hidden behind its high walls. And now that I am inside, I begin to revel in its delights and responsibilities. And then I glance back at that door by which I entered. I see, written on the inside of the door, 'All that the Father gives me will come to me.' And I recognise that way behind my choice of him, was his choice of me. I do not begin to understand why he should have set his love on me and called me. But I realise that he has, and that this divine election is more significant than my frail human response. It is the ground on which my response is possible at all. It is my ultimate security. The two strands are not incompatible, but profoundly congruent. Nobody has ever solved the intellectual problem of election and free will, but we have all tasted both courses in this divine meal of salvation. It was that celebrated Anglican divine, Charles Simeon of Cambridge, who when reflecting on this matter observed: 'The truth lies neither at one extreme nor at the other, nor yet in a mean betwixt the two. It lies in holding both extremes at the same time.' He would advise the evangelist to be a Calvinist in his prayers and an Arminian in his preaching. The evangelist is called to pray as if it all depended on God, and to preach as if it all depended on him. I, for one, seek constantly to be a Calvinist on my knees and an Arminian in the pulpit. That seems to me to be a proper attitude before the great God who deigns to use me as his messenger.

But in our Western culture evangelists do not need to be encouraged to preach as if it all depended on them. They do that already! They *do* need to be recalled to the mystery of the divine working in salvation, and to the fact that we human beings can never understand it. The prophets knew this well. Reflect on this Servant Song of Isaiah's (Isa. 49:1–6, 8–9), where the two strands of election and free response are so closely interwoven:

> The Lord called me from the womb, from the body of my mother he named my name. He made my mouth like a sharp sword, in the shadow of his hand he hid me; he made me a polished arrow, in his quiver he hid me away. And he said to me, 'You are my servant, Israel, in whom I will be glorified.' But I said, 'I have laboured in vain, I have spent my strength for nothing and vanity; yet surely my right is with the Lord, and my recompense with my God.'
>
> And now the Lord says, who formed me from the womb to be his servant, to bring Jacob back to him, and that Israel might be gathered to him, for I am honoured in the eyes of the Lord, and my God has become my strength – he says: 'It is too light a thing that you should be my servant to raise up the tribes of Jacob and to restore the preserved of Israel; I will give you as a light to the nations, that my salvation may reach to the end of the earth.'

And how will it do so?

> Thus says the Lord: 'In a time of favour I have answered you, in a day of salvation I have helped you; I have kept you and given you as a covenant to the people . . . saying to the prisoners, "Come forth," to those who are in darkness, "Appear."'

The same balance is found in Isaiah 45:18–25, and most sharply in Isaiah 43:11–12: 'I, I am the Lord, and beside me there is no saviour. I declared and saved and proclaimed, when there was no strange god among you; and you are my witnesses.' Precisely the same paradox runs through the New Testament. One example must suffice. In writing to the Ephesians, Paul recalls how his readers who 'heard the word of truth, the gospel of your salvation, and . . . believed' were 'destined . . . in love to be his sons through Jesus Christ' and 'chosen in him before the foundation of the world' (Eph. 1:13, 5, 4). We do God no honour by seeking to suppress either one of these twin biblical themes – God's election and our response. Both are true. Both are important. But modern Western preachers need to be reminded of God's sovereignty in this man-centred age. If they bear it constantly in mind, it will have several most beneficial results.

First, it will save the evangelist from being either proud of success or desolated by the lack of response. Arrogance and despair are two terrible dangers in evangelism. But if there is a deep, quiet confidence in God's overarching sovereignty, peace will replace guilt-driven activism, and humility replace self-confidence.

Second, it will not allow laziness. The sovereignty of God and the need for response impose responsibility all around. God does not treat us like robots. The evangelist has the responsibility to make known the good news in every way possible. The hearer has the responsibility to decide what he will do about it.

Most important of all, reliance on the sovereign grace of God is our only hope in evangelism. Where else can we look? If we turn to human pressure, sales techniques, or filleted, packaged selections from the Christian good news, we shall get some response, but it will not last. It will not have the depth and mystery of the divine birth in the soul. It will spring from the flesh, and issue in the flesh. Faith, like grace itself, is a gift of God (Phil. 1:29; Eph. 2:8; Acts 5:31; 11:18). So, like Paul, when he was told by God that many people were awaiting conversion in Corinth, we should 'not be afraid, but speak and do not be silent; for I am with you, and no man shall attack you to harm you; for I have many people in this city' (Acts 18:9). God had the people. Paul had the commission. It made him confident, bold, patient and prayerful. It should do the same for us.

THE AUTHORITY OF SCRIPTURE

This is not the place to argue the authority of Scripture in general. It is a subject on which a great deal has been written in recent years. Almost all denominations profess to believe that the Old and New

Testament scriptures are normative for Christian belief and behaviour. But most denominations, and many ministers and people within them, sit very light to that belief in practice. Issues like democracy, abortion, marriage and divorce, raising children, capital punishment, homosexuality, and ecology are generally debated by Christians on the same terms of reference as prevail in society at large. But the Bible has a great deal to say on these matters. Equally, when it comes to the question of how mankind can get right with God, how we can know him and discover his transforming power in our lives, many churches offer remedies which owe nothing to Scripture. The message of the Bible is muted in many mainline churches, and in many of the newer churches it may be present but is often narrowly conceived and legalistically applied. In practice, subjects which figure largely in the biblical account of salvation are strangely absent from our pulpits. Who today hears much about the holiness of God, the seriousness of sin, the sheer unmerited favour of God to sinners who deserve nothing of him? You can go to church for years without ever realising that God's Spirit is available to enter your very being, that you can be justified before the Holy One, that you need to make a responsible decision which will cost you everything you have. These things are all written clear on every page of the New Testament, but at best they are muted, and at worst omitted entirely, in much modern preaching. No wonder the church is in low water in many parts of continents which used to be mainly Christian.

Christianity is founded on the conviction that God is there, and he is not silent. He has revealed himself to mankind, and the record and the locus of that revelation is Scripture. Three points are worth making in so far as this basic Christian conviction applies to evangelism.

First, the biblical writers were confident that they were speaking from God. 'Thus says the Lord' echoes throughout the Old Testament. The New Testament is no less explicit on the subject. In 1 Peter 1:10–12 the writer is crystal-clear that the same Holy Spirit who inspired the prophets was present in a unique way in Jesus of Nazareth, and was at work in 'those who preached the good news to you through the Holy Spirit sent from heaven'. Peter's second letter sees the inspired Old Testament scriptures confirmed by the coming, the transfiguration and the voice of Jesus. 'You will do well to pay attention to this', he writes. 'You must understand . . . that no prophecy of scripture is a matter of one's own interpretation, because no prophecy ever came by the impulse of man, but men moved by the Holy Spirit spoke from God' (2 Pet. 1:16–21). Paul's own confidence in the divinely revealed source for his evangelistic preaching comes out powerfully in 1 Corinthians 2:12–13: 'Now we have received not the spirit of the world, but the Spirit which is from God, that we might understand the gifts bestowed on us by God. And we impart this in words not taught by human wisdom but taught by the Spirit.' That is the authority behind Paul's spoken word. He was no less clear about the written word: 'All scripture is inspired by God and profitable for teaching, for reproof, for correction, and for training in righteousness, that the man of God may be complete, equipped for every good work' (2 Tim. 3:16). Those are only sample texts demonstrating the conviction of the first Christians that they were speaking from God. They could be multiplied many times over. The words of these first Christians were rooted in the divine Word which had come in many forms down the ages, but was most fully, exhaustively and personally expressed in God's Son (Heb. 1:1–2).

Second, the preaching of the New Testament evangelists shared a common content. This has been made the subject of a careful study by one of the greatest New Testament scholars of this century, C. H. Dodd. His book *The Apostolic Preaching and Its Developments* shows that the evangelists of the early church used a basic outline which can be recovered from various strands in the New Testament. They did not follow it slavishly, but it provided a valuable framework, of which they made good use. It ran something like this:

> The age of fulfilment has dawned, as the Scriptures foretold. God has sent his Messiah, Jesus. He died in shame upon the cross. God raised him again from the tomb. He is now Lord, at God's right hand. The proof of this is the Holy Spirit, whose effects you see. This Jesus will come again at the end of history. Repent, believe, and be baptised.

Such was the essence of what the first Christians preached. It is very far from what you hear in most churches. An archbishop recently gathered his clergy together to discuss evangelism, and he himself taught on the subject without mentioning any of the points in this typical apostolic kerygma. He is not an aberrant exception. If Kirsopp Lake was right in maintaining that 'modern man does not believe in any form of salvation known to ancient Christianity', the same could be said of many clergy and ministers. It shows in their preaching. But the ancient Christians thought very differently. They believed that this message which they tirelessly pressed upon their hearers was vital for their eternal security. 'When you received the word of God which you heard from us,' writes Paul to his friends and converts at Thessalonica, 'you accepted it not as the word of men but as what it really is, the word of God, which is at work in you believers' (1 Thess. 2:13).

The third point is very obvious when you look round the world. Many people do not like it being pointed out, but it is important to do so. The fact of the matter is that churches which believe the Bible, teach the Bible, allow their outlook and attitudes to be moulded by the Bible, are the growing churches in the world. That holds good for First World countries and Third World countries. It makes no difference. There is a power in biblical preaching which is never present in the minister who can do no more than say, 'Scholars are agreed . . .', or 'It seems to me . . .', or 'Modern man cannot accept . . .' Some churchmen of a different outlook try to explain the growth of the biblical churches by alleging the *naiveté* of the recipients or their hunger for some form of security. Neither explanation carries conviction. It is interesting to note that in Oxford and Cambridge universities, two of the most prestigious and intellectually alive universities in the world, the largest student societies are the Christian Unions, men and women who are committed to biblical Christianity. The same is true of the churches in those university cities which are most thronged by intelligent undergraduates. It is unconvincing to accuse them of *naiveté*. And as for seeking security from a puzzling world in biblical Christianity, that may be true of some people, but overall it is a pathetically weak and evasive explanation of the growth of a Bible-based Christianity, both in the Catholic and Protestant churches in our modern world. Has it not occurred to those who make such strictures that the growth may be due not to escapism, but to truth?

The fact of the matter is that there is power in scriptural Christianity. It has power to build up believers, and enable them to face the temptations, problems, and crises of this mortal life. It also has a unique power to convert. God's word is alive and powerful and sharper than a two-edged sword (Heb. 4:12), and time and again the evangelist who makes good use of it will find that it has pierced to the hearts of his hearers in a way that his own words could never do. This has always been the experience of the church. Back in the second century, Justin Martyr wrote, 'The Scriptures and the words of Jesus possess a terrible power in themselves and a wonderful sweetness. Straightaway a flame was kindled in my soul, and a love of the prophets and of those men who were friends of

Christ possessed me' (*Dialogue*, 8). It was the same with Tatian, his friend and pupil:

> I sought how I might be able to discover the truth, and I happened to meet with certain barbaric writings, too old to be compared with the opinions of the Greeks, and too divine to be compared with their errors. And I was led to put faith in these by the unpretentious cast of the language, the genuine character of the writers, their intelligible account of creation, the foreknowledge they displayed of future events, the excellent quality of the precepts, and their declaration that the government of the world is centred in one Being. (*Oration*, 29)

The Bible Society has many modern examples of the converting power of Scripture on record. Here is one. Towards the end of the last century a young Malagasy woman of a slave-owning family purchased a slave girl in the market at Mandritsara, in northern Madagascar. In the days that followed, the slave girl relieved her loneliness by reading the one book she had – a Malagasy New Testament. Her mistress was intrigued to find the girl could read: she herself could not. So the slave girl taught her mistress to read, and the text-book was the Malagasy New Testament. Others were soon invited to the reading, and before long a small crowd of seekers gathered round the slave girl, and a church was born. It is vigorously alive today, with daughter churches in the surrounding countryside. One of the impressive facts about the Bible in relation to evangelism is that its influence rarely stops with the individual. When a person finds new life through its message he almost invariably shares his discovery with someone else.

All this has some important things to say to those who preach the gospel. The most important question we have to decide for ourselves is whether or not we will accept the Bible's claim to bring us God's own word. Upon that critical foundation all else depends. It is a difficult question for those who have received the currently acceptable theological education, for so much in that education is affected by the secularisation of our thought since the Enlightenment. But the authority of Scripture can be rationally held and competently defended by modern, critical theologians. It is a question which must be answered by modern evangelists. Can they, or can they not, trust the biblical teaching about man, God, and salvation? If they can, they must have good reasons for doing so. If they cannot, they had better give up evangelism. For evangelism is nothing other than the proclamation in word and deed of the good news contained in the Bible, the good news of what God is like and of what he has done to rescue a rebel creation. We could never dream up the wonder of God's generosity. It is either true or it is not. That is the decision the evangelist must make. I recall hearing Billy Graham once telling theological students of the tussle he had over this issue. When he came clearly to trust the Scriptures, he began to preach with the power and authority that has made him far and away the most effective evangelist in the twentieth century.

If we are persuaded that the Scriptures do indeed come to mankind marked with the stamp of God's authority, that will have a number of implications for our evangelistic ministry.

We will not be embarrassed about opening the Scriptures. We will turn to them with the same naturalness with which we would turn to any other book. The Bible is the world's best-seller, but it is an unread best-seller. People are ignorant of its contents. And there need be no hint of Bible-thumping if we turn to its pages and show people what it actually says. That is, in any discipline, a thoroughly reputable procedure: get back to the primary sources.

We will take any opportunities to lend the Scriptures. The loan or gift of an attractively presented Gospel in a modern translation is often extremely influential in the reader's life. I recall the story of Tikichi Ishii, a Second World War criminal of almost unmatched cruelty, who was awaiting execution in his cell. With fiendish brutality this Japanese guard had murdered men, women and children, and had revelled in it. Two Canadian women visited him in his cell, and told him of the salvation which Christ had achieved even for such as he. He glared at them, cursing, and they went away without apparently having achieved anything. But they left him a New Testament. He began to read it during the long hours of enforced solitude. He was fascinated by the person of Jesus, who was tortured so brutally, but without a word of resentment. Rather, he had prayed for his tormenters, 'Father, forgive them; for they know not what they do' (Luke 23:34).

Ishii said later, 'I stopped. I could not go on. I was stabbed to the heart, as by a five-inch nail. Was it the love of Christ? Was it his compassion? I do not know what it was. I only know that I believed, and the hardness of my heart was changed.' And when the executioner came to Ishii he found not the hardened brute he had anticipated, but a smiling, radiant man whose remaining days in that prison had been utterly transformed by the new life he had found in Christ. We may have confidence in lending the Scriptures to others. It is a quiet but very powerful means of evangelism.

The evangelist should also be prepared to challenge people with the Scriptures. Not only in public preaching, but also in personal conversation. Often I have said to an enquirer with whom I have been talking, 'Here is a copy of St John's Gospel. It tells us that it was written to bring people like you to the intellectual belief that Jesus was the Son of God, and to the experience of a new life through him. Why not read it with an open mind, prepared to commit yourself to the cause of Christ if, and only if, you are convinced? Pray as you read, "O God, if you are real (and I am not sure you are), show me what is true in this account, and I promise that if I am persuaded, I will entrust my life to Christ."' Often he has returned to tell me that the experiment has had a powerful effect on him. He has read it with an open mind. He has been convinced. And he has begun the life of Christian discipleship.

The evangelist will select Scripture with care. He will choose passages which speak to the condition of the people he is with. There is an immense flexibility in the way Jesus addressed different types of people, and there is no excuse for woodenness in his followers.

We must seek, too, to translate Scripture into terms people can readily understand. I do not merely mean the use of a modern translation. The very concepts of Scripture need to be put into fresh dress for many people. We find this process taking place in the pages of the New Testament itself. For example, among the gospel writers, John almost entirely replaces the synoptic Gospels' use of the phrase 'the Kingdom of God' by 'eternal life', which made more sense to the Greeks to whom he primarily directed his Gospel, and was also devoid of unhelpful socio-political overtones. Also, the apostle Paul takes the non-Jewish idea of 'adoption', which was very common in Roman circles, and uses this as a brilliant description of what God has done for us in Christ. Neither evangelist was woodenly bound to the terms of the tradition he inherited. Both were true to the content of that tradition, but they felt free to clothe the message in appropriate dress that would enable their hearers to understand. Modern evangelists should do likewise. Our language should be arresting and illustrative, like new-minted coinage; but it should be true to the gold standard! It must not relinquish the message enshrined in the New Testament, though it may properly alter the terms in which that message is presented.

Most of all, those who are seeking to share the good news need to trust the Scriptures. They have a power our words do not. Any experienced minister will have known occasions when some verse of Scripture read in a lesson has pierced to the very heart of a hearer, or when a word of Scripture which he passed over lightly in his address has totally grabbed the attention of someone in the congregation, closing their mind and ears to all else, and has subsequently made a real change in the direction of that person's life. There are times when the preacher who is exposing people to the message of the Bible can almost stand outside himself and watch the divine chemistry at work. It is so obviously not the work of the preacher himself. One person will be moved to tears by his address: the person sitting next to him will be looking at his watch, waiting for the sermon to stop!

THE POWER OF THE SPIRIT

The third area where it is so obvious that God, and God alone, is the evangelist is found in the work of the Holy Spirit. For the Holy Spirit is the prime agent in Christian mission.

The New Testament plainly teaches that Christ has a plan for the continuation of his work in the world. In the famous Marcan apocalypse, Jesus tells us that the period between his death and the end of the world will be marked by hard times, the mission of the church, and the empowering of the Holy Spirit (Mark 13:9–13). In the farewell discourses in John's Gospel, Jesus tells his followers that three things will follow his departure to the Father's side: the Holy Spirit will come to bear witness to him, they themselves will bear witness, and life will be tough (John 15:26–16:2). In Luke's account of Jesus' farewell to his disciples before the ascension, the same three things are presaged. They will bear witness, in ever-widening circles; they will be able to do nothing until they are empowered by the coming of the Spirit into their lives; and the whole story of Acts is the story of hard times.

So the time between the two advents is not an empty time of waiting. It is full of the Holy Spirit and evangelism. These two belong together. They are the two main instruments for the Kingdom's advance until the return of the King.

As the story of Acts unfolds we find the Holy Spirit taking the lead. It is he who drives the infant church on to the streets, in chapter 2. It is he who sparks the new initiative in chapters 6–8 with the Hellenists. It is he who leads the church into what was once the 'No-go' land of the Samaritans, in chapter 8. It is he who makes Peter reach out to a Roman 'godfearer', in chapter 10; he who founds the first Gentile church, in chapter 11; and he who inaugurates world mission, in chapter 13. It was not the apostles who were responsible for any of these initiatives. It was the Holy Spirit who spurred his reluctant people into action.

It is fascinating to read books, flooding from the presses these days, which bear witness to exciting new advances, and the way the Holy Spirit has prompted them. Some which have inspired me are Michael Cassidy's *Bursting the Wineskins*, John White's *When the Spirit Comes with Power*, Eileen Vincent's *God Can Do It Here*, and Archbishop Bill Burnett's collection of contributions from around the world, *By My Spirit*. But those are merely the tip of a very large iceberg.

The Holy Spirit loves to start small and build something beautiful for God. This pattern is exemplified in Acts. That is how he began on the day of Pentecost – with just a handful of people. That is how he built the church at Philippi – with a jailer, a commercial traveller and ex-medium. That is how he founded the church at Corinth – with a discouraged apostle, the companionship of Aquila and Priscilla, opportunities opening up in the workplace and in the synagogue, some significant conversions, and a whole city eventually touched by the gospel. Time and again in church history that pattern has been reproduced. God has begun small, often prompting just one person to launch out in the power of his Spirit, and the result has been remarkable.

Just recently I read the story of such a man, Nicholas Rivett-Carnac, an admiral's son turned vicar in a tough part of London. It is the remarkable account of one man, with no special expertise or clear plans, who learned to listen to the Spirit of God and has seen a large and influential ministry come to life. The book is called *On This Rock*, and it makes exciting reading because it is so obviously the work of God's Spirit.

The same is true of Robert Warren's ministry in Sheffield. St Thomas, Crookes, is now one of the most celebrated churches in Britain, but it was a fairly small concern when he was made vicar; and, as he tells in his book *In the Crucible*, he was himself well aware of the failure of his own ministry. But the Spirit of God moved upon him, and, beginning small, that church has grown into something wonderful. I well recall once going to preach for him, in the early days, and his showing me a map of the parish with the first three house groups, marked by coloured pins!

The Holy Spirit clearly attracted large numbers of people in the days of the early church by the sheer quality of life exhibited in the church. Luke gives us two cameos of their love, their generosity, unity, prayer and courageous witness, along with a touching example of the ministry of encouragement which was so notable among them, at the end of Acts 2 and 4. These are still among his prime ways of working, as we saw in chapter 4. We can all think of churches which have an outstanding impact on the society around them, because of the quality of life which the Holy Spirit has fashioned in the hearts of the believers and the structures of their church. University Presbyterian in Seattle, USA, is such a church, as is Holy Trinity, Brompton, or All Souls, Langham Place, or All Saints, Margaret Street, in England – to take four churches of very different traditions. I believe that one of the main ways in which the Spirit evangelises is through the impact of Christians living together in his joy and in his power. It is immensely attractive, and people are attracted to Christ more often by a joyous holy community than they are driven to him by a powerful evangelist.

The Holy Spirit empowers fearful disciples to bear witness to Jesus. He did so with Ananias, terrified of what that zealot, Saul of Tarsus, might do to him if he plucked up courage to go and visit him. Time and again I have seen that scenario repeated. A timorous Christian has asked the Spirit of God to give him courage, and has launched out. To his amazement, he has found that he gets mightily used by the Spirit.

An extremely interesting and very amusing example of this has just been provided by Peter Lawrence, in his first book, *Hotline*. It is the story of how he, a rather cynical young curate, more expert at cricket and golf than at evangelism or listening to God, entered into the power and fruitfulness of the Holy Spirit, and has seen a ministry open up not only in the tough city of Birmingham, where he works, but far beyond the shores of his native England. I taught Peter Lawrence long ago, so I am all the more sensitive to the remarkable change that the Spirit of God has brought about in him!

There is a remarkable example in Acts 10 of how the Spirit of God sometimes works without human intermediaries. It depicts two men, based respectively at Joppa and Caesarea, miles apart from one another. The Spirit longs to break out from the confines of Judaism into wider circles. So as these two men, Cornelius and

Peter, are praying, he gives two visions: one to each of them. They were identical in import. They led to the two men meeting. They led to the conversion of Cornelius and his household. They led to the eruption of the gospel into a whole new section of ancient society. The Spirit still speaks through dreams, and he still acts in total independence of human initiatives. One of the most remarkable examples I ever heard was told me by the Rev. Samuel Kameleson, a distinguished Indian Christian. A courageous colporteur of his acquaintance was prevailed on to go and preach Christ in a Hindu temple in the heart of Brahmin country in South India. He felt under strong compulsion to take this unusual action, but he feared it would cost him his life. He was, to his utter surprise, almost immediately joined by a woman. Later he heard her story. She was rich, and belonged to a high caste. She suffered from terminal cancer, and had gone to Madras to die. To all intents and purposes she did die, and was placed in the mortuary. She was, in fact, deeply unconscious, and in a vision the Lord met her, with an expression of intense love on his features. She was so attracted by this figure whom she instinctively recognised but did not know, that in her vision she cried out, 'If you will give me back my life, Lord, I will live it out for you.'

A mortuary assistant happened to notice that this woman displayed slight signs of breathing. He immediately went to a doctor, who took blood for transfusion from a passing crossing-sweeper, who happened to be a Christian. The patient revived. Her cancer was gone. She realised that she owed her life to the crossing-sweeper, and sought her out. She became a Christian, and renounced Hinduism. Coming from such a family, this produced the most violent reaction. Her brothers kicked her to within an inch of death. Her teeth were knocked out of her mouth. Yet in the long run she led those five brothers to Christ. This woman had no Bible. She engaged in no preaching. The whole thing was the work of the sovereign Holy Spirit of God. He gave her the vision. He revived her. He led her to faith. He gave her courage to witness. He gave her fruit for her labours.

That story is far from unique. We may expect, and we may pray, that God the Evangelist will sometimes allow us to see what he is doing in glorifying Christ without any human instrumentality at all.

But that same Spirit often chooses to channel his divine message through the agency of his people. The trouble is that these people of his have often been so conditioned by the secular outlook of the Western world that they have ceased to expect, pray for, or even believe in his powerful intervention. We read of exorcism, dreams, visions, prophecy, healing and tongues in the New Testament, but have a mental block which says: 'That could never happen here. That was for New Testament days only.' We rationalise our disbelief by telling ourselves that New Testament Christianity was a different dispensation of God's grace, and that these gifts of the Spirit were intended for the inauguration of the church, but not for today.

There really is no excuse for such scepticism, though I confess to having shared it myself, in days past. During the past thirty years a mighty movement of the Holy Spirit has touched a great many churches in the world. It may be that nothing parallel has happened since the Reformation: I do not know. But it is beyond doubt that some three hundred and fifty million Christians throughout the world can bear witness to the fact that these gifts of the Spirit have not died out, and are powerful aids to evangelism today. I am only a mere beginner in experiencing these gifts, but I have seen people brought to faith through tongues and interpretation going to the very root of their being; or after being pierced to the heart by a prophetic utterance which they knew was for them. I have seen people healed by prayer and the laying on of hands, not once but many times, and often this has led to their conversion. I have witnessed the power of the Spirit coming to drive out demons, sometimes several of them, from a life they have been infesting, and I have seen that life transformed by the new power which the Spirit has brought them.

I was not brought up to expect these things. I never heard about them in my theological seminary. I was not led to expect them in my ministry. I was highly suspicious of them, as a theological teacher myself, when they first began to impinge upon my experience. But now I know that they are real. Now I know that the Spirit uses these things as agencies in spreading the gospel. I have written more fully about the subject in three books, *I Believe in the Holy Spirit*, *To Corinth with Love*, and *I Believe in Satan's Downfall*.

A church that is sensitive to God's Spirit will expect him to intervene in sovereign power from time to time. There is no knowing when those times will be. Ours not to reason why: our task is to be prayerful, open, and always ready to see what God may do in a situation. I think this is the most important change in my own attitude. I now *expect* God to act. I follow the gentle nudges he gives me, even if they seem foolish. They sometimes are foolish, and I fall flat on my face: I have not learned to discern my

Lord's voice very clearly yet, in contrast to all the other voices that clamour for a hearing in my heart.

But often those nudges do turn out to be promptings from him, and they do lead to conversions. I have written elsewhere of a nudge I received when shaving one morning. It was 24 December, and what with the preparations for Christmas at home and in the church on that busy day in the year, I did nothing about it. The nudge was to go and visit an old man across the street who had had ample opportunity to respond to the gospel but had not done so. Imagine my chagrin, therefore, the next morning, when I heard he had been rushed to hospital during the night with a stroke! I dashed to the hospital that Christmas morning, and was very relieved to find him alive. He died not many weeks later, but not before he had put his faith firmly in the Lord. I just dread to think how many such nudges I have never noticed or never obeyed.

We need to pay serious attention to new initiatives that are tentatively suggested from perhaps an unexpected quarter in the church. That suggestion may come from God. The same applies to 'pictures' which some people receive and which may contain a message for the church or for an individual. We are told to test all these things, to be sure: but we are not told to reject them out of hand. The same Holy Spirit who convicts people of their need, makes Christ real to them, enables them to confess him as Lord, assures them they belong, and grows in them his beautiful fruit – that same Spirit gives gifts for service, and he is grieved if they are spurned. They are an important part of evangelism, and this is increasingly being recognised by even very traditional churches such as the Roman Catholic, the Anglican and the Lutheran.

WORD AND SPIRIT

In the last two sections we have been looking at two very different manifestations of God's mysterious work as evangelist. On the one hand he works through the authority of his Word. On the other he works through the power of his Spirit. But are these two not antithetical to one another?

There is certainly a great deal of tension in modern Christianity between those who rely mainly on the Spirit and those who rely on the Word. The enthusiasts for the Spirit are often disappointed by the formalism, apparent lack of expectancy, and predictability of the churches which major on the Word. The latter, confident of their doctrinal soundness, are suspicious of the weaknesses they perceive in the charismatic Christians, particularly their emotionalism, their gullibility, and their sitting loose to Scripture.

But surely this antithesis is more fancied than real. It is certainly not necessary. Charismatics are not claiming, if they are in their right senses, anything that is not to be found in the Bible which the evangelicals cherish. There is a tremendously strong link in the Old Testament between the *dabar Yahweh* and the *ruach Adonai*. You cannot divorce the 'word' of God from the 'breath' or 'Spirit' of the Lord. 'The Spirit of the Lord speaks by me, his word is upon my tongue' (2 Sam. 23:2). That is how closely the two are intertwined. So close is the link that when Saul disobeys God, and is rejected as king of Israel, we read, 'You have rejected the word of the Lord . . . [and so] the Spirit of the Lord departed from Saul' (1 Sam. 15:26; 16:14). The Old Testament shows the message of the Lord being brought to mankind in a variety of ways by God's Spirit, including dreams, visions, prophecy, didactic history, proverb and psalmody. The message comes in many forms, but is inspired by the one Spirit.

It is the same in the New Testament. The Spirit inspires both the Old and the New Testament scriptures (1 Pet. 1:10–13; 2 Pet. 3:16), and makes them luminous (2 Cor. 3:12–18). It is the same in preaching. The Spirit inspired the original passage of Scripture. The Spirit lives in the hearts of the preacher who proclaims and of the congregation who hear God's Word. The Spirit applies the Word, now here, now there, as he wills. It is the special prerogative of the Spirit to use the Word. It is, indeed, his sword.

It should be obvious by now that the Spirit and the Word are friends, not foes. It is therefore tragic to see charismatics and evangelicals in tension with one another on this issue. Charismatics should be saying, 'Back to Scripture. Get thrilled with it. Obey it. Test all claims by it.' Evangelicals, for their part, should be saying, 'Let us not be satisfied until we see vital Christianity in our church, the gifts of the Spirit as well as his fruit.' They belong together.

I believe that the power of the Word has greatly influenced the renewal movement in recent years. There is now much less stress on tongues than there used to be, and it is no longer seen in most quarters as the yardstick of having received 'the blessing'. Rather, tongues has returned to its biblical position as just one of the gifts of the Spirit, not the sign that the Spirit is in residence.

There is also much less insistence on a once-for-all 'baptism with the Spirit' as a second experience after conversion. This is now seen to have little in Scripture to commend it, and the language of 'baptism' is unhelpfully divisive. I sense less pride in renewal circles. In the early days there was a good deal of arrogance in the claim, 'I've got it. Have you?' And the sinless perfectionism, on which the early renewal movement bordered, is less in evidence these days. There is generally less preoccupation with gifts, and more with responsibilities. There is less triumphalism, less anti-intellectualism, and less pan-demonism. And there is less inward orientation within renewal circles. Instead, there is a widespread determination to allow the Spirit to thrust his people out in evangelism and service. All this is solid gain.

Equally, I believe the renewal movement has highlighted several aspects of biblical religion that were being neglected by evangelicals, as well as other sectors of the church. It has provided a challenge to the institutionalism and formalism of the church. It has shown the barrenness of the intellectualism of the church. It has disclosed the poverty of one-man leadership in the church. Those seem to me to be some of the major areas where the charismatic renewal throughout Christendom will be seen to have made lasting contributions, when all the arm-waving and tongues-speaking has been recognised as the froth on the top of a very rich mixture.

Yes, the Word and the Spirit are indeed friends.

POWER EVANGELISM

The emphasis on the Holy Spirit in recent years has been remarkable. It has produced, in the early part of the century, the Pentecostal Church, by far the fastest-growing part of Christendom. In mid-century it led to the charismatic renewal which affected practically all sections of the world-wide church, and merited Cardinal Suenens' title of *A New Pentecost?* More recently, what has been called the 'Third Wave' of this mighty movement of the Spirit of God has broken upon the Christian world. It is associated with a genial Californian, John Wimber, and his emphasis on 'signs and wonders'. After his colourful conversion, Wimber was surprised by the contrast he noticed between the Christianity he found in the

New Testament, and what was practised in the churches. He asked his now famous question, 'When are you goin' to start doin' the stuff?' 'The stuff' was the healing, the deliverance, the super-natural insight that seemed to be commonplace in the days of the apostles.

How John Wimber himself became gifted in these areas, after a good deal of fruitless searching, is by now well known throughout the Christian world. His own books, *Power Evangelism* and *Power Healing*, tell something of the story, provide reasons for his convictions, and provide a model for others to follow. Many have done so, all over the world. His own seminars on healing, prayer, signs and wonders, and holiness have seen enormous numbers coming to them and being changed by them. But this stress on signs and wonders is by no means restricted to John Wimber. It has long been prevalent, indeed taken for granted, by Third World churches, unhampered by the Western scepticism which goes back to the Enlightenment. They read of the power of God's Spirit in the New Testament, and they take him at his word.

The main assumptions of Power Evangelism, as evangelism accompanied by reliance on these spiritual gifts has come to be known, are as follows.

First, a world-view in which God and the spiritual world are seen as active and able to intervene.

Second, a belief that the gifts of the Spirit mentioned in the New Testament are still available today.

Third, a conviction that every Christian has the Spirit, and that therefore he may, if he pleases, manifest himself through any Christian in a particular situation. This marks a divergence from earlier elements in the charismatic movement, which had tended to stress that particular gifts are given by the Spirit as a permanent possession to particular people.

Fourth, a willingness to risk, and to step out, on the basis of what you believe God wants you to do in a given situation. There is a deep assumption, too, that God's will is wholeness in every aspect of our lives: that conviction, coupled with faith and compassion, are the preconditions which God is keen to honour.

A good deal of emphasis is laid on what is called 'Kingdom theology', which, in line with the synoptic Gospels (but not John), maintains that Jesus came to inaugurate the Kingdom of God on earth. He realised this partially during his ministry, and he broke the back of the opposition by his death upon the cross. While the Kingdom will not be fully established until his return, we can experience a foretaste of it now. It is this reality of the Kingdom which the church is called to live out.

Further, it is pointed out that Jesus did not operate on his own, but in dependence on the Father and in the power of the Spirit. In all this he was our model. He demonstrated both the words of the Kingdom, and its works: these were never separated in his mind, nor should they be in ours. Jesus commissioned the twelve and the seventy to do just what he did: preach the word, accompanied by the signs of the Kingdom. That is what Power Evangelism sets out to do, noting that this is precisely what the early Christians, as recorded in the Acts of the Apostles, made their own priority.

What are we to make of this emphasis?

The wonder-working of God

First, it is plain that the God of the Bible does make powerful use of signs and wonders. He did in Old Testament days, particularly in the great rescue from Egypt. The whole history of Israel is studded with signs and wonders – to Pharaoh, at the Red Sea, with the pillars of cloud and fire, with manna in the wilderness, and so forth. It continues throughout the Old Testament. God is 'majestic in holiness, terrible in glorious deeds, doing wonders' (Exod. 15:11).

The same is clearly true of Jesus Christ, who came to bring about the new Exodus. Almost a third of the gospel story is taken up with his miracles. He was indeed, as Peter said at Pentecost, 'a man attested to you by God with mighty works and wonders and signs which God did through him in your midst' (Acts 2:22).

When Joel's prophecy was fulfilled, and the Spirit was poured out on the disciples at Pentecost, we find a marvellous succession of signs and wonders beginning to emerge. These were not, of course, for show, but for the furtherance of the gospel. The early church was born in signs and wonders – wonderful healings, wonderful tongues, wonderful prophets. We read of amazing conversions, amazing unity, amazing deliverances from prison and from the power of evil spirits, and amazing divine direction as this tiny movement from the edge of the map spread to the heart of the capital of the empire, Rome itself. Luke makes a special point of this, because he has a particular purpose in Acts. He wants to show that the Christian faith is the truth, and he stresses three main grounds for this conviction. They come frequently in Acts, and are a regular feature in Christian writers of the next two centuries. The

Christian gospel is attested as true, Luke believes, through the fulfilment of prophecy, through signs and wonders, and through the irresistible progress of the gospel. Be that as it may, there can be no doubt that signs and wonders mark the trinitarian God we worship. Whether we look at the work of the Father in the Old Testament, the work of Jesus in the Gospels, or the work of the Spirit in Acts, signs and wonders are very prominent.

Signs and wonders in the New Testament

God works wonders: that is clear from Scripture. But the record is far from straightforward. In a handful of references, notably Romans 15:19, Hebrews 2:4 and the longer ending to Mark (16:9–20), they are brought before us as aids to evangelism, palpable marks of the Lord's presence. In my own ministry I can think of several such cases. But it is wrong to suppose that this is the main New Testament emphasis. It is not. Three factors need to be borne in mind.

First, the signs are primarily Christocentric. In the synoptic Gospels, miracles are called 'acts of power'. In John's Gospel they are 'signs', signs of who Jesus is and what he can do. He who feeds the multitude *is* the Bread of Life; he who raises Lazarus *is* the Resurrection and the Life. There are seven such signs in John, and they interweave act and interpretation. The first twelve chapters of John contain the book of signs: it is followed, and balanced, by 'the book of the passion'. Not either one without the other: together they take us to the heart of Jesus' person and work. The signs in the Fourth Gospel are expressly and exclusively keys to who Jesus is. They are not models for disciples to follow. This needs to be borne in mind when excessive emphasis is laid on the missions of the twelve and the seventy in the synoptic Gospels, where they are told to extend the work of the Messiah's Kingdom by signs and wonders.

Second, signs and wonders do not necessarily lead to faith. Indeed, if we look at the Gospels and Acts, we see that they normally spring from faith rather than induce it. Matthew 12:38–9 is a case in point. The people to whom Jesus was speaking had seen miracle after miracle. Between Matthew 8:1 and 9:8 there are no less than seven of them, followed by more in Matthew 9–11. In Matthew 12 itself, three 'signs and wonders' have been recorded; and still, with cynical hardness of heart, the Pharisees say, 'Show us a sign.' Jesus' reply is very instructive. He tells them that their attitude is wrong: they belong to an 'adulterous' generation, unfaithful to God, their Husband. He goes on to show that no sign can *compel* faith: it is always possible to explain it away, if you are determined enough. And his reference to Jonah alerts us to the fact that the cross and resurrection constitute the supreme sign. It is there that you meet God, not necessarily in any sign.

A large number of gospel references, therefore, dissuade us from sign-seeking, Mark 8:11–12, John 4:48 and Matthew 16:1–4 among them. Clearly, in the days of Jesus' flesh, it was an incredulous and rebellious generation that was so keen to see signs. This suggests that, though there will be supernatural signs from time to time if God is at work, we would be unwise to major on them. People can all too easily look for the wrong thing, and while seeking sensation, remain locked in rebellion.

Third, signs and wonders do not necessarily come from God. They did not in the days of the Pharaoh's magicians. They did not when charismatic Pharisees cast out demons (Matt. 12:27). They did not when Simon Magus effected his cures (Acts 8:11). The Gospels warn us against regarding signs and wonders as the mark of authentic ministry: 'False Christs and false prophets will arise and show signs and wonders, to lead astray, if possible, the elect. But take heed; I have told you all things beforehand' (Mark 13:22). Matthew 24:24 is equally explicit, as is 2 Thessalonians 2:9, 'The coming of the lawless one by the activity of Satan will be with all power and with pretended signs and wonders.'

I have seen something of that. I have been assailed by demonic tongues, counterfeiting the real thing. I have been present at demonic visions. I have had an ex-medium recount to me his experience of demonic healings in his pre-Christian days. So perhaps it is not surprising that the Bible deprecates resting our faith too much on signs. The supreme sign to which it points us is not God's power in miracle: rather, it is to God's 'weakness' on a cross.

The place of signs and wonders in the church

In the light of this ambivalent attitude towards the miraculous in the Gospels and the epistles, what is the right place for signs and wonders in today's church? The answer is nowhere more clearly given than in the Corinthian epistles: they speak to a situation very like ours. The Corinthians clearly saw God's power in miracles as the most desirable thing in the Christian life. Paul did not. To him, Christlikeness is the most important thing. He expects to see miracles among them, but most of all he longs for holiness of life, and willingness to suffer. The power and the glory are inextricably interlaced with the obedience and the suffering.

Some years ago, a book was published with the intriguing title *Living in the Banana Shape*. It drew attention to an important truth. There is an overlap where 'the age to come' has invaded 'this present age'. That overlap is, if you like, banana-shaped. This age is dominated by sin and failure, suffering and death. The age to come is marked by the Spirit of beauty, joy, and power. And we, we are living in the banana: open to the powers of the age to come, but also subject to the powers of sin, suffering and death. To be sure, we have been released from the tyrannical grip of these giant forces, but we are not yet out of their clutches. We have been set free so that we may fight them. And fight them we do, in the power of the Holy Spirit. He is the first instalment of the age to come, not its ultimate fulfilment. There is no final fulfilment in this life. We live between the ages. We live not in 'No Man's Land', but in 'Both Man's Land'. And one day we shall be for ever in that land where 'death shall be no more, neither shall there be mourning nor crying nor pain any more, for the former things have passed away' (Rev. 21:4). But not yet.

In the meantime there is a fight to be fought, and a race to be run. We must expect hardships and reverses as well as signal marks of God's supernatural power in our world. There is no place for triumphalism in the Christian life, least of all in the ministry of the evangelist. Equally, there is no place for defeatism. We are not left to the mercy of the old powers which hold sway in this age. We taste the powers of the age to come. We believe in both the cross and the resurrection.

Much Western Christianity has concentrated too much on the cross, symbolising the suffering, weakness and sorrow of our earthly existence. There is truth in that, but not exhaustive truth. Charismatic Christianity, on the other hand, has concentrated too much on the resurrection, on the transcendental power of the new life, its signs and wonders and excitement. A realistic Christianity will hold equally fast to *both*. And that is what you see in Paul, who claims that 'The signs of a true apostle were performed among you in all patience, with signs and wonders and mighty works' (2 Cor. 12:12); but almost in the same breath confides, 'I am content with weaknesses, insults, hardships, persecutions, and calamities; for when I am weak, then I am strong' (2 Cor. 12:10).

Power in weakness. That is the place of signs and wonders in today's church in general, and in evangelism in particular. We should expect God the Evangelist to be signally at work among us, as we set out in his name to storm the citadels of unbelief. We should expect and encourage spiritual gifts. We should expect God to heal physical, emotional and spiritual disease. We should 'resist the devil' when a person is manifestly in bondage to dark forces, and we should, in the name of Christ, claim his deliverance. We should trust God to show us in general, and in particular, his will for our service in his cause: it may be through common counsel, or the impact of a piece of Scripture, or maybe through a dream, a vision or a prophetic utterance. But we must never forget that the best is yet to be. We live in a fallen world. We inherit a fallen nature. Inevitably, sin, suffering, failure and death will play a part in our experience. If Jesus Christ, our head, suffered and died, there is no way in which his followers can escape hardship. And if Jesus Christ, our head, is risen from the dead, there is no way in which he will fail to display in our midst the power of his resurrection as he takes us into partnership in his mission.

FURTHER READING

Bill Burnett (ed.), *By My Spirit* (Hodder & Stoughton)
Michael Cassidy, *Bursting the Wineskins* (Hodder & Stoughton)
John Dawson, *Taking Our Cities for God* (Creation House)
C. H. Dodd, *The Apostolic Preaching and its Developments* (Hodder & Stoughton)
Michael Green, *I Believe in the Holy Spirit* (Hodder & Stoughton)
Michael Green, *I Believe in Satan's Downfall* (Hodder & Stoughton)
J. I. Packer, *Evangelism and the Sovereignty of God* (Inter-Varsity Press)
J. I. Packer, *God Has Spoken* (Hodder & Stoughton)
Frank Peretti, *Piercing the Darkness* (Kingsway Publications)
Frank Peretti, *This Present Darkness* (Kingsway Publications)
Nicholas Rivett-Carnac, *On this Rock* (Hodder & Stoughton)
Robert Warren, *In the Crucible* (Hodder & Stoughton)
David Wells, *God the Evangelist* (Eerdmans)
John White, *When the Spirit Comes with Power* (Hodder & Stoughton)
John Wimber, *Power Evangelism* (Hodder & Stoughton)
John Wimber, *Power Healing* (Hodder & Stoughton)

15
Evangelism Through the Local Church

This book has covered a good deal of ground, and it may be useful in a final chapter to draw some of the threads together. How is it possible to take an average, somewhat sleepy church in the post-Christian Western World, and turn it into a warm, vital body of loving Christians who engage in continuous evangelism? We Christians have become very settled in our ways, and those ways no longer reach out effectively to our society.

HINDRANCES

As we have seen, our churches are organised for maintenance, not for mission. They are inward looking, and the ministry is expected to nourish the faithful, not to reach out into the chill waters of contemporary unbelief to draw new members in. Many clergy have never led anyone to faith. It is not a requirement for ordination in most denominations. Theological colleges and seminaries may well not even include any instruction in evangelism in their curriculum. Students can graduate from them without ever having been on an outreach project, in some instances without even having preached a sermon. But if they had trained in Jakarta, for example, these ordinands would have faced a very different preparation for their future work. They might know less about textual criticism and patristics, but they would not have been allowed to graduate until they had personally brought into being a new church of not less than thirty baptised members. No wonder there is a fantastic explosion of new churches in Indonesia, when evangelism is given such priority.

Not only are most churches inward looking, and our ministers ill-equipped for evangelism, but there are other very serious hindrances in the way of churches becoming evangelistic in orientation. Church members are not in good spiritual health. Ask yourself whether it is not the case in your local church that many of the members show scant signs of any vibrant relationship with Jesus Christ. If that is so, and one must never judge, then it is evident why there is no evangelism. You cannot introduce someone to a person you do not know. It is as basic as that.

Lack of Christian confidence and assurance is another debilitating sickness in many of our churches. Its presence is fatal if you are looking for advance. If I am not sure whether I am a Christian at all, how can I be of much use to others? What is more, in many of the mainline churches the level of teaching is so low and so ill-focused that many of the congregation would have the utmost difficulty in leading any seeker to faith, let alone in answering basic objections. They have simply never been taught. Training the laity for mission never enters the minds of many ministers: and if it did, they would not know where to start. It is apparent that we are facing massive hindrances to evangelism in the local church. But there are more that can be mentioned. The prevailing secularism and relativism of our hedonistic culture have eroded our attitudes, and the motivation to be up and doing in our Master's service eludes us. Many churches have never been exposed to the fresh oxygen of new converts coming into the still waters of their congregation. As a consequence, they do not expect it, and the wick of faith and expectancy burns low. Worship becomes bondage to tradition, not openness to God, and stagnation sets in. One of the most serious problems of all is the ghetto mentality which increasingly seems to mark Christian communities, as their numbers shrink. They cling together for warmth. They have less and less friends who are not church people. Instead, they are taken up with a round of in-church activities. If an evangelistic event took place in their church, there is, frankly, nobody they could hope to bring along.

IMPERATIVES

If the hindrances are massive, the imperatives for evangelism are stark. In many parts of the country the church will fade away if evangelism does not take place. A sociological survey has recently been conducted into the state of Canadian Christianity. It shows decline at every level. Many of the churches I visit have congregations so elderly that it is clear that within twenty years they will have vanished, unless there is a massive turn round in the priorities and membership of the church.

The absence of evangelism in so many local churches has another serious consequence. It means that the spiritual and intellectual muscles of church members do not get exercised, and are never strong. Church life without evangelism breeds weak and feeble Christians.

And how are weakened Christians going to cope with the massive needs in society all around them? The growth of urbanisation, the escalation of crime, the sexual shambles of our day, the moral decay in public life, the corruption in government circles, the destruction of the environment, the signs of our decadence and insensate selfishness on every side: how are we to make an impact on these things with an enfeebled church? Nor is the world population standing still. Global figures released in 1987 give an added note of urgency to world evangelisation – in which the local churches must play their part. Estimates indicate that by the end of this century the world population will increase by 1.3 billion to a total of 6.2 billion. That increase of ninety-three million will exceed the population of Mexico, the eleventh most populous country in the world! Leighton Ford, the Canadian evangelist, when commenting on these figures, remarked: 'It is imperative that we communicate this challenge to people in the pews. Comfortable Christians can too easily become preoccupied with secondary concerns.'

But for a genuine disciple of Jesus Christ there is one overriding imperative: and that is Jesus' final command to go into all the world and make disciples. That is what he died for. That is the supreme passion of the loving, rescuing God he came to reveal. Evangelism is very close to the heart of God. And that should be imperative enough for us.

REFLECTION

If we feel overwhelmed by all this, some reflections comparing the initial attitudes of the church with its current practices may be in order.

The early church made evangelism its number-one priority. Today it comes far down the list. Many local churches have, I suspect, never once debated it in their decision-making body.

The early church had a deep compassion for people without Christ. Many sections of the modern church are far from convinced that it much matters whether you know Christ or not. Other religions are nearly, if not quite as good. Humanists live blameless lives. And in any case, God is far too loving to damn anyone.

The early church was very flexible in the ways it preached the good news, but was utterly opposed to syncretism of any sort. Many churches today are rigid in their preaching methods but thoroughly open to syncretism.

The early church was very sensitive to the leading of the Holy Spirit. In the modern churches of the West, managerial skills, committee meetings, and endless discussion generally replace serious dependence on the guidance of God.

The early church was not unduly minister-conscious. There is notorious difficulty in attempting to derive definitively any modern ministerial patterns from the New Testament records. Yet today, everything hinges on the minister. The paid servant of the church is expected to engage in God-talk. Others are not.

The early church expected every member to be a witness to Christ and his risen presence and power. Today witness is at a discount compared with dialogue; and it is only expected of certain gifted clergy at best, not of run-of-the-mill lay people.

In the early church, buildings were unimportant: they did not own any during the period of the church's greatest advance. Today, buildings seem all-important. Their upkeep consumes the money and the interest of the members, often plunges them into debt, and insulates them from those who do not go to church. The very word 'church' has changed its meaning. It no longer denotes a company of people: it means a building.

In the early church, evangelism was the spontaneous, natural chattering of good news. It was engaged in continuously by all types of Christians as a matter of course and privilege. Today, it is spasmodic, highly organised, expensive, and usually dependent on the skills and the enthusiasm of visiting specialists.

In the early church, the policy was to go out to where people were, and make disciples of them. Today, it is to invite people along to churches, where they feel ill at ease, and subject them to sermons. Today's church attempts suction, invitation, in-drag. The early church practised explosion, invasion, outreach.

In the early church, the gospel was frequently argued about in the philosophical schools, discussed in the streets, talked over in the laundry. Today, it is not discussed very much at all, and especially not on secular ground. It belongs in church, on a Sunday, and a properly ordained minister should do all the talking.

In the early church, whole communities seem to have come over to the faith together. In the atomised church of the West, individualism has run riot, and evangelism, like much else, tends to reach its climax in one-to-one encounter.

In the early church, the maximum impact was made by the changed lives and quality of community among the Christians. Today, much Christian lifestyle is almost indistinguishable from that of those who profess no Christian faith, and much church fellowship is conspicuous for its coolness.

It is worth reflecting on these remarkable contrasts, along with the no less striking contrasts in effectiveness between the early Christians and ourselves. If we want to take evangelism seriously in the local church, we could do worse than go back to our roots.

WHAT CAN A MINISTER DO TO MOBILISE THE LOCAL CHURCH FOR EVANGELISM?

He can do a great deal. But it will be costly. If you are a minister, here, I suggest, are some of the things that are needed.

First, you must gain a passion for evangelism. This is more often caught than taught. It may be caught from the Lord, caught from going on a mission with others, caught, too, from someone in your congregation. But unless you have a passion for reaching out with the good news to those who do not know it, it will be hard to mobilise your church.

Second, you need to teach about it. You need to teach the importance of evangelism. Along with worship, it is, in some shape or form, the primary calling of all Christians. We do not live for ourselves. Our Christianity is meant to be infectious.

Third, you need to model it. You need to start preaching evangelistically from time to time in church. You must try to help individuals to faith, both in your personal study and in the occasional services, at birth, death and marriage, which offer important opportunities. If you model evangelism, however bad you may feel you are at it, it will catch on in the church.

Fourth, you need to review the worship of your church. Are its friendliness, its prayerfulness, its concern for the locality, its music, its facilities such as would convince the casual visitor of its relevance to real life? If not, changes are called for. And they will be resisted from within!

Fifth, you need to build up a core of committed people, renewed by the Holy Spirit and actively concerned to allow his leading and Lordship in their lives and the church. You need to love them, to invest yourself in them, to train them, to encourage them. They will become the front-line troops in evangelism.

Sixth, you need to take great care in staff appointments. Do not appoint men and women who are like you and will agree with all your policies. Appoint people who are different from you, men and women with different gifts who appeal to different kinds of people. The youth pastor, the music director and the assistant pastor are three of the key posts. You need to become a fellowship of leadership. You need a unity that is born of diversity.

Seventh, you need to teach the church the importance of the spiritual weapons God has given us, rather than the material resources we think so vital. Prayer, spiritual warfare, Scripture, openness to the Spirit, holiness, love: these are the things that will make your church evangelistic. It will not be the techniques or the finance or the manuals on evangelism or the revival campaigns.

You would be wise, too, to make room in your worship for modern music as well as traditional: not the one in opposition to the other, but a blend. You could explore the use of dance in worship. You could get a drama workshop going. You could begin to do more and more in homes, thus encouraging the use of hospitality in Christ's cause. You could ensure that Christian literature in given a proper place.

You need to involve lay people with you in outreach. In this way you model body life, gain from the gifts they develop, and spread the enthusiasm that is such an attractive part of evangelism. The team may consist of one, or one hundred: I often use both. The important thing is to share the experience of evangelism with one or more partners. In this way you are building up your own congregation while serving others.

This will inevitably involve you in training. The actual equipping may be done by others. But you need to see that it happens: training in speaking, in personal evangelism, in organisation, in youth work, and in the nurture of new Christians. It can be done by teaching, by reading, by role-play, and by apprenticeship. But training is a vital part of developing an evangelistic ministry in a church. A fascinating video course called *Person to Person* has been devised jointly by the Bible Society, Campus Crusade and the Scripture Union in England. This is a very flexible instrument, using talk, video, Bible study, literature and practical experience. It is designed to 'motivate, equip, and mobilise your church for evangelism', and it has not only won a prestigious award but has effectively trained thousands of people in evangelism (write to *Person to Person*, Box 240, Swindon, SN5 7HA, England, for further details).

As a minister, you will be able to make maximum use of the great festivals of the church. You will be able to co-operate with other church leaders in the town in wider outreach. You will be able to suggest ways in which the congregation can engage in some of the varied forms of evangelism suggested in chapter 12. Most of all, you will develop the instinct for godly opportunism. You will find yourself sensing when a new initiative is possible that may be fruitful in evangelism. It will become not a chore, not a project, but a way of life.

WHAT CAN A LAY PERSON DO TO PROMOTE EVANGELISM THROUGH HIS LOCAL CHURCH?

It is sad but true that many lay people are frustrated by their local church. Frustrated, maybe, by the introversion, or by the worship, or by the way the minister keeps everything in his own hands, or by the maintenance mentality. People have told me, with tears, of the years of waiting and praying for things to change. Sometimes their patience is rewarded. Sometimes it is not, and they tend either to lose heart or to go elsewhere. That is sad, but understandable. What is most sad of all is if they drop out of active Christian membership anywhere, as a result of their bad experience of the church.

If you find yourself a lay person in a lively church, with an emphasis on the ministry of the whole Christian body to the surrounding locality, you will have no problems except where to inject your limited time and energies. But if your local church is a disappointment to you, what then? What can you do to further the spread of the good news?

The first thing is to maintain your spiritual glow. Jesus looks above all for our first love, the love of the newly engaged, the love of the honeymoon couple (Rev. 2:4). It is so important to maintain that. It can be done partly through prayer, partly through the reading of Scripture, partly through conferences and spiritual books. One of the most helpful and expedient devices is to find one other person who can become a prayer partner. The stimulus of a friend can do wonders in maintaining our own spiritual vitality when there is not too much to encourage at church.

But don't give up on the church. Who knows? God may plan to revitalise it through you. And that can never happen if you are judgemental and critical. All your love and tact and perseverance are going to be required. If the minister himself seems to lack vitality, go out of your way to encourage him. He may have had decades of unresponsive work, and have lost his sparkle as a result. It is salutary to remember that few people enter the ordained ministry these days for wrong reasons. They want – or at least they once wanted – the best. They may not have had many encouragements during their career. They may not have had a good training. They may not have had many spiritual high-points which stimulated their faith. Their own devotional life may have suffered erosion. But with love and encouragement from yourself and others in the congregation whose faith burns brightly, you may well see a real revival of faith, joy and usefulness in your minister. Don't give up on him.

The church services may not be the most exciting either. But that is no reason for absenting yourself. You can do a great deal on your own initiative. Take pains to prepare yourself before you go to worship. Determine to meet the Lord, whatever the obstacles in your surroundings. Pray fervently. Sing with joy in your heart to God. Listen attentively to the Word of God when it is read. Seek to obey what God is saying to you through the sermon, rather than criticise the shortcomings of the preacher. And be on the lookout for someone you can invite back to lunch. Offer your services judiciously when you see strategic areas where you could serve. It may well be right to stand for office in the church, because from that position you can probably effect change. Seek to be an encourager of others, and you may win love and trust in due course. Be faithful to your church, so that the dependability of your Christian life shines out. You may need to go away for a silent retreat from time to time, or to another church for the worship and teaching at their evening service. But loyalty and enterprise, bathed in prayer, and offered in humility, may well transform your church situation over the years.

Another very obvious, but neglected, area is this. Make friends outside the church. Do not surrender to the ghetto mentality. You are called to be salt and light, and like your Master to have lots of friends among 'the outcasts and sinners'. Your job, your sport, your leisure interests can all be magnetic. Pray that God will draw people to you through these very natural avenues. He will, if you will let him. Your friendliness, your hospitality, your sense of discovery will inevitably cause interest and bring seekers across your path.

There is a new surge of interest in the impact of an attractive Christian life these days, as a major instrument in evangelism. They call it lifestyle evangelism, and it is written about most amusingly and attractively in Becky Pippert's *Out of the Saltshaker* and Don Posterski's *Reinventing Evangelism*. If folk are not impressed by the people we are, they are not going to want to know what makes us tick. But if they are intrigued, they may well want to find out, and we shall have earned the right to speak. Sheer friendship is at the heart of it, friendship for people whether they come to faith or not. And we take into that friendship a vibrant, though unvocalised, friendship with Christ. In due course it is bound to show.

We can all think of people like that. They laugh at problems. Their lives have clearly been transformed. They are fun to be with. They are wholehearted in everything they do. They are outward-looking people, not taken up all the time with their own concerns. There is a warm, unostentatious, practical love about them. They are concerned for justice. They care about the poor and those who are hurting. They are not enslaved by past custom. They are great people to have as friends.

That is what lifestyle evangelism is all about. And it is eminently open to you, however unhelpful you feel your church may be. It is actually one of the very best ways of evangelism, because it is personal and authentic. It is absolutely indispensable if we are going to help our friends to Christ. We have got to be living close to him ourselves, and that simply has to show in the way we behave.

It is absolutely indispensable, but by itself it is absolutely inadequate. For none of us could ever fully embody all that the gospel of Jesus Christ means. And unless we are willing to speak, and tell our friend the source of the difference that intrigues him or her, they are likely simply to think we are nice people. Real evangelism demands Christian presence and Christian proclamation. They are not alternatives. They belong together, and together they bring others into the family.

So you need to practise telling your story. We have all got a story, of what God has done in our lives. And if our friendship has been real, people will want to hear us on this subject as well as others. We have nothing to be embarrassed about. It is quite unthreatening for the hearer. And it is unthreatening for you, too. Because, unlike a debate or an argument, nobody is going to be able to deny your experience. So it is an easy way in, and a very natural one, to developing a conversation which could help your friend to Christ, as we saw in chapter 10.

There are all sorts of other ways in which Christians who do not have much support or pastoral oversight in their local church can operate effectively in the cause of the good news. They may find openings along the lines of their natural talents. They may be drawn into some para-church organisation. Nor should they see that as a second best. Often para-church agencies are the best ones for the particular work they are called to do. Christian work in Muslim countries, for example, is often more effective through literature and radio than through the local church. Effective work in universities is often carried out more naturally and imaginatively by fellow students than by the local church, which is inevitably further removed. If you pray and yield your talents to the Lord, he is likely to take you up on your offer. You may find that you are very good with young people, or with helping prisoners after their release from jail, or with overseas students, or, as is one lady I met recently, with beauty queens! Whatever your gift, offer it to the Lord and he will not only accept it, and give you joy and fulfilment in it, but make it an avenue for his love to flow through you to others. Yes, there is a tremendous lot a lay Christian can do, even if things are not good at the church.

WHAT CAN CHURCH LIFE DO TO PROMOTE EVANGELISM THROUGH THE LOCAL CHURCH?

Once again, the answer is 'much every way'. Any who have a share in the formation of church life can bring influence to bear at the congregational level.

The quality of Sunday worship is obviously a top priority. Arriving in good time, preparation before the time of worship, genuine welcome, hospitality through coffee after the service, and lots of lunch parties to which newcomers can be invited: all of these things help to turn the attitudes of a congregation outwards – and that is where evangelism begins. In planning the services, the place of silence, the mix of old and new in hymnody and liturgy, the opening of the service for the vocal participation of members, the imagination given to the music and the preaching, the starting of an adult Sunday school, the formation of a banner group to make bright hangings for the church which embody the faith and love of the congregation: all these things can help. Concern for the social and financial needs within the congregation, opportunities for people to be prayed for after services, and to give thanks in public when prayers have been answered, the development of every member ministry – if these things are happening in church life, evangelism is almost sure to follow as summer follows spring. And people will stay around after services to chat and to be prayed with. Groups will congregate in homes and will want to talk over issues in their Christian lives. Pre-planned projects like evangelistic sermons, open-air witness, concerts or supper parties will emerge at the initiative of the members of the church, provided that the atmosphere is right. But that atmosphere has to be loving and encouraging.

When love reigns in a church, everything begins to take off. It is like when the sun shines in our garden: everything starts to grow. When there is love, members of the church will be prepared to risk making mistakes, knowing that it will not matter, and that they will be loved all the same. Love like that will become infectious. It cannot be held back by church doors. It will flow out into the community. Real love – unselfish love, Calvary love – is in very short supply in our bleeding world. And once God's own love takes hold of a congregation people are bound to be drawn to its source in God himself. That is the most powerful and effective evangelism. And nowhere is that evangelism better demonstrated than in the local church. It is here that the gospel's impact becomes visible. It is here that people are seen to be real by those who live among them. It is here that social issues can be addressed – issues that everyone knows about, because they live in the locality. It is in the local church that people see a focal point for Christianity and can be persuaded to investigate it – if they are intrigued enough.

I am convinced that there is no evangelistic force so powerful as a really loving, outward-looking local church. It is the key to evangelism in this age which is suspicious of the high-powered sales-technique and at the same time well aware of the emptiness of materialism, the breakdown of relationships, and the shortness of life. There is plenty of spiritual hunger out there. We do not have to make people hungry; we do have to persuade them that we have bread. And the only way that will be done will be by individuals and churches being so full of the love of God that it is palpable. People will see it in the worship. They will see it in the caring. They will see it as the good news is explained against such a background.

'You shall love the Lord your God with all your heart, and with all your soul, and with all your mind, and with all your strength' (Mark 12:30). That is worship. 'You shall love your neighbour as yourself' (Mark 12:31). That is evangelism. And it is best embodied in a local church, warts and all. 'A new commandment I give to you, that you love one another; even as I have loved you, that you also love one another,' said Jesus (John 13:34). When that is embodied in a local church, it is profoundly attractive. For, as Disraeli recognised, 'We are all born for love . . . It is the principle of existence and its only end.' John Milton once called love 'the golden key that opens the palace of eternity'. That key is in the hand of every local church. And it was fashioned in that same eternity to which it summons us all, 'For God so loved the world that he gave his only Son, that whoever believes in him should not perish but have eternal life' (John 3:16).

FURTHER READING

Michael Green, *Freed to Serve* (Hodder & Stoughton)
Don Posterski, *Reinventing Evangelism* (Inter-Varsity Press)
Howard Snyder, *Liberating the Church* (Inter-Varsity Press)
Paul Stevens, *Liberating the Laity* (Inter-Varsity Press)
David Watson, *I Believe in the Church* (Hodder & Stoughton)
David Watson, *I Believe in Evangelism* (Hodder & Stoughton)

PART FOUR

PRACTICAL APPENDICES

Appendix A
A Course for Enquirers
Michael Green

ADVANTAGES

The advantages of running such a course are considerable.

a. You immediately demonstrate by your willingness to hold such a group that your Christian faith has nothing to fear from honest enquiry.

b. You attract people who would not be willing to sit in church and listen to a sermon. A group where open encounter and disagreement are welcomed is very attractive to some people.

c. You will tend to draw contacts you have made personally, or those who are already closely linked to someone in the congregation – a wife, husband, boyfriend. Therefore you will have support and prayer in the background.

d. If you are successful in introducing members of your group to Christ, they are likely to become articulate and courageous Christians. If not, they will leave with a lot more respect for an intelligent Christian faith than they had when they came.

e. You will challenge some very unchurched people, often opinionated and ignorant about Christianity, to examine the basic evidence for themselves.

f. Remember that the same is true of agnostics as of footballers: 'The bigger they are, the harder they fall.' There is no need therefore to fear handling a group like that. The Holy Spirit is well able to transform the most awkward and belligerent among them.

PRINCIPLES

a. *Relationships are vital*, between the leader(s) and the members of the group, and between each other. Warm relationships help to facilitate good, honest discussion and to avoid quarrels.

b. *The invitation is vital*. The persons invited need to be made to feel that they are special, that their views will be taken seriously, that there need be no feeling of embarrassment, and that no pressure will be exerted. I often find it is best, therefore, to have only two Christians present, hosting and leading the group (i.e., to be in a manifest minority, cheerful and unabashed!).

c. *The aim is vital*. It should be made abundantly clear before people come that their aim is to assess the truth or otherwise of Christianity, that the heart of Christianity is Christ, and that therefore consideration, however wide-ranging, will constantly focus on him. It is emphatically not going to be a talk shop about the religions of the world. If the aim is not made plain to the participants, and adhered to in the discussions, the coherence and usefulness of the group will dissipate. Discovery will be replaced by opinion. The possibility of encounter will be shut out by talk.

d. *The ambience of the meeting is vital*. There is all the world of difference between meeting in a cold church hall and in the relaxed atmosphere of a home. Open up your home. Go to some trouble over the arrangements. Always have food and drink available as a mark of hospitality, and if the first meeting can be over a good meal, so much the better. You aim to get to know each other, not simply each other's views. You want to be fellow travellers down the road of enquiring into truth, not antagonists trading intellectual punches.

e. *Scripture is vital*. It has a power all its own. They are likely to be ignorant of it. Make it plain from the outset that if they are enquiring into the truth of Christianity they will need to look at the foundation documents, not necessarily as 'inspired Scripture', but at least as honest testimony which has to be taken into account by any serious students of the subject. So have some copies of a modern translation of the Bible available for them to borrow and look into. You cannot expect them to bring their own.

f. *Exposure is vital*. They, like yourself, need to be willing to face honest exposure if they are to advance. This exposure will be fourfold.

First, exposure to reason: in the debates which will follow, people need to feel free to advance their views without fear, but to have them assailed without taking umbrage.

Second, exposure to evidence is crucial. Refusal to do that leads to obscurantism. So they need to be willing to read the occasional book, perhaps hear an occasional exceptional speaker, and, most important of all, to read one of the Gospels or preferably the whole New Testament while engaged on this enquiry into Christian truth.

Third, they need to be exposed to experience. Christianity is not a collection of dogmas, but the worship of a person. Christians believe Christ can be met, both individually and corporately. Therefore members will need to listen to and weigh the testimonies to experience of Christ which may emerge during the life of the group. Indeed they will, as members, begin to discover him for themselves: and testimony from newly convinced fellow seekers is powerful among the rest of the group. At least once or twice during the life of the group, they should also be strongly urged to experience the quality of Christians at worship. Needless to say, some churches are more suited for this than others.

Finally, they need to be exposed to prayer. Make no bones about it. If there is a living God, he can be met and communicated with. Do not be in the least embarrassed, for instance, at ending a meeting with prayer for God to make himself known and to guide those who are seeking him. As with Scripture, testimony and worship, prayer has a powerful, implicit authenticity (and indeed authority) which may get people further in three minutes than they got in three hours of discussion earlier in the evening.

g. *Method is vital.* Make it plain that you will moderate the discussion, but will not dominate it. Encourage people to come regularly each week for the limited duration of the course. No views are forbidden: open discussion is the order of the day. But as the moderator of the discussion, keep veering back to Jesus and the resurrection, the two really powerful evidential grounds for Christianity.

COURSES

I suggest that a course for enquirers should be of about eight weeks' duration. Much shorter will be sketchy and superficial; much longer will lose members.

There are many ways of running such a course. Here are four.

a. Use a video series such as David Watson's *Jesus Then and Now*, referred to in chapter eleven. This is designed to give a twenty-minute input on a subject central to the Christian claim, to be followed by discussion. Before each session, make sure you have seen the video a couple of times. Decide how you are going to handle the discussion. Prepare some good diagnostic questions in case the discussion dries up.

Next week show the succeeding segment of the video, on some other aspect of Christian belief and behaviour, and take the discussion on from there. By the end of a few sessions people will be hungry to find out more, and will become familiar with looking at New Testament evidence; they may even be wanting to join you in short prayers, even before having come to an explicit faith in Christ.

b. Use an inductive Bible study. The Revd Dick Lucas at St Helen's Church, Bishopsgate, London, has made extensive and effective use of a course based on St Mark's Gospel, entitled *Read, Mark, Learn!*

The Navigators, a Christian organisation specialising in thoughtful outreach among agnostics, do this sort of thing particularly well. I recommend Jim Petersen's *Evangelism for our Generation*, which has an excellent Appendix containing a step-by-step investigative study of the Gospel of John, entitled 'Twenty-Four Hours with John', which he has used extensively. It would be a good tool to use, or to inspire you to devise a similar course of your own.

c. Make the whole procedure inductive. Start the first session with introductions, make plain the ground-rules, and then say: 'Right, now let's see what is the most serious obstacle each of us has to becoming a committed disciple of Christ. What one thing is there which, if it could be resolved to your satisfaction, would leave you open to respond to his claims?'

If you put it in some such way, you will probably avoid the hot air that would otherwise emerge; you will concentrate people's thoughts on the one really big thing that is standing in their way; and you will be keeping rigorously before them the goal of Christian commitment to which you are unashamedly hoping to direct them. Be joyfully unembarrassed about your own Christian faith and your desire that they share it: 'You tell me what you don't believe, and I'll tell you what I do believe about Jesus, and why.'

They will come up with all sorts of attacks on the hypocrisy and failures of the church, together with a variety of other chips on the shoulder. Many of these will have much justice to them, and this must, of course, be readily acknowledged. The church may have failed them. Some Christians may be hypocrites. Their prayers may not have been answered. They may have had too much 'religion' when young . . . and all the rest of it. But constantly make them face up to Jesus, and the grounds we have for believing who he is, what he has done for us, and how he can be met.

You may take one or even two sessions clearing the ground of brambles of this sort. But having done so you are likely to come up with half a dozen critical issues which people have raised, to which you can address yourselves in an ordered way in the weeks that follow, ensuring that you cover the major evidence for the existence of God, the person and work of Jesus, the resurrection, and the steps to faith.

d. Plan your own course, perhaps as follows. Maybe call it 'Questions Worth Asking'?

QUESTIONS WORTH ASKING

WEEK ONE: 'WHY BELIEVE ANYTHING AT ALL?'

The emphasis here is on welcome, warmth and openness. Get each person to introduce themselves and their main difficulty about becoming a Christian. Speak for a few minutes on the heart of authentic Christianity, and how you found it. Encourage them to seek: 'Seek, and you will find.' Ask each one to read through a Gospel with an open mind in the course of the next two weeks.

Perhaps close the evening by examining the nature of belief. Dr James Sire does this very effectively by holding discussion seminars on 'Why Believe Anything At All?' which could well be adapted for this evening. Everyone believes something: but why *should* they believe what they *do* believe?

Inductively discover from the group two important issues which will bring much clarity to subsequent discussions. First, *why do* people believe? The answer may be sociological ('Because I was raised that way'), psychological ('In reaction against my parents'), philosophical ('It seems to be the most reasonable possibility') – or a variety of other possibilities. The second question is the important one: *Why should* people believe? Every reason but one can be shown to be inadequate. Truth is the only adequate basis for belief.

Go on to show them that Christianity ought only to be believed if it is true; that it makes precisely that claim; and that there are ways of checking it out. Sire gives seven such: the inherent attractiveness of Jesus; the internal consistency and coherence of the Christian view of reality; the explanatory power of the Christian world-view; the empirical evidence for the reliability of the New Testament; the obvious accuracy of the biblical account of human beings and their problems; the witness of the Christian church down the ages (there is a St Luke's Hospital in practically every country in the world!); and the testimony of Christianity's adherents to its life-changing power. You do not need to use Sire's evidences: create your own. But this would be a powerful way to close the first evening.

WEEK TWO: 'IS ANYONE THERE?'

There will be lots of discussion arising from last week. But as you move on to today's topic, outline the options about God. Will they settle for atheism, or for polytheism (like the ancient Romans), or for animism (like the spirit-worshippers), or for monism (like the New Agers and Hindus)? Keep them asking what gives the most convincing explanation for ourselves and our world. Acknowledge that pluralism, meaninglessness, suffering and technological success have all blunted belief in God, but suggest to them seven facts which, taken together, make belief in a living personal God highly probable:

a. The fact of the world. What accounts for life here? If chance, how can they explain the cause and effect principle which is everywhere apparent?

b. The fact of design in the world. Design is even more notable in nature than in the artifacts intelligent humans design. 'The heavens are telling the glory of God; and the firmament proclaims his handiwork' (Ps. 19:1).

c. The fact of personality. A live person is utterly different from a dead corpse or a robot. Can the personal spring from the impersonal? Can the higher (human personality) come from the lower (brute stuff, devoid of a Creator)?

d. The fact of values. We all have them, however we explain it.

How do you derive values out of time, chance and the impersonal? And that is what we are left with if there is no Creator.

e. The fact of conscience. It is universal, however we argue against it. It is not an infallible guide, but it points to standards which we 'ought' (i.e. 'owe it' . . . but to what or to whom?) to keep. It cannot be explained away as social conditioning, for it often points us away from what is to what should be. This inner law strongly suggests a Law-giver.

f. The fact of religion. Man is a religious animal. He must worship God or create his own idol, and this has always been the case. Is the universal religious instinct the only one of our instincts that has no reality to satisfy it? If so, what accounts for its prevalence and power?

g. But an intelligent Creator, personal, moral, the source of values, concerned for our worship and companionship, remains an unknown God unless he chooses to reveal himself. This he has done in Jesus Christ (John 1:1–5, 14; Heb. 1:1–2; Col. 2:9).

That should stir discussion! Tell them that you will move on to Jesus Christ next week.

WEEK THREE: 'WHO IS JESUS?'

So much rubbish about Jesus is currently on sale or on view that you may well need to establish the existence of the founder of Christianity from secular sources, such as Tacitus' *Annals* 15.44, Josephus' *Antiquities* 18.3, and Suetonius' *Claudius* 25. You may like to loan them my *World on the Run*, which conveniently leads them into the non-Christian evidence for Jesus. That he existed and was crucified is incontrovertible. But the crux is – was he more than man?

Jews, the original people among whom he came, were passionate monotheists, the hardest people in the world to convince that he was more than man. Yet they became convinced by seven factors:

a. His character. It has dominated mankind from that day to this, appealing equally to men and women, young and old, all types and nationalities. Show them his balance, his qualities, his attractiveness. What is there in his heredity and environment that explains such a character?

b. His teaching. It is the most wonderful the world has ever known. Nothing like it has emerged before or since. Its authority, its pungency, its profundity, its clarity set it apart from all other teaching. Take the Sermon on the Mount, and expose them to some of it, especially its conclusion.

c. His behaviour. He taught the highest standards of conduct, and, unlike any other human being before or since, he kept them. He claimed to be without sin. Every strand of the New Testament shows that his followers, who knew him intimately, agreed. Even his enemies, Judas, Pilate and the Pharisees, could not uphold an alternative claim.

d. His miracles. These are not an embarrassment to Christians. They were never done for selfish ends. They are embedded in almost all strands of the tradition about Jesus, reaching back as it does to within a few years of his life: there is Jewish attestation to them as well. They do not prove his deity, but they are highly congruous with it. All the miracles of his life are secondary to those of his incarnation and resurrection.

e. His fulfilment of prophecy. Different strands of the Old Testament were fulfilled in him: Son of Man, Son of God, Son of David, Suffering Servant, Melchizedek, the ultimate prophet, priest and king; a greater than the temple, a greater than Moses, a greater than Solomon, etc. He is even portrayed as the replacer of the Torah and the embodiment of the *shekinah* glory of God. Such a claim to fulfilment, concentrated in a single individual, is unparalleled. Many prophecies concerned his birth and his death, the two areas of life where it is hardest to fake fulfilment!

f. His claims. He claimed God as his 'Abba' (an utterly unique filial relationship). He claimed to forgive sins, to be worshipped, to rise from the grave, to judge mankind, to be the way to God, the truth about God and to embody the very life of God himself. What are we to make of claims like these?

g. His death. The unselfishness of it, the sacrifice of it, the sin-bearing of it, the victory of it, drew all sorts of people to him, and still do. The fact that such a person went willingly to such a fate, and the interpretation of it which he gave, convinced them. The resurrection put the cap on it. To it you will turn with them next week. In the meantime Jesus' own question is pertinent: 'But who do you say that I am?'

WEEK FOUR: 'IS THE RESURRECTION JUST A LOVELY STORY?'

The resurrection is the crux of Christianity. Above all else it enables us to determine whether or not Jesus was more than man. If it is true, it puts him in a class by himself. If it is false, the whole Christian faith collapses.

As you consider the resurrection, you may have to work your way through prejudice of various sorts. Scientific prejudice may have persuaded them that miracles do not happen; theological prejudice may have suggested to them that the origins of Easter are shrouded in inscrutable mystery; personal prejudice may have prevented them from ever looking at the evidence. So take them to it. There are basically two important questions to address.

First, is it true?

Five facts cohere and point in the same direction.

a. The man was dead. The public execution, the centurion's certificate, the blood and water, Pilate's ceding the corpse to Jesus' followers after the execution, all show that no 'Passover Plot' will do. Jesus was really dead. The Romans were expert at crucifixions: their victims did not survive.

b. The tomb was empty. That is agreed all around. It was empty because of either divine or human action. If the latter, then either the friends or the enemies of Jesus would have done it. The friends could not: they were psychologically incapable of it, and they could not have got past the stone and the guard. The enemies of Jesus would not: they were only too delighted to have him dead, and intended to do nothing to disturb that situation. The only alternative is that God raised Jesus from the dead. And that is congruous with the empty tomb, the state of the grave clothes, the flight of the guard, and the dawning of Easter faith.

c. The church was born. They had nothing initially to distinguish them from orthodox Judaism apart from their convictions about Jesus and the resurrection. Their three major innovations, baptism, the Eucharist and Sunday, are all incomprehensible without the resurrection.

d. Jesus appeared over a period of forty days to a wide cross-section of people: the twelve, James, Paul, Thomas, the five hundred, Mary Magdalene and the Virgin Mary, his mother. No hallucination theory will bear serious investigation. The resurrection appearances have no parallel in all history.

e. The lives of those who met Jesus after the resurrection were transformed. Lives of people who today come into contact with him are changed too. No 'myth' theory will hold water.

All five strands of evidence point the same way. Their impact is cumulative. And the assurance that Jesus is risen and alive has not grown more speculative and remote but has deepened and spread worldwide in the succeeding centuries. Nowadays a third of all mankind profess to subscribe to it.

Second, is it relevant?

It has relevance at three points.

a. It is relevant to the mind. It answers our deepest questions, such as 'Does God exist?' (Rom. 1:4), 'Do all religions lead to God?' (John 14:6) and 'After death – what?' (1 Cor. 15:20).

b. It is relevant to the heart. It speaks to our human condition of guilt (Acts 2:36; 10:40), depression (1 Pet. 1:3), fear (2 Tim. 1:12; Rom. 8:32), loneliness (Matt. 28:18–20) and moral defeat (Phil. 4:13).

c. It is relevant to the will. We need to make an informed decision about Christ in the light of it. Show them the logic (and the background) of Acts 17:31.

WEEK FIVE: 'WHAT SAY YOU . . . ?'

It is good to have something quite different this week. You have been giving a lot of input, albeit inductively and by means of discussion. It is time to major on two or three things, with the group members taking the lead.

First, you might ask one of them the previous week to see if he can answer a book like *Basic Christianity* by John Stott, or *Who Moved the Stone?* by Frank Morison. He or she could take the first part of the evening, seeking to present a rebuttal, and facing the questions which will emerge from the others in the room.

Alternatively, if by now some of the group have actually come to faith, you could encourage them to say so. It will make an enormous impact, and move the others in the same direction, despite their initial scepticism.

Another way of doing it is to ask them the week before to list their remaining outstanding obstacles in the way of faith. You will then prepare to respond to those when the meeting takes place. You will know that you are hitting the nail on the head, because you are answering their own questions. That gives them, too, a sense of being taken seriously. I always try to give away as much as I can, with integrity, to a questioner. He is sure to have some truth in what he says. If I can recognise that, it will help him to take on board my reply to his own sticking-point.

At all events, however you handle it, this is an important week to see how people are getting on in the course, and what movement has been made since the starting-positions etched out in the first session. You will also find that the more question-and-answer work you do, the more they will tend to argue against the weak points put forward by their colleagues. So it is not you and your fellow leader versus the rest, but a genuine, shared search after truth, coupled with an unwillingness to allow sloppy thinking to be tolerated, from whatever quarter. And remember, if you are worsted in a point, always be generous in acknowledging it and quick to apologise or retract it, as the case may be.

WEEK SIX: 'BUT WHAT ABOUT . . . ?'

If they have not already arisen, it is time to tackle two of the major intellectual objections to Christian belief: What about other faiths? and What about the problem of suffering?

You might care to refer to chapters 3 and 7 for fuller consideration of these points. Remember that these two issues may be massive problems keeping people from faith, or else massive smokescreens to hide the real reason for their refusal to turn to Christ. So be sensitive to the dynamics of the group and the individual members; be in earnest, be courteous, be honest, be biblical and be prepared to listen.

'Don't all religions lead to God?'

All religions certainly bear witness to the universal need and
sometimes-felt hunger for God (Acts 17:27). Most religions reflect
something of truth. However, though widely believed, the idea
that all religions are much the same, and go the same way, is
ludicrous.

First, it is probably uninformed. If he or she knew much about
other religions, your group member would not come up with so
simplistic an idea. It is a good idea to find out what they actually
know about any other faith, and then allow it to stand alongside
what the Bible teaches about God and man.

Second, it is certainly illogical. When compared, the world's
religions contradict each other on every topic that they teach. They
have contradictory doctrines of God, man, sin, salvation, ethics
and destiny. They are incompatible not in peripheral matters but
on essentials. Hinduism is polytheistic; Christianity is monotheistic. Buddhism is atheistic, while Christianity believes in a personal
God. Christianity believes in a God who has revealed himself in
the loving incarnation and atonement of Jesus, his Son; Islam
vehemently repudiates that, does not believe in atonement for sins
(you have to work it off in hell), and is clear that God never reveals
himself, only his commands. In Eastern monism your destiny is to
be eliminated as a sentient being, and after many reincarnations to
be incorporated in the impersonal One or Monad; in Christianity it
is to be raised to eternal life where you know God and enjoy him
for ever. By no stretch of the imagination can these various 'ways'
lead to the same destination. And the more the group knows about
the tenets of other faiths, the more clearly will the illogicality of
that assertion stand out.

Third, it is impossible spiritually. And for two reasons. One is
that we human beings can never pierce through to fully understand
the inscrutable God who made us and all the world. If we are to
know anything, it must be because he has revealed it. He *has*, in the
twin books of nature and Scripture.

What is more, we are finite and God is infinite. We are sinful and
he is holy. The 'shopper's mart' attitude to faiths masks the fact
that the person concerned has not begun to face up to his or her
bankruptcy before a holy God. Take such folk to Jeremiah 17:9,
Romans 3:10–20, Matthew 7:21–7, and Luke 13:3. Walk them
through the ethical sections of the Sermon on the Mount (Matt.
5–7) or the ten commandments (Exod. 20). That may well remove

their smugness and bring them low before the holy God who offers them mercy.

It is often very helpful to take your group to the explicit claims of Jesus and the early Christians: they have an inherent power (see Matt. 7:22–3; 11:25–30; 25:31–46; Mark 8:27–38; 14:61–2; Luke 4:16–21; 14:12–24; 19:1–10; John 1:14, 18; 3:10–21; 10:7–8; 11:25; 14:6, etc.). No wonder the apostles were convinced of Acts 4:12.

Other religions do *not* all equally lead to God. But be ready to meet a further objection on this contentious issue. They may well say, 'If you are right, all other religions are wrong.' Not completely. They may well have much that is good and true in them. But they are to the gospel of Christ as candles to the sun. You will not find in all of them put together any light which you cannot find in Jesus, and you will find in them much that is unworthy. Nowhere else will you hear of a personal God who values you so much that he came to seek you, allowed himself to be crucified for you (rebel though you are), rose triumphant over sin and suffering, and offers you new life now and hereafter. Compare Genesis 11:1–9 with John 14:6: it is the contrast between man-centred religion climbing ineffectually up to God, and God-centred salvation coming in personal form down to man.

'I can't believe in God with all this suffering in the world'

We have looked at this problem in some detail in chapter 7. You might get them to read (or yourself summarise) Peter Kreeft's book *Making Sense Out of Suffering*, bringing, as he does, clues from the prophets, the artists and the philosophers, before facing the reader not with the answer to suffering but with the Answerer, the man of sorrows who was acquainted with grief.

You might look with the group at the limitations which face a loving, powerful God in this area of suffering. First, the nature of our planet, with its physical, biological and moral laws which inevitably bring suffering if they are broken. Second, the existence of Satan, the great outside artificer of evil and suffering: reject him, and the biblical account of suffering becomes incredible. Third, the fact of free will, and its misuse, accounts for nine-tenths of the world's suffering. And then fourthly, there is that mysterious intertwining of the food chain, and indeed the web of all life.

Interdependence marks our world, a world which is marred by the fall.

You will certainly want to look with the group at the heart of the Bible's answer to evil and suffering. It is concentrated in Jesus, Jesus crucified and risen. Our gaze, so mystified by evil and pain, needs to fasten on to the cross of the Son of God. It shows several vital things.

First, the ultimate paradox of innocent suffering. Never was it so stark and scandalous as at Calvary. God has felt its anguish from the inside.

Second, the fact that God is no stranger to pain. He has taken his own medicine. He understands, for he has been through it with an intensity we cannot ever share.

Third, the continuing love of the Father for the Son upon that cross shows that even if we have no sense of his love in times of darkest agony, it is never absent. God loves on through pain. It is no sign of his rejection.

Fourth, the cross shows that God uses pain and suffering. He uses pain to reach us, to teach us, to equip us for the service of others, and to refine our characters. He uses pain, though he does not deliberately will it.

Fifth, the cross shows God going to the tap-root of pain and evil, by taking personal responsibility for human wickedness, the ultimate source of so much of the world's suffering.

Sixth, the cross and resurrection show God triumphing over pain and evil. Because of Easter, Romans 8:17–23, Revelation 21:4 and Philippians 1:29 are not far-fetched. They are sober, realistic inferences from the triumph of Good Friday and Easter Day.

Ask your group if this does not give the noblest explanation of suffering and evil they have ever met, although it is incomplete. Ask them if they cannot safely surrender their lives to a God who loves them that much and is prepared to endure so much for them. A fitting way to end the evening might be to read and meditate on Isaiah 53, perhaps capped by 1 Peter 2:21–5 and 3:17–18.

WEEK SEVEN: 'BEING A CHRISTIAN — WHAT WOULD IT MEAN?'

Often people thinking about the Christian life are made to pause because of two basic hesitations: What would it cost? and Could they be sure? They do not want to commit themselves thoughtlessly to what they sense is profoundly important, nor do they want to risk a flash in the pan.

What would it cost?

Show them that there is a cost to everything that is worthwhile in life. And Christian discipleship is no exception. 'The entrance fee to the Christian life is nothing at all, but the annual subscription is everything you have got.' For being a Christian is being a disciple of Jesus, and that is costly. It always has been. Make sure that you talk over with them what it will cost.

It will cost them their sins. Genuine repentance is vital, both initially and as the years go by. It is a deliberate change of direction. It means handing over the keys of your life to Christ and letting him clear up the mess. It is his job to clean it up. It is our job to let him. That 'letting' is a major part of repentance.

It will cost them their self-centredness. He becomes Master. And that is costly. He becomes Master of all the different sides of marriage or singleness, career or unemployment, life or death, wealth or poverty. He will guide us if, and only if, we surrender to him and trust him wholeheartedly. It means no less than a change of power at the centre. We abdicate, and he takes up the reins of government.

It will cost them their independence. It has been convenient hitherto to paddle their own canoe, and to keep up the myth of independence and comparative invulnerability. But not from now on. A Christian is a member of a body, a sheep in a flock, a brick in a building, a branch in a tree. For a Christian there is no such thing as spiritual independence. We belong together in the family of God, and that means that time has to be spent in developing the new relationship both with the Father and with the other members of the family. In a word, it means that devotional life (prayer, Bible reading, abiding in Christ) will be matched by congregational life (church, Communion, informal fellowship). And it will issue in some form or other of costly, unselfish service for others.

It will cost them their secrecy. Jesus made it plain that if we would not confess him before men, he would not confess us as his followers before his heavenly Father (Matt. 10:32–3). He wants us to be like a candle on a candlestick, not hidden under a bed (Matt. 5:15–16). He expects his soldiers to wear the uniform, his ships to fly their colours. And there will be times when that is very inconvenient.

It will cost them their quiet life. They will be relentlessly attacked by the desires of the flesh, the pressures of the world, and the direct opposition of the devil. Christ will provide the power to handle this, but it is sure to come.

That is what it costs to be a Christian. They should reflect, though, on what it costs to turn their backs on Jesus: they miss out on his forgiveness, his power, his companionship, the purpose he gives to life and the destiny he offers after death.

Could they be sure?

That is the other question which keeps a lot of people on the outer fringes of the Kingdom of God. Show the group from the New Testament that God does not mean us to be agnostic on this vital matter. The whole Trinity combines to assure believers of their standing with almighty God.

There is the word of God the Father – 'justified', 'acquitted': see Romans 8:1 and 1 John 5:10–13. God gives us his word, and he cannot break it.

There is the work of God the Son: see John 3:16 and 1 John 3:9–10. He took responsibility for all the sins of all the sinners in the world. Those who offer their lives to him in grateful trust will never have those sins raised again. 'It is finished' (John 19:30).

There is the witness of God the Holy Spirit (Rom. 8:16–17). He makes his presence felt (1 John 3:24), and he does so in a number of ways. There is a whole list of them in 1 John:

> There's a new sense of pardon (1 John 2:1–2)
> There's a new desire to please God (1 John 2:5–6)
> There's a new attitude to other people (1 John 3:10,17)
> There's a new appreciation of Christian fellowship (1 John 3:14)
> There's a new power over evil (1 John 3:6; 4:4)
> There's a new joy and confidence (1 John 1:3–4; 5:20)
> There's a new experience of answered prayer (1 John 5:14–15).

These things do not all grow at once in the garden of our lives, but once the sunshine of the Spirit touches the cold earth they tend to spring to life. We are meant not just to feel or hope that we are disciples of Christ, however unworthy (and we remain that). We are meant to *know*. Hence the assurance of 1 John 5:13.

WEEK EIGHT: 'BECOMING A CHRISTIAN – HOW COULD I START?'

It may be helpful to have given a copy of *Becoming a Christian* or *Come, Follow Me* to each member of the group who so desires at the end of the seventh session, and to build discussion around it on this, the last evening. It would be good to have a celebratory meal together, and a frank evaluation of what the course has meant to everybody in the group.

The leader will then want to make the way to Christ crystal clear, and to allow the challenge of commitment to Christ to bite deep.

I have given a detailed explanation of the role of the Christian 'midwife' in bringing new children to birth in chapter 9.

This is the point where your own sensitivity and your own favourite way of explaining the good news is going to be most apt. I suggested earlier two simple outlines (pp. 268–81). The first is:

Repent . . . not just for your sins, but for the great sin of proud rebellion and for keeping your Lord at bay for so long.
Realise . . . what he has done for you through Bethlehem, Calvary, Easter, and Pentecost.
Reflect . . . on the cost of discipleship. It is commitment for life. It is going public. It is becoming no. 2 to Jesus. It is joining the church. It is working for God.
Receive . . . not just the truth into your head but the Spirit of Jesus himself into your heart and life.

Alternatively, one could show them that there are essentially four steps to a personal faith. They are as basic as ABCD:

Something to *admit* . . . our failure to love God and obey him; and the plight that has got us into – alienation from God and bondage to evil.
Something to *believe* . . . the coming, the death and the resurrection of God's Son, and the gift of his Spirit in order to deal with our plight.
Something to *consider* . . . the cost of discipleship. It is commitment for life. It is going public. It is being no. 2 to Jesus. It is joining the church. It is living and working for God, whatever your job.
Something to *do* . . . Salvation cannot be earned, but it has to be received, or else it does us no good. We have to say 'Yes' to the Lord who says 'Yes' to us. We have to make room for the entry of his Spirit and actually ask him to come and take over.

Helpful verses might include the following:

On the need . . . Romans 3:23; 6:23; 1 John 1:5–6; Isaiah 59:1–2; John 8:34, together with the implications of Matthew 22:37–9 and James 2:10.
On what God has done . . . Matthew 1:21; Romans 5:8; 1 Peter 2:24; 3:18; Isaiah 53:6; John 8:36; 1 Peter 1:5; Philippians 4:13.
On the cost of discipleship . . . Matthew 6:24; Galatians 2:20; Romans 10:9–10.
On the step of faith . . . John 1:12; 3:16; Revelation 3:20; 1 John 5:11–13.

You have explained the way. You have wrestled with intellectual problems. Throughout these eight weeks you have constantly sought to bring them back to Jesus and the resurrection. You have perhaps gently uncovered, in private conversation, the personal sins which are often the real reason for rejection of Christianity. And now you need to challenge each of them to declare his hand publicly: just as Jesus did. By this time the group members will know and trust each other enough. Ask who will join you in a prayer of commitment then and there. It will be a moving moment. And it will be a powerful challenge to those who are not yet ready.

There remain plans for the future. Those who have come to faith will need to be enrolled at once in a Discovery Group. You need to find ways either of continuing for a while with the rump of the group, if they wish, or of seeing them personally from time to time, as well as encouraging them to come to worship. They are actually in a dangerous position now. Having looked into the face of Jesus, they will get hardened if they turn away without responding, and it will be much more difficult for them subsequently. Seek by all means in your power to improve the opportunity which membership of this group has given them to respond to Christ. Some, of course, as in the days of Jesus' own ministry, will be determined to have none of it once they see what Christianity is and what it calls for. Jesus sorrowfully let such 'rich young rulers' go away empty, and we may have to do the same. But always seek to keep the channels open. Who knows? In a time of crisis that person who left the group unconvinced may well turn to you for help, and another opportunity to turn his eyes towards Jesus may occur.

Appendix B
'Discovery Groups' for New Christians
Michael Green and Jane Holloway

SETTING UP DISCOVERY GROUPS

Whatever event you are planning, whether it is a guest service, a small supper party, a church mission, a town-wide mission, always plan for the follow-up ahead of time.

a. Decide on what the follow-up should be – a Discovery Group, an enquiry group, and how many groups you think you will need.

b. Prayerfully recruit the leaders.

c. Train them in how to use whatever course material has been chosen, how to lead a small group meeting, how to care for the group pastorally and how to lead someone to faith.

d. Find out from the leaders what times of day they are available, and where the group will be held.

e. Put this information on a response card (if used) or clearly announce it at the meeting or service, so people know how to join.

f. Ensure that the leaders have met together before the first meeting of the group, both to get to know each other and to plan ahead.

g. If leaders can act as 'counsellors' at the end of the event, this gives them a chance to meet prospective group members.

h. Make sure the groups start as soon as possible after the evangelistic event. Keep in contact with the leaders, and help with the integration of members into Bible study groups at the end of the Discovery Group.

(See Appendix C's section on the role of a Follow-up Co-ordinator for more details.)

RESPONSE CARDS

These can be very useful when the invitation is made at a larger service or meeting to find out more about the Christian faith and/or join a Discovery Group. These cards need to be designed in a clear, concise way, enabling information to be gathered as easily as possible. They could be included in the service sheet with a tear-off slip, or could be printed separately.

To help with the design, think over what information is needed.

a. What is the form designed to do? To give people an opportunity to indicate they have made a decision for Christ, to join a group, to find out more about the Christian faith, to ask for a visit, to request a book?

b. If people are given the opportunity to join a Discovery Group, should the description of what it is be given verbally or on the card?

c. Will there be a choice of time and day? This should be on the card if possible.

d. Is it intended that people will fill out these cards themselves, or will they be used with a counsellor? If the former, it is wise to ask for the minimum of information, whereas if they will be used by a counsellor it is easier to ask for more information.

e. What information is needed, apart from name, address, phone and the appropriate box ticked? If used in an event which includes more than one church, or if working with young people, it might be good to have space for name of church or school/college to be inserted.

f. Will people be asked to give comments on the meeting? If so, then leave room on the card so that the speaker can ask for comments during the meeting.

g. How should these cards be returned? In the offering, in a box at the back, to a counsellor? Include a return address if used during a larger event.

h. Example of a response card – to be used without a counsellor:

Church name or mission title

☐ Count me in! I'd like to join a Discovery Group
Please indicate 1st and 2nd choice of day and time

	Mon	Tues	Wed	Thur	Fri	Sat
Morning						
Afternoon						
Evening						

☐ Tell me more! I'd like more information about the Christian faith

Name _____

Address _____

Phone _____

Church (if any) _____ School (if any) _____

Please give us your comments on the meeting:

Suggestions for counsellors when filling in a response card

a. Be natural as you speak to your 'new friend'. You need to explain why you are asking them for the details you need. If you want to invite them to a Discovery Group, explain clearly what it is. Encourage them to join even if they have not made a commitment, because a group will be able to help answer some questions. Alternatively, it may be that follow-up should be handled individually and not in a group.

b. Ask for name, address and phone, remembering to write legibly.

c. If they go to another church, or attend a school or college, put that down on the card.

d. If they want to join a Discovery Group, find out when. Remember they haven't come along expecting to need to know this information! Help them to think through their week. Get one or two preferences if you are dealing with a few choices of time and day. Assure them that they will be contacted soon with details.

e. If they don't want to join a group, but want a visit, or more information, either plan to see them again yourself, or indicate what is required on the card.

f. Offer your phone number, and give them a ring in the next day or so, even if just to say 'hello'.

g. Complete other details on the form as needed. There may be space to indicate whether this is a first-time commitment or a rededication. If there is an age grouping, it may be appropriate to make an educated guess after you have parted company. If you find out any details that would be useful to those organising the placing of people in groups or to the leaders, make appropriate notes on the back of the card before handing it in (e.g., 'Needs transport', 'Don't ring at home', 'Would like to be in the same group as a friend').

h. Make time to talk and pray together and help them with any difficulties.

i. Remember to hand in the card promptly to the organisers of the follow-up work.

NOTES FOR LEADERS OF DISCOVERY GROUPS

This is a short-term group, lasting for eight or nine weeks, which provides intensive support to help new Christians (and those who are not yet Christians) get rooted in the faith. The aim of the group is to begin the process of 'presenting everyone mature in Christ'. It is not a lecture, or a debate, but a time of informal corporate learning in someone's home. It will vary in membership, in that some will have professed faith, others will have rededicated themselves, others will be thinking seriously, and others will not be sure why they are there at all!

The course can be used for individual as well as for group use. The material tries to cover major aspects of Christian living: the foundations, Jesus, assurance, reading the Bible, learning to pray, the Holy Spirit, Christian fellowship, temptation, and serving Christ. The course should be adapted to whatever order would best suit the group.

The notes for each session are broken down into five sections:

a. Material to help the leader give a short talk on the theme.

b. A verse for members of the group to memorise. This will help them to begin to learn and use Scripture.

c. A passage for group Bible study – and some questions to stimulate discussion.

d. Some suggestions as to the way the prayer time might be directed. This teaches members to pray with and for other people, and to look for answers over the next few weeks in the group.

e. A few books are listed on each week's theme. These can be on loan, or they can be for sale, so that members can start a small Christian library for their own use and for lending to others.

Practical details

Timing
These groups can happen at any time of day. The length of each meeting will vary. In order to allow members of the group to get to know each other and have time for questions, allow between two and two and a half hours.

Meeting place
The setting should be informal and relaxed. A room in someone's house is best. Church halls are not ideal locations! Somewhere is needed to enable members to relax, feel unthreatened and able to raise questions on any issue. One room is sufficient to meet in for the first half of the meeting, but if there is another room (e.g., a kitchen or a study) then the group can split in half for the Bible study time if the group is large.

Size of the group
This will depend on the number of leaders available and the demand for the group. Two leaders for a group of six; three or four leaders for a group of ten to twelve.

Refreshments
These are not essential, but it does help people to relax on arrival when handed a cup of coffee. As the group gets to know each other, the leaders could lay on a simple meal, or have a bring-and-share meal together.

Books
Bibles are needed, especially at the first meeting. Make sure you have enough of the same version for each person expected (perhaps they could be borrowed from the church). Members should be encouraged to buy a Bible, but it is best not to assume they own one. Bible reading notes should also be available (e.g., *Come Alive to God*), either as a gift from the church or for sale. Do

have some books available for sale, or form a lending library by getting the group leaders to pool their own books. Remember to have short books which answer questions that any non-Christians in the group might be asking.

Course notes
These can be given out each week, preferably at the *end* of the meeting. These may be helpful to group members if they want to go back to a particular issue on their own.

The leaders

The people
It is important for the leaders to be able to relate to how a new believer (or an almost new believer) is thinking, to understand what their problems are, and to be able to be a sympathetic listener and supporter. Leaders do not need to know the answer to every question; one may be more gifted in the teaching role, while another may be better at personal conversation. They need to be themselves (using their different gifts accordingly), to be unshock-able, and to be able to encourage group members. People may well not have had the experience of running a group for new believers before, but if they have had experience in leading small home groups and therefore know something of the dynamics of en-couraging group participation, they can often easily slot into this role. A group like this takes time – time for meeting and planning with the leaders, time preparing for each meeting, time for the group meeting itself, as well as time with individuals themselves. Those currently involved in a Bible study group may need to be released from that for the duration of the Discovery Group. Leaders need to have basic training on how to lead someone to Christ, how to run a small group, and how to use the course material.

General responsibilities
Each group will have one leader and two or three co-leaders, so that each leader can be pastorally responsible for two or three members of the group. Before the group starts:
  a. Arrange to meet up to pray and get to know each other.
  b. Plan the first evening, by sharing the leadership. One will be responsible for hosting (books, coffee), one for teaching, one for Bible study and prayer time.

c. Pray for individual group members, for yourselves and for the group.

d. Liaise with whoever is setting up the group, to get the list of those expected and to work out who will be inviting them.

e. Meet up weekly during the course to pray and plan.

Pastoral care
Share out the members of the group among the leadership (after the first meeting), and seek to have at least two unhurried times with each one before the course is over. The first will be to ensure that they clearly understand the way of salvation, to help them with any difficulties, and to help them begin a regular pattern of Bible reading, prayer and church attendance. The second session will be to see where they are going to be incorporated into the life of the church when the group has ended. It needs to enable them to look ahead to some area of ministry and practical service they may become involved in, and also to help with any problems. No leader should have more than three people to look after: it can be very demanding. Friendships can build up within the group, and even when the group is over members will often come back to their leaders for advice and encouragement.

General hints

It is best not to attempt to cover all the aspects of the subject each week, as topics are large. The teaching session should be short – fifteen minutes maximum – leaving people wanting to know more, and allowing time for questions.

a. Try to facilitate a varied meeting each week. It may include worship (if there is a musician in the group). Allow people to share experiences and talk about difficulties. Have a shared meal, or perhaps go to a concert, once in the course of the group's life.

b. The course notes are given as suggestions. Change the material according to the needs of the group (e.g., use different Bible passages, or change the order).

c. To facilitate good discussion in a group, ask guiding questions that require more than a yes/no answer (e.g., What do we mean by this? How does this relate to our lives today? Has anyone experienced this?).

d. After a discussion, summarise: either have one of the leaders list the main ideas so that all can remember them, or ask one of the group to do so.

e. The leaders may well feel apprehensive and out of their depth, but often the group members are even more terrified at the first meeting.

The first meeting (see chapter 11)

Welcome
This is important. The leaders may know who is expected, but the visitors don't know what to expect. Aim to make people feel at ease. Have the room ready (coffee made, books out, chairs ready – but not in neat rows). Have a ten-minute circulating time.

Who is there?
The leaders need to begin to get to know the group. It is a good idea for the leader to introduce himself, briefly explaining what brought him to Christ, and then asking the others present to say what brings them along to the group and what they hope to gain from it. This may take quite a long time, but it gives valuable information to the leaders. They discover where in their spiritual pilgrimage each person thinks they are. So it proves helpful in dividing the group up into sub-groups for the Bible study part of the evening, where it helps to have a mix of those who are already committed and those who are not yet sure. This needs to be a relaxed time of sharing, and the leader needs to welcome each contribution so that from the outset people get the feeling that anything they want to say is okay. This section may well take up most of the first evening.

Talk
This sharing time will probably be followed by a short talk on laying the foundations, or on assurance. Remember not to assume any knowledge of the Bible, and try not to use 'jargon' phrases.

Questions
Some groups will be silent, others not. Questions can form an important part of the meeting, giving a way of seeing where people are, and a chance for problems to be aired.

Verse learning
This can be slotted in here, before the Bible study.

Bible study and prayer time
See that the Bible study groups are small enough to enable everyone to take a full part. This may require subdivision into two

groups for this part of the meeting, each under one of the leaders. If necessary, have questions about the Bible passage copied on to separate sheets for the convenience of the group members.

Prayer time is usually best in the smaller groups at first, in order to encourage people to pray out loud and for each other.

End of meeting

This is a good time to hand out course notes and Bible reading material. Mention the book table and issue an invitation to meet at 'same place, same time' next week.

When the meeting has finished, the leaders will want to debrief, plan next week, and sort out who is pastoring whom.

Follow up

Visit those who did not attend the first meeting, giving them the notes of the meeting and a warm invitation to the next. Or put a note in the post, or give them a phone call. Naturally a visit is best.

Subsequent meetings

These will be slightly different, in that there is no need to have that extended time of sharing at the beginning. Do leave time for catching up on news over the past week, sharing answers to prayer, and generally having fun together – perhaps going out to a film, theatre, picnic together later in the week.

At the end of the course

Leaders need to be in touch with whoever set up the group, so that handover to a regular home fellowship in the church can be smooth. They need to:

a. Encourage group members to attend Sunday worship regularly.

b. Inform the minister of their church.

c. Encourage members to do some form of service in the church, using the gifts God has given them.

d. Keep in contact with members who will need continued love and support even though the group has ended.

e. Write a brief assessment of each person to hand to the leader of the small group they are joining and to their minister.

f. Remember, the biggest danger of 'fall out' is after the Discovery Group, before the person gets settled in a new set of Christian friendships.

DISCOVERY GROUP COURSE

1. LAYING FOUNDATIONS

Getting acquainted

This is the first meeting of the group. We all need to get acquainted so that we can be open with one another in the weeks ahead. What brings us here?

Teaching section

If we are going to lay a satisfactory foundation for the house of Christian living, there are four preliminary questions we need to ask and answer from the Bible, which is the handbook of Christianity. We shall be using it each week.

What is Christianity?
There is great confusion here. It is not a religion, at all, but a revelation and a rescue. It sets out to reveal to us what God is like – Creator (Gen. 1:1), holy (Isa. 6:3), love (1 John 4:8). And it shows us the lengths he is willing to go to in order to rescue us (John 3:16; Mark 10:33–4). Christianity is not therefore a matter of church-going, ceremonies, creeds or conduct, though it embraces all four: Christianity is Christ.

Who is Jesus Christ?
He is a man like us. He was born, lived, suffered, died. Very human. But he was more than man. He was, as his name Jesus means, 'God to the rescue' (Matt. 1:21). He was the fulfilment of all God had been showing his people Israel for centuries (Heb. 1:1–4). He is God's 'Word' or message to us in the terms of a human life (see John 1:1–4, 14, 18).

What did he come for?
To liberate us from the mess we had got into. The Bible is frank about our sinfulness (Rom. 3:23; Jer. 17:9), which matters because he is 'light and in him is no darkness at all' (1 John 1:5). All humans have this disease of sin or self-centredness. It spoils lives, imposes a

bondage, separates from God, and will be fatal if it is not dealt with (John 8:34; Rom. 3:23; Isa. 59:1–2). His death on the cross dealt with the guilt of sin (1 Pet. 3:18). His rising from the tomb released the endless power of his Spirit to come and live in the lives of believers (Phil. 4:13, 19).

How do I get in touch?

If we want relationships restored, there are four steps we need to take. As simple as ABCD – but tough to take:

There is something to *a*dmit: that I am not in touch with him, that I am on my own self-centred path, and that I need a radical change which the Bible calls repentance. What is more, I need a new power to break the chains of all selfishness.

There is something to *b*elieve: that God cares enough about me to come and find me. He did it by coming to this earth, by dying on the cross to take responsibility for my wrong deeds, and by rising again to a new life that he is willing to share with me.

There is something to *c*onsider: the cost of discipleship (see Luke 14:25–33). It will involve putting Jesus no. 1, not being ashamed to be known as his follower, and allowing him to get to work cleaning up our lives. We shall need to spend time regularly with him and with his followers.

There is something to *d*o: to invite this risen Jesus Christ to come and inhabit the life he made, and for which he died (Rev. 3:20). If we ask him in, he will come. He has promised. Until then we remain out of touch.

If you like then, there are three sides to becoming a Christian: the believing side (faith), the belonging side (baptism) and the divine side (welcoming his Spirit into our lives). NB: Romans 8:9 – you are only a Christian when the Holy Spirit has been welcomed aboard. When better to begin than right away? There is no middle ground in allegiance to Jesus Christ. It's a powerful either-or! See Ephesians 2:1; Matthew 7:24–7; 25:46; 1 John 5:12.

Verse to learn

Learn Revelation 3:20 (NIV): 'Here I am! I stand at the door and knock. If anyone hears my voice and opens the door, I will come in and eat with him, and he with me.'

Bible study section

The Bible passage for study is Luke 19:1–10
1. Why do you think Zacchaeus felt the need to meet Jesus? Why do we?
2. Why did Jesus bother about Zacchaeus? How long do you think it was since anyone had gone to dinner with Zacchaeus?
3. Did Zacchaeus have to smarten up his life before Jesus would enter his home?
4. What does Jesus bring when he comes into someone's life?
5. What difference did Jesus' visit make to Zacchaeus?

Bookshelf

Copies of Bibles and New Testaments in the New International Version, and copies of the Scripture Union introductory Bible reading notes, *Come Alive to God*, together with:
Michael Green, *Come, Follow Me*
Michael Green, *The Day Death Died*
C. S. Lewis, *Mere Christianity*
David Watson, *Is Anyone There*?

2. THE HEART OF THE MATTER – JESUS

Teaching section

Jesus was fully human
Born in a humble family, attested by secular sources, he shared a human body (he was tired, hungry, tough – John 4:6; Matt. 4:2; John 19:5). He shared human experiences (he grew up in a big family, worked for a living, and knew the force of temptation – Matt. 12:46; Mark 6:3; Matt. 4:1–11; Heb. 4:15).

Jesus was more than human
Jews were the last people in the world, with their strict monotheism, to allow that any human being could be one with God. Yet they were convinced. Why?

They listened to his teaching (Matt. 5:44; Acts 20:35; John 7:16). Nothing like it had appeared before or since.

They watched his behaviour. It was utterly sinless. His own claims (John 8:28) and the evidence of his friends (1 Pet. 1:18–22; 1 John 3:5; Heb. 4:15), his enemies (Luke 23:13–16, 47; John 8:46) and onlookers (Matt. 27:4, 19, 54) show that his life was utterly unique, a moral miracle.

They witnessed his miracles. If recorded of someone else, they would be bizarre. With Jesus they fit. Never for selfish ends, never to show off, they were signs, dramatic illustrations, of who he was. Feeding the crowd (John 6), raising the dead (John 11:43–4), healing disease (Luke 4:39), controlling nature (Mark 6:47–52) highlight his claims and stand or fall with them. 'The only Christ for whom there is a shred of evidence is a miraculous figure making stupendous claims' (C. S. Lewis).

They assessed his claims. He claimed to forgive sins (Mark 2:1–12), to accept worship (John 20:26–9), to be the final Judge of men (Matt. 7:21–3; 25:31–46), to be the only bridge between God and man (Matt. 11:27; John 14:6). They could not believe he was either deluded or a deceiver. Could he be what he claimed?

They saw him die. He went there voluntarily (Luke 9:51). His innocence, his care for his murderers, and the way he died, convinced them that he had come to give his life a ransom for the world's sin, that he was the suffering servant of God foreshadowed in the Old Testament (Mark 10:45; Isa. 53) – that he was indeed 'Jesus', God the Saviour (Matt. 1:21).

They met him risen. Both Jesus and his followers based their convictions about him on his resurrection (Matt. 12:39–41; Rom. 1:3–4). The evidence is compelling: the empty tomb (all the gospels), the resurrection appearances (1 Cor. 15:3–11), the emergence of the church with its three special things (baptism, Eucharist and Sunday) all rooted in the resurrection, and the experience of believers ever since (1 Pet. 1:3; Eph. 1:19–20).

Jesus demands a verdict

There are only three options. He was either a deceiver (Matt. 27:63) or mad (John 8:52) or 'My Lord and my God' (John 20:28). The one thing that is not open to us is to say he was just a good man. The challenge was well understood by Pilate, though he made the wrong choice: 'What shall I do with Jesus?' (Matt. 27:22). The wise response is to 'receive him', and so enter the family of God (John 1:12–13).

Verse to learn

Learn Matthew 16:16 (NIV): 'You are the Christ, the Son of the living God'

Bible study section

The Bible passage for study is Philippians 2:1–13
1. What does this passage tell us of Jesus before his birth?
2. What does it mean that 'he made himself nothing' (v.7) and 'humbled himself' (v.8)?
3. Look up Isaiah 45:22–3. There it is 'at the name of God' that every knee will bow. What is that saying when applied, as here (v.10), to Jesus?
4. What difference should the example of Jesus make to us in practical behaviour?
5. When did your knee bow, and your tongue confess that Jesus is Lord?

Prayer time

It might be good for everyone to choose a verse that has struck them tonight, mention it, and pray either that God will make it true for themselves or thank him for it.

Bookshelf

Richard Bewes, *The Resurrection – Fact or Fiction?*
John Drane, *Jesus and the Four Gospels*
Michael Green, *Why Bother With Jesus?*
Val Grieve, *Your Verdict*

3. CHRISTIAN ASSURANCE

Teaching section

When we have 'come to know' Christ (Phil. 3:10) 'received' him
(Rev. 3:20; John 1:12) or 'come to him' (John 6:37) – they are all
pictures of Jesus and ourselves getting in touch – we need to know
where we stand. You cannot build a satisfactory house on an
insecure foundation.

Scripture anticipates – and answers – the immediate questions
which assail us:

Can I be sure I am accepted? (John 6:37)
Will God hold my past failures against me? (Rom. 8:1)
When I fail, do I get thrown out of the Christian family? (1 John
1:9)
Can I keep it up? (2 Cor. 12:9)
How can I overcome temptation? (1 Cor. 10:13)

One of the most pressing early problems is doubt. How can I be
sure I am accepted? Here are three grounds for a quiet confidence,
which will grow with experience:

What the Father promises us (1 John 5:10–12)
What the Son achieved for us (1 John 4:10; 1 Pet. 3:18)
What the Spirit does in us (1 John 4:13).

And what does the Spirit begin to grow in the garden of our lives,
once he has been planted there? Gradually we shall find clear marks
of his presence, if we have asked him in. They will not all come at
once or in any special order, but they *will* come! And it will all be
wonderfully new. The first letter of John tells what they are:

A new desire to please God (2:5)
A new assurance of pardon (2:1–2)
A new willingness to face opposition (3:13)
A new delight in the company of fellow Christians (3:14)
A new generosity of spirit (3:17)
A new experience of victory over temptations (4:4; 5:4)
A new discovery of answers to prayer (3:22)
A new understanding and set of priorities (5:20–1).

We are not meant to guess or hope that we belong; we are meant
to be sure of it (5:12–13).

Verse to learn

Learn 1 John 5:12 (NIV): 'He who has the Son has life; he who does not have the Son of God does not have life'

Bible study section

The Bible passage for study is Acts 9:1–22
Much of the story of Saul's conversion was unique, but much applies to every person who discovers Jesus for himself.
1. Saul of Tarsus was intelligent, religious, virtuous, enthusiastic and sincere. Surely such a man needs no conversion, then or now?
2. Later on Saul called his conversion, 'an example' (1 Tim. 1:16). In what ways is this true?
3. Was any 'Ananias' a help to you in your discovery of Jesus?
4. What differences began to be seen in Saul's life to convince him and others that the change was real?
5. What struck you most in this story?

Prayer time

God has no dumb children. He wants us to talk to him as naturally as we talk to each other. Many of you will not have joined in a time of open prayer before. Praying silently is just as valuable as praying aloud, but it helps to concentrate our own prayers and it enables others to say 'Amen' if we pray out loud. Just a one-sentence prayer of thanks, of request, or praying about some thought from the Bible study. Incidentally, it helps your concentration if you pray out loud when alone.

Bookshelf

Michael Green, *Come, Follow Me*
Michael Green, *New Life, New Lifestyle*
Michael Green, *World on the Run*
John Stott, *Becoming a Christian*
John Stott, *Being a Christian*
John White, *The Fight*
A biography or two about the power of God to change lives (e.g., Charles Colson, *Born Again*) would also be helpful.

4. READING THE BIBLE

Teaching section

What is the Bible?

Christians find that one of the great ways of developing their discipleship is the regular practice of daily Bible reading and prayer. The Bible is a collection of sixty-six books, written by some forty different authors in three languages over a period of more than a thousand years. It contains a wide variety of literary genres, yet it has an amazing unity of outlook and purpose. This is because it is a uniquely 'God-breathed' book (2 Tim. 3:14–17; 2 Pet. 1:21) designed to impart the truth about God to all men in all ages (Matt. 5:18; Mark 13:31). It is not primarily a history book, or a textbook, or a handbook of ethics, though it contains elements of all three. It has a single main theme: God's intervention into our world to rescue us from our self-centredness. In a word, it is about salvation.

Why read it?

See what it claims to do for us. It is a mirror (Jas. 1:22–5) to show us what we are like. It is a sword to be used in temptation (Eph. 6:17). It is a hammer to break us down (Jer. 23:29). It is sweet as honey, nourishing as milk or meat (Ezek. 3:3; 1 Pet. 2:2; Heb. 5:12–14). It can cleanse us, guide us, give peace and wisdom (Ps. 119:9, 105, 165; Prov. 4:4–6). No wonder we cannot grow without it (Ps. 119:162; Josh. 1:8–9; 2 Tim. 3:14–17). It is a prime way of keeping in touch with the Lord (John 15:7).

How read it?

Get a Bible you can value: RSV or NIV are probably best. Get some Bible reading notes to help you (e.g., *Daily Bread*, or *Daily Notes*). Later branch out on character studies, word studies, studies of great themes or of a whole book. But keep it regular. And apply it to yourself. Look for a promise to claim, a command to obey, new light to rejoice in, a warning to heed, a prayer to use, an example to follow. Ask yourself a) What did this mean to the original recipients? b) How does it apply to me? Then turn what you have found into prayer and thanksgiving.

Verse to learn

Learn Psalm 119:105 (NIV): 'Your word is a lamp to my feet and a light for my path'

Bible study section

The Bible passage for study is Acts 8:26–40
1. What was the traveller doing as he rode along? Why did he need help?
2. How exactly did Philip help him? What might be the modern equivalent of the help Philip offered?
3. What effect did his dawning understanding of God's truth have on the Ethiopian's life?
4. What effect should a fresh understanding of the Bible have on us as we expose ourselves to it?
5. Where does the Holy Spirit come into all this?

At the foot of the page there is a practical outline for spending time daily in Bible study and prayer. Try to use this every day for the coming week, in conjunction with the Bible reading notes, and we will discuss next time what we have found helpful, and any problems we have encountered.

Prayer time

Take a verse or a phrase from a verse in Acts 8:26–40 and turn it into a prayer, first for yourself and then for a friend.

Bookshelf

William Barclay, *Introducing the Bible*
E. Heike and P. Toon, *NIV Bible Study Guide*
Paul Little, *Know Why You Believe*
John Stott, *Understanding the Bible*
Daily Bread and *Daily Notes* Bible reading notes

Daily Quiet Times

Turn to God
Find a quiet place and time where you can be alone, and then deliberately try to set aside the business and distractions of the day in order to focus your mind on God, his truth and his goodness. Remember that he loves you, and wants to communicate with you, and that he is not trying to make the whole thing difficult! He is with you, and only wants to see you open yourself to him.

Turn to the Bible

Using the Bible reading notes you have been given, open the Bible at the passage for the day. Read it through carefully, preferably twice – once to get the feel of it, and once more carefully to pick up the details. Ask yourself what new truths this passage teaches you, and what particular relevance it has to your own life. See if there is a promise, a warning, an example, a prayer you could use.

Turn to your notebook

Without spending too much time, jot down in a notebook the main truths and lessons which have struck you from the passage before you as you think about it and chew it over.

Turn to your notes

At this point – and not sooner – have a look at the Bible reading notes you are using, as they will probably help you with background information, difficult questions, and suggestions for personal application. Read them through, and if necessary jot further in your notebook.

Turn to prayer

Remember this is a conversation with a friend! Simply turn your heart to God and (silently or out loud) talk over with him the scripture passage you have been studying, thanking him for new light and praying for help to implement any suggestions for your daily life which you may have received. Then you can turn to other needs, personal matters, family, friends and work, the needs of the church, and other issues on your mind. This may not take long to begin with, but the list of people you care about is likely to grow, so you may need a separate page or two in your notebook to jot down people you don't want to forget to pray for.

Turn to the day

Choose from the Bible passage a few words which you have found helpful, and take them with you into the day. You may well find yourself returning to them as the day wears on, and that will lift your eyes to your Lord.

5. LEARNING TO PRAY

Teaching section

Prayer

There is all the difference in the world between knowing about a person and knowing a person. A man who never prays can know a lot about God, but only a prayerful man can know God (Ps. 73:25–6; John 10:27–30). We are called to an ever-deepening life of knowing the Lord who loves us and wants us to share our whole lives with him (1 Thess. 5:10). Any mature relationship involves 'give' and 'take'. Because of who God is, we receive far more than we can ever give, but he asks us to offer:

Praise   – appreciating and enjoying him for what he is (Ps. 96:7–8)
Confession – getting rid of blotches on the page (Ps. 32:3–5; 51:1–2)
Thanks   – for his gifts, his rescue and his answers to prayer (Ps. 103:1–5)
Meditation – reflecting on his Scriptures (Josh. 1:8)
Ourselves – willingly, gladly for his service (Rom. 12:1–2).

Prayer is not twisting the arm of God. Rather it is co-operating with him in his purposes for the world. In prayer we discover his mind (Eph. 5:10, 17) and join in his purpose (Matt. 9:38; 10:5). So praying and working go together (Jas. 2:18–26).

Learning to pray

Though prayer is as natural as speech, like speech it has to be learned.

Learn by doing. Make regular times for prayer (Dan. 6:10). Pray alone (Mark 1:35) and with others (Matt. 18:20) because, as in a family, we do not learn to speak in isolation. Learn, too, to pray brief 'arrow' prayers as need arises (Matt. 14:30; Neh. 2:4–5).

Learn from Jesus, starting from his great 'pattern' prayer (Luke 11:1–13) and going on to his meditation in John 17.

Learn from books – e.g. Michel Quoist's *Prayers*, and supremely the Psalms. Hymn and song books, as well as the Prayerbook, can be an inspiration, too.

Learn from the Holy Spirit, who is given to us to help us pray (Rom. 8:15–16, 26–7).

Unanswered prayer

And if your prayers aren't getting answered: Do you actually pray

(Jas. 4:2)? And mean it (Matt. 7:7)? Are your goals selfish (Jas. 4:3)? Is there unconfessed sin in the way (Jas. 4:8)? Do you persevere in prayer (Luke 18:1–8)? Are you seeking God's will (Mark 14:36)?

Remember that answers do not always come in the form we expect, or at the time we demand: we may be meant to answer our own prayer (Matt. 14:15–16); the answer may be 'No'; and sometimes, if he appears not to answer, maybe he wants us to start loving him for who he is, not for what we can get out of him!

Verse to learn

Learn John 15:7 (NIV): 'If you remain in me and my words remain in you, ask whatever you wish, and it will be given you'

Bible study section

The Bible passage for study is Colossians 1:3–14
1. What are the main things for which Paul thanks God in the lives of these people he had never seen?
2. Why is thanksgiving such an important part of prayer?
3. Paul is not slow to ask God for things in prayer – but what are the main things he asks for? How should we pray for our friends?
4. Paul prays that they may know God's power: what sort of things is that power to do?
5. What are the main marks of Christian discipleship in this passage?

Prayer time

Go back over some of the particular matters concerning prayer that struck you during the Bible study or the Teaching Section, and wrap your time of prayer around those things.

Bookshelf

Brother Andrew, *God's Smuggler*
Richard Foster, *Celebration of Discipline*
O. Hallesby, *Prayer*
J. I. Packer, *Knowing God*
John White, *People in Prayer*

6. THE HOLY SPIRIT

Teaching section

The Holy Spirit

The Holy Spirit was not initiated by Jesus. He is the life of God in the world of men. He was there at the beginning (Gen. 1:2–3; 2:7). In the Old Testament he was bestowed on special men for special tasks: in particular the prophets, priests and kings of Israel were gifted by the Spirit. The Old Testament looked for the day when the Spirit would be widely available (Ezek. 36:25–7; Jer. 31:31–4) when the Messiah came (Isa. 11:1ff.; 61:1ff.; Joel 2:28–32). Jesus was the person uniquely filled with the Holy Spirit (John 1:32ff.; 7:37–9). He promised that after his death the Spirit, his 'other self', would come and live in believers (John 14:15–18; 16:7–15). That is just what happened at Pentecost (Acts 2). Now, in contrast to Old Testament days, the Spirit is for all believers, not some; he is not fitful, but remains with us unwithdrawn; and he is no longer impersonal, but marked with the imprint of Jesus.

The fruit of the Spirit

The Holy Spirit enters our lives at conversion (Gal. 4:6). He then sets to work getting lovely fruit to grow in the garden of our lives (Gal. 5:22–4). As the branches stay in the vine the sap of God's Spirit slowly but surely produces fruit (John 15:1–15). We cannot make these fruits of character. But we can prevent them, if we grieve or quench the Spirit (Eph. 4:30; 1 Thess. 5:19).

The gifts of the Spirit

The Holy Spirit is a great giver. He gave inspiration to the Scriptures (2 Tim. 3:16; 2 Peter 1:21), incarnation to Jesus (Luke 1:35;4:14, 18), and new life to men and women under sentence of death (Rom. 6:23; Ezek. 37:1–14). He also equips the people of God to live the life of heaven here on earth (see 1 Cor. 12:4–13; Rom. 12:3–13). His supreme aim is to make us like Christ (2 Cor. 3:18).

Current questions about the Spirit

    a. Who has the 'baptism' of the Spirit (1 Cor. 12:3, 13; cf. Rom. 8:9)?

    b. Can we tell the Spirit what gifts he must give to us (1 Cor. 12:7–11)?

    c. What is the purpose of spiritual gifts (1 Cor. 12:7; 14:5)?

    d. What is the supreme spiritual gift (1 Cor. 13)?

e. What would it be like to be 'filled' with the Spirit (Eph. 5:15–20)?

f. How can we be filled with the Spirit (Acts 5:32; Luke 11:13)?

Verse to learn

Learn Luke 11:13 (NIV): 'If you then, though you are evil, know how to give good gifts to your children, how much more will your Father in heaven give the Holy Spirit to those who ask him?'

Bible study section

The Bible passage for study is 1 Corinthians 12:1–13
1. How does verse 3 link Jesus and the Holy Spirit?
2. What do you learn from the variety of gifts, and their unified source?
3. What do verses 8–10 teach about the kind of ministries we should be exercising in our churches?
4. What is meant by 'being given one Spirit to drink' (see John 7:37–9)?
5. Does this passage give any support to the idea that there are two kinds of Christian – ordinary and 'Spirit-filled'?
6. Will you ask the Spirit to fill you and equip you for service with whatever gifts he sees to be needed? 'Ask, and you shall receive, that your joy may be full.'

Prayer time

Get each member of the group to write down two main things he wants the Spirit to do in him. If he feels free to do so, ask him to share them with the other members of the group. The group should then pray for one another.

Bookshelf

Billy Graham, *The Holy Spirit*
Michael Green, *I Believe in the Holy Spirit*
Philip Keller, *A Gardener Looks at the Fruits of the Spirit*

7. CHRISTIAN FELLOWSHIP

Teaching section

Christian living is not an isolated affair, but a matter of belonging with others in God's alternative society, the church. The church has a bad image in many people's eyes, but the Bible idea is, by way of contrast, exciting.

Images of the church in the New Testament
Each of these images emphasises a different aspect of Christian belonging. What do those images imply?

> The family of God (Gal. 4:4–7; Eph. 2:17–19)
> The bride of Christ (2 Cor. 11:1–3; Eph. 5:25–33; Rev. 21:2–8)
> The temple of the Spirit (Eph. 2:19–22; 1 Cor. 3:16; 6:19)
> The colony of Heaven (Phil. 3:17–21)
> The body of Christ (1 Cor. 12:12–28; Rom. 12:1–14)
> God's army (Eph. 6:10–20)

Functions of the church
Worship – our responsibility to God
Fellowship – our responsibility to each other
Witness and Service – our responsibility to the world for which Christ died

Read 1 Peter 2:1–12 and see how all three functions interlock.

The unity of the church
Jesus prayed for his followers to be one (John 17:20–1), and they (more or less) managed it in the early days. In due course human frailty and particular emphases led to denominations. But God hates division in his people. Despite appearances, there *is* a God-given unity among all Christians (Eph. 4:4–6). We must seek to preserve and regain that unity.

The New Testament does not know anything of clergy–laity divisions. It does not know anything of denominations. And it is very clear that nominal membership is not enough. The church is a one-class society, transcending all barriers of sex, education, class and nationality (Eph. 2:14–18; Gal. 3:28). It knows no differing status among Christians, only differing functions (Eph. 4:11–12). Love is the bond which should unite us all (Col. 3:14).

The church is both universal (Matt. 16:18) and local (e.g. Col. 1:2). It is both invisible and visible. Repentance-and-faith is the gateway into God's invisible church (1 Pet. 2:4) and baptism is the mark of members of the visible church (Acts 16:30–1). Outward profession does not guarantee inward commitment, but should accompany it (Rom. 10:9–10). If you have not been baptised, you should request it (Matt. 28:19; Gal. 3:26–7). Then you will be able to take part in the family meal, the Holy Communion, which Jesus enjoined on his followers in memory of his death, as a means of growing in his grace, and as a foretaste of heaven (1 Cor. 11:23–6).

Verse to learn

Learn 1 Corinthians 12:27 (NIV): 'Now you are the body of Christ, and each one of you is a part of it'

Bible study section

The Bible passage for study is Romans 12:1–13
1. What does true worship involve?
2. The church is Christ's body on earth. What implications flow from this? Do you see them in your local church?
3. If 'each member belongs to all the others' (v.5), what does this mean for our relationships?
4. According to Paul we all have different gifts and abilities. What do each of you think you have? What do others in the group think you have? How is it being used for the common good in your church or college group?
5. Examine the practical fruits mentioned in this passage which flow from wholehearted surrender to the Lord. Is anything holding you back from 'presenting your body as a living sacrifice'?

Prayer time

Get into pairs. Pray over the use of each other's gifts. Then think of one thing you would like to see happen in your church. Pray for it and commit yourself to do so each day throughout the coming week.

Bookshelf

David Watson, *I Believe in the Church*
Frank Tillapaugh, *Unleashing the Church*
Paul Stevens, *Liberating the Laity*

8. DEFEATING EVIL

Teaching section

Temptation is a universal experience, and it increases rather than decreases once we have become Christians: naturally – because we have changed sides. Temptation comes at us through

'the world'   ie. society which leaves God out (1 John 2:15–16)
'the flesh'   i.e. our own fallen nature (Rom. 7:21–3)
'the devil'   i.e. the anti-God force of evil (1 Thess. 3:5).

Genesis 3 gives a wonderfully clear insight into the way temptation operates. Think of it as picture language if you will, but don't miss the important truths it has to teach.

Why should there be temptation?
Because we have a great outside enemy, Satan: no figure of fun with cloven hooves, but the concentration of evil, one of God's creatures who rebelled against God and wants to wreck all that is good in God's world. Does this seem incredible? Jesus clearly believed the devil existed (Matt. 4:1–11). Experience points the same way (1 Pet. 5:8–9).

How does temptation come?
Carefully disguised (Gen. 3:1). It never wears its true colours. It seeks to catch us by surprise. Satan cannot create – only spoil. He attacks through

the body – twisting its proper desires (v.6)
the mind – causing doubt about God's goodness (v.1), his word (v.1), his holiness (v.4)
the ambition – the itch to be top dog (vv.3–4).

All are designed to reach the will – disobedience (v.6).
Only when we yield does temptation turn into sin.

What are the results?
When we give in to temptation
    – it makes us feel guilty (vv.7, 9–10)
    – if often affects other people (v.6)
    – it makes God seem unreal and unwelcome (vv.8–9). See Isaiah 59:1–2
    – it produces fear and moral cowardice (vv.10–12)
    – it brings God's judgement (vv.14–19).

Where is the answer?

Verse 15: Jesus, 'the woman's seed', did crush the serpent's head on Calvary. He endured the full force of temptation, and overcame it. He is alive and lives within us as conqueror (Col. 2:15). He offers us his moral power to turn our defeats progressively into victories (Rom. 8:37).

Things to remember

    a. Temptation is not sin. Yielding to it is.

    b. Jesus was tempted more than we are: he never gave in (Heb. 4:15).

    c. Because Jesus won the war on Calvary, he can win our battles too (Heb. 2:18).

    d. There is always a way through – if you will take it (1 Cor. 10:13). Ask for his strength when temptation strikes.

    e. You can lose a battle – many battles – and still win the war. Take heart, he hasn't finished with you yet (1 John 3:2–3).

Things to avoid

    a. Don't flirt with the world – society, films, magazines, talk, attitudes, ambitions which dull your love for Christ.

    b. Don't spare the flesh – that selfish 'you' needs keeping on the cross daily so that the Spirit of Jesus can shine through you (Gal. 2:20; Rom. 8:13).

    c. Don't compromise with Satan. Resist him (Jas. 4:7; 1 Pet. 5:9). Have nothing to do with the occult – occult books and practices need to be confessed and got rid of (Acts 19:18–20). There is nothing so miserable as a half-hearted Christian life.

Verse to learn

Learn Philippians 4:13 (NIV): 'I can do everything through him who gives me strength'

Bible study section

The Bible passage for study is Luke 4:1–13

    1. To what temptations was Jesus subject? How would those temptations be translated into our day?

    2. Is there anything significant about the time and place when temptation struck?

    3. Jesus quoted various scriptures when handling these

temptations (they came from Deuteronomy 8:3; 6:13; 6:16). What do you learn from that?
4. In Eden (Gen. 3), man fell. In the desert, Jesus overcame. What comparisons and contrasts do you see in these two events?
5. The first and the last words of the passage are highly significant . . .

Prayer time

The group may care to share areas of weakness in their own lives, where temptation is particularly attractive, and pray for one another. God looks for holiness in us . . . and offers us his Holy Spirit.

Bookshelf

Michael Green, *I Believe in Satan's Downfall*
C. S. Lewis, *The Screwtape Letters*
Jackie Pullinger, *Chasing the Dragon*
John White, *The Fight*

9. SERVING CHRIST

Teaching section

The whole ministry of Jesus was one of service. He came not to be served but to serve (Mark 10:45). He found this theme in the Old Testament, particularly in Isaiah 40–55.

There three themes predominate. Obedience (Isa. 44:1), witness (Isa. 43:12), and endurance (Isa. 43:1–6). Israel failed these tests. How do you make out on them? This was the pattern of leadership Jesus adopted: service, not status. And he told his followers to do the same (John 13:12–17; Mark 10:43–4; Luke 22:24–7). Every Christian is called to serve. Every Christian has a ministry. It is impossible to be a Christian without becoming a minister of Christ. Don't keep the word for clergy and missionaries. It includes you!

There are three main words for 'servant' in the New Testament, and all three are applied to every Christian.

The first means 'slave' (1 Pet. 2:16; Rev. 1:1). It describes the total surrender of every part of our lives – home, work, love life, ambitions, the lot, to Jesus who gave all for us. Ponder Romans 12:1–2 and 1 Corinthians 6:19–20. In ancient society the slave had no rights, but was totally at the command of his master. The New Testament writers deliberately chose this word 'slave' to describe their relation to Jesus. How does it fit you?

The second means 'worship leader' (the word from which we get 'liturgy'). It speaks of our worship (Acts 13:2). Worship is a big word. It includes our giving (2 Cor. 9:12), our faith (Phil. 2:17), the proper doing of our job (Rom. 13:6), even evangelism (Rom. 15:16). How important is worship to you? What does it cost you? Does it spill over into telling others about your Lord? If not, it will certainly grow stale.

The third means 'helper'; our word 'deacon' is derived from it. It is widely used of practical help of all kinds. It describes our relationship to those who are fellow Christians and to those who as yet are not (2 Cor. 4:5). Prison visiting and personal service (Phlm. 13; Acts 19:22), handing out the soup and preaching, are all called by this word, 'service' (Acts 6:1, 4). Since the coming of Jesus into our world we must no longer insulate the sacred from the secular.

'This is how one should regard us, as servants of Christ' (1 Cor. 4:1). Ask yourself what differences becoming a Christian has brought to you in these areas of wholeheartedness, worship and practical service.

Verse to learn

Learn Romans 12:1 (NIV): 'Therefore, I urge you, brothers, in view of God's mercy, to offer your bodies as living sacrifices, holy and pleasing to God – this is your spiritual act of worship'

Bible study section

The Bible passage for study is Acts 5:40–6:8
1. What motivated these people to want to serve the Lord? How about you?
2. How many forms of service are mentioned here?
3. Are the 'spiritual' jobs more important than the practical ones?
4. What spiritual qualifications were necessary for those who wanted to serve lunches? Apply this to your church or group.
5. How was it that the disciples 'multiplied' in Jerusalem?
6. What service are you now engaged in which you would not be if you were not a Christian?
7. What new area of fellowship and service is each of you going to commit yourself to now that this short course has ended? Be specific!

Prayer time

Members of the group should share with one another the areas in which they feel themselves called to serve Christ (see question 7, above), and pray for each other as they move from this group to new areas of fellowship and service.

Bookshelf

David Watson, *Discipleship*
Biographies such as Charles Colson's *Born Again*

Appendix C
Evangelistic Missions in Church and City

PREPARING FOR A SINGLE-CHURCH MISSION

If you are thinking of organising a mission, here are some basic guidelines which have proved themselves in experience.

Clarify the aim

This is the first essential. Is this event to be directed within the church, to renew the life of the community and to sharpen church-going into joyful commitment to Christ? Or is it aimed at the wider community who have little or no links with the church? Clarity on this issue will determine all that follows. Confusion at this point will have disastrous results.

Once you are clear on the aim, you can then proceed to the closely allied issues of the length of the mission and its content. Should it last for a week, two weeks, or one or two weekends? Should it be based in a church or in a neutral location? Should it concentrate on large meetings, or rather seek to approach different interest groups in the milieu where they are most at home? Alternatively, should the focus be a series of small home meetings?

The time of year may well be critical. Once an answer has been found to these questions a church is well placed to move on to the next imperative.

Choose the missioner

This is of vital importance, and you need to bear in mind the church's strengths and weaknesses, along with its ambience, as you make the decision and issue the invitation. Usually the missioner will be known to the local minister, either personally or through books and videos.

Once he has been approached, it is important to invite him over for an exploratory meeting with the church leadership, ordained and lay. It is helpful to combine his visit with a main Sunday service if at all possible, so that the congregation can begin to get to know and trust him. People in the church need to be clear what the aims of the mission are, how it fits in with the ongoing life of the church, and roughly what is envisaged. They will also need to be taught the value of his bringing a team with him on the mission. After his visit, there needs to be a firmly backed decision by the leadership of the church to invite him and to support the mission at all levels. Meanwhile, the mission needs to be given a high profile in the notices of the church so that all church members begin to grasp the vision and see where they fit in. It is no bad idea to get someone other than the minister to do this, so that the mission does not look like his personal hobby. Now is the time to begin detailed planning. It should start at least nine months before the mission itself.

Plan the build-up

The sequence of events may helpfully be as follows:

a. Form the Mission Committee and get members active on their portfolios.

b. Make sure the goals (and dates) of the mission are crystal clear to all concerned.

c. Choose a title, in co-operation with the missioner. It needs to be short, attractive, descriptive and related to the locality, not to the visiting missioner. It must be designed to communicate to people outside the church.

d. Distribute a short information document to the congregation.

e. Plan the training and teaching programmes leading up to the mission.

f. Organise a rough outline for the mission week.

g. Recruit people for counselling and follow-up.

h. Publicise the mission widely.

i. Start the training course(s).

j. Make careful final preparations for the team, the programme and the publicity, and move into the mission itself.

k. Start the follow-up immediately the mission is over.

l. A few weeks after the end of the mission, new members will be transferred from Discovery Groups into the small home groups of the church. Enthusiasm may even run so high that the church's own mission team is formed.

Such is the overall build-up. Let us look at some aspects of it in greater detail.

Form the Mission Task Force

Once the mission invitation has been accepted, it is time to set up the administrative framework to enable the church to be fully mobilised, informed and trained. It is sheer folly to rely on one person, especially the minister, to be responsible for the many tasks that need to be done. It is best to form a small lay Mission Task Force from among your church leadership. This may well mean temporarily releasing them from regular church commitments in order to allow time for preparing for the mission, without unduly encroaching on their family time or work load.

This must be a working committee. Choose people who have the necessary gifts, not because of their standing in the church. Certain areas have to be covered: prayer, finance, publicity, youth work, counselling and follow-up. Other areas may well emerge as plans develop. Some of these tasks can be handled by a single individual, but there is much to be said for forming small sub-groups, composed of two or three people, who can handle different sides of the enterprise. Each of these sub-groups works in its own area, and is represented by its co-ordinator on the Mission Task Force.

The Chairperson needs to be selected with especial care. Such a person needs to enjoy widespread respect, and to be able to motivate the congregation and envisage the course which the mission may take. He or she also needs to be able to maintain oversight over the whole development of events leading to the mission.

A Vice-chairperson is also often very important, to work alongside the Chairperson, and to share the load of responsibility. If the Chairperson is ordained, the Vice-chairperson should be a layperson. One of these two needs to charged with the task of keeping in regular touch with the missioner.

A Mission Secretary is essential, to record minutes and handle correspondence. This could well be the church secretary. But if so, then extra help will be needed in the church office before the mission, to ensure that church matters are not neglected. The Mission Secretary could be the ideal person to co-ordinate the mission programme.

Assign the responsibilities

Small sub-groups, or individuals, will need to attend to a number of different areas.

Prayer
This needs to start first, for without prayer, nothing is accomplished. There are a number of ways in which prayer can be encouraged:

a. Introduce 'prayer triplets', encouraging three friends to meet weekly and each to pray for three of their friends who are not yet Christians.

b. Design a prayer card with the mission title on it. On one side encourage people to pray for a specific number of people. On the other, give general prayer needs for the mission, preferably arranged under the days of the week. This could be in the form of a book-marker.

c. Mention the major prayer needs for the mission in church each week, and get them prayed for.

d. Inform and encourage any prayer groups in the church, and engage their prayer backing.

e. Supply details and news, as it emerges, in the weekly news sheet, giving both requests for prayer and answers to prayer.

f. Organise special prayer meetings, concerts of prayer or half nights of prayer for the mission.

Finance
A draft budget will need to be drawn up. Church members may be asked to contribute, using specially designated envelopes in the services for this purpose. One Sunday could be set aside both for prayer and for all the offerings for the mission expenses. Try to raise all the necessary finance before the mission, so as to avoid having to ask for money at any of the mission meetings. The most costly items are usually the hiring of any special meeting rooms, technical equipment, travelling expenses for the visiting team, and materials used for counselling and follow-up.

Publicity

This might possibly be handled by one person, but it is better dealt with by a small sub-group of people skilled in publicity.

It will be needed both within the church congregation, and also for alerting the wider community. This group will need to work in close liaison with the rest of the committee, producing art work as required, and handling all the designing and posters required for the mission. Three areas are particularly important:

a. Design a simple sheet for church members, giving information about what the mission is and how they can be involved.

b. Approach the local newspapers, radio and TV as appropriate, for advertising and with news items. If the missioner can be interviewed, so much the better.

c. Design small, attractive cards, inviting people to various mission events, which could also be useful in door-to-door visiting.

Youth

The Youth Leader of the church should be involved from the outset. He or she needs to create a programme for the young people of the church and their friends. The leader(s) need to work in close co-operation with the older members of the youth group to plan, pray for, and facilitate the programme.

They could organise a concert with a Christian guest artist who has skills not only in music but also in presenting the challenge of Christ. They could plan and host a sports event, a film evening, a pizza party, a barbecue, or whatever might be the way in to the lives and interests of the young people in the area who are currently strangers to Christ. They may well be able to publicise these events in local schools. The visiting team, of course, is likely to comprise several members who have expertise in youth work, and this needs to be explored and taken into account early on in planning the programme.

It may be right to plan some events for the younger children, if these are within the plan of the mission. It may sometimes be possible to visit classes, take an assembly, or do lunchtime events in a local school.

Counselling

Members of the congregation could profitably be trained in how to act as counsellors for those who have responded during a mission. They need to know how to lead someone to Christ and how to deal with the more common objections and difficulties that are usually encountered.

It is wise, therefore, to devise a short training course in personal counselling, to publicise it widely in the church, and personally to invite those whom you feel ought to be involved. If a public invitation for volunteers in this area is issued, those who apply need to be screened for suitability at the end of the course.

As the mission draws near, make a rota for each main meeting so that counsellors do not have to feel they are on duty every night, but can be encouraged to invite friends. See that they know exactly what will be required of them, are familiar with the materials which they will be giving out, and that they have a session with the missioner at the outset of the mission to ensure that all is in place for them to operate confidently and naturally. Do not have a special meeting for counsellors (even a prayer meeting) just before the mission event where they expect to be used, as this can discourage them from bringing friends; and they are probably the most highly motivated members of the congregation to do just this. You will need to ensure that all briefing is complete at the final training session.

Discovery Groups

The plans for the nurture of new believers need to be in place well before the actual mission. This will require the oversight of a couple of people who have great spiritual sensitivity and organisational skills. They will need to work closely both with the Counselling Group and with the Chairperson of the Mission Task Force. They will need to decide what follow-up materials to use, and to familiarise all the leaders of these Discovery Groups with the materials.

But more is needed. They will need to train leaders for these Discovery Groups, which will emerge as people come to faith in Christ during the mission. However skilled the leaders may be in home Bible studies, they will need at least two careful training sessions in the handling of these groups for new Christians, for they present particular challenges and call for love, dedication and considerable skill.

Those responsible will need to find out what time of day the leaders of Discovery Groups can offer, and organise these leaders into little teams accordingly, putting a more experienced leader alongside one or two who have had little or no experience of running groups with new Christians.

During the mission itself the leaders of the follow-up will need to monitor the response cards as they are handed in, and immediately after the mission they must ensure that the names are sorted out sensitively into appropriate Discovery Groups, and that the leaders of those groups are immediately informed who is in their group, so that a start can be made in the week immediately following the mission.

The person in charge of follow-up needs to keep in the closest contact with the Discovery Group leaders, so as to effect any necessary changes of personnel. He or she will retain a master list of all the groups, and also be responsible for ensuring that there is a smooth transfer of members from the Discovery Groups to the regular home fellowship groups of the church, at the end of the course.

The above portfolios will always be needed. Depending on the size of the church, a small sub-group may also be needed to co-ordinate hospitality for the visiting missioner and his team, and another to handle the musical requirements if, for example, both a singing group and a traditional choir – let alone a small orchestra – are to be involved. It may be wise, also, to have a small and skilled group, rather than one individual, in charge of the technical aspects of the mission, such as PA systems, staging and seating.

Plan the programme

It will only come together nearer the time, but it is wise to get the main thrust of the mission preparation in hand early on.

As the Mission Task Force approaches this responsibility, it will need to compile a profile of the church in its surrounding neighbourhood, so as to assess the strengths and weaknesses of the church and the extent to which it relates to the needs of the community. Not only the Mission Task Force but the missioner will find this invaluable.

First, the Mission Task Force will need to determine general policy, then move into specific planning, and in all this ensure congregational involvement to a high degree.

General policy
It is important to decide how best the team can be used, to find out how often the missioner is willing to speak each day, to determine

whether you are going to major on main meetings in the church each evening, whether you are going to make meetings in the homes of the congregation the main objective, or whether, perhaps, it would be best to go for sectors of society – professional people, business people, night workers, working people and so forth. It may be possible to get involved with some local event such as a music festival taking place the same week as the mission. Or there may be some imaginative means of reaching the community through tackling some obvious need in the community with the whole team. Issues like these will determine the whole thrust of the mission and need to be carefully thought through, and prayed over. Throughout, the views of the congregation need to be considered: they will expect the Mission Task Force to take the initiative over the mission, but they will naturally want to have a say in what goes on.

Specific planning
The programme could well include: special Sunday services led by the team; home meetings; meetings for young people, for doctors, lawyers and other peer groups; debates; special meetings in a neutral location; Rotary meetings; church mid-week meetings opened up to guests; open-air work on the streets and in shopping centres.

Congregational involvement
The mission will be ineffective unless the congregation is behind it. Every effort therefore needs to be made to involve them at all levels. Constant publicity and regular prayer are vital, and it is helpful to offer some training to the congregation in hosting home meetings and helping an enquirer to faith. It is best to devise and circulate a response form to the whole congregation, highlighting the main areas where personnel are needed, and inviting volunteers. These could include visiting, helping to counsel, leading a Discovery Group, offering meals or accommodation, offering creative gifts in music, drama or dance, technical skills, etc. It would be good to hold a congregational meeting early on, preferably with the missioner present, to clarify vision, answer hesitations, maximise participation and arouse enthusiasm for the project. Out of this enthusiasm imaginative ideas will flow, and the Mission Task Force will find their job immeasurably eased.

Launch the mission

All too soon, in view of all that needs to be done, the mission will be upon you. Careful thought needs to be given to the accommodation and transport of the team throughout the mission, and the visitors will need to have a complete list of their engagements in their hands a few days before they come. Daily meetings for prayer will need to be arranged in the church, and the visiting team will need time to meet daily, pray, plan and be encouraged, for this is tough work. It may be good to get a leading church dignitary to come and commission the team for their task. At all events a gala launch, preferably at the main service on Sunday, is an enormous help in getting the mission really well supported in the parish.

Ensure that someone well informed about the mission is available to answer the church phone throughout the week. The daily time for team worship, news and teaching can be opened to members of the congregation, who will be thrilled as news of answers to prayer emerges and be drawn even more closely into the whole enterprise.

It is impossible to know in advance how the mission will turn out. Everyone involved needs to be closely attuned to the Lord, seeking to discern his will in the unfolding events of the week, and ready to adapt plans as required, even at the last moment. Always the team will have exciting stories to tell of how they found the guidance of God time and again throughout the mission, often when they had no time for preparation or were intending to do something quite different! A mission will not only be fruitful outside the church: it will bring great blessing to a congregation which throws itself into the enterprise, and most of all to the team who accompany the missioner. It is often no less than life-transforming.

Before the team leaves, it is important for the local leadership to have a time of debriefing and a look at the way ahead. Encourage such debriefing meetings in other sectors of the church's life, in order to learn from mistakes and to implement lessons learned. A few weeks or months after the mission, it is very helpful if a duly considered appraisal is sent to the missioner, and if he responds with a similar evaluation of the efforts of the local church.

PREPARING FOR A CITY-WIDE OR TOWN-WIDE MISSION

Many of the same principles apply. However, a longer time of preparation is needed (say eighteen months), so that the participating churches can begin to work together closely and create a programme which can reach widely into society.

Our experience suggests that a mission on this scale is only effective when there is already a high degree of trust and co-operation between the ministers of the different churches, when almost all churches can be involved, from Roman Catholic to Baptist, and when there is already some evangelism going on to which the arrival of a large visiting team can offer both a focus and a boost.

The possibility of jointly hosting a city-wide event should be raised at the regular meeting of all the ministers, and its implications spelled out. If it is judged that the time is ripe for such a venture, a missioner needs to be invited to meet a special gathering of ministers and lay leaders from all the churches involved.

The missioner will need first to impart the vision: not a one-man crusade, but an enterprise unambiguously owned by the participating churches, to whom he and his team will offer their sevices for the duration of the mission. He will not come with a package: the local churches will determine how best they can be served by the visiting team, and the programme will be developed accordingly. And it needs to be made abundantly plain that the mission will not be based on the missioner, speaking in a central location each evening, but instead on a visiting team of lay people working alongside the local Christians to penetrate society at every level with literally a score or more meetings every day.

Second, the missioner will explain what is required of participating churches. This will include the backing of their decision-making body, financial support appropriate to the size of the church, the willingness to allow mission team members to be involved in all services and midweek meetings during the mission, the organising of special meetings in homes designed to welcome neighbours who are unchurched, the provision of a lay representative to work alongside the minister to promote the mission, the acceptance of inter-church mission training prior to the event and inter-church Discovery Groups for new believers after the mission. That is quite a tall order: but it is essential if teeth are to be given to professions of unity and support for the venture. When each participating church has signed an invitation to the missioner based on these conditions, the preparation can begin in earnest.

The Executive Committee

An Executive Committee should be formed, drawn from the participating churches. It is responsible for the formulation and execution of all mission policy. It needs to keep in close touch with the ministers corporately, but experience shows that it often works most efficiently if staffed primarily by lay persons. The choice of Chairperson is crucial: he or she must have vision, gifts of leadership, and enjoy widespread respect and support. The Chairperson, usually in consultation with the body of ministers, then selects the Committee, whose members should be chosen primarily for specialised gifts and only secondarily as representatives of a particular church.

The Committee should include a Vice-chairperson and the co-ordinators of the following: programme, prayer, finance, publicity, youth, counselling, follow-up, facilities, hospitality, small meetings, special events and possibly also music, literature and transport. One member should be commissioned to keep in regular touch with the missioner and with the body of ministers.

The Committee will need to meet at least monthly to begin with, and more frequently as the mission approaches. It is responsible for deciding goals, titles, speakers, budget, larger programme events, mission training and counselling, along with policies about youth and the nurture of new Christians.

The Chairperson needs to steer the Committee meetings: these can become occasions when deep friendships are made across the denominations. Good decisions come out of good relationships. He will need to get short reports on progress from each subcommittee, and ensure that prayer does not get squeezed out.

The Vice-chairperson's job will vary with each mission, but it is wise to have someone sharing the load with the Chairperson. One of them needs to keep in close communication both with the ministers and the missioner.

The Programme Co-ordinator needs both pastoral and organisational gifts. He will be responsible for keeping in touch with all those planning programme events, imaginatively facilitating major occasions in the mission, drawing the whole programme together and keeping the missioner in touch with it, as well as recruiting and shepherding the 'lay representatives' (see below).

The Prayer Co-ordinator will be a person with a real gift of prayer, who can inspire and mobilise others to pray – as soon as the mission is agreed. All else hangs on prayer. It is absolutely crucial. So he (or she) will introduce prayer triplets and a prayer card, and give them a high-profile launch in the churches. He or his colleagues will visit all the churches and speak on prayer. He will draw up a list of the prayer groups in the town and see that they are kept informed of topics for prayer. He will organise inter-church prayer meetings, as well as chains of prayer and a city-wide 'concert of prayer' prior to the mission. He needs to devise a simple news sheet to go in the bulletins of the churches with prayer needs and answers to prayer included. If joint corporate prayer catches fire, the churches in the town will never be the same again.

The Finance Co-ordinator will first need to draw up a budget. It will depend on whether or not premises need to be hired, what the publicity will entail, and what the financial requirements of the team will be. They may often come free, but their travelling expenses will be considerable, as will the phone and correspondence bills; and of course the team will need to be fed during the mission. Each sub-committee should be asked for an estimate of its costs. The Executive should then decide how the finance should be raised among the participating churches. A copy of the budget and the financial responsibilities of each church should be circulated, indicating when the first contributions are needed. Avoid asking for contributions at the mission itself, but you can well do so in pre-mission meetings.

The Publicity Co-ordinator is concerned with publicity both within the churches and town-wide. Can the Mayor be encouraged to declare it a special week? Would some big fiesta be a good idea? Should a logo be produced and used on bumper stickers, sweatshirts and badges as well as mission notepaper and posters? Should invitation cards be printed for the various events? What free publicity is available on local radio and TV? Should a small Christian book be delivered free to every household, or could a newspaper about the mission be produced? This portfolio gives endless scope for imagination, allied to efficiency. Its main task is to provide attractive and clear answers to the questions most people will need to know: What is a mission? Who are these visitors? What is going to happen? Needless to say, the best form of advertising is personal invitation by one friend to another.

The Hospitality Co-ordinator will be responsible for the accommodation of the team and its meals. The missioner will supply a list of the team, with details of their denomination, age, sex and any personal allergies. It is best to recruit hosts from among the more fringe members of the churches, as the committed core are likely to be involved in hosting meetings. Clarify to hosts what is expected of them (especially whether or not they are providing the evening meal), and send the addresses of hosts to the missioner before the mission team comes.

As for meals, many of the team will be out working at lunch time, so it is best to have a packed lunch, provided by different churches on different days, rather than a sit-down meal. Coffee needs to be provided mid morning, and it may be good to place team members in strategic homes for evening meals, if they are not eating with their hosts. The holder of this portfolio is also responsible for giving thought to how the team will get around town (borrow cars or bicycles?) and for providing each member with a clear map upon arrival.

The Small Meetings Co-ordinator, through the lay representatives, needs to enable scores, preferably hundreds, of small meetings in homes to spring to life. The concept will be new for many, and probably frightening. He has therefore to show that it is simply a matter of inviting a few friends round to meet a couple of the visiting team, who will have been trained to handle the situation. The total impact of the mission will probably depend on the number and quality of these home meetings, so no trouble should be spared in setting them up. Each church should be asked to set a goal of how many such meetings, hosted by members for their unchurched friends, they could expect to lay on. The Co-ordinator will be wise to devise a form, requesting information about each event, which will ensure that adequate and correct information is on the main programme: this will help the missioner or Team Administrator to allocate appropriate team members to the event.

MISSION TITLE

I would like to host a meeting:

Name of host _____ Phone _____

Day _____ Date _____ Time _____

Address _____

Church affiliation _____

Directions to meeting:

Is it a regular church meeting, or set up for the mission?

What type of meeting is it? (i.e. in a home, restaurant, church).

Please give an indication of who is likely to be there – mostly men, mostly women, young people, singles, young parents, retired people?

Two team members will come, unless you request otherwise.

Can you give any other information that will be useful to help the team prepare?

Please return to: give name of mission office and phone

The Special Events Co-ordinator may be needed to organise some of the larger events, such as a concert or a praise march, a debate or a drop-in centre. His would also naturally be the responsibility for any central worship meetings.

The Counselling Co-ordinator will recruit suitable members of the churches to act as counsellors, alongside the mission team, at the larger events. This will involve preparing a training course, in co-operation with the Follow-up Co-ordinator. Bear in mind that the role of counsellors at main meetings will differ from that performed by hosts of small home meetings who will be in regular contact with their friends afterwards. Decide with the missioner how he is likely to use the counsellors, how they are to be identified (name badge, ribbon, etc.), what material would be most appropriate for them to use, and how the response cards are to be handled.

The Follow-up Co-ordinator has the same oversight of Discovery Group leaders as in the single-church mission, but the task is more complex because of the interdenominational nature of the mission. Leaders need to be drawn from the various churches, trained, and have their suitability confirmed. Once leaders are in place, find out what time of day they can manage, so that times can be printed on the response card. The leadership of the Discovery Groups should be interdenominational, and the Co-ordinator should ensure that the leaders have met and are comfortable with each other before the first meeting with the group.

At the end of the mission finalise the groups, being careful to get a balance in age, sex and denomination. Decide whether it is important for members to be in a group near home. Inform the leaders and get them to invite members to the first meeting, which should start as soon as possible after the formal mission ends.

The Co-ordinator needs to be available to act as the central person during the week or two after the mission. Leaders should be asked to phone in lists after the first meeting so that the central list can be kept up to date. Some people, having been allocated to one group, find that they need to change. The Co-ordinator will want to ensure that leaders follow through on all non-attenders. He will also be available to help leaders with any problems, and will help to ensure a smooth transition to small midweek groups in the church of people's choice at the end of the Discovery Group. There will always be some people who for some reason cannot be fitted into a Discovery Group. The Co-ordinator needs to see that they are appropriately followed up through personal contact.

The Youth Co-ordinator should be someone who is already working among young people in the city, and can work alongside other youth leaders from different churches. He needs to set up a regular meeting for all youth workers involved in the mission. Together they will clarify the age range which is being targeted, and determine the best way to reach them with the gospel. They will probably need to arrange some event for every night of the mission. Youth counsellors need to be trained, and preparations made for special Youth Discovery Groups after the mission. Prior to the mission, have some joint youth events, and plan for some to follow the mission. If, during the mission itself, you decide to go for a well-known Christian musician, remember that such people are both heavily booked up, and expensive.

One of the most effective mission activities among young people is coffee-house evangelism. This requires a visionary and energetic team of leaders and a praying group of young people who are willing to put in a lot of hard work to set this up and invite their friends. Let them suggest possible places which are central and are on neutral ground. The Co-ordinator should accompany the young people to meet the owner of the place and hire it from him. Once the place has been found, the young people will have a big part in decorating it appropriately and deciding what equipment is necessary. It needs to be made congenial for unchurched kids. Large fish nets and subdued lighting have proved effective. There needs to be a coffee bar, music both taped and live, and suitable light and sound systems. Space needs to be left for any dramatic or musical presentations which might form part of the evening's programme. The programme itself will need to focus on issues of importance to young people: sex, sport, parents, suicide, relationships, and Jesus the friend. Videos or films may have a place. So may panel discussions, and the invitation of a Christian sports star. Music is sure to figure prominently. Food and coffee should be plentiful, and whatever happens in the programme should be fun, fast moving, and varied.

Prayer is vital at all levels, particularly among the young people themselves as they invite their friends and publicise the events in their schools. The first night is particularly crucial: you must have a speaker who is really at home in the youth culture and whom they will like. A Christian music group goes down well, and can often get into schools beforehand and give a flavour of what is to be expected at the coffee house. Continuity in the presentations night after night is important. Often kids will come to the first night, keep coming, and find a personal faith by the end of the week. The youth leaders need, of course, to mix naturally with the young people and set about building long-term relationships with the newcomers. Young people are very responsive to the claims of Christ once their interest is engaged and their hearts touched. Win their trust, and it will not be hard to lead them to faith. They will then need careful nurture, and they will only accept it from the hands of those they trust.

Finally, since the young people will have come together from across the various denominations and are likely to want to see some continuance of the friendships they have made, it might be helpful for the youth leaders to plan a monthly or quarterly joint event supported by all the youth groups of the town to supplement what goes on weekly in the different churches.

The lay representatives

Occasional mention has been made above of 'lay representatives'. Ideally a lay representative from each church needs to be working alongside the minister, encouraging and informing the congregation. They need to take the detailed planning of the mission off the back of the minister, who has many other responsibilities to keep going as well as attend to the mission. They will take every opportunity to motivate members of the congregation to get involved with hospitality, home meetings, and the offering of their skills in other areas. They will be in regular touch with the Programme Co-ordinator, and therefore be up to date with progress and able to keep the congregation informed through the bulletin or a 'spot' in the Sunday services. And they will be invaluable to the Programme Co-ordinator as his eyes and ears in the different congregations of the city, not least in advising him of possible people willing to serve in various areas of the mission.

The months of preparation

The local ministers are the key to the success of the whole enterprise. If they throw their weight behind it, the congregations will follow. If they are lax in passing on information to the congregation, cool in enthusiasm, or lacking in mutual love, trust and prayer, the mission is unlikely to prosper. So the Executive Committee must give top priority to building up relationships within the Ministers' Fraternal, and to encouraging care, sharing and prayer with one another. Prayer for the mission needs to become a central part of their meetings. A day conference for all the ministers, led by the missioner, is indispensable. This will enable them both to voice hesitations and to gain confidence in the whole enterprise. It will be no small task to mobilise each local church for the mission, and the fullest co-operation of the ministers is crucial. They need to give special emphasis to building up home groups for Bible study, prayer, mutual encouragement and service. It is into such home groups that new believers from the Discovery Groups will be transferred. Where churches do not have any such home groups, new believers tend to migrate to churches which have! The ministers also have an important role in encouraging the congregation to take part in the mission in a variety of ways: by joining a prayer triplet, hosting a small meeting, having a team member to stay, attending a pre-mission training course, leading a Discovery Group, lending a car or a bicycle to a team member, or offering creative gifts such as banner-making or music.

Having bestowed a lot of care on the ministers, the Executive Committee will need to see that its sub-committees are active, and will need to ensure that firm decisions are made, on time, about the aims of the mission, its title, the broad outlines of the programme, and the dissemination of information throughout the participating churches. They must ensure that the lay representatives and the training course are in place and functioning properly.

They will give attention to building bridges in two directions. First, between participating churches in the city, by organising occasional united celebrations of faith and inter-church prayer concerts, as well as by encouraging Christians from different churches living in the same area to get acquainted.

Second, they will want to build bridges between the mission team and the host city. The missioner and some of his team do not merely need to spend a day with the local ministers. They need the minimum of a day and preferably a weekend conference with a wide cross section of the participating congregations. This will enable people to develop confidence in the missioner and the visiting team. It will enable them to iron out misunderstandings and raise problems. It will enable them to spark ideas. And it is a marvellous opportunity for good, inspiring teaching to be given by the missioner and his colleagues.

Another way of building confidence is for individual participating churches to have a small group of the mission team members down for a weekend in preparation for the mission. This begins to build both relationships and enthusiasm, and it helps lay members of local congregations to own the mission. Some of them may even want to take the week off work and join the mission team. This is all to the good.

The missioner will need to be kept closely in touch with all these developments. He will welcome from the Executive Committee a profile of the area, covering all main aspects of city life, and outlining the major areas of resistance to the gospel, and the other religions and cults which he and his team are likely to encounter as they come. He will be no less interested in a short profile of each participating church. This is not difficult to compile. A form can be circulated, asking for the size, times and types of Sunday services, the arrangements for children, the midweek activities and home fellowships, whether creative arts are used in worship, and how the church caters for its teens. He would also be glad to know if there are any local drama teams or musicians who might become a resource for the mission itself.

The mission programme

Possible events will include the following:

Home meetings – informal groups of friends or neighbours where the good news of Christ can be discussed and questions asked in a relaxed atmosphere. The hosts will invite, produce refreshments, and brief the team: the team will lead the meeting.

Sectional meetings – where local Christians in a particular profession or group organise a special event for their colleagues during the mission.

Larger evening meetings – these serve as a gathering focus both at the start and at the end of the week of mission. They comprise worship and preaching, drama, dance and testimony, and they make use of a blend of contemporary and traditional music.

Sunday services – where members of the team take a significant part in the regular worship of each participating church.

Open-air work – taking the gospel out on to the streets, beach, or market-place, and using drama, speaking, testimony, circle-dancing, mime, music, Scripture-reading or other means to intrigue and draw a crowd, while other members of the team chat to those who stand and watch. The elements of surprise, joy and confidence are essential. So is permission from the police!

A praise march – this gives a chance for the local Christian community to turn out *en masse*, singing and praising God on the streets, with balloons, children on skateboards and general expressions of joy. The route needs to be agreed with the authorities. It certainly causes a stir in the local community, and is often the first time some Christians have identified themselves publicly.

Drop-in centres – these can be aimed at either adults or youth and can be very effective. They provide a chance for people to drop in off the street to have a coffee, talk, listen to music, meet Christians face to face, and maybe watch drama or take part in a debate or question time.

But to list possible events is not enough: careful planning is needed. The profile of the city will need to be studied. See where the main areas of need are, and consider whether or not the mission team would be useful in trying to meet them. Identify community groupings, find Christians within them, and encourage them first to pray and then to create an event during the mission. Decide whether the start and the finish of the mission should be in some big church or on neutral ground. Plan the youth programme and the main programme systematically, and in partnership with the missioner, ensuring that the final programme is in his hands before the mission so that allocation of team members can at least be pencilled in and talks prepared. A central church needs to be available for the team as a base which is open at all times and has several phone lines and a photocopier. If you are going to use a hall for large evening meetings, ensure that its amenities and decor are checked in good time. Finally, make sure that a good supply of Christian books is on hand. A local bookshop could supply books on a sale or return basis, thus enabling the team to take them into small house meetings, as well as running a bookstall at the larger events.

The mission week

During the mission itself the missioner, the team administrator, the Chairman and the Programme Co-ordinator of the Executive Committee need to have daily meetings to keep on course. The programme, though set in advance, is likely to have a good many last-minute changes and additions as the week proceeds.

It is often useful for the missioner to have a time with the local ministers during the course of the week, and to schedule in another time with the leaders of the Discovery Groups towards the end of the week, when they are probably beginning to get anxious as it becomes apparent that names are coming in and that they really will be called upon to lead groups!

After the mission

It is all too easy to collapse exhausted after the mission. But there is much to be done. There will be many names to follow up. It is important to ensure that nobody who has expressed interest on a response form is ignored. The Executive Committee will need to debrief, write an appraisal to the missioner, and decide whether they should stay in suspended animation for some future joint event. Indeed, they should consider whether there are more immediate joint ventures which may be appropriate: a Pentecost praise march, 'Advent praise' or some meeting of social need which could better be addressed by the churches acting together rather than separately. At all events, the churches need to maintain the forward impetus. The mission has been no more than a focus and a catalyst on the path of corporate ministry by the church in and to the community.

Appendix D
Leading a Mission and Training a Team
Michael Green and Jane Holloway

LEADING A MISSION

Working with a team, whatever the size, has many advantages over the single-missioner approach.

THE TEAM

Importance

    a. Meetings can happen in more sections of the community.

    b. Team members learn much and return home able to contribute more to their own church.

    c. Host church members realise that it is not necessary to be a 'professional Christian worker' in order to speak about Christ, and will want to take part in their own evangelistic projects.

    d. A team demonstrates what the body of Christ can do in a church or a community when it is seeking to 'love God and love our neighbours as ourselves' – and people notice.

Qualifications

None – except a personal knowledge of Christ and a willingness to speak about him and try out new things. Members should make the training sessions a priority and come for the whole mission. Some will have had experience, whereas others may not. The team should work in pairs, with the team-leader ensuring that those with less experience work with those who have had more.

Recruitment

As the missioner will probably take people from his own church, then a personal invitation, along with an announcement in a Sunday service, should be enough.

a. The missioner should spend time individually with all prospective team members, in order to find out what particular gifts, interests and experience they have.

b. Depending on the size of the team, it may be appropriate to devise a form asking for name, address, phone, age, work experience, length of Christian commitment, any previous experience of mission, denomination (for a city-wide event), a brief personal profile (which could be sent to the host church or city), any allergies or dietary requests to be passed on to their hosts, and whether they have a car to bring.

Size

This will depend very much on whether this is a single church or a city-wide event. Estimate the number of proposed meetings and decide accordingly.

TEAM TRAINING SESSIONS

These are important to enable members to get to know and trust one another, and to be trained for what lies ahead. Allow time for relationship building.

Worship

Worship is vital and should be a central focus of the meetings. Time for singing, silence, meditation, teaching from Scripture – all ensure that the team acknowledges its dependence on God before it seeks to do or say anything.

Prayer

Prayer is needed.

   a. It is needed for individual needs as well as for specific areas of the mission.

   b. The home church needs to pray, whether there is just one person or a whole team going. Information should be given in church bulletins, and special prayer meetings organised.

   c. Each person on the team should be encouraged to find a prayer sponsor, for before, during and after the mission.

   d. Team members should pledge to pray with and for each other.

The value of the team

Whatever the size of the team, and whether people are experienced or not, there will be some who say, 'Where do I fit in?' Members need to be encouraged to 'be themselves' and contribute different gifts (cf. 1 Cor. 12). Some will be used more publicly (e.g., speaking, acting); whereas others will use their gifts in listening, praying and encouraging.

Briefing

Take time to keep the team informed about the mission and up-to-date on the programme, special prayer requests, etc. It may be good to give a brief written update for each meeting if working in a large team.

Teaching

In the training sessions cover topics like: how to give a testimony, how to lead someone to Christ, how to counsel, how to use Scripture, how to give a short talk, how to lead a small home meeting (see below). It is important to make the sessions practical. The use of role play (when two members pair up to try out their skills) works well in highlighting weak areas, and it helps members get to know each other. Teach about the reality of spiritual warfare before going into the front line of the battle.

Personal preparation

Encourage the team:

a. To make use of books such as Paul Little's *How to Give Away Your Faith*, Leighton Ford's *Good News is for Sharing*, Michael Green's *You Must be Joking, World on the Run, Why Bother with Jesus?* and *Ten Myths About Christianity*, and David Watson's *Is Anyone There?*

b. To prepare ahead of time a couple of outline talks.

c. To practise talking to people they do not yet know (i.e. at the end of a Sunday service).

d. To get used to talking about their faith, initially with friends and then with others.

Specialist preparation may be needed in the areas of music, drama and dance. Certainly any musicians should meet together, and preliminary planning needs to be done to decide how the team's resources can best be deployed. Drama needs much preparation time, and the missioner needs to do advance planning on themes and subjects so that material can be chosen and rehearsed. Any dance in the worship services may be in the hands of a small dance group, but circle dancing can be done by anyone, and it is good to teach a few dances to the whole team, so that if a dance needs to happen spontaneously, as it may in the open air, anyone can join in.

It is in the team training sessions that the teaching is given, and on the mission itself that the lessons are learned.

THE MISSIONER AND/OR TEAM ADMINISTRATOR

This may be one or two people. If two people are involved, they need to work closely together at all stages during the preparation for the mission, in getting to know and equip the team, as well as being in close touch with the host city or church. Their responsibilities include five major areas.

Discerning the gifts of the team

Many gifts will emerge during the mission, but use those you already know (e.g., if you have someone good at leading worship, playing an instrument, teaching, then use them in the team meetings). Individual time spent with team members will give many insights as to where their strengths and weaknesses lie. It is good to have a few experienced members to boost the team initially in confidence and numbers.

Training and teaching the team

This involves specific training and teaching in preparation for the particular mission ahead. See below.

Liaising regularly with the host church or city

a. Keep the host church informed about the team. Send short profiles of the team members ahead of time, and perhaps a team photograph.

b. On the basis of the profile received from the host church or town, adjust the training of the team accordingly (e.g., if the team needs specialist information about a particular cult).

c. The missioner or team administrator need to make at least two or three visits (depending on the distance) to attend Committee meetings and get to know the Committee, as well as speaking at some pre-mission meetings or training days. They need to be able to get to know the church or town.

d. The programme needs overseeing as the planning develops. A visitor can often perceive local needs more easily than can a resident. It is important to ensure that the team can cope with what is outlined on the programme, that there is time built in for regular team meeting times, and, if the mission is over a week, that a complete day off is insisted upon for all the visiting team. The programme should be available at least a week before the mission starts.

e. The missioner should give advance thought to what titles should be given to any of the larger meetings, and agree these with the Committee in good time for publicity to be printed.

Caring for the team

Often, especially when the programme is busy, team members can easily go at the whole thing in their own strength for the first two or three days and then collapse. They will need love and encouragement to finish the task, and a fresh infilling of the Holy Spirit. Depending on the size of the team, it may be best to divide the team up into small groups of five or six around a more experienced member to pray together, both before and during the mission. Do encourage team members to look after each other.

Practical planning matters

Attention needs to be given to practical arrangements such as the provision of transport and the organisation of a team base in the host town.

MISSION DETAILS

Counselling

As all of the team will have been trained in counselling skills, they are available to act as counsellors, whether in an informal home setting or in a larger meeting. Outline to the team what is expected of them at each event, and how they will work alongside any locally trained counsellors.

Literature

Ensure that whatever counselling literature is to be used on the mission is made available to team members beforehand, so that specific instructions can be given and they can know how to use the material.

The team will need a supply of Christian literature (mainly evangelistic books), which can be used to supplement the spoken message at all the different meetings. A local bookshop may be asked to supply these, on a sale or return basis, and they can be set up in a large bookstall at the team's base. The team will then be able to take a small number of books to each of the meetings they attend. Detailed instructions need to be given on which are available for sale and which can be given away, to ensure that the money is accounted for at the end of the week.

Response forms

These will need to be circulated to the team in advance, and detailed instructions given as to how to fill them in (see Appendix B). The team needs to know what are the follow-up procedures for the mission, and what a Discovery and Enquiry Group is, so as to be able to explain them to people they meet. Clear instructions should be given to the team as to what their responsibilities are in contacting those they have counselled. In some cases it may be that team members need personally to follow-up each person within twenty-four hours; but in some cases, by agreement, the local counsellors will do that.

Accommodation arrangements

Staying with hosts during the mission can be daunting for some team members. Mention needs to be made of the need for punctuality, friendliness and helpfulness at all times! Practical matters like asking for a key to the house (in case they need access when hosts are out), and giving plenty of advance warning if an evening meal is not needed, should be highlighted. It may be appropriate to remind team members to buy their host a small gift too, before they leave, and to write a thank-you letter afterwards.

Do not assume that your hosts are keen Christians, and be sensitive to their children. Ministry with hosts, formal or informal, may be the most useful thing team members do on a mission.

ALLOCATING THE PROGRAMME

a. Ensure that a complete programme has reached the team administrator well in advance of the mission. There may, of course, be additions or deletions, but it enables preliminary allocation to be done.

b. Prayerfully allocate the team to events, matching experienced members with less experienced members; also, using the completed information sheets (see above), match people with suitable gifts to particular events.

c. Plan who will speak at the larger meetings. Obviously the missioner will address a fair proportion of these, using experienced team members for others.

d. For youth events, choose the most experienced youth speaker. If working with a musician or group, ensure that both parties have had a chance to talk over the event.

e. The Sunday service during the mission is important. If more than one church is involved, allocate the preachers at least two weeks or so in advance, so that it can be announced in the services the week before. Then build a small team around the speaker, to read lessons, give testimony, do a children's spot, act, dance or sing. The service is usually geared towards people inviting friends and guests.

f. For the smaller home meetings, try to match age and background with those who will be attending.

g. Team members would probably do about two meetings a day, and the missioner probably not more than two evangelistic addresses in a day, in addition to the regular team meetings.

h. Stress to team members that it is all right to take some time out for quiet and for rest.

THE MISSION WEEK

a. Allow time for the team to be briefed on local details after arrival.

b. Have daily team meetings. Obviously the length of time needed will depend on the size of the team. Ensure that no events are put into the programme when the team is scheduled to meet. Have an open session of worship, news sharing, prayer, and a short 'thought for the day', followed, after coffee, by time for detailed planning and allocation of people to events.

c. If working with a large team in a city-wide event, suggest that the first part of the meeting (i.e. worship, news sharing, prayer and 'thought for the day') is open to anyone in the community – this encourages involvement by local Christians.

d. For a large team (fifty plus), a starting time of 8.45, with a half hour coffee break, should mean that the team is available for events from 11.30 a.m. onwards. A few members may need to arrive late if involved in breakfast meetings.

e. Daily meetings for the missioner, team administrator and chairman of the Mission Committee are needed, to ensure that all is on course for that day and to deal with any last minute changes. This meeting is often best held before the team meets together.

f. All the local ministers need to be invited to meet with the missioner towards the end of the mission, to look back over the mission and to encourage the unity among the different churches in the community after the mission is over.

g. Discovery Group leaders should have a final training session towards the end of the mission to which the missioner can go and give some input and encouragement before the groups start in the week following the mission.

h. At the last team meeting warn team members about the difficulties, when tired and excited, of re-entry into the normal world, and of relating to those at home who have been praying.

DE-BRIEFING AFTER THE MISSION

a. Plan a time after the mission is over for the whole team to meet again, to de-brief, to share what personal lessons have been learned and what new gifts have been discovered, and to praise and to pray. This will also be a valuable way of learning lessons on general mission administration for the next time!

b. Have a detailed reporting back slot in the Sunday services of churches from which the team members come, to encourage those who have been praying.

c. Think ahead to the next mission!

TRAINING A TEAM

Here is a basic course, designed specifically for use on a mission that involves a team working alongside the missioner. It can be adapted for use in equipping both the visiting team and the congregation of the church hosting a mission.

Hints for course leaders

a. Use both lecture style and role-play methods. Be practical as much as possible.

b. Use other literature, videos, books as appropriate.

c. Encourage homework.

d. Amend the course to suit the mission in question.

Topics for a training course

1. *Giving a testimony*
2. *Helping people to faith*
3. *Handling problems*
4. *Giving an evangelistic talk*
5. *Using Scripture*
6. *Leading a house meeting*
7. *Hosting a house meeting*
8. *Open-air work*
9. *Visiting during missions*
10. *How to fill in and use response forms* (see Appendix B)

---

1. GIVING A TESTIMONY

One of the most important things we have to offer on a mission is our own 'story'. There will be many different opportunities in which to share it – at both smaller and larger events. Here are some tips to keep in mind.

What is testimony?

It is not about yourself. Those testimonies which give the impression 'once I was very bad, and now I am very good' are sickly.

It is not about the past. Many people, when asked to give a testimony, tend to speak about their past experience, when they first met Christ. That could seem stale. People will be much more helped by what Christ means to you today.

Witness in the New Testament means *testimony to Jesus* and the fact that he is alive. This is so important, because most people have no idea that Jesus (as opposed to creeds, churchgoing or ethical conduct) is the centre of Christianity, and less still that he is risen and can make a difference to the lives of ordinary people. So your testimony is quite simply telling in your own words the life-changing reality of Jesus. The spotlight of what you have to say should focus on him, and only incidentally on yourself.

What is the value of testimony?

There are many values in it.

First, it is intriguing. Just imagine the impact that the testimony of the woman of Samaria made among her colleagues when she ran back and told them about Jesus (John 4:28–30). It was the major feature in starting a Samaritan movement towards Jesus (John 4:39–42).

Second, it is a very natural thing to do. When we have found treasure it is only natural to want to share it. It is not like a pre-planned address. It is spontaneous, shaped towards the circumstances of the person we are talking to.

Third, it is simple. This is something everyone can do. We all have a story about the impact on our lives which Christ has made. Testimony is simply sharing that with one person or with a crowd. It is always first person singular: 'I have found . . .'

Fourth, it opens up conversation. You have only to say, in the course of a supper party, 'May I share with you the greatest discovery of my life?' and they will inevitably say 'Please do.' You respond: 'It is that Jesus Christ is alive, and he has come to make a massive difference to my life.' I can promise you an interesting supper party!

Fifth, it brings Christianity out of the expected area, of the church building, the church book, the church professional. It comes right into the real world. And here you are, a perfectly ordinary person, telling them of the difference that Jesus can make. It will be likely to take their breath away.

Finally, it is unanswerable. There is a lovely story in John 9 about the blind man whom Jesus healed on the sabbath day. The Pharisees were furious, and grilled first his parents and then the man himself. They posed him difficult theological issues like: 'This man is not from God, for he does not keep the Sabbath' (John 9:16, NIV). But the man was very wise. He did not attempt to answer their theological point. He simply stuck to what he knew: 'Whether he is a sinner or not, I don't know. One thing I do know. I was blind but now I see!' (John 9:25, NIV). This kind of thing is unanswerable. People cannot controvert our experience. Let's make the most of it.

General principles for giving your testimony

a. Pray and ask the Lord for guidance as you prepare and as you speak.

b. Centre it on the person of Jesus, not on yourself. What was life like before you met Christ? How did you meet him? What are the main benefits you have discovered?

c. Be selective. Try to assess the position of your hearers, and leave out details that will not mean much to them. Prune the irrelevant.

d. Be disciplined. Stop when you have finished and stick within the time allotted.

e. Be warm and natural. The way you speak and your body language is just as important as what you say. Smile. Testimony is not meant to be something to get apprehensive about. It is simply overflow. That is what Paul recognised in his Thessalonian converts. He speaks of their 'assurance' (1 Thess. 1:5), which literally means their being so filled with the Lord that they spill over.

f. Total honesty is vital. Never claim that faith in Christ has done more for you than it has . . . we all have a long way to go.

g. Be courteous, but bold. Many people have simply not heard that Jesus Christ is alive and can be met today.

h. Be intriguing! When Jesus met the woman in John 4 he

fascinated her with the idea of water that could well up within her very empty heart (v.10, 'If you knew . . .').

Things to avoid:
  i. The use of Christian jargon.
 ii. Preaching to your listeners: 'I have found' is what you are there to say, not 'You should'.
iii. Too many references to Scripture.
 iv. Speaking critically of another church, denomination, or individual.
  v. Giving the impression that the Christian life is easy.
 vi. The use of notes while speaking (though it may be wise to make some notes beforehand).

Specific mission situations

In a larger meeting, or church service
The aim here is to show that the aspect of Christian reality which the speaker is concentrating on is something which really does make a difference in the lives of ordinary people. Accordingly, you will need to work closely with the speaker and see that your testimony chimes in with the thrust of the message.

Spend time together beforehand. Decide which are the areas you should concentrate on, how much time you have, where you will stand, whether you will use a microphone (and if so, know how to use it), and where in the meeting you are expected to come and take part. Sorting these things out saves possible confusion in the meeting itself.

It is often best and most natural to get yourself interviewed with two or three questions which you know beforehand will be asked, and round which you can build what you want to say.

Remember not to over-run the time allotted to you.

In a smaller meeting (e.g., a house meeting)
Here the situation is different. You are not the icing on the cake of someone else's talk. You *are* the presentation! It is very easy to move into testimony in a house meeting on a mission. After all, you are visitors and have been invited to give some input into the meeting.

Your testimony will often form the beginning of such an event. Start off in an informal way, introducing yourself and your team member, explaining that you are not professionals, but are just here on the mission because you want to share something of the joy of knowing Jesus Christ. Then go on to explain what you have found, about this joy. Keep it short. Select those parts of your story with which your hearers are mostly likely to be able to identify.

Depending on how you have planned the meeting, you may want to open it up for questions or for other people to share their 'spiritual stories'. Your other team member can keep gentle control on the ensuing discussion, to ensure that you finish at the advertised time. Emphasise that no two individuals come to Christ through identical routes.

Be watchful for opportunities to change the subject and move into spiritual things. We are called to 'redeem the time' (Eph. 5:16), to snap up the opportunities like bargains in the market. That requires imagination and enterprise. And it can all stem from your testimony!

2. HELPING PEOPLE TO FAITH

Here are some suggestions for a mission situation where talk of Christian commitment is very much in the air, and where an opportunity has arisen to talk to a friend (or even a stranger) about Christ after one of the meetings.

Preparation

The basic requirements are not very many or very exacting:

a. We must know Christ personally. Without that we can never introduce anyone to him.

b. We must be thrilled with him; enthusiasm communicates. See how in John 1:41 a sense of discovery proved a vital evangelistic tool. It still does.

c. We must have the love of the Lord flowing through us. Without that, it will all be hard and professional. Compare John 3:16 with 1 John 3:16.

d. We must be flexible, allowing our friend to make the running, and all the time drawing him back towards Jesus and the resurrection. It may well not be the classic 'sense of need' that leads him to stay behind: it could be a sense of the presence of God, a sense that here is something different, a search for fulfilment and meaning, or an awareness of deep loneliness. Your job is to see where he is, and apply to his situation that aspect of our many-sided Lord which is most appropriate to him at that time.

Specific preparation

Granted those general preparations, on the evening itself:

a. Come with a Bible, pen and paper, and pick up a booklet and a counselling form. Try to come accompanied by someone who is not yet a believer. The fact that you are going to be available for counselling need not deter you. Simply, at the end of the meeting, slip your counsellor's badge on unobtrusively, smile at your friend and say, 'I've been asked to help with people who want to join those Discovery Groups he was talking about. Why don't you join one? I can strongly recommend them.' In this way you may well find yourself counselling the friend you brought with you!

b. Be much in prayer for the speaker, for yourself, and for anyone with whom the Lord might use you that night. But be prepared for anything. One night you may not be used at all.

Another night you might have two or three people to handle. Put your counsellor's badge or identification on only at the very end of the meeting.

c. Be alert to the way the speaker is closing the meeting. He may call for response in a variety of ways. It is up to you to act accordingly.

He may call people to the front or to another room: in that case, move promptly, and keep your eye open for someone else of your own background who is not wearing a counsellor's badge. Get alongside, and approach them naturally. 'Good evening, I'm Jenny Jones. What's your name?'

He may ask people to stand while others have their eyes closed in prayer. In that case have your own eyes open, and scan the area around you, so that afterwards you can go up to someone who stood and ask if he or she would like a short chat. Alertness is essential here: otherwise people can be missed who most need help. This approach by the speaker is designed to bring counsellor and en-quirer in contact with the minimum of movement and fuss, but it leaves much to the initiative and alertness of the counsellor.

He may ask people to raise a hand and then to seek out one of the counsellors afterwards. So keep your eyes skinned, and your badge prominent. He may even say, 'Everyone chat to one of the people next to you about Christ.' Then the ball will be in your court. On such occasions it is not difficult to be charmingly direct, 'Tell me, do you know Christ?' or 'What does Jesus Christ mean to you, I wonder?'

Pointing the way

Once you are sitting with your friend (and it does not matter where: it is amazing how intimate you can be in the midst of a room full of talking people), introduce yourself, and establish friendly relations fast. 'Is this the first time you have been along, John? What was it that struck you tonight? Would you say that you had put your faith in Christ personally, or are you still thinking about it?'

Such questions should get him talking. And you need that. It is fatal to prescribe before diagnosing. There is great value in asking, 'Would you say that you had put your faith in Christ [or "accepted Christ" or "come to Christ" – stick to whatever metaphor the speaker is using that night], or are you still thinking about it?'

If he has not got there yet, you can be sure that he will gratefully cling to your alternative option, and say, 'I'm still thinking about it.'

You reply with another diagnostic question, 'Would that be because there is something in all this that you don't understand, or is it that you are not yet willing for all that it involves?'

This will probably land you in summarising the steps to faith and seeing where the sticking-point is. You will need to have some rough outline in your head, around which you can build the verses which have most helped you.

You will have seen explicit suggestions on how to introduce an enquirer to Christ on pages 268–73 and 279–81 above. There are many other simple outlines, such as 'the bridge diagram', widely used by the Navigators, or the 'four spiritual laws' beloved by Campus Crusade. Choose what you find congenial. Helpful verses to keep in mind during such conversations include the following:

On the need . . . Romans 3:23; 6:23; 1 John 1:5; Isaiah 59:1–2; John 8:34, together with the implications of Matthew 22:37–9 and James 2:10.

On what God has done . . . Matthew 1:21; Romans 5:8; 1 Peter 2:24; 3:18; Isaiah 53:6; John 8:36; 1 Peter 1:5; Philippians 4:13.

On the cost of discipleship . . . Matthew 6:24; Galatians 2:20; Romans 10:9–10.

On the step of faith . . . John 1:12; 3:16; Revelation 3:20; 1 John 5:11–12.

Encouraging response

When faced with the powerful personal challenge of the gospel, you will probably get one of three main reactions. He may say 'Yes', 'No' or 'Not yet'. We have looked at common commitment anxieties and difficulties on pages 273–9 above. You may wish to refresh your memory of them. But if he says that he has entrusted his life to Christ, rejoice with him, and get him to thank God there and then. It will help him to praise God out loud with you, however haltingly.

a. Get him to explain back to you the essense of what he has done. This will help him to get it as clear as can be hoped for at that stage.

b. Tell him about the Discovery Groups that are being planned, and find out if there are any nights he cannot manage.

c. Get his details carefully on to the counselling form, and give him your own address and phone number.

d. Advise him on the inevitable initial doubts that will come, and show him how to meet doubt with promise (e.g. Rom. 6:23; John 10:10; Rev. 3:20; 1 John 5:12–13).

e. Introduce him to the speaker or some other Christian leader, and put him in the position where he can 'confess with the mouth the Lord Jesus' straight away. This will be a real help to him (Rom. 10:9–10).

f. Encourage him to come back the next night with a friend in

tow. He can be useful to the Lord straight away, and should expect
to be.

g. If the Discovery Group is some days away, arrange to meet
him within forty-eight hours to cope with initial problems.

h. Hand in your counsellor's form before leaving the building.
Make sure it is completely filled out.

But do not imagine, just because he has come to the front after an
evangelistic address, that the person you are talking with has
necessarily come to faith. People come up for all manner of reasons,
and you may need patiently to sift through problems and difficulties
which are proving to be stumbling-blocks. Some of the more
common ones are dealt with in the next section, and also on pages
268–81 above. You will need all your flexibility and sensitivity at
this point.

It may well be, however, that after you have spent time with him,
patiently answering his doubts from the Bible and experience, he is
ready to take a step of faith. He wasn't quite there at the end of the
preaching, but your conversation with him has made all the difference. You will need to handle him very much as if he was in our first
category of response, the person who says 'Yes'.

So, after things seem to be pretty clear, say to him, 'Do you think
you are ready to say "Yes" to the Lord now?' or 'Is there anything
that is still keeping you back from him?' If he can't think of
anything, say, 'Right, then let's kneel down right away and ask him
to come into your life' [or whatever imagery you use]. He may
prefer to do it on his own, and tell you when he has done so; but he
may want your help and presence at this important time. Probably
he will opt for your help (though respect the other way if he chooses
it). If so, sit or kneel together. Pray for him that he may be truly
brought into the family of God. Then encourage him to pray for
himself, admitting his sins, and asking Christ to come into his life.
Use some promise like John 3:16, John 1:12 or Revelation 3:20, and
get him to claim it. It is no better if he prays out loud, of course, but
Christians do, and he might as well start as he means to continue!
More, it will be an aid in precision, and it will break the sound
barrier. It will also help you to be aware of what is going on. If he
says, 'I can't pray aloud,' say, 'Then let's ask God together that he
will open your lips.' You pray for him, and he will probably find that
he can then pray out loud. It is a great privilege to be around as these
broken, sometimes sobbing words of commitment and repentance
and faith come out. You will often find yourself weeping too, in
empathy. Then pray for him, that the Holy Spirit will baptise him,
deeply into Christ, fill him with spiritual gifts, and never leave him.

It is a most moving time. But do not omit to complete the
counselling form, to get the phone number and fix a day very soon
for a chat. Remember that the bond between a new believer and the

person who led him to faith is very special, and he will take things from you that he will take from nobody else (see 1 Cor. 4:15). When you have handed in your form, you have technically completed your responsibilities. But you will probably want to see such people again, help them on in the early days of their Christian life, and see them settled in a Discovery Group and a church where they can be fed. You will want to ensure that they get some initial Bible reading notes (e.g. *Come Alive to God*) before going on to one of the well-known systems of Bible reading. You will certainly want to pray regularly for him or her. And having tasted the joy of this ministry, you will want to be in it till your dying day, mission or no mission. Rejoice, you may do just that!

3. HANDLING PROBLEMS

We human beings are a very varied bunch! So it is quite impossible
to give advice on every type of situation you may have let yourself in
for when you offered to help in counselling. Here, however, are
some suggestions.

*You may find yourself talking to someone who actually is a Christian,
but is very unsure of it*
'It doesn't work,' or 'I've tried it all before,' 'I think I am a Christian'
are classic expressions of this. It is a mistake to urge decisions on
what may be an indecisive person. Rather

> Go for the promises – John 6:37; Revelation 3:20; Romans 8:1;
> Ephesians 2:1.
> Point to the cross – Hebrews 10:10–14. It is sufficient, and never
> needs to be repeated. Bills do not have to be paid twice!
> Look for the signs of the new birth. He is meant to *know* (1 John
> 5:13).

Some of the marks of new life as indicated in 1 John are worth
pointing out. If he can begin to see some of them growing in his life,
it will be an enormous encouragement. There will gradually
emerge, as we saw above (pp. 275, 443), a new sense of pardon, a
new desire to please God, a new attitude to other people, a new love
for fellow Christians, new power over evil, new joy and confidence
and a new experience of answered prayer (1 John 2:1–2; 2:4, 6;
3:10; 3:14, 16; 4:4; 1:3–4; 4:16–19; 5:14–15). We are meant not just
to hope but humbly to be confident that we are in God's family and
have eternal life (1 John 5:13).

*You may find yourself in conversation with someone from a Catholic
or other strongly liturgical background*
Here the concept of responding to Christ in the faith which grasps
salvation is often confused with receiving Christ regularly afresh in
word and sacrament. Do nothing to disturb the background, but
stress the areas that may have been obscured through it: such a
background may have been weak on the person of Jesus (the saints
and the Virgin may have been more prominent) and weak on the
assurance of salvation (Rom. 5:1, 8). He may have had the frame of
Christianity without the portrait. Don't worry about the frame:
bring the portrait back to life. And this is best done by majoring on
personal response to the gracious offer of Christ to come and take
up residence within our lives, so that we really begin to experience
the reality of the faith we have been nourished in. Liturgy can be an
escape from commitment: quite possibly our friend has been using it
in that way. But it can also become a very rich channel down which

true commitment can flow. It is your privilege to help him to 'possess his possessions'. Show him or her how they can be sure where they stand with God.

You may find yourself caught up in spiritual warfare

We are warned in Scripture that there is a war on. We do not wrestle only against flesh and blood, but against spiritual forces of great power and evil (Eph. 6:10–18; 2 Cor. 11:3; 1 Pet. 5:8). These forces are often stirred up in a mission and present themselves in ways that would normally be unfamiliar.

The New Testament has a lot to say about being affected by demonic forces, and while we should not look for this, we dare not discount it, particularly when faced by violent reaction against the name of Jesus, against a cross, a Bible, or worship; or when the person breaks out into wild hysterical laughter, or displays manic strength. Jesus told how Satan is like a strong man who has such a person 'bound', but the Stronger than the strong can subdue him. If the person has been involved, as many have these days, in black or white magic, astrology, tarot cards, automatic writing, levitation, or has seen a lot of psychic films or literature, or has been involved in Eastern cults, he or she may well need specialised ministry. Don't handle it yourself if you have not seen people been set free from these dark forces. Go with your contact to someone who has had that experience, maybe the speaker.

Some parts of the country are particularly heavy in this area, since there is a great deal of occult practice going on there. Prayer, confident claiming of the name of Jesus, praise and worship, and a life where no unconfessed sin has a hold, are the best ways to combat it. You may be given some prophetic insight into a particular source of the trouble; in which case see the team leader. If you are experienced in this whole area, please also see the team leader so that he may be able to draw you in if any such ministry is required.

You may find someone who has problems about the Holy Spirit

Certain churches are very dogmatic, either in asserting that unless you speak in tongues you are grossly inadequate; or, alternatively, that if you do, you must be acting under psychological or even demonic influence. Because of this polarisation (some churches even asserting that spiritual gifts died in the second century) it is unwise to get involved too much in such a debate unless the person is especially keen to follow it through. One helpful piece of information is that whereas we are enjoined to be filled with the Spirit (Eph. 5:18 – a present continuous tense is used: it is not a once-for-all experience), nowhere in the New Testament is the phrase 'baptism in the Holy Spirit' used of a second stage in Christian initiation. All its seven references are concerned with the initial bringing into the realm of the Spirit when we became Christians (Matt. 3:11; Mark 1:8; Luke 3:16; John 1:33; Acts 1:5; 11:16; I Cor.

12:13). Of course many Christians have times of going deeper with
the Holy Spirit, sometimes very life-changing, but there is no New
Testament evidence that there are two sorts of Christians, those
who have and those who have not been baptised with the Spirit. 'If
any one does not have the Spirit, he is not a Christian' (Rom. 8:9).
We need to encourage people to go deeper in the life of the Spirit, to
ask the Spirit to give them any gifts they need for service, and to
cultivate the fruit of the Spirit.

You may find someone who is highly critical of their church
Don't lend too sympathetic an ear to that sort of complaint. Ask the
person if they have had it out with the minister, and if not, direct
them to him in person. All churches have failings, and we are not
there to take sides. It may be a matter that you could take in
confidence to the team leader, who in turn could raise it with the
appropriate person in the church as something which the team has
run across.

You may find someone whose reactions appear illogical
If someone's reaction is out of proportion to the event; if there seem
to be unwarranted emotions being shown; if there are apparently
irrational thoughts or feelings; if God is unreal, or distant; if success
is all-important or failure seems all-pervading, then suspect that
some event from the past (recent, middle-distance, or early in life) is
clouding the ability to think objectively or to feel appropriately.
Often the climate in which a person was brought up (even, in fact,
often in a Christian home) has moulded attitudes so deeply that
there is a lot of garbage to clear away before God's re-education can
take root. Gently explore whether this is a long-term attitude or
feeling, and this may lead you to the roots of the problem. The key
tools in helping are the two directions of forgiveness: a) *Being
forgiven*: confession, claiming God's forgiveness, and change (1
John 1:8–9) and b) *Forgiving others*. Deliberate forgiveness, expressed in prayer, will in due course change the feelings of resentment (Matt. 5:43–4; 6:14–15). Don't do all the praying. Expect the
other person to pray aloud.

You may hit marriage problems
There is no quick solution. Listen, be alongside – but don't over-
sympathise. Remember that you are listening to only one person's
perspective. The most helpful thing you can do in a short time is to
show the need to forgive the spouse repeatedly (Matt. 18:21–2) and
to ask the Lord to show his truth. Show that we must always be
willing to pray, 'Lord, please change me,' before we ask him to
change the spouse or the situation.

4. GIVING AN EVANGELISTIC TALK

(The notes which follow are designed to help inexperienced members of a mission team, who will find themselves thrown into an unaccustomed and rather frightening role of preaching or speaking at a significant mission event.)

Many of you will be giving a talk, perhaps for the first time, during the mission and you will be all too well aware that it is an important occasion. We are looking for many people to come to faith. How can they hear without a preacher? What if that preacher is you?

There will be many different situations in which you may be asked to speak: in a house meeting, in a school, at a youth rally, in a church service. We need to be as carefully prepared as possible. Here are some suggestions.

Find out

What sort of event is it? Are they churchgoers, enquirers, fellow Christians? Is it a large or small meeting? Will it be in a home or in a larger building? How do you fit in with the rest of the meeting or service? If others are speaking, singing or acting, what are their themes?

How long should you speak for? It is very important to find out – and keep to. Most people tend to over-run.

What is your aim? Be clear on your aim and stick to it. This is of utmost importance. Say to yourself, 'What is this talk intended to do?' Put that aim down on your paper as you prepare, and make sure that everything is subservient to it. Cut out all that is not, however precious it may be. Make sure the aim arises naturally from the passage itself and is not read into it. If *you* are not clear about the aim, nobody else will be. Do not have a split aim. It must be simple, and it must be expressible in a single sentence. This is vitally important.

Remember

Do not make the mistake of underestimating the great difficulty of preaching the good news in such a way that people may have their whole lives transformed. Mercifully, it is God's work, not ours. Only God can reveal God. Only he can shine in blinded hearts. But he has deigned to use us in partnership with him. We are his ambassadors, his messengers, his heralds.

We will be operating in a godless city in a post-Christian age. Preaching in the churches is at a low ebb. There is often little sense of authority in many a pulpit, little biblical content, little attractiveness in the message, little variety in the presentations. The structure of many sermons can be hard to follow. They are often not bathed in prayer. They do not have the seriousness of a dying man pointing another dying man the path to rescue.

Our preaching has got to be different. It has got to be striking. It has got to reach to the heart. And all this in an age which is eaten up with selfishness and materialism, has little belief, rejects authority, has sold out to relativism, is ignorant of the Bible, and is dominated by TV.

One further thing. If God is the evangelist, so are you! This is not a mission based on a big preacher; this mission is multi-faceted, and depends on you. In many a meeting, if people do not hear the good news from you they will not hear it at all.

General preparation

Be open to God. Offer yourself wholly to him. Ask him to rekindle that first love of yours. Open yourself to any gift and equipping that the Holy Spirit can give you. Open yourself to wait on God and see how he will direct you. Open yourself to the possibility that he means to use even you! You need to come to God for your message, not to dream it up and then ask his blessing.

Soak yourself in Scripture. It is dynamite. Let it speak. It will be far more effective than your own best thoughts. Present it without apology, so that it lives for your hearers. No dry bones. They must see in it a taste of new wine. It is through the word of God that people are in fact born again. Use it. Let it be a sword in your hand. Hide behind it. Break it up memorably and attractively so that people sense its power and see its truth.

On the whole you will thrill others most with what has thrilled you. So if you have the opportunity for free choice of subject, choose something that has spoken to you in your own devotional times recently.

Be a modern person and relate to felt needs. Learn from plays, sport, music, films, and sense where people are at. You need to be firmly rooted both in Scripture and in the modern world if you are going to win people from the modern world for Christ. Attack areas where modern man is vulnerable: lack of meaning, lack of love, lack of moral power, hunger for fulfilment, relationships, loneliness, etc.

Don't start with a text, but let your handling of the theme be biblical.

Be Christ-centred. That is what people need. They will never really be helped unless they are brought face to face with Jesus, divine, human, atoning, risen and challenging. Show who he is. Show what he has done. Show that he is alive. Show the difference he can make. Show that a decision is required.

Specific preparation

a. *Read* the passage you have been given, or have chosen, again and again.

b. Make random *notes* of things that strike you. Arrange them in coherent order.

c. *Prune* everything that does not subserve the aim.

d. Get memorable *headings* and arrange material under them. Clarity needs bold headings. You know what you are going to say. They don't. All headings should be crystal clear.

e. Make sure all your *points* come from the scripture. Seek to unfold the scripture and let each point lead on to the next. Thus John 3:16 lends itself to the analysis: God's great love . . . man's great need . . . your great decision (believe). Three main points is about right!

f. Use *illustration* wherever appropriate. Try to have a good illustration for each main point, but don't contrive this. Good illustrations do not draw attention to themselves, they shed light on the path. They are drawn from what is familiar to the hearers. They are not verbose. They are not too highly coloured (so that folk remember the illustration but not what it means). They serve both to let the light in and to rest the concentration as you pause in the argument.

g. Make sure your talk is *applied* to the needs of the hearers, and not left hanging in the air. The challenge to do something about it may well come at the end, but need not be restricted to that. God's truth always challenges response. So should your exposition of it.

h. Prepare your *ending*. The conclusion is critical. The issues of man's need, God's provision, and the need for a step of commitment must be made crystal clear. Give yourself time to plead with people, to challenge them, to tell them that you are going to invite them to open up their lives to the Lord. You then need to anticipate the more obvious objections they may have, and deal with them briskly: 'Are you afraid? Not surprisingly. Many are. But you need have no fear. Perfect love casts out fear, and you are about to invite Perfect Love on board!' Then repeat your challenge.

j. Have your *notes* on cards small enough to fit into your Bible –
large enough for you to see, but not obvious to your hearers.

As you speak

a. Your *manner* is important. As an ambassador of Christ you
should dress unostentatiously, speak naturally, clearly and loud
enough to reach everyone. You should have your Bible out in front
of you, as if to show it is your authority. Practise in a full-length
mirror. Avoid mannerisms and anything that will distract attention
from your message.

b. Be *enthusiastic*. It is unusual in a laid-back society, but is very
attractive. That enthusiasm comes from having found treasure in
Christ. It is sustained by keeping close to him in the face of
disappointment and opposition. It is sustained also by a sober
recognition of the issues. Evangelistic preaching is no optional
extra, but a matter of life and death.

c. Be *bold*. Most inexperienced preachers are not. They are
embarrassed to put the knife in, to say 'you' when they mean 'you',
and to challenge people to decision. You can be modest but bold at
the same time. You have nothing to be ashamed about.

d. Give yourself *time to end*. You may well do so in silence and
prayer.

Silence is powerful. Do not be afraid to use it. Let them consider
what you have said for two minutes of silence. And then tell them
that you are about to lead them in a prayer of commitment: those
who feel ready to take this step can be invited to join in, under their
breath or out loud. Suggest some such prayer as this:

'Lord, I have kept you out of my life for far too long. It is amazing
that you should bother about me when I have bothered so little
about you. Thank you for showing me I need you. Thank you for
dealing with the rotten things in my life on the cross. Thank you
that you are alive, and willing to come and share my life. Lord, I
want to ask you in, here and now. Come in, and never leave me.
And I will seek to be your loyal servant for the rest of my life.'

Gathering up the results

Some of the results will not be known until eternity. But some will
be there to be collected at once. Make room for this.

a. Ask people either to come and see you afterwards or to chat
to one of the team, and sign up for an Enquirers' or Discovery
Group.

b. Challenge undecided people to read one of the Gospels, to be open to the challenge of what it contains, and to be prepared to follow wherever it may lead.

c. Draw people's attention to appropriate material on the book-table.

Finally, be open to opportunities to speak. Don't just wait for the set piece. Evangelistic 'preaching' may happen on a bus or a ferry, in a bar or at a party. Don't wait for the formal occasion. And if it comes, don't let it be formal. 'Redeem the time . . .'

5. USING SCRIPTURE

'Do your best to present yourself to God as . . . a workman who does not need to be ashamed and who correctly handles the word of truth' (2 Tim. 2:15, NIV).

Scripture is that 'word of truth', and we do not need to be apologetic about relying on its inherent truth. It is 'useful for teaching, rebuking, correcting and training in righteousness' (2 Tim. 3:16, NIV). One of those purposes is directed towards our understanding, the others primarily towards our behaviour. But we need to know how to handle this powerful tool well, as skilful workmen. So these hints are offered for those giving talks, and in dealing one-on-one with problems as they arise.

Some things to avoid

a. *Dullness.* This is a living, exciting book, and it is criminal if we reinforce the idea, which many already hold, that it is dull and irrelevant.

b. *Jargon.* It can be fascinating to listen to a specialist on a topic on which we are totally ignorant laymen – but only if that specialist can explain his subject in language that is used in ordinary life. Too often the Christian is not actually sure enough about what he believes to be able to explain it simply, or without Christian jargon. For instance, who, in normal life, understands the word 'grace'? It is totally outside everyday experience, and so it fails to communicate.

c. *Complexity.* Do not cause confusion by using a multitude of cross-references. Seek to use passages of the Bible that will encompass most of what you say.

d. *Assuming much Bible knowledge.* Do not expect your hearers, in most instances, to know anything of biblical background. Even the most intelligent people are often utterly ignorant of the Bible (listen to erudite radio or TV quiz programmes to be aware of this), and even long-term churchgoers are often exceedingly hazy about their faith.

e. *Irrelevance.* The Bible is not just for theoretical undersanding, but to lead us to a change in lifestyle. Consequently, it needs to be applied and seen to be practical for everyday life.

Some things to do

a. It is usually a help if listeners can see the words, as well as listen. Therefore, have the Bible passage printed on service sheets, or use on overhead projector.

b. Bring it to life by putting it into context, using simple, vivid, colloquial language. This helps to show that it is up-to-date and relevant, not just a book of 2,000 years ago.

c. Explain (or get them to explain) what it means. Scrutinise your language, and think, 'If I were an ordinary non-Christian, would I understand these words? Would I understand this line of thought?'

d. Illustrate. Make sure that the illustration really does highlight one aspect of the Bible verse you are using – and ensure that the illustration itself doesn't have to be explained.

e. Maybe use a brief personal testimony to underline the relevance of the scripture passage you are using.

f. Apply what you are saying to the daily life of your audience.

For one-to-one encounters

You are not giving a sermon, but think of it as if you are leading a group Bible study, with a group of one. Use the same principles that you would use in a small group, not doing all the talking, but drawing the thoughts out from the other person.

a. Ask the other person to read the verses out loud, usually not more than two or three at a time.

b. Ask, 'What did that say to you?'

c. Gently ask questions, to help the other person to dig, explore, understand for him/herself.

d. Then add what may be necessary by way of further explanation to bring understanding.

e. When there is understanding, there needs to be a choice about whether this truth is to be applied to life.

f. Prayer that grasps the new truth and deliberately discards the old confusion can ask for the Holy Spirit to help us to live out the consequences of this newly understood truth.

Some useful tips

a. Personalise the text. For example, having looked at 1 John 1:8, ask your client to read it in the first person: 'If I claim to be without sin, I deceive myself . . .' Be very logical. For example, on

Romans 5:6–8, 'What words do you identify with?' 'Powerless, ungodly, sinners.' 'What did Christ do for those people?' 'He died for them.' 'What is that demonstrating?' 'His love.' 'Whom does he love?' 'The sinners.' 'What did you say you are?' 'Powerless, a sinner.' 'Whom does he love?' 'Well, I suppose it means he loves me.' 'Now, read those verses again in the first person.' 'When I was still powerless, Christ died for me, the ungodly, etc.' The truth may not yet have sunk through to the heart, but it has been affirmed through scripture: 'God demonstrates his own love for me in this . . .'

b. When a verse has an 'all' or equivalent, write it down, with some space to be specific. For example, Philippians 4:6, 'Do not be anxious about anything [not even . . . and get your client to list the things that are causing anxiety], but in everything [including . . . and list the same things!), by prayer . . .' etc. Or Matthew 19:26, 'With God all things are possible [except . . . and write down the things that feelings, apparent circumstances, etc., say are impossible. Then delete the word *except* and replace it with *including*] . . .'

c. Carry a Bible, or at least a New Testament, with you at most times. You never know when it may come in handy.

6. LEADING A HOUSE MEETING

Many smaller meetings happen on a mission. Local Christians invite friends or colleagues to meet team members to hear about the mission and the Christian faith. These meetings are hosted by the local Christians, but usually the main input is given by team members, who work closely with their hosts.

A 'home meeting' format can take place in a workplace or in a restaurant as well as in a home. It may be for a group of neighbours, work colleagues, or a specialist group.

These smaller meetings constitute the main part of a mission programme. They enable team members to meet with people in a context where it is easier to talk one-to-one about the Christian faith.

What happens at a home meeting?

These meetings can take place over breakfast, coffee, lunch, supper, a BBQ, in a sauna – i.e., anywhere and anytime! After people have been served whatever food or drink is being offered, the host will usually welcome them, announce the shape of the meeting, and then hand over to the team. One of them will then speak on the relevance of Jesus Christ; discussion will follow, and the meeting be drawn to an end by the stated finishing time. The whole thing needs to be informal, relaxed and Christ-centred.

The host's responsibilities

a. To pray and decide what sort of meeting is appropriate.

b. To make it clear to guests that this is a gathering where the Christian faith will be discussed.

c. To select the place, and the time of day, to suit those invited.

d. To organise all the practical details (layout of room, food and drink).

e. To communicate to the mission organisers as much information as possible about the meeting, particularly the numbers and sort of people.

f. To work closely with team members.

g. To pray for the meeting itself.

h. To be involved in the follow-up of their guests.

The role of the team members

Contacting the hosts

Once the programme has been allocated, it is the responsibility of team members to contact the host, if possible forty-eight hours ahead of the event. This enables the host to get to know them, as well as to co-ordinate plans for the meeting.

a. Introduce yourselves to your hosts. This may need to happen over the phone if time does not permit a visit. Give them confidence. They may be Christians, or church-people, or completely outside the church. Don't expect them to know how to run such a gathering. They will look to you.

b. Find out as much as you can about those who have been invited.

c. Agree with the hosts the specific aim of the meeting. Some meetings will be much more pre-evangelistic (i.e., raising questions, and inviting on to other mission events), while others will be directly evangelistic.

d. Decide whether the refreshment should precede or follow the meeting. It may be best to have something both on arrival, to help people relax, and afterwards, to encourage personal conversations around the room. Stress that nothing elaborate is needed, just simple food.

e. Discover the layout of the room where the meeting will be held. Try to avoid the hosts setting out rows of chairs beforehand.

f. Hosts are not always sure about *who* is actually coming, even if they have received firm acceptances. Reassure them. Encourage them to call their friends or neighbours. Most important, keep them praying.

Preparing to lead the meeting

This can feel daunting, especially the first time. However, the team will work in pairs, one of whom will have had some experience.

a. Meet up with your partner, as you may not know each other. Introduce yourselves, and briefly share your story. Pray together for each other and for the meeting.

b. Find out from each other your strengths and weaknesses, for instance, one might be good at guiding a discussion, rather than giving a formal 'talk'.

c. Decide which of you will open the meeting, give the testimony, do the talk, how the meeting should end, who will bring the bookstall. Be clear on transport, and arrange if possible to meet up to pray with the hosts before people arrive.

d. Go armed with the outlines of two short talks: one for a mixed group, consisting of believers and others; another in case all the

guests turn out to be Christians. In this case something to encourage
them and show them ways in which they could reach out would be
valuable. Remember that you can always discard what you have,
but it is hard to do a succinct off-the-cuff presentation.

Suggestions for topics and format

On the basis of the information received from the hosts (and
sometimes it is very limited), prayerfully decide on what you think
would be appropriate in the meeting. You could:

Use a short talk (10 mins maximum), as a discussion starter. This
can help people to relax, and at the same time thrill them with the
person of Jesus, prompt questions and initiate conversation. You
could deal with:

    a. One of the mission titles
    b. What is so special about Jesus?
    c. What's wrong with the world?
    d. What is a Christian?
    e. Why bother?

Try to start from questions which people are really asking, and
move from there into the relevance of the gospel to those questions.

Use testimony – from each of yourselves, your hosts and perhaps
others in the meeting. It may be that your hosts take more of a lead,
introducing their own 'stories', and then asking their friends to say
where they stand, with the team members coming last. One of them
can then give a succinct challenge to faith.

Use a book that you know, and think will help to answer questions
people are asking. Have some copies available; you might use some
thoughts from a chapter to start a discussion.

Use a video – if you know, or your hosts know, of a short arresting
presentation which would start a discussion.

As suggested above, always go prepared with two talks – one for
those who do not yet know the Lord, and one for Christians. Don't
be downcast if nobody but Christians are present. This can often
happen. What do you do? One possibility is to go through what
Christianity is not – not creeds, conduct, ceremonies, churchgoing
(though it embraces all four) and then show what it is: Jesus Christ
himself, and a vital relationship with him. Then you could ask round
the room what Jesus means to each person. It should warm the
hearts of those present, and it should not be difficult to encourage
them afresh to reach out to others with the good news of Jesus. You
may well find among them those who know about Christianity, but

do not know Christ. They need to be encouraged to open up their lives to him and to join a Discovery Group after the mission.

Alternatively, you could develop the headings for two brief talks: one of encouragement (such as the growth of the faith in Corinth from one man to a lively church, Acts 18:1–11), and one of challenge (such as the differences which happen to people when the Holy Spirit is welcomed among them, e.g. Acts 2:37–47). Choose which to use. Then get discussion going. Trust God to make you a blessing, even if it is only the hosts of the home meeting that are present. Time spent in encouraging or challenging dispirited church people is never wasted. Gently turn their orientation outward. It is sometimes most rewarding to discuss with them how they might share their faith at work. And if only Christians are present, why not encourage them to pray out loud? This could be the opportunity for some to 'break the sound barrier'.

Leading the meeting

a. Arrive ahead of time to pray with the host. Perhaps not many people are expected, and it may even be appropriate to go out and invite the neighbours yourselves. Try to chat, however briefly, with each guest as they come through the door so that you do not come over as an invasion from Mars!

b. Come with a bookstall; arrange that and other mission materials on a small obvious table. Work out where you will stand, or sit. You need to be able to have eye contact with everyone.

c. Encourage the host to introduce you both and to indicate when the meeting will end.

d. Be at ease, full of the Holy Spirit. Then you will put others at ease. Have your team member pray for you constantly as you speak, and vice versa. Expect God to work. A little humour at the outset works wonders if it is natural.

e. Treat spiritual things as the most natural in the world. Be prepared to move easily from natural to spiritual things and vice versa.

f. Use the Bible naturally, without apology or explanation, as the sourcebook for Christianity, and use your own experience as 'icing on the biblical cake'.

g. Your talk should be seen as a discussion-starter. Do not go on for more than ten minutes. You want to see where they are, and that will emerge through the discussion. Your opening needs to be arresting.

Hints on working in small groups

a. No two groups are the same. The same 'formula' will not necessarily succeed because it worked with a previous group. Team members must quickly try to get a 'feel' of the group and continue to be sensitive to its character.

b. People will attend the meeting for a variety of reasons, and many of the guests will be nervous and apprehensive. Team members should try to put them at ease. This will enable more people to contribute in sharing or discussion.

c. Team members should identify the main characters in the group (i.e., the dominant, the talkative, the humorist, the deviant, the angry, the confused, the silent, the co-operative), and act accordingly. Remember that most will bring with them some burden of soul or body, however well disguised.

d. Do not make quick decisions about people – you could be terribly wrong.

e. Do not get into an argument or allow others to do so. There is a great difference between unprofitable argument and lively discussion. Relationships with the people is more important than winning the point at issue. You may well allow several unprofitable issues to pass you by until you find one which will open up profitable discussion.

The discussion

a. Try not to dominate the discussion, but be ready to change direction if needed.

b. If possible, use your colleague, who has not done the talk, to steer the discussion; but work very much together.

c. Do not be embarrassed to answer questions from Scripture. It is powerful and carries its own ring of truth.

d. Avoid the situation where all the remarks are directed exclusively to team members. Open it up for others to contribute. Do not let one person dominate the meeting, or allow the discussion to wander into irrelevance.

e. Never try to impress: ask yourself, 'What answer would be most helpful for the state where the questioner is right now?'

f. Keep in touch with the Spirit. Expect the unexpected. Keep the discussion on Jesus.

g. At some point the way of salvation will almost certainly need to be covered in simple, well-illustrated and non-theological language.

Closing a meeting

a. Close by the pre-announced time. If discussion is still going on, then it can continue as some leave and more coffee is brought in.

b. A closing prayer may be inappropriate, but that depends on how the meeting has gone. For some it could be the time of decision. Have a simple prayer prepared and encourage people, if they feel they are ready, to repeat it silently after you.

c. A useful way of concluding might be to say, 'We want to be of help to you and to encourage you in every way possible. Before we leave today I'm going to pass round these blank cards and pencils, because we'd like to know what you thought of what we had to say.' Get these items passed round. Ask for three things to be put on the card: 'Please write 1) your name, 2) a comment on what you thought about what we had to say, and 3) if you have opened up your life to Christ, just put a tick in the top right-hand corner. We would like to give you some material that will be of help in developing that relationship with Christ and invite you to join a Discovery Group.' Not everyone will fill in such a card, and no pressure must be exerted, but some will. Collect the cards, and afterwards go through them with the hosts.

d. Personally invite all the group to another mission meeting, and have information ready to hand out about dates, times and places.

e. Use literature to sell, give, or lend as appropriate.

Afterwards

a. Circulate. You may well have noticed that some of the group have been touched by what has been said. Try to make sure everyone has a personal word. Team members should take the initiative in approaching people. Such conversations after the meeting are usually the most profitable of all.

b. Offer to pray with people about their situation then and there, as you sit or stand.

c. It may be appropriate to arrange another house meeting later on in the week for further discussion. Sometimes a guest who has been intrigued by this meeting will offer to invite a group of friends round for a similar evening.

d. After the guests have gone, assess with the hosts how the evening went. Go through the response cards. Pray together. Talk about the strengths and weaknesses of the meeting. Learn from it. Encourage the hosts in following through with their friends in the next day or two.

e. If anyone has responded wanting a Discovery Group, remember to take the form with all the information to the next team meeting.

A word about other types of meetings

Specialist groups

It may be that you will be assigned to a grief support group, or a meeting with parents of handicapped children. Remember, you are not expected to be an expert on this subject. Team members will be allocated on the basis that one of you will have had some experience in the area. The aim is to draw alongside, to be understanding, and all the time to show people how Jesus Christ is applicable to their situation – however hopeless they may think it to be.

Restaurant meetings

If your meeting is held in a restaurant, plan the seating arrangements with your hosts, where the team members should sit, who is paying for the meal, how it will be ordered, and at what time in the meal the team members should give some input. Try not to get stuck in conversation with those on your left and right. At the end of the meal, leave your seats and be available for personal conversation.

7. HOSTING A HOUSE MEETING

(These notes are intended for those considering hosting a meeting in their home.)

What actually is a house meeting?

During a mission a house meeting provides the main means of reaching people who would not otherwise come near a church. It is the name given to a gathering of people in someone's home to hear more about the Christian faith. It is not a formal supper party – though food may be included. It does not need best china, nor does it mean that the house has to be clean, tidy and especially neat. It does not mean that you need a big house, or a big room, or that you need elegant furniture – it is informal. The team will provide the main input.

What happens at a house meeting?

After people have arrived and been served with refreshments, get everyone seated, with the team members clearly visible and audible.

Then welcome everyone who has turned up, and introduce the team members, who will take over at that point, usually giving a short thought-provoking talk, interspersed with testimony and questions. The meeting is then brought to a close, and personal conversation goes on throughout the room.

What if I am a member of a small Bible study group, fellowship group or prayer group?

Good news if so, because for the purposes of this mission week the group can be split in half, so that you can make enough room for each member to invite a non-Christian friend. It is a good idea if you can get the half of the group that is not meeting first to pray for the other half, and vice versa.

How do I go about setting up a house meeting?

a. *Pray*. If you are able to run a house meeting with another member of your household (or with a friend), then get together to pray about it. Pray about what you should do, whom you might invite, what sort of meeting you will run. Prayer triplets could be set up now, specifically to pray for those you could invite.

b. *Plan*. Whose home will the meeting be in? What sort of meeting will it be? What time would suit people best? Nearer the time, these questions need to be sorted out.

c. *Invite*. Your aim is to invite non-Christian friends, acquaintances from the neighbourhood and/or from work, social contacts, children's friends' parents, etc. It may well be right to include some people from other churches who may or may not be committed to Christ.

How should I go about inviting people?

Whether you ask people face to face, by phone or by written request, be natural when you issue the invitation, and make it clear what you are inviting people to (e.g., 'To a talk by a member of the team on . . .' or 'To a short talk on . . . by . . . , with an opportunity for questions and discussion,' or whatever). Experience has shown that you need to aim for a definite 'yes' or 'no' reply to the invitation, rather than an 'I might'.

What about contact with members of the team?

The team will be involved in many of these meetings. Once the details of the house meeting date, time and place have been given to the church representative and he has assured you that it is on the programme, then rest assured that members of the team will be assigned to you.

Normally two members of the team will come to your home, though it may be that you are more than willing and able to co-lead the meeting with a team member, thus enabling more house meetings to take place.

One of the team members will be in contact a day or two before the meeting, to introduce themselves. Together you can finalise the exact order of what is happening, when the refreshments are to be served, etc. Allow time before the meeting starts to pray with your team members.

What about the day itself?

a. Follow up your invitations by phone a day or so before the meeting is due to take place.

b. Be clear beforehand about the seating arrangements (not rows of chairs, please!), and allow time and space for people to mix as they arrive and to meet the team members.

c. Be clear who will be serving the refreshments, and when.

d. Have a small table for the bookstall that the team members will bring.

e. Pray before, during and after the meeting.

f. Avoid Christian jargon at all times.

g. End the meeting in a natural way, inviting people to stay on for coffee and to deal with any unanswered questions.

What about follow-up?

It is the hosts' responsibility to follow-up those who attend the house meeting. It is therefore very important that the hosts think about what events or groups they can invite people to after the meeting. Aim to get everyone who came to your house meeting to go to another event, church service, or Discovery Group.

The team will have brought with them a small bookstall in case people would like to buy booklets or books. You may want to provide a small number of books you could lend yourself. Make a note of the borrowers, and follow them up later, when the book is returned.

The team may hand out blank response cards for people to jot down what they thought of the evening. That will be talked through with you. The information on these cards can help you to carry out follow-up work.

8. OPEN-AIR WORK

The term 'open-air work' is used to describe the many ways we can communicate our faith on streets, beaches and shopping malls in attractive and thought-provoking ways, to people who do not normally go near a church. The manner in which this is conducted is just as important as what is said, sung or acted.

Background preparation

a. Permission needs to be obtained for most open-air work from local authorities, shopping mall managers, etc. Many cities are willing to allow a mission team to do something once and see how it goes down with the local shopkeepers. Each mall manager will have his own special instructions. Make sure all the team is aware of what these are.

b. You need to choose a time of day when many people are around. This is important. It is not worthwhile planning something, and just hoping people will turn up. We need to be where people are: for example, in the middle of a busy shopping day, a place where people eat their lunch is good.

Different types of open-air work

The 'set piece' presentation
This can use whatever medium is appropriate – drama, music, circle dancing, puppets, juggling, sketch-board. It usually requires a small 'stage area', which focuses people's concentration on a planned programme.

There are two different groups of people in such a presentation. The 'up front' people (musicians, dramatists, speakers), who need to remain free from engaging in conversation while the programme is going on; and the 'crowd', who will gather around the performers, watch, and engage in conversation with those who stop and watch. Contrary to what is often thought, the 'crowd' is more important than the 'up front' people.

The performers will have planned a programme (usually no more than twenty minutes), so that the material follows in a logical sequence, presenting different sides of the gospel. Every sketch, testimony or song is linked by a speaker. The idea is to have a fast-moving programme (with no pauses) that will attract a crowd.

a. The team needs to meet together for prayer and praise before going out on to the streets. We are entering hostile territory whenever we take the gospel out, and we need the cleansing and protection of the Lord before we go.

b. Each team member needs to have an ample supply of literature that advertises the mission.

c. At the time arranged, all involved will meet to start the presentation. The 'crowd' should form a fairly close circle around where the presentation is to be done, allowing enough space for actors, and yet not blocking walkways.

d. When in the 'crowd', watch, pray and be sensitive to those who gather around you. After a sketch it is often a good idea to turn to some person and ask, 'What did you think of that drama?', wait for the reply and take it from there. You may well not be used to speaking to complete strangers – nor are they! You will get both friendly and hostile responses. Keep your conversation light, and yet be bold in handing out literature and inviting people to a mission meeting.

e. Other 'crowd' members may well stand further away, handing out mission literature and engaging in conversation. Be alert to those around you. Allow people space to stop and watch before going up to them. Never pester passers-by. Smile!

f. Be sensitive to the ending of the presentation. That is the time for all to get involved in one-to-one conversations. If people have indicated an interest in coming along to a main meeting, look out for them when it happens.

The use of questionnaires

This is another quite different approach that is sometimes helpful in the open air. Singly or in twos, team members go out with a simple questionnaire and conduct a random sample of views which can sometimes develop into really good conversations. At the very least, such encounters will give the person you are talking to a close-up view of a committed Christian chatting on the street, which may be unusual to him or her! It will also develop your own skills in chatting informally about important issues with complete strangers.

Here is a simple questionnaire used during a city-wide mission called 'Celebration of Hope'. It had these three questions in it:

a. Do you think there are any solid grounds for hope these days?

b. Do you think the Christian church has any real hope to hold out to people?

c. If you could meet Jesus Christ, would you want to?

The encounter might go somewhat like this:

Q: Excuse me, but I wonder if you could spare a moment to help us with a short questionnaire we are conducting from Celebration of Hope here this week?

A: Very well, but I haven't long to spare.

Q: I quite understand. Here, then, is the first question: 'Do you think there are any solid grounds for hope these days?'

A: Well, I suppose we have a great country – and our homes mean a lot to us.

Q: Right. But of course many people live wretched lives without much hope. So here's the next question on my list: 'Do you think that the Christian church has any real hope to hold out to people?'

A: Well, I'd never thought about that. They seem to keep themselves to themselves.

Q: Alas, that is often true. But Jesus wasn't like that. He was always moving out among people, offering them the most wonderful things to celebrate, and the most solid grounds for hope. So here's my third question: 'If you could meet Jesus Christ, would you want to?'

. . . and if that does not open up the chance for personal testimony to the living Jesus, I should be surprised!

There is of course no knowing how people will respond to your questions. But you can see how a simple three-question questionnaire like this can be used (with a minimum of imagination) to lead to a conversation which could be profitable. There is a progression about the questions. They start where you are – Celebration of Hope, which is happening as they speak to you; and with a question about the hopes which everyone must cherish in their hearts one way or another – for nobody can live long without hope. You then find your way to a narrower front in your second question, asking as it does what they feel about the church, but more specifically planting in their minds the possibility that it might have some hope to offer and something to celebrate. No matter what the response to that, it is easy to move on to the source of hope, and the solid grounds we have for it in the historical Jesus, crucified and risen.

Remember the following points:

a. Your manner is more important than what you say.

b. You are not there to argue, but to invite the person to answer questions which may gently lead them towards the light.

c. You must not delay people long – unless they want to, and a good conversation develops.

d. Your aim is to point them decisively to the hope that Jesus offers, and to show why it is so solidly grounded.

e. You want to leave them with an invitation to join you and attend some mission event – and maybe after a good encounter, you could leave them with something to read.

Bookstalls

Hosting a booktable – often in a shopping mall – is another way to publicise a mission and engage in conversation with those who are interested. Posters and leaflets about the mission would also be needed. Free cups of coffee go down well.

A praise march

This is a very powerful way to make a statement to a city, by drawing the local Christians and the team together. All are encouraged to join in, from children on bikes, to seniors, as the march moves slowly along a pre-arranged route, usually following a music group, singing and praising God. Banners can be carried. Leaflets can be distributed to those who watch. People can be invited to join in. At one or more points along the route there could be a pause to give time for more singing, some drama, music, circle dancing and possibly a short message aimed at those who have joined in.

Open-air work can be enjoyable, if rather terrifying. Remember God's encouragement to Paul: 'Do not be afraid; keep on speaking, do not be silent. For I am with you, and no-one is going to attack and harm you, because I have many people in this city' (Acts 18:9–10, NIV).

9. VISITING DURING MISSIONS

Visiting is largely neglected by the churches, and left to the sects and the travelling salesmen. There is therefore considerable resistance among householders to those who just turn up on their doorstep. We may be asked to visit selected people, or to visit down a street. In either case, we would be wise to keep these considerations in mind.

The preparation

Preparation is needed even for something so unpredictable as visiting.

We need a warm heart

We need a heart full of Jesus' love, before we will give ourselves to such a daunting task. Maybe read Luke 15, or 2 Corinthians 4 or 5 or John 21 before going out. I often go back to Acts 9:11, the story of the reluctant visitor!

    a. The Lord called Ananias because he needed him (v.10).

    b. The Lord told him to go and visit a home (v.11).

    c. There was someone in that home in deep need (v.11).

    d. God had already prepared that person to be receptive (v.11).

    e. Ananias was reluctant: this man was too prejudiced, too tough, too hostile (v.13).

    f. At the second attempt, Ananias went, no doubt in fear and trembling (v.17).

    g. His approach was natural, friendly, direct (v.17).

    h. His message was of Jesus, who can open blind eyes and fill an empty life (v.17).

    i. He found a very practical ministry was awaiting him in that house (vv.18–19).

    j. His obedience was rewarded in the conversion of Saul and his filling with the Spirit.

We need a cool head

We need to listen carefully to the instructions we have been given, familiarise ourselves with the geography, and if possible know the names of those to be visited. Go equipped with a pen, a notebook (to take down the details of each visit), and a few tracts, booklets or Gospels which could come in handy, along with a leaflet about the mission. Have a good grasp of what goes on in the local church for all ages, so that you can offer appropriate suggestions for the household.

The approach

You may feel happier visiting two by two: there is a precedent!

a. Don't work your way down one side of the street consistently: people will see you coming and not let you in.

b. It is easiest to fill in information about your last visit when you are standing in your next doorway, before you actually knock. You are practically invisible then.

c. Pray on the doorstep; pray for your initial impact, humour, self-forgetfulness, and warmth.

d. Remember, if you are afraid, that you have the initial advantage. They are not expecting you, and may be busy, defensive, suspicious. So smile. God loves you!

e. If a child opens the door, ask him to go get one of his parents, and if the child accompanies the adult, make sure you involve him in the conversation.

f. First impressions are crucial. So introduce yourself with a friendly 'Hi' or 'Hello'. Announce your name, your authority (from the church or the mission) and your purpose.

g. Be cheerful, be unfailingly courteous, be natural. Make it plain you are not out to con them or get something out of them, but to love them and give something to them.

h. Don't be dismayed if you are seldom invited in. But get in if you can. Don't outstay your welcome.

The visit

There is, of course, no blueprint. Keep your eyes open for any lead, any common ground. Here are some possible aims you might bear in mind:

a. Aim to establish a good relationship. Let them see you are not odd. Never argue, never be rude. Open the way for a return visit, which will often be much easier.

b. Aim to gather information about the house and family which could be handy for future use – are there kids who could be invited to a Sunday school party, is there a one-parent family which could do with some practical assistance, etc.?

c. Aim to impart information about the mission. Concentrate on a single event, and see if they would like you to pick them up before going to it – they might well not bother (or dare) to come on their own. 'Come with me' is powerful. 'Do go' is not.

d. Aim to speak of Jesus, to mention his name one way or another. It is he who can meet their need. He is indeed the only card in our pack! And many people do not know that the heart of Christianity is not a system but the person of Jesus. It is at this juncture that a word of testimony can be so effective.

e. It may be suitable to pray for the house, or the person, or some need you have discovered. People often value this even if they do not pray themselves. NB: Use a natural voice!

f. It could be good to leave a bit of literature behind, along with information about the mission.

The questions

These are sure to emerge if you get into a conversation of any length. Sometimes they will be excuses: 'The minister has never called . . . I went to church too much when I was young . . . I can worship God in my back yard.' Sometimes they will be real difficulties, such as the divided state of the church, the New Age movement, the implausibility of Christianity in a secular age, the problem of suffering, the aching heart of a battered wife or a single mother. Try to analyse whether it is *an excuse* or *a problem* you are dealing with. Excuses come from hard hearts. Problems come from confused minds. I sometimes say, 'If I were able to answer this to your satisfaction, do you think that the way would be clear to your opening up your life to Christ?' If not, don't bother with the excuse. Answering it won't help. Showing that you have seen through it may.

Always be courteous, humble and loving. Never seek to score points. Always seek to find out and maximise any common ground.

The sequel

a. When out of sight, jot down any comments you have, any information that is not confidential which might be passed back to those who sent you.

b. Pray for the house you have just visited.

c. Decide if a further visit in a day or two's time would be fruitful.

d. Do not be discouraged. If you are, it will show in your manner, and you will not be a good witness. Read Isaiah 55:11. Claim Christ's power as you go. Claim Christ's presence, and as he bade you, go (Matt. 28:18–20).

10. FILLING IN RESPONSE FORMS

It might be thought utterly unnecessary to spend time in a
training course on so apparently insignificant a detail as this.
But experience shows that the filling in of these cards is of the
utmost importance. It is the only written record which survives the departure of the mission team, who are certain to
have made a great many contacts in town that the churches
know nothing of. They need to be filled in with great care,
which is why we have devoted considerable detail to this
matter at the start of Appendix B. It is not only the front of the
form which needs to be filled in. When a team member has
gleaned any additional information about the person concerned or their circumstances, he should note it on the back of
the card before handing it in to those in charge of follow-up. It
is often also a help to add a note of the occasion at which the
card was filled in. At all events, it will pay to assimilate
Appendix B on the matter. It comes out of a lot of experience,
much of it frustrating simply because we ourselves did not do
what we there have come to recommend!

Appendix E
Drama and Movement in Evangelism
Jane Holloway

The truth of the gospel can be powerfully communicated using creative arts such as drama, movement and mime. However, it is important to realise that although for some people this form of expression seems very natural, it is viewed by others as inappropriate. We need to remain sensitive to this tension and do all that is possible to ensure that these art forms are used to glorify God and not man. The incarnational significance of using the whole body in worship (cf. John 1:14) is being grasped afresh in many parts of the Christian church. Worship need not be restricted to our minds and hearts. In Romans 12:1 Paul reminds us 'in view of God's mercy, to offer your bodies as living sacrifices, holy and pleasing to God – this is your spiritual act of worship'. Such is the attitude in which to use these creative art forms in our churches and for reaching out to others. The limelight should go not to the performers, but to God himself in centre stage.

For background information concerning the use of these arts, please refer to the books listed at the end of chapter 4, on page 104.

CONTEXTS IN WHICH DRAMA AND MOVEMENT CAN BE USED

In worship services

a. *Call to worship* – Scripture can be read by different voices; responsive readings can involve the whole congregation; an interpretative dance can introduce the theme; or a simple procession can carry in some symbol, such as a cross or a candle.

b. *Children's time* – read a story, then get them to act it out and dress up; involve other children in reading parts; teach simple arm movements to their favourite action songs, or a circle dance; use visual aids, sketch boards, puppets, mime.

c. *Scripture reading* – use different readers for different characters in a passage; act (or dance) out the whole passage using biblical narrative; update a parable for today's world.

Encourage those involved in the public reading of Scripture to

i. Prepare prayerfully.

ii. Find the version which is needed for the occasion and be familiar with the passage. What does it say? How should it be read? Use punctuation, pauses. Practise reading it out loud.

iii. Speak clearly and don't mumble. Learn how to treat a microphone as a friend and not an enemy. Look as though you believe what you are reading.

d. *Congregational prayer time* – different prayers can be led by different people, and simple arm movements to familiar prayers (or responses) like the Lord's Prayer can be taught to the whole congregation.

e. *Communion* – without detracting from the holiness of the meal, the elements can be carried in by those doing processional dance steps. The movements of the minister during the consecration are important too.

f. *Worship time* – dances can be prepared for particular hymns or songs that are to be used in the service, and can be danced while the congregation is singing.

g. *Work with the preacher* – either to illustrate the theme of the service with a sketch or a dance, or to dramatise a particular theme of the talk by using a short sketch.

In teaching

a. In Sunday school – whether for adults or children – use opportunities to get people to act out the Bible passage under discussion. Also encourage the use of the whole body to express lessons learned.

b. Workshops can be used to teach more about the art forms themselves, to encourage anyone interested to have a go, as well as to identify people who may be willing to give more time to using drama and movement in the life of the church.

In outreach

a. Guest services in the church, incorporating any of the above suggestions into a service, can often communicate much of the joy and vitality of the Christian faith.

b. Special church events, such as picnics and barbecues, often have a slot for a 'talk'; so why not insert something different?

c. Church holidays, children's camps – these are ideal opportunities to introduce drama.

d. Local schools – many churches have connections with schools. Offer to go in and do an assembly using drama, or lay on a presentation of music and drama in the lunch hour.

e. Open-air work – out in shopping centres, on housing estates, on the streets, and in praise marches: a mixture of testimony, drama, circle dancing, juggling, puppetry, and speaking can lead people to find out more about the Christian faith.

f. Local arts festivals, community centres, amateur dramatics – maybe those interested in acting and dance could work together to produce something for a community event like this.

HOW TO INTRODUCE THE USE OF
DRAMA AND MOVEMENT

It will need much prayer and sensitivity, but it can be done.

a. *Be open to God.* He is the source of all creativity, and creative arts stem from him. An interest in drama or dance may not mean you should use it in public performance. Your role might be that of an enabler of others. But be open to God, and open to have a go!

b. *Be open with the minister.* Keep him informed of plans as they emerge. Is the church ready for the use of drama or movement? Is the leadership sympathetic?

c. *Share the vision with like-minded friends*, and start praying together.

d. *Explore the possibilities.* Where are the places that drama or dance could be used in the church or for outreach? Are there any local resources in terms of people already involved, or a neighbouring church which could help? Investigate books on the subject.

e. *Prepare the congregation.* Some teaching will be necessary on how the arts can be integrated with worship and outreach. Otherwise you are courting shock, and rejection.

f. *Choose a suitable occasion*. For example, a special festival – Advent, Easter, Harvest.

g. *Start with the children* – they so often show adults the way!

TYPES OF DRAMA

a. Readings and storytelling – taking a passage of Scripture, a Bible narrative, a poem.

b. Short sketches – essentially concentrating on one theme, using a minimum of props, designed to be part of a 'bigger picture'.

c. One-act plays – less demanding in terms of equipment and actors than a full-length play, but enabling a plot to be developed.

d. Full-length plays – using full stage facilities. The theme could be either secular (with an underlying Christian message) or explicitly Christian.

Most of these different types of drama use words as the main means of communication; however, mime, which replaces words with stylised movements, can often be even more powerful, and is invaluable in an international context, because it needs no words.

TYPES OF MOVEMENT OR DANCE

a. Simple arm movements, or gestures, to children's songs, and to prayers.

b. Folk dances or Israeli-type circle dances.

c. Congregational dances – where the whole congregation might process out to the last song or hymn.

d. Set pieces by a smaller dance group:

i. dance/mime – to a piece of music, song or narration;

ii. presentation dance – done as a ministry for healing or meditation or as sheer worship.

e. Spontaneous movement done without any prior choreography, in response to God's love.

STARTING A DRAMA OR DANCE GROUP

In order to produce good quality pieces of drama or dance, time is needed for creation, practice and rehearsal before presenting them in front of others. Forming a small group specifically to work on this needs careful consideration.

a. *What type of group?* It could be one that meets occasionally, as and when opportunities come to present a piece. It could be a more long-term group, meeting regularly, and committed to the regular production of material.

b. *The aim of a group* would be to please God (and not the church, the minister or those involved), to serve the church, and to communicate the gospel to those outside the church. Ideally the aim would be a mixture of all three.

c. *Leadership* involves commitment to the group's priorities and aims; being prepared to be involved as well as to learn; encouraging and caring for group members; discovering and developing creative gifts in others; and putting in time to organise and delegate scriptwriting and publicity. Some previous experience would be helpful.

d. *The group* can comprise people with and without experience. The most important thing is commitment – to God, to the work, and to each other. As the group gets to know each other, prays, worships and studies the Bible together, new gifts will emerge, creativity will flow, and great love and trust will develop. Try not to have too large a group: between three and ten members can work well; anything larger tends to get a bit impersonal. However, for special productions others may need to be drawn in.

e. *Each meeting* should include prayer, worship and sharing. Other elements would be: time to learn new things; drama games and movements; exercises to improve muscles and breathing, body movement, balance, and weight transference; working together as a group and synchronisation; working on different techniques; improvisation and work on new material. You could also invite outside speakers to teach, and you could go to plays, concerts and dance productions. Obviously the content will depend on how much group members know at the start.

f. *Starting off.* Decide when and where to meet. Choose a large carpeted room if possible. Break down barriers gently and gradually (e.g., embarrassment at moving, or at being watched, and uncertainty as to what to expect). Relax and have fun. Worship and pray together. Clarify the leadership, the aims of the group, and how often you will meet.

INTEGRATING DRAMA OR DANCE INTO
AN EVENT OR SERVICE

a. Work closely with the leaders.

b. Find out the theme, and plan a piece to fit as appropriate.

c. What is the aim of your piece? How does it start and finish? What should precede and follow it?

d. Does the piece need introduction and/or linking from the previous item to the following item?

e. Try not to introduce too many new ingredients into one event.

f. If drama or dance is to be used for the first time, a short word of explanation is imperative.

PRACTICAL DETAILS

a. Performance space. This will often need to be cleared beforehand. Plan what area is needed, and who will clear away chairs, microphones, etc.

b. Visibility. Sit in the seats and find out what is visible from different places and angles.

c. Audibility. Try not to use microphones in drama for smaller events. Teach people to throw their voices. If microphones are needed, do voice checks prior to the event, and work with the sound technician.

d. Technical resources. If using taped music, get it all set up and have it tried beforehand. Carefully brief whoever is working the sound desk. Plan the positioning of any props.

e. Dress. For dance, it needs to allow for full movement, and should also be modest. For drama, keep it simple but uniform.

f. Ensure that the final rehearsal takes place where the performance is due to happen.

MOVING FORWARD

Resources

Make use of available resources (see book list in chapter 4, p. 104). Get in contact with others working in the same areas. Share ideas. Much of the drama published is governed by copyright laws. Check these out and get the church or organisation to purchase the appropriate licences (either for a one-off performance in a worship or mission context, or for a situation where the audience is paying to see the work).

Creating new material

Whether it is writing a new sketch or choreographing a fresh dance, God is the creator and will give the creativity.

a. As a group or as an individual, pray over the piece of music, song, theme or biblical passage. Write down ideas. Share these with others.

b. The material needs to be relevant and appropriate to the place and the event. Find out what that is. Spend time with the speaker if it is to be integrated with the talk.

c. One can begin the creative process by having several people improvise, and getting one person to write down the precise lines or movements. Or one can identify choreography or sketch writing gifts in one or two individuals and send them off to come up with the piece.

d. There is a danger in 'writing by committee', although on more than one occasion it has been known to work.

e. The hardest part is when a dance or a sketch is produced and does not seem to work. Do not use it just because it was created by the group. Talk and pray about it, and take what is good from it and work from there.

Handling the responses

These will be many and varied. The same piece can evoke praise from one and severe criticism from another. Listen to where the comments are coming from, and:

a. Direct any praise back to the Lord.

b. Weigh the criticism, pray about it in the group, and learn from it.

c. Be prepared to have no reaction whatsoever to a piece. Your most funny piece of drama can fall flat, without a single laugh, especially in another culture or in a context where drama is not often used. Equally, a hard-hitting serious piece of drama can evoke laughter when you are least expecting it.

Work out how you wish applause to be handled, and educate the congregation as to how they can show their appreciation of these newer art forms when they are used in the context of worship.

Most important – have fun!

Appendix F
Leading Worship in Evangelism
Neale Fong

INTRODUCTION

Leading worship in church is a great responsibility. You are seeking to bring the whole congregation to the place where there is real communication with God both at an individual and at a corporate level.

It is a ministry with skills which differ from, yet complement those of a pastor, priest, elder, or even musician. It is also a ministry that requires certain gifts. It should not be seen as one where everyone has 'a go' to develop leadership; nor as a requisite for everyone involved in leadership; nor as a 'stepping-stone' to other ministries within the church.

Those who lead worship need to realise the awesome responsibility in doing so, understanding the spiritual dimensions of what they are involved in, the skills of communication that need to be practised, and the variety of music and worship forms that can be accommodated.

FUNCTIONS OF A WORSHIP LEADER

a. To lead the congregation into the presence of God, so that they may both worship him and receive from him in every service.

When leading an evangelistic service, the goal would be to ensure that the service itself, the type of music and form of worship used, and the manner of the worship leader, should all bear witness to the life-changing reality and presence of Jesus Christ.

b. To co-ordinate the instrumentalists, singers and other participants in their ministry within the service.

GENERAL CONSIDERATIONS IN LEADING WORSHIP

a. The main aim is to make people feel comfortable and relaxed in a warm and joyful atmosphere. People who are ill-at-ease will not worship. Remember, non-churchgoers will be faced with a whole new world when they walk in the front door of the church. In general, people will find it harder to respond to the worship leader and preacher in a tense and overformal atmosphere.

b. At the same time as putting people at ease and making them feel comfortable, to be truly effective a service needs to have a built-in sense of expectation; of waiting to see the 'unexpected' happen; of realising that God, through his Spirit, is present and at work. Leadership of the service at this point requires courage and sensitivity.

c. Paradoxically, the worship leader needs to be as unobtrusive as possible, but also to give strong leadership. You have done a good job, if at the close of the service people did not realise that you were actually leading. Yet a good leader will maintain control of the participants and gently but firmly lead the congregation into worship, encouraging them to be sensitive to the presence and guidance of the Spirit.

d. The analogy from Anne Ortlund's book *Up With Worship* is a good one on which to model our services: the audience or congregation is God; the participants are the worshippers; the prompters in the wings are the worship leaders.

People need to be involved in giving worship to God, and not mere spectators at some 'holy event'. The worship leader tries to see that this happens.

ESSENTIALS IN WORSHIP LEADING

Preparation
a. The worship leader must know the type of service (e.g.,

evangelistic, thanksgiving, baptismal), the theme of the service (e.g., God's forgiveness, discipleship), and the order of service (what follows what!). These aspects must be discussed and prayed through prior to the service, with a worship team or committee who meet on a regular basis.

b. During the week much time should be spent in thinking and praying through the service. Worship leaders need the anointing of the Holy Spirit as much as the preacher does.

c. It is a good idea (especially if you are new to leading worship) to know basically what you will be saying at different points during the service. There is nothing wrong with working unobtrusively from notes that you have made in preparation.

d. Be early to the service and have the programmes, music, books, overhead transparencies and participants organised prior to the start of the service. This type of preparation gives a calmness to the worship leader and all involved.

e. To pray with the participants is of paramount importance. You are entering a time of spiritual battle.

f. Always be prepared for last-minute alterations. Be sensitive that the Holy Spirit may be leading you or others into inserting or deleting some part of the service.

Projection

a. Be enthusiastic and friendly. Regular worshippers are coming to celebrate many things about their faith, and joy and expectancy should at least be sensed in the gathering. The non-churchgoer may not agree with the content or sentiments of what is being expressed, but at least he expects the leader to believe in and be enthusiastic about the things he is talking about.

b. There is a great need to be sensitive (both to the type of service and to the people present), and to be warm and genuine in manner and attitude. Never overdo this by becoming 'gushy'.

c. If you are new to whatever task you are doing, do not apologise for yourself. Often it makes people feel insecure and adds to the tension they may already have. If you make a mistake, people understand. They don't need an explanation.

d. A good worship leader does not attempt to be the star attraction; but with the Spirit he simply acts as a facilitator. The aim of the service is for people to come into contact with the living God, not with the worship leader or the preacher.

e. Be confident in your own ability and the Spirit's help.

Confidence
When leading a meeting of any type, the leader will require
confidence. Some seem to be born with confidence: others need to
develop it. Here are some ways to develop confidence in worship
leading.

a. Realise that your ministry is from God, for the purpose of
glorifying him and bearing witness to him. Beware of any arrogance about your own ability, but at the same time repent of any
false humility that God is not able to use you.

b. Realise that your ministry is a significant one in the life of the
body of Christ. You are not just the 'song-leader' or someone
whose turn on the rota has come round this week.

c. Develop a loving and vital relationship with God. It sounds
basic. But how can you be confident in leading others in worship if
your own walk with God is not right?

d. Be prepared for whatever you do. If you don't know what
you are doing or where you are going, you will be timid and lack
confidence. Moreover, the congregation will not follow you.

e. Develop the gift of leadership by getting involved in the
leading of a smaller and less threatening group than the main
congregation, and train yourself there in the use of your skills.

STARTING SERVICES

a. Be prompt in starting. Starting late gives a bad impression to
newcomers (especially non-churchgoers), and it breeds bad habits
among the regular worshippers.

b. Use a variety of methods. These may include: a call to
worship, using Scripture; an introduction to the service and a
personal general welcome (usually best for an evangelistic service);
a musical selection; spontaneous singing (though it can be confusing for an evangelistic service where people are not used to
singing); or the Prayer Book, suitably introduced and, perhaps,
'filleted'.

c. It is essential to make people feel accepted and welcomed.
Have the instrumentalists and singers lead songs before the 'official
start'; this will help to create a welcoming, worshipping atmosphere for people to come into.

d. Encourage the 'psychology of bigness'. Never apologise for the numbers that may be present. The size of the meeting does not matter. Be positive in welcoming people and enthusiastic about what is going to occur in this time together.

FACTORS IN LEADING WORSHIP

a. Be careful how much talking you do. As you grow in experience, there will be a tendency to talk less. A leader usually talks more when he feels insecure. The worship leader needs to lead worship, not preach. The leader should never use his position to make a point, or to lobby for certain things.

b. Be enthusiastic and clear in giving instructions. This is especially necessary when using a book the congregation may not be familiar with, or when and where to go for counselling.

c. Be wary of jokes. They can often back-fire, and not everyone may share your sense of humour.

d. In most types of services, do not be afraid of periods of silence. It is during these times that God may wish to break in, revealing something that was unexpected. However, be careful to introduce the silent periods, as silence can indicate the leader has lost his way, or make the congregation feel uncomfortable. In an evangelistic service, people may feel especially uncomfortable with long periods of silence or reflection.

e. Be encouraging. Never chastise people about how they worship, or how they sing.

f. Be careful of the use of jargon. For Christians there is a whole dictionary of terminology that we are comfortable with. However, when leading worship (especially in evangelistic services), avoid it like the plague, and go for simple everyday language.

Songleading

a. For the regular worshipper, singing is a normal, uninhibiting activity. However, for the average non-churchgoer, the idea of singing songs out loud, with a group of largely unknown people and often with unfamiliar words and tunes, can be quite daunting. It is very important to make the 'uninitiated' feel relaxed in the worship atmosphere. Avoid making people feel guilty if they do not wish to sing.

b. It is important for the worship leader to lead with the voice, though this does not mean being a great singer himself. The first note or word of each song is the most important, as it gives a clean start which people can follow.

c. As the songleader, you must know the songs you select, and it is always best to sing the melody. If you sing harmonies it can be off-putting. Encourage worshipping as a 'whole' person: that is, body (with actions and movement, if appropriate, though it rarely is appropriate in an evangelistic meeting), soul (with mind, emotions and will) and spirit (with openness to the Spirit of God). But never pressurise a congregation into 'doing' worship, or into doing anything that they will not feel comfortable with (e.g., raising hands).

d. As you lead, be relaxed, smile, and enjoy the experience. If you are enjoying it, others will.

Voice

The worship leader's vocal expression should be varied, enthusiastic, joyous, and dignified. As much as possible, the leader should be uplifting in content and tone. Care should be taken not to mumble, get too low or 'bassy', or to be too shrill. The leader should speak clearly, and not too fast. It is occasionally helpful to listen to tapes of oneself, to hear what others are hearing.

Body language

a. When addressing the congregation, look at the people, and make eye contact. There is nothing more disconcerting to a listener than someone who does not 'connect' with them visually.

b. The worship leader does not have to stay behind a pulpit. Often pulpits (especially if they are large) are a barrier to communication with the congregation.

c. Most people have idiosyncrasies of some type, and the worship leader should be aware of them, and minimise them. Fidgeting is distracting.

d. A picture paints a thousand words. The leader should be enjoying the experience, and expressing it on his face by smiling.

Choice of hymns and songs

a. Select hymns and songs which help develop the theme for the service. It is best to group hymns and songs with themes and styles (e.g., don't move from songs about warfare to adoration, to commitment). Also, be aware of key changes for the instrumentalists.

b. If it is a meeting where there are casual attenders, try to have songs that are very well known or easy to learn. If it is a trans-denominational event or rally, select hymns and songs that will have broad appeal.

c. For an evangelistic service, it is a good idea to have songs with fairly objective content. We must not embarrass visitors by asking them to sing subjective material which may not ring true to their experience.

Teaching new songs

a. Always ensure that *you* know the new hymn or song. Never practise it on the congregation.

b. There is nothing wrong in teaching a new song at an evangelistic service. In fact it puts people on an equal standing. The only danger is that the song may not go over well, and thus may not enhance the service.

c. Use the singers and instrumentalists as a tool for teaching – have the singers singing in unison, until the hymn or song is learned.

Introducing guests

a. Always know the guest's name and find out a little of their background prior to the service.

b. If the guest is a singer, pay attention to them by looking at them as they minister. Never make facial expressions that show what you think of the artist. People are watching your face for a reaction.

c. It is always polite to acknowledge the guests and thank them.

Musicians

a. There are great advantages in developing a team of musicians who see their involvement as a ministry to the Lord, and not as a job to be done.

b. The greater the teamwork, the more effective the group will be in leading the praise and worship times. Practising *and praying together* is essential.

c. As the worship leader, never chastise the musicians publicly. This destroys teamwork and confidence.

d. If possible, develop and use hand signals to facilitate movement through songs without having to interrupt to give verbal directions.

Use of an overhead projector

a. In contemporary worship services, there is much to be said for guiding the singing by means of the overhead projector. It enables people to look up; frees their hands of books; saves telling people to turn to particular numbers; and it enables songs to be sung in medleys without interruption.

b. Before the service, make sure the overhead transparencies are in order.

c. It is important to have an experienced operator handling the transparencies.

POPULAR HERESIES

About leading worship
a. Everyone can lead worship.
b. Every elder, pastor or 'good speaker' can lead worship.
c. Everyone who understands and reads music can lead worship. But it helps if you do.
d. If you can't sing well, you can't lead worship. But it helps if you can.

About the form of worship
a. The Prayer Book is no good.
b. Hymns are out of date.

c. Hymns and choruses are not compatible.

d. No chorus is 'anointed' unless it is sung at least twice.

e. The order of service cannot be changed.

f. The organ is the only instrument for leading the singing.

MARKS OF A GOOD WORSHIP LEADER

a. Commitment to Jesus Christ: if you do not know him, you cannot lead others in worshipping him.

b. A sense of rhythm: a high degree of musical ability is not necessary, but rhythm is.

c. A good speaking voice: you should be able to speak clearly and be understood.

d. Enthusiasm: it is infectious.

e. Sincerity: both in your life and performance. People are quick to spot hypocrisy and half-heartedness.

f. Dignity: there is a delicate balance between enthusiasm and dignity. Both are essential and complement each other. Be buoyant and cheerful, but never at the expense of dignity.

g. Being an encourager: you need the ability to enable a congregation to enter into worship.

h. Being prepared to be vulnerable.

Appendix G
Sports Ministry from the Local Church
Andrew Wingfield Digby

BACKGROUND

In recent years the Christian public has got used to well-known sports personalities speaking openly of their faith in Jesus. In many countries there is a sophisticated organised ministry evangelising and pastoring specific sports people – a tennis ministry serves the needs of pro-players around the world, regular Bible studies are held on the golf tours, chaplains are available at the great sports festivals of the world, chaplains have been appointed to teams in many sports in many countries. The testimonies of Julius 'Dr J' Erving, Stan Smith, Andre Agassi, Larry Nelson, Glenn Hoddle, Rudi Hartarno and numerous others are readily available. The local church has used these stories in their own periodicals, and often the secular media have picked them up too. All this has had an evangelistic impact in the local church. Large para-church movements like Athletes in Action and the Fellowship of Christian Athletes have reached and nurtured literally thousands of athletes.

But there has been a negative side too. Is sports ministry only about exploiting famous people to 'sell' the gospel? Are Christians guilty of an élitist approach in singling out sportspeople for special treatment? Are Christians compromising dangerously in having anything to do with the 'seedy' materialistic world of professional sport? Some have even asked whether Christians should be involved in 'play' at all – especially if it involves the possibility of playing on Sunday.

A BIBLICAL RESPONSE

Those of us working in sport face these questions on a daily basis, and realise the intensity of feelings that can be aroused. Recently, the Rev. Leonard Browne spent a year studying the place of sport in the local church ('Sport and Recreation, and Evangelism in the Local Church' – available from Christians in Sport, PO Box 93, Oxford, UK OX1 1QX). He concluded that 'play' is part of God's will for humanity. In Zechariah 8:5 part of God's plan for restored Israel is that 'the streets shall be full of boys and girls *playing*'. Play and recreation are seen in Scripture as gifts of God, Browne asserts. Play is analysed as being the basis of culture, essential to the cognitive development of children, essential in retaining the best of the past through festivals and ceremonies, and a means of creating fantasy to help understand and prepare for the future.

THE ROLE OF THE LOCAL CHURCH

Much more could be said, but it is my contention that the local church must take play and recreation more seriously in order to involve and evangelise the community in which it is placed.

The fact is that in the Western world people are experiencing more and more leisure time. Leisure is big business, as we all know. In Britain farmers are rushing to turn their agricultural land into amusement parks and wildlife sanctuaries. The TV commercials extol the virtues of holidays, health programmes and happy retirements at an early age. The church can, indeed I would say must, grasp the opportunity this increase in leisure time provides.

THE PRIORITY OF EVANGELISM

If you have read this book carefully you will be convinced by now that fulfilment of Christ's great commission to proclaim the gospel is the urgent priority. We Christians are 'ambassadors for Christ'. We have been entrusted with the message of reconciliation. It is our task. The problem is that many Christians simply don't know unbelievers well enough to pass on the message. They meet people in the shops, or in the street, but they feel they do not know them well enough to talk about Jesus, or perhaps they have lost confidence in the power of the message about Jesus because they have used it so rarely. So, too often evangelism only happens in 'set-up' situations – street preaching, door-to-door work, big crusades and missions, guest service, etc. All have their place, of course, but surely the way to develop relationships with people with whom you can share trustingly is by doing something together which is fun.

SOME MODELS

Perhaps some examples will be of help. In Oxford, where I live, 250 'pubs' put teams into the local 'Aunt Sally' league. 'Aunt Sally' is a traditional Oxfordshire game, which involves throwing a wooden beam at a wooden 'dolly' ten metres away. The team that knocks over 'Aunt Sally' the most times is the winner. Every Wednesday evening approximately 2500 unreached, serious drinking men engage in this game. The vast majority would not go near a church or consider the claims of Christ. But a local church made contact with a pub which had no team, asked if they could put a team into the league, were granted permission, and have begun to evangelise the 'Aunt Sally' world.

Another unreached group engages in the serious recreational pursuit of clay-pigeon shooting. So a few Christians who were prepared to give it a go invited some non-Christian friends to an evening's clay-pigeon shooting at the local shooting club. Tremendous fun was had by all, and over an informal meal afterwards it was the most natural thing in the world to talk about Jesus.

One church was situated at a sea-fishing resort. Many people spent many hours bobbing up and down in the middle of the sea trying to catch fish. So the church chartered a boat, invited church members who enjoyed fishing to bring a friend, and had twelve uninterrupted hours in the middle of the sea with nothing else to do except discuss Christian things.

So seriously did the Peninsula Covenant Church in California view the possibility of evangelism through sport and recreation that they purchased the local sports centre, staffed it with Christians, and now run it as a top-quality recreational centre, but use it to proclaim Christ to the members, 95% of whom are not Christians.

Children's and youth work is another obvious area where coaching can be effectively allied to evangelism. Certainly in England there is less and less instruction in sport being provided in schools. What is available in local clubs and teams often emphasises winning, over against skills and personal development. The church that provides a caring concern for the child along with decent coaching will be very popular with most parents. We do this, with my church in Oxford, and in one year our group of children has grown eightfold and now includes at least two-thirds from non-church families – the programme provides a wonderful bridge between the church and the local community.

A WARNING

In all these activities there is a great danger which has not always been avoided in the infant local church sports ministries in North America and Britain. The danger is that your programme creates a Christian sub-culture, rather than a Christian counter-culture. I vividly recall a conversation I had with a young lady at a large church in Dallas. She was watching her husband play basketball for their young marrieds Sunday school class against the singles class in the beautiful church gymnasium. This was Christians 'recreating' in the church sports programme. I asked her if the basketball provided an opportunity to invite their non-Christian friends to a church activity. She said it did not. When I enquired as politely as I could why this was, she told me that they did not have any non-Christian friends because they spent their leisure time with the Sunday school basketball team!

Those responsible for a local church sports programme must maintain the evangelistic emphasis, or the very thing that they set themselves up to do becomes impossible. The Christians previously playing in non-Christian teams head for the church programme like little ships caught in a gale head for port. Fearful of witnessing to their friends, Christians crowd into the safety of the church ghetto where there is no danger of having to witness because everyone is a believer already. So leadership is vital, and all programmes that lose their evangelistic impact must be closed down.

But how do you start, and what is available to help?

GETTING STARTED

Let me suggest a ten-point plan:

1. PRAY – with the church leadership that God would open the way, and overcome potential problems, so that through a sports ministry people would come to faith. Start praying for friends now!

2. APPOINT – someone to head up the work. Perhaps the pastor, but probably a member who has a *vision for evangelism*, rather than a sports fanatic (though a keen interest in sport will obviously help).

3. ASSESS – your church's and the community's facilities (e.g., halls, crypts, parks, leisure centres, etc.), along with financial resources (if any), to see what might be possible. Link this in with what is already on offer in your locality and with what your non-Christian friends would be interested in. Discover by a questionnaire how your church members use their leisure time.

4. BEGIN – but be realistic. Be prepared for a long-term build-up from small, well-planned, well-prayed-through activities. Depending on facilities and resources (as well as the time of year), a few approaches might be as follows:

5. INTRODUCTORY – obtain the use of a local leisure centre/ school gym, or assemble in a local park for a *family fun day*. Invite all your non-Christian friends with their families. Have lots of different activities, with the emph-

asis very much on fun. End with refreshments, and perhaps a very brief hello from the church. Repeat, when appropriate, with many variations.

6. OCCASIONAL – organise a *fun run*, again for the family (or youth, etc.), perhaps to raise money for a charity. Have certificates for *all* participants, with details of the church on the reverse side. End with refreshments or a barbeque/picnic, and, if appropriate, a word from the pastor.

7. REGULAR – start a keep fit/aerobics class for mums. Hold it in the church hall, and make sure you also have a creche. Have a Christian lead it, someone who knows what they are doing. The leader must be properly qualified. Use the regularity to build up friendships.

8. TEAMWORK – form a football/hockey/netball/bowls team with the majority being Christians. Invite non-Christians to join. Play some friendly games or join the local league. Again, use the time spent together to establish relationships.

9. CLINICS – teaching the skills of particular games will always attract people, especially if your teacher is competent. Organise sports clinics for particular sports (and probably age groups.) Again, have certificates available at the end, with the possibility of some information about other church activities. Variations can include on-going teaching and coaching of different games, especially for youth, which could include appropriate epilogues.

10. EVANGELISE – All the above examples have been shown to bring people within the orbit of the church. If appropriate, people can simply be invited to church, or to an already established evangelistic programme. This can work in conjunction with the organizing of regular 'sports dinners', barbeques or buffets.

where you can invite your particular group (e.g., the football team) to have a meal, listen to a Christian footballer being interviewed, and have the pastor give an appropriate evangelistic talk; or the church can invite all those who are involved in the different sports to a similar event with a more general appeal. Remember, though, many will come to faith primarily through *our friendship* and *our prayers*, as *they* are used by God.

RESOURCES AVAILABLE

Sports ministry is now a worldwide movement co-ordinated by the International Sports Coalition. Full details of existing sports ministries in many countries and programmes for existing local church ministries are available from: ISC, PO Box 878, Newhall, Ca. 91322-0878, USA. Readers in the UK might like to contact Christians in Sport, which is based at St Aldate's Church in Oxford (PO Box 93, OXFORD, OX1 1QX – (0865) 311211).

Appendix H
Social Justice and Evangelism
Ron Dart

When you spread out your hands in prayer, I will hide my eyes from you; even if you offer many prayers, I will not listen. Your hands are full of blood; wash and make yourselves clean. Take your evil deeds out of my sight! Stop doing wrong, learn to do right! Seek justice, encourage the oppressed. Defend the cause of the fatherless, plead the case of the widow.

(Isaiah 1:15–17, NIV)

The greatest evil today is indifference. To know and not to act is a way of consenting to injustice. The planet has become a very small place. What happens in other countries affects us.

(Elie Wiesel)

If they come for the innocents without first having to step over your body, then a curse on your life and a curse on your religion.

(Philip Berrigan)

The thing that keeps coming back to me is, what is Christianity, and, indeed, what is Christ, for us today?

(Dietrich Bonhoeffer)

Many evangelicals have had their knuckles constantly rapped by their brothers and sisters in the mainline churches throughout most of this century. Some thoughtful evangelicals are also seriously questioning the methods and message of many modern evangelists. Those who support large crusades and friendship evangelism are faithful in proclaiming the name of Christ, but they often distort or deny the character of Christ by the type of Christ they proclaim.

Jesus Christ came to bring good news, but the good news announced by many evangelists is, unfortunately, often a soothing defence of the social and political status quo. The challenge of the prophetic tradition and the gripping demand of the Sermon on the

Mount are either conveniently ignored, muted or tranquillised by many of our modern heralds of the good news.

Many modern Christians are asking tough questions about what their faith means when confronted with the warlords of militarism, the crushing reality of poverty, millions of refugees, disappearing indigenous cultures, the growing brutality of human rights violations, environmental genocide, the crumbling of the family, the legality of abortion and systemic injustice in our courts, palaces and cathedrals.

There are those who choose not to look at injustice, and they close their hearts to the cries of the oppressed. Then there are those who, momentarily, allow the scales to fall from their eyes, and they begin to see, but the price of seeing is too great, so they retreat from the fray. There are others who enter the struggle, but they become overwhelmed by the immensity of the issues, and they sense that nothing can be done, and for various reasons they become cynical, and their cynicism paralyses them. Then there are some who enter the battle, ripe with the finest enthusiasm and highest idealism, but their experiences make them bitter. These people continue to work in the area of peace and justice, but their attitudes and the means they use undermine the message they speak and the goal they are striving to reach. Finally, there are those, keenly aware of the dangers of burnout, wary of naive optimists and paralysed cynics, sensitive to the pains of bitter activists, who do serve the risen Christ; but they realise the good news often comforts the afflicted and afflicts the comfortable.

If evangelism in the church is going to have any significant meaning, other than adding a few more members to the Christian community, those who are concerned about spreading the good news of Jesus Christ must ask what the good news is all about. Since Christ is the bearer of the good news, this leads us to ask, again and again, 'Who is Christ?' All serious evangelism begins with this question, and this question, inevitably, leads to the question, 'What is the Kingdom of God?', and 'What are the responsibilities of the citizens of the Kingdom as they pilgrimage through time and history?' Naturally, there are different approaches and answers to these questions, but we do need to discern the relationship between proclaiming the good news and issues of peace and justice.

In my work over the years in the area of peace and justice, I have found that many well-meaning Christians have mistakenly identified some political regime or cause group with the Kingdom of

God. This inevitably leads to disappointment, because the Kingdom of God is much greater than any of the groups we might place our highest hopes in. Does this mean, then, that we should not get involved with peace and justice groups? A tragedy of Christianity in the twentieth century has been that those who claim to be evangelicals have turned aside from the task of being hewers of justice and makers of peace, and those who have been committed to justice and peace have consequently walked away from evangelical Christianity. I might also add that there are many committed people working in a sacrificial way in peace and justice issues, and they have a profound spiritual hunger, but they are sceptical of the church; and there are many people in the church who make a big thing of worship, prayer, Bible studies and devotional times, but they are totally apathetic when it comes to peace and justice concerns.

The time has come when we must remember the richness of the Christian tradition, and as we remember this ancient yet ever new tradition, we will realise that the redemptive message of Jesus Christ necessarily means that we must be agents and ambassadors of divine justice and peace, and protectors of creation. If the Jesus we proclaim has nothing to say in these areas, then we have slipped into a modern and more sophisticated form of Gnosticism in which we worship and announce a spiritual Christ that has little to do with matter, time and history.

When people witness suffering, their first reaction, if they are the least bit sensitive, is to try to relieve it as soon as possible. This reaction is understandable, and we must always remember and encourage such a response. This type of response justifies the importance of charity, acts of mercy and all sorts of relief and development agencies. But acts of mercy and emotive responses to suffering must never blind or restrain our concern for justice. Oscar Romero once said, 'When I feed the poor I am called a saint, but when I ask why the poor are poor, I am called a communist.' The task of justice and peace begins when the questions of 'why' are asked. Works of mercy deal with symptoms, and aid can, potentially, be an obstacle to the development of a just society. In the name of progress, many wealthy countries, using relief, aid or development as their mercy flag, often create greater injustice in the countries they claim to care for. The prophets spoke strong words to those in power who created and maintained personal and structural power that led to oppression for widows, the fatherless and the vulnerable. If we are going to seek justice, we must aid the victims of injustice; but we must also ask why there are victims, and who is profiting from the victims' situation. If Moses, for example, had only built a first-aid station to assist the Jewish slaves in Egypt, then there would have been no serious liberation from the oppression from Egyptian bondage. Moses spoke to Pharoah and his religious pundits, and this was an act of serious justice. When we move in the areas of justice with the good news, we discover that the good news of the Kingdom is bad news for those with important vested interests. Powers will clash, and it is in that clash that the depth, breadth and height of the living Christ will be experienced in a totally new way.

I have listed below eight areas to think about and discuss as you or your group attempt to think and pray through the meaning of the good news as it relates to peace, justice and the integrity of creation.

First, a desire to share the good news must be rooted in the soil of prayer. It is in prayer, or contemplation if you will, that we experience our union with Christ in an ever-deepening way. In contemplation, the roots of our new person go deep into the character of Christ, and from the nourishment of the divine soul we are energised and empowered to live the full demands of divine love; and as C. S. Lewis reminds us, 'Love is as tough as nails.' It is in prayer that we awaken to our gifts, our calling, our vocation; and as we learn to discern these important aspects of our emerging selves, we are less likely to be blown about by all sorts of fads and passing interests. It is also in prayer that we learn, particularly through unitive prayer, how to be centred and focused; and as we grow in this area, we discern our route, our path in the midst of a myriad of conflicting possibilities. One of the first questions that is often asked by those concerned about peace and justice is, 'There are so many groups, so many issues – what can I do?' As we wait on God, as we learn how to be quiet and centred, the still, small voice will break through the static of many conflicting voices and whisper, 'This is the way, walk you in it.' As we learn to attune ourselves and, as Simone Weil insists, be attentive to the still, small voice, the way will become clear to us, although we will often feel as if we are wandering in a cloud of unknowing. I cannot emphasise enough the importance of prayer as the basis of peace and justice activities. As we learn what it means to be 'oned' in Christ, Christ's love will open up to us the path each of us must walk; but we must be willing to be open.

Second, we should try to soak ourselves in the prophetic tradition of the Bible, the Sermon on the Mount, and other texts: there are many of them that deal with issues of justice and peace. As you read the Bible, try to imagine what a prophet would say to our situation today. It is too easy to isolate Scripture, reduce its contents to a bygone age, and never ask what its prophetic word is for us today. It is also important to read good literature in the Christian tradition from men and women who have spent their lives hungering after justice and seeking peace. The great cloud of witnesses can teach us much, if we are willing to look back, remember our history and listen. The combination of biblical insight and tradition can form in us, if we allow it, a Christian mind; and this mind, if it is truly united with the heart of Christ, will feel the pain of this world and long to end it. We should also read some good contemporary literature that deals with the relationship of the good news to justice and peace, and we should try to read books that probe the meaning of justice in our time. I have listed a few books at the end of this article that are fine primers for some of these issues.

Third, we should try to join a group or community of people who are struggling with these issues. It can be lonely and alienating if we try to make sense of these issues alone, and we always need the broader community to bounce ideas off and to check any of our personal heresies or odd leanings. One of the most important issues of justice and peace is that we live it, and we need one another to challenge us on whether we are living a just life rather than merely talking about it. Each group will have its own texture or quality, and it will change as new members come and go, but the challenge of living the good news begins, first, at home, with our immediate families, then with the groups we are trying to grow with. Lanza del Vasto once said:

> We cannot have peace in the world if we do not have peace in our nation, and we cannot have peace in our nation if we do not have it in our communities, and we will not have peace in our community if we do not have it in our family, and we will not have peace in our family if we do not have it within ourselves.

The quest for justice and peace begins in the deep, inner life of the individual; this is why prayer is so crucial, because God gives the divine peace. The individual then attempts to live out authentic and honest relationships in the immediate family and community. There is little point in thinking about macro issues of injustice if the micro issues of self, family and community are in a state of disarray; but there is a danger of reducing justice and peace issues to a relational level and ignoring the bigger, structural macro issues. A healthy concern for justice and peace will wed micro and macro issues, relational integrity and political justice.

Fourth, each group should attempt to discern what issues are important for them, and how they are going to deal with them. Some groups only concentrate on local issues, and they do a fine job, whereas other groups are concerned with national issues of justice, and some groups have a broader concern for international issues. The people in each group will usually determine the concerns of the group, and it is important for this to happen rather than imposing some agenda from an outside source. Many churches have national peace and justice units, but at the local level the direction the group takes is usually up to its members. I would recommend, if possible, working with an international or national group that has some sort of local representation. The larger the group, the more effective it can be in assisting those who most need it, and the more compelling it can be in asking the tougher questions. The bigger the group, also, the richer the resources available, hence much unnecessary work can be avoided by tapping what is there. I think it is wise to try (and this is an ongoing activity) to think through the interrelationship between international, national and local issues. The more a group asks tougher questions about, for example, local housing problems or unemployment, the more they will discover such questions take them to a national level, and further still, to an international discussion of economics and, in the West, the World Bank and the International Monetary Fund.

Fifth, since the spreading of the good news is crucial, and we are to be light and salt in our world, I would recommend joining justice and peace groups that have little or no religious orientation. It is valuable to work with religious groups that are concerned with justice and peace, but the danger of this is that the light stays within the religious household. It is important to go out, to reach out, to work with others who think and live differently, and in that activity to discern how the light of Christ should shine. This reaching out will raise all sorts of tough and demanding questions and issues, and the danger for many religious people is that the questions become too demanding, and they run back to the womb of their religious friends, never to leave again. If people wish to mature in their faith, they must face issues which at times threaten to topple their faith; but as they do this, they will discover that their faith grows deeper rather than dissolving.

Sixth, I think it is important to contact (either by phone, letter or personal visit) those whom we admire in this area. All of us are at different stages of our journey, and we have all been helped by those further along the path. Sometimes those who have assisted us by the books or articles they have written, or by the talks they have given, can be a greater support when we meet them personally. Information is one thing, but personal support is another thing; and those who care the deepest for justice and peace are usually as deeply concerned for informational integrity as they are to support others in a personal way. Never be afraid to reach out to those who have assisted you. Jesus always had time for people, and if he did not have the time, he made it. And if those who claim to follow Christ do not have time to care for others in a personal way, because they are too busy in the information industry, then perhaps they need to remember, in a deeper way, the Christ who is their personal Lord, and how he took time in his busy schedule for people who came to him.

Seventh, as we struggle to make sense of various levels of the good news, we must remember that we are on a journey, and our understanding will therefore expand the deeper we probe in the area. This means we must be aware that we are in process, so what we know and do should always be open for correction. We see through a glass darkly, and as we act on what we know, our knowledge and understanding of things will deepen and change. We must always press our knowledge through the sieve of action, and as we do this, what is essential will remain, while the unnecessary will be trapped and thrown away. It is crucial to act on what we know and to check our knowledge by our actions, then check our type of activity by the new knowledge gained. Paulo Freire has some important things to say in this area, and for those who are interested in his ideas of critical awareness or 'conscientisation', his books are readily available.

Eighth, conflict resolution is an important issue. Groups inevitably conflict with other groups who differ with them in methods or aims, and often members within groups will butt horns. We must always struggle to remember that our visions are finite, and we must respect the other, even though we may disagree with him or her. It is easy to back oneself into a corner, refuse to acknowledge personal failures, and defend oneself, right or wrong. If we are truly going to be bearers of the good news, the means we use must line up with the end we hope to attain. We must always be sensitive and kind to the other, even though we might disagree with them. We must also be prepared to acknowledge our errors and realise that we can learn much from people from whom we differ. Conflicts are an inevitable part of life, but how we resolve them demonstrates the extent to which we understand the richness of God's reconciling love.

Forty thousand children a day die of starvation or malnutrition. There are about twelve million refugees in the world today; most of them are women or children. There are at least eight hundred million people living in a state of absolute poverty, and the number is expected to rise to one billion by the end of the century. The environment is being devastated by those who lust for greater profits. Meanwhile, the money spent throughout the world on arms research, production and deployment, if redirected, could provide adequate food, water, education, health care and housing for each individual on earth. What does the good news of Jesus Christ have to say to these realities and to those who sustain and profit by them? If it has nothing to say, then the good news is only good for a privileged élite in our feudal world order. But it was such folk who killed Christ in his time, and things have not changed. If renewal is ever going to come, our lives must be one in Christ, we must be a people of relational integrity, we must be a people who proclaim justice and peace in the political sphere, and we must announce how Christ is the Lord of all life, well aware that this announcement will bring us into conflict with the principalities and powers.

SUGGESTED READING

J. Bennet, with Susan George, *The Hunger Machine* (Polity Press)
Charles Elliot, *Praying the Kingdom* (Darton, Longman & Todd)
Charles Elliot, *Comfortable Compassion* (Hodder & Stoughton)
Susan George, *How the Other Half Dies: The Real Reason for World Hunger* (Penguin Books)
Alan Kreider, *Social Holiness* (Marshall Pickering)
E. Peters, *Torture* (Basil Blackwell)
Anthony Sampson, *The Money Lenders* (Hodder & Stoughton)
R. Sider and R. Taylor (eds), *Nuclear Holocaust and Christian Hope* (Hodder & Stoughton)
John Stott (eds), *Decide for Peace: Evangelicals Against the Bomb* (Marshall Pickering)

N. Twose, *Cultivating Hunger* (Oxfam)
Jim Wallis, *The Call to Conversion* (Harper & Row/Lion)

ORGANISATIONS

Amnesty International
Christian Aid
Evangelicals for Social Action
Fellowship of Reconciliation
Greenpeace
Oxfam
Pax Christi
Project Ploughshares
United Nations High Commission for Refugees
World Council of Churches – Human Rights Committee

NOTES ON CONTRIBUTORS

Notes on Contributors

Ron Dart is at present National Religious Communities Co-ordinator for Amnesty International in Canada, and he is also the Regional Development Officer for Amnesty in British Columbia and the Yukon. Over the years he has been active with various groups that have dealt with the relationship between militarism and poverty. He has published three books, *Adam: Rationalism, Romanticism and Propheticism*; *Contemplation and Politics*; *The Lute and the Anvil*; and articles on religion and human rights. Ron is married with two children and lives in Vancouver, Canada.

Neale Fong graduated in medicine and surgery from the University of Western Australia. He has had experience in local church ministry as a lay youth pastor, elder and worship leader. He has led services in city-wide missions both in Australia and Canada, conducted worship leaders' seminars and led evangelistic missions in rural Western Australia for six years with youth choirs. He is now completing a Masters Degree in Theological Studies at Regent College, and is presently Music Director and lay preacher at Holy Trinity Anglican Church in Vancouver. Neale is married to Peta, who is an Australian Christian vocalist.

Jane Holloway trained as a secretary and worked in biochemical research and publishing before joining the staff of St Aldate's Church in Oxford. During her eight years there she was involved in secretarial work, church administration, drama and dance, taking teams on missions and pastoral work among students. In 1987 she moved to Vancouver to take up the post of Outreach and Field Work Co-ordinator at Regent College. She is now responsible for the administration, and much of the training, of the mission teams which go out from Regent into various cities and universities in Canada. She also runs the College Drama Group and has taught at the Regent College Summer School on using the arts in worship.

Andrew Wingfield Digby is an Anglican clergyman, trained at Oxford, where he was a distinguished cricketer. After two curacies he returned to Oxford as full-time Director of Christians in Sport, a Christian ministry to sports people all over Britain, which has grown enormously under his leadership. He was a British chaplain to the Olympic Games, and is an influential member of the International Sports Coalition. He, his wife Sue, and their family are members of St Aldate's Church, Oxford.

BIBLIOGRAPHY

Bibliography

The following are works that have been mentioned in the main text, the suggestions for further reading and the Appendices.

J. C. Aldrich, *Lifestyle Evangelism* (Multnomah Press)

Roland Allen, *Missionary Methods – St Paul's or Ours?* (Eerdmans)

J. N. D. Anderson, *Christianity and World Religions* (Inter-Varsity Press)

J. N. D. Anderson, *The Evidence for the Resurrection* (Inter-Varsity Press)

J. N. D. Anderson, *God's Word for God's World* (Hodder & Stoughton)

J. N. D. Anderson, *A Lawyer Among the Theologians* (Hodder & Stoughton)

J. N. D. Anderson, *The Mystery of the Incarnation* (Hodder & Stoughton)

Brother Andrew, *God's Smuggler* (Hodder & Stoughton)

R. S. Armstrong, *The Pastor as Evangelist* (Westminster Press)

R. S. Armstrong, *Service Evangelism* (Westminster Press)

D. M. Baillie, *God Was in Christ* (Faber & Faber)

J. A. Baker, *The Foolishness of God* (Darton, Longman & Todd)

Ray Bakke, *The Urban Christian* (Inter-Varsity Press)

Robert Banks, *Paul's Idea of Community* (Paternoster Press)

William Barclay, *Introducing the Bible* (International Bible Reading Association)

Paul Barnett, *Is the New Testament History?* (Hodder & Stoughton)

Patricia Beall, *The Folk Arts in God's Family* (Hodder & Stoughton)

J. Bennet, with Susan George, *The Hunger Machine* (Polity Press)

Peter Berger, *The Heretical Imperative* (Doubleday Anchor)

Peter Berger, *A Rumour of Angels: Modern Society and the Rediscovery of the Supernatural* (Penguin Books)

Peter Berger, *The Sacred Canopy* (Doubleday Anchor)

Madeleine Berry, *Know How to Use Dance in Worship* (Scripture Union)

Richard Bewes, *The Resurrection – Fact or Fiction?* (Lion)

H. Blamires, *The Christian Mind* (SPCK)

D. G. Bloesch, *Faith and Its Counterfeits* (Inter-Varsity Press)
Board for Mission and Unity, *The Measure of Mission* (Church House Publishing)
Dietrich Bonhoeffer, *Spiritual Care* (Fortress Press)
Michael Bourdeaux (ed.), *Ten Growing Soviet Churches* (MARC Europe)
Bill Bright, *Revolution Now* (Campus Crusade)
Bill Bright, *Witnessing Without Fear* (Campus Crusade)
Leonard Browne, 'Sport and Recreation, and Evangelism in the Local Church' (Christians in Sport)
F. F. Bruce, *Jesus and Christian Origins Outside the New Testament* (Hodder & Stoughton)
F. F. Bruce, *The New Testament Documents: Are They Reliable?* (Inter-Varsity Press)
F. F. Bruce, *The Real Jesus* (Hodder & Stoughton)
Paul Burbridge and Murray Watts, *Lightning Sketches* (Hodder & Stoughton)
Paul Burbridge and Murray Watts, *Red Letter Days* (Hodder & Stoughton)
Paul Burbridge and Murray Watts, *Time to Act* (Hodder & Stoughton)
Bill Burnett (ed.), *By My Spirit* (Hodder & Stoughton)
Anthony Campolo, *A Reasonable Faith: Responding to Secularism* (Word Books)
George Carey, *The Great God Robbery* (Collins Fount)
George Carey, *I Believe in Man* (Hodder & Stoughton)
Caring for New Christians (Bible Society/Scripture Union)
Langmead Casserley, *Graceful Reason: The Contribution of Reason to Theology* (University Press of America)
Michael Cassidy, *Bursting the Wineskins* (Hodder & Stoughton)
Colin Chapman, *The Case for Christianity* (Lion)
John Chapman, *Know and Tell the Gospel* (Navpress)
Robert Coleman, *The Master Plan of Evangelism* (Fleming Revell)
Charles Colson, *Against the Night* (Hodder & Stoughton)
Charles Colson, *Born Again* (Hodder & Stoughton)
Charles Colson, *Kingdoms in Conflict* (Hodder & Stoughton)
Church Family Worship (Hodder & Stoughton)
Come Alive to God (Scripture Union) – introductory, undated Bible reading notes
Harvie Conn, *A Clarified Vision for Urban Mission* (Zondervan)
Orlando Costas, *Liberating News* (Eerdmans)
Peter Cotterell, *Church Alive* (Inter-Varsity Press)
Daily Bread (Scripture Union) – dated Bible reading notes
Daily Notes (Scripture Union) – dated Bible reading notes
Charles Darwin, *The Origin of Species* (Penguin Books)
Richard Dawkins, *The Selfish Gene* (Oxford University Press)
John Dawson, *Taking Our Cities for God* (Creation House)

C. H. Dodd, *The Apostolic Preaching and its Developments* (Hodder & Stoughton)
C. H. Dodd, *The Founder of Christianity* (Collins Fount)
J. D. Douglas (ed.), *Let the Earth Hear His Voice* (World Wide Publications)
J. D. Douglas (ed.), *Proclaim Christ Until He Comes* (World Wide Publications)
J. D. Douglas (ed.), *The Work of an Evangelist* (World Wide Publications)
John Drane, *Jesus and the Four Gospels* (Lion)
James Dunn, *The Evidence for Jesus* (SCM Press)
William Dyrness, *Christian Apologetics in a World Community* (Inter-Varsity Press)
David Edwards, with John Stott, *Essentials* (Hodder & Stoughton)
T. N. Eisenmann, *Everyday Evangelism* (Inter-Varsity Press)
Charles Elliot, *Comfortable Compassion* (Hodder & Stoughton)
Charles Elliot, *Praying the Kingdom* (Darton, Longman & Todd)
Jacques Ellul, *The New Demons* (Seabury Press)
C. Stephen Evans, *Thinking About Faith* (Inter-Varsity Press)
Antony Flew, *Hume's Philosophy of Belief* (Routledge)
Leighton Ford, *Good News is For Sharing* (Cook)
Richard Foster, *Celebration of Discipline* (Hodder & Stoughton)
R. T. France, *The Evidence for Jesus* (Hodder & Stoughton)
R. T. France, *Jesus and the Old Testament* (Tyndale Press)
R. Gagne, T. Kane, R. VerEecke, *Dance in Christian Worship* (Pastoral)
R. Gange, *Origins and Destiny* (Word Books)
Susan George, *How the Other Half Dies: The Real Reason for World Hunger* (Penguin Books)
Eddie Gibbs, *I Believe in Church Growth* (Hodder & Stoughton)
Eddie Gibbs (ed.), *Ten Growing Churches* (MARC Europe)
Billy Graham, *The Holy Spirit* (Collins Fount)
Billy Graham, *Steps to Peace with God* (Billy Graham Evangelistic Organization)
Winston Graham, *The Sleeping Partner* (Bodley Head)
Michael Green, *The Authority of Scripture* (Falcon)
Michael Green, *Baptism* (Hodder & Stoughton)
Michael Green, *To Corinth with Love* (Hodder & Stoughton)
Michael Green, *Come, Follow Me* (Inter-Varsity Press)
Michael Green, *The Day Death Died* (Inter-Varsity Press)
Michael Green, *The Empty Cross of Jesus* (Hodder & Stoughton)
Michael Green, *Evangelism in the Early Church* (Hodder & Stoughton)
Michael Green, *Evangelism Now and Then* (Inter-Varsity Press)
Michael Green, *Freed to Serve* (Hodder & Stoughton)
Michael Green, *I Believe in the Holy Spirit* (Hodder & Stoughton)
Michael Green, *I Believe in Satan's Downfall* (Hodder & Stoughton)
Michael Green, *The Meaning of Salvation* (Hodder & Stoughton)

Michael Green, *New Life, New Lifestyle* (Hodder & Stoughton)
Michael Green, *The Ten Myths About Christianity* (Lion)
Michael Green (ed.), *The Truth of God Incarnate* (Hodder & Stoughton)
Michael Green, *Was Jesus Who He Said He Was?* (Servant Books)
Michael Green, *Why Bother With Jesus?* (Hodder & Stoughton)
Michael Green, *World on the Run* (Inter-Varsity Press)
Michael Green, *You Must Be Joking* (Hodder & Stoughton)
S. L. Greenslade, *Shepherding the Flock* (SCM Press)
Roger Greenway and Timothy Mousma, *Cities: God's New Frontier* (Baker Books)
Val Grieve, *Your Verdict* (Inter-Varsity Press)
E. Griffin, *Getting Together* (Inter-Varsity Press)
E. M. Griffin, *The Mind Changers* (Tyndale Press)
Michael Griffiths (ed.), *Ten Sending Churches* (MARC Europe)
A. Guillaume, *Islam* (Penguin Books)
Os Guinness, *The Dust of Death* (Inter-Varsity Press)
Os Guinness, *The Gravedigger File* (Hodder & Stoughton)
C. K. Hadaway, S. A. Wright and F. M. DuBose, *Home Cell Groups and House Churches* (Broadmore)
O. Hallesby, *Prayer* (Inter-Varsity Press)
Anthony Hanson (ed.), *Vindications* (SCM Press)
Elizabeth Heike and Peter Toon, *NIV Bible Study Guide* (Hodder & Stoughton)
William Hocking, *Rethinking Missions* (Harper & Row)
H. T. Hoekstra, *Evangelism in Eclipse* (Paternoster Press)
A. Huxley, *Ends and Means* (Chatto)
Hymns for Today's Church (Hodder & Stoughton)
Bob and Betty Jacks, *Your Home a Lighthouse* (Navpress)
Philip Keller, *A Gardener Looks at the Fruits of the Spirit* (Pickering & Inglis)
Graham Kendrick (ed.), *Ten Worshipping Churches* (MARC Europe)
Graham Kendrick, *Worship* (Kingsway Publications)
James Kennedy, *Evangelism Explosion* (Tyndale Press)
Philip King, *Leadership Explosion* (Hodder & Stoughton)
Cliffe Knechtle, *Give Me an Answer* (Inter-Varsity Press)
Paul Knitter, *No Other Name?* (Orbis Books)
Donald B. Kraybill, *The Upside Down Kingdom* (Marshalls)
Peter Kreeft, *Making Sense Out of Suffering* (Hodder & Stoughton)
Alan Kreider, *Social Holiness* (Marshall Pickering)
Hans Küng, *Christianity and World Religions* (Collins Fount)
Hans Küng, *On Being a Christian* (Collins Fount)
J. E. Kyle (ed.), *Urban Mission* (Inter-Varsity Press)
Christopher Lamb, *Belief in a Mixed Society* (Lion)
The Lamb's Players, *Developing a Drama Group* (World Wide Publications)